Essentials of Children's Literature

A Story Is a Doorway

A story is a doorway
That opens on a wider place.
A story is a mirror
To reflect the reader's face.

A story is a question
You hadn't thought to ponder,
A story is a pathway,
Inviting you to wander.

A story is a window,
A story is a key,
A story is a lighthouse,
Beaming out to sea.

A story's a beginning,
A story is an end,
And in the story's middle,
You just might find a friend.

—Richard Peck

Eighth Edition

Essentials of Children's Literature

Kathy G. Short
University of Arizona

Carol Lynch-Brown
Florida State University

Carl M. Tomlinson
Northern Illinois University

PEARSON

Boston Columbus Indianapolis New York San Francisco Upper Saddle River
Amsterdam Cape Town Dubai London Madrid Milan Munich Paris Montréal Toronto
Delhi Mexico City São Paulo Sydney Hong Kong Seoul Singapore Taipei Tokyo

Vice President, Editor-in-Chief: Aurora Martínez Ramos
Acquisitions Editor: Kathryn Boice
Development Editor: Jennifer Gessner
Editorial Assistant: Michelle Hochberg
Executive Marketing Manager: Krista Clark
Production Editor: Cynthia DeRocco
Projection Coordination, Editorial Services, and Text Design: Electronic Publishing Services, Inc., NYC
Manufacturing Buyer: Linda Sager
Art Rendering and Electronic Page Makeup: Jouve
Cover Designer: Diane Lorenzo

Text and illustration credits are located on pages 403–404.

Library of Congress Cataloging-in-Publication Data

Short, Kathy Gnagey.
   Essentials of children's literature / Kathy G. Short, University of Arizona, Carol Lynch-Brown, Florida State University, Carl M. Tomlinson, Northern Illinois University.—Eighth edition.
     pages   cm
   Includes bibliographical references and index.
   ISBN 978-0-13-306673-9
   1. Children's literature—Study and teaching (Higher)   2. Children's literature—History and criticism.   3. Children's literature—Bibliography.   I. Lynch-Brown, Carol.   II. Tomlinson, Carl M.   III. Title.
   PN1009.A1L96   2013
   809'.892820711—dc23

          2012048611

4   16

ISBN 10: 0-13-306673-8
ISBN 13: 978-0-13-306673-9

Contents

Chapter Eight   Realistic Fiction   145

Chapter Nine   Historical Fiction and Biography   165

Chapter Ten   Informational Books   193

Part Three   Literature in the School   245

Chapter Twelve   Literature in the Curriculum   247

Chapter Thirteen   Engaging Children with Literature   275

Features

Figures and Tables

Figures

Tables

About the Authors

Kathy G. Short teaches graduate courses in children's literature, inquiry, and curriculum at the University of Arizona and taught elementary school in Indiana and Ohio. Her books include *Creating Classrooms for Authors and Inquirers, Literature as a Way of Knowing,* and *Stories Matter: The Complexity of Cultural Authenticity.* She is director of Worlds of Words (www.wowlit.org), an initiative to encourage the use of literature to explore global cultures. She is on the 2014 Caldecott Committee and is the Vice President of NCTE.

Carol Lynch-Brown taught graduate and undergraduate courses in children's and young adult literature, reading, and language arts education at Florida State University. She was a teacher in elementary school and middle school in St. Paul and Minneapolis Public Schools, and taught English in French Public Schools. She co-authored with Carl M. Tomlinson *Essentials of Young Adult Literature,* second edition, published by Pearson in 2010 and is a former editor of *The Reading Teacher,* a journal of the International Reading Association.

Carl M. Tomlinson taught graduate and undergraduate courses in children's literature and language arts at Northern Illinois University. He was an elementary and middle school teacher in Thomasville, Georgia, public schools, and taught classes in English in Norway. He co-authored with Carol Lynch-Brown *Essentials of Young Adult Literature,* second edition, published by Pearson in 2010, and is the editor of *Children's Books from Other Countries,* published by USBBY and Scarecrow Press in 1998.

Preface

Essentials of Children's Literature is a brief, affordable, comprehensive textbook with rich resources—a true compendium of information about children's literature. It is tailored to a survey course in children's literature but is also suitable as a companion text in an integrated language arts course because of its brevity and affordability.

The primary focus of a survey course in children's literature should be reading children's trade books, not reading an exhaustive textbook about children's books. Students in such a course need direct experience with books—reading independently, reading aloud, discussing, writing, comparing, criticizing, evaluating, and connecting to their lives as well as exploring ways of sharing books with children.

One of our goals is to awaken or reawaken the joy of reading for college-level students. This reawakening can happen only by experiencing the pleasure and excitement of reading excellent trade books. At the same time, the body of knowledge about literature and about teaching literature to children can be conveyed most efficiently through a textbook. *Essentials of Children's Literature* presents this body of knowledge in a clear, concise, direct narrative along with brief lists, examples, figures, and tables, thus freeing class time for involvement with literature.

The eighth edition of *Essentials of Children's Literature* heralds two milestones. It was over two decades ago that we began conceptualizing and planning this book. Much has changed since the first edition to influence the world of children's literature, and although successive editions have reflected these changes, the book remains, in essence, true to our initial concept—a comprehensive but brief alternative to compendium textbooks. The second milestone is that Kathy G. Short, professor of children's literature at the University of Arizona, has moved into the role of senior author for this edition. Kathy's research in global children's literature and intercultural understanding, children's dialogue about literature, and inquiry-based curriculum is internationally known.

New to This Edition

Our goals in revising this book were twofold: to make it as fresh and current as possible and to produce a brief text without sacrificing content. We have added many new children's book titles and retained older titles most likely to be known and appreciated by students. Features within chapters—Milestones, Excellent Books to Read Aloud, Notable Authors and Illustrators, and Invitations for Further Investigation—have been updated to include important developments, recent outstanding children's titles, outstanding new creators of children's books, and current issues and topics related to the field. We have reorganized some of the content in the chapters and moved sections from one chapter to another to create a stronger structure and flow to the text.

We have also integrated a strong focus on global and multicultural titles and authors throughout all of the chapters.

The most important revision is integrating connections to the Common Core State Standards throughout the chapters. For example, we have added a focus on a specific literary element and a reader connection to each of the genre chapters to encourage close reading, a discussion of text complexity, an expanded discussion of informational books, and an analysis of how the standards connect to the use of literature in classrooms. In addition, the Invitations for Further Investigation have been expanded to provide suggestions for close reading and text analysis related to the focus of that chapter. Revisions to individual chapters are as follows:

Chapter 1: Learning about Story and Literature

- Added a discussion of the role of story in making meaning of our lives
- Updated sections on the value of literature in children's lives and in their learning
- Moved the section on why reading and literature are at risk in our society from Chapter 2 to Chapter 1

Chapter 2: Learning about Children and Literature

- Reorganized the chapter to focus on strategies for knowing the child and for knowing books
- Included new examples of children's literature titles appropriate for the various stages of children's development
- Added information on text complexity as defined by the Common Core State Standards
- Moved information on book awards, review journals, and professional organizations from Chapter 3 to Chapter 2
- Moved the description of the political context and standards to Chapter 12

Chapter 3: Learning about Literature

- Updated the discussion of New Criticism and Reader Response as related to Common Core State Standards
- Included new book titles in the literary elements section
- Added a new section on knowledge of literature as a discipline as a frame for the features in the chapters

Chapter 4: Picture Books and Illustration

- Updated discussion of the visual elements, artistic media, artistic styles, and book design
- Added a section on the Postmodern Picture Book
- Updated titles of picture books throughout the chapter and in the Recommended Picture Books list
- Updated Recommended Lists of Transitional Books and Easy-to-Read Books due to their emphasis within Common Core State Standards

Chapter 5: Poetry

- Updated examples of poems and types of poetry books
- Updated Recommended Poetry Books list
- Added Reader Connections section on reading and writing poetry in the classroom

Chapter 6: Traditional Literature

- Revised discussion of evaluation and selection with an additional focus on plot
- Updated Recommended Traditional Literature list
- Added Reader Connections section on storytelling in the classroom

Chapter 7: Modern Fantasy

- Revised discussion of evaluation and selection with an additional focus on theme
- Updated discussion of fantasy books often challenged by censors
- Updated examples of types of modern fantasy and titles for recommended book lists
- Included Reader Connections section on censorship (moved from Chapter 12)

Chapter 8: Realistic Fiction

- Revised discussion of evaluation and selection with an additional focus on character
- Updated examples of types of realistic fiction and of titles in Recommended Realistic Fiction Books list
- Added Reader Connections section on character education with examples of paired texts to examine character traits

Chapter 9: Historical Fiction and Biography

- Revised discussion of evaluation and selection with an additional focus on setting and point of view
- Added Reader Connections section on developing an understanding of historical contexts using jackdaws
- Updated Recommended Historical Fiction and Biography Books lists by historical time period

Chapter 10: Informational Books

- Expanded discussion of types of informational books and their features and structures
- Revised discussion of evaluation and selection with an additional focus on style
- Added Reader Connections section on pairing informational books with a fiction book
- Updated examples of types of informational books and Recommended Informational Books list

Chapter 11: Literature for a Diverse Society

- Highlighted curriculum that is culturally responsive (finding one's own culture within education), culturally expansive (going beyond one's own culture), and culturally critical (addressing critical literacy and social justice education)
- Updated Recommended Book lists for Multicultural and International Literature

Chapter 12: Literature in the Curriculum

- Completely reorganized chapter with a major section on the Politics of Literacy and Literature that addresses Common Core State Standards and common misunderstandings of these standards
- Revised and updated sections on planning a literature curriculum, integrating literature into a literacy curriculum, and evaluating a literature curriculum
- Updated tables on important studies on literature and reading and literature and writing
- Added conceptual planning webs on journeys and refugees

Chapter 13: Engaging Children with Literature

- Organized chapter into sections on Reading Widely for Personal Purposes, Reading Critically to Inquire about the World, and Reading Strategically to Learn about Literacy
- Added more discussion of plays and resources for plays
- Updated discussion of digital books and e-books
- Updated children's book examples and websites

Appendixes

- Appendix A, Children's Book Awards, updated to include award winners and honor books for the years 2009–2012
- Appendix B, Professional Resources, updated to reflect the latest titles and editions
- Appendix C, Children's Magazines, updated to include new magazines and to reflect current magazine content, intended audience, website, and ordering information

Supplements for Instructors and Students

The following supplements comprise an outstanding array of resources that facilitate learning about children's literature. For more information, ask your local Allyn & Bacon Merrill Education representative or contact the Allyn & Bacon Merrill Faculty Field Support Department at 1-800-526-0485. For technology support, please contact technical support directly at 1-800-677-6337 or http://247.pearsoned.com.

Instructor's Manual and Test Bank

The instructor's manual features multiple syllabi of typical survey courses in children's literature. The test bank includes multiple-choice, matching, fill-in-the-blank, short answer, and essay questions. This supplement has been written by the text authors. (Available for download from the Instructor Resource Center at www.pearsonhighered.com/irc.)

Acknowledgments

We particularly want to acknowledge the contributions of Desiree W. Cueto at the University of Arizona to this edition. Desiree did the background research on new book titles, research, and trends that provided the basis for updating and revising this edition, as well as serving as a sounding board for reorganizing and revising the chapters. Her thinking and ideas are woven throughout this text and made an invaluable contribution to our writing and consideration of new potentials and structures.

We gratefully acknowledge the reviewers of the eighth edition: Terry Diana Benton, Youngstown State University; Brenda Cole, Columbia College; Gail Ditchman, Moraine Valley Community College; Renee L. Funke, Jamestown Community College; and Karen Guerrero, Mesa Community College.

We are also indebted to David Wiesner for the cover art for this edition of *Essentials of Children's Literature*. His art underscores the wonder and flights of imagination that books inspire in the lives of children.

Part One

Children and Literature

Part 1 introduces you to the field of children's literature. These chapters will support you in learning how to read, select, and evaluate children's books.

Chapter 1 defines children's literature and examines the role of story and books in the lives of children. Stories fill our daily lives and are the way in which we make sense of our experiences. Literature thus plays an essential role in children's lives, inviting children into new experiences that provide them with important connections and understandings that go beyond entertainment and instruction. Overlooking this personal purpose for reading can have personal and societal implications.

Chapter 2 emphasizes the need to know both children and books in order to connect children with books that are significant in their lives and learning. Knowing children includes general guidelines for the types of literature likely to appeal to children as they develop from year to year, strategies for determining children's reading interests, and the factors to consider in evaluating text complexity. Knowing books involves building a knowledge of resources for book selection, including review journals, professional websites, and major awards, in order to select a balance and variety of books for children as well as understanding why children resist reading.

Approaches to studying and interpreting literature, elements of fiction, and categories of literature are treated extensively in Chapter 3. The chapter concludes with a table of literary genres and their locations within this text.

Examples of notable books are provided throughout this text, but we do not include lengthy plot summaries or book reviews. We believe that more is gained from reading and discussing children's books themselves than reading *about* the books in a lengthy text.

Chapter One

Learning about Story and Literature

Reading

We get no good
By being ungenerous even to a book,
And calculating profits . . . so much help
By so much reading. It is rather when
We gloriously forget ourselves and plunge
Soul-forward, headlong, into a book's profound,
Impassioned for its beauty and salt of truth—
'Tis then we get the right good from a book.

—*Elizabeth Browning*

A child leans forward, head cupped in hands, eyes wide with anticipation, listening to a story. Whether that child is seated beside an open fire in ancient times, on a rough bench in a medieval fairground, or on the story rug in a modern-day classroom, this image signals the same message—children love a good story.

Definition of Children's Literature

This book is about literature for children from infancy to early adolescence, written for you as teachers, librarians, and parents. In these roles, you will have many opportunities to invite children to engage with good books. This text will help you become acquainted with these books and the criteria to consider in selecting a range of books for children.

Children's books, first and foremost, are literature. Literature is not written to teach something, but to illuminate what it means to be human and to make accessible the most fundamental experiences of life—love, hope, loneliness, despair, fear, and belonging. Literature is the imaginative shaping of experience and thought into the forms and structures of language. Children read literature to experience life, and their experiences inside the world of a story challenge them to think in new ways about their lives and world.

More specifically, **children's literature** is good-quality trade books for children from birth to early adolescence, covering topics of relevance and interest to children through prose and poetry, fiction and nonfiction. They are the books that children see as reflecting their life experiences, understandings, and emotions. This definition contains key concepts that will help you find your way around the more than 250,000 children's titles published in the last decade and currently in print (*Children's Books In Print,* 2012) and the more than 20,000 new children's titles being published annually in the U.S. (*Library and Book Trade Almanac,* 2012), as well as the additional thousands of children's books published worldwide each year. In addition, children's books are now being published in a range of electronic formats, including interactive digital books, books on e-readers, and applications on smartphones and tablets. These formats are not in competition with print books, but instead offer different kinds of experiences and potentials for children to connect with literature.

Content

Children's books are about the full range of experiences of childhood from the difficult to the exciting. Whether these experiences are set in the past, present, or future, they should be relevant to children today. The content of children's books includes amazingly diverse and interesting topics, including dinosaurs, Egyptian mummies, and world records. This content can be expressed in prose or poetry. If the literary work is prose, it can be in the form of fiction (an invented story), nonfiction (factual), or a combination of the two.

The manner in which content is treated is significant to children. Childhood stories that are forthright, humorous, or suspenseful are appropriate for young readers; stories *about* childhood that are nostalgic or overly sentimental are inappropriate and written for adults. The content should authentically reflect diverse cultural experiences and not contain stereotypical images. When stories show children as victims of natural and human-made disasters, they should contain some hint of hope for a better future rather than only depict the hopelessness and despair of the moment. An element of hope does not mean that all stories have "happy endings" where all turns out well at the end. Many children have experienced difficult life situations and know that always having a happy ending is unrealistic.

Teachers and librarians distinguish between the terms *textbook* and *trade book*. A **textbook**, by design and content, is for the purpose of instruction, such as the basal reader used in many classrooms for reading instruction. In contrast, a **trade book**, by design and content, is primarily for the purposes of entertainment and information. Trade books are often referred to as *library books* and *storybooks*. The books highlighted in this text are trade books, not textbooks.

Quality

Not all trade books aimed at young readers are worth close attention. Books ranging in quality from excellent to poor are readily available in bookstores and libraries as well as online. Racks of children's books can be found in department stores, drugstores, and even grocery stores. But the question is: Are they *high-quality* children's books?

Quality in writing and illustration has to do with originality and importance of ideas, imaginative use of language and image, and beauty of literary and artistic style that enable a work to remain fresh, interesting, and meaningful for many years. The best children's books offer readers enjoyment as well as memorable characters and situations and valuable insights into the human condition. These books have permanent value and stay in our memories.

This is not to say that books of good-but-not-great quality, such as series books, have no value. These books do not win literary prizes, but they are enjoyed by young readers and encourage more reading. However, you will probably not want to select series books to read aloud to your students. Read-alouds should challenge readers to consider new possibilities rather than focus on the easy and enjoyable books they are already reading independently.

Many recent so-called children's books are nothing more than advertisements for film and television characters and associated products, such as candy, clothing, and toys. These books represent the low end of the quality spectrum and focus on the child as a consumer, rather than a reader and human being.

The Value of Story in Making Meaning of Our Lives

This text focuses on literature; but we need to remember that books connect to broader notions of story as meaning making. Stories of all kinds are woven so tightly into the fabric of our everyday lives that it's easy to overlook their significance in framing how we think about ourselves and the world. They fill every part of daily life as we talk about events and people, read books, browse online news reports, send text messages, listen to music, watch video clips, check in with friends on Facebook, and catch up on a favorite television show. We live storied lives.

Stories are thus much more than a book—they are the way our minds make sense of our lives and world. Stories allow us to move from the chaotic "stuff" of daily life into understanding. An endless flow of experiences surround us on a daily basis, and we create stories to impose order and coherence on those experiences and to work out their significance (Rosen, 1986). Stories provide a means of structuring and reflecting on our experiences. We tell our stories to invite others to consider our meanings and to construct their own, as well as to better understand those experiences ourselves. We listen to other's stories to try on another perspective or way of living in the world.

Story is thus a mode of knowing—one of the primary ways in which we think and construct meaning from our experiences. Our views of the world are a web of interconnected stories: a distillation of all the stories we have shared. This web of stories becomes our interpretive lens for new experiences and is culturally based. Our human need to story about our experiences may be universal but there is no one way to tell stories. Our stories are always interwoven with the stories that exist within our own cultures both in content and in the style and structure of the telling. All children come to school with stories, although the types of stories that they are familiar with and the ways in which they tell stories may be quite different from school norms.

We also construct stories to make sense of information. Theories are just bigger stories. Scientists create a theory by using current information to tell a story that provides an explanation of a natural phenomenon, such as black holes. They change their stories over time as new information and perspectives become available. A story is thus a theory of something—what we tell and how we tell it reveals what we believe (Rosen, 1986).

Story is at the heart of who we each are as human beings and who we might become. We often treat books for young children as "cute" or as instructional lessons rather than recognizing their broader role as story. The values of literature for children, both inside and outside of school, are interwoven with story as meaning making.

The Value of Literature in Children's Lives

Descriptions of children's literature in elementary schools typically focus on how to *use* children's books to teach something else. Literature is viewed as a material that is used to teach reading, math, science, or social studies or to teach comprehension skills or writing strategies. We are often so focused on using literature for other purposes that we lose sight of literature as having value in and of itself for children's lives as well as serving the purpose of enhancing their academic learning.

Enjoyment

First and foremost, good books offer enjoyment. Those of you who read widely as children will never forget the stories that were so funny that you laughed out loud, the poem that was so lilting that you chanted it from memory, the mystery that was so scary that your heart thumped with apprehension, and the characters who became your best friends or family. These positive early experiences often lead to a lifetime of reading enjoyment.

Personal and Cultural Identity

Stories that are handed down from one generation to the next connect us to our past, to the roots of our cultural identities and national heritage, and to the general human condition. Readers grow in their own identities by finding themselves and their families and communities within books and exploring the multiple connections of their identities, including race, ethnicity, nationality, gender, religion, language, disability, region, family structures, and social class.

Stories are also the repositories of culture. Knowing the tales, characters, and expressions that are part of our cultural heritage is part of being culturally literate. In addition, stories based on events in the past provide a connection to the people, both ordinary and extraordinary, who made history.

Imagination and Transformation

By seeing the world around them in new ways and by considering ways of living other than their own, children are encouraged to think creatively and divergently. Stories can provide children with alternative pathways for understanding their past or imagining their future. As children enter a world through stories that differ from the present, they develop their imaginations and are inspired to overcome obstacles, consider different perspectives, and formulate personal goals. They transform their understandings of the possibilities for themselves and the world.

Often, story characters are placed in situations that require them to make difficult life decisions. As the story unfolds and a character's decision and the consequences of that choice become apparent, readers can critically consider their own decisions and develop their own moral concepts and values.

Knowledge and Insights

Good books offer information and wisdom and so combine the heart and mind, reason and emotion. Informational books provide factual knowledge, whereas fiction and poetry offer insights into life along with information. When a story is so convincingly written that readers feel as though they have lived through an experience or been in the place and time of that story, the book has given them a valuable personal experience that takes them beyond the constraints of their current lives. These experiences encourage children to view situations from perspectives other than their own.

Understanding and Empathy

Literature helps children gain an appreciation of the universality of human needs across history, which makes it possible for them to understand what connects all of us as human beings as well as what makes each of us unique. Living someone else's life through a story can help children develop a sense of social justice and a greater capacity to empathize with others. All children can benefit from stories that involve them in the lives of characters who struggle with disabilities, politics, or difficult circumstances or whose lives differ because of culture or geography. Literature plays an essential role in building intercultural understanding as children immerse themselves in the lives and thinking of characters within global cultures. Likewise, children can relate on a more personal level with the events and people of history when reading historical fiction which focuses on characters who are their own age.

Literary and Artistic Preferences

Another valuable result of children's interactions with literature is that they come to recognize the literary and artistic styles of many authors and illustrators. Children who read regularly from a wide variety of books develop their own personal preferences for types of books and select favorite authors and illustrators. Personal preference and interest as expressed through self-selection of reading materials are powerful motivators for becoming a lifelong reader.

The more children know about their world, the more they discover about themselves—who they are, what they value, and what they stand for. These insights alone are sufficient to warrant making good books an essential part of any child's home and school experiences. But literature is also valuable for learning in school contexts as well.

The Value of Literature for Children's Learning

Literature is of tremendous value for children's learning across the curriculum in schools. Literature provides interesting texts that support students in learning about text structures, literary elements, and reading/writing strategies, and in exploring important concepts, perspectives, and ideas in science and social studies.

Reading and Writing

Reading, like any other skill, improves by engaging in the actual process. Many teachers and librarians believe that regular reading of excellent appropriate literature can foster language development and help young children learn to read and value reading. Reading is devalued if we only give children beginning reading materials that aren't worth the effort of reading them and don't read aloud to them from books that engage their interest and minds.

Reading aloud to children at home and in the classroom greatly benefits children's acquisition of reading strategies and their attitudes toward reading. The landmark study *Becoming a Nation of Readers* (Anderson, Hiebert, Scott, & Wilkinson, 1985) noted that "the single most important activity for building the knowledge required for eventual success in reading is reading aloud to children" (p. 23). This report also noted that the greatest gains in vocabulary, fluency, and comprehension came from independent reading by children. So the two most important engagements we can provide on a daily basis is to read aloud excellent literature and schedule time for silent independent reading of free-choice materials and books. Table 1.1 provides a summary of the landmark studies supporting these practices.

By listening to and reading excellent literature, children are exposed to rich vocabulary and excellent writing styles, which serve as good mentor texts for their own speaking and writing voices. Books that use particular literary devices such as dialect, dialogue, and precise description provide demonstrations of options for students' writing.

Government policies have had a tremendous effect on the teaching of reading and writing in classrooms and thus on the use of literature within literacy instruction. The specific policies change over time with the Common Core State Standards and assessments most recently affecting classrooms. Connections to these standards have been integrated throughout the chapters in this book, but are addressed in depth as part of text complexity in Chapter 2 and the political context of reading in Chapter 12.

Literature across the Curriculum

Literature across the curriculum refers to using literature as teaching materials in social studies and history, science, health, and mathematics. Many trade books contain information that is relevant to the topics, issues, and themes that are explored in schools. Moreover, this information is often presented through captivating, beautifully illustrated narratives that are interesting and are more comprehensible and memorable to students. When using literature across the curriculum, teachers and students are not confined to a dry pedantic textbook as the sole resource. Using several sources of information provides fuller factual coverage of topics and leads to more informed consideration of issues and perspectives. The abundance of well-written informational books for children provides rich resources for inquiries in the content areas. Teachers support the teaching

Table 1.1   Landmark Studies on Literature and Reading

Researcher(s)	Participants	Findings
Carlsen & Sherrill (1988)	College students who become committed readers	Conditions that promote a love of reading in childhood include: • Freedom of choice in reading material • Availability of books and magazines • Family members who read aloud • Adults and peers who read • Role models who value reading • Sharing and discussing books • Owning books • Availability of libraries and librarians
Eldredge & Butterfield (1986)	1,149 beginning readers in 50 classrooms	Use of children's literature to teach reading has a much greater positive effect on students' reading achievement and attitudes than does use of basal readers with traditional homogeneous grouping.
Fielding, Wilson, & Anderson (1986)	Middle-graders	Students who read a lot at home show larger gains on reading achievement tests.
Leinhardt, Zigmond, & Cooley (1981)	Elementary-grade children	The amount of time children spend reading silently in school is associated with their year-to-year gains in reading achievement. Children improve their reading ability by increasing their reading.
Applebee (1978)	Children ages 2 to 17	Children's sense of story grows as they mature. Hearing and reading literature has a positive effect on children's language development.
Butler (1975)	Cushla, a severely disabled child from ages 4 months to 3 years	Reading aloud daily from picture books enabled this child to learn to read.
Durkin (1966)	Children who learned to read before attending school	Children who learned to read before attending school were read to regularly from the age of 3. Early reading and early writing are often linked.

of mathematics, social studies, and science through engaging students in nonfiction and by pairing fiction with informational texts.

Art Appreciation and Visual Literacy

Illustrations in children's picture books can be appreciated for their cognitive value in helping to tell the story and for their aesthetic value as art. Picture books provide a means of understanding art as a meaning-making process and appreciating art for its own sake. By calling attention to particularly striking and unusual illustrations as you read aloud to children, you show that you value art. Students gain an understanding of art by discussing the artist's style, medium (watercolor, oils, pastels, etc.), and use of color, line, and shape as well as by using picture books as demonstrations of media, techniques, and topics for their own artwork.

In addition, children can learn to critically read visual images through interactions with picture books and so develop their visual literacy. Visual literacy is essential to acquiring the ability to critique the pervasive images of popular culture and mass media.

So Why Are Literature and Reading at Risk in Our Society?

Given the significant values of story and literature, you might assume that engaging with all kinds of books for personal reading would be a valued activity in our society. Research indicates that the opposite is true and that voluntary reading is at risk. Newspaper headlines put a spotlight on illiteracy, the number of people who cannot read and write at the levels needed to function in our society, when the much bigger problem is aliteracy, the number of people who can read and choose not to. They read work-related materials, but reading books for personal purposes is not part of their lives.

Voluntary reading of literature in the U.S. has been monitored by the U.S. Bureau of the Census and the National Endowment for the Arts (NEA) since 1982. From 1982 to 2002, NEA reports show a steady decline in voluntary reading across all age groups in the U.S., but particularly among young adults ages 18–24. The NEA's 2008 report shows that this slide has finally reversed itself and that, for the first time in twenty-five years, our love of literature has been rekindled with a 7 percent rise in adults reading literature, particularly novels and short stories. Despite this slight rise, there is still cause for concern because only 50.2 percent of Americans report reading *any literature* in 2008 and only 54.3 percent read *any book* that was not related to school or work. The U.S. population now breaks into almost equally sized groups of readers and nonreaders, not because the nonreaders cannot read but because they are choosing not to read books, either electronic or print. The NEA (2008) believes that one reason for the recent slight rise in reading is that parents, teachers, librarians, and civic leaders took action and created thousands of programs for families, schools, and communities based on publicity about the major declines in earlier reports.

The NEA's 2007 report found a correlation between the decline in reading and increased participation in a variety of electronic media, including the Internet, video games, and portable digital devices. This correlation is a concern because reading books supports the development of the focused attention and contemplation essential to complex communication and insight. The report also noted that the percentage of 17-year-olds who read nothing for pleasure doubled over a twenty-year period while the amount they read for school (15 or fewer pages a day) stayed the same. There was also a significant decline from childhood to adolescence from 54 percent to 22 percent for those who read almost daily for pleasure. College attendance is no longer a guarantee of active reading habits; one in three college seniors read nothing for pleasure in a given week. Our assumption is that high school and college students stop reading for personal purposes because reading becomes associated with textbooks and school work—hardly motivating reading!

The NEA 2007 report details the consequences of the loss of reading for pleasure, noting that voluntary reading correlates strongly with academic achievement in reading and that proficient readers have more financially rewarding jobs and opportunities for career growth. Literary readers are three times more likely than nonreaders to visit museums, attend plays or concerts, and create artwork, and twice as likely to exercise, volunteer, and vote. The greater academic, professional, and civic benefits associated with higher levels of leisure reading and reading comprehension point to the significance of your role as a parent, teacher, or librarian in the lives of children.

Books do change lives for the better, but *you* need to be a reader to engage children as readers. Many of you are likely to be among those college students who stopped reading due to the lack of relevance in teacher-selected reading materials, dull textbooks, boring instructional practices, lack of time, peer pressure, past failures, a preference for electronic media, and a perception of reading as hard work. Due to the heavy load of course work and textbook reading, you are much more likely to watch television or YouTube videos and surf the Internet, activities that require passive participation, when you have free time. One of our goals is that you rediscover the joys of reading for pleasure and gain insight through reading lots of children's books (electronic and print): graphic novels and novels in verse, fantasy in new worlds and fiction about the past, information about the world and fiction about the struggles of daily life. If you are to immerse children in reading good books that add to their lives, not put them to sleep, you need to find those books for your life as well.

As you learn *about* literature in the chapters of this textbook be sure that you immerse yourself in interesting books. Read picture books and novels, fiction and nonfiction, stories and poems, to reclaim these values for yourself and for the children with whom you will interact. We have kept this textbook concise with many invitations for you as a reader to encourage you to reclaim your reading life. We want you to experience reading as life—not school work.

 # Invitations for Further Investigation

- Document the types of stories that you use across a single day and the different ways in which you tell those stories. Share your data with a small group and create a list of roles that stories play in your lives.

- Create a time line of stories that you remember from your childhood at home and at school. What kinds of stories were significant (oral, written, film, etc.)? What specific stories do you remember interacting with over and over? Were there memorable people with whom you interacted around these stories? Why were those stories important to you as a child? Write or draw one of your literacy memories to share,

- Reflect on your reading life as an adult. What types of books or materials do you read as an adult? If you do not read for pleasure as an adult, trace why reading does not play a role in your life.

- Read one of the landmark studies and reflect on the significance of this study for the role of literature in the lives of children today. Another option is to divide into six groups with each group reading and discussing one of the landmark studies. Then form a new group with one person representing each study. Brainstorm a list of implications for your own work as a parent or educator.

References

Anderson, R. C., Hiebert, E. H., Scott, J. A., & Wilkinson, I. A. G. (1985). *Becoming a nation of readers: The report of the Commission on Reading.* Washington, DC: National Institute of Education.

Applebee, A. N. (1978). *The child's concept of story.* Chicago, IL: University of Chicago.

Bogart, Dave (Ed.). (2012) *Library and book trade almanac* (57th ed.). Medford, NJ: Information Today.

Browning, E. B. (1902). Reading. In K. D. Wiggins & N. A. Smith (Eds.), *Golden numbers.* New York: Doubleday.

Butler, D. (1975). *Cushla and her books.* Boston, MA: Horn Book.

Carlsen, G. R., & Sherrill, A. (1988). *Voices of readers: How we come to love books.* Urbana, IL: NCTE.

Children's books in print, 2011. (2012). Armenia, NY: Grey House Publishing.

Durkin, D. (1966). *Children who read early.* New York: Columbia Teachers College Press.

Eldredge, J. L., & Butterfield, D. (1986). Alternatives to traditional reading instruction. *The Reading Teacher, 40,* 32–37.

Fielding, L. G., Wilson, P. T., & Anderson, R. C. (1986). A new focus on free reading: The role of trade books in reading instruction. In T. Raphael (Ed.), *The contexts of school-based literacy* (pp. 149–160). New York: Random House.

Leinhardt, G., Zigmond, N., & Cooley, W. W. (1981). Reading instruction and its effects. *American Educational Research Journal, 18,* 343–361.

National Endowment for the Arts. (2004). *Reading at risk: A survey of literary reading in America.* Research Division Report #46. Washington, DC: National Endowment for the Arts.

National Endowment for the Arts. (2007). *To read or not to read: A question of national significance.* Research Division Report #47. Washington, DC: National Endowment for the Arts.

National Endowment for the Arts. (2008). *Reading on the rise: A new chapter in American literacy.* Retrieved from www.arts.gov/research/Research_brochures.php

Rosen, H. (1986). *Stories and meanings.* London, England: NATE.

Rosenblatt, L. (1938). *Literature as exploration.* Chicago, IL: Modern Language Association.

Chapter Two

Learning about Children and Literature

My Book!

I did it!
I did it!
Come and look
At what I've done!
I read a book!
When someone wrote it
Long ago
For me to read,
How did he know
That this was the book
I'd take from the shelf

And lie on the floor
And read by myself?
I really read it!
Just like that!
Word by word,
From first to last!
I'm sleeping with
This book in bed,
This is the FIRST book
I've ever read!

—*David L. Harrison*

We can engage children as readers by not only placing reading materials in their hands that interest them and are appropriate for their reading abilities but that also challenge them as inquirers. Finding the right book is always a combination of knowing the child and knowing the books. This intersection of books and readers is based on building our knowledge of children and developing our strategies for selecting books.

Connecting Children with Books: Know the Child

The best teachers know their students well—their long-term and short-term interests, their home environment and families, their friends and social activities, their hobbies, their skills, their hopes or plans for the future, and the kind of books they currently select in free-choice situations. Children's interests have been shown to be one of the most powerful motivating forces available to teachers. Because there are now books on almost every topic conceivable and written at varying degrees of difficulty, you should be able to assemble a collection of books from which your students can make satisfying selections.

You will also want to have a grasp of your students' reading and listening levels. Young children, in particular, are able to listen to and comprehend more difficult material than they are able to read and comprehend. For these children, teachers can read aloud more challenging books while providing a choice of easier reading material for independent reading.

Considering the Age-Level Characteristics of Children

Teachers and librarians who are consistently successful in helping children find books narrow the field of choices by first considering general factors such as the types of books and topics appropriate for children of a particular age level. Children's physical, cognitive, language, and moral development are important considerations, as is their developing concept of story. Teachers and librarians also consider personal and cultural factors such as the child's interests, experiences, and reading ability to select specific titles. Knowing children's general reading preferences provides some guidance in book selection, but there is no substitute for personally knowing each child.

Ages 0 to 2   In choosing books for infants, consider the practical aspects of physical development, such as how well infants can see the illustrations and how long they will sit still for a book experience. Often these books are collections of nursery rhymes, concept books, board books, and interactive books. Common features of these book types and formats are simplicity of content or story; repetitive text or language patterns; clearly defined, brightly colored illustrations, usually on a plain background; physical durability; and opportunities for the child to participate or interact with the book.

A classic example of a book for children ages 0 to 2 is Dorothy Kunhardt's interactive book *Pat the Bunny* (1962/2001). More recent examples are Harriet Ziefert's (2002) *Who Said Moo?* illustrated by Simms Taback, an interactive board book with lift-the-flaps and repetitive phrases, and *Hello Baby!* by Mem Fox (2009), illustrated by Steve Jenkins, composed of rhymes that are a call-and-response between the adult and child. The best baby books, whether wordless or with brief text, invite the reader and listener to "talk" their way through the book, which promotes oral language development—a child's first step toward literacy.

Ages 2 to 4   Many of the book types enjoyed by babies are also enjoyed by toddlers, but with slight differences in emphasis. Nursery rhymes, for example, are often committed to memory by toddlers. Concept books can now include letters (ABC books), numbers (counting books), and more complex concepts such as opposites. Word books, another type of concept book that encourages labeling, promote vocabulary development and can include creative options as in *Seymour Chwast Says—Get Dressed* (2012) with foldout pages of labeled types of clothing for all kinds of adventures.

Picture storybooks that appeal to this age group feature simple plots, illustrations that tell part of the story, and characters who exhibit the physical skills (running, whistling, buttoning clothes, tying shoes) that 2- to 4-year-olds take pride in accomplishing. A perennial favorite, *Owen* by Kevin Henkes (1993), and a more recent book, *Will Sheila Share?* by Elivia Savadier (2008), feature protagonists who overcome problems typical of children at this age. Children also enjoy wordless books because they can "read" the pictures and enjoy the books independently, and folktales because of their relatively simple plots, repetitive aspects, and two-dimensional, easy-to-understand characters.

Ages 4 to 7 Increasing independence and enthusiasm for finding out about the world are characteristics of 4- to 7-year-olds. Stories in which children interact with other children, spend time away from home, begin school, and learn interesting facts are popular. Picture storybooks, folktales, and informational picture books will be at the heart of literature experiences during these years. Rosemary Wells's (2008) *Yoko Writes Her Name* and Marla Frazee's (2008) *A Couple of Boys Have the Best Week Ever* are excellent books as is the informational book *What Do You Do with a Tail Like This?* by Steve Jenkins and Robin Page (2003).

Most children become emergent readers at this age level. Easy-to-read books and predictable books make use of familiar words, word and sentence patterns, illustration clues, and rhyme to make the text easier to read. Often these books appear in a series. Books for beginning readers should connect to children's interests, experiences, and reading abilities to support them in their initial reading experiences. The classic, easy-to-read Frog and Toad series by Arnold Lobel has been enjoyed by young children for forty years and can be used alongside more recent series like Cynthia Rylant's Henry and Mudge books and Wong Herbert Yee's Mouse and Mole books.

Ages 7 to 9 Most 7- to 9-year-old children become readers as they are beginning to understand and accept others' perspectives, recognize that life and people do not fit into neat categories, and develop an understanding of time in the past and future. They also start to assert their growing abilities to meet their own needs. With these skills they enjoy reading or listening to books about the lives of children of the past and present in picture books, transitional books, and some novels. Fittingly, these books often center on the adventures of young characters within their neighborhoods and communities, such as Lenore Look's Ruby Lu and Alvin Ho books, Nikki Grimes's Dyamonde Daniel series, Sara Pennypacker's Clementine series, and Annie Barrows' Ivy and Bean series.

Ages 9 to 14 With their rapidly developing physical and mental skills and abilities, 9- to 14-year-olds are ready for more complicated story plots, including such devices as flashback, symbolism, and dialects of earlier times or different cultures. Both historical fiction and science fiction, which are set in the distant past and the distant future, respectively, are understood and enjoyed. They also enjoy stories about their peers who are growing up, asserting themselves, using their newfound skills, moving toward independence, and meeting challenges, as in survival stories. They are better able to recognize the legitimacy of opinions, mores, and lifestyles different from their own and so enjoy stories that present alternative points of view, nontraditional characters, and moral dilemmas. Some good examples include *Inside Out and Back Again* (historical fiction, Vietnamese immigrant) by Thanhha Lai (2011), *The Arrival* (fantasy, wordless novel) by Shaun Tan (2007), and *Red Kayak* (realistic fiction with a moral dilemma) by Priscilla Cummings (2004).

Considering Research on Children's Reading Interests

Research studies on reading interest, reading preference, and reading choice provide useful information for selecting books for collections and children. These studies try to infer what students like to read. Generally, a **reading interest** suggests a feeling one has toward particular reading material; a **reading preference** implies making a choice from two or more options; a **reading choice** study investigates the materials that children select and read from a specific collection. These studies do not always provide an opportunity for students to express their interests and children can only select from the books offered by the researcher as an option. Although the findings from this body of research can be useful, the results of these studies reflect the reading interests of groups of students, not individuals.

Many studies of children's reading interests have been conducted during the past fifty years. Differences in the choices offered to children and in the ways data were gathered make generalization difficult, but a few patterns have emerged from these studies:

- There are no significant differences between the reading preferences of boys and girls before age 9. The greatest differences in reading preferences of boys and girls occur between ages 10 and 13, a result of socialization and media images.

- Boys and girls in the middle grades (ages 10 to 13) share a pronounced preference for mysteries along with humor, adventure, and animals.

- Preferences of boys in the middle grades include nonfiction, adventure, sports, science fiction, and fantasy stories, while the preferences of girls at this age include fantasy stories, animal stories, romance, and stories about people.

Certain characteristics of books may matter as much to a young reader as the topic. The patterns across studies (Langerman, 1990; Worthy, 1996; Worthy, Moorman, & Turner, 1999) include the appeal of:

- Short books or books with short sections or chapters
- Picture books, illustrated books, comic books, and novels in which illustrations are interspersed throughout the book
- Cover illustrations that suggest the topic of the story
- Episodic plots or progressive chronological plots that can be easily followed
- Quick start to the story with action beginning on the first or second page to hook the reader
- Rapid introduction to main characters and a focus on only a few main characters
- Characters that are the age of the reader or slightly older
- Books based on movies and television

In addition, trivia books such as the *Guinness Book of World Records,* sports statistics books, joke books, and guides for video and computer games are appealing to some readers. Although you will want to encourage children to read books of excellent quality, the first step is to create an enthusiasm about books and reading and so start with high appeal books. Once children are willing readers, you can find many opportunities to booktalk and read aloud excellent books that they will come to love and want to read.

These studies support adults in making general predictions about the types of books students of a certain age might enjoy, but general reading preferences do not capture individual reading interests. Since most teachers and school librarians work with particular groups of children over an extended time, they can learn the interests of each child and gain the knowledge needed to successfully match children and books.

Discovering Reading Interests of Individual Students

Learning students' reading interests can be accomplished by observing and keeping a record of students' choices of books from the classroom collection or from the school library media center. You can also learn about children's interests through their free-choice writing and journal writing or by directly asking children to list their interests or the type of books they like to read. You can get to know students by talking and listening to them in whole-class sharing and in one-to-one conferences. The following questions might start a dialogue between you and a child:

1. Who is in your family? Tell me about each family member.
2. What are your favorite things to do?
3. Are you good at doing something? Tell me about it.
4. What would you like to learn more about?
5. What do you like to spend most of your free time doing? What do you do after school? On weekends?
6. Do you like fiction (stories) or nonfiction (information books) better?
7. What kinds of stories do you like to hear?
8. Which topics do you enjoy reading about in information books?
9. Are there some kinds of books you don't enjoy reading? If so, why?
10. Tell me about a book that you especially enjoyed and why you enjoyed it.

Yet another way for teachers and librarians to keep current on students' reading interests is to conduct *reading interest inventories* several times a year. These steps are one way to conduct a classroom reading interest inventory:

1. Collect thirty to forty appropriate books that are new to your students and represent a wide variety of genres and topics.
2. Number the books by inserting paper markers with numbers at the top.
3. Note the number and genre of each book on a master list.
4. Design a response form for students (Would You Like to Read This Book?), where children circle yes or no next to each number.
5. Place the books in numerical order on tables and shelves around the classroom or media center.
6. Give students 20–30 minutes to make the circuit, browse the books, and mark their response forms.
7. Collect and tally their responses and compare to your master list to arrive at the types of books which seem to most interest students.

Classroom reading interest inventories provide teachers and librarians with helpful information about students' current interests and introduce children to new genres, topics, and books. Many students will discover a book that they want to read from the books set out in this manner. Common sense tells us that children will engage more vigorously to reading or learning something that they are interested in than something that they find boring. Interest generates engagement, and so introducing students to good books on topics that satisfy their individual interests is essential.

Evaluating Text Complexity

Teachers and librarians typically consider the readability and conceptual difficulty of books in selecting books to meet the reading needs of the children with whom they work. *Readability* is an estimate of a text's difficulty based on its vocabulary (common versus uncommon words) and sentence structure (short, simple sentences versus long, complex sentences). *Conceptual difficulty* is related to the complexity of ideas in the book and how these ideas are presented. Symbolism and lengthy description contribute to the complexity of ideas, just as the use of flashback contributes to the complexity of plot presentation.

Students' reading levels differ greatly in most classrooms, making it important to provide materials of varying difficulty. Being able to assess the difficulty of reading materials is helpful; however, for independent, leisure reading, students should be encouraged to read books of interest to them regardless of the level, so long as they are capable of comprehending the material and want to read it. As adults, we would not appreciate being told that we cannot read a book because someone else thinks it's too easy for us. We should respect the rights of children to select their own books for leisure reading if our goal is that they become lifelong readers. Their selections for personal reading are balanced with teachers' selections of complex texts for instructional purposes.

The Common Core State Standards (CCSS) focus attention on *text complexity* and the need for children to engage with texts that gradually increase in difficulty of ideas and textual structures. This focus on rigor in reading is based on the goal that students understand the level of texts necessary for success in college and careers by the time they graduate from high school (Fisher, Frey, & Lapp, 2012). Text complexity is determined by consideration of three dimensions discussed in the Common Core State Standards (National Governors Association Center for Best Practices and Council of Chief State School Officers, 2010).

1. **Qualitative dimensions of text complexity**—informed decisions by teachers and librarians about the difficulty of a text based on their judgments about the influences of these aspects on a specific reader:

    a. **Levels of meaning and purpose.** Determining greater or less complexity based on how many layers of meaning are in the text and whether the purpose of the text is implicit or clearly stated.

    b. **Structure.** Examining if the text is organized around a simple, well-marked, and conventional structure that readers will quickly recognize or a structure that is unusual and seldom used, involving elements such as flashbacks or complex graphics.

    c. **Language conventionality and clarity.** Examining whether the text uses clear, literal, contemporary language or relies on figurative, ambiguous, archaic, academic, or unfamiliar language.

    d. **Knowledge demands.** Evaluating assumptions about the types of life experiences and cultural or content knowledge that readers will bring to a particular text.

2. **Quantitative dimensions of text complexity**—computerized readability formulas that rate a text on word familiarity, word length, and sentence length, based on the assumption that unfamiliar words, long words, and long sentences increase complexity.

   a. **Possible formulas** include the Fry Readability Graph, the Dale-Chall Readability Formula, the Lexile Framework, the Accelerated Reader ATOS formula, and Coh-Metrix.

   b. **CCSS recommends the Lexile Framework** (www.lexile.com; Schnick, 2000), but notes that this framework does not provide accurate levels for K–1 reading materials, poetry, and complex narrative fiction for young adults.

3. **Reader and task considerations related to the texts**—considering the fit between a text and a specific reader who is engaging in a particular task with that text.

   a. **Experiences and strategies of the reader** including cognitive abilities, motivation, interest, knowledge, and experiences.

   b. **Task** that the reader is asked to engage in with a particular text.

Considering all three dimensions of text complexity, instead of relying only on quantitative leveling of texts, such as the Lexile levels, is essential. Readability formulas may be helpful in selecting books but they have drawbacks. Although sentence length and word choice are important, a student's prior knowledge or interest in a topic cannot be factored into a formula. The formulas also have difficulty measuring conceptual difficulty, the complexity of the ideas in a book, and how these ideas are presented. Symbolism, abstraction, and figurative language contribute to the complexity of ideas, just as the use of nonlinear plots or shifting points of view contribute to the complexity of the plot. *Skellig* (Almond, 1999) is a novel of magical realism in which two children become involved with an otherworldly being hidden in a garage. The text has easy vocabulary and short sentences with a readability of around grade 3.5. Yet the concepts of spirituality, faith, and prejudice cast the conceptual level of this novel at a higher level, making it more appropriate for students who are 11 to 15, depending on the background of the specific student. Another example is John Stenbeck's *Grapes of Wrath* (1939), which scores at a second to third grade level on quantitative measures because it uses familiar words and short sentences through dialogue. Teachers, however, note that the many layers of meaning and mature themes indicate that this book is meant for grades 6 and above.

Information on readability can be found on some book covers and many online databases list the Lexile reading levels. Teachers can also estimate difficulty by selecting a page of uninterrupted text, reading the first sentence, counting the words in the sentence, and looking to see if this length appears to be typical of the rest of the page. The page can then be read for word difficulty, noting the frequency of words students will likely not know.

The Common Core State Standards include a list of Text Exemplars consisting of stories, poems, and informational texts at each grade level. Excerpts from these texts are provided to help educators explore text complexity. This list of texts is not intended as books for all students to read; instead these texts are provided as exemplars for teachers to use in understanding text complexity so they can make more effective selections for their students. Teachers would never want to limit children to reading only the books on these lists since many are classics that are dated and do not reflect the multicultural or global nature of the world.

Connecting Children with Books: Know the Books

Teachers and librarians who read children's books regularly and who are familiar with a wide variety of genres as well as informed about recently published books are more likely to know the right book for the right moment and purpose in a child's life. Reading widely also allows you to share your reactions to a book with children and engage with them as a reader, rather than as an expert. Other ways to become familiar with a variety of books include sharing information about books with colleagues, reading book reviews, and consulting award lists. The resources you can consult in developing knowledge of books and reference sources are integrated throughout the chapters in this text.

After you have read a number of books from a genre, particularly notable examples, you will develop a framework for thinking about that type of book, whether or not you have read an individual title. You will also develop a sense of how to evaluate the ways in which authors use literary and visual elements within particular genres. Criteria for evaluating literary and visual elements of literature within specific genres are discussed throughout the chapters in this text and so you will gradually develop your own understandings and internal sense of these criteria.

Balance and Variety in Book Selections

In your work with children, you will need to know many kinds of books because all classrooms include children with a wide range of reading abilities and interests. You have your own reading preferences but need to go beyond those interests to gain familiarity with many different types of books, including picture books, easy-to-read books, short chapter books, longer books, and books of prose, poetry, fiction, and nonfiction. Balance among the *genres of literature* as well as *variety in topics* are essential. The chapters in this text will help you build this range and balance.

The books available in the classrooms and chosen as read-alouds also need to be varied in order to challenge students and enhance their language and cognitive development. The *mood* of the books should include stories that are sad, humorous, silly, serious, reflective, boisterous, suspenseful, or scary. A steady diet of light, humorous books might appeal to students at first, but eventually, the sameness will become boring. Reading aloud books with the same predominant emotion ignores the rapid change and growth in personal lives and choices that are the hallmark of youth.

A balance between male and female main characters over the course of a year is necessary to meet the needs of children and to help members of each gender understand more fully the perspectives, problems, and feelings of members of the opposite gender. Classroom and school library collections need to have a wide range of topics with a balance of male and female main characters. In addition, understanding and empathy for people with physical, emotional, mental, and behavioral disabilities can be gained through portrayals in books. When a positive image of people with disabilities is conveyed through books, children with disabilities encounter characters like themselves.

The representation of people of color as main characters is essential to presenting a realistic view of society and the world and to challenging stereotypes. Through well-written **multicultural literature,** children of color can see characters from backgrounds similar to their own in leading roles. Characters with whom one can identify permit a deeper involvement in literature and help children understand situations in their own lives. Children also need to see that someone from a different race, ethnic group, or religion has many of the same needs and feelings as they do, as well as come to recognize and value differences in experiences and cultural views. Literature by and about people different from oneself can develop an understanding and appreciation for difference as a resource, not a problem.

Global and international literature, literature from nations and regions of the world, should also be included in read-aloud choices and in classroom and library collections in order to encourage the development of global understanding. Through reading or listening to books about the lives of children from global cultures, children will experience cultural literacy on a worldwide basis.

Finding this range of books and staying current with new releases involves familiarity with the major book awards and review journals as well as attending professional conferences to meet authors and illustrators and attend sessions on literature. These resources will allow you to locate the best in books being published for children and books that meet specific needs for diversity in collections.

Book Awards

Book award programs have been established to elevate and maintain the literary and artistic standards of children's books and honor the authors whose work is judged by experts in the field to have the greatest merit. These awards provide teachers and librarians with one source for selecting excellent works of literature to share with children. Table 2.1 lists the major awards for children's books in the U.S., Canada, and Great Britain. The winners of these major children's book awards and other awards for specific genres or topics are found in Appendix A.

Table 2.1 Major U.S., Canadian, and British Children's Book Awards		
Award/Country	**Period**	**For/Year Established**
Newbery Medal/U.S.	Annual	The most distinguished contribution to children's literature published in the previous year. Given to a U.S. author. Established 1922.
Caldecott Medal/U.S.	Annual	The most distinguished picture book for children published in the previous year. Given to a U.S. illustrator. Established 1938.
National Book Award for Young People's Literature/U.S.	Annual	Outstanding contribution to children's literature in terms of literary merit published in the previous year. Given to a U.S. writer. Established 1996.
Coretta Scott King Awards for Writing and for Illustration/U.S.	Annual, two awards	Outstanding contribution to literature for children and young people by an African-American author and illustrator published in the previous year. Established 1970 (author award)/1974 (illustrator award).
Pura Belpré Awards for Writing and Illustration/U.S.	Annual, two awards	Writing and illustration in a work of literature for youth published in the previous year by a Latino writer and illustrator whose work portrays, affirms, and celebrates Latino cultural experiences. Established 1996.
Governor General's Literature for Children Award for Writing/Canada	Annual	Best book for children published in the previous year. Separate prizes for works in English and French. Established 1987.

(Continued)

Table 2.1 Continued		
Award/Country	**Period**	**For/Year Established**
Governor General's Literature for Children Award for Illustration/ Canada	Annual	Best illustration in a children's work published in the previous year. Separate prizes for works in English and French. Established 1987.
Carnegie Medal/Great Britain	Annual	The most distinguished contribution to children's literature first published in the United Kingdom in the previous year. Given to an author. Established 1936.
Kate Greenaway Medal/ Great Britain	Annual	The most distinguished picture book for children first published in the United Kingdom in the previous year. Given to an illustrator. Established 1956.

Some book award programs involve children in the selection process. The Children's Choices Project, sponsored by the International Reading Association/Children's Book Council Joint Committee, features newly published books selected by children around the country. The list of winners appears each October in *The Reading Teacher* and is available at www.reading.org.

Most states also have their own children's choices award and programs. Usually a ballot of book titles is generated for certain age ranges, such as 5–8 and 9–12, based on nominations from teachers, librarians, or children. The list is circulated across the state for children to vote on their favorites. Balloting usually occurs in the spring to permit reading time over the course of a school year. More information on state children's book awards and programs, including websites for many of the state programs, can be found at www.childrensbooks.about.com/cs/stateawards.

Another book award program, Teachers' Choices Project, sponsored by the International Reading Association, also develops an annual list of winners. Teachers read and vote for recently published books worthy of use in the classroom, then develop the Teachers' Choices Booklist. The list appears in the November issue of *The Reading Teacher* and is available at www.reading.org.

Review Journals

Journals that review children's books and feature current topics in the field of children's literature are an important source of information for teachers and librarians. Professional teacher journals on literacy for elementary teachers, such as *The Reading Teacher* (www.reading.org) and *Language Arts* (www.ncte.org), have columns that review new children's books. *The Journal of Children's Literature* (www.childrensliteratureassembly.org), a journal dedicated to children's literature and those involved in it, also has review sections of new children's books. In addition, these journals contain articles discussing effective strategies for incorporating literature into reading and content-area instruction and for bringing children and books together.

The following review journals offer evaluative reviews and suggested grade-level ranges for books. These reviews primarily come from the perspectives of librarians and literary critics. These journals are readily available in most university libraries as well as some school and public libraries.

- *Booklist* (www.ala.org/offices/publishing/booklist). This journal reviews current print and nonprint materials for children and adults that are worthy of consideration for purchase by public libraries and school media centers. It also has a free online version at www.booklistonline.com.
- *The Bulletin of the Center for Children's Books* (http://bccb.lis.illinois.edu). This publication reviews current children's books, assigning a recommendation code to each.
- *The Horn Book Magazine* (www.hbook.com). This magazine includes detailed reviews of high quality children's books. The Newbery and Caldecott acceptance speeches are featured in the July/August issue.
- *Kirkus Reviews* (www.kirkusreviews.com). This publication annually reviews approximately 5,000 titles of prepublication books for adults and children.
- *School Library Journal* (www.schoollibraryjournal.com). This journal includes both negative and positive reviews of most children's books published. It also includes articles of interest to school librarians.

Professional Associations and Websites

Major professional associations that have strong connections to the field of children's literature and so provide a range of services, projects, and resources of use to teachers and librarians include:

- **Association for Library Service to Children** (ALSC; www.ala.org/alsc). This professional group is a division of the American Library Association and provides services primarily to librarians and media specialists as well as supports major book awards in children's literature.
- **International Reading Association** (IRA; www.reading.org and clrsig.org). This professional organization offers services to teachers of language, literacy, and literature. Its Children's Literature and Reading Special Interest Group has a website, awards, activities, and journal, *The Dragon Lode*.
- **National Council of Teachers of English** (NCTE; www.ncte.org and www.childrens literatureassembly.org). This professional association addresses teaching and research in language and literature from preschool through college. The Children's Literature Assembly at NCTE promotes literature in the lives of children, supports several awards, provides a forum for exchange among teachers of children's literature, and publishes the *Journal of Children's Literature*.
- **Children's Literature Association** (ChLA; www.childlitassn.org). This professional group has many members from the field of English and addresses criticism, research, and teaching of children's literature through its journal the *Children's Literature Association Quarterly*.
- **United States Board of Books for Young People** (USBBY; www.usbby.org and www.ibby .org). This professional group of publishers, authors, educators, and librarians promotes the use of literature to build international understanding and the right of all children to have books in their own language and culture. The U.S. national section is part of the international organization, IBBY, which publishes *Bookbird: A Journal of International Children's Literature*.

The following websites are helpful in locating professional information about children's literature:

- **Carol Hurst's Children's Literature Site** (www.carolhurst.com). This educational consultant provides book reviews, curriculum ideas, themes, and professional topics.

- **Children's Book Council** (CBC; www.cbcbooks.org). This nonprofit association of children's book publishers offers book-related literacy materials for children and information on National Children's Book Week in May.

- **Children's Literature Comprehensive Database** (www.clcd.com). This independent media site gathers the reviews from a range of journals and websites for each book and provides readability ratings for books.

- **Cooperative Children's Book Center** (CCBC; www.education.wisc.edu/ccbc). This children's literature research library site provides information about collections, upcoming events, and publications. CCBC publishes an annual report of trends in children's literature and recommended books.

- **Worlds of Words** (wowlit.org). This initiative focuses on the use of literature to build global and cultural understanding and includes a searchable database, an online book review journal that highlights cultural authenticity, an online journal of classroom vignettes about global literature, book lists and resources, and a regular blog of current issues.

Connecting Resistant Readers with Books: Know the Books *and* the Readers

Children and adolescents resist or reject reading for many reasons. Reaching these *resistant readers* who can read but choose not to requires that parents, teachers, and librarians know books as well as those readers in order to find just the right books for them. Because children resist reading for different reasons, the types of books we offer also need to vary.

Some children who have good to excellent comprehension, few difficulties in decoding, and average reading rates by third or fourth grade rarely read or do not like to read. With little or no reading practice, these children eventually lose their former reading achievement levels. Sometimes these children perceive the books they are forced to read in school as irrelevant to their lives and therefore boring. They may lack encouragement at home to read for recreational reasons. They seldom or never go to public or school libraries to select books for their reading enjoyment because the emphasis by their teachers and parents is almost exclusively on improving their reading skills. Neither their parents nor their teachers serve as reading role models, nor do they persist in their efforts to foster a love of reading because their focus is on raising test scores to the detriment of other aspects of reading. These children desperately need books that relate closely to their interests and lives in all kinds of formats.

Some children struggle with reading from the earliest grades and become discouraged. Most of them can decode, but this skill remains a conscious cognitive act rather than an automatic process. The act of concentrating on decoding words slows the reading rate and fluency of these children, hampers their ability to recall what they have read to make sense of the text, and tires them mentally. Others in this group are fluent decoders who have difficulty comprehending what they read. Experiencing ridicule by their peers and embarrassment in class for their reading difficulties has taught them to avoid reading whenever possible. These are the children for whom regular immersion in reading whole books for pleasure is especially important to develop reading fluency. They need books that are more supportive, such as easy-to-read books, transitional chapter books, graphic novels, and informational books heavy in visuals.

Some children resist reading because the books they are asked to read do not depict their lives or the lives of those who are significant to them in their families and communities. Children's books are more multiculturally and globally diverse today than in years past, but books that reflect the true range of cultural diversity of our society are still underrepresented in the broader body of children's books. Unless adults make a conscious effort to search out books reflecting a range of cultural identities, children may not find themselves in books and so resist reading because they see these books as threatening and demeaning to their identities and irrelevant to their lives.

Students learning English as a second language sometimes encounter difficulties in reading because they lack strong vocabularies and well-developed sentence structures in English to draw on when encountering English language texts. They are also often asked to read texts that portray unfamiliar experiences and cultural norms and thus avoid reading whenever possible. This group is large and growing and so teachers need to be familiar with predictable books, concept books, and wordless books as well as books from a range of global cultures.

Boys who resist reading may do so in part because of the preponderance of female teachers in U.S. schools (75% in grades K–12) who tend to select reading materials that do not always appeal to boys (Brozo, 2005). Their resistance to reading also may stem from the perception that reading, because it is quiet and passive, is a female activity, or because teachers ask them to read silently from fiction when they prefer to interact socially with peers around an informational book. On average, boys exhibit more difficulty in reading and other language areas than girls. Some boys are avid readers, but of materials that schools do not traditionally recognize, such as magazines, Internet websites, and informational books. Informative sources about boys and reading are *Reading Don't Fix No Chevys: Literacy in the Lives of Young Men* (Smith & Wilhelm, 2002); *Teaching Reading to Black Adolescent Males: Closing the Achievement Gap* (Tatum, 2005); *Reluctant Readers: Connecting Students and Books for Successful Reading Experiences* (Jobe & Dayton-Sakari, 1999); and *Connecting Boys with Books 2: Closing the Reading Gap* (Sullivan, 2009).

By connecting books with readers we can inspire young people to love reading and to become aware of its power to inform, entertain, educate, and transform as well as help them develop the habits of lifelong readers.

Invitations for Further Investigation

- Conduct a reading interest inventory with a group of students. Analyze your findings, then suggest appropriate titles to children for independent reading from books available in the school.
- Observe and document the reading habits and literary selections of three children over a period of several weeks. Select one avid reader, one typical reader, and one resistant reader for your observations.
- Create a list of favorite books that you remember reading as a child and use a database to look up the Lexile ratings for those texts. Consider the quantitative ratings for these books and how they match up with when you actually read them as a child. What factors in your own characteristics as a reader influenced your ability to read and understand these books?
- Explore a book review journal or website that interests you and provide a description of the resources and services available on that site for class members.
- Locate your state's children's choices book award and read some of the current nominees or recent winners of the award. Evaluate their student appeal, literary quality, complexity, curricular value, and illustration quality.
- Read some of the research on boys as readers and create a list of the types of books and reading materials and practices that may be more appealing and engaging for boys who resist reading.

References

Almond, D. (1999). *Skellig*. New York: Delacorte.

Brozo, W. G. (2005). Gender and reading literacy. *Reading Today, 22*(4), 18.

Chwast, S. (2012). *Seymour Chwast says—Get dressed!* New York: Appleseed.

Cummings, P. (2004). *Red kayak*. New York: Dutton.

Fisher, D., Frey, N., & Lapp, D. (2012). *Text complexity: Raising rigor in reading*. Newark, DE: IRA.

Fox, M. (2009). *Hello baby!* Jenkins, S. (Illus.) New York: Beach Lane.

Frazee, M. (2008). *A couple of boys have the best week ever*. New York: Harcourt.

Harrison, D. L. (1993). My book! In D. L. Harrison (Ed.), *Somebody catch my homework*. Lewin, B. (Illus.). Honesdale, PA: Boyds Mills.

Henkes, K. (1993). *Owen*. New York: Greenwillow.

Jenkins, S., & Page, R. (2003). *What do you do with a tail like this?* New York: Houghton.

Jobe, R., & Dayton-Sakari, M. (1999). *Reluctant readers: Connecting students and books for successful reading experiences*. Markham, ON: Pembroke.

Kunhardt, D. (1962/2001). *Pat the bunny*. New York: Golden.

Lai, T. (2011). *Inside out and back again*. New York: HarperCollins.

Langerman, D. (1990). Books and boys: Gender preferences and book selection. *School Library Journal 36*(3), 132–136.

National Governors Association Center for Best Practices & Council of Chief School Officers. (2010).

Common Core State Standards for English language arts and literacy in history/social studies, science and technical subjects. Washington, DC: Authors. Available from http://www.corestandards.org/

Savadier, E. (2008). *Will Sheila share?* New York: Roaring Brook.

Schnick, T. (2000). *The Lexile framework: An introduction for educators*. Durham, NC: MetaMetrics.

Smith, M. W., & Wilhelm, J. D. (2002). *Reading don't fix no Chevys: Literacy in the lives of young men*. Portsmouth, NH: Heinemann.

Steinbeck, J. (1939). *The grapes of wrath*. New York: Viking.

Sullivan, M. (2009). *Connecting boys with books 2: Closing the reading gap*. Chicago, IL: American Library Association.

Tan, S. (2007). *The arrival*. New York: Scholastic.

Tatum, A. (2005). *Teaching reading to black adolescent males: Closing the achievement gap*. Portland, ME: Stenhouse.

Wells, R. (2008). *Yoko writes her name*. New York: Hyperion.

Worthy, J. (1996). Removing barriers to voluntary reading: The role of school and classroom libraries. *Language Arts 73*, 483–492.

Worthy, J., Moorman, M., & Turner, M. (1999). What Johnny likes to read is hard to find in school. *Reading Research Quarterly 34*(1), 12–27.

Ziefert, H. (2002). *Who said moo?* Tabak, S. (Illus). Brooklyn, NY: Handprint Books.

Chapter Three

earning
about
Literature

A Book

I'm a strange contradiction; I'm new and I'm old,
I'm often in tatters, and oft deck'd in gold;
Though I never could read, yet letter'd I'm found;
Though blind, I enlighten; though loose, I am bound—
I am always in black, and I'm always in white;
I am grave and I'm gay, I am heavy and light.
In form too I differ—I'm thick and I'm thin,
I've no flesh, and no bones, yet I'm covered with skin;
I've more points than the compass, more stops than the flute—
I sing without voice, without speaking confute;
I'm English, I'm German, I'm French and I'm Dutch;
Some love me too fondly; some slight me too much;
I often die soon, though I sometimes live ages,
And no monarch alive has so many pages.

—*Hannah More*

The ways in which you study literature with children can either encourage them to share their connections and engage in dialogue and analysis or cause them to lose confidence in their abilities to construct the "correct" interpretation. You can organize your approach by genres, literary elements, themes and topics, authors and illustrators, and notable books. An understanding of literary elements and genre is particularly significant for you in reading widely and learning to evaluate the quality and range of literature for children.

Approaches to Studying and Interpreting Literature

The scholarly study of literature focuses on the meanings found in a work of literature and how readers construct that meaning. These approaches recognize literature as a discipline and separate course of study, a common focus in high schools and universities. What is often overlooked in elementary contexts is that literature is itself a content area; a way of knowing the world that differs from other ways of knowing such as science or history. Instead literature in elementary classrooms is usually viewed only as a material used to teach reading, math, science, or social studies.

Although teachers of literature in secondary schools and universities view literature as a field of study, their focus has often been on teaching the formal art of words and texts and introducing students to the classics and a literary heritage rather than on experiencing literature as life. When readers subject a work to deep analysis through exact and careful reading, it is referred to as **New Criticism** or **structural criticism.** In this approach, the analysis of the words and structure of a work is the focus; the goal is to find the "correct" interpretation.

Structural criticism dominated literature classrooms until the 1960s; many teachers continue to use this method today. Most teachers using this approach take the view that there is one correct interpretation of any work of literature and so reading is a process of taking from the text only what was put there by the author. Successful readers of literature are determined by how closely their interpretations match the "authorized" interpretation. Students' responses are thus limited to naming (or guessing) the "right" answers to teachers' questions.

Many of you experienced this approach as students and know the frustration and apathy that can result from trying to replicate the teacher's interpretation. You may have even been one of many readers who did not bother with reading the actual book and instead consulted Cliff Note study guides. Structural approaches do not encourage students to see reading as relevant to their lives outside of school or help students develop confidence in their abilities to construct meaning and connect those meanings to their lives. Often these experiences are so painful that students stop reading books other than to meet school assignments.

Louise Rosenblatt introduced **reader response theory** or the **transactional view of reading** in 1938. She asserted that what the reader brings to the reading act—his or her world of experience, personality, cultural views, and current frame of mind—is just as important in interpreting the text as what the author writes. Reading is thus a fusion of text and reader. Consequently, any text's meaning will vary from reader to reader and, indeed, from reading to reading of the same text by the same reader. Most of us have experienced reading a book only to discover that a friend has reacted to or interpreted the same book quite differently. Rosenblatt (1978) argues the text of any book guides and constrains the interpretation that is made, but that a range of personal interpretations are valid and desirable as long as readers can support an interpretation by citing evidence from the text and their own lives.

Readers bring connections from their worlds of experience to a book, including (1) knowledge of various genres and literary forms gained from previous reading that help them understand new, similar books; (2) social relationships that help them understand and evaluate characters' actions and motivations; (3) cultural knowledge that influences their attitudes toward self and others and their responses to story events; and (4) knowledge of the world or topic that can deepen readers' understanding of a text and enrich their response (Beach & Marshall, 1990).

Another aspect of Rosenblatt's theory is her focus on the importance of the stance that readers choose related to their purpose for reading. Efferent reading focuses on taking knowledge or information from the text, while aesthetic reading involves living through a literary experience and immersing yourself within the world of the story. Whether people read efferently or aesthetically depends on what they are reading (e.g., a want ad versus a mystery novel) and why they are reading it (e.g., for information versus for pleasure). The problem is that many teachers encourage an efferent stance toward literature by asking questions on specific details, and readers are so preoccupied with reading for those details that they fail to engage with or understand the story itself.

Rosenblatt's view of reading has important implications for the way teachers encourage students to respond to literature. Readers first need an opportunity for personal response to literature as they make connections between their lives and the text to construct their initial interpretations. The first discussion of a book should focus on sharing these personal connections. If readers instead are first asked to answer literal-level questions or provide book summaries or book reports, they read for the details but miss the story. Many teachers believe that readers need to start with literal comprehension and then move to higher levels of thinking, not realizing that this approach limits students' understandings and interest in a book. If you participate in adult book groups, you probably have experienced understanding deep themes and issues in a book, while forgetting specific details of names or events that are clarified in the process of the group discussion.

Rosenblatt (1991) points out that personal response is necessary but not sufficient. Readers need to move from sharing personal responses into dialogue with other readers. Through dialogue readers critique their individual responses by returning to the text and their lives for evidence to support their interpretations and to deepen their understandings. This approach honors the individual voices of readers while also holding them responsible to the group and remaining open to other interpretations.

Many educators have misunderstood Rosenblatt's theories and believe that reader response only promotes personal connections and so lacks rigor. Instead of an either/or approach, Rosenblatt points out that teachers and students can choose to engage in close textual analysis of particular aspects of the text *after* first creating personal meaning and significance from their reading.

The Common Core State Standards encourage a return to the close text analysis of New Criticism and an initial emphasis on literal comprehension, dismissing the importance of personal response as part of close reading. Teachers who understand reader response realize that they do not need to choose between these approaches but can begin with personal connections and then move to text analysis and finding evidence to support interpretations. The danger of only focusing on text analysis is that readers will again be subjected to the search for "correct" interpretations and move away from personal significance and dialogue that engages and challenges their thinking.

The literary elements provide a way to heighten your awareness of literary criticism and provide a shared vocabulary for talking with children about your responses to books. These literary terms are tools that your students can use to initiate and sustain conversations about literature with each other. In using these terms in the classroom you help children acquire a literary vocabulary and support them in meeting the standards of text analysis highlighted in the Common Core.

Elements of Fiction

Learning to evaluate children's books can best be accomplished by reading as many excellent books as possible. Gradually, you will develop your ability to make judgments on the merits of individual books. Discussing your responses to these books with children, teachers, and other students and listening to their responses will also allow you to become more critical and appreciative. Understanding the different parts, or elements, of a piece of fiction and how they work together can help you become more analytical about literary works; and this, too, can improve your judgment of literature. The elements of fiction are discussed separately in the following sections, but it is the unity of all of these elements that produces the story.

Plot

The events of the story and the sequence in which they are told constitute the *plot* of the story. The plot is what happens in the story and so is an important element of fiction for children. Often, adults believe that a story for children only needs to present familiar, everyday activities—the daily routines of life. Perhaps 2- and 3-year-olds enjoy hearing narratives such as this, but by age 4, children want to find more excitement in books. A good plot produces conflict to build the excitement and suspense that are needed to keep the reader involved.

The nature of the *conflict* within the plot can arise from different sources. The basic conflict may be one that occurs within the main character, called *person-against-self*. In this type of story, the main character struggles against inner drives and personal tendencies to achieve some goal or overcome a traumatic event. In *City Boy* by Jan Michael, Sam loses his sense of identity when he moves from the city to a rural village in Malawi after the death of his mother. He lashes out at family and friends while struggling with his own internal conflict. Katherine Paterson's *The Great Gilly Hopkins* is another story of a character who is struggling to cope with her longings and fears as she schemes against anyone who attempts to show her friendship or caring.

A conflict usually found in survival stories is the struggle the character has with the forces of nature. This conflict is called *person-against-nature* and is often exemplified in survival novels such as *Hatchet* by Gary Paulsen where Brian's plane goes down in the wilderness and *Eight Days: A Story of Haiti* by Edwidge Danticat about a young boy trapped by the hurricane disaster.

In other stories, the source of the conflict is found between two characters. Conflicts with peers, problems with sibling rivalries, and stories of children rebelling against an adult are *person-against-person* conflicts. An example of this plot device is Max's conflict with his mother in *Where the Wild Things Are* by Maurice Sendak, and Lucy's conflict with her great-aunt from China with whom she is forced to share her bedroom in *The Great Wall of Lucy Wu* by Wendy Wan Long Shang.

Occasionally, a story for children presents the main character in conflict with society. This conflict is most often either about the environment being destroyed by new technology or changing times or about children caught up in a political upheaval such as war. The conflict is then called *person-against-society* as in stories of war, such as *Yellow Star* by Jennifer Roy and *Tropical*

Secrets by Margarita Engle. In the mystery *Hoot* by Carl Hiaasen, the conflict is between those who want to develop and destroy natural areas and wildlife and those who want to preserve them.

In some stories, the protagonist faces **multiple conflicts** in which, for example, a character may be in conflict with society and also in a conflict with self. In Jean Craighead George's *Julie of the Wolves,* Julie/Miyax rebels against the societal changes that threaten the wildlife in her native Alaska while at the same time seeking to resolve her own conflicting thoughts about her Inuit traditions and modern society.

Plots are constructed in many different ways. The most common plot structures in children's stories are **chronological plots,** which cover a particular period of time and relate the events in order within that time period instead of moving back and forth across time. *Lizzie Bright and the Buckminster Boy* by Gary Schmidt and *Charlotte's Web* by E. B. White have chronological plots.

Two distinct types of chronological plots are progressive plots and episodic plots. In books with **progressive plots,** the first few chapters are the exposition, in which the characters, setting, and basic conflict are established. Following the expository chapters, the story builds through rising action to a climax. The climax occurs, a satisfactory conclusion (or dénouement) is reached, and the story ends. Figure 3.1 suggests how a progressive, chronological plot might be visualized.

An **episodic plot** ties together separate short stories or episodes, each an entity in itself with its own conflict and resolution. These episodes are typically unified by the same cast of characters and the same setting and each episode comprises a chapter. Although the episodes are usually chronological, time relationships among the episodes may be nonexistent or loosely connected by "during that same year" or "later that month." Examples of short chapter books with an episodic plot structure are *Ramona Quimby, Age 8* by Beverly Cleary and *My One Hundred Adventures* by Polly Horvath. Because episodic plots are less complex, they tend to be easier to read and often involve recounting humorous escapades. Thus, the reader who is making the transition from picture books to chapter books may find these plots appealing. Many easy-to-read books for beginning readers are also structured in this way, such as in *Frog and Toad Are Friends* by Arnold Lobel and *Mr. Putter and Tabby Feed the Fish* by Cynthia Rylant. Figure 3.2 on the following page suggests how a chronological, episodic plot might be visualized.

Authors use a **flashback** to convey information about events that occurred earlier, often before the beginning of the first chapter. The chronology of events is disrupted, and the reader is taken back to an earlier time. Flashbacks can occur more than once and in different parts of a story. The use of a flashback permits authors to begin the story in the midst of the action but later fill in the background for fuller understanding of present events. Flashbacks in children's books are mostly in chapter books for older readers because such plots can confuse young children.

Figure 3.1 Diagram of a Progressive Plot

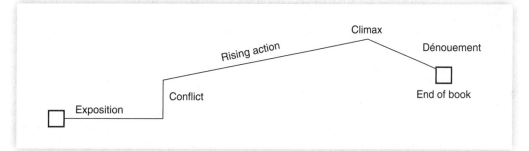

Figure 3.2 Diagram of an Episodic Plot

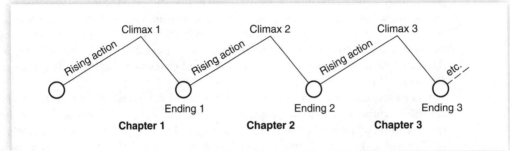

Figure 3.3 Diagram of a Flashback

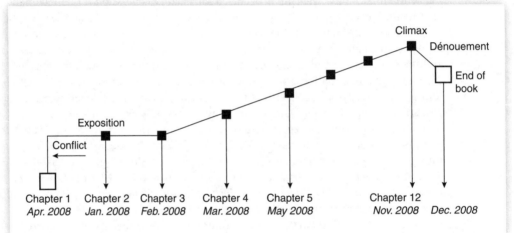

Teachers can help students understand this plot structure by reading aloud good examples of this type of story, such as Jean Craighead George's *My Side of the Mountain* and *Because of Winn-Dixie* by Kate DiCamillo. Class discussion can focus on the sequence of events and why the author has chosen to relate the events in this manner. Figure 3.3 illustrates the structure of a flashback in a book in which some events occurred before the beginning of the book.

More children's novels are appearing with new plot formulations such as *complex multiple plots* in which the traditional chronology is replaced by nonlinear plots that occur simultaneously. In Louis Sachar's *Holes,* a humorous mystery and survival story, two apparently unrelated stories set in two different time periods are developed, yet are gradually revealed to be connected to one another through the unraveling of the mystery. Kathi Appelt's *The Underneath* relates the events of an animal story set in present-day Louisiana bayou country, while interweaving a fantasy about a centuries-old story of love, betrayal, and revenge.

A stylistic plot device that prepares readers for coming events in a story is *foreshadowing.* This device gives clues to a later event, possibly even the climax of the story. For example, the first illustration of Max's bedroom in *Where the Wild Things Are* by Maurice Sendak shows a picture of a "wild thing" on the wall, while the classic *Tuck Everlasting* by Natalie Babbitt uses a detailed description of the long yellow road in the first chapter to foreshadow the long journey the Tuck family members must travel in their lives.

Plot is an important element to all readers, but especially to young readers, who enjoy fast-moving, exciting stories. A well-constructed plot contributes substantially to children's acceptance and enjoyment of stories.

Characters

Memorable characters populate the world of children's literature. Ferdinand the bull, Charlotte the spider, Frances the badger, Little Toot the young tugboat, and Peter and his dog, Willie, are all remembered fondly by generations of readers.

Characters, the "actors" in a story, are vital to the enjoyment of a story. A well-portrayed character can become a friend, a role model, or a temporary parent. Although young readers enjoy exciting events, the characters involved in those events must matter or the events no longer seem significant. How characters are depicted and develop in the course of the story is important to readers, who can study a character through characterization and character development.

Characterization refers to the way an author helps the reader know a character. The most obvious way an author can do this is to describe the character's physical appearance and personality. Portraying the character's emotional and moral traits or revealing her relationships with other characters are more subtle and effective techniques. In the most convincing characterizations, the character comes alive through a combination of actions and dialogue, the responses of other characters, and the narrator's descriptions.

Character development refers to the changes the character undergoes during the course of events in the story. If a character experiences significant, life-altering events, readers expect that the character will somehow be different as a result of those events. For example, Bud runs away from both an orphanage and his foster family in *Bud, Not Buddy* by Christopher Paul Curtis to search for his real father during the Great Depression. He encounters danger and violence as well as kindness in a journey that changes his sense of identity and hopes for the future. Minli undergoes a quest to change her family's future in the fantasy *Where the Mountain Meets the Moon* by Grace Lin. Along the way she find excitement and danger, wisdom and magic in her encounters with dragons, talking fish, and peddlers that gradually change her understandings of family, friendship, and faith.

Usually one or two main characters and some minor characters are included in books for children. Ideally, each main character, sometimes called the *protagonist,* is fully described and is a complex individual with both good and bad traits, like a real person. Such a character is called a *round character.* For example, in the historical fiction novel *Catherine, Called Birdy* by Karen Cushman, Birdy, the protagonist whose father is seeking a suitable husband for her, is presented as a complex character with many strengths and weaknesses. In the realistic fiction novel *Inside Out and Back Again* by Thanhha Lai, the protagonist, whose Vietnamese family are refugees, is presented as a round, complex character dealing with the many challenges of immigration.

Minor, or *secondary, characters* may be described in a partial or less complete manner. The extent of description depends on what the reader needs to know about the character for a full understanding of the story. Some of the minor character's traits are described fully, whereas other facets of the character's personality may remain obscure. Because the purpose is to build the story and make it comprehensible, fragmentary knowledge of a minor character may suffice. In *Heat*

(2006) by Mike Lupica, the secondary character Manny is depicted as the catcher and a loyal mate to talented pitcher Michael Arroyo, the protagonist whose struggles and home situation are portrayed in depth through dialogue and action. Parents are often secondary characters, such as Michael's mother in *Skellig* by David Almond, who moves believably between frustration and sympathy for Michael as the family deals with a very sick baby, but who is too distracted to be fully present in his life.

Occasionally, an author will insert a ***flat character***—that is, a character described in a one-sided or underdeveloped manner. Although such people do not exist in real life, they may be justified within the story to propel the plot. For example, in Susan R. Vaught's *Big Fat Manifesto*, self-assured and overweight Jamie seeks to be taken seriously in a thin world by writing in the school newspaper about her attitudes about her weight. Other students in the story lack depth and appear as somewhat flat stereotypes. The current importance of the topic presented by a character as well-developed as Jamie will make this an appealing book for many middle-school readers. Sometimes the character is all-evil or all-frivolous; for instance, folktales present flat characters as symbols of good and evil.

In some stories, a flat character plays the role of ***character foil,*** a person in direct juxtaposition to another character (usually the protagonist) who serves to highlight the characteristics of the other individual. A character foil may occur as a flat or round character. The character or force that is in direct opposition to the main character is called the ***antagonist.*** In Avi's *The True Confessions of Charlotte Doyle,* the ship's captain is a frightening antagonist to Charlotte. In *Now Is the Time for Running* by Michael Williams, Deo encounters a greedy farmer and a drug dealer who serve as antagonists as he flees his home in Zimbabwe and looks for a place of safety in South Africa.

The main characters in an excellent work of fiction for children are rounded, fully developed characters who undergo change in response to life-altering events. Because children generally prefer personified animals or children of their own age or slightly older as the main characters of their stories, authors of children's books often face a dilemma. Although in real life children usually have restricted freedom of action and decision making within the confines of a family, the author can develop a more vivid and exciting story if the main characters are "on their own." Thus, in many children's stories, parents are absent, no longer living, or no longer functioning, as in Jeanne Birdsall's *The Penderwicks,* in which four sisters and their absentminded dad spend the summer in a cottage in rural Massachusetts. The spirited, lovable girls' many adventures and near mishaps could not occur without a preoccupied father. Furthermore, by making up situations, authors can focus on just one aspect of life, enabling young readers to see and understand this facet of life more clearly.

Setting

The time and place in which the story occurs constitute the setting of a story. The setting's importance depends on the story. For example, in historical fiction the authentic re-creation of the period is essential to the comprehension of the events. In this situation, the setting, fully described in both time and place, is called an ***integral setting.*** The story could not be the same if placed in another setting. For example, in the historical fiction mystery novel *The Case of the Missing Marquess* by Nancy Springer, 14-year-old Enola Holmes, the much younger sister of Sherlock Holmes, unravels the disappearance of her missing mother. Historical facts, British dialect and vocabulary, and Victorian customs create a believable work of historical fiction. The novel, set in nineteenth-century England, also depicts the English countryside and the filth of Victorian London through imagery.

By contrast, the setting in folktales is often vague and general. For example, "long ago in a cottage in the deep woods" is meant to convey a universal, timeless tale, one that could have happened anywhere and almost anytime except the present or very recent past. This type of setting is called a *backdrop setting* and is used to set the stage and the mood.

Theme

The literary themes of a story are the underlying meanings or significance. Although we sometimes think of the literary *theme* as the message or moral of the story, it can just as easily be an aesthetic understanding, such as an appreciation for nature or a viewpoint on a societal issue. To identify the theme, consider the author's purpose in writing the story or what the author is saying through this story along with your own thinking about how this book connects to larger understandings of life.

A theme is usually better expressed by means of a complete sentence than by a single word. For example, students often suggest that a theme found in *Charlotte's Web* by E. B. White is friendship. A better statement of the theme is "Friendship is one of the most satisfying things in the world," as Wilbur tells us in the story. The single word *friendship* may be a topic within the story, but it is not an expression of a theme. Similarly, the phrase "race relations during Reconstruction" incompletely expresses the theme of *When I Crossed No-Bob* by Margaret McMullan. Set in Mississippi ten years after the Civil War, 12-year-old Addy makes a difficult decision when faced with the dilemma of testifying against her own father or keeping silent and letting someone else be hurt. "Doing good is hard, doing nothing is the easiest of all" more clearly reflects the theme.

Themes in children's books should be worthy of children's attention and convey important life understandings. A theme must not overpower the plot and characters of the story, however; children read fiction for enjoyment, not for enlightenment. If the theme is expressed in a heavy-handed, obvious fashion, then the pleasure of the reading experience is diminished. Likewise, overly "teachy" or didactic themes detract from a reader's enjoyment of a story. Certainly a well-written book may convey a moral message, but it should also tell a good story from which the message evolves so that the theme is subtly conveyed to the reader. In the novel *Smiles to Go* by Jerry Spinelli, 14-year-old, self-absorbed perfectionist Will, as a result of a serious accident involving his little sister, discovers that it is worth risking love and friendship even if he can't always be the one in control.

Often, adults write stories to teach morality lessons rather than for children's pleasure. Although stories of this sort are associated with the thinly disguised religious tracts in the early history of children's literature, some current authors use children's literature as a platform to preach about drug abuse, animal rights, and other contemporary issues. If the literary quality of these so-called problem novels is weakened, then the story and characters become secondary to the issue or problem. However, when moral values are embedded within the fabric of a powerful story, children can develop a sense of right and wrong without feeling as if they are being indoctrinated.

Style

Style is the way an author tells the story; it can be viewed as the writing itself, as opposed to the content of the book. However, the style must suit the content of the particular book so that the two are intertwined.

Different aspects of style are considered in evaluating a work of fiction. Most obviously, you can look at the **words** chosen to tell the story and whether they are long or short, common or uncommon, rhyming or melodic, boring and hackneyed or rich and challenging, unemotional or emotional, standard dialect or regional/minority dialect. The words should be appropriate to the story; so ask yourself, Why did the author choose these words? What effect was the author trying to achieve?

The **sentences** may also be considered as to whether they read easily and flow without the reader needing to reread to gain the meaning of the text. Sometimes an author chooses to limit the word choices in a book for beginning readers. Yet in the hands of a gifted writer, the sentences will remain melodic, varied in length and structure, and enjoyable to read and hear as in Arnold Lobel's *Frog and Toad Are Friends,* Mo Willems's *I Will Surprise My Friend!* and Annie Barrows's *Ivy and Bean.*

The **organization** of the book may be considered by noting the paragraphs and transitions, length of chapters, headings and chapter titles, preface, endnotes, prologue, epilogue, and length of the book. For the beginning reader it is important whether a story is divided into chapters. After years of looking at, listening to, and reading books without chapters, it is quite an accomplishment for a 6-year-old to move up to so-called chapter books, even if each chapter is only three pages long.

Chapter titles can provoke interest in what will follow, as well as provide the reader with clues to predict story events. Some books provide a **prologue,** an introductory statement telling events that precede the start of the story, or an **epilogue,** a concluding statement telling events that occur after the story has ended. Ying Chang Compestine in *A Banquet for Hungry Ghosts* provides a prologue about the importance of food in her life and in Chinese culture along with an explanation of the tradition of hungry ghosts as a frame for the frightening tales. Each ghostly tale is followed by a recipe and a short historical note that provides a context for the reader instead of placing these notes in an extended epilogue at the end that would be read by only a few readers.

In *Kipling's Choice* by Geert Spillebeen, an epilogue has been included to provide information on the historical context of World War I in France. Other times, an epilogue resolves questions readers may have regarding what happened after the story's conclusion, as in Marion Dane Bauer's *A Bear Named Trouble,* a story of companionship between a wild bear cub and a lonely boy.

Point of view is another aspect of an author's style. If the story is told through the eyes and voice of a **third-person narrator** (the use of *he, she, it*), then the reader can know whatever the narrator knows about the events of the story. In many stories, the narrator is **omniscient** and can see into the minds of all characters and be at many places at the same time. The reader of Lynne Rae Perkins's *Criss Cross* can understand and interpret the story from many different perspectives because she uses an omniscient point of view. In *Loser,* Jerry Spinelli also draws on the omniscient narrative point of view to relate the story of Donald Zinkoff, whose enthusiasm and exuberance are unabated in spite of being seen as a loser by classmates.

Other stories are narrated from the perspective of only one character in the story. In this case, the story is still told in the third person, but the reader knows only what that particular character can see and understand. This latter technique is called **limited omniscient** point of view. Beverly Cleary's *Dear Mr. Henshaw* is a realistic story told from the perspective of Leigh, a boy troubled by family difficulties and changes at school, who corresponds with Mr. Henshaw, an author. In *Clay* by David Almond, disturbing events are told through the point of view of altar boy Davie, who becomes part of those events.

Other times, authors choose to tell the story through a **first-person narrator** (the use of *I*), generally the main character of the story. The reader gains a sense of closeness to the main character but is not privy to any information unavailable to this character. Some authors have accomplished a first-person point of view by writing as though their main character is writing a diary or letters, as in *Flight to Freedom* by Ana Veciana-Suarez, or through narrative poems composed by the main character, as in *Diamond Willow* by Helen Frost. The story is both an exciting survival adventure and dog story set in Alaska and related through diamond-shaped concrete poems. Occasionally, a story is told in first person through the eyes of a minor character. For example, *We Can't All Be Rattlesnakes* by Paul Jennings is a humorous animal fantasy about a boy, Gunnar, and his troubled life told through the point of view of a captured rattlesnake, Crusher.

A *shifting point of view* permits the reader to see events from different characters' points of view. This technique is demanding for young readers. When the point of view shifts, the author must carefully cue readers to the changing point of view, as Avi does in *Nothing but the Truth* by identifying sender, receiver, or discussants at the beginning of each letter, memorandum, telephone call, or face-to-face conversation. Beverley Naidoo's *Web of Lies* relates the story of the school experiences of two Nigerian refugees in London by shifting between their two points of view.

Symbolism is an artistic invention that authors use to suggest invisible or intangible meanings by analogy to something else through association, resemblance, or convention. Often, a symbol—a person, object, or situation—represents an abstract or figurative meaning in the story in addition to its literal meaning. Some symbols are universal and can be found repeatedly in literary works; others may be particular to the story. For example, a farm usually represents love and security in literature, as in E. B. White's *Charlotte's Web*. Children often read on a literal level, but can be helped to note more obvious symbols in the books they are reading. If the symbolic feature recurs in the story, it is referred to as a *motif.* The number 3 is a common motif in folktales, for example.

A story for children must be more than a plot and a character study; a story must integrate all the elements of fiction into a pleasing whole. In drawing together these elements, authors create new worlds for young readers. The role of literary elements represents only one aspect of the knowledge needed to understand literature as a discipline.

Building Your Knowledge of Literature as a Discipline

The purpose of this text is to introduce you to literature as a discipline so that you become familiar with genres, literary and visual elements, evaluation and selection criteria, critical issues, and resources along with reading widely from children's books so as to interact with a range of authors, illustrators, poets, and titles. An *inquiry approach* is encouraged through the Invitations for Further Investigations at the end of each chapter and the Reader Connections that suggest a response engagement to encourage you to pursue your own questions and connections within a particular set of books and to think collaboratively with peers.

A literature curriculum can be organized by genre, theme or topic, author or illustrator, literary element or device, or notable books. We have organized this text by genre to encourage you to read broadly, but within that genre structure, each chapter is organized around themes and topics and includes discussions of literary elements and lists of authors and notable books and awards.

Genre provides a context for you to learn about the various types of books and their characteristics, such as historical fiction, fantasy, poetry, etc. The goal is to expose you to a wide variety of literature and to explore the evaluation and selection criteria for excellent books within each genre.

Theme or topic focuses attention on a book's meaning and is the primary approach you will use with literature in your classroom or library. Organizing a set of books around particular themes, such as alienation and acceptance by peers or the tension of dependence/independence as children grow older, encourages critical thinking and in-depth consideration of issues along with more thoughtful connections across books. Organizing books by topics, such as pets or World War II, can help students find books that interest them for independent reading but is less useful for in-depth discussion and inquiry. You are encouraged to explore both themes and topics within the chapters.

An *author or illustrator* approach involves organizing books around the people who create books and becoming familiar with their books, creative processes, and life experiences. A list of notable authors and illustrators for each genre is included in the chapters and you are encouraged to inquire into the life and work of people whose books particularly intrigue you. Excellent reference sources such as *Something about the Author* provide information about children's book authors and illustrators, and many biographies and autobiographies are available as well. An author/illustrator inquiry involves reading books by particular authors or illustrators, examining their writing or artistic style and use of visual and literary elements, noting the themes they explore in their books, locating interviews or articles about their lives, books, and creative process, and exploring the ways in which their lives have influenced their books.

Literary and visual elements and devices are another way to organize a literature curriculum and focus on the literary elements presented in this chapter along with the visual elements of illustration in the chapter on picture books. Literary devices are particular techniques used by authors for a special effect, such as irony, symbolism, or parody, or techniques by illustrators in their use of a particular medium like watercolor. Each genre chapter highlights a particular literary element to provide an opportunity for you to revisit these elements and explore them in greater depth in a set of books. Examining these elements will give you a better understanding of the craft of writing and are essential to engaging in the close text analysis encouraged by the Common Core State Standards.

Organizing around *notable books* involves an in-depth focus on award-winning books or other exemplary classic or contemporary books. The emphasis is on reading a few books closely and engaging in discussions with other readers about your personal connections and the issues you find significant in those books. You can then analyze the features that contribute to their excellence, such as their relevance to readers, unique perspectives or insights, memorable characters, or illustration style. Each chapter includes a list of recommended books for reading aloud, a reader connection that encourages you to interact closely with a set of books, and references to award lists that you can consult. You are encouraged to engage in literature discussions around an exemplary book or set of books for each genre to deepen your understandings and ability to evaluate literature.

The Organization of This Text

In Chapters 4 to 11, the main categories of children's books are defined and explained, followed by book titles recommended for reading in each category. Chapters 5 through 10 focus on the literary genres. An overview of the genres, subtopics, and their relationships to one another is displayed in Table 3.1. We recognize that a genre organization is a more traditional, though admittedly imperfect, way of grouping literature, but view it as the most practical structure for your learning and to help you make balanced choices for your reading. As noted, other ways to organize books have been integrated within the chapters.

Table 3.1   Genres and Topics of Children's Literature

Poetry (Ch. 5)	Prose				
	FICTION				**NONFICTION**
	Fantasy		**Realism**		
	Traditional Literature (Ch. 6)	*Modern Fantasy (Ch. 7)*	*Realistic Fiction (Ch. 8)*	*Historical Fiction and Biographies (Ch. 9)*	*Informational Books (Ch. 10)*
Nursery rhymes

Lyric poems

Narrative poems | Myths

Epics and Legends

Folktales

Fables

Religious stories | Modern folktales

Animal fantasy

Personified toys and objects

Unusual characters and strange situations

Worlds of little people

Supernatural events and mystery fantasy

Historical fantasy

Quest stories

Science fiction and science fantasy | Families

Peers

Physical, emotional, mental, and behavioral challenges

Local and global communities

Animals

Sports and mysteries

Romance and sexuality

Adventure and survival

Difficult life decisions and coming of age | Beginnings of civilization

Civilizations of the ancient world

Civilizations of the medieval world

Emergence of modern nations

Development of industrial society

World wars in the twentieth century

Post–World War II | Biological science

Physical science

Applied science

Social science

Humanities |

Understanding genre characteristics builds a frame of reference for readers of a particular genre and can facilitate comprehension. Many authors are playing with the traditional boundaries of a genre, and knowledge of the traditional literary forms will help you understand what authors are doing and gain new understandings from this shift. These explorations include creating postmodern picture books and novels that use multiple nonlinear narratives and characters who come off the page to speak to authors and readers. These books are discussed in the chapter on picture books.

Authors have also been experimenting with books that blend characteristics of several genres, and so genre boundaries are increasingly blurred. Novels for children are being written as free verse and other verse forms are occurring with greater frequency across genres. An example of a *novel in verse* is Karen Hesse's *Out of the Dust,* awarded the Newbery Medal and the Scott O'Dell Award for Historical Fiction. Novels in verse are listed in this textbook under their particular narrative genre, such as historical fiction, rather than in the chapter about poetry. Books of magical realism combine realism and fantasy, such as *Sweet Whispers, Brother Rush* by Virginia Hamilton and *Skellig* by David Almond. Magical realism offers readers new ways to perceive the world and is discussed in the fantasy chapter. Historical fantasy blends historical fiction and modern fantasy, as Rebecca Stead does in *When You Reach Me* with moving time frames; these books are included in the fantasy chapter. Other blended genres include works of fictionalized biography and informational books that contain elements of fiction and nonfiction, as in Russell Freedman's *Confucius: The Golden Rule* and David Macaulay's *Mosque.* These blended-genre works offer readers new ways to perceive the world and often heighten the interest of readers. Another trend is multigenre books where several distinct genres are included in the same book, such as poetry along with a separate box of information on each page as in *Where in the Wild?* by David Schwartz and Yael Schy. The Magic School Bus series by Joanna Cole and Bruce Degen is a well-known example of multigenre.

One other variation in genre is that nonfiction includes both biography and informational books. We have grouped biography with historical fiction since biography typically uses a more narrative writing style and reflects historical eras and placed informational books in their own chapter.

Chapters 4 and 11 diverge from the organization of genre and present books that go across genres around a particular focus. Chapter 4 focuses on picture books and includes an in-depth discussion of illustrations as well as the types of books that are particularly appropriate for young children. These books actually fit into a range of genres but are grouped to reflect the distinct needs of young children. Chapter 11 is organized by culture. Although multicultural and international books have been placed in a separate chapter for emphasis and ready access, many multicultural and international titles are included in the genre chapters.

Chapters 12 and 13 focus on literature in the curriculum and the ways in which you might organize a curriculum around children's literature as well as strategies for engaging children in responding to literature. In addition, these chapters include a discussion of the political context of policies, tests, and standards that affect the ways in which literature is used in classrooms, with a particular emphasis on the Common Core State Standards and their connection to literature.

Invitations for Further Investigation

- Revisit a book that you remember loving as a child. Before you reread the book, write about your remembered response and connections to that book—what was it about the book that was significant for you as a child? Reread the book and write about your response as an adult. Compare the two responses.
- Read a multilayered novel, such as *Skellig* (Almond, 1999) or *Lizzie Bright and the Buckminster Boy* (Schmidt, 2004), and share your responses and connections with other readers. Revisit the book in another class session with each small group taking on a different literary element to analyze how that element plays out in the novel. Develop a visual diagram or image to share your insights with the other groups.

References

Almond, D. (1999). *Skellig.* New York: Delacorte.

Almond, D. (2006). *Clay.* New York: Delacorte.

Appelt, K. (2008). *The underneath.* New York: Atheneum.

Avi. (1990). *The true confessions of Charlotte Doyle.* New York: Orchard.

Avi. (1991). *Nothing but the truth.* New York: Orchard.

Babbitt, N. (1975). *Tuck everlasting.* New York: Farrar.

Barrows, A. (2006). *Ivy and Bean.* Blackall, S. (Illus.). San Francisco, CA: Chronicle.

Bauer, M. D. (2005). *A bear named Trouble.* New York: Clarion.

Beach, R. W., & Marshall, J. D. (1990). *Teaching literature in the secondary school.* Belmont, CA: Wadsworth.

Birdsall, J. (2005). *The Penderwicks.* New York: Knopf.

Cleary, B. (1981). *Ramona Quimby, age 8.* Tiegreen, A. (Illus.). New York: Morrow.

Cleary, B. (1983). *Dear Mr. Henshaw.* Zelinsky, P. (Illus.). Orlando, FL: Harcourt.

Compestine, Y. C. (2009). *A banquet for hungry ghosts.* New York: Holt.

Cushman, K. (1994). *Catherine, called Birdy.* New York: Clarion.

Danticot, D. (2010). *Eight days: A story of Haiti.* Delinois, A. (Illus.). New York: Orchard.

DiCamillo, K. (2000). *Because of Winn-Dixie.* Cambridge, MA: Candlewick.

Engle, M. (2009). *Tropical secrets: Holocaust refugees in Cuba.* New York: Holt.

Freedman, R. (2002). *Confucius: The golden rule.* Clément, F. (Illus). New York: Arthur A. Levine.

Frost, H. (2008). *Diamond willow.* New York: Farrar.

George, J. C. (1959). *My side of the mountain.* New York: Dutton.

George, J. C. (1972). *Julie of the wolves.* Schoenherr, J. (Illus.). New York: Harper.

Hamilton, V. (1982). *Sweet whispers, Brother Rush.* New York: Philomel.

Hesse, K. (1997). *Out of the dust.* New York: Scholastic.

Hiaasen, C. (2002). *Hoot.* New York: Knopf.

Horvath, P. (2008). *My one hundred adventures.* New York: Schwartz & Wade.

Jennings, P. (2009). *We can't all be rattlesnakes.* New York: HarperCollins.

Lai, T. (2011). *Inside out and back again.* New York: Harper.

Lin, G. (2010). *Where the mountain meets the moon.* New York: Little, Brown.

Lobel, A. (1970). *Frog and toad are friends.* New York: Harper.

Lupica, M. (2006). *Heat.* New York: Philomel.

Macaulay, D. (2003). *Mosque.* Boston, MA: Houghton.

McMullan, M. (2007). *When I crossed No-Bob.* Boston, MA: Houghton.

Michael, Jan. (2009). *City boy.* New York: Clarion.

More, H. (1961). A book. In W. Cole (Ed.), *Poems for seasons and celebrations.* Cleveland, OH: World Publishing.

Naidoo, B. (2006). *Web of lies.* New York: HarperCollins.

Paterson, Katherine. (1978). *The great Gilly Hopkins.* New York: HarperColllins.

Paulsen, G. (1987). *Hatchet.* New York: Bradbury.

Perkins, L. R. (2005). *Criss cross.* New York: Greenwillow.

Rosenblatt, L. (1978). *The reader, the text, the poem.* Carbondale, IL: Southern Illinois University.

Rosenblatt, L. (1991). Literature—S.O.S.! *Language Arts, 68,* 444–448.

Roy, J. (2006). *Yellow star.* New York: Marshall Cavendish.

Rylant, C. (2001). *Mr. Putter & Tabby feed the fish.* Howard, A. (Illus.). San Diego, CA: Harcourt.

Sachar, L. (1998). *Holes.* New York: Farrar.

Schmidt, G. D. (2004). *Lizzie Bright and the Buckminster boy.* New York: Clarion.

Schwartz, D., & Schwy, Y. (2007*). Where in the wild?* Kuhn, D. (Photos). New York: Tricycle Press.

Sendak, M. (1963). *Where the wild things are.* New York: HarperCollins.

Shang, W. W. L. (2011). *The great wall of Lucy Wu.* New York: Scholastic.

Spillebeen, G. (2005). *Kipling's choice.* Edelstein, T. (Illus.). Boston, MA: Houghton.

Spinelli, J. (2002). *Loser.* New York: HarperCollins.

Spinelli, J. (2008). *Smiles to go.* New York: Joanna Cotler.

Springer, N. (2006). *The case of the missing marquess.* New York: Philomel.

Stead, R. (2009). *When you reach me.* New York: Wendy Lamb.

Vaught, S. R. (2008). *Big fat manifesto.* New York: Bloomsbury.

Veciana-Suarez, A. (2002). *Flight to freedom.* New York: Orchard.

White, E. B. (1952). *Charlotte's web.* Williams, G. (Illus.). New York: Harper.

Willems, M. (2008). *I will surprise my friend!* New York: Hyperion.

Wlliams, M. (2011). *Now is the time for running.* New York: Little, Brown.

Part Two

Categories of Literature

Part II presents a broad spectrum of the genres of literature. Organizing by genres, topics, and historical eras is a convenient way to locate books and to encourage broad reading, even though literary genres do not have absolute definitions and some books fall between or go across genres. A genre organization also provides criteria for evaluating books and understanding how the literary elements play out within a particular type of literature—an important understanding given the focus on close textual analysis in the Common Core State Standards. In addition, each genre chapter highlights a literary element of significance to that genre and includes Reader Connections that invite readers into a thoughtful consideration of that genre.

The special features in each chapter of Part II include a Milestones feature that overviews the history of the development of each genre. The lists of Notable Authors will familiarize you with well-known creators of literature and help you make choices for in-depth author studies, just as the Excellent

Books to Read Aloud features provide help in selecting good read-alouds. The Invitations for Further Investigation suggest aspects of each chapter's content for in-depth study, issues for discussion, and literature-related inquiries.

The Recommended Books sections have been updated at the end of each genre chapter. Our goal is to include the best books from the recent past as well as some older titles that continue to hold wide appeal. Inevitably some titles must be dropped from edition to edition to make room for newer books. Titles in the Recommended Books lists are organized by the same topics or historical eras as presented in the body of the chapter to make finding specific types of books easier. A brief list of films related to each genre follows the Recommended Book lists.

Chapter 4 focuses on picture books and goes across genres to the types of books that appeal to young children as well as the visual elements, techniques, and styles of illustration. Chapter 11 goes across genres to overview current issues, trends, and recommended books that are multicultural and international in order to highlight the importance of these areas. Multicultural and international titles are also integrated into all of the genre chapters.

Other recommended children's literature titles may be found in Appendix A (Children's Book Awards). Appendix C lists good magazines available for children. Information on the genre of plays in children's literature is found in Chapter 13.

Chapter Four

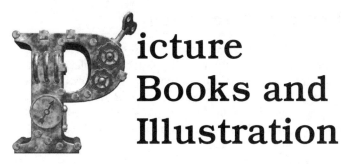

Picture Books and Illustration

Picture This

I'm the belle of the ball!
I'm the star of the show!
When you open a book
I'm the place your eyes go.

I'm colors and shapes.
I'm an actor on stage,
worth one thousand words
that just sit on the page!

I'm scattered throughout.
I'm the best part to see.
I know when you read
you are hoping for me!

—*Laura Purdie Salas*

In an era when picture books abound and provide children with a delightful introduction to the world of books, it is difficult to imagine a time when books had no illustrations. The picture book is actually a product of the twentieth century; different types of picture books developed in response to a growing awareness of the importance of early learning. The picture book, however, is not just for young children. Many sophisticated and complex picture books are being published for older readers for whom visual image has a strong appeal due to their daily immersion in images from mass media and technology. Picture books can provide a means of developing visual literacy—the ability to read and critique these images—as well as provide a thought-provoking story.

Definition and Description

Picture books are books in which both words and illustrations are *essential* to the story's meaning. In a true picture book, the illustrations are integral to the reader's experience of the book and the story would be diminished or confusing without the illustrations. Picture books are written in all genres and typically have illustrations on every page or every other page. As a general rule, they are thirty-two pages long. *Where the Wild Things Are* by Maurice Sendak is often cited as an exemplary picture book because of the fusion of word and image into a seamless whole. Sendak's use of space conveys emotion and movement as the illustrations break out of their borders and take over the white space to signal the story's climax during Max's imaginary journey to the "wild things" and then shrink back within their borders when Max returns home to find his supper waiting for him. The dreamlike story setting is signaled through the subdued watercolor washes over delicate line drawings, while the crosshatched lines set up emotional tension that shifts across the pages.

Books with occasional illustrations that serve to break up or decorate the text, add interest, or depict specific incidents are not picture books, but are called **illustrated books.** Illustrations in these books are not essential to understanding the content but may enhance the content and bring visual interest for readers. *The Curious Adventures of the Abandoned Toys* by Julian Fellowes, illustrated by S. D. Schindler, has full-page, full-color illustrations that occur on every seventh page and pen-and-ink vignettes on every other page. These illustrations represent what is given in the text, but do not add new information to the story, as would be true in a picture book.

Evaluation and Selection of Picture Books

Children's first experiences with books must be enjoyable and meaningful to create an interest and involvement with literacy and books. Evaluation and selection of picture books involves a balance between what children naturally enjoy and invitations to extend their interests as readers. The following criteria will help identify the best picture books:

- **Is the picture book on a topic that children enjoy or find intriguing?** Avoid picture books that are *about* childhood, in the sense of nostalgia for or reminiscence of childhood. These books are for adults, not children.

- **Does the book avoid racial, ethnic, or sexual stereotyping in text and illustrations**? Subtle forms of stereotyping are often embedded within the illustrations of picture books in depicting hairstyles or homes or other aspects of a character's appearance and context.

- **Is the language and writing style rich and varied but not so complicated as to be incomprehensible to the child?** New or unusual vocabulary should be featured within the context of interesting situations and complementary illustrations. Books with overly sentimental and trite language should be avoided.

- **Are the illustrations appropriate in complexity to the age of the intended audience?** In picture books for infants, look for relatively uncomplicated pages showing outlined figures against a plain background. Unusual perspectives or page designs in which only parts of a figure are shown may not be readily understood by children younger than age 2.

- **Are the illustrations appropriate to the story?** Although children prefer color in illustrations, color is not essential. The more important point to consider is whether color or black and white is right for the story. Also, consider whether the artistic medium, style, and book design/format are appropriate to the content of the book.

- **Does the book offer connections for both children and adults in a read-aloud experience?** Picture books selected for reading aloud, especially by parents and preschool and kindergarten teachers, should offer something to both listener and reader and promote interaction. Multiple layers of meaning, child and adult perspectives, and humor are sources of enjoyment in books that adults willingly read and reread to children. Generally, picture storybooks lend themselves to being read aloud.

- **Is the amount of text on a page appropriate to the child audience?** The amount of text on the pages of a picture book determines how long it will take to read. Generally, the longer the text, the older the intended audience. Children's willingness to listen to stories grows with experience, which may result in a younger child who has been read to regularly having a much longer attention span than an older child with no story experience.

Excellent Picture Books to Read Aloud

Agee, Jon. *Terrific.* Ages 5–8.

Brown, Peter. *Children Make Terrible Pets.* Ages 5–8.

Cole, Brock. *Good Enough to Eat.* Ages 4–8.

DiCamillo, Kate. *Louise, the Adventures of a Chicken.* Illustrated by Harry Bliss. Ages 5–8.

Kasza, Keiko. *The Dog Who Cried Wolf.* Ages 4–7.

Klassen, Jon. *I Want My Hat Back.* Ages 6–9.

Larochelle, David. *The End.* Illustrated by Richard Egielski. Ages 4–8.

MacLennan, Cathy. *Chicky Chicky Chook Chook.* Ages 3–6.

McCarthy, Meghan. *Aliens Are Coming! The True Account of the 1938 War of the Worlds Radio Broadcast.* Ages 8–12.

Ryan, Candace. *Moo Hoo.* Illustrated by Mike Lowery. Ages 4–8.

Stead, Phillip. *A Sick Day for Amos McGee.* Illustrated by Erin Stead. Ages 5–8.

Stein, David. *Interrupting Chicken.* Ages 5–8.

Willems, Mo. *Knuffle Bunny: A Cautionary Tale.* Ages 3–5.

Willis, Jeanne. *Tadpole's Promise.* Illustrated by Tony Ross. Ages 5–9.

Several key awards provide access to the outstanding picture books. The most prestigious picture book award in the U.S. is the Caldecott Medal, sponsored by the Association for Library Service to Children division of the American Library Association. The equivalent award in Great Britain is the Kate Greenaway Medal; in Canada, the Governor General's Award for Illustration; and in Australia, the Picture Book of the Year Award (see Appendix A). Another source of excellent picture books is "The New York Times Best Illustrated Children's Books of the Year," published in early November in the *New York Times Book Review Supplement.*

Visual Elements

Understanding the contributions of illustrations begins with knowing the *visual elements,* the basic elements that reflect the choices made by illustrators as they decide what and how to illustrate parts of the story and how to move the illustrations from page to page. These visual elements are line, shape, color, light, space, perspective, and texture as they come together to create a composition. Knowledge of these elements is essential to understanding and selecting high-quality picture books.

The Common Core State Standards put a strong emphasis on children being able to provide evidence from the text to support their responses and analysis. The illustrations in picture books often contain the details regarding setting, tone, and characters, and so children need to be able to use the visual elements as well as the literary elements to create meaning and analyze a text.

Line and Shape

Lines are the continuous stroke marks in a picture that define shapes and create texture. Artists may choose to use lines that are dark or pale, heavy or light, solid or broken, wide or thin, straight or curved. The lines may be mostly *vertical, horizontal,* or on a *diagonal.* In pictures of the ocean and open prairies, the lines are predominantly horizontal to give an impression of calm and tranquility. If the ocean is stormy, then the lines are more likely diagonal and upward moving, suggesting action or emotion. The lines may be vertical on a sailboat mast or a tall tree to convey stability and strength. An *implied line* is not an actual stroke mark, but an arrangement of objects to create the illusion of a line, such as a row of trees along a pathway, to encourage the reader's eye to move to a focal point in the illustration. Each of these choices results in a different visual effect and can help set a different mood.

Lines should help create and convey the meaning and the feeling of the story. David Shannon's jagged, diagonal lines in *No, David!* convey the constant motion of an exuberant toddler and the resulting chaos (Illustration 1). The horizontal lines in *Song of the Water Boatmen & Other Pond Poems* by Joyce Sidman, on the other hand, suggest peace and tranquility (Illustration 9), while the policeman in *Officer Buckle and Gloria,* by Peggy Rathmann, has a strong vertical line suggesting stability (Illustration 10). The diagonal placement of the mice and their line of sight creates an *implied line* in Barbara Reid's *The Subway Mouse* that focuses readers on the interaction between the two mice (Illustration 11).

Shape, or the spatial forms of a picture, is produced by lines and areas of color joining and intersecting to suggest outlines of forms. Shapes can be simple or complex, large or small, clearly defined or amorphous, and rigid (geometric shapes) or flexible (organic shapes). Shape helps to create moods and carry messages. Distinctly outlined figures can project security, reality, or permanence, whereas broken or thin outlines might suggest instability, make-believe, or transience. The proportion of one object to another in an illustration and the spaces surrounding the shapes carry nonverbal messages—the bigger, the more important.

Notable Authors and Illustrators of Picture Books

Eric Carle, author/illustrator. Unusually formatted picture storybooks and concept books about insects and animals. *The Grouchy Ladybug; The Very Busy Spider.* www.eric-carle.com

Lois Ehlert, author/illustrator. Bold color, collage, and engineered pages characterize her informational and concept books. *Color Zoo; Leaf Man; In My World; Ten Little Caterpillars; Hands: Growing Up to Be an Artist.*

Denise Fleming, author/illustrator. Pattern books of handmade paper. *In the Small, Small Pond; The Cow Who Clucked; Buster Goes to Cowboy Camp.* www.denisefleming.com

Kevin Henkes, author/illustrator. Family situation fantasies featuring mice and simple, touching picture books about the wonder of life. *Lilly's Purple Plastic Purse; A Good Day; Kitten's First Full Moon.* www.kevinhenkes.com

Yumi Heo, author/illustrator. Picture books highlighting Korean-American experiences. *Ten Days and Nine Nights: An Adoption Story; Lady Hahn and Her Seven Friends; One Sunday Morning; Henry's First Moon Birthday.*

Barbara Lehman, illustrator. Uses an uncluttered cartoon style in wordless picture books in which real and imagined worlds blend. *The Red Book; Museum Trip; Rainstorm.*

E. B. Lewis, illustrator. Detailed watercolor illustrations in picture books, many historical fiction works based in African American experiences. *The Other Side; Night Boat to Freedom.* www.eblewis.com/illustration/books.html

Helen Oxenbury, author/illustrator. British watercolorist best known for baby books in board book format. *I Can; I See; I Touch; I Hear.* Also illustrator of *Ten Little Fingers and Ten Little Toes; There's Going to Be a Baby.*

Chris Raschka, illustrator. Spare, expressionist watercolors and brief texts elegantly capture mood. Two-time Caldecott medalist. *Yo! Yes?;*

Mysterious Thelonious; The Hello, Goodbye Window; A Ball for Daisy.

Cynthia Rylant, author. Author of Newbery, Newbery Honor, and Caldecott Honor award-winning books and several easy-to-read series. *Henry and Mudge* series; *Mr. Putter and Tabby* series; *Annie and Snowball* series.

Robert Sabuda, pop-up book artist and paper engineer. Intricate award-winning pop-up books based in children's classics, folklore, and prehistorical animals. Often works with Matthew Reinhart. *Alice's Adventures in Wonderland; Encyclopedia Prehistorica: Dinosaurs.* www.robertsabuda.com/

Jon Scieszka, author. Fractured folktales, transitional series books, and a truck series for young children focusing on encouraging boys as readers. *The Stinky Cheese Man and Other Fairly Stupid Tales; Robot Zot, Welcome to Trucktown;* Time Warp Trio series. www.jsworldwide.com

Laura Vaccaro Seeger, author/illustrator. Concept and beginning reader books characterized by bold lines, bright colors, and die-cuts. *First the Egg; One Boy; Lemons Are not Red; Green.* www.studiolvs.com

Brian Selznick, author/illustrator. Attention to period detail and unusual perspectives in groundbreaking picture books for older readers. *The Invention of Hugo Cabret; Wonderstruck.* www.theinventionofhugocabret.com

Maurice Sendak, author/illustrator. Explores the dreams and imagination of children in complex picture storybooks. Caldecott Medal for *Where the Wild Things Are; Outside Over There.* Final book is *Bumble-Ardy.*

Uri Shulevitz, author/illustrator. Rich but subtle watercolor illustrations create long-ago settings and exemplify interplay between text and pictures. *Snow; The Treasure; How I Learned Geography; So Sleepy Story.*

(Continued)

Notable Authors and Illustrators of Picture Books (Continued)

Peter Sís, author/illustrator. Noted for intricate pen and ink and watercolor illustrations in picture book biographies for older readers. *The Wall; Starry Messenger; Tibet through the Red Box.* www.petersis.com

Chris Van Allsburg, author/illustrator. Uses shadow and unusual perspectives to create mysterious moods in picture storybooks for intermediate-grade readers. *Jumanji; The Polar Express.* www .chrisvanallsburg.com/flash.html

Sara Varon, illustrator and comics artist. Wordless graphic novels that focus on the nature of friendship, using a range of characters. *Robot Dreams; Bake Sale; Chicken and Cat.* www .chickenopolis.com/

Rosemary Wells, author/illustrator. Picture books, concept books, baby books, and beginning readers featuring personified animals. *Max's ABC; Max and Ruby's Bedtime Book; Yoko Writes Her Name.* www.rosemarywells.com

David Wiesner, author/illustrator. Wordless fantasy stories and postmodern picture books. Three-time Caldecott medalist. *Tuesday; Sector 7; Flotsam; The Three Pigs; Art and Max.* www .hmhbooks.com/wiesner

Mo Willems, author/illustrator. Picture books for preschoolers featuring minimalist, childlike art, much humor, and action. *Don't Let the Pigeon Drive the Bus!; Knuffle Bunny: A Cautionary Tale.* www.mowillems.com

Color and Light

Hue and intensity are significant in considering *color*. Hue is the color itself, with predominant colors ranging from the cool end of the spectrum (the blues, greens, and gray-violets) or from the warm end (the reds, oranges, and yellows). The colors may be bright and intense or pale and dull (that is, more or less saturated) and range from diaphanous to opaque. The colors must complement the text, as in the use of cool, muted blues, grays, black, and white to convey the still, quiet mood and cold, dark setting of *Polar Bear Night* by Lauren Thompson (Illustration 7). In contrast, the bright, loud colors in *Officer Buckle and Gloria* project a jovial, emotionally warm mood and establish the noisy school setting (Illustration 10). If the events and mood of the text change during the story, then the colors will change to reflect and signal the shift occurring in the story. Sometimes illustrators choose not to use color or use color to focus our attention, such as in *Baseball Hour* by Carol Nevius, illustrated by Bill Thomson, where the reader's attention is drawn to the brilliant white and red baseball surrounded with muted shades of gray and cream (Illustration 4).

The amount of **light and dark** that artists use in an illustration is known as **value** and combines with color to bring a sense of drama and a three-dimensional effect to the illustrations. The illustration of David jumping on the bed clearly involves a lamp that provides shadows and establishes that this event is occurring at night (Illustration 1), while the shadows of Office Buckle and Gloria indicate the presence of spotlights on a stage (Illustration 10).

Space and Perspective

Space refers to the distance from one point to another in illustrations, with some illustrations appearing shallow with little depth and others creating the illusion of deep space. The father and daughter in *Knuffle Bunny* by Mo Willems are in the foreground, highlighted with color, while the buildings behind them in sepia tones create depth and background. The two are also in the center of the page, the point of greatest attention (Illustration 5). The use of negative space or blank space can highlight an object or show isolation or loneliness. For example, the proportions of the baseball relative to the human figure in *Baseball Hour* and the placement of the pitcher on a blank background emphasize the importance of the ball (Illustration 4). Another use of space is that the center of the page is typically the point of greatest attention.

Perspective is an aspect of space used by illustrators to highlight particular aspects of their visual images. Perspective creates the point of view from which an artist observes a scene and gives a sense of action by varying perspectives from far away views to close-ups and from a bird's-eye view looking down at a scene, a worm's-eye view looking up, or at eye level looking straight at the scene. Kadir Nelson is a master of using perspectives that range from close-ups of clenched fists to a faraway bird's-eye view that pans the entire boxing scene in *A Nation's Hope: The Story of Boxing Legend Joe Louis*. *Officer Buckle and Gloria* offers a worm's-eye audience view of the main characters on the stage, while *Baseball Hour* provides a dramatic close-up of the baseball (Illustrations 4 and 10).

Texture

The tactile surface characteristics of pictured objects comprise the ***texture*** of a picture. The reader's impression of how a pictured object feels is its texture. Sometimes young children will reach out to touch the surface of an illustration expecting to physically feel texture. Texture can also be implied through crosshatching or the use of lines in the beaver dam in *Song of the Waterboatman* (Illustration 9). Textures may be rough or slick, firm or spongy, hard or soft, jagged or smooth. The effects of texture can offer a greater sense of reality to a picture, as in *The Subway Mouse,* which features slightly rounded and textured plasticine for the mice's furry bodies and found objects such as a feather, scraps of newspaper, buttons, and old food labels in their nests (Illustration 11).

Composition

Composition refers to the arrangement of all of these visual elements and the way in which the visual elements relate one to the other and combine to make the picture. Many artists arrange each illustration around a single focal point, which is often a key to understanding composition. The artist decides on proportion, movement, balance, harmony, and dissonance within the various elements to produce the desired visual impact. The total effect should not overpower the story but rather extend and enrich the meaning and mood of the text. In *Knuffle Bunny: A Cautionary Tale,* Mo Willems places the main characters at the center of the illustration and then emphasizes them by using color against a nearly monochromatic sepia background. He draws the pair holding hands and sharing a loving look, and he places them in a calm, sunny, urban setting that is a digitally-altered photograph. The use of white space and the placement of the tree also serve to focus attention on the pair as does the directionality of their eyes toward each other (Illustration 5). Although it is not mentioned in the text, the little girl is clutching her stuffed rabbit. This composition indicates that the story will be about a happy little girl who trusts her father and that what happens to them could actually occur in the real world.

The details in the illustrations should not conflict with those in the text, but they can add another storyline and additional details, emotions, and events. Children are keenly observant of contradictions between the text and illustrations (e.g., a character or object missing from the illustration) and find them distracting. Although children accept illustrations that are varied in visual elements and artistic styles, they have little tolerance for inaccuracies.

Artistic Media

The *artistic media* refer to the materials and technical means used by artists to create pictures. *Technique* refers to *how* an illustrator uses a particular material, like watercolor. Although the variety of techniques and materials used by book illustrators is virtually unlimited, some of the more common media found in children's books are:

- *Drawing:* Pen and ink, colored pencils, pastels, charcoal pencils, scratchboard. Two excellent examples of drawing are Peter Sís's autobiographical *The Wall: Growing Up behind the Iron Curtain,* in which he uses pen and ink and colored markers, and Brian Selznick's *The Invention of Hugo Cabret,* in which he uses charcoal pencil. Brian Pinkney and Beth Krommes use scratchboard, where artists scratch white lines through the surface of a special paper with a black coating and then add color into the scratched areas using an oil pigment.

- *Collage:* An assemblage of materials such as real objects, cut or torn paper, fabric, and clay. The illustration from *The Subway Mouse* includes found objects—a feather, torn newspaper, a crayon, fabric, twine, a button (Illustration 11). Steve Jenkins uses cut papers to assemble his dazzling animal collages in such books as *Dogs and Cats* and *Prehistoric: Actual Size.*

- *Printmaking:* Woodcuts, linoleum prints, lithography, etching. Beckie Prange's hand-colored woodcuts in *Song of the Water Boatman & Other Pond Poems* perfectly capture the woodsy spirit of nature and wetland wildlife (Illustration 9). The linocut technique used to make the illustrations in *Polar Bear Night* resembles that of woodcuts, but uses linoleum as the relief surface (Illustration 7). Arthur Geisert is known for a related medium, etching, where he draws a design on a waxed metal plate and dips the plate in acid. The acid eats thin lines into the metal that is used as an inked plate for printing.

- *Photography:* Black and white, color. The large, close-up photographs used by Walter Wick in *A Drop of Water* support the factual nature of its contents and signal "This is real" (Illustration 12). Photographs are often used in concept books to help young children make the connection to their world.

- *Painting:* Oils, acrylics, watercolors, gouache, tempera. Oils, acrylics, tempera, and gouache paints produce an opaque surface with the possibility of brilliant, rich colors and a solid appearance. Watercolors are more transparent and prized for the luminosity achieved by the white paper surface shining through the paint. The tools with which the artist applies the paint affect its look and can be as varied as brushes, airbrushes, and sponges to apply paint. The bold colors in David Shannon's acrylic illustration from *No, David!* enhance the chaotic scene and the character's ebullient personality—a close look at the painting reveals the artist's actual brush strokes (Illustration 1).

- *Computer:* Digital painting, digital application of color to hand-drawn art, digital manipulation of images such as photographs. Using software, drawing pads, and scanners, artists can achieve unique artistic effects. In *Knuffle Bunny: A Cautionary Tale,* Mo Willems used a computer to color his hand-drawn characters, create the sepia tone of the background photographs, and remove unwanted items from the photographs (Illustration 5).

Then fielders field and pitchers pitch,

4

5

SNIP!

6

7

8

9

10

11

12

Guide to Illustrations

	Source of Book Illustration	Artistic Style; Media	Visual Elements	Elements of Fiction Complemented by Illustrations
1	Shannon, David. *No, David!* Scholastic, 1998.	Expressionist; acrylic paint, colored pencil	Line, shape, color	Character, plot, mood, theme, style
2	Smith, Chris. *One City, Two Brothers.* Illustrated by Aurélia Fronty. Barefoot, 2007.	Folk; acrylic paint	Line, shape/space, color	Setting, theme
3	Imai, Ayano. *Chester.* Penguin, 2007.	Surreal; watercolor with mineral pigments	Composition, color, line	Mood, theme, plot
4	Nevius, Carol. *Baseball Hour.* Illustrated by Bill Thomson. Marshall Cavendish, 2008.	Realistic; oil and acrylic paints, kneaded eraser, colored pencils	Shape/space, line, composition, texture, color	Character, setting, mood
5	Willems, Mo. *Knuffle Bunny: A Cautionary Tale.* Hyperion, 2004.	Cartoon/Realistic; pen and ink, digital photography, computer	Line, color	Character, setting, theme, mood
6	Hale, Shannon, and Dean Hale. *Rapunzel's Revenge.* Illustrated by Nathan Hale. Bloomsbury USA, 2008.	Cartoon/graphic novel format; pencil, ink colored with Photoshop	Line, color	Plot, character, setting, theme, style

Guide to Illustrations

Source of Book Illustration	Artistic Style; Media	Visual Elements	Elements of Fiction Complemented by Illustrations
7 Thompson, Lauren. *Polar Bear Night*. Illustrated by Stephen Savage. Scholastic, 2004.	Abstract; linocut prints	Color, shape, composition	Setting, characters, theme
8 Juster, Norton. *The Hello, Goodbye Window*. Illustrated by Chris Raschka. Hyperion, 2005.	Impressionistic; watercolors, oil pastels, pen and ink, charcoals	Composition, color, line	Character, setting, mood, style
9 Sidman, Joyce. *Song of the Water Boatman & Other Pond Poems*. Illustrated by Beckie Prange. Houghton, 2005.	Woodcut; watercolors	Composition, line, color, mood	Setting, theme
10 Rathmann, Peggy. *Officer Buckle and Gloria*. Putnam, 1995.	Cartoon; watercolors, pen and ink	Line, composition, mood	Plot, character, theme
11 Reid, Barbara. *The Subway Mouse*. Scholastic, 2003.	Cartoon; collage	Texture, color, mood	Character, setting, style
12 Wick, Walter. *A Drop of Water: A Book of Science and Wonder*. Scholastic, 1997.	Realistic; photography	Composition, space	Style, theme

Artists generally use one predominant medium in a picture book, drawing from other media for special effects. Multimedia is a recent trend, with more artists combining media to achieve the desired effect, often using digital scans to combine and manipulate the various media in order to create an effective illustration. Brief explanations of the artist's techniques and materials are often included in the copyright information, on the dust jacket, or in an illustrator note. See the column of "Artistic Style: Media" in the Guide to Illustrations for examples of illustrations in a range of mediums.

Artistic Styles

Children can identify the distinctive features that identify the work of their favorite illustrators, like Mo Willems. Although the style of a picture is individual to each artist, artwork in general can be grouped by style similarities. Five broad categories of artistic styles recognized in the Western world are realistic, impressionistic, expressionistic, abstract, and surrealistic. Another set of categories relate to particular cultural styles, reflecting traditional ways of creating visual images within a specific cultural group. Although an artist's works seldom fit neatly into one single art style, facets of these styles may be merged into the artist's personal expression of the world.

- *Realistic art* represents natural forms and provides accurate representations without idealization. Bill Thomson's almost photographic paintings and Mo Willems's use of actual photographs as backgrounds are excellent examples of realistic art (Illustrations 4 and 5).

- *Impressionistic art* depicts natural appearances of objects by rendering fleeting visual impressions with an emphasis on light. Chris Raschka's rendering of the house in Norton Juster's *The Hello, Goodbye Window* exhibits these qualities with extensive use of white space to create light and lack of detail to suggest a fleeting image (Illustration 8).

- *Expressionistic art* communicates an emotional experience more than an external reality. The artist draws attention to the central message by exaggeration and by eliminating competing details. David Shannon distorts the figure of the boy to emphasize his noisy exuberance and keeps background details to a minimum in *No, David!* (Illustration 1).

- *Abstract art* uses intrinsic geometric forms and surface qualities with little direct representation of objects to emphasize mood and feeling. Some abstract art is considered **graphic design,** adapted from the field of commercial art, as seen in Stephen Savage's economy of line and emphasis on elemental triangles and circles in *Polar Bear Night* to suggest the harsh, barren, frozen landscape of the Arctic in winter (Illustration 7).

- *Surrealistic art* emphasizes the subconscious by juxtaposing incongruous dreamlike and fantasy images with realistic ones. In *Chester,* Ayano Imai juxtaposes the relatively realistic images of a dog and two humans against the fantasy of flowers growing out of the table, suggesting a positive outcome and a bright future, along with depicting smoke coming from the chimney of the dog's house, a visual metaphor for finding a happy home (Illustration 3).

- *Folk art,* usually seen in picture books set in the distant past or in rural and preindustrial societies, is often representative of the artistic style prevalent in the culture of that story. Folk art thus varies by culture but typically involves flat, stylized figures. Folktales are sometimes illustrated in folk art style to give a sense of the culture and the ancient setting of the story, such as the illustration from Chris Smith's *One City, Two Brothers,* a story based on a folktale shared by Israelis and Palestinians (Illustration 2). Authors can also use elements of folk art, as David Diaz did in the backgrounds and endpapers of *Going Home,* by Eve Bunting.

- **Cartoon art** often features rounded figures, exaggerated action, and simplified backgrounds. Peggy Rathmann's humorous illustrations for *Officer Buckle and Gloria* are reminiscent of those found in comic books (Illustration 10). Nathan Hale uses a more sophisticated cartoon style in the graphic novel *Rapunzel's Revenge* (Illustration 6).

- **Cultural styles** developed over time within the traditions of particular cultures, such as the use of simplified forms and bright colors in African art and painting on silk and rice papers with flat designs for scenes in traditional Japanese art. These styles are particularly important in traditional literature or picture books of historical time periods dominated by that style within a culture. Modern artists from these cultures use a wide range of styles but may embed specific cultural elements from traditional styles into their illustrations. The Come Look with Me art series focuses on cultures, such as Asian, Latin American, American Indian, and African American, and provides an introduction to the range of styles within each of these cultural traditions.

Book Design

Book design is the artful orchestration of all components of a book into a coherent whole. Children's books are more than text or text and pictures and use a range of design features:

- The **dust jacket** is a removable paper cover wrapped around the book to protect against soiling. It also attracts purchasers and readers as well as informs them about the book, author, and illustrator.

- The **covers** of a book are usually made of two boards, which make the book more durable and allow it to stand on a shelf. When no dust jacket is on a book, the front cover provides a first impression of the story.

- The **title** is usually first seen on the dust jacket or front cover along with an illustration to communicate the nature of the story to readers. Many titles suggest the topic of the story and help readers decide whether to read the book. Other titles and covers may not offer much information, and so a booktalk by a teacher or librarian is needed to entice readers.

- The **endpapers** are the pages glued to the inside front and back boards of the cover and the *flyleaf* is the page facing each endpaper. The endpaper and flyleaf are often used to provoke curiosity in the reader for what follows, to set a mood, to evoke an affective response in preparation for the story, or to act as a visual prologue and epilogue, as in Emily Gravett's *Wolves* and Jerry Pinkney's *The Lion and the Mouse.*

- The **title page** tells the book's full title and subtitle, if there is one; the names of the author(s) and illustrator(s); and the name and location of the publisher. Occasionally, a book will include a *frontispiece,* an illustration facing the title page, which is intended to establish the tone and to entice the reader to begin the story.

- On the reverse side of the title page, called the **verso** of the title page, is the **publishing history** of the book. On this page is the copyright notice, a legal right giving the holder permission to produce and sell the work. The copyright is indicated by the international symbol ©, followed by the name of the person(s) holding the copyright and the date it takes effect, which is the year the book is first published. Later publications are also listed. The country in which the book was printed, the number assigned to the book by the Library of Congress, the International Standard Book Number (ISBN), and the edition of the book are also included. Many publishers include cataloguing information for libraries, a very brief annotation of the story, and a statement on the media and techniques used in the illustrations.

- The title page typically presents the *typeface,* the style of print, used throughout the book. The size and legibility of the typeface must be suited to the book's intended audience. Books for the young child who is just learning to read should have large, well-spaced print for easy eye scanning. The print style for an easy-to-read book should be a somewhat larger-than-average standard block print with easily distinguishable and recognizable uppercase and lowercase letters. Legibility is diminished when background colors are used behind the text, leaving insufficient contrast for easy reading.

- The size, shape, and darkness of the *print type* can be heavy and strong or light and willowy. The choice of print type should enhance the overall visual message of the illustrations and fit the visual style and mood. The placement of the print on the pages in relation to the illustrations can subtly guide the reader and become a functional part of the story.

- Unusual *print styles* are sometimes selected, such as script print to give the impression of handwriting in a book with diary entries. Some illustrators choose to hand-letter the text. Examples of lettering as part of design are the classic *Millions of Cats* by Wanda Gág and David Larochelle's *The End,* illustrated by Richard Egielski.

- The *page layout* can vary from illustrations being placed one on a page, on facing pages, on alternating pages, or on parts of pages. A picture that extends across the two facing pages is called a *doublespread* and gives the effect of motion, drawing the eye to the next page. It can also give a feeling of grandeur, openness, and expansiveness. Sometimes, a picture will begin on a right-hand page and spill over to the following page, the reverse side. This offers a strong sense of continuity from one part of the story to the next.

- Some pictures have a *frame* or *border.* Framing an illustration can distance the reader from the action, lend a sense of order to the story, or make the mood more formal. The frame itself may be a simple line or a broad, ornately decorated ribbon of information or another storyline. Decorations on a frame may repeat certain images or symbols to reinforce the meaning of the story.

- *Paper* is another part of the book makeup. The paper should be thick enough to be durable and sometimes involves the use of textured or colored paper to enhance the story. Similarly, the shape of the pages should be in keeping with the story or concept, particularly if it is unique or unusual (e.g., in the shape of a concrete object or as a fold out).

- The *size* of the book is an important design feature. Large picture books are well suited for reading aloud to a class. Smaller picture books are usually not satisfactory choices for class read-alouds, but support interaction with one child.

- *Book binding,* or the way the pages are held together, determines a book's durability. Books may be bound in hardcover, paperback, or in some special-purpose material. Books for babies are frequently bound in sturdy cardboard or vinyl to withstand the dual role of toy and book. Carefully open the book at its midpoint to determine whether the binding of a hardcover book is glued or sewn. Stitches in the gutter of the book can be seen in a book binding that is sewn. Sewn bindings last much longer than glued ones. Durability relative to cost is the usual trade-off in selecting paper or hardcover bindings for classroom or school libraries, with the cost of hardcover books justified for fairly heavy use.

Observing the Role of Illustrations in Picture Books

The role of illustrations in picture books can best be understood as the intersection of visual elements, artistic styles, and artistic media with literary elements (e.g., character, setting, theme, and plot). These roles vary in importance, depending on the type of picture book. In wordless picture books, the illustrations tell the whole story; in picture storybooks, they tell part of the story; in illustrated books, they may serve as decoration to enhance the book.

The Guide to Illustrations at the beginning and end of the color insert gives a brief analysis of each illustration and how it contributes to the story. To better understand the examples, locate the books from which the illustrations were taken and use the guide as an aid to understanding how artistic styles, visual elements, and elements of fiction contribute to each story's meaning. For example, in David Shannon's *No, David!* (Illustration 1), a pajama-clad little boy, instead of quietly preparing for sleep, careens off his bed imagining that he is a superhero. His mother's presence is found only in her words, "Settle down!" For child and adult reader alike, the boy's exaggerated expression and motion provide humor. David Shannon's use of an expressionistic style, bold colors, and jagged, diagonal lines emphasize the child's energy, motion, and zest for life. Seen from his mother's perspective, however, these same artistic attributes could be interpreted as emphasizing the child's mischievousness and disobedience.

The key to understanding and appreciating the role of illustrations in picture books is to look carefully at illustrations for the messages they contain. You need to be able to "read" the ways in which pictures "mean." Table 4.1 offers tips about what to look for as you read picture storybooks.

Table 4.1 How Illustrations Contribute to Picture Book Stories: A Summary

Artistic and Literary Aspects		Contributions of Illustrations to Stories
Literary Elements	Plot	Convey story events not in the text.
	Character	Show characters not in the text; contribute to characterization by showing physical appearance and actions.
	Setting	Show the setting and time period. Indicate the passing of time in a day or seasons.
	Theme	Accentuate the book's theme. Indicate the theme in wordless books.
	Style	Show author's stance toward the protagonist by viewing the world from the protagonist's perspective. Support a book's literary style to faithfully represent an era or culture.
Visual Elements	Line	Indicate motion or action, story mood (e.g., calm vs. agitated), aspects of plot (e.g., real vs. dreamed), and character (e.g., fragile vs. strong).
	Color	Indicate characters' emotions and personalities, story mood, and aspects of setting (e.g., lush vs. arid, cold vs. warm).

Artistic and Literary Aspects		Contributions of Illustrations to Stories
	Shape and Space	Indicate what is most important by relative size. Emphasize contrast by juxtaposing large and small objects. Use of blank space to highlight an object or show isolation.
	Perspective and Light	Create a sense of drama and action by taking points of view from above, below, or at eye level. Use of a light source to focus attention or to establish time of day and reality.
	Texture	Intensify a sense of character or setting by indicating the feel of objects or surroundings.
	Composition	Focus the eye on what is most important (usually in the center). Indicate a character's perspective (how the character sees the world).
Artistic Styles	Realistic	Emphasize that information in nonfiction is real and that realistic fiction could be true or based on fact.
	Impressionistic	Contribute to settings through light-filled scenes of nature.
	Expressionistic	Express characters' feelings and emotions through exaggeration.
	Abstract	Emphasize basic, shared traits of characters; create a nonspecific setting.
	Surrealistic	Help connect characters' conscious and unconscious thoughts, emotions, and concerns.
	Folk	Establish and develop settings in the past or in particular cultural traditions.
	Cartoon	Provide humor through exaggeration of character appearance and actions.
	Cultural	Provide connections to traditions that developed over time within particular cultures.

Historical Overview of Picture Books

Orbis Pictus (The World in Pictures), an ABC book written and illustrated by John Amos Comenius in Moravia in 1657, is considered to be the first children's picture book. Comenius was the first to emphasize using pictures to explain and expand the meaning of the text in books for young people. Since early books were rare and prohibitively expensive, very few children had access to them. Moreover, until well into the nineteenth century, Europeans and Americans believed that books were for the serious business of educating and soul saving—not enjoyment!

Today's full-color, beautifully illustrated, humorous picture books are the result of these important developments:

- Technological advances in color printing made high-quality illustrations more affordable.
- A more understanding attitude toward childhood evolved. During the nineteenth century, society began to accept the notion of childhood as a time for playing and learning and the economy could support the leisure time these activities require for the average child.
- Higher standards of excellence in picture book illustrations developed through the beauty and charm of nineteenth-century illustrators Randolph Caldecott, Kate Greenaway, and Walter Crane, gaining the attention of the general public.
- The establishment of national awards for excellence in children's book illustration in the twentieth century encouraged more artists to enter the children's book field.
- The growth of public school systems and public and school library systems increased the demand for books. In addition, reading came to be recognized as one of the child's best tools for learning and for gaining a worthy source of entertainment.

Today, the picture book genre is well established, with an ever-widening audience and a focus on multicultural and global themes on more realistic issues such as the effects of war, poverty, immigration, and disabilities on the lives of children. Greater diversity in formats and more illustrated retellings of folktales are available. A trend of the 1990s was to publish picture books with high levels of conceptual difficulty and artistic sophistication intended for middle-grade students. The twenty-first century has witnessed the growth of the graphic novel, a novel-length comic book originally created for adults that now includes books for elementary- and middle-grade students.

Types of Picture Books

Today's picture books differ in intended audience, purpose, format, and relative amount of text and illustration. These differences are not absolute, but picture books can be grouped according to characteristics into several specific types. Although overlap between types is inevitable, the following kinds of picture books are available for children today. The types here are organized by the intended age of the audience from youngest to oldest. Note that poems, nursery rhymes, and songbooks in picture book format are included in the chapter on Poetry, folktale picture books are discussed in Traditional Literature, and informational picture books are covered in Informational Books.

Baby Books

Baby books are simply designed, brightly illustrated, durable picture books that are intended for use with children ages 0 to 2, such as *Global Babies* by Maya Ajmera. Safety is ensured by rounded corners, nontoxic materials, washable pages, and no loose attachments. The types of baby books are based on the material used in their construction, such as *vinyl books* and *cloth books*. *Board books* are constructed of heavy, laminated cardboard and are either bound as a book with pages or made to fold out in an accordion fashion. These books have little or no text, mostly simple, clear illustrations that are easy to label, such as the classic *Goodnight Moon* by Margaret Wise Brown, which many parents have read over and over and over again. Their content, which deals with the objects and routines that are familiar to the infant and toddler, is presented mainly in the illustrations. The best

MILESTONES in the Development of Picture Books

Date	Event	Significance
1484	*Aesop's Fables,* illustrated by William Caxton	One of the first-known illustrated books enjoyed by children
1657	*Orbis Pictus,* written and illustrated by John Amos Comenius	Considered the first picture book for children
1860–1900	Golden Age of children's book illustration in Great Britain, led by Randolph Caldecott, Walter Crane, and Kate Greenaway	Increased awareness, stature, popularity, and appreciation of children's picture books
1902	*The Tale of Peter Rabbit* by Beatrix Potter	Early important modern picture storybook in English
1928	*Millions of Cats* by Wanda Gág	Early important modern American picture storybook
1938	First Caldecott Award for illustration in children's books in U.S.	Promoted excellence in illustrating for children and encouraged talented artists to illustrate children's books
1940	*Pat the Bunny* by Dorothy Kunhardt	One of the first books for babies; began the move to different types of picture books for different child audiences
1957	*The Cat in the Hat,* written and illustrated by Dr. Seuss, and *Little Bear,* written by Else Minarik and illustrated by Maurice Sendak	Introduced the easy-to-read genre of picture books
1967	*A Boy, a Dog, and a Frog,* illustrated by Mercer Mayer	Popularized the wordless book genre
1972	*Push Pull, Empty Full* by Tana Hoban	Signaled the growing popularity of the concept picture book
1981	"The Baby Board Books" by Helen Oxenbury	Established baby books as a distinct and important type of picture book
1990	*Color Zoo* by Lois Ehlert wins a Caldecott Honor Award	Recognition of the engineered book genre
1991	*Black and White* by David Macaulay wins Caldecott Medal	Denoted influence of postmodernism and acceptance of nontraditional picture book formats
2006	First Theodor Seuss Geisel Award	Promoted excellence in books for beginning readers

baby books, such as those produced by Helen Oxenbury, are thoughtfully designed to emphasize patterns and associations to promote dialogue between the caregiver and the young child.

Interactive Books

Interactive books are picture books that invite a child's verbal or physical participation as the book is read. These books ask the child direct questions, invite unison recitation of chants or repeated lines, encourage clapping or moving to the rhythm of the words, or require the child to touch or manipulate the book or find objects in the illustrations. The intended audience is usually children ages 2 to 6, and the books are seen as an extension of their world of play. One classic example of this type of book that is still greatly enjoyed by toddlers is Dorothy Kunhardt's *Pat the Bunny.* A recent example is Mem Fox's *Ten Little Fingers and Ten Little Toes,* illustrated by Helen Oxenbury.

Toy Books

Sometimes called *engineered books, toy books* use paper that has been engineered (i.e., cut, folded, constructed) to provide pop-up, see-through, movable, changeable, foldout, or three-dimensional illustrations. Toy books can be found for all ages, but only those that have the simpler types of engineering, such as pages of varying widths or drilled holes for see-through effects (as in Eric Carle's classic *The Very Hungry Caterpillar,* or Laura Seeger's *First the Egg*), are appropriate for most young children. Toy books with fragile or elaborate pop-up features, such as Robert Sabuda's amazing pop-up versions of *Alice's Adventures in Wonderland* or his *Encyclopedia Prehistoria: Dinosaurs,* would not last in the hands of a young child, but delight older children (and adults).

Wordless Books

The *wordless book* depends entirely on carefully sequenced illustrations to present the story. There is either no text or the text is limited to one or two pages in the book, so the illustrations must carry the narrative, such as in Jerry Pinkney's *The Lion and the Mouse* and Chris Raschka's *A Ball for Daisy,* both Caldecott Medal winners. Wordless books are often targeted at young emergent readers or English language learners, but many sophisticated wordless books exist for older readers, such as David Wiesner's *Flotsam* and Shaun Tan's *The Arrival.* When children "read" these illustrations in their own words, they benefit from the book's visual story structure in several ways:

- They develop a concept of story as a cohesive narrative with a beginning and an end.
- They use language inventively, which promotes language development.
- They learn the front-to-back, left-to-right page progression in reading.
- They begin to understand that stories can be found not only in books but in themselves.
- They develop an understanding of the complexity of visual images in telling a story.

Alphabet Books

The *alphabet,* or *ABC, book* presents the alphabet letter by letter to acquaint young children with the shapes, names, and, in some cases, the sounds of the twenty-six letters, as in *ABC: A Child's First Alphabet Book* by Alison Jay. Almost all ABC book authors and illustrators choose a theme (animals, elves, fruit, etc.) or device (finding the many objects in the accompanying illustration beginning with the featured letter) to give their books cohesion. In choosing an ABC book, consider the appropriateness of the theme or device for students, whether both uppercase and lowercase letters are displayed, and the use of a simple, easy-to-read style of print.

Most ABC books are intended for emergent readers. Some authors and illustrators use the alphabet itself as a device for presenting information or wordplay, and so the intended audience are older children who already know the alphabet. In *Superhero ABC*, Bob McLeod presents imaginative and wacky superheroes whose names and descriptions begin with the featured letter, inviting readers to invent such characters of their own.

Counting Books

The *counting book* presents numbers, usually 1 through 10, to acquaint young children with the numerals and their shapes (1, 2, 3), the number names (one, two, three), the sense of what quantity each numeral represents, and the counting sequence. *Teeth, Tails, & Tentacles: An Animal Counting Book* by Christopher Wormell, with its bold linocut prints clearly depicting the numerals and the objects to be counted, presents lessons in counting and zoology simultaneously. As with alphabet books, authors and illustrators employ themes or devices to make counting books more cohesive and interesting. Specific considerations include the appeal to children of the theme and objects chosen to illustrate the number concepts and the clarity with which the illustrator presents the concept of number. Some counting books are meant for older readers, either because of the sophistication of the number concepts or the use of counting as an organizing structure to present information aimed at older readers, as in *Ten Birds* by Cybele Young.

Illustrators often fill their alphabet and counting books with unusual and intriguing objects for children to name and count, such as aardvarks, barracudas, and chameleons, inviting children to pick up a great deal of interesting information and vocabulary. You will be in the best position to decide whether the novelty of these objects will be motivating or confusing to your students.

Concept Books

A *concept book* is a picture book that explores or explains an idea or concept (e.g., opposites), an object (e.g., a train), or an activity (e.g., working) rather than telling a story. Many concept books have no plot but use repeated elements in the illustrations and text to tie the book together. Concept books are a form of informational book that focuses on a specific concept appropriate for young children, such as the innovative *Hippopposites* by French illustrator Janik Coat. Laura Seeger combines a simple format, well-known but unexpected objects, and paper cutouts to create interesting books about color in *Lemons Are Not Red* and *Green*. The concepts are not necessarily simplistic as in *More* by I. C. Springman, which explores excessive materialism through the antics of a magpie who hoards too much stuff and the mice who show that less is more. Limited text and clearly understood illustrations encourage children's exploratory talk about the concepts, objects, and activities.

Alphabet and counting books are considered types of concept books. Another variety of the concept book that is popular with 2- to 4-year-olds is the *naming book,* which presents simple pictures of people, animals, and objects that are labeled for young children to identify, such as *The Big Book of Words and Pictures* by Ole Konnecke.

Picture Storybooks

The *picture storybook* is a book in which a story is told through both the words and pictures. Text and illustration occur with equal frequency in these books, and both are in view on most double spreads. Most people associate the term *picture book* with this type of book and it is the most common type. An enduring favorite picture storybook is Chris Van Allsburg's *The Polar Express*. Recent examples that are Caldecott Medal winners include Kevin Henkes's *Kitten's First Full Moon* and Philip and Erin Stead's *A Sick Day for Amos McGee*. The information found in Table 4.1 is particularly applicable to picture storybooks.

The text of most picture storybooks is meant to be read aloud to the intended audience of 4- to 7-year-olds, at least for the first time or two, and often includes challenging vocabulary. Many of the best picture storybooks are also read and enjoyed independently by children 8 years old and up. Picture storybooks reflect a range of genres and so examples are included in the genre chapters of Traditional Literature, Modern Fantasy, Realistic Fiction, and Historical Fiction and Biography.

Predictable Books

Predictable, or *pattern, books* have repeated language patterns, story patterns, or familiar sequences that encourage children to chime in on repeating phrases, as in Bill Martin Jr. and Eric Carle's perennial favorite *Brown Bear, Brown Bear, What Do You See?* and Emily Gravett's *Monkey and Me*. These books support readers through meaning and illustration clues and the use of repeating refrains or phrases. Some predictable books use language regularities and repeat certain phonological features, as is the line, "Is this the bus for us, Gus?" in Suzanne Bloom's *The Bus for Us* or the entertaining story of friendship, *Moo Hoo* by Candace Ryan and Mike Lowery, which utilizes rhymed sound words to express the emotional content of the book.

Easy-to-Read Books

Easy-to-read books help the beginning reader read independently with success. These books have limited text on a page, large print, double-spacing, short sentences, and often occur in series. There is usually an illustration on every other page. Language is often, but not always, controlled, and words are short and familiar. Laura McGee Kvasnosky's *Zelda and Ivy: The Runaways* emphasizes familiar family situations and gentle humor, while Mo Willems's *Are You Ready to Play Outside?* focuses on friendship and tells the story in dialogue balloons. Easy-to-read books can be used with children whenever they want to learn to read, but the audience is usually 5- to 7-year-olds.

The easy-to-read book differs in appearance from the picture storybook in several obvious ways. Because they are intended for independent reading, they do not have to be seen from a distance and may be smaller, the text takes up a greater proportion of each page, and the text is often divided into short chapters. *Billy & Milly, Short & Silly* by Eve Feldman plays with this format, telling thirteen short stories of only three or four words each of the adventures of two friends.

The importance of easy-to-read books was recognized with the establishment of the Theodor Seuss Geisel Award in 2004. This annual award, named for the renowned Dr. Seuss and sponsored by the American Library Association, is given to the author and illustrator of the most distinguished American book for beginning readers. Mo Willems has won this award multiple times for his Elephant and Piggy series as has Kate DiCamillo for her Mercy Watson series and her Bink and Gollie series and Tedd Arnold for his Fly Guy series. Theodor Seuss Geisel believed that easy-to-read books with their limited vocabulary could engage young readers with imagination and creativity instead of forcing them to read the pedantic stories found in many early reading materials. These award winners are excellent examples of books that invite children to eagerly engage as readers.

Transitional Books

Transitional books are books for children who can read but have not yet become fluent readers. They are not picture books, but lie somewhere between picture books and full-length novels. Characteristics of transitional books are an uncomplicated writing style and vocabulary, illustrations on about every third page, division of text into chapters, slightly enlarged print, and an average length of 100 pages. The Ruby Lu and Alvin Ho books by Lenore Look, the Nikki and Deja books by Karen English, and the Tia Lola books by Julía Alavarez reflect a trend toward more multicultural content in these books. Often, books for the transitional reader occur in series, as Donald J. Sobol's much-loved Encyclopedia Brown books and the more recent Ivy and Bean series by Annie Barrows and Martin Bridge series by Jessica Kerrin. *The No. 1 Car Spotter* and the Anna Hibiscus series by Atinuke based on her Nigerian childhood provide a global connection.

The Center for Children's Books at the University of Illinois at Urbana–Champaign established the Gryphon Award for transitional books in 2004. This prize is given to fiction or nonfiction that best exemplifies qualities that successfully bridge the gap in difficulty between picture books and full-length books. The 2012 winner, Julie Sternberg's *Like Pickle Juice on a Cookie,* captures a first experience of loss and reflects the range of life experiences depicted in transitional books.

Picture Books for Older Readers

Picture books for older readers are generally more sophisticated, abstract, or complex in themes, stories, and illustrations and are suitable for children age 10 and older. This type of picture book began to appear in the 1970s in response to increasingly visual modes of communication and is being created by artists such as Anthony Browne, D. B. Johnson, David Macaulay, Shaun Tan, and Peter Sís. Peter Sís's autobiographical *The Wall: Growing Up behind the Iron Curtain* has aspects of both picture books and graphic novels and its serious content and factual historical base are aimed at older students. Another groundbreaking book that blurs genres is Brian Selznick's *The Invention of Hugo Cabret,* which won the Caldecott as a picture book but is over 500 pages long. The book contains long sequences of black and white illustrations without any text in between sections of text that do not have illustrations. Because the illustrations are essential to the telling of the story, the book is considered a picture book, although it also has characteristics of a graphic novel or stills from a film presented in a slow motion sequence.

Picture books for older readers lend themselves to use across the middle- and high-school curriculum, including social studies, science, language arts, mathematics, art, music, and physical education (Albright, 2002). The possible uses for readers in middle and secondary schools include:

- Teacher read-alouds for introductions and supplements to textbook units of instruction.
- Text sets (several books on the same topic or theme) for small group in-class reading and discussion and to provide background for a novel, event, or time period.
- Models of excellent writing to be used within mini-lessons and writing inquiries.
- Source of humor and interest in a topic, and as a way to provoke discussion, which can result in a deeper understanding of the content.

- Demonstration of practical applications of difficult concepts.
- Factual content that reinforces or adds to that found in textbooks.
- Source of different perspectives on issues and historical events, particularly those of underrepresented groups.

The traditional notion that picture books are only for younger children no longer applies. Although some adults may persist in guiding older children away from picture books, teachers and librarians find that picture books for older readers offer an effective way to thoughtfully engage students.

Graphic Novels

The last decade has seen the emergence and popularity of *graphic novels* as a book format related to picture books. These novel-length books feature text written in speech bubbles or as captions similar to comic-book illustrations. The term *graphic* refers to stories told through images and not the nature of the content. These books have become so popular that they are found across all genres and so are incorporated throughout the genre chapters, with a GR note in the recommended book lists.

Graphic novels appeal to young people and to reluctant readers because they are visually oriented, emphasize dialogue, often occur in series, and have close ties to popular culture such as films and comic-book superheroes. Shannon and Dean Hale and illustrator Nathan Hale created the graphic novel *Rapunzel's Revenge* (Illustration 6) by recasting the demure folktale heroine as a proactive superwoman and changing the setting to the outlaw-ridden U.S. Wild West. Barry Deutsch has created a superhero tale involving a young Orthodox Jew in the series, Hereville. A graphic novel appropriate for younger readers is *Babymouse: Queen of the World!* by Jennifer L. Holm and illustrated by her brother, Matthew Holm.

Postmodern Picture Books

A number of authors and illustrators are playing with multiple storylines, voices, and perspectives to create *postmodern picture books* that are exciting because of their unpredictability. These books reflect the fragmented and multimodal nature of modern society, with frequent changes in attitudes, styles, and knowledge: everything is constantly shifting. This uncertainty is used in picture books to create playful, unexpected and sometimes cynical books that delight in breaking the rules of convention and giving greater power to the reader. Most are meant for older readers because of their sophistication, sarcasm, and reference to other texts.

David Wiesner's *The Three Pigs* is viewed as an exemplar of postmodern picture books. This book is *not* a traditional folktale as his pigs step off the page of the book to peer at the reader and fold up the page to create a paper airplane to fly into other stories. The characteristics of postmodern picture books (Goldstone, 2004) include:

- **Multiple storylines**. The text may move back and forth in time, jumble up time, or interrupt a story that then goes in multiple directions as occurs when Wiesner's pig steps off the page. In Emily Gravett's *Wolves,* the text reads like a simple information book on wolves, but the illustrations reveal a different narrative as a menacing wolf looms over the rabbit immersed in reading information on the eating habits of wolves.
- **Multiple perspectives and page planes**. Different characters may tell their side of the story or the narrator's story maybe interrupted by characters, as in Melanie Watt's *Chester,* where the

cat changes the author's story about a mouse. Multiple planes can be revealed in the illustrations where the characters break outside the surface plane of the page and move into the reader's space or suddenly move underneath or above the page. Wiesner's pigs talk to each other, to the reader, and to themselves, as they step off pages, fold up pages, and look behind and over pages.

- **Irony and contradiction**. A sarcastic or mocking tone can be found in fractured and spoofed fairy tales, as in Jon Scieszka's *The Stinky Cheese Man,* or may occur through discrepancies, unexpected elements, and other storylines in the illustrations. The illustrations are sometimes purposefully in complete contradiction to the text.

- **Uncovering the artistic process of bookmaking**. The act of making the book is revealed by having the characters argue with the illustrator or author or the author and illustrator may argue with each other as in *Chloe and the Lion* by Mac Barnett and Adam Rex. Sometimes readers are invited to step into a story world but are spoken to by the characters about creating the story as occurs in Mordecai Gerstein's *A Book*.

These same characteristics are also used to create postmodern novels, as in Kate DiCamillo's *The Tale of Despereaux* with its multiple parallel stories and a narrator who directly addresses the reader.

During the twentieth century the picture book developed as a genre, diversified to meet the demands of an ever-expanding audience and market, and improved as a result of printing technology. As researchers came to realize the connections between positive early experiences with good literature, reading, and school success, new types of picture books were developed. Today, high-quality picture books on nearly every imaginable topic can enrich the lives and imaginations of children.

Invitations for Further Investigation

- Read Molly Bang's *Picture This: How Pictures Work* (2000) about the elements that make up a picture and the ways images work to tell a story that engages the emotions. Apply her principles of color, line, and shape to create a scary picture using simple geometric shapes and four basic colors (red, black, white, and purple). Explore books that Molly Bang has written and illustrated to examine how she uses these principles in her own books.

- Investigate visual symbolism in art through online sites such as the Dictionary of Symbolism. Then read a book noted for its use of visual symbols, such as the Grimm brothers' *Snow White and the Seven Dwarfs,* translated by Randall Jarrell and illustrated by Nancy Ekholm Burkert (1972), or books by Anthony Browne, such as *Piggybook* (1990) or *The Tunnel* (1989). How does awareness of visual symbolism influence a reader's appreciation and understanding of stories presented in picture storybook format?

- Select a picture storybook appropriate for a particular group of students. Read the book aloud to the students and invite them to share their connections and responses to the book. Then ask them how the illustrations contribute to their understandings of the story. If possible, share several books by the illustrator so students can see patterns. Use Table 4.1 for ideas.

- Investigate the ways in which graphic novels can be used with students and the strategies that students use in reading these books in such articles as Brenner's (2006) "Graphic

Novels 101: FAQ" and Rudiger's (2006) "Graphic Novels 101: Reading Lessons." Explore several graphic novels and keep a record of your reading strategies.

- Read several postmodern picture books along with the article by Goldstone (2004). Identify the postmodern features of these books and consider their appeal for older readers.

References

Albright, L. K. (2002). Bringing the Ice Maiden to life: Engaging adolescents in learning through picture book read-alouds in content areas. *Journal of Adolescent and Adult Literacy, 45*(5), 418–428.

Brenner, R. (2006). Graphic novels 101: FAQ. *Horn Book Magazine, 82*(2), 123–125.

Fellowes, J. (2007). *The curious adventures of the abandoned toys.* Schindler, S. D. (Illus.). New York: Holt.

Goldstone, B. (2004). The postmodern picture book: A new subgenre. *Language Arts 81*(3), 196–204.

Grimm, J., & Grimm, W. (1972). *Snow White and the seven dwarfs.* (R. Jarrell, Trans.). Burkert, N. E. (Illus.). New York: Farrar.

Hearn, M. P. (1984). In the library. In J. Cole (Ed.), *A new treasury of children's poetry.* New York: Doubleday.

Rudiger, H. M. (2006). Graphic novels 101: Reading lessons. *Horn Book Magazine, 82*(2), 126–134.

Recommended Picture Books

Ages indicated refer to approximate concept and interest levels.

Baby Books

Ajmera, Maya, and Global Fund for Children. **Global Babies**. Charlesbridge, 2007. Ages 0–2. (Board book).

Ashman, Linda. **Babies on the Go**. Illus. Jane Dyer. Harcourt, 2003. Ages 2–4.

Cousins, Lucy. **Maisy's Snuggle Book**. Candlewick, 2011. Ages 1–3. (Cloth book).

Fox, Mem. **Hello Baby!** Illus. Steve Jenkins. Beach Lane, 2009. Ages 1–3. (Also in a board book).

Frazee, Marla. **Walk On! A Guide for Babies of All Ages**. Harcourt, 2006. Ages 1–2.

Henderson, Kathy. **Look at You! A Baby Body Book**. Illus. Paul Howard. Candlewick, 2007. Ages 2–4. (Interactive).

Katz, Karen. **Counting Kisses**. Little Simon, 2010. Ages 0–2. (Board book).

Lobel, Anita. **Hello, Day!** Greenwillow, 2008. Ages 2–4.

Oxenbury, Helen. **I Can**. Walker, 2000. Ages 0–3. Also **I See; I Touch; I Hear**. (Board book).

Wildsmith, Brian. **Brian Wildsmith's Animal Colors**. Star Bright, 2008. Ages 1–3. (Board book).

Yoon, Salina. **One, Two, Buckle My Shoe: A Counting Nursery Rhyme**. Robin Corey, 2011. Ages 1–3. (Board book).

Ziefert, Harriet. **Who Said Moo?** Illus. Simms Taback. Blue Apple, 2010. Ages 1–3. (Board book).

Interactive Books

Beaumont, Karen. **I Ain't Gonna Paint No More!** Illus. David Catrow. Harcourt, 2005. Ages 3–7.

Chwast, Seymour. **Seymour Chwast Says—Get Dressed!** Appleseed, 2012. Ages 2–6. (Flaps).

Fox, Mem. **Ten Little Fingers and Ten Little Toes**. Illus. Helen Oxenbury. Harcourt, 2008. Ages 3–5.

Kunhardt, Dorothy. **Pat the Bunny**. Golden, 2001 (1940). Ages 2–4.

Ljungkvist, Laura. **Follow the Line through the House**. Viking, 2007. Ages 3–7.

Schwartz, Amy. **What James Likes Best**. Simon & Schuster, 2003. Ages 3–5.

Slater, Dashka. **Baby Shoes**. Illus. Hiroe Nakata. Bloomsbury, 2006. Ages 1–3.

Tullet, Herve. **Press Here**. Handprint, 2010. Ages 3–8. Translated from French.

Whybrow, Ian. **The Noisy Way to Bed**. Illus. Tiphanie Beeke. Scholastic, 2004. Ages 2–4.

Yee, Wong H. *Who Likes Rain?* Holt, 2007. Ages 3–6.

Yolen, Jane, editor. *This Little Piggy: Lap Songs, Finger Plays, Clapping Games, and Pantomime Rhymes.* Illus. Will Hillenbrand. Candlewick, 2006. Ages 2–4.

Toy Books

Campbell, Rod. *Dear Zoo: A Lift-the-Flap Book*. Little Simon, 2007 (1982). Ages 1–4.

Carle, Eric. *The Very Hungry Caterpillar.* Philomel, 1968. Ages 4–6. (Die-cut pages). Predictable book.

Carter, David. *White Noise*. Little Simon, 2009. Ages 6–12. (Pop-up).

Crowther, Robert. *Opposites.* Candlewick, 2005. Ages 4–8. (Pull tabs and lift flaps). Concept book.

Ehlert, Lois. *Leaf Man.* Harcourt, 2005. Ages 5–8. Also *In My World* (2002). (Die-cut pages).

Gravett, Emily. *The Rabbit Problem*. Simon & Schuster, 2010. Ages 5-8. (Pop-up).

Polhemus, Coleman. *The Crocodile Blues.* Candlewick, 2007. Ages 3–7. (Lift flaps). Picture storybook.

Sabuda, Robert. *Alice's Adventures in Wonderland.* Simon & Schuster, 2003. Ages 8–12. (Pop-up).

Sabuda Robert, and Matthew Reinhart. *Encyclopedia Prehistorica: Dinosaurs.* Candlewick, 2005. Ages 5–9. (Pop-up).

Seeger, Laura V. *First the Egg.* Roaring Brook, 2007. Ages 3–5. (Die-cut pages). Concept and pattern book.

Walsh, Melanie. *Living with Mom and Living with Dad.* Candlewick, 2012. Ages 2–6. (Lift-the-flap).

Yorinks, Arthur. *Mommy?* Illus. Maurice Sendak. Engineer Matthew Reinhart. Scholastic, 2006. Ages 5–10. (Pop-up).

Zelinsky, Paul, adapter. *Knick-Knack Paddywhack! A Moving Parts Book.* Dutton, 2002. Ages 5–8. (Pop-up).

Wordless Books

Devernay, Laetitia. *The Conductor*. Chronicle, 2011. Ages 5–9. (France).

Faller, Régis. *The Adventures of Polo.* Roaring Brook, 2006. Ages 4–8. Also *Polo: The Runaway Book.* (France).

Fleischman, Paul. *Sidewalk Circus.* Illus. Kevin Hawkes. Candlewick, 2004. Ages 5–10.

Geisert, Arthur. *Lights Out.* Houghton, 2005. Ages 5–10.

Judge, Lita. *Red Sled.* Atheneum, 2011. Ages 3–7.

Lee, Suzy. *Wave.* Chronicle, 2008. Ages 5–8. Also *Shadow* (2010) and *Mirror (*2010). (Korea).

Lehman, Barbara. *Museum Trip.* Houghton, 2006. Ages 5–8. Also *Rainstorm* (2007) and *The Red Book* (2004).

McPhail, David. *No!* Roaring Brook, 2009. Ages 4–8.

Newgarden, Mark. *Bow-Wow Bugs a Bug.* Illus. Megan M. Cash. Harcourt, 2007. Ages 6–8.

Raschka, Chris. *A Ball for Daisy*. Schwartz & Wade, 2011. Ages 5–8.

Savage, Stephen. *Where's Walrus*? Scholastic, 2011. Ages 4–7.

Tolman, Marije and Ronald. *The Tree House*. Lemniscaat, 2010. Ages 4–8. (Netherlands).

Varon, Sara. *Chicken and Cat.* Scholastic, 2006. Graphic novel. Ages 4–7.

Wiesner, David. *Flotsam.* Clarion, 2006. Ages 6–10. Also *Sector 7* (1999) and *Tuesday* (1991).

Yum, Hyewon. *Last Night.* Farrar, 2008. Ages 3–6.

Alphabet Books

Ernst, Lisa Campbell. *The Turn-Around, Upside-Down Alphabet Book.* Simon & Schuster, 2004. Ages 3–6.

Floca, Brian. *The Racecar Alphabet.* Atheneum, 2003. Ages 4–8.

Jay, Alison. *ABC: A Child's First Alphabet Book.* Dutton, 2003. Ages 4–7.

Johnson, Stephen. *A is for Art: An Abstract Alphabet.* Simon & Schuster, 2008. Ages 9–12.

Lear, Edward. *A Was Once an Apple Pie.* Illus. Suse MacDonald. Orchard, 2005. Ages 3–7.

Martin, Bill, & John Archambault. *Chicka Chicka Boom Boom.* Illus. Lois Ehlert. Simon & Schuster, 1989. Ages 3–6.

McGuirk, Leslie. *If Rocks Could Sing: A Discovered Alphabet*. Tricycle, 2011. Ages 4–8.

McLeod, Bob. *Superhero ABC.* HarperCollins, 2006. Ages 4–8.

McLimans, David. *Gone Wild: An Endangered Animal Alphabet*. Walker, 2006. Ages 6–9.

Seeger, Laura Vaccaro. *The Hidden Alphabet.* Roaring Brook, 2003. Ages 4–7.

Sierra, Judy. *The Sleepy Little Alphabet: A Bedtime Story*. Illus. Melissa Sweet. Knopf, 2009. Ages 3–6.

Spirin, Gennady. *A Apple Pie.* Philomel, 2005. Ages 4–7.

Wells, Rosemary. *Max's ABC.* Viking, 2006. Ages 3–7.

Woop Studios. *A Zeal of Zebras: An Alphabet of Collective Nouns*. Chronicle, 2011. Ages 5–10.

Counting Books

Carle, Eric. *10 Little Rubber Ducks.* HarperCollins, 2005. Ages 3–6.

Hines, Anna Grossnickle. *1, 2, Buckle My Shoe.* Harcourt, 2008. Ages 2–5.

Jay, Alison. *123: A Child's First Counting Book.* Dutton, 2007. Ages 4–7.

Martin, Bill, Jr. *Ten Little Caterpillars.* Illus. Lois Ehlert. Beach Lane, 2011. Ages 3–6.

McLimans, David. *Gone Fishing: Ocean Life by the Numbers.* Walker, 2008. Ages 6–9.

McMullan, Kate. *I'm Dirty.* Illus. Jim McMullan. HarperCollins, 2006. Ages 4–7.

Menotti, Andrea. *How Many Jelly Beans?* Illus. Yancey Labat. Chronicle, 2012. Ages 4–8.

Morales, Yuyi. *Just a Minute: A Trickster Tale and Counting Book.* Cbronicle, 2003. Ages 6–8. (Mexico).

Reiser, Lynn. *Hardworking Puppies.* Harcourt, 2006. Ages 3–7.

Seeger, Laura Vaccaro. *One Boy.* Roaring Brook, 2008. Ages 3–8. (Also a toy and easy-to-read book).

Wells, Rosemary. *Max Counts His Chickens.* Viking, 2007. Ages 3–5.

Wong, Janet S. *Hide and Seek.* Illus. Margaret Chodos-Irvine. Harcourt, 2005. Ages 4–8.

Wormell, Christopher. *Teeth, Tails, & Tentacles: An Animal Counting Book.* Running Press, 2004. Ages 3–8.

Young, Cybele. *Ten Birds.* Kids Can Press, 2011. Ages 6–9. (Canada).

Concept Books

Bernhard, Durga. *While You Are Sleeping: A Lift-the-Flap Book of Time Around the World.* Charlesbridge, 2011. Ages 5–8.

Blexbolex. *Seasons.* Trans. Claudia Bedrick. Enchanted Lion, 2010. Ages 5–12. (France).

Coat, Janik. *Hippopposites.* Appleseed, 2012. Ages 2–5.

Coffelt, Nancy. *Big, Bigger, Biggest.* Holt, 2009. Ages 3–7.

Ehlert, Lois. *Color Zoo.* Lippincott, 1989. Ages 3–6.

Freymann, Saxton. *Food for Thought: The Complete Book of Concepts for Growing Minds.* Scholastic, 2005. Ages 3–5.

Freymann, Saxton, and Joost Elffers. *Fast Food.* Illus. Saxton Freymann. Scholastic, 2006. Ages 3–7.

Gravett, Emily. *Orange Pear Apple Bear.* Simon & Schuster, 2007. Ages 2–4.

Hutchins, Hazel. *A Second Is a Hiccup: A Child's Book of Time.* Illus. Kady M. Denton. Scholastic, 2007. Ages 3–7.

Jenkins, Emily. *Five Creatures.* Illus. Tomek Bogacki. Farrar, 2001. Ages 4–7.

Konnecke, Ole. *The Big Book of Words and Pictures.* Gecko Press, 2012. Ages 2–5. (Germany).

Mayo, Margaret. *Choo Choo Clickety Clack!* Illus. Alex Ayliffe. Carolrhoda, 2005. Ages 2–5.

Messner, Kate. *Over and Under the Snow.* Illus. Christopher S. Neal. Chronicle, 2011. Ages 4–8.

Ogburn, Jacqueline. *Little Treasures: Endearments from Around the World.* Houghton, 2011. Ages 4–8.

Otoshi, Kathryn. *One.* KO Kids Books, 2008. Ages 4–6.

Padmanabhan, Manjula. *I Am Different! Can You Find Me?* Charlesbridge, 2011. Ages 6–9. (India).

Prince, April Jones. *What Do Wheels Do All Day?* Illus. Giles Laroche. Houghton, 2006. Ages 3–7.

Rosenthal, Amy Krouse. *Cookies! Bite Size Life Lessons.* Illus. Jane Dyer. HarperCollins, 2006. Ages 4–7.

Savadier, Elivia. *Will Sheila Share?* Roaring Brook, 2008. Ages 3–5.

Seeger, Laura Vaccaro. *Lemons Are Not Red.* Roaring Brook, 2004. Ages 3–7. Also *Green* (2012).

Seeger, Laura Vaccaro. *Black? White! Day? Night!* Roaring Brook, 2006. Ages 3–7.

Springman, I. C. *More.* Illus. Brian Lee. Houghton, 2012. Ages 4–9.

Underwood, Deborah. *The Loud Book.* Houghton, 2011. Ages 4–8. Also *The Quiet Book* (2010).

Picture Storybooks

Agee, Jon. *Nothing.* Hyperion, 2007. Ages 4–8. Also *Terrific* (2005). Ages 5–8.

Ahlberg, Allan. *The Pencil.* Illus. Bruce Ingman. Candlewick, 2008. Ages 4–7. (England).

Arnosky, Jim. *Grandfather Buffalo.* Putnam, 2006. Ages 5–8.

Barasch, Lynne. *First Come the Zebra.* Lee & Low, 2009. Ages 5–9. (Kenya).

Barnett, Mac. *Extra Yarn.* Illus. Jon Klassen. Balzer, 2012. Ages 5–9.

Bean, Jonathan. *At Night.* Farrar, 2007. Ages 5–7.

Billingsley, Franny. *Big Bad Bunny.* Illus. G. Brian Karas. Atheneum, 2008. Ages 4–7.

Black, Michael Ian. *Chicken Cheeks.* Illus. Kevin Hawkes. Simon & Schuster, 2009. Ages 4–8.

Bley, Anette. *A Friend*. Translated from German. Kane/Miller, 2009. Ages 4–10.

Bloom, Suzanne. *A Splendid Friend, Indeed*. Boyds Mills, 2005. Ages 2–5.

Brown, Peter. *Children Make Terrible Pets*. Little, Brown, 2006. Ages 5–8.

Burningham, John. *Edwardo: The Horriblest Boy in the Whole Wide World*. Knopf, 2007. Ages 4–8. (England).

Carle, Eric. *The Grouchy Ladybug*. Crowell, 1971. Ages 5–7. Also *The Very Busy Spider* (1984).

Charlip, Remy. *A Perfect Day*. Greenwillow, 2007. Ages 4–7.

Chen, Zhiyuan. *Artie and Julie*. Heryin, 2008. Ages 6–9. (Taiwan).

Child, Lauren. *But Excuse Me That Is My Book*. Dial, 2006. Ages 4–6. (England).

Chocolate, Deborah N. *El barrio*. Illus. David Diaz. Holt, 2009. Ages 4–8.

Chodos-Irvine, Margaret. *Best Best Friends*. Harcourt, 2006. Ages 3–6.

Coffelt, Nancy. *Fred Stays with Me!* Illus. Tricia Tusa. Little, Brown, 2007. Ages 5–7.

Cohen, Miriam. *My Big Brother*. Illus. Ronald Himler. Star Bright, 2004. Ages 4–7.

Cole, Brock. *Good Enough to Eat*. Farrar, 2007. Ages 4–8.

Cole, Henry. *On Meadowview Street*. Greenwillow, 2007. Ages 5–8.

Cooper, Elisha. *A Good Night Walk*. Orchard, 2005. Ages 3–6.

Cordsen, Carol Foskett. *The Milkman*. Illus. Douglas B. Jones. Dutton, 2005. Ages 3–7.

Cottin, Menena. *The Black Book of Colors*. Illus. Rosana Faria. Trans. Elisa Amado. Groundwood, 2008. Ages 5–8. (Mexico).

Cronin, Doreen. *Click, Clack, Moo: Cows That Type*. Illus. Betsy Lewin. Simon & Schuster, 2000. Ages 4–7.

Cronin, Doreen. *Diary of a Fly*. Illus. Harry Bliss. HarperCollins, 2007. Ages 3–8.

Cruise, Robin. *Little Mama Forgets*. Illus. Stacey Dressen-McQueen. Farrar, 2006. Ages 3–7.

Crum, Shutta. *Thunder-Boomer!* Illus. Carol Thompson. Clarion, 2009. Ages 4–8.

Cunnane, Kelly. *For You Are a Kenyan Child*. Illus. Ana Juan. Atheneum, 2006. Ages 5–8. (Kenya).

D'Amico, Carmela. *Ella Takes the Cake*. Illus. Steven D'Amico. Scholastic, 2005. Ages 4–6.

Deacon, Alexis. *Beegu*. Farrar, 2003. Ages 3–6. (England).

Dubuc, Marianne. *In Front of My House*. Translated from French. Kids Can, 2010. Ages 6–9. (Canada).

DiCamillo, Kate. *Louise, the Adventures of a Chicken*. Illus. Harry Bliss. HarperCollins, 2008. Ages 5–8.

Dillon, Leo, and Diane Dillon. *Jazz on a Saturday Night*. Scholastic, 2007. Ages 5–9.

Dodds, Dayle Ann. *The Prince Won't Go to Bed!* Illus. Krysten Brooker. Farrar, 2007. Ages 3–6.

Dunrea, Olivier. *Gossie*. Houghton, 2002. Ages 3–5. Also *Gossie and Gertie*. (2002).

Falconer, Ian. *Olivia*. Atheneum, 2000. Ages 4–7. Also *Olivia Forms a Band* (2006). Ages 3–7.

Flatharta, Antoine Ó. *Hurry and the Monarch*. Illus. Meilo So. Knopf, 2005. Ages 4–7.

Fleming, Candace. *Muncha! Muncha! Muncha!* Illus. G. Brian Karas. Simon & Schuster, 2002. Ages 3–7.

Foley, Greg. *Thank You, Bear*. Viking, 2007. Ages 3–6.

Ford, Bernette. *First Snow*. Illus. Sebastian Braun. Holiday, 2005. Ages 3–7.

Foreman, Jack. *Say Hello*. Illus. Michael Foreman. Candlewick, 2008. (England).

Frazee, Marla. *A Couple of Boys Have the Best Week Ever*. Harcourt, 2008. Ages 5–8. Also *Roller Coaster* (2003).

Freeman, Don. *A Pocket for Corduroy*. Viking, 1978. Ages 3–5.

Friend, Catherine. *The Perfect Nest*. Illus. John Manders. Candlewick, 2007. Ages 5–7.

Fromental, Jean-Luc. *Oops!* Illus. Joelle Jolivet. Translated from French. Abrams, 2010. Ages 5–10. (France).

Gág, Wanda. *Millions of Cats*. Coward-McCann, 1928. Ages 4–6.

Gerstein, Mordicai. *The Man Who Walked between the Towers*. Millbrook, 2003. Ages 5–8.

Goode, Diane. *The Most Perfect Spot*. HarperCollins, 2006. Ages 5–7.

Graham, Bob. *Dimity Dumpty: The Story of Humpty's Little Sister*. Candlewick, 2007. Ages 4–7. (Australia).

Grey, Mini. *Traction Man Is Here!* Knopf, 2005. Ages 5–7. Also *Traction Man Meets Turbodog* (2008). (England).

Haas, Irene. *Bess and Bella*. Simon & Schuster, 2006. Ages 4–7.

Hamilton, Kersten. *Red Truck*. Illus. Valeria Petrone. Viking, 2008. Ages 3–5.

Harper, Charise M. *When Randolph Turned Rotten*. Knopf, 2007. Ages 3–7.

Harrington, Janice N. *The Chicken-Chasing Queen of Lamar County.* Illus. Shelley Jackson. Farrar, 2007. Ages 5–7.

Harris, Robie. *Maybe a Bear Ate It!* Illus. Michael Emberley. Orchard, 2008. Ages 3–8.

Henkes, Kevin. *Kitten's First Full Moon.* Greenwillow, 2004. Ages 3–5.

Henkes, Kevin. *Lilly's Big Day.* Greenwillow, 2006. Ages 4–7. Also *Lilly's Purple Plastic Purse.* (1996).

Henkes, Kevin. *A Good Day.* Greenwillow, 2007. Ages 3–5. Also *Old Bear* (2008) and *Birds* (2009).

Hest, Amy. *The Dog Who Belonged to No One.* Illus. Amy Bates. Abrams, 2008. Ages 3–6.

Hurst, Carol Otis. *Terrible Storm.* Illus. S. D. Schindler. Greenwillow, 2007. Ages 5–7.

Imai, Ayano. *Chester.* Penguin, 2007. Ages 4–6. (Japan).

Isadora, Rachel. *Yo, Jo!* Harcourt, 2007. Ages 4–7.

Jarrett, Clare. *Arabella Miller's Tiny Caterpillar.* Candlewick, 2008. Ages 4–7.

Jeffers, Oliver. *The Incredible Book Eating Boy.* Philomel, 2007. Ages 4–8. (Northern Ireland).

Jenkins, Emily. *That New Animal.* Illus. Pierre Pratt. Farrar, 2005. Ages 3–7.

Jenkins, Emily. *What Happens on Wednesdays.* Illus. Lauren Castillo. Farrar, 2007. Ages 4–6.

Juan, Ana. *The Night Eater.* Scholastic, 2004. Ages 4–7. (Spain).

Juster, Norton. *The Hello, Goodbye Window.* Illus. Chris Raschka. Hyperion, 2005. Ages 4–7.

Kajikawa, Kimiko. *Tsunami!* Illus. Ed Young. Philomel, 2009. Ages 4–7. (Japan).

Kasza, Keiko. *The Dog Who Cried Wolf.* Putnam, 2005. Ages 4–7.

Kimmel, Elizabeth C. *The Top Job.* Illus. Robert Neubecker. Dutton, 2007. Ages 5–8.

Kinsey-Warnock, Natalie. *Nora's Ark.* Illus. Emily Arnold McCully. HarperCollins, 2005. Ages 5–8.

Klassen, Jon. *I Want My Hat Back.* Candlewick, 2011. Ages 6–9. (Canada).

Kleven, Elisa. *The Apple Doll.* Farrar, 2007. Ages 4–7.

Kloske, Geoffrey. *Once Upon a Time, The End (Asleep in 60 Seconds).* Illus. Barry Blitt. Simon & Schuster, 2005. Ages 5–8.

Knudsen, Michelle. *Library Lion.* Illus. Kevin Hawkes. Candlewick, 2006. Ages 4–7.

Kohara, Kazuno. *Ghosts in the House!* Roaring Brook, 2008. Ages 3–7.

Kolar, Bob. *Big Kicks.* Candlewick, 2008. Ages 4–8.

Krauss, Ruth. *The Growing Story.* Illus. Helen Oxenbury. HarperCollins, 2007. Ages 3–5.

Kulka, Joe. *Wolf's Coming!* Carolrhoda, 2007. Ages 3–7.

Larochelle, David. *The End.* Illus. Richard Egielski. Scholastic, 2007. Ages 4–8.

Lee, Ho Baek. *While We Were Out.* Translated from Korean. Kane/Miller, 2003. Ages 4–7. (Korea).

Lee, Hyun Young. *Something for School.* Translated from Korean. Kane/Miller, 2008. Ages 4–8. (Korea).

Lipp, Frederick. *Running Shoes.* Illus. Jason Gaillard. Charlesbridge, 2008. Ages 6–9. (Cambodia).

Lloyd, Sam. *Mr. Pusskins: A Love Story.* Simon & Schuster, 2006. Ages 4–7.

Lobel, Anita. *Nini Here and There.* Greenwillow, 2007. Ages 3–5.

Long, Melinda. *How I Became a Pirate.* Illus. David Shannon. Harcourt, 2003. Ages 5–8.

MacDonald, Ross. *Bad Baby.* Roaring Brook, 2005. Ages 5–8.

Madison, Alan. *Velma Gratch and the Way Cool Butterfly.* Illus. Kevin Hawkes. Random, 2007. Ages 5–8.

Mahy, Margaret. *Bubble Trouble.* Illus. Polly Dunbar. Ages 4–8. (New Zealand).

Manning, Maurice. *Laundry Day.* Clarion, 2012. Ages 5–9.

Markes, Julie. *Shhhhh! Everybody's Sleeping.* Illus. David Parkins. HarperCollins, 2005. Ages 4–6.

McCarty, Peter. *Moon Plane.* Holt, 2006. Ages 3–5.

McClintock, Barbara. *Adèle and Simon.* Farrar, 2006. Ages 5–8. (France).

McDonnell, Patrick. *Me . . . Jane.* Little, Brown, 2011. Ages 4–10. (Biography).

McElmurry, Jill. *I'm Not a Baby!* Random, 2006. Ages 4–7.

McMillan, Bruce. *The Problem with Chickens.* Illus. Gunnella. Houghton, 2005. Ages 4–8. (Iceland).

McMullan, Kate. *I Stink!* Illus. Jim McMullan. HarperCollins, 2002. Ages 4–7.

McNulty, Faith. *If You Decide to Go to the Moon.* Illus. Steven Kellogg. Scholastic, 2005. Ages 5–8.

Meddaugh, Susan. *The Witch's Walking Stick.* Houghton, 2005. Ages 5–7.

Melling, David. *The Scallywags.* Barron's, 2006. Ages 5–8.

Milgrim, David. *Time to Get Up, Time to Go.* Clarion, 2006. Ages 3–6.

Nakagawa, Chihiro. *Who Made This Cake?* Illus. Junji Koyose. Front Street, 2008. Ages 3–5. (Japan).

Nevius, Carol. *Baseball Hour.* Illus. Bill Thomson. Marshall Cavendish, 2008. Ages 7–9.

Ogburn, Jacqueline. *The Bake Shop Ghost.* Illus. Marjorie Priceman. Houghton, 2005. Ages 5–8.

O'Malley, Kevin. *Gimme Cracked Corn & I Will Share.* Walker, 2007. Ages 7–9.

Palatini, Margie. *Three French Hens.* Illus. Richard Egielski. Hyperion, 2005. Ages 5–7.

Pearson, Susan. *Slugs in Love.* Illus. Kevin O'Malley. Marshall Cavendish, 2006. Ages 5–7.

Pennypacker, Sara. *Pierre in Love.* Illus. Petra Mathers. Scholastic, 2007. Ages 4–7.

Perkins, Lynne Rae. *Pictures from Our Vacation.* Greenwillow, 2007. Ages 5–7.

Perl, Erica S. *Chicken Bedtime Is Really Early.* Illus. George Bates. Abrams, 2005. Ages 3–5.

Pitzer, Susanna. *Not Afraid of Dogs.* Illus. Larry Day. Walker, 2006. Ages 5–8.

Pullen, Zachery. *Friday My Radio Flyer Flew.* Simon & Schuster, 2008. Ages 4–7.

Rathmann, Peggy. *Officer Buckle and Gloria.* Putnam, 1995. Ages 6–8. Also *10 Minutes till Bedtime* (1998).

Raven, Margot T. *Night Boat to Freedom.* Illus. E. B. Lewis. Farrar, 2006. Ages 6–8. (Historical fiction).

Ray, Jane. *The Apple-Pip Princess.* Candlewick, 2008. Ages 4–7.

Reid, Barbara. *The Subway Mouse.* Scholastic, 2005. Ages 5–7. (Canada).

Richards, Beah E. *Keep Climbing, Girls.* Illus. R. Gregory Christie. Simon & Schuster, 2006. Ages 5–8.

Richardson, Justin, & Peter Parnell. *And Tango Makes Three.* Illus. Henry Cole. Simon & Schuster, 2005. Ages 5–8.

Rocco, John. *Blackout.* Hyperion, 2012. Ages 5–8.

Rodman, Mary Ann. *My Best Friend.* Illus. E. B. Lewis. Viking, 2005. Ages 5–7.

Rohmann, Eric. *My Friend Rabbit.* Roaring Brook, 2002. Ages 4–8.

Roth, Susan L. *Great Big Guinea Pigs.* Bloomsbury, 2006. Ages 5–7.

Rumford, James. *Silent Music: A Story of Baghdad.* Roaring Brook, 2008. Ages 6–10. (Iraq).

Sakai, Komako. *Emily's Balloon.* Chronicle, 2006. Ages 2–4.

San Souci, Daniel. *Space Station Mars.* Tricycle, 2005. Ages 6–9.

Scanlon, Elizabeth G. *All the World.* Illus. Marla Frazee. Beach Lane, 2009. Ages 3–6.

Schotter, Roni. *The Boy Who Loved Words.* Illus. Giselle Potter. Random, 2006. Ages 6–10.

Schwartz, Amy. *Starring Miss Darlene.* Roaring Brook, 2007. Ages 5–7.

Scieszka, Jon. *Cowboy & Octopus.* Illus. Lane Smith. Viking, 2007. Ages 5–10.

Scieszka, Jon. *Welcome to Trucktown!* Illus. David Shannon, Loren Long, David Gordon. Simon & Schuster, 2008. Ages 3–7. Also *Robot Zot!* (2009).

Seeger, Laura V. *What If?* Roaring Brook, 2008. Ages 5–9.

Sendak, Maurice. *Where the Wild Things Are.* Harper, 1963. Ages 5–7.

Sendak, Maurice. *Outside Over There.* Harper, 1981. Ages 7–10.

Shannon, David. *David Gets in Trouble.* Scholastic, 2002. Ages 4–6. Also *Duck on a Bike* (2002).

Shannon, George. *Tippy-Toe Chick, Go!* Illus. Laura Dronzek. Greenwillow, 2003. Ages 4–6.

Shulevitz, Uri. *How I Learned Geography.* Farrar, 2008. Ages 5–10. Also *So Sleepy Story* (2006).

Sís, Peter. *Madlenka.* Farrar, 2000. Ages 5–8. Also *Madlenka's Dog* (2002).

Smith, Chris. *One City, Two Brothers.* Illus. Aurélia Fronty. Barefoot, 2007. Ages 5–8.

Smith, Lane. *Madam President.* Hyperion, 2008. Ages 5–7.

Smith, Lane. *It's a Book.* Roaring Brook, 2010. Ages 8–11. Also *Grandpa Green* (2011).

Stead, Philip. *A Sick Day for Amos McGee.* Illus. Erin Stead. Roaring Brook, 2010. Ages 5–8.

Stein, David E. *Leaves.* Putnam, 2007. Ages 3–7. Also *Interrupting Chicken* (2010).

Stevens, Janet, and Susan Stevens Crummel. *The Great Fuzz Frenzy.* Illus. Janet Stevens. Harcourt, 2005. Ages 4–7.

Stewart, Sarah. *The Gardener.* Illus. David Small. Farrar, 1997. Ages 4–7.

Stuve-Bodeen, Stephanie. *Elizabeti's Doll.* Illus. Christy Hale. Lee & Low, 1998. Ages 3–7. (Tanzania).

Teckentrup, Britta. *Grumpy Cat.* Boxer, 2008. Ages 2–5. (Germany).

Thompson, Lauren. *Polar Bear Night.* Illus. Stephen Savage. Scholastic, 2004. Ages 2–5.

Van Allsburg, Chris. *Jumanji.* Houghton, 1981. Ages 6–10. Also *The Polar Express* (1995).

Van Leeuwen, Jean. *Benny & Beautiful Baby Delilah.* Illus. LeUyen Pham. Dial, 2006. Ages 3–5.

Viva, Frank. *Along a Long Road.* Little, Brown, 2011. Ages 5–8. (Canada).

Waddell, Martin. *Hi, Harry! The Moving Story of How One Slow Tortoise Slowly Made a Friend.* Illus. Barbara Firth. Candlewick, 2003. Ages 3–5. (Ireland).

Wells, Rosemary. *Yoko Writes Her Name.* Hyperion, 2008. Ages 3–7.

Wheeler, Lisa. *Castaway Cats.* Illus. Ponder Goembel. Atheneum, 2006. Ages 4–7.

Wheeler, Lisa. *Boogie Knights.* Illus. Mark Siegel. Atheneum, 2008. Ages 5–8.

Wiesner, David. *Art & Max.* Clarion, 2010. Ages 4–10.

Willems, Mo. *Don't Let the Pigeon Drive the Bus!* Hyperion, 2003. Ages 4–7. Also *Don't Let the Pigeon Stay Up Late* (2006).

Willems, Mo. *Knuffle Bunny: A Cautionary Tale.* Hyperion, 2004. Ages 3–5. Also *Knuffle Bunny Too: A Case of Mistaken Identity* (2007) and *Knuffle Bunny Free: An Unexpected Diversion* (2010).

Willems, Mo. *City Dog, Country Frog.* Illus. Jon J. Muth. Hyperion, 2010. Ages 5–8.

Williams, Karen Lynn, and Khadra Mohammed. *My Name is Sangoel.* Illus. Catherine Stock. Eerdmans, 2009. Ages 7–9. (Sudanese refugee).

Willis, Jeanne. *Tadpole's Promise.* Illus. Tony Ross. Atheneum, 2005. Ages 5–9. (England).

Winters, Jonah. *Here Comes the Garbage Barge!* Illus. Red Nose Studio. Schwartz & Wade, 2010. Ages 4–8.

Winthrop, Elizabeth. *Squashed in the Middle.* Illus. Pat Cummings. Holt, 2005. Ages 5–8.

Wong, Janet S. *Buzz.* Harcourt, 2000. Ages 3–5.

Predictable Books

Arnold, Marsha Diane. *Roar of a Snore.* Illus. Pierre Pratt. Dial, 2006. Ages 2–4.

Becker, Bonny. *A Visitor for Bear.* Illus. Kady MacDonald Denton. Candlewick, 2008. Ages 4–7.

Bloom, Suzanne. *The Bus for Us.* Boyds Mills, 2001. Ages 3–6.

Bunting, Eve. *Hurry! Hurry!* Illus. Jeff Mack. Harcourt, 2007. Ages 3–6.

Chodos-Irvine, Margaret. *Ella Sarah Gets Dressed.* Harcourt, 2003. Ages 2–5.

Fleming, Denise. *The Cow Who Clucked.* Holt, 2006. Ages 3–6. Also *In the Small, Small Pond.* Holt (1993).

Fox, Mem. *Where Is the Green Sheep?* Illus. Judy Horacek. Harcourt, 2004. Ages 2–5. (Australia).

Gravett, Emily. *Monkey and Me.* Simon & Schuster, 2008. Ages 4–6. (England).

MacLennan, Cathy. *Chicky Chicky Chook Chook.* Boxer, 2007. Ages 3–6. (Zimbabwe).

Martin, Bill, Jr. *Brown Bear, Brown Bear, What Do You See?* Illus. Eric Carle. Holt, 1983. Ages 3–6.

Martin, Bill, Jr. *Panda Bear, Panda Bear, What Do You See?* Illus. Eric Carle. Holt, 2003. Ages 3–6.

Meisel, Paul. *See Me Run.* Holiday, 2011. Ages 5–7. I Like to Read series.

Patricelli, Leslie. *Higher! Higher!* Candlewick, 2009. Ages 3–7.

Peck, Jan. *Way Down Deep in the Deep Blue Sea.* Illus. Valeria Petrone. Simon & Schuster, 2004. Ages 3–6.

Rohmann, Eric. *A Kitten Tale.* Knopf, 2008. Ages 2–4.

Ryan, Candace. *Moo Hoo.* Illus. Mike Lowery. Walker, 2012. Ages 4–8.

Shannon, David. *No, David!* Scholastic, 1998. Ages 2–5.

Smee, Nicola. *Clip-Clop.* Boxer, 2006. Ages 3–5. (England).

Swanson, Susan. *The House in the Night.* Illus. Beth Krommes. Houghton, 2008. Ages 3–7.

Wickenburg, Susan. *Hey Mr. Choo-Choo, Where Are You Going?* Illus. Yumi Heo. Putnam, 2008. Ages 3–6.

Wild, Margaret. *Piglet and Papa.* Illus. Stephen M. King. Abrams, 2007. Ages 3–5. (Australia).

Wood, Audrey. *The Napping House.* Illus. Don Wood. Harcourt, 1984. Ages 3–7.

Easy-to-Read Books

Adler, David A. *Young Cam Jansen and the Substitute Mystery.* Illus. Susanna Natti. Viking, 2005. Ages 5–7. Series.

Ahlberg, Allan. *The Children Who Smelled a Rat.* Illus. Katharine McEwen. Candlewick, 2005. Ages 6–9. (England).

Arnold, Tedd. *Hi! Fly Guy.* Cartwheel Books/Scholastic, 2005. Ages 5–7. Series.

Bang-Campbell, Monika. *Little Rat Makes Music.* Illus. Molly Bang. Harcourt, 2007. Ages 5–7. Series.

Brown, Marc, and Stephen Krensky. *Arthur and the Big Blow-Up.* Illus. Marc Brown. Little, Brown, 2000. Ages 5–7.

Cammuso, Frank, and Jay Lynch. *Otto's Orange Day.* Illus. Frank Cammuso. TOON, 2008. Graphic novel. Ages 5–7.

Cowley, Joy. *Snake and Lizard.* Illus. Gavin Bishop. Kane/Miller, 2008. Ages 6–9. (Australia).

Danziger, Paula. *Get Ready for Second Grade, Amber Brown.* Illus. Tony Ross. Putnam, 2002. Ages 5–7.

Davis, Eleanor. *Stinky: A Toon Book.* Toon, 2008. Ages 5–8.

DiCamillo, Kate. *Mercy Watson Goes for a Ride.* Illus. Chris Van Dusen. Candlewick, 2006. Ages 5–7. Series.

DiCamillo, Kate, and Alison McGhee. *Bink & Gollie.* Illus. Tony Fucile. Candlewick, 2010. Ages 5–8.

Edwards, Michelle. *Stinky Stern Forever.* Harcourt, 2005. Ages 6–9.

Feldman, Eve. *Billy & Milly, Short & Silly.* Illus. Tuesday Mourning. Putnam, 2009. Ages 5–7.

Fine, Anne. *The Jamie and Angus Stories.* Illus. Penny Dale. Candlewick, 2002. Ages 5–7. (England).

George, Jean Craighead. *Goose and Duck.* Illus. Priscilla Lamont. HarperCollins, 2008. Ages 5–7.

Grant, Judyann A. *Chicken Said, "Cluck!"* Illus. Sue Truesdell. HarperCollins, 2008. Ages 5–7.

Greene, Stephanie. *Princess Posey and the First Grade Parade.* Illus. Stephanie Sisson. Putnam, 2010. Ages 6–8.

Guest, Elissa Haden. *Iris and Walter and the Field Trip.* Illus. Christine Davenier. Harcourt, 2005. Ages 6–8. Series.

Harper, Jessica. *Uh-Oh, Cleo.* Illus. Jon Berkeley. Putnam, 2008. Ages 5–8.

Hayes, Geoffrey. *Benny and Penny in the Big No-No!* Toon, 2009. Graphic novel. Ages 5–7. Series.

Hoberman, Mary Ann. *You Read to Me, I'll Read to You: Very Short Stories to Read Together.* Illus. Michael Emberley. Little, Brown, 2001. Ages 5–7. Also *Very Short Fables to Read Together* (2010).

Howe, James. *Pinky and Rex and the New Baby.* Illus. Melissa Sweet. Aladdin, 2006. Ages 6–8.

Jacobson, Jennifer Richard. *Andy Shane and the Very Bossy Dolores Starbuckle.* Illus. Abby Carter. Candlewick, 2005. Ages 5–8.

Kvasnosky, Laura McGee. *Zelda and Ivy: The Runaways.* Candlewick, 2006. Ages 5–8. Series.

Lin, Grace. *Ling & Ting: Not Exactly the Same!* Little Brown, 2010. Ages 5–8.

Lobel, Arnold. *Frog and Toad Together.* HarperColllins, 1972. Ages 5–8. Also *Owl at Home* (1975). Series.

McMullan, Kate. *Pearl and Wagner: One Funny Day.* Dial, 2009. Ages 5–8. Series.

Ries, Lori. *Aggie and Ben: Three Stories.* Illus. Frank W. Dormer. Charlesbridge, 2006. Ages 4–7.

Rylant, Cynthia. *Henry and Mudge and the Great Grandpas.* Illus. Suçie Stevenson. Simon & Schuster, 2005. Ages 5–7. Series.

Rylant, Cynthia. *Mr. Putter and Tabby See the Stars.* Illus. Arthur Howard. Harcourt, 2007. Ages 5–7. Series.

Schneider, Josh. *Tales for Very Picky Eaters.* Clarion, 2011. Ages 5–9.

Seeger, Laura. *Dog and Bear: Two Friends, Three Stories.* Roaring Brook, 2007. Ages 4–7. Also *Two's Company* (2008).

Silverman, Erica. *Cowgirl Kate and Cocoa.* Illus. Betsy Lewin. Harcourt, 2005. Ages 5–7. Series.

Smith, Jeff. *Little Mouse Gets Ready.* Toon, 2009. Graphic novel. Ages 4–7.

Van Leeuwen, Jean. *Amanda Pig and the Really Hot Day.* Illus. Ann Schweninger. Dial, 2005. Ages 5–7. Series.

Willems, Mo. *There Is a Bird on Your Head!* Hyperion, 2007. Ages 5–7. Elephant and Piggy Series.

Willems, Mo. *Are You Ready to Play Outside?* Hyperion, 2008. Ages 5–7.

Yee, Wong Herbert. *Mouse and Mole: Fine Feathered Friends.* Houghton, 2009. Ages 5–8. Series.

Transitional Books

Alvarez, Julía. *How Tia Lola Ended Up Starting Over.* Knopf, 2011. Ages 8–11. Series.

Barrows, Annie. *Ivy and Bean.* Illus. Sophie Blackall. Chronicle, 2006. Ages 6–9. Series.

Benton, Jim. *Franny K. Stein, Mad Scientist: Lunch Walks among Us.* Simon & Schuster, 2003. Ages 6–9. Series.

dePaola, Tomie. *26 Fairmount Avenue.* Putnam, 1999. Ages 6–9. Also *For the Duration* (2009). Series.

English, Karen. *Nikki & Deja: Birthday Blues.* Illus. Laura Freeman. Clarion, 2009. Ages 6–10. Series.

Fenner, Carol. *Snowed in with Grandmother Silk.* Illus. Amanda Harvey. Dial, 2003. Ages 5–7.

Greenwald, Sheila. *Rosy Cole's Memoir Explosion.* Farrar, 2006. Ages 7–10. Series.

Grimes, Nikki. *Make Way for Dyamonde Daniel.* Illus. R. Gregory Christie. Putnam, 2009.

Grindley, Sally. *Dear Max.* Illus. Tony Ross. Simon & Schuster, 2006. Ages 6–9. (England).

Haas, Jessie. *Jigsaw Pony.* Illus. Ying-Hwa Hu. Greenwillow, 2005. Ages 7–10.

Han, Jenny. *Clara Lee and the Apple Pie Dream.* Illus. Julie Kao. Little Brown, 2011. Ages 7–10.

Harper, Charise M. *Just Grace.* Houghton, 2007. Ages 7–9. Series.

Jenkins, Emily. *Toys Go Out: Being the Adventures of a Knowledgeable Stingray, a Tough Little Buffalo, and Someone Called Plastic.* Illus. Paul Zelinsky. Random, 2006. Ages 6–9. Sequels.

Kerrin, Jessica. *Martin Bridge: Ready for Takeoff!* Illus. Joseph Kelly. Kids Can, 2005. Ages 7–10. Series.

Look, Lenore. *Ruby Lu, Brave and True.* Illus. Anne Wilsdorf. Simon & Schuster, 2004. Ages 6–9. Series.

MacLachlan, Patricia. *Waiting for the Magic.* Illus. Amy June Bates. Atheneum, 2011. Ages 8–11.

Marsden, Carolyn. *The Gold-Threaded Dress.* Cambridge, MA: Candlewick, 2002. Ages 6–9.

McEwan, Jamie. *Rufus the Scrub Does Not Wear a Tutu.* Illus. John Margeson. Darby Creek, 2007. Ages 7–10.

Pennypacker, Sara. *Clementine.* Illus. Marla Frazee. Hyperion, 2006. Ages 6–9. Series.

Roberts, Ken. *Thumb and the Bad Guys.* Illus. Leanne Franson. Groundwood, 2009. Ages 8–11. Series. (Canada).

Sachar, Louis. *Marvin Redpost: Class President.* Illus. Amy Wummer. Random House, 1999. Ages 7–10. Series.

Scieszka, Jon. *Marco? Polo!* Illus. Adam McCauley. Viking, 2006. Ages 7–10. Time Warp Trio Series.

Sobol, Donald J. *Encyclopedia Brown: Boy Detective.* Illus. Leonard Shortall. Bantam, 1985. Ages 7–10. Series.

Sternberg, Julie. *Like Pickle Juice on a Cookie.* Amulet, 2011. Ages 7–10.

Picture Books for Older Readers

Avi. *Silent Movie.* Illus. C. B. Mordan. Atheneum, 2003. Ages 8–12.

de la Peña, Matt. *A Nation's Hope: The Story of Boxing Legend Joe Louis.* Illus. Kadir Nelson. Dial, 2011. Ages 8–11.

Gaiman, Neil. *The Wolves in the Walls.* Illus. Dave McKean. HarperCollins, 2003. Ages 9–12.

Greder. Armin. *The Island.* Allen & Unwin, 2008. Ages 9–12. (Australia).

Johnson, D. B. *Henry Builds a Cabin.* Houghton, 2002. Ages 9–13. Also *Henry Climbs a Mountain* (2003) and *Henry Hikes to Fitchburg* (2000).

Johnson, D. B. *Magritte's Marvelous Hat: A Picture Book.* Houghton, 2012. Ages 5–10.

Lee, Milly. *Landed.* Illus. Yangsook Choi. Farrar, 2006. Ages 8–12.

Lewis, J. Patrick. *And the Soldiers Sang.* Illus. Gary Kelley. Creative Editions, 2011. Ages 9–12.

Macaulay, David. *The Way We Work.* Houghton, 2008. Ages 13–18.

McCarthy, Meghan. *Aliens Are Coming! The True Account of the 1938 War of the Worlds Radio Broadcast.* Knopf, 2006. Ages 8–12.

Milway, Katie Smith. *One Hen: How One Small Loan Made a Big Difference.* Illus. Eugenie Fernandez. Kids Can, 2008. Ages 9–12. (Ghana).

Myers, Walter Dean. *Blues Journey.* Illus. Christopher Myers. Holiday, 2003. Ages 10–14.

Polacco, Patricia. *Pink and Say.* Philomel, 1994. Ages 9–12.

Raven, Margot T. *Night Boat to Freedom.* Illus. E. B. Lewis. Farrar, 2006. Ages 8–12.

Reibstein, Mark. *Wabi Sabi.* Illus. Ed Young. Little, Brown, 2008. Ages 7–11.

Rogers, Gregory. *The Boy, the Bear, the Baron, the Bard.* Roaring Brook, 2004. Ages 8–12. Wordless. (England).

Selznick, Brian. *The Invention of Hugo Cabret.* Scholastic, 2007. Ages 9–12. Also **Wonderstruck** (2011).

Sidman, Joyce. *Song of the Water Boatman & Other Pond Poems.* Illus. Beckie Prange. Houghton, 2005. Ages 7–12.

Sís, Peter. *Starry Messenger.* Farrar, 1996. Ages 9–14. Italy. Also *Tibet through the Red Box* (1998). (Tibet).

Sis, Peter. *The Wall: Growing Up behind the Iron Curtain.* Farrar, 2007. Ages 9–14. (Czechoslovakia).

Uhlberg, Myron. *A Storm Called Katrina.* Illus. Colin Bootman. Peachtree, 2011. Ages 8–12.

Graphic Novels

Atagan, Patrick. *The Yellow Jar: Vol. I: Two Tales from Japanese Tradition.* NBM, 2002. Ages 11–14.

Cammuso, Frank. *Knights of the Lunch Table, Book 1.* Scholastic, 2008. Ages 9–13.

Crane, Jordan. *The Clouds Above.* Fantagraphics, 2005. Ages 7–9.

Czekaj, Jef. *Grampa and Julie: Shark Hunters.* Top Shelf, 2004. Ages 9–14.

Dembiki, Matt, editor. *Trickster: Native American Tales.* Fulcrum, 2010. Ages 10–14.

Eisner, Will. *Sundiata: A Legend of Africa.* NBM, 2003. Ages 10–14.

Frampton, Otis. *Oddly Normal, Vol. 1.* Viper, 2006. Ages 9–12.

Friesen, Ray. *Lookit! A Cheese Related Mishap and Other Stories.* Don't Eat Any Bugs, 2005. Ages 10–13.

Gaiman, Neil. *Coraline: Graphic Novel.* Illus. P. Craig Russell. HarperCollins, 2008. Ages 9–12.

Gownley, Jimmy. *Amelia Rules! What Makes You Happy.* ibooks, 2004. Ages 8–12.

Hale, Shannon, and Dean Hale. *Rapunzel's Revenge.* Illus. Nathan Hale. Bloomsbury, 2008. Ages 10–14.

Harper, Charisse M. *Fashion Kitty.* Hyperion, 2005. Ages 9–13.

Hatke, Ben. *Zita the Spacegirl: Far from Home*. First Second, 2010. Ages 9–12.

Hartman, Rachel. *Amy Unbounded: Belondweg Blossoming.* Pug House, 2002. Ages 9–14.

Hayes, Geoffrey. *Benny and Penny: In Just Pretend.* TOON, 2008. Ages 4–6.

Holm, Jennifer L. *Babymouse: Queen of the World!* Illus. Matthew Holm. Random, 2005. Ages 9–12. Series.

Huey, Debbie. *Bumperboy and the Loud, Loud Mountain.* Adhouse, 2006. Ages 7–9.

Irwin, Jane, and Jeff Verndt. *Vögelein: A Clockwork Faerie.* Fiery Studio, 2003. Ages 12–16.

Kobayashi, Makoto. *What's Michael? Vol. 10: Sleepless Nights.* Dark Horse, 2005. Ages 10–13.

Kochalka, James. *Monkey vs. Robot and the Crystal of Power.* Top Shelf, 2003. Ages 8–12.

Lat. *Kampung Boy.* First Second, 2006. Ages 9–14. Autobiography. (Malaysia; Muslim).

Morse, Scott. *Magic Pickle.* Scholastic, 2008. Ages 7–9.

Neri, Greg. *Yummy: The Last Days of a Southside Shorty*. Illus. Randy DuBurke. Lee & Low, 2010. Ages 10–14.

O'Malley, Kevin. *Captain Raptor and the Space Pirates.* Illus. Patrick O'Brien. Walker, 2007. Ages 5–9.

Phelan, Matt. *The Storm in the Barn.* Candlewick, 2009. Ages 11–14.

Renier, Aaron. *Spiral-Bound: Top Secret Summer.* Top Shelf, 2005. Ages 9–12.

Rodi, Rob. *Crossovers.* CrossGeneration, 2003. Ages 11–16.

Runton, Andy. *Owly, Vol. I: The Way Home & the Bittersweet Summer.* Top Shelf, 2004. Ages 5–9.

Sfar, Joann. *Little Vampire Does Kung Fu!* Translated from French by Mark and Alexis Siegel. Simon & Schuster, 2003. Ages 9–13. (France).

Siegel, Siena Cherson. *To Dance: A Ballerina's Graphic Novel.* Illus. Mark Siegel. Simon & Schuster, 2006. Ages 10–14.

Smith, Jeff. *Bone: Out from Boneville.* Graphix, 2005. Ages 9–14.

Stamaty, Mark Alan. *Alia's Mission: Saving the Books of Iraq.* Knopf, 2004. Ages 9–13.

Steinberg, D. J. *Sound Off!* Illus. Brian Smith. Grosset, 2008. Ages 8–10.

Tan, Shaun. *The Arrival.* Scholastic, 2007. Ages 12–18. Wordless. (Australia).

Varon, Sara. *Robot Dreams.* First Second, 2007. Ages 8–14. Also *Bake Sale* (2011).

Weigel, Jeff. *Atomic Ace (He's Just My Dad).* Albert Whitman, 2004. Ages 9–12.

Yang, Gene L. *American Born Chinese.* First Second, 2006. Ages 12–16. (Chinese American).

Postmodern Picture Books

Barnett, Mac. *Chloe and the Lion.* Illus. Adam Rex. Hyperion, 2012. Ages 6–9.

Browne, Anthony. *Voices in the Park.* DK Ink, 1998. Ages 6–10. Also *Me and You* (2010). (England).

Burningham, John. *Granpa.* Red Fox, 2003. Ages 6–9. Also *Come Away from the Water, Shirley* (2000). (England).

Chin, Jason. *Redwoods*. Flash Point, 2009. Ages 6–9.

Gerstein, Mordicai. *A Book*. Roaring Brook, 2009. Ages 6–9.

Gravett, Emily. *Wolves.* Simon & Schuster, 2006. Ages 6–9. (England).

Lendler, Ian. *An Undone Fairy Tale.* Illus. Whitney Martin. Simon & Schuster, 2005. Ages 6–9.

Macaulay, David. *Black and White.* Houghton, 1990. Ages 7–10.

Scieszka, Jon. *The Stinky Cheese Man & Other Fairly Stupid Tales*. Illus. Lane Smith. Viking, 1992. Ages 7–10. Also *The True Story of the 3 Little Pigs* (1989).

Van Allsburg, Chris. *Bad Day at Riverbend*. Houghton, 1995. Ages 6–9.

Watt, Melanie. *Chester*. Kids Can, 2007. Ages 5–8. Also *Chester's Masterpiece* (2010). (Canada).

Whatley, Bruce. *Wait! No Paint!* HarperCollins, 2001. Ages 6–9.

Wiesner, David. *The Three Pigs*. Clarion, 2001. Ages 6–12.

Willems, Mo. *We Are in a Book*. Hyperion, 2010. Ages 6–9.

Related Films, Videos, and DVDs

Children Make Terrible Pets (2011). Author/Illustrator: Peter Brown (2010). 8 minutes.

Diary of a Spider. (2006). Author: Doreen Cronin (2005). Illustrator: Harry Bliss. 9 minutes.

Don't Let the Pigeon Drive the Bus (2009). Author/Illustrator: Mo Willems (2003). 7 minutes.

The Dot. (2004). Author/Illustrator: Peter H. Reynolds (2003). 7.5 minutes.

Hugo (2012). Author/Illustrator: Brian Selznick (2007). 126 minutes.

I Stink! (2009). Authors/Illustrators: Kate and Jim McMullan (2002). 9 minutes.

Jumanji. (1995). Author/Illustrator: Chris Van Allsburg (1981). 104 minutes.

Just a Minute: A Trickster Tale and Counting Book (2003). Author/Illustrator: Yuyi Morales (2003). 12 minutes.

Knuffle Bunny: A Cautionary Tale. (2006). Author/Illustrator: Mo Willems (2004). 10 minutes.

The Man Who Walked between the Towers. (2005). Author/Illustrator: Mordicai Gerstein (2003). 60 minutes.

Chapter Five

Poetry

What's a Poem?

A whisper,
a shout,
thoughts turned
inside out.

A laugh,
a sigh,
an echo
passing by.

A rhythm,
a rhyme,
a moment
caught in time.

A moon,
A star,
a glimpse
of who you are.

—*Charles Ghigna*

Poetry is a natural beginning to literature for young children and an enjoyable literary form for all ages. In their earliest years, children acquire language and knowledge of the world around them through listening and observing. Poetry is primarily an oral form of literature that draws heavily on the auditory perceptions of listeners and so is ideally suited to young children. Throughout elementary and middle school, poetry that relates to topics and issues being explored in the classroom can be shared orally, providing a flash of humor or a new perspective.

Definition and Description

Poetry is the concentrated expression of ideas and feelings through precise and imaginative words carefully selected for their sonorous and rhythmical effects. Originally, poetry was oral, recited by minstrels as they traversed the countryside, sharing poems and songs with listeners of all ages. The musicality of poetry makes it an especially suitable literary form for teachers to read aloud.

Children often believe that rhyme is an essential ingredient of poetry, yet some types of poetry do not rhyme. What distinguishes poetry from prose is the concentration of thought and feeling expressed in succinct, exact, and beautiful language, as well as an underlying pulse or rhythm.

Not all rhyming, rhythmical language merits the label of poetry. **Verse** is a language form in which simple thoughts or stories are told in rhyme with a distinct beat or meter. Mother Goose and nursery rhymes are good examples of well-known, simple verses. And, of course, we are all aware of the **jingle,** a catchy repetition of sounds heard so often in commercials. The most important feature of verses and jingles is their strong rhyme and rhythm with light or silly content. Although verses and jingles are enjoyable and engage children, poetry enriches children's lives by giving new insights and fresh views on life's experiences and inviting strong emotional responses.

A recent trend is **novels in verse,** which are novel-length narratives told through poetry rather than prose using different kinds of verse forms. These novels in verse focus less on the structure or individuality of single poems that relate to each other, as found in a themed poetry collection like Joyce Sidman's *Dark Emperor,* and more on the use of the verse format to serve the structure of a novel, such as Karen Hesse's *Out of the Dust.* The verses in these novels work together to create character development and setting, convey a story, and establish a strong voice. Novels in verse are therefore not included in this chapter but are integrated into the relevant genre chapters.

The term *poetry* is used in this chapter both to refer to a form of language that can evoke great depth of feeling and provoke new insights through imaginative and beautiful language and to refer to favorite verses of childhood.

Types of Poetry Books

Poetry touches our minds and hearts by drawing on all five senses. Children respond to poetry, even though the themes that move them may differ from those that move adults. A wide variety of poetry books are available for students and teachers. Selecting books of poetry for use in the classroom as bridges between classroom activities, as materials for reading, and as literature for enjoyment will require teachers to review and evaluate the many types of poetry books, including anthologies, Mother Goose and nursery rhyme books, books of poems on special topics and by favorite poets, and single illustrated poems in picture book formats.

Mother Goose, Nursery Rhymes and Songs

Mother Goose and *nursery rhymes* are heavily illustrated collections of traditional verse. Often, a familiar illustration is all a child needs to begin reciting one of these well-loved verses. Collected nursery rhymes first appeared in Charles Perrault's *Tales of Mother Goose* in France in the early eighteenth century. These verses are now part of children's literary heritage and are a wonderful introduction to the world of literature for young children. In Western societies in which countless allusions are made every day to the characters and situations found in nursery rhymes, knowledge of this literature is a mark of being culturally literate. In China, classic Chinese poetry plays this same cultural role, as noted in the collection by Siyu Liu, *A Thousand Peaks*.

Because so many of these verses exist, the better collections include large numbers of rhymes organized thoughtfully around themes or topics and indexed by titles or first lines. Favorites include *Tomie dePaola's Mother Goose* and *The Arnold Lobel Book of Mother Goose*. Modern versions of rhymes can be found in *Nursery Rhyme Comics,* edited by Chris Duffy, in which fifty cartoonists give their take on traditional rhymes, and *Spinster Goose,* by Lisa Wheeler, which satirizes traditional rhymes with a focus on the consequences of bad behavior. Cultural connections can be expanded by collections from other traditions, such as *My Village: Rhymes from around the World,* by Danielle Wright, and *Arrorró, mi niño: Latino Lullabies and Gentle Games,* collected by Lulu Delacre.

Nursery songs are heavily illustrated collections of traditional and modern verses with musical notation. Melody emphasizes the innate musicality of these verses and turns some verses into games ("Ring around the Roses") and others into lullabies ("Rock-a-Bye Baby") and finger plays ("Eensy, Weensy Spider"). Collections of songs, like José-Luis Orozco's *Diez Deditos and Other Play Rhymes and Action Songs from Latin America,* appeal to young children. Single illustrated versions of familiar songs provide innovative interpretations, such as the two picture book versions of *Hush, Little Baby* by Brian Pinkney and Marla Frazee.

Anthologies of Poetry

A large, comprehensive *anthology of poetry* for children is a must in every classroom. Anthologies should be organized by subject for easy retrieval of poems appropriate for almost any occasion. In addition, indexes of poets and titles or first lines are usually provided in these texts. Works by contemporary and traditional poets can be found in most of these anthologies; they appeal to a wide age range, providing nursery rhymes for toddlers as well as longer, narrative poems for older readers. Examples include *The Random House Book of Poetry for Children,* edited by Jack Prelutsky, and *The Bill Martin Jr. Big Book of Poetry,* edited by Bill Martin Jr. and Michael Sampson.

Specialized Poetry Books

Specialized poetry books, in which the poems are by one poet, on one topic, or of one poetic form, are readily available. These specialized collections support teachers and children in exploring specific topics, poets, and types of poetry. Beautifully illustrated collections are especially enjoyed by children for independent reading of poetry. Examples include *Dinothesaurus: Prehistoric Poems and Paintings* by Douglas Florian and *Sharing the Seasons,* edited by Lee Bennett Hopkins.

Single Illustrated Poems

Single illustrated poems can be presented in a picture book format. These editions make poetry more appealing and accessible for children, but in some cases the illustrations may get in the way of children forming their own mental images from poetic language. *My People,* with photographs by Charles Smith, is a visual metaphor of Langston Hughes's classic poem, while Joyce Sidman's poem *Swirl by Swirl: Spirals in Nature* is illustrated in striking scratchboards by Beth Krommes.

Evaluation and Selection of Poetry

The criteria to keep in mind in evaluating a poem for use with children are as follows:

- **Are the ideas and feelings expressed in authentic, fresh, and imaginative ways?**
- **Is the expression of the ideas and feelings unique in order to encourage readers to perceive ordinary things in new ways?**
- **Is the poem appropriate to the experiences of children, instead of preaching to them?**
- **Does the poem present the world through a child's perspective?** The poem should focus on children's lives as well as activities all ages can relate to.
- **What is the quality of choices within a poetry collection?** Also examine the illustrations and the appearance of the book, remembering that beautiful illustrations do not ensure a good collection.

In selecting poems to read to students, start with the Golden Age poets listed in the Milestones feature, the list of Notable Authors of Poetry, or the list of poets who have won the National Council of Teachers of English (NCTE) Award. The NCTE Award was established in 1977 to honor living U.S. poets whose poetry has contributed substantially to children's lives. This award is given to poets for their body of writing for children ages 3 through 13. In addition, the Poetry Foundation established a Children's Poet Laureate in 2006, naming Jack Prelutsky, Mary Ann Hoberman,

NCTE Excellence in Poetry for Children Award Winners

Year	Winner	Year	Winner
1977	David McCord	1991	Valerie Worth
1978	Aileen Fisher	1994	Barbara Juster Esbensen
1979	Karla Kuskin	1997	Eloise Greenfield
1980	Myra Cohn Livingston	2000	X. J. Kennedy
1981	Eve Merriam	2003	Mary Ann Hoberman
1982	John Ciardi	2006	Nikki Grimes
1985	Lilian Moore	2009	Lee Bennett Hopkins
1988	Arnold Adoff	2011	J. Patrick Lewis

and J. Patrick Lewis to serve two-year terms, and the Lee Bennett Hopkins Poetry Award, given annually to an American poet or anthologist for the most outstanding new book of poetry for children.

Although more poetry for children is being written, published, and enjoyed by many teachers and students, some teachers are uncertain about how to select poems for their students. By learning about students' preferences in poetry and exploring some of the best-loved poems and poets, a teacher can become more confident about selecting poems that engage students.

Children's Poetry Preferences

The findings from surveys of children's poetry preferences can be helpful in selecting poems for a new group of students. Fisher and Natarella (1982) surveyed primary-grade children and their teachers, while Terry (1974) and Kutiper and Wilson (1993) studied intermediate-grade children. These findings include:

- A preference for narrative poems over lyric poems and modern over classics.
- An enjoyment of limericks and dislike of haiku.
- A preference for poems with pronounced sound patterns, especially poems that rhyme or have a regular, distinctive rhythm.
- An interest in humorous poems, poems about animals, and poems about enjoyable, familiar experiences.
- Primary-grade children preferred poems about strange and fantastic events, animals, and children. Older children preferred poems on humor, familiar experiences, unusual people, moments of crisis, and social problems.
- Figurative language in poetry was initially confusing to children and interfered with their attempts to understand the poems.

The humorous contemporary poetry of Shel Silverstein and Jack Prelutsky continues to dominate students' choices and so their poetry is a good place to start in order to create an interest in poetry. Teachers can then read poetry from collections by NCTE award winners and other notable poets to move students from light verse into poems with a high quality of language and poetic arrangement. Students need exposure to an array of poetry and poets that build on their interests.

Children's appreciation of poetry can be broadened and deepened in classrooms, by starting with the kinds of poems that students enjoy and then moving them to the other types of poetry. A good selection of rhyming, narrative poems with distinct rhythms about humorous events and familiar experiences is a good starting point for students who have little experience with poetry.

The Significance of Style and Word Choice in Poetry

Just as with a work of fiction, the elements of a poem should be considered if the reader is to understand and evaluate the poem. Each of these parts—meaning, rhythm, sound patterns, figurative language, and sense imagery—work together to express ideas and feelings. Emotion, imagery, and the music of poetry are at the heart of poems that touch our hearts and minds.

• *Meaning* is the underlying idea, feeling, or mood conveyed through the poem. As with other literary forms, poetry is a form of communication; it is the way a poet chooses to express emotions and thoughts through the choice and arrangement of words.

• *Rhythm* is the beat or regular cadence of the poem. Poetry, usually an oral form of literature, relies on rhythm to help communicate meaning. A fast rhythm is effected through short lines; clipped syllables; sharp, high vowel sounds, such as the sounds represented by the letters *a, e,* and *i;* and abrupt consonant sounds, such as the sounds represented by the letters *k, t, w,* and *p.* A fast rhythm can provide the listener with a feeling of happiness, excitement, drama, and even tension and suspense. A slow rhythm is effected by longer lines, multisyllabic words, full or low vowel sounds such as the sounds represented by the letters *o* and *u,* and resonating consonant sounds such as the sounds represented by the letters *m, n,* and *r.* A slow rhythm can evoke languor, tranquillity, inevitability, and harmony, among other feelings. A change in rhythm during a poem signals the listener to a change in meaning.

The following poems reflect the use of rhythm to either exhibit a sense of speed or to communicate the calm and quiet of summer.

The Pickety Fence

The pickety fence.
Give it a lick it's
The pickety fence
Give it a lick it's
A clickety fence
Give it a lick it's
A lickety fence
Give it a lick
Give it a lick
Pickety
Pickety
Pickety
Pick

—David McCord

Slowly

Slowly the tide creeps up the sand,
Slowly the shadows cross the land.
Slowly the cart-horse pulls his mile,
Slowly the old man mounts the stile.
Slowly the hands move round the clock,
Slowly the dew dries on the dock.
Slow is the snail—but slowest of all
The green moss spreads on the old brick wall.

—James Reeves

- *Sound patterns* are made by repeated sounds and combinations of sounds in the words. Words, phrases, or lines are sometimes repeated in their entirety. Also, parts of words may be repeated—as with rhyme, a sound device that children most recognize and enjoy.

  - *Rhyme* occurs when the ends of words (the last vowel sound and any consonant sound that may follow it) have the same sounds, such as *fat, vat, brat* or *hay, they, stray,* and *obey.*
  - *Assonance* is a pattern where the same vowel sound is heard repeatedly within a line or a few lines of poetry, such as *hoop, gloom, moon, moot,* and *boots.*
  - *Alliteration* is a pattern in which initial consonant sounds are heard frequently within a few lines of poetry, such as *ship, shy,* and *shape.*
  - *Consonance* is similar to alliteration but usually refers to a close juxtaposition of similar final consonant sounds, as in fla*ck*e, chu*ck,* and stro*ck*e.
  - *Onomatopoeia* is the device in which the sound of a word imitates its real-world sound, such as *buzz* for the sound of a bee and *hiss* for the sound a snake makes.

- *Figurative language* takes different forms and involves comparing or contrasting one object, idea, or feeling with another one.

  - A *simile* is a direct comparison, typically using *like* or *as* to point out the similarities. The familiar poem "The Star" includes a simile comparing a star to a diamond.

The Star

> Twinkle, twinkle little star,
> How I wonder what you are!
> Up above the world so high,
> Like a diamond in the sky.

—Jane Taylor

  - A *metaphor* is an implied comparison without a signal word to evoke the similarities. In "The Night Is a Big Black Cat," the metaphor implies a comparison between the night sky and a black cat.

The Night Is a Big Black Cat

> The Night is a big black cat
> The Moon is her topaz eye,
> The stars are the mice she hunts at night,
> In the field of the sultry sky.

—G. Orr Clark

- *Personification* is the attribution of human qualities to animals or to inanimate objects for the purpose of drawing a comparison between the animal or object and human beings. In "The Sun Has a Tail," the sun is personified by human/animal actions.

The Sun Has a Tail

> The sun has a tail
> that reaches under the earth
> and tickles seeds.
> That's what grandmother
> once told me.
> She says things grow
> in laughter.

—Emanuel di Pasquale

- *Hyperbole* is an exaggeration to highlight reality or to point out ridiculousness. Children often delight in hyperbole because it appeals to their strong sense of the absurd. To show a boy's reluctance to go to school John Ciardi uses hyperbole in this stanza from "Speed Adjustments."

> Why does a boy who's fast as a jet
> Take all day—and sometimes two—
> To get to school?

- *Sense imagery* is the way in which a poet plays with one or more of the five senses in descriptive and narrative language. *Sight* may be awakened through the depiction of beauty; *hearing* may be evoked by the sounds of a city street; *smell* and *taste* may be recalled through the description of a fish left too long in the sun; and *touch* can be sensitized through describing the gritty discomfort of a wet swimsuit caked with sand from the beach. After listening to a poem, children can think about which of the senses the poet is appealing to.

These elements of poetry may be considered to select varied types of poems and to group them for presentation. However, little is gained by teaching each of these elements as a separate item to be memorized or analyzed. Poetic analysis has caused many students to dislike poetry. Students whose teachers love poetry, select it wisely, read it aloud well, and share it often and in many enjoyable ways will come to appreciate poetry.

Historical Overview of Poetry

Poetry for children began centuries ago in the form of nursery rhymes that were recited to babies and toddlers by caregivers. These verses were passed along via the oral tradition. The earliest published collection of nursery rhymes that survives today is *Tommy Thumb's Pretty Song Book* (1744), containing familiar rhymes such as "Hickory Dickory Dock" and "Mary Mary Quite Contrary." The term *Mother Goose* was first used in France by Charles Perrault in his *Stories and Tales of Past Times with Morals; or, Tales of Mother Goose* (1697) to refer to his collection of fairy tales. Later editions contained nursery rhymes, which were so popular that Mother Goose became a general name for nursery rhymes. For many, nursery rhymes and poems were the first forms of literature experienced and came to symbolize the reassuring sounds of childhood.

Notable Authors of Poetry

Arnold Adoff, recipient of the National Council of Teachers of English (NCTE) Award for Excellence in Poetry. Many poems about relationships across racial groups. *All the Colors of the Race; Roots and Blues: A Celebration.* www.arnoldadoff.com

Paul Fleischman, winner of the Newbery Medal for his *Joyful Noise: Poems for Two Voices.* This book and *I Am Phoenix* have poems composed for two to four readers to read lines in unison and solo. www.paulfleischman.net

Douglas Florian, poet and illustrator, blends irresistible wordplay, free-flowing poems, interesting facts, and vibrant collage art to create picture book poetry collections. *Dinothesaurus; Comets, Stars, the Moon and Mars; Autumnblings.* www.douglasflorian.com or see his blog, www.floriancafe.blogspot.com

Kristine O'Connell George, noted for poetry on children's everyday lives and interests that use different poetic forms. *Emma Dilemma: Big Sister Poems; Swimming Upstream: Fold Me a Poem.* www.kristinegeorge.com

Nikki Grimes, African-American poet whose poetry celebrates children's friendships and families; NCTE Award for Excellence in Poetry. *Danitra Brown: Class Clown; A Pocketful of Poems.* www.nikkigrimes.com

Mary Ann Hoberman, recipient of the NCTE Award for Excellence in Poetry, known for humorous, colorful poetry. *Fathers, Mothers, Sisters, Brothers: A Collection of Family Poems; You Read to Me, I'll Read to You.* www.maryannhoberman.com

Lee Bennett Hopkins, poet and award-winning anthologist of many children's poetry collections on a wide range of topics. *Amazing Faces; America at War; Behind the Museum Door.* www.leebennetthopkins.com

Paul B. Janeczko, contemporary poet and anthologist of poetry that invites children to enjoy and learn about poetry. *A Poke in the I; A Foot in the Mouth; A Kick in the Head.* www.pauljaneczko.com

Marilyn Nelson, a poet who uses a range of poetic forms from requiem to sonnets as reflections on African-American history. *Fortune's Bones; A Wreath for Emmet Till.* www.blueflowerarts.com/marilyn-nelson

Naomi Shihab Nye, a poet and anthologist whose poems offer global perspectives and whose edited collections include Mexican, Native American, and Middle Eastern poetry. *This Same Sky: A Collection of Poems from around the World; 19 Varieties of Gazelle: Poems of the Middle East.*

Joyce Sidman, an award-winning poet of picture book collections who uses a range of poetic forms from riddles to concrete poems in celebration of nature. *Song of the Water Boatman and Other Pond Poems; Butterfly Eyes and Other Secrets of the Meadow; Meow Ruff; Red Sings from Treetops; Dark Emperor.* www.joycesidman.com

Janet Wong, a poet who writes about contemporary American culture and creates free-verse poems based on life experiences, ranging from dreams to growing up Asian American. *Good Luck Gold and Other Poems; A Suitcase of Seaweed and Other Poems.* www.janetwong.com

Poems with a moral and religious bent were shared with obvious didactic intent, reflecting the strict attitude toward the rearing of children that held sway in the Western world from the Middle Ages to the late nineteenth century. Fear of death and punishment was used to gain obedience to authority. Ann and Jane Taylor's *Original Poems, for Infant Minds, by Several Young Persons* (1804) provided poems, such as "The Idle Boy," "Greedy Richard," and "Meddlesome Matty."

Poetry for children flourished from the middle of the nineteenth century through the 1920s, a period considered the Golden Age of Poetry for Children. The Golden Age of Poetry moved away from moralistic poetry to poems about the beauty of life and nature; poems of humor, nonsense,

MILESTONES in the Development of Poetry

Date	Poet	Landmark Work	Country	Characteristic
1846	Edward Lear	A Book of Nonsense	England	Father of nonsense poetry, limericks
1864	Lewis Carroll	"Jabberwocky"	England	Nonsense verses, such as those in *Alice's Adventures in Wonderland*
1872	Christina Rossetti	*Sing Song*	England	Poems on children and the small things around them
1885	Robert Louis Stevenson	*A Child's Garden of Verses*	England	Descriptive poems of childhood memories
1888	Ernest Thayer	"Casey at the Bat"	U.S.	Famous ballad on baseball
1890	Laura E. Richards	*In My Nursery*	U.S.	Poems with hilarious situations, wordplay, and strong rhythm
1896	Eugene Field	*Poems of Childhood*	U.S.	Poems reflecting on children and child life
1902	Walter de la Mare	*Songs of Childhood*	England	Musical and imaginative poetry
1920	Rose Fyleman	*Fairies and Chimneys*	England	Imaginative poems about fairies
1922	A. A. Milne	*When We Were Very Young*	England	Poems of fun and observations of a child's world
1926	Rachel Field	*Taxis and Toadstools*	U.S.	Poems about city and country through the child's eyes

and word play; and imaginative poems that interpreted life from a child's perspective. Much of the Golden Age poetry retains its appeal today; for example, *A Child's Garden of Verses* (1885) by Robert Louis Stevenson remains a favorite collection.

In the 1960s and 1970s, the trend toward realism in children's literature was also reflected in poetry. More topics were considered suitable for children, resulting in protest poetry, poems about girls in nontraditional roles, and irreverent poems. Parents, teachers, and other adults became fair game for ridicule and mockery and poets from diverse cultures were more frequently published.

Poems became more popular in classrooms beginning in the 1980s. Publishers continue to present both single poems and collections of poems in beautifully illustrated book formats. In the 1980s, Nancy Willard's *A Visit to William Blake's Inn: Poems for Innocent and Experienced Travelers* and Paul Fleischman's *Joyful Noise: Poems for Two Voices* received Newbery Medals, indicating greater recognition of poetry for young people in the U.S. An increase in the publication of anthologies of poems by and about people of color, such as *Pass It On*, edited by Wade

Hudson, and *Cool Salsa,* edited by Lori Carlson, appeared in the 1990s. This increased publication also resulted in greater attention to earlier African-American poets, such as Paul Laurence Dunbar and Langston Hughes. A current trend is using poetry to create novels in verse, as by authors such as Karen Hesse, Helen Frost, Jacqueline Woodson, and Margarita Engle.

Poetry Types and Forms

Poetry can be classified in many ways; one way is to consider two main types that generally differ in purpose. *Lyric poetry* captures a moment, a feeling, or a scene and is descriptive in nature, whereas *narrative poetry* tells a story or includes a sequence of events. This example is a lyric poem.

Giraffes

Stilted creatures,
Features fashioned as a joke,
Boned and buckled,
Finger painted,
They stand in the field
On long-pronged legs
As if thrust there.
They airily feed,
Slightly swaying,
Like hammer-headed flowers.

Bizarre they are,
Built silent and high,
Ornaments against the sky.
Ears like leaves
To hear the silken
Brushing of the clouds.

—Sy Kahn

Although many narrative poems are quite lengthy in telling a story, the next selection is a very succinct narrative:

The Little Turtle

There was a little turtle.
He lived in a box.
He swam in a puddle.
He climbed on the rocks.

He snapped at a mosquito.
He snapped at a flea.
He snapped at a minnow.
And he snapped at me.

He caught the mosquito.
He caught the flea.

He caught the minnow.
But he didn't catch me.

—Vachel Lindsay

Poetry can also be categorized by its *poetic form,* which refers to the way the poem is structured or put together. *Couplets, tercets, quatrains,* and *cinquains* refer to the number (two, three, four, and five) of lines of poetry in a stanza—a set of lines of poetry grouped together. Couplets, tercets, quatrains, and cinquains usually rhyme, though the rhyme scheme may vary. These poetic forms may constitute an entire poem, or a poem may comprise a few stanzas of couplets, tercets, and so on. "Higglety, Pigglety, Pop!" is an example of the cinquain poetic form in a traditional nursery rhyme.

Higglety, Pigglety, Pop!

Higglety, pigglety, pop!
The dog has eaten the mop.
The pig's in a hurry,
The cat's in a flurry,
Higglety, pigglety, pop!

—Samuel Goodrich

Other specific poetic forms frequently found in children's poetry are limericks, ballads, haiku, sijo, free verse, and concrete poetry. Paul Janeczko's *A Kick in the Head* is a poetry anthology with examples of poetic forms along with brief explanations of the form.

A *limerick* is a humorous one-stanza, five-line verse form (usually a narrative), in which lines 1, 2, and 5 rhyme and are of the same length and lines 3 and 4 rhyme and are of the same length but shorter than the other lines. The following is an example of a limerick by Edward Lear, the poet who popularized this poetic form in the nineteenth century.

Limerick

There was an Old Man with a beard
Who said, "It is just as I feared!—
Two Owls and a Hen
Two Larks and a Wren
Have all built their nests in my beard!"

—Edward Lear

A *ballad* is a fairly long narrative poem of popular origin, usually adapted to singing. These traditional story poems are often romantic or heroic, such as "Robin Hood" or "John Henry."

Haiku is a lyric unrhymed poem of Japanese origin with seventeen syllables, arranged on three lines with a syllable count of five, seven, and five. Haiku is highly evocative poetry that frequently espouses harmony with and appreciation of nature.

The wind and I play
tug-of-war with my new kite.
The wind is winning.

—Bob Raczka

Sijo is a traditional Korean poetry form with three lines, each with fourteen to sixteen syllables. The first line introduces the topic, the second develops the topic, and the third contains some kind of twist. Unlike haiku, sijo can focus on many topics, including relationships and everyday moments.

Pockets

What's in your pockets right now? I hope they're not empty;
Empty pockets, unread books, lunches left on the bus—all a waste.
In mine: One horse chestnut. One gum wrapper. One dime. One hamster.

—Linda Sue Park

Free verse is unrhymed poetry with little or light rhythm. Sometimes words within a line will rhyme. The subjects of free verse are often abstract and philosophical; they are always reflective.

Autumn Leaves

gather in gutters,
pile on walks,
tumble
    from the tips
of toes,
crunching
fall hellos
to back-to-school feet.

—Rebecca Kai Dotlich

Concrete poetry is written and printed in a shape that signifies the subject of the poem. Concrete poems are a form of poetry that must be seen as well as heard to be fully appreciated. These poems do not usually have rhyme or definite rhythm; they rely mostly on the words, their meanings and shapes, and the way the words are arranged on the page to evoke images. In "Concrete Cat" note the position of the word that suggests that the mouse has met with an accident.

Concrete Cat

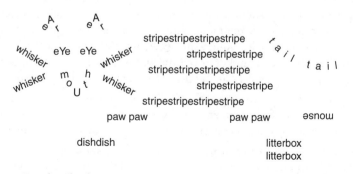

—Dorthi Charles

Reader Connections: Poetry in the Classroom

Young children delight in the sounds and language play of poetry—yet by fifth grade, students typically indicate that poetry is their least favorite genre. The cause of this huge shift is school. Poetry is the most misused genre in classrooms, often chosen for memorization and handwriting practice. Poetry tends to be neglected, seldom shared until the dreaded poetry unit comes along and students are bombarded with abstract poems that they are expected to analyze in order to uncover the "hidden meanings." The result is that students often build a lifelong dislike of poetry instead of being provided with experiences that create a lifelong love of poetry.

Reading Poetry Aloud

Poetry should be introduced first and often to children in an oral form. Poetry was originally an oral form of literature and so still relies heavily on the auditory perceptions of listeners. Moreover, children's oral language is the basis for their acquisition of literacy. These two facts make listening to and saying poems a natural early introduction to literature for children.

Poetry should be read aloud to students on a daily basis. Elster and Hanauer (2002) found that reading poetry aloud with expression is effective in drawing children's attention to literate language. Brief, positive encounters with one to three poems at a time are best. Too many poems in one sitting can overwhelm students or make the reading tedious. Introduce the poem to the class before reading it aloud, either by tying the poem in with something else or by briefly telling why you chose the poem. Then state the title of the poem and the poet and begin to read. Because poetry tends to be brief and conceptually dense, reading the poem several times is often necessary for students to make connections and construct understandings. By practicing a poem ahead of time and reading poetry frequently, teachers can become effective in sharing poetry with students. Some points to keep in mind in learning to read poetry well include:

- Read poetry for its meaning. Stress the meaning elements of the poem just as when reading a story. Pauses should be determined by the meaning units of the poem, not by the end of the lines.

- Do not overemphasize the beat of the poem. Doing so results in an annoying singsong effect. Let the poetic language provide the rhythm.

- Enunciate the poem clearly. Each sound and each syllable are important and need to be heard to be appreciated. Slow down your normal reading pace to give full value to each sound. Poetry requires a willingness to listen with an expectation that the sounds will be pleasing and meaningful.

- Poetry begs to be performed and dramatized. Try out different effects (using different voices, elongating words, singing, shouting, whispering, pausing dramatically) as you read poems aloud. Your voice is a powerful tool: You may change it from louder to softer to only a whisper; start at a deep, low pitch and rise to a medium and eventually high pitch; speak very quickly in a clipped fashion and then slow down and draw out the words. Sara Holbrook's *Wham! It's a Poetry Jam: Discovering Performance Poetry* (2002) offers good suggestions for performing poetry.

- Some poems may need to be read aloud a number of times for the meaning to be fully understood by listeners. Also, favorite poems can be enjoyed again and again, as teachers and students savor one more reading and linger over the musicality of poetry and appreciate the word choice.

- Read poems in pairs that relate by theme or topic to put the poems in conversation with each other so that the ideas resonate with each other and illuminate the experience of being in the poem.

• Consider recording poems and making the recordings available along with the poem on a chart or in a book for the student to listen to and read. Commercial recordings of popular poets reading their works, accompanied by music, are popular with children. You might ask parents to peruse a poetry anthology, select a favorite poem, and record their reading of the poem.

• After reading a poem aloud, response can extend students' enjoyment through choral reading, discussion, art, drama, etc. Do not begin with analysis, but with responding to the emotional or imaginative aspects of the poem. Students can share how the poem made them feel or what it made them think about by discussing, "How did this poem make you feel? What meaning does this poem have for you?"

• Overanalyzing the form, figurative language, and meaning of poems has led to a dislike of poetry. Often, just reading and enjoying the poem is all that is needed. Other times, students can respond to the emotional impact of a poem. Once students have experience with poetry, a careful look at form is appropriate occasionally but only *after* they have an opportunity for personal response. Children can be asked to point out parts of the poem that they like and talk about why. They can also be encouraged to explore metaphor, imagery and sensory language in poems. An analysis of form and language can be integrated into mini-lessons as students write their own poetry and want to make their poems more effective. The major focus, however, should always be on the meaning and emotional impact of a poem.

Choral Poetry   Choral reading of poetry provides an opportunity to say and hear poems over and over again as a form of reader response. *Choral poetry* consists of orally interpreting the poem through your voice by saying a poem together as a group activity. These poems may be practiced and recited or read aloud. Students enjoy this way of experiencing poetry because they have a participatory role in the activity. Most poetry, intended to be listened to, is suitable for choral presentation. The following sections explain how to select choral poems and teach them to students.

1. **Selection.** At first, select short poems (from one to four stanzas) until students develop skill in reciting and performing poems. Humorous narrative poems are good first choices, leading later to longer poems. Provide students with a copy of the poem.

2. **Arrangements.** Options for reading a poem chorally include unison, two- or three-part, solo voices, cumulative build-up, and simultaneous voices.

   • In unison choral speaking, the students recite the poem together as a group. Two-part or three-part choral poetry is usually based on arranging students into voice types (e.g., high, medium, and low) to achieve different effects and by selecting lines of the poem for each group to recite or read.

   • Solo voices can be added to either of these presentations and are sometimes used for asking a question or making an exclamation.

   • Some poems lend themselves to cumulative build-up presentations, such as voices saying the first line, then two more joining in on the second, and then two more, gradually building to a crescendo until the entire class says the last line or stanza.

   • Poems can be presented by simultaneous recitation, which forms a presentation similar to a musical round. Group one begins the poem and recites it all the way through. When group one begins the third line, then group two starts the first line, and the two groups recite simultaneously until the end. Other groups can, of course, be added.

- Poetry selected and arranged for dramatic choral readings on a particular theme infuses an interesting variation into choral poetry. Paul Fleischman's *Joyful Noise: Poems for Two Voices*; *I Am Phoenix: Poems for Two Voices*; and *Big Talk: Poems for Four Voices* are collections of poetry written in a manner suitable for choral reading. These collections were written to be read aloud by two readers at once, one reading the left half of the page and one reading the right half, as well as certain lines simultaneously. Pairs of students may each take a different poem from the collection.

Many other variations can be developed for choral readings. Let imagination be your guide. Words and lines can be spun into ghostly moans, or barked, or sung, or repeated. Choreography adds visual impact, as do simple props. As soon as children learn that poems do not have to be read sedately exactly as written, they will find excitement and deeper meaning in poetry.

3. **Performance.** Incorporating action, gestures, body movements, and finger plays can produce interesting and enjoyable presentations. Many of these performances will be informal, with a focus on playing with various arrangements of a poem in a small group or class. More formal performances involve memorizing a well-loved poem, trying out various arrangements, and rehearsing the final arrangement for presentation to an audience.

Students' Reading and Writing Poems

Learning to Read Poetry   Children enjoy reading poetry silently and aloud to others. The classroom library corner should have one or two comprehensive poetry anthologies for students to browse. In addition, specialized collections by a single poet, such as Jack Prelutsky's *I've Lost My Hippopotamus,* and books of poems on a single topic, such as *Around the World in Eighty Poems* edited by James Berry, are needed. Students can be encouraged to make copies of favorite poems from these collections to develop personal, individual anthologies. Many students choose to illustrate and arrange the poems in new and inventive ways. Rotating poetry books occasionally over the course of the school year will spark renewed interest in reading poetry. Consider these additional other activities to encourage the reading of poetry:

- Students can take turns reading favorite poems to one another in pairs. Make video or audio recordings of these readings so students can watch or listen to their readings.

- Ask each student to select three poems by one poet (e.g., a Golden Age poet or an NCTE poet) and find something out about the poet; then place students in groups of five or six to tell briefly about the poet and read the three poems aloud. Paul B. Janeczko's *The Place My Words Are Looking For: What Poets Say about and through Their Work* (1990) and Sylvia Vardell's *Poetry People* (2007) are excellent resources. Information about children's authors can also be found on many websites, including www.childrenslit.com.

- Have students find three poems on the same topic or theme, such as dinosaurs, baseball, or the value of friendship, to read aloud in small groups.

- Encourage students to find poems that are of the same poetic form (cinquains, limericks, etc.), or that exhibit similar poetic elements (rhyme, alliteration, onomatopoeia, etc.), or that have fast or slow rhythms. These poems can be used for reading aloud that day or week.

- Students can bring their collections of poems to class to share. One way to extend this sharing is to have each small group select a poem for a multimodal response by creating a Cin(E)-Poem

(Stuart, 2010). Students sketch a storyboard of the poem that integrates images with the language of the poem. They then collect or create digital images, words, sounds, and music to construct a visual interpretation and experience of their poem to present to the class.

• An excellent site for ideas and resources for finding and sharing poetry with children is Sylvia Vardell's blog, http://poetryforchildren.blogspot.com/.

• Georgia Heard (2012) provides suggestions for encouraging students to read and appreciate poetry in order to address the Common Core State Standards as related to exemplar poems.

Do	Don't
Read poetry aloud every day	Limit poetry choices to one or two poets or types of poems
Practice reading a poem before reading it aloud for the first time to students	Read poems in a singsong style
Choose poetry the students will like	Choose all poems from one anthology
Have a variety of poetry anthologies and specialized poetry books in the classroom	Have a poetry marathon for days or weeks to make up for not sharing poetry regularly
Encourage students to recite and write poems	Force students to memorize and recite poems
Facilitate choral readings of poetry	Make analysis the focus of poetry study
Invite responses to poetry through art, music, and movement	Have students copy poems for handwriting practice
Feature a notable poet each month	Emphasize the writing of formula poems
Begin and end each day with a poem	Read poems only during the annual poetry unit

Learning to Write Poetry   A rich poetry environment stimulates children's interest in writing their own poems. Children need to be familiar with poetry of many kinds and by many poets before they are asked to compose poems. The collection of poems *Inner Chimes: Poems on Poetry,* selected by Bobbye S. Goldstein, may be a natural starting place for helping students to think about what poetry is. This collection contains poems by well-known children's poets writing about creating poetry. Other books that provide suggestions on poetry in the classroom are *Awakening the Heart* (1999) by Georgia Heard and *Poetry Aloud Here!* (2006) by Sylvia Vardell.

One way to start writing poetry is through a collaborative effort. The class brainstorms ideas and composes the poem orally as the teacher writes it on the board or on chart paper. As students become comfortable with writing group poetry, they can branch off and compose poems in pairs or individually. Georgia Heard has collections of poems created from lists and pieces of print found on signs and slips of paper that provide fun ways to ease into writing poetry.

Poetry is a form of communication and so encourage children to think of an idea, feeling, or event to write about. They should be reminded that poetry does not have to rhyme and that they may write about something of interest to them. Children's poetry follows no absolute rules; perfection of form should not be a goal. Other suggestions to encourage poetry writing include:

• Have students compile personal and class anthologies of their favorite poems. Another type of anthology is to collect poems that reflect their own identities and interests.

- Design bulletin boards with displays of students' poems as well as copies of poems by favorite poets. Students may also design posters, individually or in groups, to illustrate a favorite poem.

- Encourage students to model the works of professional poets by imitating a whole poem or specific techniques.

- Read aloud many poems of one poetic form; then analyze the form with the students to reveal the characteristics of its structure. Quatrains, cinquains, haiku, concrete poems, and limericks can be used as models with students once they have an appreciation for poetry and for the specific poetic form.

Some poets have suggested other models and patterns for students to follow in writing poetry. Kenneth Koch's *Wishes, Lies, and Dreams: Teaching Children to Write Poetry* (1999/1970); Myra Cohn Livingston's *Poem Making: Ways to Begin Writing Poetry* (1991); Paul Janeczko's *How to Write Poetry* (1999) and *Poetry from A to Z: A Guide for Young Writers* (1994); Ralph Fletcher's *Poetry Matters: Writing a Poem from the Inside Out* (2002); and Jack Prelutsky's *Pizza, Pigs, and Poetry: How to Write a Poem* (2008) are useful resources for teachers who want to encourage students to compose poems.

Invitations for Further Investigation

- Create a self-portrait anthology by collecting poems that celebrate and explore the different aspects of who you are and what you are doing, thinking, and feeling. Open the anthology by selecting a signature poem that reflects your sense of self. Georgia Heard's *Songs of Myself* is a useful resource as an example of this type of anthology.

- Share your collections of favorite poems and select a poem as a small group to explore through the multimodal approach of Cin(E)-Poetry (Stuart, 2010).

- Research the history of Mother Goose or nursery rhymes within a particular culture.

- Some children see poetry as sentimental and irrelevant to their lives. One way to challenge this viewpoint is to read poetry that provokes feelings and ideas about issues of social justice. Consider this role for poetry by reading about the experiences of children in a classroom (Damico, 2005) and collecting poems that address complex social issues.

- Pair sets of poems with each other or pair a poem with a picture book, novel, or song so the ideas in these texts play off of each other to provide diverse perspectives.

References

Charles, D. (1982). Concrete cat. In X. J. Kennedy & D. M. Kennedy (Eds.), *Knock at a star*. Weinhaus, K. A. (Illus.). Boston, MA: Little, Brown.

Ciardi, J. (1996). *The monster den*. Philadelphia, PA: Lippincott.

Clark, G. O. (1983). The night is a big black cat. In J. Prelutsky (Ed.), *The Random House book of poetry for children*. Lobel, A. (Illus.). New York: Random House.

Crane, W. (1983). The crocus. In J. Prelutsky (Ed.), *The Random House book of poetry for children*. Lobel, A. (Illus.). New York: Random House.

Damico, J. (2005). Evoking hearts and heads: Exploring issues of social justice through poetry. *Language Arts, 83*(2), 137–146.

Dotlich, R. K. (2003). Autumn leaves. In R. K. Dotlich (Ed.), *In the spin of things: Poetry of motion*. Dugan, K. (Illus.). Honesdale, PA: Boyds Mills.

Elster, C. A., & Hanauer, D. I. (2002). Voicing texts, voices around texts: Reading poems in elementary school classrooms. *Research in the Teaching of English, 37*(1), 89–134.

Fisher, C. J., & Natarella, M. A. (1982). Young children's preferences in poetry: A national survey of first, second and third graders. *Research in the Teaching of English, 16*(4), 339–354.

Fletcher, R. (2002). *Poetry matters: Writing a poem from the inside out.* New York: HarperCollins.

Ghigna, C. (2003). What's a poem? In C. Ghigna (Ed.), *A fury of motion: Poems for boys.* Honesdale, PA: Boyds Mills.

Heard, G. (1999). *Awakening the heart: Exploring poetry in elementary and middle school.* Portsmouth, NH: Heinemann.

Heard, G. (2000). *Songs of myself: An anthology of poems and art.* New York: Mondo.

Heard, G. (2013). *Poetry lessons to meet the Common Core State Standards.* New York: Scholastic.

Holbrook, S. (2002). *Wham! It's a poetry jam: Discovering performance poetry.* Honesdale, PA: Boyds Mills.

Janeczko, P. B., selector. (1990). *The place my words are looking for: What poets say about and through their work.* New York: Bradbury.

Janeczko, P. B. (1994). *Poetry from A to Z: A guide for young writers.* New York: Bradbury.

Janeczko, P. B. (1999). *How to write poetry.* New York: Scholastic.

Kahn, S. (1967). Giraffes. In S. Dunning, E. Lueders, & H. Smith (Eds.), *Reflections on a gift of watermelon pickle.* New York: Lothrop, Lee and Shepard.

Koch, K. (1999/1970). *Wishes, lies, and dreams: Teaching children to write poetry.* New York: Random.

Kutiper, K., & Wilson, P. (1993). Updating poetry preferences: A look at the poetry children really like. *The Reading Teacher, 47*(1), 28–35.

Lear, E. (1946). *The complete nonsense book.* New York: Dodd, Mead.

Lindsay, V. (1920). The Little Turtle. *The Golden whales of California and other rhymes in the American language.* New York: The Macmillan Company.

Livingston, M. C. (1991). *Poem making: Ways to begin writing poetry.* New York: HarperCollins.

McCord, David. (1977). *One at a Time.* Boston: Little, Brown.

Park, L. S. (2007). Pockets. In L. S. Park, *Tap dancing on the roof: Sijo (poems).* Banyai (Illus.). New York, NY: Clarion.

Prelutsky, J. (2008). *Pizza, pigs, and poetry: How to write a poem.* New York: Greenwillow.

Reeves, J. (1963). Slowly. In E. Blishen (Ed.), *Oxford book of poetry for children.* Wildsmith, B. (Illus.). Oxford, England: Oxford University Press.

Stuart, D. (2010). Cin(E)-Poetry: Engaging the digital generation in 21st-century response. *Voices from the Middle.* 17 (3), 27–35.

Taylor, J. (1983). The star. In J. Prelutsky (Ed.), *The Random House book of poetry for children.* Illus. A. Lobel. New York: Random House.

Terry, A. C. (1974). *Children's poetry preferences: A national survey of upper elementary grades.* Urbana, IL: National Council of Teachers of English.

Vardell, S. (2006). *Poetry aloud here! Sharing poetry with children.* Chicago, IL: American Library Association.

Vardell, S. (2007). *Poetry people: A practical guide to children's poets.* Santa Barbara, CA: Libraries Unlimited.

Wise, W. (1931/1932). After the party. In W. Wise, *Jonathan Blake.* New York: Knopf.

Recommended Poetry Books

Because poetry is usually of interest to a broad age group, entries of poetry books indicate age only for books mainly suitable for older readers.

Mother Goose, Nursery Rhymes and Songs

Chorao, Kay, compiler. ***Rhymes 'Round the World.*** Dutton, 2009.

Crews, Nina. *The Neighborhood Mother Goose.* Greenwillow, 2004. Photographs in a city setting.

Delacre, Lulu, selector. *Arrorró, mi niño: Latino Lullabies and Gentle Games.* Lee & Low, 2004.

dePaola, Tomie, compiler. *Tomie dePaola's Mother Goose.* Putnam, 1985.

Dillon, Leo, and Diane Dillon, compilers. *Mother Goose: Numbers on the Loose.* Harcourt, 2007.

Duffy, Chris, editor. *Nursery Rhyme Comics: 50 Times Rhymes from 50 Celebrated Cartoonists.* First Second, 2011. Graphic novel.

Frazee, Marla. *Hush, Little Baby.* Harcourt, 2003.

Lobel, Arnold, selector. *The Arnold Lobel Book of Mother Goose.* Knopf, 1997.

Opie, Iona, editor. *Mother Goose's Little Treasures.* Illus. Rosemary Wells. Candlewick, 2007.

Orozco, José-Luis, selector and translator. *Diez Deditos and Other Play Rhymes and Action Songs from Latin America.* Illus. Elisa Kleven. Dutton, 1997.

Pinkney, Brian. *Hush, Little Baby.* Greenwillow, 2006.

Taylor, Jane. *Twinkle, Twinkle, Little Star.* Illus. Jerry Pinkney. Little, Brown, 2011.

Wheeler, Lisa. *Spinster Goose*. Illus. Sophie Blackwell. Atheneum, 2011. Parodies of traditional rhymes.

Wright, Danielle. *My Village: Rhymes from around the World*. Illus. Mique Moriuchi. Frances Lincoln, 2010.

Yolen, Jane, editor. *Trot, Trot to Boston: Lap Songs, Finger Plays, Clapping Games, and Pantomime Rhymes.* Illus. Will Hillenbrand. Candlewick, 2005.

Anthologies of Poetry

Driscoll, Michael. *A Child's Introduction to Poetry.* Illus. Meredith Hamilton. Black Dog & Leventhal, 2003. Poetic forms and individual poets.

Ferris, Helen, compiler. *Favorite Poems Old and New.* Illus. Leonard Weisgard. Doubleday, 1957.

Hall, Donald, editor. *The Oxford Illustrated Book of American Children's Poems.* Oxford University Press, 1999.

Hoberman, Mary Ann, compiler. *Forget-Me-Nots: Poems to Learn by Heart*. Illus. Michael Emberley. Little Brown, 2012.

Kennedy, X. J., and Dorothy Kennedy, editors. *Knock at a Star: A Child's Introduction to Poetry.* Illus. Karen Lee Baher. Little, Brown, 1999.

Martin, Bill, Jr., and Michael Sampson, editors. *The Bill Martin Jr. Big Book of Poetry.* Simon & Schuster, 2008.

Prelutsky, Jack, editor. *The Random House Book of Poetry for Children.* Illus. Arnold Lobel. Random House, 1983.

Yolen, Jane, and Andrew Peters, collectors. *Here's a Little Poem: A Very First Book of Poetry.* Illus. Polly Dunbar. Candlewick, 2007.

Specialized Poetry Books

Poetry books by a single poet and thematic poetry books are included.

Adoff, Arnold. *All the Colors of the Race.* Illus. John Steptoe. Lothrop, 1982.

Adoff, Arnold. *Roots and Blues: A Celebration*. Illus. R. Gregory Christie. Clarion, 2011.

Agee, Jon. *Orangutan Tongs: Poems to Tangle Your Tongue.* Disney/Hyperion, 2009.

Appelt, Kathi. *Poems from Homeroom: A Writer's Place to Start.* Holt, 2002. Ages 12–18. Includes a bibliography of adult books on writing poems and stories.

Ashman, Linda. *The Essential Worldwide Monster Guide.* Illus. David Small. Simon & Schuster, 2003.

Berry, James. *A Nest Full of Stars: Poems.* Illus. Ashley Bryan. Greenwillow, 2004. Caribbean.

Berry, James, editor. *Around the World in Eighty Poems.* Illus. Katherine Lucas. Chronicle, 2002. Fifty countries.

Brooks, Gwendolyn. *Bronzeville Boys and Girls.* Illus. Faith Ringgold. HarperCollins, 2007.

Carlson, Lori, editor. *Red Hot Salsa: Bilingual Poems on Being Young and Latino in the United States.* Holt, 2005. Ages 10–16. Also *Cool Salsa* (1994).

Clinton, Catherine, editor. *A Poem of Her Own: Voices of American Women Yesterday and Today.* Illus. Stephen Alcorn. Abrams, 2003. Ages 10–16.

Cullinan, Bernice, and Deborah Wooten, editors. *Another Jar of Tiny Stars: Poems by More NCTE Award–Winning Poets.* Wordsong, 2009. Also *A Jar of Tiny Stars* (1995).

Durango, Julia. *Under the Mambo Moon.* Illus. Fabricio Vanden Broeck. Charlesbridge, 2011. Latin America.

Elliott, David. *In the Wild*. Illus. Holly Meade. Candlewick, 2010. Also *In the Sea* (2012). Animals.

Fleischman, Paul. *I Am Phoenix: Poems for Two Voices*. Illus. Eric Beddows. Harper, 1985.

Fleischman, Paul. *Joyful Noise: Poems for Two Voices*. Illus. Eric Beddows. Harper, 1988.

Florian, Douglas. *Autumnblings*. Greenwillow, 2003. One of his cycles of seasons, including *Handsprings*, 2006; *Summersaults*, 2002; and *Winter Eyes*, 1999.

Florian, Douglas. *Comets, Stars, the Moon, and Mars: Space Poems and Paintings*. Harcourt, 2006.

Florian, Douglas. *Dinothesaurus: Prehistoric Poems and Paintings*. Atheneum, 2009.

Franco, Betsy. *Mathematickles*. Illus. Steven Salerno. Simon & Schuster, 2003.

Franco, Betsy. *A Dazzling Display of Dogs: Concrete Poems*. Illus. Michael Wertz. Tricycle, 2011. Also *A Curious Collection of Cats* (2009).

George, Kristine O'Connell. *Hummingbird Nest: A Journal of Poems*. Illus. Barry Moser. Harcourt, 2004.

George, Kristine O'Connell. *Fold Me a Poem*. Illus. Lauren Stringer. Harcourt, 2005.

George, Kristine O'Connell. *Emma Dilemma: Big Sister Poems*. Illus. Nancy Carpenter. Clarion, 2011.

Ghigna, Charles. *A Fury of Motion: Poems for Boys*. Boyds Mills, 2003. Ages 12–18.

Giovanni, Nikki, editor. *Hip Hop Speaks to Children: A Celebration of Poetry with a Beat*. Illus. K. Balouch. Sourcebooks, 2008.

Goldstein, Bobbye S., editor. *Inner Chimes: Poems on Poetry*. Illus. Jane Breskin Zalben. Wordsong, 1992.

Grady, Cynthia. *I Lay My Stitches Down: Poems of American Slavery*. Illus. Michele Wood. Eerdmans, 2012.

Grandits, John. *Technically, It's Not My Fault: Concrete Poems*. Clarion, 2004. Ages 9–13.

Greenberg, Jan, editor. *Heart to Heart: New Poems Inspired by Twentieth-Century American Art*. Abrams, 2001. Ages 11–15. Also *Side by Side: New Poems Inspired by Art from Around the World* (2008).

Greenfield, Eloise. *Honey, I Love, and Other Love Poems*. Illus. Leo & Diane Dillon. HarperCollins, 1978.

Greenfield, Eloise. *The Great Migration: Journeys to the North*. Illus. Jan Spivey Gilchrist. Amistad, 2011.

Grimes, Nikki. *A Pocketful of Poems*. Illus. Javaka Steptoe. Clarion, 2001.

Grimes, Nikki. *Danitra Brown: Class Clown*. Illus. E. B. Lewis. HarperCollins, 2005. Ages 7–10.

Harley, Avia. *African Acrostics: A Word in Edgeways*. Photos Deborah Noyes. Candlewick, 2009. Animals.

Heard, Georgia, editor. *Falling Down the Page*. Roaring Brook, 2009.

Heard, Georgia, editor. *The Arrow Finds Its Mark: A Book of Found Poems*. Illus. Antoine Guilloppe. Roaring Brook, 2012.

Hines, Anna Grossnickle. *Peaceful Pieces: Poems and Quilts about Peace*. Holt, 2011.

Hoberman, Mary Ann. *Fathers, Mothers, Sisters, Brothers: A Collection of Family Poems*. Illus. Marylin Hafner. Little, 1991.

Holbrook, Sara. *By Definition: Poems of Feelings*. Illus. Scott Mattern. Boyds Mills, 2003.

Hopkins, Lee Bennett, selector. *Behind the Museum Door: Poems to Celebrate the Wonders of Museums*. Illus. Stacey Dressen-McQueen. Abrams, 2007.

Hopkins, Lee Bennett, selector. *America at War*. Illus. Stephen Alcorn. M. K. McElderry, 2008.

Hopkins, Lee Bennett. *Sharing the Seasons: A Book of Poems*. Illus. David Diaz. M. K. McElderry, 2010.

Hudson, Wade, editor. *Pass It On: African American Poetry for Children*. Illus. Floyd Cooper. Scholastic, 1993.

Janeczko, Paul B., editor. *A Poke in the I: A Collection of Concrete Poems*. Illus. Chris Raschka. Candlewick, 2000.

Janeczko, Paul B., editor. *A Kick in the Head: An Everyday Guide to Poetic Forms*. Illus. Chris Raschka. Candlewick, 2005. Ages 9–14. Poems of various forms with brief explanations of each form.

Janeczko, Paul B., editor. *A Foot in the Mouth: Poems to Speak, Sing, and Shout*. Illus. Chris Raschka. Candlewick, 2009. Poems to read aloud in voices; some are bilingual.

Katz, Bobbi. *We, the People*. Illus. Nina Crews. Greenwillow, 2000. First-person monologues, U.S. history.

Katz, Bobbi, editor. *Pocket Poems*. Illus. Marylin Hafner. Dutton, 2004.

Katz, Susan. *Looking for Jaguar and Other Rainforest Poems*. Illus. Lee Christiansen. Greenwillow, 2005.

Kennedy, Caroline, editor. *My Favorite Poetry for Children.* Illus. Jon J. Muth. Hyperion, 2005.

Kennedy, X. J. *Fresh Brats.* Illus. James Watts. Macmillan, 1990.

Kuskin, Karla. *Green as a Bean.* Illus. Melissa Iwai. HarperCollins, 2007.

Lear, Edward. *His Shoes Were Far Too Tight.* Selected by Daniel Pinkwater. Illus. Calef Brown. Chronicle,2011.

Lewis, J. Patrick. *Doodle Dandies: Poems That Take Shape.* Illus. Lisa Desimini. Simon & Schuster, 1998.

Lewis, J. Patrick. *Vherses: A Celebration of Outstanding Women.* Illus. Mark Summers. Creative, 2005. Ages 9–14.

Lewis, J. Patrick. *Edgar Allan Poe's Pies: Math Puzzlers in Classic Poems.* Illus. Michael Slack. Harcourt, 2012.

Liu, Siyu, and Orel Protopopescu. *A Thousand Peaks: Poems from China.* Illus. Siyu Liu. Pacific View Press, 2001. Ages 10–18.

Mak, Kam. *My Chinatown.* Illus. Kam Mak. Harper-Collins, 2002.

Mora, Pat. *Yum! Mmmm! Que rico!: America's Sproutings.* Illus. Rafael Lopez. Lee & Low, 2007. Ages 7–12.

Morrison, Lillian, compiler. *It Rained All Day That Night: Autographs, Rhymes & Inscriptions.* Illus. Christy Hale. August House, 2003.

Myers, Walter Dean. *Blues Journey.* Illus. Christopher Myers. Holiday, 2003. See also *Jazz* (2006).

Myers, Walter Dean. *Here in Harlem: Poems in Many Voices.* Holiday, 2004. Ages 12–18.

Nelson, Marilyn. *Fortune's Bones: The Manumission Requiem.* Front Street, 2004. Ages 12–16. Poetic memorial of an enslaved man who died in 1798.

Nelson, Marilyn. *A Wreath for Emmett Till.* Illus. Philippe Lardy. Houghton, 2005. Ages 12–18. Interlocking sonnets.

Nelson, Marilyn. *Sweethearts of Rhythm: The Story of the Greatest All-Girl Swinging Band in the World.* Illus. Jerry Pinkney. Dial, 2009. Ages 10–14. World War II female jazz band, poems in the voices of instruments.

Nye, Naomi, Shihab, editor. *This Same Sky: A Collection of Poems from around the World.* Four Winds, 1992. Ages 11–18.

Nye, Naomi Shihab, editor. *The Space between Our Footsteps: Poems and Paintings from the Middle East.* Simon & Schuster, 1998.

Nye, Naomi Shihab, editor. *19 Varieties of Gazelle: Poems of the Middle East.* HarperCollins, 2002. Ages 11–18.

Nye, Naomi Shihab, editor. *A Maze Me: Poems for Girls.* Illus. Terre Maher. Greenwillow, 2005. Ages 11–18.

Park, Linda Sue. *Tap Dancing on the Roof: Sijo (Poems).* Illus. Istvan Banyai. Clarion, 2007.

Pearson, Susan. *The Drowsy Hours: Poems for Bedtime.* Illus. Peter Malone. HarperCollins, 2002.

Peters, Lisa Westberg. *Earthshake: Poems from the Ground Up.* Illus. Cathie Felstead. Greenwillow, 2003.

Prelutsky, Jack. *If Not for the Cat.* Illus. Ted Rand. Greenwillow, 2004. Animals described in haiku.

Prelutsky, Jack. *Behold the Bold Umbrellaphant and Other Poems.* Illus. Carin Berger. HarperCollins, 2006.

Prelutsky, Jack. *I've Lost My Hippopotamus.* Illus. Jackie Urbanovic. Greenwillow, 2012.

Prelutsky, Jack, editor. *Read a Rhyme, Write a Rhyme.* Illus.Meilo So. Knopf, 2005.

Raczka, Bob. *Lemonade: And Other Poems Squeezed from a Single Word.* Illus. Nancy Doniger. Roaring Brook, 2011. Word-puzzles about daily life.

Rex, Adam. *Frankenstein Makes a Sandwich.* Harcourt, 2006. Ages 9–12.

Rochelle, Belinda. *Words with Wings: A Treasury of African-American Poetry and Art.* HarperCollins, 2001.

Roessel, David, and Arnold Rampersad, editors. *Langston Hughes.* Illus. Benny Andrews. Sterling, 2006.

Ruddell, Deborah. *Today at the Bluebird Cafe: A Branchful of Birds.* Illus. Joan Rankin. M. K. McElderry, 2007.

Ruddell, Deborah. *A Whiff of Pine, a Hint of Skunk: A Forest of Poems.* Illus. Joan Rankin. M. K. McElderry, 2009.

Salas, Laura P. *Bookspeak: Poems about Books.* Illus. Josee Bisaillon. Clarion, 2011.

Schertle, Alice. *Button Up! Wrinkled Rhymes.* Illus. Petra Mathers. Harcourt, 2009.

Shange, Ntozake. *We Troubled the Waters.* Illus. Rod Brown. Collins, 2009. Racism in the United States. Ages 10–14.

Sidman, Joyce. *Song of the Water Boatman and Other Pond Poems.* Illus. Beckie Prange. Houghton, 2005.

Sidman, Joyce. *Butterfly Eyes and Other Secrets of the Meadow.* Illus. Beth Krommes. Houghton Mifflin, 2006.

Sidman, Joyce. *Meow Ruff.* Illus. Michelle Berg. Houghton Mifflin, 2006. Concrete poems.

Sidman, Joyce. *Red Sings from Treetops: A Year in Colors.* Illus. Pamela Zagarenski. Houghton Mifflin, 2009.

Sidman, Joyce. *Dark Emperor & Other Poems of the Night.* Illus. Rick Allen. Houghton Mifflin, 2010.

Siebert, Diane. *Tour America: A Journey through Poems and Art.* Illus. Stephen T. Johnson. Chronicle, 2006.

Silverstein, Shel. *Where the Sidewalk Ends.* Harper, 1974. Also *The Light in the Attic* (1981).

Singer, Marilyn. *Mirror Mirror: A Book of Reversible Verse.* Illus. Josee Masse. Dutton, 2010. Fairy tale characters.

Singer, Marilyn. *A Full Moon Is Rising.* Illus. Julia Cairns. Lee & Low, 2011. Global journey.

Soto, Gary. *Neighborhood Odes.* Illus. David Diaz. Harcourt, 1992. Ages 10–15. Mexican-American neighborhood.

Soto, Gary. *Worlds Apart: Traveling with Fernie and Me.* Illus. Greg Clarke. Putnam, 2005. Ages 9–13.

Steptoe, Javaka. *In Daddy's Arms I Am Tall: African Americans Celebrating Fathers.* Illus. Javaka Steptoe. Lee & Low, 1997.

Tadjo, Véronique, editor. *Talking Drums: A Selection of Poems from Africa South of the Sahara.* Bloomsbury, 2004. Ages 9–14. Seventy-five poems from sixteen African countries.

Thomas, Joyce Carol. *The Blacker the Berry.* Illus. Floyd Cooper. Joanna Cutler, 2008.

Updike, John. *A Child's Calendar.* Illus. Trina Schart Hyman. Holiday, 1999.

Wardlaw, Lee. *Won-Ton: A Cat Tale Told in Haiku.* Illus. Eugene Yelchin. Holt, 2011.

Weatherford, Carole Boston. *Remember the Bridge: Poems of a People.* Philomel, 2002. Ages 10–16.

Willard, Nancy. *A Visit to William Blake's Inn: Poems for Innocent and Experienced Travelers.* Illus. Alice and Martin Provensen. Harcourt, 1981.

Wong, Janet. *Good Luck Gold and Other Poems.* M. K. McElderry, 1994. See also *A Suitcase of Seaweed* (1996).

Worth, Valerie. *Animal Poems.* Illus. Steve Jenkins. Farrar, 2007.

Yolen, Jane. *Birds of a Feather.* Photos Jason Stemple. Wordsong, 2011. Also *An Egret's Day* (2010).

Zolotow, Charlotte. *Seasons: A Book of Poems.* Illus. Erik Blegvad. HarperCollins, 2002. Easy-to-read book.

Single Illustrated Poems

Illustrated poems are listed here. Illustrated stories in verse and rhyme are included in the chapter on Picture Books.

Bartoletti, Susan. *Naamah and the Ark at Night.* Illus. Holly Meade. Candlewick, 2011. Arabic ghazel verse form.

Carroll, Lewis. *Jabberwocky.* Illus. Christopher Myers. Jump at the Sun/Hyperion, 2007.

Frost, Helen. *Step Gently Out.* Photos Rick Lieder. Candlewick, 2012. Insects.

Hughes, Langston. *My People.* Photos Charles R. Smith Jr. Atheneum, 2009.

Hughes, Langston. *The Negro Speaks of Rivers.* Illus. E. B. Lewis. Disney/Jump at the Sun, 2009.

Janeczko, Paul, and J. Patrick Lewis. *Birds on a Wire: A Renga 'round Town.* Illus. Gary Lippincott. Wordsong, 2008.

Longfellow, Henry W. *Paul Revere's Ride: The Landlord's Tale.* Illus. Charles Santore. HarperCollins, 2003.

Shange, Ntozake. *Ellington Was Not a Street.* Illus. Kadir Nelson. Simon & Schuster, 2004. Ages 9–13. Harlem.

Shore, Diane, and Jessica Alexander. *This Is the Dream.* Illus. James Ransome. Amistad, 2006.

Sidman, Joyce. *Swirl by Swirl: Spirals in Nature.* Illus. Beth Krommes. Houghton Mifflin, 2011.

Siebert, Diane. *Motorcycle Song.* Illus. Leonard Jenkins. HarperCollins, 2002.

Stevenson, Robert Louis. *The Moon.* Illus. Tracey C. Pearson. Farrar, 2006.

Thayer, Ernest L. *Casey at the Bat: A Ballad of the Republic Sung in the Year 1888.* Illus. C. F. Payne. Simon & Schuster, 2003.

Thayer, Ernest L. *Casey at the Bat.* Illus. Joe Morse. Kids Can, 2006. Ages 9–13. Urban setting.

Chapter Six

Traditional Literature

There Is a Land

There is a land—
a marvelous land—
where trolls and giants dwell;
Where witches
With their bitter brew
Can cast a magic spell;
Where mermaids sing,
Where carpets fly,
Where, in the midst of night,
Brownies dance

To cricket tunes;
And ghosts, all shivery white,
Prowl and moan.
There is a land
Of magic folks and deeds,
And anyone
Can visit there
Who reads and reads and reads.

—*Leland B. Jacobs*

Visual narratives on ancient cave paintings in Europe, Asia, and Australia indicate that prehistoric humans had stories to tell long before they had a written language. For thousands of years, the best of these stories were preserved through the art of storytelling from one generation to the next. These stories survived because people enjoyed hearing them and used them to make sense of their lives and world. Our most ancient stories are folk literature, providing a priceless literary and cultural heritage that links us to our beginnings as thinking beings.

Definition and Description

Traditional literature is the body of ancient stories and poems that grew out of the oral tradition of storytelling before being eventually written down. Having no known or identifiable authors, these stories and poems are attributed to entire groups of people or cultures. Although some traditional stories are told as cultural or spiritual truths or may contain factual elements, most are considered make-believe and not based in real historical events.

Because these stories have been preserved over time, they provide insights into the underlying values and beliefs of particular cultural groups and opportunities for comparisons across cultures. Most are considered imaginative stories that provide a window into human nature and cultural beliefs. These traditional stories also provide the basis for many works of modern literature and drama and so children need a strong background in these stories.

Folklore is still being created, particularly in cultures and countries where the oral tradition remains an important means of communication. In the U.S., urban legends, jokes, and jump-rope rhymes are part of the constantly evolving body of modern folklore.

Evaluation and Selection of Traditional Literature

For thousands of years, people of all ages were the intended audience for traditional stories. In our contemporary society with a strong focus on scientific fact, these stories of the supernatural and magic are relegated to children. Traditional literature includes several different types of stories, but because they were all shared orally for so long, they have many features in common.

- *Plots* are short, simple, and direct; all but the essentials disappeared during countless retellings.
- *Action* is concentrated and fast paced, adding interest.
- *Characters* are two-dimensional and easily identified as good or bad.
- *Settings* are unimportant and vague ("In the beginning" or "Long ago in a land far away").
- *Literary style* is characterized by standard beginnings and endings ("Once upon a time"), *motifs* (recurring features such as the number 3), and repeated refrains ("Mirror, mirror, on the wall").
- *Themes* are limited (e.g., good overcomes evil, the small and powerless overcome the powerful, explanations for the ways of the world).
- *Endings* are almost always happy ("and they lived happily ever after").

The following list of evaluation criteria was developed with a child audience in mind.

- **Does the tale reflect a narrative storytelling style?** A traditional tale should sound as though it is being told even though it is written down.

- **Does the tale preserve the flavor of the culture or country of its origin?** Techniques involve the use of unusual speech patterns and the integration of terms or proper names common to the culture.

- **Do the illustrations match the tone of the text and help to capture the essence of the culture?** Some illustrators use traditional art forms or folk art, while others use a style that is more contemporary but that still captures the tone of the story and the cultural context.

- **Does the tale employ a rich literary style?** Children are fascinated by the chants, stylistic flourishes, and colorful vocabulary that are characteristic of masterful storytelling.

In evaluating collections of traditional literature, consider the number and variety of tales in the collection and the reference aids, such as a table of contents and index to help readers locate tales. One issue raised by some adults in evaluating traditional literature is their concern that the gruesome violence in some traditional stories will harm or traumatize children. Many traditional stories have been rewritten to omit the violence, as in the Disney versions of folktales. In a "softened" version of "Snow White," the evil stepmother is forgiven by the heroine or banished from the kingdom instead of dancing to her death in red-hot iron shoes, her fate in early Grimm versions. Critics of the softened versions claim that altering the stories robs them of their power, appeal, and psychological benefit to children, who are reassured that the evil force is gone forever and cannot come back to hurt them.

Another critique has been that many traditional tales reflect male chauvinism and poor feminine role models, from ever-sinister stepmothers to ever-helpless princesses. These stories reflect the values of past societies and of the male collectors who selected which tales to immortalize in written form. Instead of continuing to evolve through oral retellings to reflect societal changes as they had for thousands of years, the written stories are frozen in time.

The Significance of Plot in Traditional Literature

Because traditional literature highlights simple direct plots, these stories provide an opportunity for students to explore plot as a sequence of events that show characters in conflict. Traditional literature uses chronological or time order in *rising action,* where the events rise by building suspense to a peak or *climax,* and then quickly conclude with *falling action.* The conclusion is a *closed ending,* where the reader is assured that all is well. These explorations of the patterns in plot can be made visible by having children create plot lines to depict the exposition, the initial explanation of the situation and character, the rising action of the events, the climax, and the denouement or ending after the climax.

Historical Overview of Traditional Literature

The world's first stories probably grew out of the dreams, wishes, ritual chants, or retellings of the notable exploits of our earliest ancestors. Little can be said about the early history of this genre except that these stories existed in oral form for thousands of years.

Folklorists are intrigued by the startling similarity of traditional tales around the world. Cinderella-type tales, for example, can be found in every culture. One explanation for this is that the first humans created these stories and took them along as they populated the globe. This theory is called *monogenesis,* or "single origin." Another theory credits the fundamental psychological

Excellent Traditional Literature to Read Aloud

Andrews, Jan. *When Apples Grew Noses and White Horses Flew: Tales of Ti-Jean.* Illustrated by Dusan Petricic. Ages 9–11. French-Canadian humorous fool tales.

Chen, Jiang Hong. *The Magic Horse of Han Gan.* Ages 5–9. Chinese legend.

dePaola, Tomie. *Strega Nona.* Ages 5–8. Italian folktale.

Emberley, Rebecca. *Chicken Little.* Illustrated by Ed Emberley. Ages 4–7. Aesop fable.

Fleischman, Paul. *Glass Slipper, Gold Sandal: A Worldwide Cinderella.* Ages 5–9. Global folktale variants.

Hamilton, Virginia, reteller. *In the Beginning: Creation Stories from Around the World.* Illustrated by Barry Moser. Ages 9–12. Myths.

Hennessy, B. G. *The Boy Who Cried Wolf.* Illustrated by Boris Kulikov. Ages 4–7. Aesop fable.

Karas, Brian. *Young Zeus.* Ages 5–8. Greek myth.

McGill, Alice. *Way Up and Over Everything.* Illustrated by Jude Daly. Ages 8–12. African-American folktale.

Pinkney, Jerry. *Little Red Riding Hood.* Ages 5–9. German folktale.

similarity of humans for the similarity of their stories. *Polygenesis,* or "many origins," holds that early humans had similar urges and motives, asked similar fundamental questions about themselves and the world around them, and logically created similar stories in response. Both theories have merit, and since the answer lies hidden in ancient prehistory, neither theory has prevailed.

The popularity of traditional literature with children has continued to grow, owing in part to a renewed interest in storytelling. Other trends contributing to the popularity of this genre are the publication of single illustrated retellings of traditional literature, cultural variants of traditional tales from around the world, and folk literature of ethnic minorities from Canada and the U.S.

Types of Traditional Literature

Classification of traditional literature can be confusing, particularly since scholars use different terms for certain types of traditional stories. Also, modern stories written by known authors in the style of the traditional ones, but are not of ancient and unknown origin, are not "traditional" in the strict sense. These stories are considered fantasy because they did not originate orally and have an identified author, such as the tales created by Hans Christian Andersen, and so are included in the chapter on fantasy.

The following terms are commonly used when referring to traditional literature:

- *Traditional literature.* The body of stories passed down from ancient times by oral tradition. The term *folktales* is sometime used synonymously, but we see it as a subcategory.

- *Retold tale.* A *version* of a tale written in a style that will appeal to a contemporary audience but otherwise remains true to the ancient tale.

- *Variant.* A story that shares elements of plot or character with stories in the same "story family" but differs mainly by culture. Some tales, such as "Cinderella," have hundreds of variants from around the world that originated in the ancient past. Modern variants where an author uses these elements to create an original story in a new time and place are considered fantasy.

Myths

Myths are stories that recount and explain the origins of the world and the phenomena of nature. They are sometimes referred to as **creation stories.** The characters are mainly gods and goddesses, with occasional mention of humans, and the setting is high above earth in the home of the gods. Although often violent, myths mirror human nature and the essence of our sometimes primitive emotions, instincts, and desires. Some folklorists believe that myths are the foundation of all other ancient stories. The best-known mythologies are of Greek, Roman, and Norse origin. Many myths are published in collections like Katrin Tchana's *Changing Woman and Her Sisters,* which focuses on goddesses from around the world.

The complexity and symbolism often found in myths make them appropriate for older children. Some myths have been simplified for a younger audience, but oversimplification can rob these stories of their power and appeal.

Epics and Legends

Epics are long stories of human adventure and heroism recounted in many episodes, sometimes in verse. Epics are grounded in mythology, and their characters can be both human and divine. However, the hero is always human or, in some cases, superhuman, as was Ulysses and Beowulf. The setting is earthly but not always realistic. Because of their length and complexity, epics are perhaps more suitable for adolescents. Some epics have been successfully adapted and shortened for younger audiences due to their compelling characters and events. A good example is Beowulf, retold in three vividly illustrated versions by James Rumford, Gareth Hinds, and Nicky Raven.

Legends are stories based on real or supposedly real individuals and their marvelous deeds. Legendary characters such as King Arthur and Robin Hood and legendary settings such as Camelot are a tantalizing mix of realism and fantasy. Although the feats of these heroes defy belief today, in ancient times these stories were considered factual. Some legendary characters, such as Johnny Appleseed and John Henry, also appear in tall tales.

Folktales

Folktales are stories that grew out of the lives and imaginations of the people, or folk. Folktales have always been a favorite for children from age 3 and up. Folktales vary in content as to their original intended audiences. Long ago, the nobility and their courtiers heard stories of the heroism and benevolence of people like themselves—the ruling classes. In contrast, the stories heard by the common people portrayed the ruling classes as unjust or hard taskmasters whose riches were fair game for quick-witted or strong common folk. These class-conscious tales are referred to as **castle** and **cottage** tales, respectively.

Some people use the terms **folktale** and **fairy tale** interchangeably. In fact, the majority of folktales have no fairies or magic characters, so to use one term in place of the other can be

MILESTONES in the Development of Traditional Literature

Date	Event	Significance
Prehistory–1500s	Oral storytelling	Kept ancient stories alive and provided literature to common people
500 B.C.E.	Aesop, a supposed Greek slave, wrote classic fables	Established the fable as a type of traditional literature
1484	*Aesop's Fables* published by William Caxton in England	First known publication of traditional literature
1500–1700	Puritan movement and chapbooks	Prevented the publication of traditional literature by the legitimate press. Chapbooks encourage interest in traditional heroes.
Late 1600s	Jean de la Fontaine of France adapted earlier fables in verse form	Popularized the fable
1697	*Tales of Mother Goose* published by Charles Perrault in France	First written version of folktales
1700s	Romantic Movement	Traditional fantasy promoted and embraced in Europe
1812	Wilhelm and Jakob Grimm collected *Nursery and Household Tales* in Germany	Helped popularize folk literature
1851	Asbjørnsen and Moe collected *The Norwegian Folktales* in Norway	Helped popularize folk literature
1889–1894	Andrew Lang collected four volumes of world folktales	Growing popularity and knowledge of folktales worldwide
1894	Joseph Jacobs collected *English Fairy Tales* in England; adapted many tales for a child audience	Helped popularize folk literature and made the tales accessible for children

confusing and erroneous. Fairy tales are categorized here as a type of folktale that has magic characters such as fairies.

The following is a list of the most prevalent kinds of folktales. Note that some folktales have characteristics of two or more folktale categories.

Cumulative　The *cumulative tale* uses repetition, accumulation, and rhythm to make an entertaining story out of the barest of plots. Because of its simplicity, rhythm, and humor, the cumulative tale has special appeal to young children. "The Gingerbread Man," with its runaway cookie and growing host of pursuers, is a good example of this kind of tale.

Humorous   The *humorous tale* revolves around a character's incredibly stupid and funny mistakes. These tales are also known as *noodleheads, sillies, drolls,* and *numbskulls.* They have endured for their comic appeal and the laughter they evoke. Some famous noodleheads are the Norwegian husband who kept house (and nearly demolished it) and Clever Elsie, who was so addle-brained that she got herself confused with someone else and was never heard from again.

Beast   *Beast tales* feature talking animals and overstated action with occasional human characters, such as "Goldilocks and the Three Bears." Young children accept and enjoy these talking animals, and older children understand that the animals symbolize humans. Trickster tales are a specific type of beast tale that feature an animal character who outsmarts everyone else, such as Br'er Rabbit, Anansi the Spider, and Coyote.

Magic   *Fairy tales* contain elements of magic or enchantment in characters, plots, or settings. Fairies, elves, pixies, brownies, witches, magicians, genies, and fairy godparents are pivotal characters and they use magic objects or words to weave their enchantments. Talking mirrors, hundred-year naps, glass palaces, enchanted forests, thumb-sized heroines, and magic kisses are the stuff of magic tales, such as "The Princess and the Frog."

Pourquoi   *Pourquoi tales* explain phenomena of nature as in "Why the Sun and Moon Live in the Sky." The word *pourquoi* is French for *why,* and these tales can be understood as explanations for the many "why" questions asked by early humans. The strong connection between these tales and myths is obvious, which is why some folklorists identify pourquoi tales as the simplest myths. However, deities play no role in pourquoi tales as they do in myths and the setting in pourquoi tales is earthly, whereas the setting in myths is the realm of the gods.

Tall Tales   *Tall tales* are highly exaggerated accounts of the exploits of persons, both real and imagined. Over time, as each teller embroidered on the hero's abilities or deeds, the tales became outlandishly exaggerated and were valued more for their humor and braggadocio than for their factual content. Well-known North American tall-tale heroes are Pecos Bill, Paul Bunyan, John Henry, and Johnny Appleseed. Lesser-known but equally amazing are such tall-tale heroines as Sally Ann Thunder Ann Whirlwind Crockett.

Realistic   *Realistic tales* are those whose characters, plot, and setting could conceivably have occurred. There is no magic in these tales, and any exaggeration is limited to the possible. Only a few realistic tales exist, including "Dick Whittington and His Cat" and Diane Snyder's *The Boy of the Three-Year Nap.*

Fables

The *fable* is a simple story that incorporates characters—typically animals—whose actions teach a moral lesson or universal truth. Often, the moral is stated at the end of the story. Fables appeal to adults as well as to children, for these stories are simple and wise. Moreover, their use of animals as symbols for humans have made them safe, yet effective, political tools. Perhaps because of their adult appeal, fables were put into print far earlier than other forms of traditional literature.

Notable Retellers and Illustrators of Traditional Literature

Ashley Bryan, illustrator and author of African traditional literature and African-American spirituals. *Beautiful Blackbird; Ashley Bryan's African Tales, Uh-Huh; The Night Has Ears: African Proverbs; Let It Shine: Three Favorite Spirituals.*

Trina Schart Hyman, reteller and illustrator of classic European folktales. *Little Red Riding Hood; The Sleeping Beauty.*

Rafe Martin, storyteller and author who retells stories from a range of cultures. *The Shark God; The Rough-Face Girl; Foolish Rabbit's Big Mistake; The World before This One.* www.rafemartin.com

George O'Connor, graphic novelist who created Olympians, an ongoing series that retells classic Greek myths in comic form. *Athena: Grey-Eyed Goddess; Hades: Lord of the Dead.* www.olympiansrule.com

Jerry Pinkney, Caldecott medalist whose realistic watercolors invigorate folktales from many

traditions. *Noah's Ark; John Henry; The Lion and the Mouse.*

Robert D. San Souci, adapter of obscure or almost-forgotten stories from many different places and cultures. *Sister Tricksters, Cut from the Same Cloth.* www.rsansouci.com

Ed Young, illustrator and author of Chinese folklore and other global folklore. *Lon Po Po; Yeh-Shen; Seven Fathers; I, Doko: The Tale of a Basket.* www.edyoungart.com

Paul Zelinsky, illustrator whose realistic oil paintings provide insights into the meaning of folktales. *Hansel and Gretel; Rapunzel; Rumpelstiltskin.* www.paulozelinsky.com/paul.html

Lisbeth Zwerger, illustrator from Vienna with a focus on translated European traditional literature. *Little Red Cap; The Bremen Town Musicians; Aesop's Fables.*

Aesop's fables compose the best-known collection of fables in the Western world, but other collections include the **Panchatantra** tales from Persia; the **Jataka** tales from India; and the collected fables of Jean de la Fontaine from France.

Religious Stories

Stories based on religious writings or taken intact from religious manuscripts are considered to be **religious stories.** These stories may recount milestones in the development of a religion and its leadership, or they may present a piece of religious doctrine in narrative form, called **parables.**

Scholars of religion, language, and mythology have found a definite thread of continuity from myth and folk narrative to early religious thinking and writing. Many of the stories, figures, and rituals described in the sacred scriptures of Christianity, Hinduism, and Buddhism, among other religions, have their roots in ancient mythology.

Regardless of whether religious stories are considered fact or fiction, these stories are rich with cultural and spiritual narratives and provide unique perspectives for readers. Some Indigenous scholars argue that much of their traditional literature is rooted in spiritual beliefs and has been mislabeled as legend. Because religion in the classroom is potentially controversial, however, many teachers and librarians do not feel comfortable sharing stories with religious connections. The consequence is that students miss characters, sayings, situations, and stories essential to understanding particular cultures.

Reader Connections: Storytelling in the Classroom

Given that traditional literature is rooted in oral tradition, telling these stories in classrooms provides an effective and powerful means for engaging children with this literature. Children are attentive listeners when their teachers tell stories and quickly begin telling stories themselves. By bringing stories to life through personal expression and interpretation, storytellers establish a close communication with their audience and are a form of reader response.

Selection of a Story

To find stories for telling, read through collections of folktales and short stories until you find a few you especially like. Consider these two points:

- Good stories for telling usually have few characters (from two to five), high conflict, action that builds to a climax, and a quick conclusion that ties together all the threads of the story. Humorous elements are also worth seeking.
- Initially select short stories of less than ten minutes, before moving to longer stories.

Good resources for teachers and students who want to tell stories are Pellowski's *The Storytelling Handbook* (2008), McDonald's *The Storyteller's Start-Up Book* (2006), and Bruchac's *Tell Me a Tale* (1997). Websites that provide stories and storytelling resources and tips include www.storyarts .org and www.storynet.org.

Preparation for Telling

Outline the story content in terms of the plot. Many storytellers note the title and source of the tale, the characters' names and story events, and any other information that may be helpful on an index card to consult quickly just before telling a story. Another option is to tape yourself telling stories to use in refreshing your memory for retellings.

Tell the story aloud to yourself again and again. Do not memorize the story, but keep in mind the characters and sequence of main story events. Each time you tell the story, it will change a bit, becoming more and more your own story as you include personal touches. Some storytellers use simple props (a hat, a stick-on mustache, or a stuffed toy) or more elaborate ones (a mask, a puppet, or a costume). You can also tell stories through a feltboard, using pictures or objects that are moved around during the story.

Digital storytelling connects the age-old art of storytelling with children's digital worlds through the use of computer-based tools. Digital stories can be personal narratives, traditional tales, or historical recountings that are told by combining computer-based images, text, recorded audio narration, video clips, photographs, drawings, and/or music to tell a brief story. Resources include Miller's *Make Me a Story* (2010), the Center for Digital Storytelling (www.storycenter .org), and Educational Uses of Digital Storytelling (http://digitalstorytelling.coe.uh.edu).

Invitations for Further Investigation

- Explore sexism in traditional literature and the subtle messages conveyed to children. Also examine less well-known tales that portray women as leaders rather than victims, such as Jane Yolen's *Not One Damsel in Distress.*

- Create plots lines to show the action in several folktales and discuss the patterns that emerge. Compare the patterns in plot lines in folklore from different cultures.

- Engage in a cross-cultural analysis of the "Cinderella" tale. Gather variants from around the world, including Asian, Western European, and American Indian cultures. Compare plot details, themes, and gender messages.

- Disney versions of fairy tales enjoy tremendous popularity and yet are negatively critiqued as stereotyped. Watch the video *Mickey Mouse Monopoly* or locate articles that critique Disney films and books. Use the stereotypes chart in Christensen (2002) to engage in your own analysis.

- Select, learn, and tell (not read) a folktale to a group of children, using props, if appropriate. Note the differences in telling and reading a story to a young audience.

References

Bruchac, J. (1997). *Tell me a tale.* San Diego, CA: Harcourt.

Christensen, L. (2002). Unlearning the myths that bind us. In *Reading, Writing and Rising Up* (pp. 39–51). Milwaukee, WI: Rethinking Schools.

McDonald, M. R. (2006). *The storyteller's start-up book.* Atlanta, GA: August House.

Miller, L. (2010). *Make me a story: Teaching writing through digital storytelling.* Portland, ME: Stenhouse.

Pellowski, A. (2008). *The storytelling handbook: A young people's collection of unusual tales and helpful hints on how to tell them.* New York: Aladdin.

Recommended Traditional Literature

Ages refer to concept and interest levels. Formats other than novels will be coded as follows:

(PI) Picture book
(COL) Short story collection
(GR) Graphic novel
Country, continent, or culture of origin are noted after entries.

Myths

Burleigh, Robert. *Pandora.* Illus. Raúl Colón. Silver Whistle, 2002. **(PI)**. Ages 8–11. (Greek).

Byrd, Robert. *The Hero and the Minotaur: The Fantastic Adventures of Theseus.* Dutton, 2005. **(PI)**. Ages 8–12. (Greek).

d'Aulaire, Ingri, and Edgar Parin d'Aulaire. *Norse Gods and Giants.* Doubleday, 1967. (**COL**). Ages 8–10. (Norway).

Hamilton, Virginia, reteller. *In the Beginning: Creation Stories from Around the World.* Illus. Barry Moser. Harcourt, 1988. (**COL**). Ages 9–12.

Karas, G. Brian. *Young Zeus.* Scholastic, 2010. (**PI**). Ages 5–8. (Greece).

Kimmel, Eric. *The McElderry Book of Greek Myths.* Illus. Pep Montserrat. M. K. McElderry, 2008. (**COL**). Ages 9–12. (Greece).

Marshall, James V. *Stories from the Billabong.* Illus. Francis Firebrace, Frances Lincoln, 2008. (**COL**). Ages 5–9. (Australian Aboriginal).

McDermott, Gerald. *Creation.* Dutton, 2003. (**PI**). Ages 8–12. (Biblical).

Menchú, Rigoberta, and Dante Liano. *The Honey Jar.* Translated by David Unger. Illus. Domi. Groundwood, 2006. (**COL**). Ages 9–12. (Guatemala/Mayan).

O'Connor, George. *Hades: Lord of the Dead.* First Second, 2011. (**GR**). Ages 10–14. Olympians series on Greek gods. See other titles such as *Athena: Grey-Eyed Goddess* (2010).

Tchana, Katrin Hyman, *Changing Woman and Her Sisters.* Illus. Trina Schart Hyman. Holiday, 2006. (**COL**). Ages 10–14. (World).

Williams, Marcia. *Ancient Egypt: Tales of Gods and Pharaohs.* Candlewick, 2011. (**GR**). Ages 9–12. (Egypt).

Epics and Legends

Arni, Samhita. *Sita's Ramayana.* Illus. Moyna Chitraker. Goundwood, 2011. (**GR**). Ages 12–15. (India).

Chen, Jiang Hong. *The Magic Horse of Han Gan.* Translated by Claudia Zoe Bedrick. Enchanted Lion, 2006. (**PI**). Ages 5–9. (China).

Clayton, Sally. *Rama and Sita: Path of Flames.* Illus. Sophie Hersheimer. Frances Lincoln, 2010. Ages 9–12. (India).

Demi. *The Legend of Lao Tzu and Tao Te Ching.* M. K. McElderry, 2007. (**PI**). Ages 5–9. (China).

Henderson, Kathy. *Lugalbanda: The Boy Who Got Caught Up in a War.* Illus. Jane Ray. Candlewick, 2006. (**PI**). Ages 9–12. (Iraq).

Hinds, Gareth. *Beowulf.* Candlewick, 2007. (**PI**). Ages 10–14. (England).

Hinds, Gareth. *The Odyssey: A Graphic Novel.* Candlewick, 2010. (**GR**). Ages 12–15. (Greece).

Hodges, Margaret. *Saint George and the Dragon.* Illus. Trina Schart Hyman. Little, Brown, 1984. (**PI**). Ages 8–10. (England).

Kimmel, Eric. *Gershon's Monster: A Story for the Jewish New Year.* Illus. Jon J. Muth. Scholastic, 2000. (**PI**). Ages 6–11. (Jewish).

Lee, Tony. *Excalibur: The Legend of King Arthur.* Illus. Sam Hart. Candlewick, 2011. (**GR**). Ages 11–15. (England).

Mandell, Muriet. *A Donkey Reads.* Illus. Andre Letria. Star Bright, 2011. (PI). Ages 5–9. (Turkey).

Martin, Rafe. *The World before This One: A Novel Told in Legend.* Illus. Calvin Nicholls. Scholastic, 2002. Ages 12–14. (Native American, Seneca).

McCaughrean, Geraldine. *Gilgamesh the Hero.* Illus. David Parkins. Eerdmans, 2003. (**PI**). Ages 10–14. (Middle East).

Morris, Gerald. *The Legend of the King.* Houghton Mifflin, 2010. Ages 10–14. Squire's Tales series. (King Arthur, England).

Raven, Nicky. *Beowulf.* Illus. John Howe. Candlewick, 2007. Ages 10–14. (England).

Rumford, James. *Beowulf: A Hero's Tale Retold.* Houghton Mifflin, 2007. Ages 10–14. (England).

San Souci, Robert. *Cut from the Same Cloth: American Women of Myth, Legend, and Tall Tale.* Illus. Brian Pinkney. Philomel, 1993. (**COL**). Ages 8–12.

San Souci, Robert. *Robin Hood and the Golden Arrow.* Illus. E. B. Lewis. Orchard, 2010. (**PI**). Ages 7–10. (England).

Wisniewski, David. *Golem.* Clarion, 1996. (**PI**). Ages 6–12. (Prague, Jewish legend).

Folktales

Aardema, Verna. *Why Mosquitoes Buzz in People's Ears.* Illus. Leo & Diane Dillon. Dial, 1975. (**PI**). Ages 5–7. (Kenya).

Andrews, Jan. *When the Apples Grew Noses and White Horses Flew: Tales of Ti-Jean.* Illus. Dusan Petricic. Goundwood, 2011. Ages 9–11. (French Canadian).

Aylesworth, Jim. *The Mitten.* Illus. Barbara McClinktock. Scholastic, 2009. (**PI**). Ages 5–9. (Ukraine).

Brown, Marcia. *Stone Soup.* Scribner's, 1975 (1947). (**PI**). Ages 6–8. (France).

Bruchac, James, and Joseph Bruchac. *The Girl Who Helped Thunder and Other Native American Folktales.* Illus. Stefano Vitale. Sterling, 2008. (**COL**). Ages 9–12. (Native American).

Bruchac, Joseph, and James Bruchacs. *Raccoon's Last Race: A Traditional Abenaki Story.* Illus. Jose Aruego and Ariane Dewey. Dial, 2004. (**PI**). Ages 4–7. (Native American, Abenaki).

Bryan, Ashley. *Beautiful Blackbird.* Atheneum, 2003. (**PI**). Ages 5–7. (Zambia).

Cousins, Lucy. *Yummy: Eight Favorite Fairy Tales.* Candlewick, 2009. Ages 5–9. (England, Germany).

Cummings, Pat. *Ananse and the Lizard: A West African Tale.* Holt, 2002. (**PI**). Ages 4–8. (Ghana).

Dembicki, Matt, editor. *Trickster: Native American Tales.* Fulcrum, 2010. (**GR, COL**). Ages 10–14. (Native American).

Demi. *The Hungry Coat: A Tale from Turkey.* M. K. McElderry, 2004. (**PI**). Ages 5–9. (Turkey).

dePaola, Tomie. *Strega Nona.* Prentice Hall, 1975. (**PI**). Ages 5–8. (Italy).

Emberley, Rebecca. *Chicken Little.* Illus. Ed Emberley. Roaring Brook, 2009. (**PI**). Ages 4–7. (England).

Fleischman, Paul. *Glass Slipper, Gold Sandal: A Worldwide Cinderella.* Illus. Julie Paschkis. Holt, 2007. (**PI**). Ages 5–9. (World).

Galdone, Paul. *The Gingerbread Man.* Clarion, 1975. (**PI**). Ages 4–6. (England). See also *The Little Red Hen* (1973) and *The Three Billy Goats Gruff* (1973).

Gerson, Mary-Joan. *Fiesta Femenina: Celebrating Women in Mexican Folktales.* Barefoot, 2001. (**COL**). Ages 10–13. (Mexico).

Goble, Paul. *Storm Maker's Tipi.* Atheneum, 2001. (**PI**). Ages 7–12. (Native American, Siksika).

Grimm, Jakob, and Wilhelm Grimm. *Snow-White and the Seven Dwarfs.* Translated by Randall Jarrell. Illus. Nancy Ekholm Burkert. Farrar, 1972. (**PI**). Ages 8–10. (Germany).

Grimm, Jakob, and Wilhelm Grimm. *Little Red Riding Hood.* Illus. Trina Schart Hyman. Holiday, 1982. (**PI**). Ages 6–8. (Germany).

Grimm, Jakob, and Wilhelm Grimm. *Hansel and Gretel.* Illus. Anthony Browne. Knopf, 1998 (1981). (**PI**). Ages 8–14. (Germany).

Grimm, Jakob, and Wilhelm Grimm. *Little Red Cap.* Illus. Lisbeth Zwerger. Trans. Elizabeth D. Crawford. Miniedition, 2006. (**PI**). Ages 5–9. (Germany).

Grimm, Jakob, and Wilhelm Grimm. *The Bremen Town Musicians.* Translated by Anthea Bell. Illus. Lisbeth Zwerger. Miniedition, 2007. (**PI**). Ages 5–9. (Germany).

Hamilton, Virginia. *The People Could Fly: American Black Folktales.* Illus. Leo & Diane Dillon. Knopf, 1985. (**COL**). Ages 8–10. (African American).

Hamilton, Virginia. *Her Stories: African American Folktales, Fairy Tales, and True Tales.* Illus. Leo & Diane Dillon. Scholastic, 1995. (**COL**). Ages 9–15. (African American).

Hamilton, Virginia. *The Girl Who Spun Gold.* Illus. Leo & Diane Dillon. Blue Sky, 2000. (**PI**). Ages 5–8. (West Indian).

Hamilton, Virginia. *Bruh Rabbit and the Tar Baby Girl.* Illus. James Ransome. Scholastic, 2003. (**PI**). Ages 5–7. (Gullah, South Carolina).

Heo, Yumi, reteller. *The Green Frogs: A Korean Folktale.* Houghton, 1996. (**PI**). Ages 4–7. (Korea).

Hodges, Margaret, reteller. *Dick Whittington and His Cat.* Illus. Melisande Potter. Holiday, 2006. (**PI**). Ages 5–9. (England).

Hurston, Zora Neale. *Lies and Other Tall Tales.* Illus. Christopher Myers. HarperCollins, 2005. (**PI**). Ages 7–10. (Southern U.S.).

Hyman, Trina Schart. *The Sleeping Beauty.* Little, Brown, 1977. (**PI**). Ages 5–8. (Germany).

Isadora, Rachel. *The Twelve Dancing Princesses.* Putnam, 2007. (**PI**). Ages 5–9. (Germany, Africa).

Janisch, Heinz. *Fantastic Adventures of Baron Munchausen: Traditional and Newly Discovered Tales of Karl Friedrich Hieronymus van*

Munchausen. Translated by Belinda Cooper. Illus. Aljoscha Blau. Enchanted Lion, 2009. (**PI**). Ages 6–9. (Germany, tall tale).

Johnson-Davies, Denys. *Goha the Wise Fool.* Illus. Hany El Saed Ahmed and Hag Hamdy Mohamed Fattouh. Philomel, 2005. (**COL**). Ages 6–12. (Middle East).

Kellogg, Steven, reteller. *Paul Bunyan.* Morrow, 1984. (**PI**). Ages 6–8. Also *Johnny Appleseed.* (1988) and *Pecos Bill* (1986). (U.S., tall tales).

Kilaka, John. *True Friends.* Groundwood, 2006. (**PI**). Ages 5–9. (Tanzania).

Kimmel, Eric. *Three Samurai Cats.* Illus. Mordicai Gerstein. Holiday, 2003. (**PI**). Ages 4–8. (Japan).

Kimmel, Eric. *Cactus Soup.* Illus. Phil Huling. Marshall Cavendish, 2004. (**PI**). Ages 5–9. (Mexico).

Knutson, Barbara. *Love and Roast Chicken: A Trickster Tale from the Andes Mountains.* Carolrhoda, 2004. (**PI**). Ages 4–7. (Peru, Bolivia).

Laird, Elizabeth. *Pea Boy and Other Stories from Iran*. Illus. Shirin Adl. Frances Lincoln, 2010. (**COL**). Ages 9–12. (Iran).

Lesser, Rika. *Hansel and Gretel.* Illus. Paul Zelinsky. Dutton, 1999. (**PI**). Ages 5–8. (Germany).

Lester, Julius, reteller. *The Tales of Uncle Remus: The Adventures of Brer Rabbit.* Illus. Jerry Pinkney. Dial, 1987. (**COL**). Ages 7–9.

Lester, Julius, reteller. *John Henry.* Illus. Jerry Pinkney. Dial, 1994. (**PI**). Ages 8–10. (African American).

Louie, Ai-Ling. *Yeh-Shen: A Cinderella Story from China.* Illus. Ed Young. Philomel, 1982. (**PI**). Ages 7–9. (China).

Lunge-Larsen, Lise. *The Hidden Folk: Stories of Fairies, Dwarves, Selkies, and Other Secret Beings.* Illus. Beth Krommes. Houghton, 2004. (**COL**). Ages 6–12. (Northern Europe).

Marcantonio, Patricia Santos. *Red Ridin' in the Hood, and Other "Cuentos."* Illus. Renato Alarcão. Farrar, 2005. (**COL**). Ages 7–12. (Latino, U.S.).

Marshall, James. *Goldilocks and the Three Bears.* Dial, 1988. (**PI**). Ages 5–7. (England).

Martin, Rafe, reteller. *Foolish Rabbit's Big Mistake.* Illus. Ed Young. Putnam, 1985. (**PI**). Ages 6–8. (India).

Martin, Rafe, reteller. *The Rough-Face Girl.* Illus. David Shannon. Putnam, 1992. (**PI**). Ages 8–10. (Native American, Mi'kmaq).

Martin, Rafe, reteller. *The Shark God.* Illus. David Shannon. Scholastic, 2001. (**PI**). Ages 5–9. (Hawai'i).

McClintock, Barbara. *Cinderella.* Scholastic, 2005. (**PI**). Ages 5–9. (France).

McDermott, Gerald. *Monkey: A Trickster Tale from India.* Harcourt, 2011. (**PI**). Ages 6–9. (India).

McDonald, Margaret Read. *The Boy from the Dragon Palace.* Illus. Sachiko Yoshikawa. (**PI**). Ages 6–9. (Japan).

McGill, Alice. *Way Up and Over Everything.* Illus. Jude Daly. Houghton Mifflin, 2008. (**PI**). Ages 8–12. (African American).

Milligan, Bryce. *The Prince of Ireland and the Three Magic Stallions.* Illus. Preston McDaniels. Holiday, 2003. (**PI**). Ages 6–8. (Ireland).

Mollel, Tololwa. *Subira Subira.* Illus. Linda Saport. Clarion, 2000. (**PI**). Ages 5–10. (Tanzania).

Nesbit, E. *Jack and the Beanstalk.* Illus. Matt Tavares. Candlewick, 2006. (**PI**). Ages 5–9. (England).

Nshizuka, Koko. *The Beckoning Cat.* Illus. Roxanne Litzinger. (**PI**). Ages 6–9. Holiday, 2009. (Japan).

Onyefulu, Ifeoma. *The Girl Who Married a Giant and Other Tales from Nigeria.* Illus. Julia Cairns. Frances Lincoln, 2010. (**COL**). Ages 9–12. (Nigeria).

Orgel, Doris, reteller. *The Bremen Town Musicians and Other Animal Tales from Grimm.* Illus. Bert Kitchen. Roaring Brook, 2004. (**COL**). Ages 6–9. (Germany).

Osborne, Mary Pope. *American Tall Tales.* Illus. Michael McCurdy. Knopf, 1991. (**COL**). Ages 8–11.

Paterson, Katherine. *The Tale of the Mandarin Ducks.* Illus. Leo and Diane Dillon. Lodestar, 1990. (**PI**). Ages 7–9. (Japan).

Perrault, Charles. *Cinderella.* Illus. Marcia Brown. Scribner's, 1954. (**PI**). Ages 6–8. (France).

Perrault, Charles. *Puss in Boots.* Illus. Fred Marcellino. Farrar, 1990. (**PI**). Ages 6–8. (France).

Pinkney, Jerry. *Little Red Riding Hood.* Little, Brown, 2007. (**PI**). Ages 5–9. (Germany).

Powell, Patricia H. *Frog Brings Rain/Ch'at Tó Yinílo'.* Translated by Peter A. Thomas. Illus. Kendrick

Benally. Salina Bookshelf, 2006. (**PI**). Ages 5–8. (Bilingual English/Navajo).

Ramsden, Ashley. *Seven Fathers*. Illus. Ed Young. Roaring Brook, 2011. (**PI**). Ages 6–9. (Norway).

Sanderson, Ruth, reteller. *The Golden Mare, the Firebird, and the Magic Ring.* Little, Brown, 2001. (**PI**). Ages 8–12. (Russia).

San Souci, Robert. *Sister Tricksters: Rollicking Tales of Clever Females.* Illus. Daniel San Souci. August House, 2006. (**COL**). Ages 8–12. (Southern U.S.).

Sierra, Judy. *Can You Guess My Name? Traditional Tales Around the World.* Illus. Stefano Vitale. Clarion, 2002. (**COL**). Ages 8–10.

Scott, Nathan K. *The Sacred Banana Leaf: An Indonesian Trickster Tale.* Illus. Radhashyam Raut. Tara, 2008. (**PI**). Ages 6–9. (Indonesia).

Sellier, Marie. *What the Rat Told Me: A Legend of the Chinese Zodiac.* Illus. Catherine Louis and Wang Fu. North-South, 2009. (**PI**). Ages 6–9. (China).

Shelby, Anne. *The Man Who Lived in a Hollow Tree.* Illus. Cor Hazelaar. Atheneum, 2009. (**PI**). Ages 6–9. (Appalachian tall tale).

Simonds, Nina, Leslie Swartz, and the Children's Museum, Boston. *Moonbeams, Dumplings and Dragon Boats: A Treasury of Chinese Holiday Tales, Activities and Recipes.* Illus. Meilo So. Harcourt, 2002. (**COL**). Ages 9–12. (China).

Singer, Isaac Bashevis. *When Shlemiel Went to Warsaw and Other Stories.* Translated by Elizabeth Shub. Illus. Margot Zemach. Farrar, 1968. (**COL**). Ages 8–10. (Jewish).

Smith, Chris. *One City, Two Brothers.* Illus. Aurélia Fronty. Barefoot Books, 2007. (**PI**). Ages 5–9. (Middle East).

Snyder, Diane. *The Boy of the Three-Year Nap.* Illus. Allan Say. Houghton Mifflin, 1988. (**PI**). Ages 6–9. (Japan).

Stampler, Ann. *The Rooster Prince of Breslov.* Illus. Eugene Yelchin. Clarion, 2010. (**PI**). Ages 6–9. (Yiddish, Ukraine).

Steptoe, John. *Mufaro's Beautiful Daughters: An African Tale.* Lothrop, 1987. (**PI**). Ages 6–8. (Zimbabwe).

Storace, Patricia. *Sugar Cane: A Caribbean Rapunzel.* Illus. Raúl Colón. Hyperion, 2007. (**PI**). Ages 9–12. (Caribbean).

Sweet, Melissa. *Carmine: A Little More Red.* Houghton, 2005. (**PI**). Ages 4–8. (Germany; also an ABC book).

Taback, Simms, reteller. *This Is the House That Jack Built.* Putnam, 2002. (**PI**). Ages 5–7. (Hebrew).

Taback, Simms, reteller. *Kibitzers and Fools: Tales My Zayda Told Me.* Viking, 2005. (**PI**). Ages 7–12. (Eastern Europe).

Tatar, Maria. *The Story of Little Red Riding Hood.* Illus. Christopher Bing. Handprint, 2010. (**PI**). Ages 6–9. (German, 3 versions).

Tchana, Katrin. *The Serpent Slayer and Other Stories of Strong Women.* Illus. Trina Schart Hyman. Little, Brown, 2000. (**COL**). Ages 7–12. (World).

Tarnowska, Wafa, *The Arabian Nights.* Illus. Carole Henaff. Barefoot, 2010. (Arabic, Lebanon).

Taylor, Sean. *The Great Snake: Stories from the Amazon.* Illus. Fernando Vilela. Frances Lincoln, 2008. Ages 9–12. (Brazil).

Yolen, Jane. *Not One Damsel in Distress: World Folktales for Strong Girls.* Illus. Susan Guevara. Silver Whistle, 2000. (**COL**). Ages 8–13. (World).

Young, Ed. *Lon Po Po: A Red-Riding Hood Story from China.* Philomel, 1989. (**PI**). Ages 7–9. (China).

Young, Ed. *I, Doko: The Tale of a Basket.* Philomel, 2004. (**PI**). Ages 5–9. (Nepal).

Zelinsky, Paul. *Rapunzel.* Dutton, 1997. (**PI**). Ages 5–8. (Germany). See also *Rumpelstiltskin* (1986).

Zemach, Harve. *Duffy and the Devil.* Illus. Margot Zemach. Farrar, 1973. (**PI**). Ages 6–8. (England).

Zemach, Margot. *It Could Always Be Worse.* Farrar, 1977. (**PI**). Ages 6–8. (Jewish).

Fables

Aesop's Fables. Illus. Jerry Pinkney. North-South/Sea Star, 2000. (**COL**). Ages 5–9.

Brown, Marcia. *Once a Mouse.* Scribner's, 1961. (**PI**). Ages 6–8. (India).

Burkert, Rand. *Mouse & Lion.* Illus. Nancy Ekholm Burkert. Michael di Capua Books, 2011. (**PI**). Ages 5–9. (Aesop).

Hennessy, B. G. *The Boy Who Cried Wolf.* Illus. Boris Kulikov. Simon & Schuster, 2006. (**PI**). Ages 4–7. (Aesop).

Husain, Shahrukh. *The Wise Fool: Fables from the Arabic World.* Illus. Micha Archer. Barefoot, 2011. (**COL**). Ages 6–9. (Arabic).

Naidoo, Beverley. *Aesop's Fables.* Illus. Piet Grobler. Frances Lincoln, 2011. (**COL**). Ages 6–9. (Aesop/South African setting).

Pinkney, Jerry. *The Lion and the Mouse.* Little, Brown, 2009. (**PI**). Ages 5–9. (Aesop, wordless).

Uribe, Verónica, *Little Book of Fables.* Translated by Susan Ouriou. Illus. Constanza Bravo. Groundwood, 2004. (**COL**). Ages 6–12. (Aesop).

Wormell, Christopher. *Mice, Morals, & Monkey Business: Lively Lessons from Aesop's Fables.* Running Press, 2005. (**PI, COL**). Ages 5–8.

Zwerger, Lisbeth, *Aesop's Fables.* North-South Books, 2006. (**COL**). Ages 5–9.

Religious Stories

Demi. *Buddha.* Holt, 1996. (**PI**). Ages 8–12.

Goldin, Barbara Diamond. *Journeys with Elijah: Eight Tales of the Prophet.* Illus. Jerry Pinkney. Harcourt, 1999. (**COL**). Ages 7–14.

Hao, K. T. *Little Stone Buddha.* Translated by Annie Kung. Illus. Giuliano Ferri. Purple Bear, 2005. (**PI**). Ages 4–7.

Koralek, Jenny. *The Story of Queen Esther.* Illus. Grizelda Holderness. Eerdmans, 2009. (**PI**). Ages 6–9. (Jewish).

Muth, Jon J. *Zen Shorts.* Scholastic, 2005. (**PI, COL**). Ages 5–9. (Buddhist).

Oberman, Sheldon. *The Wisdom Bird: A Tale of Solomon and Sheba.* Illus. Neil Waldman. Boyds Mills, 2000. (**PI**). Ages 5–9.

Pinkney, Jerry. *Noah's Ark.* North-South, 2002. (**PI**). Ages 5–8.

Root, Phyllis. *Big Momma Makes the World.* Illus. Helen Oxenbury. Candlewick, 2003. (**PI**). Ages 4–7.

Schwartz, Howard. *Invisible Kingdoms: Jewish Tales of Angels, Spirits, and Demons.* Illus. Stephen Feiser. HarperCollins, 2002. (**COL**). Ages 8–12. (World).

Young, Ed. *Monkey King.* HarperCollins, 2001. (**PI**). Ages 5–8. (Buddhist, China).

Related Films, Videos, and DVDs

American Tall Tales (includes *John Henry, Swamp Angel*). (2006). Retellers: Julius Lester and Paul Zelinsky. Illustrators: Jerry Pinkney and Paul Zelinsky. 32 minutes.

The Boy Who Cried Wolf (2008). Reteller: B. G. Hennessy. Illustrator: Boris Kulikov. 7 minutes.

Favorite Fairy Tales, Volume II (includes *Rapunzel, Princess Furball*). (2006). Retellers: Paul Zelinsky and Charlotte Huck. Illustrators: Paul Zelinsky and Anita Lobel. 32 minutes.

Hansel and Gretel. (2005). Reteller/Illustrator: James Marshall. 16.5 minutes.

Lon Po Po. (2008). Reteller/Illustrator: Ed Young. 14 minutes.

There Was an Old Lady Who Swallowed a Fly. (2002). Illustrator: Simms Tabeck. 8 minutes.

Why Mosquitoes Buzz in People's Ears and Other Caldecott Classics (includes *Why Mosquitoes Buzz in People's Ears; The Village of Round and Square Houses; A Story, A Story: An African Tale*). (2002). Retellers: Verna Aardema, Ann Grifalconi, and Gail Haley. Illustrators: Leo and Diane Dillon, Ann Grifalconi, and Gail E. Haley. 32 minutes.

 odern Fantasy

Magic Words

In the very earliest time,
When both people and animals lived
  on earth,
a person could become an animal
  if he wanted to
and an animal could become a
  human being.
Sometimes they were people
and sometimes animals
and there was no difference.
All spoke the same language.
That was the time when words were
  like magic.
The human mind had mysterious
  powers.

A word spoken by chance
might have strange consequences.
It would suddenly become alive
and what people want to happen
  could happen—
all you had to do was say it.
Nobody could explain this:
That's the way it was.

—*Anonymous Inuit Poet*

Modern fantasy has its roots in traditional literature, from which motifs, characters, stylistic elements, and themes have been drawn. Many of the most revered works of children's literature fall into the genre of modern fantasy. *Alice's Adventures in Wonderland, The Wonderful Wizard of Oz, Winnie-the-Pooh, Pippi Longstocking,* and *Charlotte's Web* immediately come to mind along with contemporary favorites such as *Harry Potter and the Sorcerer's Stone* and *The Hunger Games.* The creation of stories that are highly imaginative—yet believable—is the hallmark of this genre.

Definition and Description

Modern fantasy refers to the body of literature in which the events, the settings, or the characters are outside the realm of possibility. A fantasy is a story that cannot happen in the real world, and for this reason this genre has been called "the literature of the fanciful impossible." In these stories, animals talk, inanimate objects come to life, people are giants or thumb-sized, imaginary worlds are inhabited, and future worlds are explored. Modern fantasies are written by known authors, and this distinguishes the genre from traditional literature, in which the tales are handed down through the oral tradition and have no known author. Although the events could not happen in real life, modern fantasies often contain truths that help the reader understand today's world.

The *cycle format,* or *series format,* in which one book is linked to another through characters and/or settings across three or four volumes, is a growing trend. Authors attempt to make each novel self-contained, but reading the entire series provides for more complex and in-depth experiences. The cycle format appeals to readers who become attached to characters and delight in reading the next book. The cycle format can be found in the Hunger Games trilogy by Suzanne Collins and the Percy Jackson and the Olympians series by Rick Riordan.

Fantasy often includes supernatural elements such as magic, witches, wizards, vampires, and other elements that some adults connect to the occult and so has been frequently censored. The Harry Potter series was on the American Library Association's Most Frequently Challenged Children's Books list for several years due to the wizardry and magic in the books. A discussion of censorship, the responsibilities of schools and teachers, and ways to address challenges are included at the end of this chapter.

Evaluation and Selection of Modern Fantasy

The usual standards for fine fiction must be met by authors of modern fantasy, including believable and well-rounded characters who develop and change, well-constructed plots, well-described settings with internal consistency, a style appropriate to the story, and worthy themes. In addition, the following criteria apply specifically to modern fantasy:

- **Does the story have an internal logic and consistency that allows the impossible to seem real?** Authors of modern fantasy must persuade readers to open themselves to believing that which is contrary to reality, strange, whimsical, or magical. This believability is dependent on authors developing a strong internal logic and consistency to their fantasy world and story. Sometimes authors begin the story in a familiar setting with typical, contemporary human beings as characters. A transition is then made from this realistic world to the fantasy world, such as in C. S. Lewis's *The Lion, the Witch and the Wardrobe,* in which the children enter a wardrobe in an old house and discover that the back of the wardrobe leads into the land of Narnia, a fantasy world with unusual characters. Other fantasies begin in the imagined world but use well-described settings and consistent well-rounded characters to make this new reality believable as in J. R. R. Tolkien's *The Hobbit*. Either way, the plot, characters, and setting must be so well developed that the reader is able to suspend disbelief and accept the impossible as real.

- **Does the author provide a unique imaginative setting? How does the author move the setting beyond the realistic?** In some stories, the setting may move beyond the realistic in both time (moving to the past or future or holding time still) and place (imagined worlds); in other stories, only one of these elements (place or time) will go beyond reality. Moreover, a modern fantasy author's creation must be original. When the Harry Potter books gained tremendous popularity, other books with similar worlds of wizards and magic quickly appeared, but were formulaic, failing to match the originality and imaginative power of the original books.

The Significance of Theme in Fantasy

One literary element of particular significance for fantasy is *theme,* the key ideas that hold a story together and allow readers to construct insights into their lives and world. Theme unifies and illuminates a story, providing the "So what?" that allows a book to be more than just an enjoyable reading experience. Theme goes beyond the specific details of the story to focus on what it means to be human in a complex world (Lukens, 2012).

The power of fantasy for many readers is that it's a safe place to explore an alternative world as a metaphor for life in their own world. Theme provides the metaphorical connection that is at the heart of the power of fantasy, encouraging readers to consider "what if" and imagine a different way of living in their own world.

Excellent Modern Fantasy to Read Aloud

Appelt, Kathi. *The Underneath.* Ages 9–14.

Avi. *The Seer of Shadows.* Ages 9–14.

Babbitt, Natalie. *Jack Plank Tells Tales.* Ages 8–12.

DiCamillo, Kate. *The Miraculous Journey of Edward Tulane.* Ages 8–12.

Graham, Bob. *April and Esme: Tooth Fairies.* Ages 5–8.

Jonell, Lynne. *Emmy and the Incredible Shrinking Rat.* Ages 8–11.

Law, Ingrid. *Savvy.* Ages 10–14.

Lin, Grace. *Where the Mountain Meets the Moon.* Ages 9–12.

Mass, Wendy. *11 Birthdays.* Ages 9–12.

Pullman, Philip. *The Scarecrow and His Servant.* Ages 9–13.

Stanley, Diane. *Bella at Midnight: The Thimble, the Ring, and the Slippers of Glass.* Ages 10–14.

Stead, Rebecca. *When You Reach Me.* Ages 10–14.

All books have a range of possible themes, since themes are constructed by readers as they interpret that book through the lens of their differing life experiences. **Primary themes** are highlighted throughout the book, while **secondary themes** are of lesser importance to the book but of significance to the lives of specific readers. Although fantasies often play with the theme of good versus evil, many variations of this theme along with other themes are found in fantasy. **Explicit themes** are directly stated by the author, often through the words of a character, while an **implicit theme** is implied through actions and events. These themes are not a single topic or concept like justice or evil, but a life understanding that raises issues and addresses complexity, such as the ways in which society treats those who are viewed as "different" or "inferior." Gathering a text set, such as Ingrid Law's *Savvy,* Shannon Hale's *Princess Academy,* Victoria Forester's *The Girl Who Could Fly,* and Okorafor Nnedi's *Akata Witch,* provides an opportunity to explore the complexities that surround this theme of societal views about difference in more depth within and across the books as well as consider the secondary themes in each book.

Historical Overview of Modern Fantasy

Imaginative literature appeared in the eighteenth century in stories intended as political satires for adults, but enjoyed by children. *Gulliver's Travels* (1726) by the Irish clergyman Jonathan Swift is an adult satire ridiculing the antics and politics of the English courts. Gulliver travels to strange, imaginary places, such as the world of the six-inch Lilliputians that are described in fascinating detail and with sufficient humor to appeal to a child audience.

In England in 1865, Charles Lutwidge Dodgson, an Oxford don who used the pen name Lewis Carroll, wrote *Alice's Adventures in Wonderland,* which tells of a fantastic journey Alice takes to an imaginary world. The total absence of didacticism—replaced by humor and fantasy—resulted in the book's lasting appeal and world fame. Other fantasies that originated in England include *The Light Princess* (1867) and *At the Back of the North Wind* (1871) by George MacDonald, and *Just So Stories* (1902) by Rudyard Kipling. This early development of modern fantasy for children in England was unrivaled by any other country and established the standard for the genre worldwide.

Modern fantasy has continued to thrive in England. Noteworthy contributions from England include *The Tale of Peter Rabbit* (1902) by Beatrix Potter, *The Wind in the Willows* (1908) by Kenneth Grahame, *The Velveteen Rabbit* (1922) by Margery Williams, *Winnie-the-Pooh* (1926) by A. A. Milne, *Mary Poppins* (1934) by Pamela Travers, *The Hobbit* (1937) by J. R. R. Tolkien, *The Lion, the Witch and the Wardrobe* (1950) by C. S. Lewis, and *The Borrowers* (1953) by Mary Norton.

Early books of modern fantasy from other countries include *The Adventures of Pinocchio* (1881) by Carlo Collodi from Italy and *Journey to the Center of the Earth* (1864) and *Twenty Thousand Leagues under the Sea* (1869) by the Frenchman Jules Verne, considered the first science fiction novels. Jean de Brunhoff wrote *The Story of Babar* (1937), the first book of a popular fantasy series about an elephant family.

Hans Christian Andersen, a Dane, published many modern folktales using the same literary elements as traditional tales, but he was the originator of most of his tales, for which his own life experiences were the inspiration. "The Ugly Duckling," "The Emperor's New Clothes," and "Thumbelina" are three of the most loved of Andersen's stories. His tales were published in 1835 and are considered the first modern fairy tales. A century later, Swedish author Astrid Lindgren produced *Pippi Longstocking* (1945). Pippi, a lively, rambunctious, and strong heroine who throws caution to the wind, lives an independent life of escapades that are envied by children the world over.

MILESTONES in the Development of Modern Fantasy

Date	Event	Significance
1726	*Gulliver's Travels* by Jonathan Swift (England)	An adult novel prototype for children's fantasy adventures
1835	*Fairy Tales* by Hans Christian Andersen (Denmark)	First modern folktales
1864	*Journey to the Center of the Earth* by Jules Verne (France)	First science fiction novel (for adults)
1865	*Alice's Adventures in Wonderland* by Lewis Carroll (England)	First children's masterpiece of modern fantasy
1881	*The Adventures of Pinocchio* by Carlo Collodi (Italy)	Early classic personified toy story
1900	*The Wonderful Wizard of Oz* by L. Frank Baum (U.S.)	First classic U.S. modern fantasy for children
1908	*The Wind in the Willows* by Kenneth Grahame (England)	Early classic animal fantasy
1910	*Tom Swift and His Airship* by Victor Appleton (U.S.)	First science fiction novel for children
1926	*Winnie-the-Pooh* by A. A. Milne (England)	Early classic personified toy story
1937	*The Hobbit* by J. R. R. Tolkien (England)	Early quest adventure with a cult following
1950	*The Lion, the Witch and the Wardrobe* by C. S. Lewis (England)	Early classic quest adventure for children; first of the Narnia series
1952	*Charlotte's Web* by E. B. White (U.S.)	Classic U.S. animal fantasy
1953	*The Borrowers* by Mary Norton (England)	Classic little people fantasy
1962	*A Wrinkle in Time* by Madeleine L'Engle (U.S.)	Classic U.S. science fiction novel for children
1993	*The Giver* by Lois Lowry (U.S.)	Popular futuristic fiction novel; Newbery Medal winner
1998	*Harry Potter and the Sorcerer's Stone* by J. K. Rowling (England)	First book in the best-selling quest fantasy series

The U.S. also produced some outstanding early modern fantasies, beginning with *The Wonderful Wizard of Oz* (1900) by L. Frank Baum, considered the first classic U.S. modern fantasy for children. Other landmark works are *Charlotte's Web* (1952) by E. B. White, the best-known and best-loved U.S. work of fantasy; the Prydain Chronicles by Lloyd Alexander; and *A Wrinkle in Time* (1962) by Madeleine L'Engle, which is considered a modern classic in science fiction for children.

Science fiction, the most recent development in modern fantasy, is based in the nineteenth-century novels of Jules Verne and H. G. Wells (*Time Machine,* 1895) for adults. It was not until the twentieth century that science fiction began to be aimed specifically at children. In the early 1900s, the Tom Swift series by Victor Appleton (collective pseudonym for the Stratemeyer Syndicate), although stilted in style and devoid of female characters, can be considered the first science fiction for children. The success of the science fiction magazine *Amazing Stories,* launched in 1926, brought formal recognition to the genre of science fiction.

In 1963, Madeleine L'Engle's *A Wrinkle in Time* was awarded the Newbery Medal. From this point forward, many science fiction novels for children began to appear. In the late 1960s and 1970s, the theme of mind control was popular in books such as John Christopher's Tripods trilogy and William Sleator's *House of Stairs* (1974). Space travel and future worlds were frequent science fiction topics in the 1980s.

Modern fantasy for children remains strong, especially in Great Britain and English-speaking countries. Although personified toys and animals remain popular in children's books, growth in this genre appears to be in stories in which fantasy is interwoven into other genres—science fiction, science fantasy, and historical fantasy. Fractured folktales, traditional tales with a contemporary twist or a tale told from a new perspective, took on new popularity with Jon Scieszka's *The True Story of the 3 Little Pigs* in the voice of A. Wolf, illustrated by Lane Smith in 1989. This blurring of traditional genres can also be seen in the interesting mixture of realistic mystery stories with supernatural elements, as in the popular mysteries of Mary Downing Hahn. One recent shift has been a cultural shift to using myths and legends from non-Western cultures within fantasy stories, such as Grace Lin's *Where the Mountain Meets the Moon.*

Modern fantasy is likely to continue to be a popular genre, as evidenced by the extraordinary popularity of the best-selling Harry Potter quest series by J. K. Rowling, whose first novel was published in 1998.

Types of Modern Fantasy

In modern fantasy, the distinctions between types are not totally discrete. These types of modern fantasy are a starting point for thinking about the variety of fantastic stories, motifs, themes, and characters created by gifted authors. Additional categories could be listed, and some stories clearly fit in more than one category. Kate DiCamillo's *The Tale of Despereaux,* for example, could be categorized as a modern fairy tale or quest fantasy as well as an animal fantasy.

Modern Folktales

Modern folktales, or **literary folktales,** are tales told in a form similar to that of a traditional tale with little character description, strong conflict, fast-moving plot with a sudden resolution, vague setting, and, in some cases, magical elements. But these modern tales have a known, identifiable author who has written the tale in this form. In other words, the tales do not spring from the cultural heritage of a group of people through the oral tradition but rather from the mind of one creator. This distinction does not matter to children, who delight in these tales.

The tales of Hans Christian Andersen are the earliest and best known of these modern tales. More recently, other authors, including Gail Carson Levine (*Ella Enchanted* and *The Fairest*) and Shannon Hale *(Goose Girl* and *Princess Academy),* have become known for their modern folktales.

Fractured folktales can be defined as traditional folktales with a contemporary twist or a tale told from a new perspective, such as Zoe Alley's *There's a Wolf at the Door* and *The Adventures of the Dish and the Spoon* by Mini Grey in which the characters of the well-known nursery rhyme run away to become vaudeville stars.

Modern folktales are an important counterbalance to traditional tales. Many traditional tales present an old-fashioned, stereotyped view of male and female characters, while modern tales present feisty resourceful female characters, such as those in modern fairy tales by Gail Carson Levine and Shannon Hale and the tall tales of Anne Isaacs.

Animal Fantasy

Animal fantasies are stories in which animals behave as human beings in that they experience emotions, talk, and have the ability to reason. Usually, the animals in fantasies retain many of their animal characteristics. In the best of these animal fantasies, the author will interpret the animal for the reader in human terms without destroying the animal's integrity or removing it from membership in the animal world. For example, a rabbit character in an animal fantasy will retain natural abilities of speed and camouflage to outsmart adversaries. At the same time, however, the reader sees human qualities, such as caring and love, through the rabbit's conversations with family members.

Animal fantasies can be read to very young children who enjoy the exciting but reassuring adventures in books. Examples are *The Tale of Peter Rabbit* by Beatrix Potter and the Elephant and Piggie series by Mo Willems. Many picture books for young children use animal characters who depict the normal interactions of families and friends, such as the Olivia books by Ian Falconer and the Max and Ruby books by Rosemary Wells.

Books for children in primary grades include somewhat longer stories, often in a humorous vein, such as Beverly Cleary's *The Mouse and the Motorcycle,* Lynne Jonell's *Emmy and the Incredible Shrinking Rat,* and the beloved pig in the Mercy Watson series by Kate DiCamillo. Enjoyable animal fantasies for the young reader often have easy-to-follow, episodic plots.

Fully developed novels of modern fantasy with subtle and complex characterizations and a progressive plot are especially suitable for reading aloud to children. *Charlotte's Web* by E. B. White remains a favorite read-aloud book; *The Tale of Despereaux* by Kate DiCamillo and *The Underneath* by Kathi Appelt are also popular as read-alouds. A classic book with richly drawn characterizations, *The Wind in the Willows* by Kenneth Grahame, describes in artistic detail the life of animal friends along a riverbank. This book features an episodic plot structure but has a challenging style appropriate for intermediate-grade students, who will also enjoy the progressive plot of *A Coyote's in the House* by Elmore Leonard, the humorous story of a coyote in Hollywood that satirizes the movie industry.

Although the interest in animal fantasy peaks at age 8 or 9, many children and adults continue to enjoy well-written animal fantasies. In animal fantasies for older readers, an entire animal world is usually created, with all of the relationships among its members that might be found in a novel portraying human behavior, such as *Watership Down* by Richard Adams and *The Amazing Maurice and His Educated Rodents* by Terry Pratchett.

Personified Toys and Objects

Stories in which admired objects or beloved toys are brought to life and believed in by a child or adult character include classics such as *The Adventures of Pinocchio* by Carlo Collodi in which a mischievous puppet comes to life and has many exciting and dangerous escapades. In these stories, the object, toy, or doll becomes real to the human protagonist and, in turn, becomes real to the child reader (who has perhaps also imagined a toy coming to life). Close family relationships are also demonstrated in *The Doll People* by Ann M. Martin and Laura Godwin. Emily Jenkins's *Toys Go Out* depicts toys who become friends with one another. In Kate DiCamillo's *The Miraculous Journey of Edward Tulane*, a vain china rabbit learns the power of love in this

Notable Authors of Modern Fantasy

David Almond, British writer noted for magical realism novels for intermediate readers. *Skellig,* Carnegie Medal winner; *Kit's Wilderness; Clay.* www.davidalmond.com

Kate DiCamillo, author of animal and toy fantasies for children in primary and intermediate grades. *The Tale of Despereaux,* winner of the Newbery Medal; *The Miraculous Journey of Edward Tulane;* the Mercy Watson series. www.katedicamillo.com

Mini Grey, an award-winning British author and illustrator of humorous picture books for young children featuring nursery rhymes and action toys. *The Adventures of the Dish and the Spoon; Traction Man and the Beach Odyssey; Into the Woods; Three by the Sea.*

Margaret Peterson Haddix, author of two popular fantasy series, the Shadow Children and the Missing, as well as numerous fantasy novels for intermediate readers. www.haddixbooks.com/home.html

Shannon Hale, author of modern folktales. *Goose Girl; Book of a Thousand Days; Rapunzel's Revenge and Calamity Jack* (cowritten with Dean Hale). www.squeetus.com

Gail Carson Levine, author of modern folktales in novels with strong female characters. *Ella Enchanted; Fairest; Ever; Fairy Dust and the Quest for the Egg.* www.gailcarsonlevine.com

Neil Gaiman, British author of novels, graphic novels, and picture books featuring unusual characters in strange situations, such as *Coraline and The Graveyard Book,* winner of both the Newbery Medal and the Carnegie Medal. www.neilgaiman.com

Anne Isaacs, author of original tall tales featuring strong women. *Swamp Angel; Dust Devil; Pancakes for Supper.* www.anneisaacs.com/content

Lois Lowry, winner of the 1994 Newbery Medal for *The Giver,* a popular work of science fiction. Giver Quartet also includes *Gathering Blue, Messenger,* and *Son.* www.loislowry.com

Nnedi Okorafor, Nigerian-American writer of fantasy and science fiction set in Nigeria, including *The Shadow Speaker* and *Akata Witch.* www.nnedi.com

Terry Pratchett, British author of Nation and the Discworld series that includes *The Wee Free Men.* Winner of the Carnegie Medal for *The Amazing Maurice and His Educated Rodents,* a work of humorous fantasy. www.terrypratchettbooks.com

Philip Pullman, British creator of His Dark Materials fantasies, a trilogy comprising *The Golden Compass, The Subtle Knife,* and *The Amber Spyglass.* www.philip-pullman.com

J. K. Rowling, British author of the best-selling series about Harry Potter, a child wizard. *Harry Potter and the Sorcerer's Stone.* www.jkrowling.com

story suitable for intermediate-grade students. Personified toy and object stories appeal to children from preschool through upper elementary grades, and is also reflected in the popularity of the Toy Story movies.

Unusual Characters and Strange Situations

Some authors approach fantasy through reality but go beyond reality to the ridiculous or exaggerated through unusual characters or strange situations. *Alice's Adventures in Wonderland* by Lewis Carroll is the best known of this type of modern fantasy. Writers of modern fantasy have described such strange situations as a boy sailing across the Atlantic Ocean in a giant peach (*James and the Giant Peach* by Roald Dahl) and a small-town girl who seems unremarkable, except when she flies (*The Girl Who Could Fly* by Virginia Forester).

Modern fantasy appeals to readers of all ages. Shaun Tan's *The Arrival,* a wordless graphic novel, features a hero who leaves his homeland and travels to a bizarre new world where he faces the struggles of being an immigrant, seeks employment, and eventually makes friends in this strange new place. In Neil Gaiman's *The Graveyard Book,* a young boy is being raised in a cemetery by its ghostly occupants. The topics of life, death, and the power of family can provoke discussion with intermediate-grade students. In *Tuck Everlasting,* Natalie Babbitt explores the theme of immortality and its consequences, a provocative theme for children and adults.

Worlds of Little People

Worlds inhabited by miniature people who have developed a culture of their own in this world or who live in another world have long been a favorite for children. In Barb Bentler Ullman's *The Fairies of Nutfolk Wood,* Willa Jane, the protagonist, defends a band of fairies living in the nearby woods who are threatened by humans. In *Toby Alone,* the Tree is populated by a society of miniature people whose world is threatened by their lifestyle. Stories of little people delight children because they identify with the indignities foisted on powerless little people and because the big people are invariably outdone by the more ingenious little people.

Supernatural Events and Mystery Fantasy

Many recent fantasies evoke the supernatural, such as ghost stories and the recent onslaught of vampire and werewolf books due to the success of Stephenie Meyer's *Twilight* and the accompanying movie series. Some ghost stories intrigue younger children, especially when the topic is treated humorously and reassuringly. The goblins of Hilari Bell's *The Goblin Wood* eventually become allies of the protagonist. Ghosts in children's books can be fearful threats or helpful protectors, as is the ghost of Cynthia DeFelice's *The Ghost of Poplar Point,* who is angry about the disturbance of sacred grounds marking a massacre of Seneca Indians. Many authors write mysteries for children in which the solution is partially supernatural or arrived at with supernatural assistance.

Witchcraft and other aspects of the occult sometimes play a role in children's fantasy books. Witches are often portrayed as the broom-wielding villains of both traditional and modern tales, such as the Russian stories of Baba Yaga. Halloween and its traditions are also frequently presented in children's stories. An example is Frances Hardinge's *Well Witched,* in which three children who steal some coins discover that a witch has endowed the coins with strange powers. Witchcraft has recently been the focus of criticism and some parents' groups have attempted to censor children's books featuring witches, Halloween, and other elements of the occult.

Magical realism, a blend of fantasy and realism, has the appearance of a work of realism but gradually introduces the fantastic as an integral, and necessary, part of the story. The fantastic is merged into these stories such that the distinction between realism and fantasy is blurred, often leaving the reader in some doubt as to what is real and what is fantasy. Magical realism with its origins in Latino literature has stories with the feel of realism, but the magical elements cause them to fall outside of the definition of realistic fiction, such as found in Meg Medina's *Milagros: Girl from Away* and David Almond's *Skellig* and *Clay.*

Historical Fantasy

Historical fantasy includes *time-warp fantasies,* a story in which a present-day protagonist goes back in time to a different era. A contrast between the two time periods is shown to readers through the modern-day protagonist's discoveries of and astonishment with earlier customs. Historical fantasies must fully and authentically develop the historical setting, both time and place, just as in a book of historical fiction. Mary Hoffman, in *Stravaganza: City of Masks,* succeeds in producing this type of mixed-genre story as does Jeanette Winterson in *Tanglewreck.* Time travel has also been used in easily accessible series books, such as the Time Warp Trio books by Jon Scieszka.

Another type of historical fantasies are fantasies that are set in a specific historical time period that is authentically represented but to which some aspect of magic or the supernatural has been added, such as Rebecca Stead's *When You Reach Me* and Avi's *The Seer of Shadows.*

Quest Stories

Quest stories are adventure stories with a search motif. The quest may be pursuit for a lofty purpose, such as justice or love, or for a rich reward, such as a magical power or a hidden treasure. Quest stories that are serious in tone are called *high fantasy.* Many of these novels are set in medieval times and are reminiscent of the search for the holy grail. In these high fantasies, an imaginary otherworld is fully portrayed: the society, its history, family trees, geographic location, population, religion, customs, and traditions. The conflict in these tales usually centers on the struggle between good and evil. *The Hobbit,* written by J. R. R. Tolkien in 1937, is one of the first of these high fantasies. Other examples are C. S. Lewis's Chronicles of Narnia series, Philip Pullman's His Dark Materials trilogy, and J. K. Rowling's Harry Potter series.

A recent trend in quest fantasies is a focus on action-packed adventures, such as in the Septimus Heap series by Angie Sage. Another trend is a move from distant medieval worlds to the contemporary world, such as found in Ingrid Law's *Savvy,* and the portrayal of a world within a world, such as *Falling In* by Frances O'Roark Dowell in which a sixth grader falls through the floor of a closet into a parallel universe.

Many quest fantasies follow a structure similar to that found in traditional myths and described by Joseph A. Campbell (1949) as a *monomyth* or *hero cycle.* In this structure, the hero starts out in the ordinary world and receives a call to enter a strange, dangerous, supernatural world where he must face daunting trials involving a struggle against external forces and internal temptations. If the hero overcomes these trials, he will receive a precious gift. He then has a choice to return to the ordinary world or to remain in the supernatural world. If he chooses to return, he will face more trials on the return journey. After returning successfully, the hero shares the gift to improve the world. The hero cycle represents a journey of self-discovery and personal growth for the protagonist.

A reader response strategy that encourages students to explore their understandings of the transformational journeys of their heroes in these fantasies is to construct **quest maps**. Students create visual maps of a favorite character's journey to show literal as well as figurative transformations. Students can develop their own creative format for the map, such as a road map, time line, graph, or the map of the character's heart or brain.

Science Fiction and Science Fantasy

Science fiction is a form of imaginative literature that provides a picture of something that could happen based on real scientific facts and principles. Therefore, story elements in science fiction must have the appearance of scientific plausibility or technical possibility. Hypotheses about the future of humankind and the universe presented in science fiction appear plausible and possible to the reader because settings and events are built on extensions of known technologies and scientific concepts.

In novels of science fiction, such topics as mind control, genetic engineering, space technologies and travel, visitors from outer space, and future political and social systems all seem possible to the readers. For example, in Margaret Peterson Haddix's novel *Double Identity,* genetic engineering and its implications are explored. These novels especially fascinate many young people because they feature characters who must learn to adjust to change and to become new people; two aspects of living that adolescents also experience. In addition, science fiction stories may portray the world that young people might one day inhabit; for this reason, science fiction has sometimes been called *futuristic fiction*. Many current futuristic fantasies focus on a *dystopia,* in which authors depict a dark future world of dehumanization and fear, such as that found in the Hunger Games trilogy by Suzanne Collins.

Science fiction is growing in popularity among children and adolescents. If you are reluctant to read science fiction or have never read it, you may want to start with some books by Nancy Farmer (*The House of the Scorpion*), Andrew Clements (*Things Not Seen*), or Lois Lowry (*The Giver; Messenger*).

The distinction between science fiction and science fantasy is not clearly defined or universally accepted. **Science fantasy** is a popularized type of science fiction in which a scientific explanation, though not necessarily plausible, is offered for imaginative leaps into the unknown. Science fantasy presents a world that often mixes elements of mythology and traditional fantasy with scientific or technological concepts, resulting in a setting that has some scientific basis but never has existed or never could exist. One example is Sylvia Waugh's *Earthborn,* in which the protagonist discovers her parents are space aliens. Science fantasy novels, which usually appear in series, appeal to adolescents and young adults and, like many series, are sometimes formulaic and of mixed quality.

Worlds of magic and monsters and dystopian worlds of the future have great appeal to children. Their lively imaginations invite them into these worlds to explore the many different kinds of fantasies and levels of conceptual understandings and themes. This openness and delight in fantasy is not always appreciated by adults, some of whom see these books as dangerous to children's minds. Fantasy, along with realistic contemporary fiction on social issues, is often the target of censorship attempts and so educators need to know how to respond to these challenges.

Reader Connection: Censorship and the First Amendment

The First Amendment to the U.S. Constitution guarantees all citizens the right to free speech and freedom of the press. Teaching children about their First Amendment rights is important because there are those who would take these rights away through censorship. **Censorship** is the removal, suppression, or restricted use of reading materials on the grounds that they are objectionable, often for moral reasons (Reichman, 2001). When someone attempts to remove material from the curriculum or library, thereby restricting the access of others, it is called a **challenge.** Most book challenges occur locally, and most fail. When a challenge is successful and materials are removed from the curriculum or library, it is called a **banning** (www.ala.org/ala/issuesadvocacy/banned/aboutbannedbooks/index.cfm).

Our position regarding censorship is:

• Teachers and schools have the right and the obligation to select reading materials suitable for the education of their students. With this right comes the professional responsibility to select good quality literature that furthers educational goals while remaining appropriate for the age and maturity level of the students.

• Parents have the right to protect their children from materials or influences they see as potentially damaging to their children. In the instance that a parent believes that material selected by a school or teacher is potentially harmful to his/her child, that parent has the right to bring this to the attention of the school and request that his/her child not be subjected to this material. Parents must indicate the reason for their concern.

• The school must take the parent's objection seriously and provide a reasonable substitute for the material of concern. If an alternative procedure is necessary in the situation (e.g., the student will listen to a different book in the library while the teacher is reading aloud), the alternative should respect the student and be sensitive to his/her feelings.

• The parent does not have the right to demand that the material in question be withheld from other students. This would interfere with the rights and professional duty of the teacher and school to educate students. Once a student is given a reasonable alternative, the school has fulfilled its obligation and should not interfere with the First Amendment rights of other students.

As adults, we cherish our right to choose our reading material and use this right nearly every day of our lives. Social studies and civics textbooks proudly proclaim the freedom of choice in the lives of citizens of the U.S. But do we, as parents, teachers, and librarians, actually extend these rights to our children? Specifically,

• Do we allow outspoken special-interest groups to influence the removal of good, but controversial, books from the library or classroom shelves, or do we stand by our convictions and book selections?

• Do we self-censor by only selecting books on "safe" topics, or do we select books on the basis of quality and age appropriateness?

• Do we listen to young readers' ideas and responses to books, or do we only ask them comprehension questions?

• Do we allow children to reject books that they do not like, or do we force them to read our selections?

- Do we engage children in critically analyzing books for authenticity and stereotyped representations?

We need to teach students, by our actions as well as by our words, about their First Amendment rights.

The censorship database of the American Library Association's Office of Intellectual Freedom (OIF) indicates that the most censorship attempts in 1990–2010 came from parents (57%), library patrons (14%), and school administrators (10%). Of the 10,676 challenges reported to the OIF in these 20 years, 30 percent were based on material perceived to be "sexually explicit"; 25 percent were based on material perceived to have "offensive language"; and 21 percent were based on material perceived to be "unsuited to the age group." It should be noted that the OIF estimates that 75 to 80 percent of censorship attempts are not reported, so these figures are approximate.

Another unlikely, but significant, source of censorship is teachers themselves. Wollman-Bonilla (1998) found that teachers often object to texts reflecting gender, ethnic, race, or class experiences that differ from their own. This subtle form of censorship is made worse by the fact that most teachers are unaware of their biases in text selection (Jipson & Paley, 1991; Luke, Cooke, & Luke, 1986). Wollman-Bonilla argued for the First Amendment rights of children, saying, "If we are to know how books actually affect children, we need to hear *children's* voices and understand *their* experiences before, during, and after reading" (p. 293).

Teaching the First Amendment

Teaching students about their First Amendment rights might begin by posting a copy of the First Amendment, having students read it, and discussing what this amendment means to them and the consequences of its loss in their lives. Lists of children's books that some have declared "objectionable" could be posted. Children who have read the books could discuss why these books might be considered objectionable and why banning these books violates their First Amendment rights. Children's and young adults' fiction about censorship could be read and discussed. Good examples for younger readers are *Arthur and the Scare-Your-Pants-Off Club* by Marc Brown and Stephen Krensky (1998) and *The Landry News* by Andrew Clements (1999); for older readers, see *Americus* by M. K. Reed (2011), *The Sledding Hill* by Chris Crutcher (2005), *The Last Safe Place on Earth* by Richard Peck (1995), and *Save Halloween!* by Stephanie Tolan (1993). As teachers and librarians, we should do everything possible to promote the kinds of books that encourage critical thinking, inquiry, and self-expression, while maintaining respect for the views of others.

Dealing with Censorship Attempts

The American Library Association's Office of Intellectual Freedom monitors the challenges made against children's books in the U.S.. Most adults and children who have read the highly regarded books that often appear on these "most challenged books" lists find the reasons given for the challenges perplexing, if not incredible. The following titles, for example, appeared on one or more of the ALA's "Top 10 Most Frequently Challenged Books of the Year" lists from 2006 to 2011:

- *And Tango Makes Three* by Justin Richardson and Peter Parnell (2005) for anti-ethnic and antifamily content, homosexuality, having a religious viewpoint, and being unsuited to the age group

- IM Series (e.g., *Ttyl; ttfn; l8r; g8r*) by Lauren Myracle for offensive language, religious views, being sexually explicit
- The Hunger Games trilogy by Suzanne Collins for anti-ethnic and antifamily content, insensitivity, offensive language, occult/satanic content, violence
- *The Absolutely True Diary of a Part-Time Indian* by Sherman Alexie for offensive language, racism, religious viewpoint, sexually explicit content, and being unsuitable for age group
- Alice (series) by Phyllis Reynolds Naylor for offensive language, being sexually explicit, and religious viewpoint
- Captain Underpants series by Dav Pilkey for antifamily content, being unsuitable for age group, violence
- His Dark Materials trilogy by Philip Pullman for political and religious viewpoints and violence
- *It's Perfectly Normal* by Robie H. Harris (1994) for sex education and being sexually explicit
- *Olive's Ocean* by Kevin Henkes (2003) for offensive language and being sexually explicit
- Scary Stories series by Alvin Schwartz for occult/satanic content, religious viewpoint, and violence

Often, individuals challenge books on the basis of a single word or phrase, or on hearsay, and have not read the book. Teachers and library media specialists have found that a written procedure is helpful for bringing order and reason into discussions with parents who want to censor school materials. Most procedures call for teachers and librarians to give would-be censors a complaint form and ask them to specify their concerns in writing. The advantages to this system is that both teachers and parents are given time to reflect on the issue and to control their emotions, and the would-be censor is given time to read the book in its entirety, if he or she has not done so already. Developing written procedures and complaint forms are important tasks for a school curriculum committee. Figure 7.1 presents a form produced by the National Council of Teachers of English (NCTE) for reconsideration of a work of literature.

The American Library Association's Office for Intellectual Freedom has several publications about censorship, such as Reichman's *Censorship and Selection: Issues and Answers for Schools* (2001), which provide important information to schools (www.ala.org.). ALA and other organizations have collaboratively established a website of resources for Banned Book Week (www .bannedbooksweek.org/). People for the American Way also provides advice in combating school censorship (www.pfaw.org).

The National Council of Teachers of English has an Anti-Censorship Center (www .ncte.org/action/anti-censorship) and offers a valuable document about censorship, *The Students' Right to Read,* which explains the nature of censorship, the stand of those opposed to it, and ways to combat it. This document and the *Citizen's Request for Reconsideration of a Work* are available free of charge at www.ncte.org/positions/statements/righttoreadguideline.

Figure 7.1 Citizen's Request for Reconsideration of a Work

Author _____ Paperback _____ Hardcover _____

Title _____

Publisher (if known) _____

Request initiated by _____

Telephone _____ Address _____ City _____ Zip Code _____

Complainant represents:

_____ Himself/Herself

_____ (Name of Organization) _____

(Identify other group) _____

1. Have you been able to discuss this work with the teacher or librarian who ordered it or used it?
   _____ Yes _____ No

2. What do you understand to be the general purpose for using this work?
   a. Provide support for a unit in the curriculum? _____ Yes _____ No
   b. Provide a learning experience for the reader in one kind of literature? _____ Yes _____ No
   c. Other _____
   _____

3. Did the general purpose for the use of the work, as described by the teacher or librarian, seem suitable to you? _____ Yes _____ No
   If not, please explain._____

4. What do you think is the general purpose of the author in this book? _____

5. In what ways do you think a work of this nature is not suitable for the use the teacher or librarian wishes to carry out? _____
   _____

6. Have you been able to learn what the students' response to this work is? _____ Yes _____ No

7. What response did the students make? _____
   _____

8. Have you been able to learn from your school library what book reviewers or other students of literature have written about this work? _____ Yes _____ No

9. Would you like the teacher or librarian to give you a written summary of what book reviewers and other students have written about this book or film? _____ Yes _____ No

(*Continued*)

Figure 7.1 Continued

10. Do you have negative reviews of the book? _____ Yes _____ No

11. Where were they published? _____

12. Would you be willing to provide summaries of the reviews you have collected?
_____ Yes _____ No

13. What would you like your library/school to do about this work?
_____ Do not assign/lend it to my child.
_____ Return it to the staff selection committee/department for reevaluation.
_____ Other—Please explain.
_____

14. What work would you recommend that would convey as valuable a picture and perspective of the subject treated in place of this book ? _____

Signature _____ Date _____

Source: Committee on the Right to Read. (1982). *The students' right to read.* Urbana, IL: National Council of Teachers of English.

 # Invitations for Further Investigation

- Select a classic work of modern fantasy for children, such as *Alice's Adventures in Wonderland, Charlotte's Web, The Wonderful Wizard of Oz,* or *The Wind in the Willows.* Read the work and review articles of literary criticism about the work. Present your perspectives and consider whether it remains a valuable book for today's children.

- Select a concept of significance to children, such as freedom, hope, beauty, or forgiveness, and put together a text set of three to five fantasies that focus on this concept. Read and discuss the books with other readers to identify the primary themes in each book. Select excerpts from each book that explicitly or implicitly state the theme. Compare the ways in which the themes play out in these books and list the secondary themes in each fantasy.

- Select a quest story from the recommended list and work with a small group to create a quest map, depicting the characters' journeys and transformations over time.

- Investigate the nature of book challenges by reading several of the American Library Association's most frequently challenged books. Analyze them for the reasons that would-be censors find them objectionable. Develop an argument for or against the censorship attempt for each book.

References

Alexie, S. (2007). *The absolutely true diary of a part-time Indian*. New York: Little, Brown.

American Library Association. (2009). *Frequently challenged books of the 21st century*. Retrieved from www.ala.org/issuesadvocacy/banned /frequentlychallenged/21stcenturychallenged /index.cfm

Campbell, J. A. (1949). *The hero with a thousand faces*. New York: Pantheon.

Brown, M., & Krensky, S. (1998). *Arthur and the scare-your-pants-off club*. (M. Brown, Illust.). New York: Little, Brown.

Clements, A. (1999). *The Landry News*. New York: Simon & Schuster.

Committee on the Right to Read. (1982). *The students' right to read*. Urbana, IL: National Council of Teachers of English.

Crutcher, C. (2005). *The sledding hill*. New York: Harper-Collins.

Harris, R. H. (1994). *It's perfectly normal: A book about changing bodies, growing up, sex, and sexual health*. (M. Emberley, Illus.). New York: Candlewick.

Henkes, K. (2003). *Olive's ocean*. New York: Greenwillow.

Jipson, J., & Paley, N. (1991). The selective tradition in children's literature: Does it exist in the elementary classroom? *English Education, 23*, 148–159.

Luke, A., Cooke, J., & Luke, C. (1986). The selective tradition in action: Gender bias in student teachers' selections of children's literature. *English Education, 18*, 209–218.

Peck, R. (1995). *The last safe place on earth*. New York: Delacorte.

Reed, M.K. (2011). *Americus*. New York: First Second/ Roaring Brook.

Reichman, H. (2001). *Censorship and selection: Issues and answers for schools*. Chicago, IL: American Library Association.

Richardson, J., & Parnell, P. (2005). *And Tango makes three*. (H. Cole, Illus.). New York: Simon & Schuster.

Tolan, S. (1993). *Save Halloween!* New York: HarperCollins.

Wollman-Bonilla, J. E. (1998). Outrageous viewpoints: Teachers' criteria for rejecting works of children's literature. *Language Arts, 75*(4), 287–295.

Recommended Modern Fantasy Books

Ages indicated refer to concept and interest levels. Formats other than novels will be coded as follows:

(PI) Picture book
(NV) Novel in Verse
(COL) Short story collection
(GR) Graphic novel

Modern Folktales

Alley, Zoe. ***There's a Wolf at the Door***. Illus. R. W. Alley. Roaring Brook, 2008. (**PI, GR**). Ages 6–8. Also ***There's a Princess in the Palace*** (2010). (Interwoven folktales).

Andersen, Hans Christian. ***The Pea Blossom***. Retold and Illus. by Amy Lowry Poole. Holiday, 2005. (**PI**). Ages 5–8. (China).

Elya, Susan Middleton. ***Rubia and the Three Osos***. Illus. Melissa Sweet. Hyperion, 2010. (**PI**). Ages 3–7. (Mexican American).

Fleming, Candace. ***Clever Jack Takes the Cake***. Illus. G. Brian Karas. Schwartz & Wade, 2010. (**PI**). Ages 5–9. (Fairy tale).

Grey, Mini. ***The Adventures of the Dish and the Spoon***. Knopf, 2006. Ages 5–9. (**PI**). (Nursery rhyme, England).

Gidwitz, Adam. ***A Tale Dark and Grimm***. Dutton, 2010. Ages 10–14. (Hansel and Gretel, Grimm tales).

Hale, Shannon. ***Princess Academy***. Bloomsbury, 2005. Ages 10–14.

Hale, Shannon. ***Book of a Thousand Days***. Bloomsbury, 2007. Ages 11–15. (Grimm, Central Asia). See also ***Goose Girl*** (2003).

Hale, Shannon, and Dean Hale. *Calamity Jack.* Illus. Nathan Hale. Bloomsbury, 2010. (**GR**). Ages 10–14.

Hopkinson, Deborah. *Apples to Oregon: Being the (Slightly) True Narrative of How a Brave Pioneer Father Brought Apples, Peaches, Pears, Plums, Grapes, and Cherries (and Children) Across the Plains.* Illus. Nancy Carpenter. Atheneum, 2004. (**PI**). Ages 6–10. (Tall tale).

Isaacs, Anne. *Pancakes for Supper.* Illus. Mark Teague. Scholastic, 2006. (**PI**). Ages 4–8. (Tall tale).

Isaacs, Anne. *Dust Devil.* Illus. Paul Zelinsky. Schwartz & Wade, 2010. (**PI**). Ages 6–9. (Tall tale). Also *Swamp Angel* (1994).

Lester, Julius. *The Old African.* Illus. Jerry Pinkney. Dial, 2005. (**PI**). Ages 9–12. (Historical legend).

Levine, Gail Carson. *Ella Enchanted.* HarperCollins, 1997. Ages 10–13. (Cinderella).

Levine, Gail Carson. *Fairy Dust and the Quest for the Egg.* Illus. David Christiana. Disney, 2005. Ages 8–11. (Peter Pan).

Levine, Gail Carson. *Fairest.* HarperCollins, 2006. Ages 11–16. (Snow White)

Lin, Grace. *Where the Mountain Meets the Moon.* Little, Brown, 2009. Ages 9–12. (Chinese folklore).

McKinley, Robin. *Spindle's End.* Putnam, 2000. Ages 12–18. (Sleeping Beauty, England).

McKissack, Patricia C. *Porch Lies: Tales of Slicksters, Tricksters, and Other Wily Creatures.* Illus. Andre Carilho. Random House, 2006. (**COL**). Ages 8–11. (African American history and legend).

Mora, Pat. *Doña Flor: A Tall Tale about a Giant Woman with a Great Big Heart.* Illus. Raúl Colón. Knopf, 2005. (**PI**) Ages 4–8. (Tall tale)

Murdock, Catherine Gilbert. *Princess Ben.* Houghton, 2008. Ages 11–16. (Fairy tale).

Napoli, Donna Jo. *Beast.* Atheneum, 2000. Ages 11–16. (Beauty and the Beast, Persia).

Napoli, Donna Jo. *Bound.* Simon & Schuster, 2004. Ages 10–18. (Cinderella, China).

Nolen, Jerdine. *Big Jabe.* Illus. Kadir Nelson. Lothrop, Lee & Shepard, 2000. (**PI**). Ages 6–9. (Tall tale, historical).

Paterson, John and Katherine. *The Flint Heart: A Fairy Story.* Illus. John Rocco. Ages 9–12. (Fairy tale).

Pattou, Edith. *East.* Harcourt, 2003. Ages 12–16. (East of the Sun and West of the Moon).

Pullman, Philip. *The Scarecrow and His Servant.* Illus. Peter Bailey. Knopf, 2005. Ages 9–13. (Folkloric, England).

Reeve, Philip. *Here Lies Arthur.* Scholastic, 2008. Ages 12–18. (King Arthur legend, England).

Stanley, Diane. *Bella at Midnight: The Thimble, the Ring, and the Slippers of Glass.* Illus. Bagram Ibatoulline. HarperCollins, 2006. Ages 10–14. (Cinderella).

Ursu, Anne. *Breadcrumbs.* Illus. Erin McGuire. Walden Pond, 2011. Ages 9–12. (Snow Queen).

Animal Fantasies

Adams, Richard. *Watership Down.* Scribner, 1972. Ages 12–15.

Anderson, M. T. *Whales on Stilts!* Harcourt, 2005. Ages 9–13. Sequel is *The Clue of the Linoleum Lederhosen,* 2006.

Appelt, Kathi. *The Underneath.* Atheneum, 2008. Ages 9–14. (Magical realism).

Armstrong, Alan. *Whittington.* Illus. S. D. Schindler. Random House, 2005. Ages 9–13.

Bruchac, Joseph. *Wabi: A Hero's Tale.* Dial, 2006. Ages 10–15. (Abenaki).

Cleary, Beverly. *The Mouse and the Motorcycle.* Illus. Louis Darling. Morrow, 1965. Ages 7–11.

Deedy, Carmen. *The Cheshire Cheese Cat: A Dickens of a Tale.* Illus. Barry Moser. Peachtree, 2011. Ages 9–12.

DiCamillo, Kate. *The Tale of Despereaux.* Illus. Timothy Basil Ering. Candlewick, 2003. Ages 7–10.

Finney, Patricia. *I, Jack.* HarperCollins, 2004. Ages 8–12.

Grahame, Kenneth. *The Wind in the Willows.* Illus. E. H. Shepard. Scribner's, 1908. Ages 8–12.

Grey, Mimi. *Three by the Sea.* Knopf, 2011. (**PI**). Ages 5–8. (England).

Jennings, Patrick. *We Can't All Be Rattlesnakes.* HarperCollins, 2009. Ages 8–12.

Johnson, D. B. *Henry Builds a Cabin.* Houghton, 2002. (**PI**). Ages 9–13. Also *Henry Hikes to Fitchburg* (2000) and *Henry Climbs a Mountain* (2003).

Jonell, Lynne. *Emmy and the Incredible Shrinking Rat.* Illus. Jonathan Bean. Holt, 2007. Ages 8–11. Series.

King-Smith, Dick. *Babe: The Gallant Pig.* Illus. Maggie Keen. Viking, 1983. Ages 8–11. (England).

Leonard, Elmore. *A Coyote's in the House.* Harper Entertainment, 2004. Ages 9–13.

Oppel, Kenneth. *Darkwing*. Illus. Keith Thompson. HarperCollins, 2007. Ages 10–14. Silverwing Series. (Canada).

Palatini, Margie. *The Web Files.* Illus. Richard Egielski. Hyperion, 2001. (**PI**). Ages 9–12.

Potter, Beatrix. *The Tale of Peter Rabbit.* Warne, 1902. (**PI**). Ages 5–9.

Pratchett, Terry. *The Amazing Maurice and His Educated Rodents.* HarperCollins, 2001. Ages 12–16.

Said, S. F. *Varjak Paw.* Illus. Dave McKean. Knopf, 2003. Ages 9–12.

Seidler, Tor. *Gully's Travels.* Illus. Brock Cole. Scholastic, 2008. Ages 9–12.

White, E. B. *Charlotte's Web.* Illus. Garth Williams. Harper, 1952. Ages 8–11.

Willems, Mo. *I Broke My Trunk!* Hyperion, 2011. (**PI**). Ages 5–8. Elephant & Piggie series.

Personified Toys and Objects

DiCamillo, Kate. *The Miraculous Journey of Edward Tulane.* Illus. Bagram Ibatoulline. Candlewick, 2006. Ages 8–12.

Fine, Anne. *The Jamie and Angus Stories.* Illus. Penny Dale. Candlewick, 2000. (**COL**). Ages 5–8. (England).

Grey, Mini. *Traction Man and the Beach Odyssey*. Knopf, 2012. (**PI**). Ages 5–8. See other Traction Man books. (England).

Jenkins, Emily. *Toys Go Out: Being the Adventures of a Knowledgeable Stingray, a Toughy Little Buffalo, and Someone Called Plastic.* Illus. Paul Zelinsky. Random, 2006. Ages 5–8. Also *Toy Dance Party* (2008) and *Toys Come Home* (2011).

Martin, Ann, and Laura Godwin. *The Doll People.* Illus. Brian Selznick. Hyperion, 2000. Ages 8–12. Also *The Meanest Doll in the World* (2003).

Unusual Characters and Strange Situations

Avi. *Strange Happenings: Five Tales of Transformations.* Harcourt, 2006. (**COL**). Ages 10–15.

Babbitt, Natalie. *Tuck Everlasting.* Farrar, 1975. Ages 10–14.

Babbitt, Natalie. *Jack Plank Tells Tales.* Scholastic, 2007. Ages 8–12. (Humorous).

Dahl, Roald. *James and the Giant Peach.* Illus. Nancy Ekholm Burkert. Knopf, 1961. Ages 8–11. (England).

Forester, Victoria. *The Girl Who Could Fly.* Feiewel & Friends, 2008. Ages 9–12.

Gaiman, Neil. *The Graveyard Book.* Illus. Dave McKean. HarperCollins, 2008. Ages 10–15. (England).

Gonzalez, Julie. *Wings.* Delacorte, 2005. Ages 12–16.

Jones, Diana Wynne. *House of Many Ways.* Greenwillow, 2008. Ages 10–14.

Tan, Shaun. *The Arrival.* Scholastic, 2007. (**GR**). Ages 11–16. (Wordless). Also *Tales from Outer Suburbia* (2009). (Australia).

Valente, Catherynne. *The Girl Who Circumvented Fairyland in a Ship of Her Own Making.* Feiwel & Friends, 2011. Ages 10–14.

Wiesner, David. *Flotsam.* Clarion, 2006 (**PI**). Ages 6–9. Also *Tuesday* (1991) and *Sector 7* (1999).

Worlds of Little People

Augarde, Steve. *The Various.* David Fickling, 2004. Ages 10–14. Also *Celandine (*2006) and *Winter Wood (*2009). (England).

Cross, Gillian. *The Dark Ground.* Dutton, 2004. Ages 11–15. Also *The Black Room* (2006). (England).

De Fombelle, Timothy. *Toby Alone.* Candlewick, 2009. Trans. Sarah Ardizzone. Ages 10–14. Also *Toby and the Secrets of the Tree* (2009). (France).

Graham, Bob. *April and Esme, Tooth Fairies.* Candlewick, 2010. (**PI**). Ages 5–8. (Australia).

Pratchett, Terry. *The Wee Free Men.* HarperCollins, 2003. Ages 10–15. Also *A Hat Full of Sky (*2004) and *Wintersmith (*2006). (England).

Ullman, Barb Bentler. *The Fairies of Nutfolk Wood.* HarperCollins, 2006. Ages 8–11.

Supernatural Events and Mystery Fantasy

Almond, David. *Clay.* Delacorte, 2006. Ages 11–18. Also *Kit's Wilderness* (2000) and *Skellig* (1999). Ages 9–12. (England).

Barry, Dave, and Ridley Pearson. *Peter and the Starcatchers.* Hyperion, 2004. Ages 9–13. (Humorous).

Bell, Hilari. *The Goblin Wood.* EOS, 2003. Ages 11–16. Also *The Goblin Gate* (2010) and *The Goblin War* (2011).

Carey, Janet Lee. *Dragon's Keep.* Harcourt, 2007. Ages 12–16.

Compestine, Ying Chang. *A Banquet for Hungry Ghosts: A Collection of Deliciously Frightening Tales*. Holt, 2009. Ages 12–15.

DeFelice, Cynthia. *The Ghost of Poplar Point.* Farrar, 2007. Agest 9–12. (Seneca Indians).

Delaney, Joseph. *Revenge of the Witch: The Last Apprentice.* Greenwillow, 2005. Ages 10–14. Series. (England).

Dickinson, Peter. *The Tears of the Salamander.* Random, 2003. Ages 11–15. (England).

DiPucchio, Kelly. *Zombie in Love.* Illus. Scott Campbell. Atheneum, 2011. (PI). Ages 6–9.

Funke, Cornelia. *The Thief Lord.* Trans. Oliver Latsch. Scholastic, 2002. Ages 10–14.

Funke, Cornelia. *Inkheart.* Trans. Anthea Bell. Scholastic, 2003. Ages 12–18. Also *Inkspell* (2005) and *Inkdeath* (2008). (Germany).

Gaiman, Neil. *Coraline: Graphic Novel.* Adapted by P. Craig Russell. HarperCollins, 2008. (**GR**). Ages 10–14.

Hahn, Mary Downing. *The Ghost of Crutchfield Hall.* Clarion, 2010. Ages 9–12.

Hardinge, Frances. *Well Witched.* HarperCollins, 2008. Ages 10–14.

Hurston, Zora Neale. *The Skull Talks Back and Other Haunting Tales.* Adapted by Joyce Carol Thomas. Illus. Leonard Jenkins. HarperCollins, 2004. (**COL, PI**). Ages 9–13.

Jones, Diana Wynne. *Enchanted Glass.* Greenwillow, 2010. Ages 10–14.

Lowry, Lois. *Gossamer.* Houghton, 2006. Ages 9–12.

Lubar, David. *Punished!* Darby Creek, 2006. Ages 8–11.

Mass, Wendy. *11 Birthdays.* Scholastic, 2009. Ages 9–12. Also *13 Gifts* (2011) and *Finally* (2010).

McKinley, Robin, and Peter Dickinson. *Water: Tales of Elemental Spirits.* Putnam, 2002. (**COL**). Ages 11–16. Series. (England).

Medina, Meg (2008*). Milagros: Girl from Away.* Holt, 2008. Ages 9–12. (Caribbean).

Meyer, Stephenie. *Twilight.* Little, Brown, 2005. Ages 13–18.

Nnedi, Okorafor. *Akata Witch.* Viking, 2011. Ages 12–15. (Nigeria).

Noyes, Deborah, editor. *Gothic! Ten Original Dark Tales.* Candlewick, 2004. (**COL**). Ages 12–18.

Phelan, Matt. *The Storm in the Barn.* Candlewick, 2009. (**GR**). Ages 10–14.

Prue, Sally. *Cold Tom.* Scholastic, 2003. Ages 10–13.

Rohmann, Eric. *Bone Dog.* Roaring Brook, 2011. (**PI**). Ages 6–9.

Slade, Arthur. *Dust.* Random House, 2003. Ages 12–16.

Stine, R. L., editor. *Beware! R. L. Stine Picks His Favorite Scary Stories.* HarperCollins, 2002. (**COL**). Ages 9–14.

Historical Fantasy

Avi. *The Seer of Shadows.* HarperCollins, 2008. Ages 9–14. (New York, 1865–1868).

Bell, Ted. *Nick of Time.* St. Martins, 2008. Ages 10–14. (WWII, UK).

Buckley-Archer, Linda. *Time Travelers.* Simon & Schuster, 2006. Ages 10–14. Gideon Trilogy. (London).

Curry, Jane Louise. *The Black Canary.* Simon & Schuster, 2005. Ages 11–14. (Biracial character, London).

Haddix, Margaret Peterson. *Found.* Simon & Schuster, 2008. Ages 10–14. Missing series.

Hoffman, Mary. *Stravaganza: City of Masks.* Bloomsbury, 2002. Ages 12–16. Sequels. (Venice, Italy).

Stead, Rebecca. *When You Reach Me.* Wendy Lamb, 2009. Ages 10–14. (1979, New York).

Winterson, Jeanette. *Tanglewreck.* Bloomsbury, 2006. Ages 10–15. (Time warps, London).

Quest Stories

Alexander, Lloyd. *The Book of Three.* Holt, 1964. Ages 10–15. The first of the Prydain Chronicles.

Alexander, Llyod. *The Golden Dreams of Carlo Chuchio.* Holt, 2007. Ages 10–14.

Collins, Suzanne. *Gregor the Overlander.* Scholastic, 2003. Ages 9–14. Underland Chronicles.

Cornish, D. M. *Foundling.* Putnam, 2006. Ages 12–16. See also *Lamplighter* (2008) and *Factotum* (2010). Trilogy.

Crossley-Holland, Kevin. *The Seeing Stone: Arthur Trilogy, Book One.* Scholastic, 2001. Ages 12–16. Arthur trilogy, includes *At the Crossing Places* (2002) and *King of the Middle March* (2004). (England).

DiCamillo, Kate. *The Magician's Elephant.* Illus. Yoko Tamaka. Candlewick, 2009. Ages 9–12.

Divakaruni, Chitra Banerjee. *The Conch Bearer.* Millbrook, 2003. Ages 10–14. (India).

Dowell, Frances O"Roark. *Falling In.* Atheneum, 2010. Ages 9–12.

Farmer, Nancy. *A Sea of Trolls.* Atheneum, 2004. Ages 9–14. (Norse mythology).

Fisher, Catherine. *Day of the Scarab.* Greenwillow, 2006. Ages 10–14. Oracle Prophecies trilogy. (Mediterranean/Egypt).

Flanagan, John. *The Ruins of Gorlan.* Philomel, 2005. Ages 11–15. Rangers Apprentice series. (Australia).

Gardner, Sally. *I, Coriander.* Dial, 2005. Ages 11–14. (England).

Gavin, Jamila. *The Blood Stone.* Farrar, 2005. Ages 12–16. (Venice to Afghanistan, 1700s).

Hodges, Margaret. *Merlin and the Making of the King.* Illus. Trina Schart Hyman. Holiday, 2004. (**PI**). Ages 9–12.

Law, Ingrid. *Savvy.* Dial, 2008. Ages 10–14. Also *Scramble* (2010).

Le Guin, Ursula K. *Gifts: Annals of the Western Shore.* Harcourt, 2007. Ages 11–16. Also *Voices* (2006) and *Powers* (2007).

Lewis, C. S. *The Lion, the Witch and the Wardrobe.* Macmillan, 1950. Ages 9–12. Chronicles of Narnia series. (England).

Morpurgo, Michael. *Sir Gawain and the Green Knight.* Illus. Michael Foreman. Candlewick, 2004. Ages 10–14. (England).

Oppel, Kenneth. *Airborn.* HarperCollins, 2004. Ages 11–14. Also *Skybreaker* (2006) and *Starclimber* (2009). (Canada).

Pratchett, Terry. *Nation.* HarperCollins, 2008. Ages 11–15. (England).

Prineas, Sarah. *The Magic Thief.* HarperCollins, 2008. Ages 9–12. Also *Lost* (2009) and *Found* (2010).

Pullman, Philip. *The Golden Compass.* Knopf, 1996. Ages 12–16. His Dark Materials trilogy.

Riordan, Rick. *The Lightning Thief.* Hyperion, 2005. Ages 10–15. Percy Jackson and the Olympians series.

Rodda, Emily. *The Key to Rondo.* Scholastic, 2007. Ages 9–12. Also *The Wizard of Rondo* (2008).

Rowling, J. K. *Harry Potter and the Sorcerer's Stone.* Scholastic, 1998. Ages 9–13. Harry Potter series. (England).

Sage, Angie. *Magyk.* Katherine Tegen, 2005. Ages 9–12. Septimus Heap series. (England).

Smith, Jeff. *Out from Boneville.* Scholastic, 2005. (**GR**). Ages 9–12. Bones Graphic series.

Stroud, Jonathan. *The Amulet of Samarkand.* Hyperion, 2003. Ages 11–18. Bartimaeus trilogy.

Thal, Lilli. *Mimus.* Trans. John Brownjohn. Annick, 2005. Ages 11–15. (German).

Thompson, Kate. *The New Policeman.* Greenwillow, 2007. Ages 12–16.

Tolkien, J. R. R. *The Hobbit.* Houghton, 1937. Ages 12–18. Also the Lord of the Rings trilogy. (England).

Turner, Megan Whalen. *The King of Attolia.* Greenwillow, 2006. Ages 11–18. Also *The Thief* (1997) and *The Queen of Attolia* (2005).

Weston, Robert. *Zorgmazoo.* Razorbill, 2008. Ages 10–14. (**NV**).

Yolen, Jane. *Sword of the Rightful King: A Novel of King Arthur.* Harcourt, 2003. Ages 11–15.

Science Fiction and Science Fantasy

Adlington, L. J. *The Diary of Pelly D.* Greenwillow, 2005. Ages 12–18. Also *Cherry Heaven* (2008). (England).

Anderson, M. T. *Feed.* Candlewick, 2002. Ages 12–18.

Bertagna, Julie. *Exodus.* Walker, 2008. Ages 12–16.

Boyce, Frank C. *Cosmic.* Walden Pond, 2008. Ages 10–14. (England).

Clements, Andrew. *Things Not Seen.* Philomel, 2002. Ages 10–14.

Collins, Suzanne. *The Hunger Games.* Scholastic, 2008. Ages 12–15. Also *Catching Fire* (2009) and *Mockingjay* (2010).

DuPrau, Jeanne. *The City of Ember.* Random House, 2003. Ages 10–14. Also *The People of Sparks* (2004).

Farmer, Nancy. *The House of the Scorpion.* Simon & Schuster, 2002. Ages 12–18.

Haddix, Margaret Peterson. *Double Identity.* Simon & Schuster, 2005. Ages 10–14.

Kostick, Conor. *Epic.* Viking, 2007. Ages 13–16.

L'Engle, Madeleine. *A Wrinkle in Time.* Farrar, 1962. Ages 11–15.

Lowry, Lois. *The Giver.* Houghton, 1993. Ages 11–15. Also *Messenger* (2004) and *Gathering Blue* (2000).

Reeve, Philip. *Mortal Engines.* HarperCollins, 2003. Ages 12–18. The first of the Hungry Cities Chronicles. (England).

Reeve, Philip. *Larklight: A Rousing Tale of Dauntless Pluck in the Farthest Reaches of Space.* Bloomsbury, 2006. Ages 10–15.

Strahan, Jonathan. *The Starry Rift: Tales of New Tomorrows.* Viking, 2008. (**COL**). Ages 13–18.

Waugh, Sylvia. *Earthborn.* Delacorte, 2002. Ages 9–13.

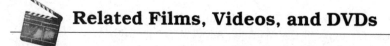

Related Films, Videos, and DVDs

Charlotte's Web. (2006). Author: E. B. White (1952). 113 minutes.

The Chronicles of Narnia: The Lion, the Witch and the Wardrobe. (2005). Author: C. S. Lewis (1955). 140 minutes.

City of Ember. (2008). Author: Jeanne DuPrau (2003). 95 minutes.

Coraline. (2009). Author: Neil Gaiman (2002). 100 minutes.

Ella Enchanted. (2004). Author: Gail Carson Levine (1997). 96 minutes.

Eragon. (2006). Author: Christopher Paolini (2003). 120 minutes.

The Golden Compass. (2007). Author: Philip Pullman (1996). 113 minutes.

Harry Potter and the Sorcerer's Stone. (2001). Author: J. K. Rowling (1998). 152 minutes. Seven others in the series also available.

The Hunger Games. (2011). Author: Suzanne Collins (2008). 144 minutes,

Inkheart. (2008). Author: Cornelia Funke (2003). 106 minutes.

The Seeker: The Dark Is Rising. (2007). Author: Susan Cooper (1973). 99 minutes.

Shrek. (2001). Author: William Steig (1990). 90 minutes. Also *Shrek 2* (2004) and *Shrek the Third* (2007).

Thief Lord. (2006). Author: Cornelia Funke (2002). 98 minutes.

Tuck Everlasting. (2002). Author: Natalie Babbitt (1975). 88 minutes.

The Water Horse. (2007). Author: Dick King-Smith. (1998). 112 minutes.

A Wrinkle in Time. (2003). Author: Madeleine L'Engle (1962). 128 minutes.

Chapter Eight

Realistic Fiction

Listening to Grownups Quarreling,

standing in the hall against the
wall with my little brother, blown
like leaves against the wall by their
voices, my head like a pingpong ball
between the paddles of their anger:
I knew what it meant
to tremble like a leaf.

Cold with their wrath, I heard
the claws of the rain
pounce. Floods
poured through the city,
skies clapped over me,
and I was shaken, shaken
like a mouse
between their jaws.

—*Ruth Whitman*

Children of all ages are drawn to stories about people who seem like themselves or who are involved in familiar activities. Realistic stories deal with the realities of children's lives, the sad and harsh situations as well as the happy and humorous. These realistic fiction stories have appealed to children for many years and continue to do so today.

Definition and Description

Realistic fiction refers to stories that could happen to people and animals. The protagonists of these stories are fictitious characters created by the author, but their actions and reactions are quite like those of real people or real animals. Sometimes events in these stories are exaggerated or outlandish; however, it is within the realm of possibility for such improbable events to occur. On the other hand, some realistic fiction incorporates actual people, places, or events, in which case these factual aspects of the story need to be recorded accurately.

Contemporary realism is a term used to describe stories that take place in the present time and portray attitudes and mores of the present culture. Unlike realistic books of several decades ago that depicted only happy families and were never controversial, today's contemporary realism often focuses on current societal issues, such as alcoholism, racism, poverty, and homelessness. Contemporary books still tell of the happy, funny times in children's lives, but they also include the harsh, unpleasant times that are a part of many children's lives.

Excellent Realistic Fiction to Read Aloud

Alvarez, Julia. *How Tia Lola Learned to Teach.* Ages 8–12.

Birdsall, Jeanne. *The Penderwicks on Gardam Street.* Ages 9–12.

Cummings, Priscilla. *Red Kayak.* Ages 11–15.

DiCamillo, Kate. *Bink & Gollie.* Illustrated by Tony Fucile. Ages 6–9.

Harper, Charise M. *Just Grace Walks the Dog.* Ages 7–9.

Horvath, Polly. *The Pepins and Their Problems.* Ages 8–12.

Lord, Cynthia. *Rules.* Ages 9–13.

Lowry, Lois. *Gooney Bird and the Room Mother.* Ages 7–9.

Nicholls, Sally. *Ways to Live Forever.* Ages 9–12.

O'Connor, Barbara. *The Small Adventure of Popeye and Elvis.* Ages 9–12.

Pennypacker, Sara. *Clementine's Letter.* Illustrated by Marla Frazee. Ages 7–10.

Resau, Laura. *Star in the Forest.* Ages 9–12.

Ritter, John H. *The Boy Who Saved Baseball.* Ages 10–13.

Smith, Hope Anita. *Keeping the Night Watch.* Illustrated by E. B. Lewis. Ages 11–15.

Tarshis, Lauren. *Emma-Jean Lazarus Fell Out of a Tree.* Ages 10–14.

Urban, Linda. *Hound Dog True.* Ages 8–12.

Because of the difficult nature of the issues in some realistic fiction, these books are often the target of censors who argue that children need to be protected from these issues. In their attempts to protect the perceived "innocence" of children, adults fail to face the reality of children's lives in today's world. Many children are dealing with complex life situations; they read to battle the real monsters in their lives or to deal with situations that seem to be outside their control. Literature provides a way for them to gain valuable perspectives on these issues, to realize that they are not alone, and to experience the strategies characters use to respond to challenging situations. They read for entertainment, but they also read because books provide them with hope as they face everyday and epic dangers. In addition, reading about other children's challenging situations can help those who are not facing these problems develop empathy. Children need perspective, not protection.

Authors of contemporary realistic fiction set their stories in the present or recent past. But, in time, features of these stories, such as dialogue and allusions to popular culture, customs, and dress, become dated and the stories are therefore no longer contemporary, though they may still be realistic. Older stories that obviously no longer describe today's world, though they may have once been contemporary realistic fiction, are now simply realistic fiction. Older realistic fiction stories that are considered modern classics are included in this chapter.

Evaluation and Selection of Realistic Fiction

The criteria for evaluating realistic fiction are the same as those for any work of fiction. Well-developed characters who manifest change as a result of significant life events, a well-structured plot with sufficient conflict and suspense to hold the reader's interest, a time and place suitable to the storyline, and a worthy theme are basic literary elements expected of any work of fiction. Specific evaluation issues in realistic fiction include:

- **Does the story permit some cause for hope?** Children need to trust that adverse and discouraging social situations can be overcome or ameliorated and that they can take action to make the world a better place in which to live. Children need hope that is realistic to their life situations, not wishful thinking.

- **Is the story a thin disguise for a heavy-handed moral lesson?** Realistic fiction often conveys values, such as kindness and generosity, but children resist stories that preach. The moral should not overwhelm the story, but be a logical outcome.

- **Is the story believable?** Are the events possible, even though all aspects are not probable? Sometimes an author goes close to the edge of the believable range to produce a more exciting, suspense-filled story, but should avoid the overuse of coincidence in order to resolve the plot.

- **Have you selected a range of stories, including humorous stories?** An aspect of writing style that children greatly appreciate is humor. Humorous stories feature characters caught up in silly situations or involved in funny escapades, such as *Bink and Gollie* by Kate DiCamillo and *The Pepins and Their Problems* by Polly Horvath.

- **Does your selection of realistic fiction offer the richness of experience to children that they deserve and provide for the varied reading interests of children?** Be sure to balance humorous stories with those dealing with serious and controversial issues.

Intermediate-grade children report on reading interest surveys that realistic fiction is their favorite genre. Although book collections need to include a range of genres to reach all children as readers, realistic fiction holds high appeal for many children at all grade levels.

The Significance of Character in Realistic Fiction

Although all of the literary elements are significant within realistic fiction, character plays a particularly critical role and often determines whether a book stays with the reader over time. As adults we frequently forget the plot of favorite childhood books, but remember characters to whom we had a strong connection. Children need to share their personal connections and discuss the issues they find significant within a particular book, and then revisit that book to consider the ways in which the author has developed intriguing characters. If literature is to help children understand life, then the portrayal of characters needs to be carefully considered by asking:

- How does the author reveal the character (e.g., by the character's actions, speech, or appearance; visual depictions in illustrations; others' comments or thoughts; the author's comments)?
- Do characters act and talk in ways that are consistent with their age, gender, and culture?
- Do the characters grow and change in a believable manner over the course of the book?
- Does the author portray a range of qualities for major and minor characters in order to avoid stereotypes?

Historical Overview of Realistic Fiction

The earliest realistic stories were didactic ones intended to teach morality and manners to young readers. The characters of the 1700s were wooden, lifeless boys and girls whose lives were spent in good works; however, in England during this period, two significant events affecting the future of children's literature occurred. *Robinson Crusoe* by Daniel Defoe, an exciting survival story, was published in 1719 for adults but became a popular book among children. Then in 1744, John Newbery began to publish, expressly for a child audience, books of realistic fiction intended to entertain as well as to educate. These two events laid the groundwork for establishing children's literature as a separate branch of literature.

The first type of realistic fiction for children that avoided the heavy didactic persuasion was the adventure story. Imitators of *Robinson Crusoe* were many, including the *Swiss Family Robinson* by Johann Wyss of Switzerland in 1812. Later adventure stories from England were *Treasure Island* (1883) and *Kidnapped* (1886) by Robert Louis Stevenson, and from the U.S., *The Adventures of Tom Sawyer* (1876) and *The Adventures of Huckleberry Finn* (1884) by Mark Twain (pseudonym of Samuel Clemens).

Realistic family stories came on the scene during the 1800s with *Little Women* (1868) by Louisa May Alcott. The family story remained a favorite in the twentieth century with such memorable books as *Anne of Green Gables* (1908) by Canadian Lucy Maud Montgomery and *The Secret Garden* (1911) by Frances Hodgson Burnett. Since their characters were orphans, these books can be considered precursors of stories that address the needs of children with problems. Stories of happy and often large families continued to thrive and peaked in the 1940s and 1950s in stories about the Moffat family by Eleanor Estes and the Melendy family by Elizabeth Enright. These happy family stories seem lighthearted compared with today's contemporary realism.

Children from other lands is another theme that can be found in many realistic stories for children. *Hans Brinker, or The Silver Skates* (1865) by Mary Mapes Dodge and *Heidi* (1880) by Johanna Spyri of Switzerland are set in Holland and Switzerland, respectively.

Realistic animal stories for children appeared in the late 1800s. *Black Beauty* (1877) by Anna Sewell was a plea for humane treatment of animals, although it is quite sentimental in places and completely personified (i.e., the animal is given human qualities). Animal stories showing the maturing of the young human protagonist who assists the animal remain popular today.

Regional stories and stories about children of minority groups appeared with more frequency in the 1940s. *Strawberry Girl* (1945) by Lois Lenski featured rural Florida and was one of the first regional stories. It was only in the 1960s and 1970s that books written by authors of

MILESTONES in the Development of Realistic Fiction

Date	Event	Significance
1719	*Robinson Crusoe* by Daniel Defoe (England)	Early survival/adventure on a desert island; many imitators
1812	*Swiss Family Robinson* by Johann Wyss (Switzerland)	Most successful imitation of *Robinson Crusoe*
1868	*Little Women* by Louisa May Alcott (U.S.)	Popular early family story
1876	*The Adventures of Tom Sawyer* by Mark Twain (U.S.)	Classic adventure story set along the Mississippi River
1877	*Black Beauty* by Anna Sewell (England)	Early horse story deploring inhumane treatment of animals
1880	*Heidi* by Johanna Spyri (Switzerland)	An early international story popular in the U.S.
1883	*Treasure Island* by Robert Louis Stevenson (England)	Classic adventure story with pirates
1908	*Anne of Green Gables* by Lucy Maud Montgomery (Canada)	Early family story about an orphan and her new family
1911	*The Secret Garden* by Frances Hodgson Burnett (U.S.)	A classic sentimental novel of two children adjusting to life
1938	*The Yearling* by Marjorie Kinnan Rawlings (U.S.)	Classic animal story and coming-of-age story
1964	*Harriet the Spy* by Louise Fitzhugh (U.S.)	The beginning of the new realism movement
1970	*Are You There, God? It's Me, Margaret* by Judy Blume (U.S.)	Early book with frank treatment of sex

color began to achieve national recognition. Two early noteworthy examples that portray African-American childhood experiences are *Zeely* (1967) by Virginia Hamilton and *Stevie* (1969) by John Steptoe.

A new era in realistic fiction was ushered in with the publication of *Harriet the Spy* by Louise Fitzhugh in 1964. This story of an unhappy and, at times, unpleasant girl depicted Harriet, her parents, and her classmates as anything but ideal or sympathetic human beings. This trend toward a more graphic and explicitly truthful portrayal of life and the inclusion of many topics that were previously considered taboo continued in children's books in the 1970s and 1980s and still prevails today. Controversial topics such as death, divorce, drugs, alcoholism, and disabilities, which have always been a part of childhood, became permissible topics in children's books. Parents and other adults were portrayed as they truly are, not as one might believe they should be. This newer, franker brand of realism, sometimes referred to as the ***new realism,*** changed the world of children's books. The new realism books may be less lighthearted than their predecessors, but they are also more truthful and real in portraying the actual lives of children.

Topics in Realistic Fiction

The subject matter of realistic fiction includes the child's whole world of relationships with self and others: the joys, sorrows, challenges, adjustments, anxieties, and satisfactions of human life. Realistic books often address more than one aspect of human life; thus, some realistic fiction books can be categorized by more than one of the following topics.

Families

Stories about the ***nuclear family***—children and their relationships with parents and siblings—are a natural subject of books for children. Childhood for most children is spent in close contact with family members. Family stories for younger children often portray a happy child with loving parents. In these stories, everyday activities from brushing teeth to cooking dinner are shown, such as in *What Happens on Wednesdays* by Emily Jenkins. Easy chapter books appealing to newly independent readers are also prevalent, often showing the child at play and exploring sibling relationships, such as in *Clementine and the Family Meeting* by Sara Pennypacker and *Ling & Ting: Not Exactly the Same!* by Grace Lin.

Extended families can frequently be found in children's books. Aunts, uncles, grandparents, stepparents, and cousins are important in the real lives of many children and are integral in stories for children, such as *Waiting for Normal* by Leslie Connor *and The Hello, Goodbye Window* by Norton Juster.

The ***alternative family*** of today's world is also depicted in family stories. Separation, divorce, single-parent families, adoptive families, foster families, same-sex parents, and reconstructed families of stepparents and stepchildren are often the backdrop of stories as in *Being Bee* by Catherine Bateson, *The Penderwicks on Gardam Street* by Jeanne Birdsall, and *Molly's Family* by Nancy Garden. The difficulty children and adults encounter in adjusting to these new family situations often is the primary conflict. It is important for children to see families other than the typical mother, father, and two children portrayed positively. They need to find themselves and their families in books.

Peers

In addition to adapting to one's family situation, children must also learn to cope with their peers. Many realistic stories show children struggling for *acceptance by peers* in a group situation, often in school settings, such as in *Just Grace* by Charise M. Harper and *Fame and Glory in Freedom, Georgia* by Barbara O'Connor.

Bullying by peers can be damaging to the self-esteem of those targeted. Angry outbursts by those being humiliated are not infrequent and, at times, can be frightening. Literature can provide an opportunity to address these issues by developing an awareness and understanding of the harm caused and by encouraging more compassion toward those who are targeted for some real or perceived difference. In Wendelin Van Draanen's *Secret Identity,* Nolan, a fifth-grade outsider, becomes fed up with the school bully and finds an ingenious way to expose the bully's misdeeds. Although the treatment is humorous, the problem can be raised in discussion of the book.

Developing *close friendships* is another focus of stories about peer relationships across gender, age, and culture. A concern for friendship and how to be a good friend are shared traits of these stories. *Bird Lake Moon* by Kevin Henkes, *The Small Adventures of Popeye and Elvis* by Barbara O'Connor, and *Emma-Jean Lazarus Fell Out of a Tree* by Lauren Tarshis are good examples of this type of book.

Physical, Emotional, Mental, and Behavioral Challenges

Many children must deal with difficult challenges in their lives. Some children have disabilities; others have a family member or a friend with a disability. These disabilities may be **physical,** such as scoliosis; **emotional,** such as bipolar disorder; **mental,** such as mental retardation or learning disabilities; **behavioral,** such as hyperactivity; or a combination of these. Authors of children's books are becoming increasingly sensitive to the need for positive portrayals of individuals with special challenges and the need for children with these challenges to find their lives reflected in books.

Well-written, honest stories of such individuals in books can help other children gain an understanding of disabilities and empathize with people who have disabilities. With the inclusion of special education students into regular classrooms, this trend in children's literature can be an important educational resource. Cynthia Lord's *Rules* includes an autistic brother and a paraplegic friend as minor characters, and in Sarah Week's *So B. It,* the central character lives with her developmentally disabled mother and is cared for by her neighbor who is agoraphobic. Recent books are written from the perspective of the character who is dealing with a disability, such as Nora Raleigh Baskin's *Anything but Typical* in the voice of an autistic boy who wants to be a writer and Sharon Draper's *Out of My Mind* in the voice of a girl with cerebral palsy who discovers a device that allows her to speak for the first time.

Local and Global Communities

Growing up includes the discovery of one's membership in a *community,* a group extending beyond the family. In some children's books, school settings are depicted in which students, teachers, administrators, and, at times, parents constitute the community. Helen Frost's novel told through twenty-two poetic forms, *Spinning through the Universe: A Novel in Poems from Room 214,* shows students, the teacher, and the custodian writing their thoughts.

In other books the community setting is the neighborhood. An old favorite, *Seedfolks* by Paul Fleischman, tells the story of a neighborhood coming together around a community garden in chapters narrated by each character. *One Day and One Amazing Morning on Orange Street* by

Joanne Rocklin and *What Happened on Fox Street* by Tricia Springstubb are recent examples of communities uniting to take action and to care for each other.

Living in a diverse community involves establishing significant relationships that go across gender and race, but this diversity can also be a source of racism and discrimination. The books that most frequently portray racism tend to be historical fiction, providing children with the false impression that racism is in the past. Books such *as The Absolutely True Diary of a Part-Time Indian* by Sherman Alexie and *The Cruisers* by Walter Dean Myers challenge this misconception.

Community extends beyond one's own country to communities around the world. With increasing interdependence among countries, young people will likely be more connected to an international community than ever before. Books set in global cultures can help children and adolescents develop an awareness and sense of connection with people from other countries and an appreciation for people whose lives differ from their own. They particularly need contemporary images of life around the world since the majority of novels are historical fiction, leading to misconceptions of these cultures as set back in time. Examples include *City Boy* by Jan Michael, set in urban and rural Malawi, *Minji's Salon* by Eun-hee Choung, set in South Korea, and *Wanting Mor* by Rukhsana Khan, set in Afghanistan.

Animals

Animal stories remain an ever-popular genre with children, with dog and horse stories being the most popular. In the strictest sense, the animal protagonist in realistic animal fiction behaves like an animal and is not personified. Usually, a child is also a protagonist in these stories, as in *Because of Winn-Dixie* by Kate DiCamillo and *How to Steal a Dog* by Barbara O'Connor.

Animals are frequently the main characters in children's picture books where the story is realistic, except that family members are visually portrayed as animals. Although technically these books are classified as fantasy, their stories focus on realistic events and they have no fantastic or magical element. Anthony Browne, for example, uses gorillas for his books about parents, *My Mom* and *My Dad,* where the characters are not talking gorillas but parents who happen to be portrayed as animals. Another example is the well-loved books of Kevin Henkes, such as *Lily's Purple Plastic Purse* and *Chrysanthemum,* with characters who act as human beings but are visually portrayed as mice. Letting animals play out human roles provides intellectual and emotional distance and opens a safe space for children to reflect on the issues and choices in their lives.

Sports and Mysteries

Sports and mysteries remain popular genres that have wide appeal, including to children who are reluctant readers. Sports stories often present a story in which a child protagonist struggles to become accepted as a member of a team and does eventually succeed through determination and hard work. *The Batboy* and other books by Mike Lupica are good examples of sports stories. Although traditionally written with boys as the main characters, some sports stories are now available that feature girls as protagonists, such as Dawn FitzGerald's *Soccer Chick Rules*

Mysteries range from simple "whodunits" to complex character stories. The element of suspense is a strong part of the appeal of these stories, such as *Chasing Vermeer* by Blue Balliett and *Flush* by Carl Hiaasen. Mysteries have won more state children's choice awards than any other type of story. The Edgar Allan Poe Award for Juvenile Mystery Novels, given to U.S. authors, can be helpful in selecting good mysteries (see Appendix A).

Notable Authors of Realistic Fiction

Julia Alvarez, author of novels about family and community, with a focus on bilingualism and immigration. *Return to Sender* and Tia Lola series, including *How Tia Lola Learned to Teach.* www.juliaalvarez.com

Sharon Creech, author of novels about girls seeking their families to find themselves. *Walk Two Moons; Ruby Holler; The Wanderer.* www .sharoncreech.com

Jack Gantos, author of Joey Pigza novels about a boy with attention deficit disorder, as well as autobiographical books. *Heads or Tails: Stories from the Sixth Grade; Joey Pigza Swallowed the Key.* www.jackgantos.com

Jean Craighead George, author of ecological fiction and survival in nature stories. *Julie of the Wolves; My Side of the Mountain.* www.jean craigheadgeorge.com

Lenore Look, author of short chapter books focusing on Chinese-American family life and relationships. *Ruby Lu, Star of the Show; Alvin Ho: Allergic to Girls, School, and Other Scary Things.*

Polly Horvath, author of realistic and often humorous family stories. *The Trolls* (Boston Globe/ Horn Book Award); *Everything on a Waffle; The Canning Season* (National Book Award); *My One Hundred Adventures.* www.pollyhorvath.com

Walter Dean Myers, author of novels about African-American adolescents in urban settings. *Scorpions; Slam!; Lockdown.* www.walterdeanmyers.net

Barbara O'Connor, author of realistic stories of families and peer relationships. *How to Steal a Dog; The Small Adventure of Popeye and Elvis; Fame and Glory in Freedom, Georgia.* www.barboconnor.com

Katherine Paterson, author of stories featuring relationships with peers and family. *The Great Gilly Hopkins; Bridge to Terabithia.* www.terabithia.com

Gary Paulsen, author of nature survival adventures often set in the northern U.S. or Canada. *Hatchet; The River.* www.garypaulsen.com

Jerry Spinelli, author of realistic novels of peers and their escapades. *Maniac Magee* (Newbery Medal); *Wringer* (Newbery Honor book). www .jerryspinelli.com

Wendelin Van Draanen, author of the popular Sammy Keyes mystery series featuring a funny and clever heroine who has to extricate herself from difficult situations. *Sammy Keyes and the Dead Giveaway; Flipped.* www.randomhouse .com/kids/vandraanen

Jacqueline Woodson, author of novels with African-American characters that often treat sensitive issues of sexuality, abuse, and race. *Locomotion; Hush; After Tupac and D Foster.* www.jacquelinewoodson.com

Three recent series of interest to mystery readers are the Bloodwater Mysteries by Pete Hautman and Mary Logue, the 39 Clues by Rick Riordan and other authors, and the Red Blazer Girls by Michael Beil. An established series with a female protagonist, the Sammy Keyes series (beginning with *Sammy Keyes and the Hotel Thief*) by Wendelin Van Draanen, remains popular.

Romance and Sexuality

Romance stories are popular with preteens and teens, especially girls. Some stories depict boy-girl friendships, as in *The Possibilities of Sainthood* by Donna Freitas, *Under the Watson's Porch* by Susan Shreve, and *Deep Down Popular* by Phoebe Stone. Since the 1990s, more stories of characters dealing with pregnancy and teenage parenting have appeared; some realistic examples are

Virginia Euwer Wolff's *Make Lemonade,* Sylvia Olsen's *The Girl with a Baby,* and Angela Johnson's *The First Part Last.*

Children become aware of their growing sexuality during preteen and teen years as they mature. Some stories for older teens show attraction between members of the opposite sex as well as members of the same sex, with the beginning of sexual activity sometimes depicted in relationships. Stories that portray the struggle of young people coming to terms with a homosexual or lesbian sexual orientation are seen more frequently than they were in the past; other stories show the cruelty of society toward young homosexuals or lesbians, such as in *The Misfits* by James Howe and *So Hard to Say* by Alex Sanchez.

Adventure and Survival

Facing physical danger, an external force, also contributes to the maturing process. Stories of *survival and adventure* are ones in which the young protagonist must rely on will and ingenuity to survive a life-threatening situation. Although most survival stories are set in isolated places, a growing number are set in cities where gangs, drug wars, and abandonment are life threatening. Adventure stories may be set in any environment where the protagonist has freedom of action, as found in *Wilderness* by Roddy Doyle and *Small as an Elephant* by Jennifer Jacobson, about a boy who has been abandoned by his mother.

A recent type of survival story is stories of immigration, particularly when the characters lack legal status and live with the constant fear of deportation, as in *Ask Me No Questions* by Marina Budhos, in which a Muslim family struggles to survive after 9-11. In *Star in the Forest* by Laura Resau, a young girl struggles with trusting anyone after her father is deported to Mexico, and in Julie Alvarez's *Return to Sender,* a farm family's survival depends on migrant Mexican workers who are also struggling to survive amidst the threat of immigration raids. Another recent trend are refugee and war stories, such as *A Long Walk to Water* by Linda Sue Park, based on the life of a boy separated from his family in the Sudan war.

Difficult Life Decisions and Coming of Age

Characters in many realistic fiction novels face moments of crisis, situations of great difficulty, or events in which a decision may change someone's life. These situations are often similar to those that children will face in their lives. Through these stories children can understand the difficult decisions faced by the character and can discuss the consequences that may result from their choices. Teachers often select these books for literature discussions. Using a book in which a character is faced with a difficult moral choice can stimulate lively discussions. An example is Priscilla Cummings's *Red Kayak,* in which a 13-year-old boy faces a conflict between telling police the truth in a tragic accidental death or remaining loyal to his friends.

From birth to age 10, most children's lives revolve around family, friends, and classmates, but during the preteen and teen years a shift toward self-discovery and independence occurs. Rapid growth and change are seen in the physical, emotional, moral, and intellectual domains of life. These changes and the struggles encountered as children move toward adulthood are referred to as *coming-of-age stories* or *rite-of-passage books*. Examples of rite-of-passage books that focus on a particular event in a child's life and signal a change from child to adult are *Olive's Ocean* by Kevin Henkes and *The Year the Swallows Came Early* by Kathryn Fitzmaurice. Often these events grow out of life situations which force the character to make difficult choices and so reach new understandings about themselves and their world.

Reader Connections: Paired Character Trait Books

Realistic stories in which characters are faced with difficult life choices can provide the foundation for programs of *character education,* a process intended to engage children in considering core values and to build awareness of these values among teachers and parents. The Josephson Institute of Ethics, in conjunction with a nonsectarian coalition, promotes the framework *Character Counts,* which consists of six values with related traits. Although this program consists of materials to use in schools, these same values are expressed in good literature as the basis for understanding and developing moral reasoning. A powerful piece of literature can address the complexities of how these values play out in actual life situations, resisting simplistic doctrines of right and wrong. Moralizing and preaching are seldom appreciated by children. If the moral or lesson overpowers the story, children will resist the obvious preaching and balk at reading such stories. They want powerful stories that excite them, amuse them, and inspire them.

The following list features a paired set of picture books for each of the six values, along with a novel that could be used for read-aloud or literature discussion groups on that value. For each value, a picture book that addresses the trait in a straightforward manner is paired with a book that raises questions about the situational complexity of the value. Reading and responding to the paired books can help children formulate their own understandings of the complexities of these values. They can be asked to provide evidence for their statements about the ways in which these values are addressed within each book, a textual analysis strategy highlighted in the Common Core State Standards.

Trustworthiness: Build trust through integrity, honesty, loyalty, promise-keeping.
- Bunting, Eve. *A Day's Work*. Illustrated by David Diaz.
- Amado, Elisa. *Tricycle*. Illustrated by Alfonso Ruano.
- Literature discussion novel: Bredsdorff, Bodil. *The Crow Girl*.

Respect: Honor the dignity and worth of each person.
- O'Neill, Alexis. *The Recess Queen*. Illustrated by Laura Huliska-Beith.
- Coffelt, Nancy. *Fred Stays with Me*. Illustrated by Tricia Tusa.
- Literature discussion novel: Draper, Sharon. *Out of My Mind*.

Responsibility: Show accountability, self-control, self-reliance, persistence, hard-working traits.
- Wyeth, Sharon. *Something Beautiful*. Illustrated by Chris Soentpiet.
- Bang, Molly. *When Sophie Gets Angry—Really, Really Angry. . . .*
- Literature discussion novel: Cummings, Priscilla. *Red Kayak*.

Fairness: Demonstrate consistent, careful decision-making, equitable treatment.
- Khan, Rukhsana. *Big Red Lollipop*. Illustrated by Sophie Blackall.
- Recorvits, Helen. *Yoon and the Jade Bracelet*. Illustrated by Gabi Swiatkowska.
- Literature discussion novel: Spinelli, Jerry. *Wringer*.

Caring: Be kind, compassionate, empathetic, forgiving, grateful.

- Fleming, Virginia. *Be Good to Eddie Lee*. Illustrated by Floyd Cooper.
- Steptoe, John. *Stevie*.
- Literature discussion novel: Ryan, Pam Muñoz. *Becoming Naomi Leon*.

Citizenship: Obey laws, improve well-being of others, engage in active participation.

- Anzaldúa, Gloria. *Friends from the Other Side*. Illustrated by Consuelo Méndez.
- McGovern, Ann. *The Lady in the Box*. Illustrated by Marni Backer.
- Literature discussion novel: Fleischman, Paul. *Seedfolks*.

Realistic fiction presents familiar situations with which children can readily identify, often reflects contemporary life, and portrays settings not so different from the homes, schools, towns, and cities of today's children. The protagonists of these stories are frequently testing themselves as they grow toward adulthood; young readers can therefore empathize and gain insight into their own predicaments. Keeping current with the many excellent realistic stories being published is essential to providing a wide range of books that will entertain, encourage, and inspire students.

 Invitations for Further Investigation

- Read and discuss a paired picture book set for one of the character values. Web descriptions of that value and the complex issues in how it plays out in different situations. Also read the novel associated with that value and add to the web.

- Create a list of favorite childhood books or stories that have stayed in your memory. Revisit one or two of those books to determine why that book had such a strong appeal for you as a child and to examine the portrayal of the characters in the book.

- Select a realistic fiction novel and create a heart map that shows the ideas, values, and people that are important to one of the main characters and that also depicts how that character changes in the novel. Create a list of devices used by the author that helped you get to know that character.

- Select and read three to five winners of the Edgar Allan Poe Award for Juvenile Mystery Novels. (See Appendix A.) Compare and contrast these novels, considering the source and type of mystery, the devices used to cause suspense, and the elements of realism and fantasy in each story.

- Select fifteen realistic fiction novels suitable for a particular grade level in which you are participating. Booktalk and display these novels for a group of eight students, then ask them to complete an interest ballot. What did you discover about their reading preferences from this activity?

- Gather a set of picture books that use animals as main characters. Consider which are based in realistic settings and situations with animals taking the role of humans and so might be considered realistic fiction and which are fantasy with talking animals. Consider the role of animals in books for children by reading Burke and Copenhaver (2004).

References

Burke, C., & Copenhaver, J. (2004). Animals as people in children's literature. *Language Arts 81*(3), 205–213.

Whitman, R. (1968). Listening to grownups quarreling. In R. Whitman (Ed.), *The marriage wig and other stories.* Orlando, FL: Harcourt.

Recommended Realistic Fiction Books

Ages indicated refer to content appropriateness and conceptual and interest levels. Formats other than novels will be coded as follows:

(PI) Picture book
(GR) Graphic novel
(COL) Short story collection
(NV) Novel in verse

Families

Acampora, Paul. *Defining Dulcie.* Dial, 2006. Ages 12–15.

Banks, Kate. *Dillon Dillon.* Farrar, 2002. Ages 10–13.

Bateson, Catherine. *Being Bee.* Holiday, 2007. Ages 8–12. (Australia).

Birdsall, Jeanne. *The Penderwicks: A Summer Tale of Four Sisters, Two Rabbits, and a Very Interesting Boy.* Knopf, 2005. Ages 9–12. Also *The Penderwicks on Gardam Street* (2008).

Browne, Anthony. *My Dad.* Grimm, 2001. **(PI).** Ages 5–9. Also *My Mom.* Grimm, (2005). **(PI).** (England).

Cohn, Rachel. *The Steps.* Simon & Schuster, 2003. Ages 9–13.

Connor, Leslie. *Waiting for Normal.* Katherine Tegan Books, 2008. Ages 10–13.

Creech, Sharon. *Ruby Holler.* HarperCollins, 2002. Ages 8–11. Also *Walk Two Moons* (1994).

Creech, Sharon. *Heartbeat.* HarperCollins, 2004. **(NV).** Ages 9–14.

Creech, Sharon. *Replay.* HarperCollins, 2005. Ages 9–13. Includes a short play featured in the story.

Fogelin, Adriana. *The Big Nothing.* Peachtree, 2004. Ages 11–14.

Fusco, Kimberly Newton. *Tending to Grace.* Knopf, 2004. Ages 12–15.

Garden, Nancy. *Molly's Family.* Illus. Sharon Wooding. Farrar, 2004. **(PI).** Ages 5–8.

Giff, Patricia Reilly. *Pictures of Hollis Woods.* Wendy Lamb, 2002. Ages 10–12.

Gonzalez, Julie. *Wings.* Delacorte, 2005. Ages 12–16. Two parallel narrators.

Goscinny, René. *Nicholas Again.* Trans. Anthea Bell. Illus. Jean Jacques Sempé. Phaidon, 2006. Ages 9–12. (France).

Grimes, Nikki. *Dark Sons.* Hyperion, 2005. Ages 11–16.

Hannigan, Katherine. *Ida B: . . . and Her Plans to Maximize Fun, Avoid Disaster, and (Possibly) Save the World.* Greenwillow, 2004. Ages 9–12.

Henkes, Kevin. *Lilly's Purple Plastic Purse.* Greenwillow, 1996. **(PI).** Ages 5–8. Also *Chrysanthemum* (1991).

Hicks, Betty. *Out of Order.* Roaring Brook, 2005. Ages 9–12.

Horvath, Polly. *The Canning Season.* Farrar, 2003. Ages 12–16.

Horvath, Polly. *The Pepins and Their Problems.* Farrar, 2004. Ages 8–12. (Humorous).

Jenkins, Emily. *What Happens on Wednesdays.* Illus. Lauren Castillo. Frances Foster Books, 2007. **(PI).** Ages 3–6.

Jones, Kimberly K. *Sand Dollar Summer.* Simon & Schuster, 2006. Ages 10–14.

Juster, Norton. *The Hello, Goodbye Window.* Illus. Chris Raschka. Hyperion, 2005. **(PI).** Ages 4–7.

Khan, Ruksana. *Big Red Lollipop.* Illus. Sophie Blackall. Viking, 2010. **(PI)**. Ages 4–8. (Pakistani Canadian).

Leavitt, Martine. *Heck Superhero.* Front Street, 2004. Ages 12–15.

Lin, Grace. *Ling & Ting: Not Exactly the Same!* Little Brown, 2010. **(COL)**. Ages 6–9.

Look, Lenore. *Ruby Lu, Star of the Show.* Atheneum, 2011. Ages 8–11.

Mason, Simon. *The Quigleys in a Spin.* Illus. Helen Stephens. Random, 2006. Ages 8–11.

McKay, Hilary. *Forever Rose.* M. K. McElderry Books, 2008. Ages 10–14. Casson Family series. (England).

Naylor, Phyllis Reynolds. *Roxie and the Hooligans.* Atheneum, 2006. Ages 7–10. (Humorous).

Nelson, Theresa. *Ruby Electric.* Simon & Schuster, 2003. Ages 10–13.

O'Connor, Barbara. *How to Steal a Dog.* Farrar, 2007. Ages 10–12.

Paterson, Katherine. *The Great Gilly Hopkins.* Crowell, 1978. Ages 9–12.

Paterson, Katherine. *The Same Stuff as Stars.* Clarion, 2002. Ages 10–13.

Pennypacker, Sara. *Clementine and the Family Meeting.* Disney/Hyperion Books, 2011. **(PI)**. Ages 7–10.

Scieszka, Jon, editor. *Guys Write for Guys Read: Boys' Favorite Authors Write about Being Boys.* Viking, 2005. **(COL)**. Ages 10–14.

Smith, Hope Anita. *The Way a Door Closes.* Illus. Shane W. Evans. Holt, 2003. **(NV)**. Ages 10–13.

Smith, Hope Anita. *Keeping the Night Watch.* Illus. E. B. Lewis. Holt, 2008. **(NV)**. Ages 11–15.

Tolan, Stephanie S. *Surviving the Applewhites.* HarperCollins, 2002. Ages 10–14.

Twice Told: Original Stories Inspired by Original Artwork. Illus. Scott Hunt. Dutton, 2006. **(COL)**. Ages 12–16. Pairs of popular, acclaimed authors respond to the same illustration.

Van Draanen, Wendelin. *Runaway.* Knopf, 2006. Ages 12–16.

Williams, Vera B. *Amber Was Brave, Essie Was Smart: The Story of Amber and Essie Told Here in Poems and Pictures.* Greenwillow, 2001. **(NV)**. Ages 6–10.

Peers

Castellucci, Cecil. *The Plain Janes.* Illus. Jim Rugg. DC Comics, 2007. **(GR)**. Ages 12–18.

Creech, Sharon. *Love That Dog.* HarperCollins, 2001. **(NV)**. Ages 9–14.

Creech, Sharon. *Granny Torrelli Makes Soup.* Illus. Chris Raschka. HarperCollins, 2003. **(NV)**. Ages 9–13.

DiCamillo, Kate, and McGhee, Alison. *Bink & Gollie.* Illus. Tony Fucile. Candlewick, 2010. **(PI)**. Ages 6–9.

Dowell, Frances O'Roark. *Chicken Boy.* Atheneum, 2005. Ages 9–13.

Fine, Anne. *Up on Cloud Nine.* Delacorte, 2002. Ages 10–13.

Gantos, Jack. *Heads or Tails: Stories from the Sixth Grade.* Farrar. 1994. Ages 10–14.

Grindley, Sally. *Dear Max.* Illus. Tony Ross. Simon & Schuster, 2006. Ages 7–10. (England).

Harper, Charise M. *Just Grace.* Houghton, 2007. Ages 7–9.

Henkes, Kevin. *Bird Lake Moon.* HarperCollins, 2008. Ages 9–12.

Howe, James. *The Misfits.* Simon & Schuster, 2001. Ages 10–13.

Kinney, Jeff. *Diary of a Wimpy Kid.* Amulet, 2007. Ages 10–14. Series.

Lombard, Jenny. *Drita, My Homegirl.* Putnam, 2006. Ages 8–11.

Look, Lenore. *Alvin Ho: Allergic to Girls, School and Other Scary Things.* Schwarz & Wade, 2008. Ages 8–11.

Lowry, Lois. *Gooney Bird Greene.* Houghton, 2002. Ages 7–9. Also *Gooney Bird Is So Absurd* (2009).

O'Connor, Barbara. *Fame and Glory in Freedom, Georgia.* Farrar, 2003. Ages 11–14.

O'Connor, Barbara. *The Small Adventure of Popeye and Elvis.* Farrar, 2009. Ages 8–12.

Paterson, Katherine. *Bridge to Terabithia.* Crowell, 1977. Ages 9–13.

Pennypacker, Sara. *Clementine.* Illus. Marla Frazee. Hyperion, 2006. Ages 7–10. (Humorous).

Perkins, Lynne Rae. *Criss Cross.* Greenwillow, 2005. Ages 11–15.

Schusterman, Neal. *Antsy Does Time.* Dutton, 2008. Ages 11–15.

Scieszka, Jon, editor. *Funny Business.* Illus. Adam Rex. Walden Pond, 2010. (**COL**). Ages 9–13.

Spinelli, Jerry. *Eggs.* Little, Brown, 2007. Ages 9–12. Also *Wringer* (1997).

Stauffacher, Sue. *Donuthead.* Knopf, 2003. Ages 9–12.

Tarshis, Lauren. *Emma-Jean Lazarus Fell out of a Tree.* Dial, 2007. Ages 10–14.

Urban, Linda. *Hound Dog True.* Harcourt, 2011. Ages 8–12.

Van Draanen, Wendelin. *Secret Identity.* Illus. Brian Biggs. Knopf, 2004. Ages 8–12.

Williams, Lori Aurelia. *When Kambia Elaine Flew In from Neptune.* Simon & Schuster, 2001. Ages 12–18.

Physical, Emotional, Mental, and Behavioral Challenges

Baskin, Nora Raleigh. *Anything but Typical.* Simon & Schuster, 2009. Ages 10–14. (Autism).

Draper, Sharon. *Out of My Mind.* Athenuem, 2010. Ages 9–12. (Cerebral palsy).

Duncan, Lois, editor. *On the Edge: Stories at the Brink.* Simon & Schuster, 2000. (**COL**) Ages 12–18. (Emotional, physical difficulties).

Erskine, Kathryn. *Mockingbird.* Philomel, 2010. Ages 8–12. (Asperger's syndrome).

Gantos, Jack. *I Am Not Joey Pigza.* Farrar, 2007. Ages 10–13. Also *Joey Pigza Loses Control* (2002), *Joey Pigza Swallowed the Key* (1998), and *What Would Joey Do?* (2002). (Attention deficit/hyperactivity).

George, Madeleine. *Looks.* Viking, 2008. Ages 12–18. (Eating disorders).

Hautman, Pete. *Invisible.* Simon & Schuster, 2005. Ages 12–16. (Mental health)

Hobbs, Valerie. *Defiance.* Farrar, 2005. Ages 10–14. (Childhood cancer).

Kerz, Anna. *Better Than Weird.* Orca, 2011. Ages 10–14. (Autism).

Konigsburg, E. L. *Silent to the Bone.* Simon & Schuster, 2000. Ages 11–15. (Mutism).

Lord, Cynthia. *Rules.* Scholastic, 2006. Ages 9–13. (Autism, paraplegia).

Morgenroth, Kate. *Echo.* Simon & Schuster, 2006. Ages 13–18. (Depression, mental health, trauma).

Nicholls, Sally. *Ways to Live Forever.* Scholastic, 2008. Ages 9–12. (Leukemia; England).

Schumacher, Julie. *Black Box.* Delacorte, 2008. Ages 12–18. (Depression).

Vaught, Susan R. *Big Fat Manifesto.* Bloomsbury, 2008. Ages 12–18. (Body image).

Weeks, Sarah. *So B. It.* HarperCollins, 2004. Ages 10–14. (Mental retardation, agoraphobia).

Communities

Alexi, Sherman. *The Absolutely True Diary of a Part-Time Indian.* Little, Brown, 2007. Ages 12–18. (Spokane Indian).

Alvarez, Julia. *How Tia Lola Learned to Teach.* Knopf, 2010. Ages 9–12. (Dominican American).

Cameron, Ann. *Colibrí.* Farrar, 2003. Ages 10–16. (Guatemala).

Canales, Viola. *The Tequila Worm.* Wendy Lamb, 2005. Ages 11–15. (Mexican American).

Choung, Eun-hee. *Minji's Salon.* Kane/Miller. Ages 6–9. (Korea).

Cofer, Judith Ortiz. *Call Me Maria.* Orchard, 2004. Ages 11–14. (Puerto Rican).

Craig, Colleen. *Afrika.* Tundra, 2008. Ages 12–15. (South Africa).

Danticat, Edwidge. *Behind the Mountains.* Orchard, 2002. Ages 11–14. (Haiti).

Fleischman, Paul. *Seedfolks.* HarperCollins, 1997. Ages 10–14.

Frost, Helen. *Spinning through the Universe: A Novel in Poems from Room 214.* Farrar, 2004. (**NV**). Ages 11–14.

Grimes, Nikki. *Bronx Masquerade.* Dial, 2002. (**NV**). Ages 12–18.

Khan, Rukhsana. *Wanting Mor.* Groundwood, 2009. Ages 12–15. (Afghanistan).

Marsden, Carolyn. *Silk Umbrellas.* Candlewick, 2004. Ages 8–12. (Thailand).

Michael, Jan. *City Boy.* Clarion, 2009. Ages 10–14. (Malawi).

Myers, Walter Dean. *The Cruisers.* Scholastic, 2010. Ages 9–13. (African American).

Na, An. *A Step from Heaven.* Front Street, 2001. Ages 13–18. (Korea).

Naidoo, Beverley. *The Other Side of Truth.* Harper-Collins, 2001. Ages 11–14. (Nigeria, London).

Naidoo, Beverley. *Out of Bounds: Seven Stories of Conflict and Hope.* HarperCollins, 2003. Ages 10–14. (South Africa).

Naidoo, Beverley. *Web of Lies.* HarperCollins, 2006. Ages 12–16. (Nigeria, London).

Ochoa, Annette, Betsy Franco, and Tracy L. Gourdine, editors. *Night Is Gone, Day Is Still Coming: Stories and Poems by American Indian Teens and Young Adults.* Candlewick, 2003. (**COL**). Ages 12–18.

Patron, Susan. *The Higher Power of Lucky.* Atheneum, 2006. Ages 9–12.

Resau, Laura. *What the Moon Saw.* Delacorte, 2006. Ages 10–15. (Mexican American).

Resau, Laura. *Red Glass.* Delacorte, 2007. Ages 11–15. (Mexico).

Rocklin, Joanne. *One Day and One Amazing Morning on Orange Street.* Amulet, 2011. Ages 8–12.

Saldaña, René, Jr. *The Jumping Tree: A Novel.* Delacorte, 2001. Ages 11–16. (Mexican American).

Springstubb, Tricia. *What Happened on Fox Street.* Balzer and Bray, 2010. Ages 8–12.

Staples, Suzanne Fisher. *Under the Persimmon Tree.* Farrar, 2005. Ages 12–16. (Pakistan, Afghanistan).

Stratton, Allan. *Chanda's Secrets.* Annick, 2004. Ages 12–18. (South Africa).

Williams-Garcia, Rita. *No Laughter Here.* HarperCollins, 2004. Ages 10–14. (Nigerian American).

Woodson, Jacqueline. *Locomotion.* Putnam, 2003. (**NV**). Ages 9–12. (African American).

Animals

Bauer, Marion Dane. *A Bear Named Trouble.* Clarion, 2005. Ages 8–11.

DiCamillo, Kate. *Because of Winn-Dixie.* Candlewick, 2000. Ages 8–11.

Foreman, Jack. *Say Hello.* Illus. Michael Foreman. Candlewick, 2008. (**PI**) Ages 5–8.

Haas, Jessie. *Jigsaw Pony.* Illus. Ying-Hwa Hu. Greenwillow, 2005. Ages 7–10.

Hearne, Betsy. *The Canine Collection: Stories about Dogs and People.* M. K. McElderry, 2003. (**COL**). Ages 10–14.

Hiaasen, Carl. *Hoot.* Knopf, 2003. Ages 10–14.

Nelson, Marilyn. *Snook Alone.* Illus. Timothy Ering. Candlewick, 2010. (**PI**). Ages 5–8.

O'Connor, Barbara. *How to Steal a Dog: A Novel.* Farrar, Straus and Giroux, 2007. Ages 8–12.

Sports

Coy, John. *Crackback.* Scholastic, 2005. Ages 12–18.

Deuker, Carl. *Gym Candy.* Houghton, 2007. Ages 13–18.

Eskilsen, Erik E. *Offsides.* Houghton, 2004. Ages 10–14.

Feinstein, John. *Vanishing Act.* Knopf, 2006. Ages 11–18.

FitzGerald, Dawn. *Soccer Chick Rules.* Roaring Brook, 2006. Ages 10–14.

Koertge, Ron. *Shakespeare Bats Cleanup.* Candlewick, 2003. Ages 11–14.

Lipsyte, Robert. *Yellow Flag.* HarperTeen, 2007. Ages 14–18.

Lupica, Mike. *The Batboy.* Philomel, 2010. Ages 10–14. Also *Heat* (2006) and *Million Dollar Throw* (2009).

Maddox, Jake. *Running Rivals.* Illus. Tuesday Mourning. Stone Arch, 2009. Ages 8–12.

Myers, Walter Dean. *Slam!* Scholastic, 1996. Ages 12–18.

Ritter, John H. *The Boy Who Saved Baseball.* Philomel, 2003. Ages 10–13.

Roberts, Kristi. *My Thirteenth Season.* Holt, 2005. Ages 10–14.

Mysteries

Abrahams, Peter. *Down the Rabbit Hole.* HarperCollins, 2005. Ages 11–15.

Allison, Jennifer. *Gilda Joyce: Psychic Investigator.* Dutton, 2005. Ages 10–14. (Humorous).

Balliett, Blue. *Chasing Vermeer.* Illus. Brett Helquist. Scholastic, 2004. Ages 9–14. Also *The Wright 3.* Illus. Brett Helquist (2006).

Beil, Michael. *The Red Blazer Girls: The Ring of Racamadour.* Knopf, 2009. Ages 10–14.

Broach, Elise. *Shakespeare's Secret.* Holt, 2005. Ages 11–15.

Cheshire, Simon. *The Treasure of Dead Man's Lane and Other Case Files.* Illus. R. W. Alley. Roaring Brook, 2009. Ages 8–12

Coman, Carolyn. *The Big House.* Illus. Rob Shepperson. Front Street, 2004. Ages 8–12.

Curtis, Christopher Paul. *Mr. Chickee's Funny Money.* Random House, 2005. Ages 9–13.

DeFelice, Cynthia. *The Missing Manatee.* Farrar, 2005. Ages 10–14.

Ehrenhaft, Daniel. *Drawing a Blank; or How I Tried to Solve a Mystery, End a Feud, and Land the Girl of My Dreams.* Illus. Trevor Ristow. HarperCollins, 2006. Ages 12–18. (Alternating chapters of first-person narratives and superhero comic-strip episodes).

Hautman, Pete, and Logue, Mary. *Snatched.* Putnam, 2006. Ages 11–15. Bloodwater Mysteries series.

Hiaasen, Carl. *Flush.* Knopf, 2005. Ages 10–14.

Montgomery, Lewis B. *The Case of Stinky Socks.* Illus. Amy Wummer. Kane, 2009. Ages 8–12.

Riordan, Rick. *The Maze of Bones.* Scholastic, 2008. Ages 9–13. 39 Clues series.

Roberts, Ken. *Thumb and the Bad Guys.* Illus. Leanne Franson. Groundwood, 2009. Ages 8–12.

Selfors, Suzanne. *Smells Like Treasure.* Little, Brown, 2011. Ages 8–12.

Springer, Nancy. *The Case of the Missing Marquess: An Enola Holmes Mystery.* Philomel, 2005. Ages 10–14.

Van Draanen, Wendelin. *Sammy Keyes and the Cold Hard Cash.* Knopf, 2008. Ages 10–13. Series.

Romance and Sexuality

Anderson, Laurie Halse. *Speak.* Farrar, 1999. Ages 12–18.

Baskin, Nora Raleigh. *The Summer before Boys.* Simon & Schuster, 2011. Ages 9–12.

Deak, Erzsi, and Kristin Embry Litchman, editors. *Period Pieces.* HarperCollins, 2003. (COL). Ages 10–14.

Flake, Sharon G. *Who Am I without Him?* Hyperion, 2004. (COL). Ages 11–18.

Freitas, Donna. *The Possibilities of Sainthood.* Farrar, 2008. Ages 12–16.

Hartinger, Brent. *Geography Club.* HarperTempest, 2003. Ages 12–18.

Howe, James. *Totally Joe.* Atheneum, 2005. Ages 10–14.

Johnson, Angela. *The First Part Last.* Simon & Schuster, 2003. Ages 12–18.

Larochelle, David. *Absolutely, Positively Not.* Scholastic, 2005. Ages 12–18. (Humorous).

Myers, Walter Dean. *What They Found: Love on 145th Street.* Wendy Lamb, 2007. (COL). Ages 13–18.

Naylor, Phyllis Reynolds. *Almost Alice.* Atheneum, 2008. Ages 10–15.

Peters, Julie Anne. *Luna.* Little, Brown, 2004. Ages 13–18.

Sanchez, Alex. *Getting It.* Simon & Schuster, 2006. Ages 13–18. Also *So Hard to Say* (2004).

Shreve, Susan. *Under the Watson's Porch.* Knopf, 2004. Ages 10–14.

Spinelli, Jerry. *Stargirl.* Knopf, 2000. Ages 11–15. Also *Love, Stargirl* (2007).

Stone, Phoebe. *Deep Down Popular.* Scholastic, 2008. Ages 10–14.

Wittlinger, Ellen. *Parrotfish.* Simon & Schuster, 2007. Ages 14–18.

Wolff, Virginia Euwer. *Make Lemonade.* Holt, 1993. Ages 12–18.

Adventure and Survival

Alvarez, Julia. *Return to Sender.* Knopf, 2009. Ages 9–12.

Budhos, Marina. *Ask Me No Questions.* Atheneum, 2006.

Couloumbis, Audrey. *The Misadventures of Maude March: or, Trouble Rides a Fast Horse.* Random House, 2005. Ages 10–13.

Creech, Sharon. *The Wanderer.* HarperCollins, 2000. Ages 11–14.

Doctorow, Cory. *Little Brother.* Tor, 2008. Ages 12–18.

Doyle, Roddy. *Wilderness.* A. A. Levine, 2007. Ages 11–16.

Ellis, Sarah. *The Several Lives of Orphan Jack.* Illus. Bruno St-Aubin. Groundwood, 2003. Ages 7–11.

George, Jean. *My Side of the Mountain.* Dutton, 1959. Ages 9–12.

George, Jean Craighead. *Julie of the Wolves.* Illus. John Schoenherr. Harper, 1972. Ages 11–15.

Hobbs, Will. *Crossing the Wire.* HarperCollins, 2006. Ages 10–15. Also *Jackie's Wild Seattle* (2003).

Horvath, Polly. *My One Hundred Adventures.* Random House, 2008. Ages 9–12.

Jacobson, Jennifer. *Small as an Elephant.* Candlewick, 2011. Ages 10–14.

Key, Watt. *Alabama Moon.* Farrar, 2006. Ages 11–15.

Lee, Tanith. *Piratica: Being a Daring Tale of a Singular Girl's Adventure Upon the High Seas.* Dutton, 2004. Ages 11–14. Presented in three acts.

McCaughrean, Geraldine. *Smile!* Illus. Ian McCaughrean. Random House, 2006. Ages 10–14. (Australia).

McCaughrean, Geraldine. *The White Darkness.* HarperTempest, 2007. Ages 12–16.

Myers, Walter Dean. *Scorpions.* Harper, 1988. Ages 10–16.

Park, Linda Sue. *A Long Walk to Water.* Clarion, 2010. Ages 10–14. (Sudan).

Paulsen, Gary. *Hatchet.* Bradbury, 1987. Ages 9–12.

Philbrick, Rodman. *The Young Man and the Sea.* Scholastic, 2004. Ages 10–14.

Resau, Laura. *Star in the Forest.* Delacorte, 2010. Ages 9–12. (Mexican American)

Rhodes, Jewell Parker. *Ninth Ward.* Little, Brown, 2010. Ages 10–14.

Salisbury, Graham. *Calvin Coconut: Hero of Hawaii.* Wendy Lamb, 2011. Ages 7–10.

Snicket, Lemony. *The End: Book the Thirteenth.* Illus. Brett Helquist. HarperCollins, 2006. Ages 10–14.

Stewart, Trenton Lee. *The Mysterious Benedict Society.* Little, Brown, 2007. Ages 10–14.

Taylor, Theodore. *Ice Drift.* Harcourt, 2004. Ages 9–13.

Wood, Don. *Into the Volcano.* Scholastic, 2008. (**GR**). Ages 9–14.

Difficult Life Decisions and Coming of Age

Amado, Elisa. *Tricycle.* Illus. Alfonso Ruano. Groundwood, 2007. (**PI**). Ages 5–9. (Guatemala).

Anzaldúa, Gloria. *Friends from the Other Side.* Illus. Consuelo Méndez. Children's Book Press, 1993. (**PI**). Ages 8–12.

Bang, Molly. *When Sophie Gets Angry—Really, Really Angry. . . .* Blue Sky, 1999. (**PI**). Ages 5–9.

Bauer, Marion Dane. *The Double-Digit Club.* Holiday, 2004. Ages 9–12.

Bredsdorff, Bodil. *The Crow-Girl: The Children of Crow Cove.* Trans. Faith Ingwersen. Farrar, 2004. Ages 9–12. (Denmark).

Bunting, Eve. *A Day's Work.* Illus. Ronald Himler. Clarion, 1994. (**PI**). Ages 5–9.

Coffelt, Nancy, *Fred Stays with Me.* Illus. Tricia Tusa. Little, Brown, 2007. (**PI**). Ages 5–9.

Cummings, Priscilla. *Red Kayak.* Dutton, 2004. Ages 11–15.

Curtis, Christopher Paul. *Bucking the Sarge.* Random House, 2004. Ages 11–16.

DeFelice, Cynthia. *Under the Same Sky.* Farrar, 2003. Ages 12–15.

Fitzmaurice, Kathryn. *The Year the Swallows Came Early.* Bowen, 2009. Ages 9–12.

Fleming, Virginia. *Be Good to Eddie Lee* Illus. Floyd Cooper. Philomel, 1993. (**PI**). Ages 5–9.

French, Simon. *Where in the World.* Peachtree, 2003. Ages 10–13.

Henkes, Kevin. *Olive's Ocean.* Greenwillow, 2003. Ages 10–13.

Jocelyn, Marthe. *How It Happened in Peach Hill.* Random House, 2007. Ages 11–16.

Leavitt, Martine. *Tom Finder.* Red Deer, 2003. Ages 12–18.

Lynch, Chris. *Me, Dear Dad & Alcatraz.* HarperCollins, 2005. Ages 13–16.

McGovern, Ann. *The Lady in the Box.* Illus. Marni Backer. Turtle, 1997. (**PI**). Ages 5–9

Myers, Walter Dean. *Lockdown.* Amistad, 2011. Ages 12–18.

O'Connor, Barbara. *Taking Care of Moses.* Farrar, 2004. Ages 9–12.

O'Neill, Alexis. *The Recess Queen.* Illus. Laura Huliska-Beith. Scholastic, 2002. (**PI**). Ages 5–9.

Oates, Joyce Carol. *Small Avalanches and Other Stories.* HarperCollins, 2003. (**COL**). Ages 14–18.

Olsen, Sylvia. *The Girl with a Baby.* Sono Nis, 2004. Ages 12–18.

Park, Linda Sue. *Project Mulberry.* Clarion, 2005. Ages 10–13.

Peters, Julie Anne. *Mom and Jo.* Little, Brown, 2006. Ages 12–14.

Polacco, Patricia. *Mr. Lincoln's Way.* Philomel, 2001. (**PI**). Ages 5–9.

Recorvits, Helen. *Yoon and the Jade Bracelet.* Illus. Gabi Swiatkowska. Farrar, 2008. (**PI**) Ages 5–9.

Ryan, Pam Munoz. *Becoming Naomi Leon.* Scholastic, 2004. Ages 10–14.

Saldaña, René, Jr. *Finding Our Way.* Wendy Lamb, 2003. (**COL**). Ages 12–16.

Salisbury, Graham. *Island Boyz: Short Stories.* Wendy Lamb, 2002. (**COL**). Ages 12–16.

Sonnenblick, Jordan. *Notes from the Midnight Driver.* Scholastic, 2006. Ages 12–16.

Spinelli, Eileen. *Three Pebbles and a Song.* Illustrated by S. D. Schindler. Dial, 2003. Ages 5–8.

Spinelli, Jerry. *Maniac Magee.* HarperCollins, 1990. Ages 9–12.

St. Anthony, Jane. *The Summer Sherman Loved Me.* Farrar, 2006. Ages 10–14.

Steptoe, John. *Stevie.* HarperCollins, 1969. (**PI**). Ages 5–9.

Woodson, Jacqueline. *After Tupac and D Foster.* Putnams, 2010. Ages 12–18. Also *Hush* (2002).

Wyeth, Sharon Dennis. *Something Beautiful.* Illus. Chris K. Soentpiet. Doubleday, 1998. (**PI**). Ages 5–9.

Related Films, Videos, and DVDs

Because of Winn-Dixie. (2005). Author: Kate DiCamillo (2000). 106 minutes.

Bink and Gollie. (2012). Author: Kate DiCamillo (2010). 14 minutes.

Bridge to Terabithia. (2007). Author: Katherine Paterson (1977). 96 minutes.

Diary of a Wimpy Kid (2010). Author: Jeff Kinney (2007). 92 minutes.

Holes. (2003). Author: Louis Sachar (1998). 117 minutes.

Hoot. (2006). Author: Carl Hiaasen (2002). 91 minutes.

Lemony Snicket's A Series of Unfortunate Events. (2004). Author: Daniel Handler, *The Bad Beginning* (1999). 107 minutes.

Maniac Magee. (1992). Author: Jerry Spinelli (1990). 30 minutes.

Shiloh. (1997). Also *Shiloh Season* and *Saving Shiloh* (1999). Author: Phyllis Reynolds Naylor (1991), (1996), and (1997). 93 minutes, 96 minutes, 90 minutes.

The Sisterhood of the Traveling Pants. (2005). Also *The Sisterhood of the Traveling Pants 2* (2008). Author: Ann Brashares (2001, 2005). 117 minutes, 119 minutes.

Whale Rider. (2002). Author: Witi Ihimaera (1987/2003). 101 minutes.

Where the Red Fern Grows. (2003). Author: Wilson Rawls (1961). 86 minutes.

Chapter Nine

Historical Fiction and Biography

Ancestors

On the wind-beaten plains
once lived my ancestors.
In the days of peaceful moods,
they wandered and hunted.
In days of need or greed,
they warred and loafed.
Beneath the lazy sun, kind winds above,
they laughed and feasted.
Through the starlit night, under the moon,
they dreamed and loved.
Now, from the wind-beaten plains,
only their dust rises.

—*Grey Cohoe*

Historical fiction and biography can make the past come alive, inviting readers to immerse themselves into another time and place. Stories of the past provide us with a sense of humanity and memory. Milton Meltzer (1981) argues that we need history to compare our current experiences with the past in order to make sense of our lives. Without history, we are locked in the current moment, blinded from understanding that moment. We need stories of the past to locate ourselves in the larger continuum of life and to envision reasons for taking action to create change.

Definition and Description of Historical Fiction

Historical fiction is realistic fiction set in a time remote enough from the present to be considered history. Stories about events that occurred at least one generation (twenty years or more) prior to the date of the original publication are included in this chapter. Authors write about time periods in which they did not live or which occurred more than twenty years prior to their books. This distance provides them with contextual perspectives from which to view the significance and interpretations of these events. Authors of historical fiction often blend historical facts with imaginary characters and an invented plot. The events in their plots must be within the realm of possibility, constructed around actual historical events, authentic period settings, and real historical figures.

In the most common form of historical fiction, the main characters are imaginary, but some secondary characters are actual historical figures. An example is the classic novel *Johnny Tremain* by Esther Forbes, the story of Johnny, a fictitious character, who is apprenticed to a silversmith during the U.S. Revolutionary War period, and who encounters Samuel Adams, John Hancock, and Paul Revere. Another example, *One Crazy Summer* by Rita Williams-Garcia, is set in Oakland, California, in the summer of 1968. Three sisters are sent to a Black Panther summer camp when they arrive to visit the mother they barely know and encounter well-known Black Panthers, such as Huey Newton, and actual events, such as the death of Bobby Hutton.

In another form of historical fiction, the social traditions, customs, and values of the relevant period are described within an accurate physical place but with no mention of an actual historical event nor actual historical figures as characters. An example is *The Witch of Blackbird Pond* by Elizabeth George Speare. The Puritan way of life in Connecticut in the 1600s is depicted in this story about young Kit from Barbados, who becomes involved in a witchcraft trial. Another example is *Tofu Quilt* by Ching Yeong Russell about a young girl who dreams of becoming a writer, but struggles with the limitations placed on her by her family and society in 1960s Hong Kong.

There are historical stories in which elements of fantasy are found, and so are not considered historical fiction. For example, time warps and other supernatural features pop up in Jonathan Stroud's *The Ring of Solomon* and in Margaret Peterson Haddix's *Found*. These stories are **historical fantasy** and are included in the chapter on fantasy.

Evaluation and Selection of Historical Fiction

In evaluating historical fiction, the criteria for any well-written story must be considered, particularly whether the book tells an engaging story with rounded complex characters with whom children can identify. Also of significance is whether the book highlights universal themes that are thought-provoking without being didactic.

Award lists provide sources of recent books that offer readers the human side of history. The Scott O'Dell Award, established in 1982, honors the most outstanding work of children's historical fiction published in the previous year. The work must be written by a U.S. citizen and be set in the New World. The Scott O'Dell Award winners found in Appendix A are a source of outstanding historical fiction. The National Council for the Social Studies publishes an annual list of the most notable trade books in the field of social studies in the May/June issue of *Social Education*. This list includes many works of historical fiction, as well as nonfiction works, and is a useful source to locate recent books.

The Significance of Setting and Point of View in Historical Fiction

Two literary elements that are particularly significant for historical fiction are *setting* and *point of view.* The story must be told within an authentic time and place that come alive for readers and that acknowledge differing perspectives on those events and times. Historical fiction depends on integral settings that are essential to understanding the story and the actions and beliefs of the characters. The following criteria should be considered:

- **Is the setting described in rich details that are accurate and authentic for that time and place**? A setting must be described in enough detail to provide an authentic sense of time and place without overwhelming the story. Details such as hair and clothing styles, home architecture and furnishings, foods and food preparation, and modes of transportation must be subtly woven into the story to provide a convincing, authentic period setting.

- **Do the characters act and think within the traditions and norms of their times?** The story must make the connections between setting and actions evident so that readers understand the ways in which the characters are influenced by time and place. In most historical fiction, setting takes on the role of clarifying the conflict by showing how the time and place affect the action. Other roles include setting as antagonist, setting that illuminates character, setting that establishes mood, and setting as a symbol (Lukens, 2012).

- **Is the dialogue authentic to the time period as well as understandable to children?** Expressing the language or dialect of the period presents a challenge for authors, especially in creating dialogue. If the speech of the period differs greatly from that of today, the author must decide whether to remain true to the language of the time, which can cause difficulties in comprehending, or change the language to modern phrasing and risk losing the authenticity of the time period. The language should not jar the reader by its obvious inappropriateness or lose the reader by its extreme difficulty. Most authors strive for a middle ground by retaining some flavor of language difference but making modifications to be understandable to the child reader.

- **Are multiple perspectives about the events and issues shared through the various characters?** Does the book highlight only one group's interpretation of that event? Many adults are unaware that the history they learned as children may have been biased or one-sided. Some authors attempt to integrate more complex interpretations of historical events by including events and facts that are typically excluded from history textbooks and adding characters who reflect differing experiences and perspectives. The challenge is to do so but still have characters act in historically authentic ways.

Reading novels with differing perspectives on the same events invites readers to closely examine how setting and perspective impact characters' actions and beliefs. For example, reading the Little House series about pioneer life by Laura Ingalls Wilder alongside Louise Erdrich's series

Excellent Historical Fiction to Read Aloud

Addy, Sharon. *Lucky Jake.* Ages 6–8.

Cushman, Karen. *The Loud Silence of Francine Green.* Ages 11–15.

Erdrich, Louise. *The Porcupine Year.* Ages 9–14.

Kadohata, Cynthia. *Kira-Kira.* Ages 11–18.

Lee, Milly. *Landed.* Illustrated by Yangsook Choi. Ages 7–11.

Levine, Ellen. *Henry's Freedom Box.* Illustrated by Kadir Nelson. Ages 7–12.

Park, Linda Sue. *When My Name Was Keoko.* Ages 10–14.

Philbrick, Rodman. *The Mostly True Adventures of Home P. Figg.* Ages 8–12.

Roy, Jennifer. *Yellow Star.* Ages 10–15.

Sheth, Kashmira. *Keeping Corner.* Ages 12–18.

Vanderpool, Clare. *Moon over Manifest.* Ages 11–15.

White, Ruth. *Little Audrey.* Ages 9–13.

on the displacement of an Ojibwa family provides a powerful contrast in experiences and viewpoints between pioneers and Native Americans. Reading *When My Name Was Keoko* by Linda Sue Park alongside *So Far from the Bamboo Grove* by Yoko Watkins offers contrasting views on the Japanese occupation of Korea—the first from the view of two Korean siblings who are forced to take on Japanese culture and language and the second from a child whose father is a Japanese soldier enforcing the occupation.

Historical Overview of Historical Fiction

Although historical stories were written for children as early as the 1800s, few titles of interest remain from those early years. The early books placed an emphasis on exciting events and idealized real-life characters—much in the style of heroic legends. Between World War I and World War II, a few historical stories appeared in which well-developed characters were portrayed in authentic period settings. Between 1932 and 1943, the first eight books of the Little House series by Laura Ingalls Wilder were published. *Johnny Tremain* by Esther Forbes was awarded the Newbery Medal in 1944 and is considered a children's classic.

The period of fifteen years right after World War II saw a flowering of historical fiction for children in both English and U.S. literature. Examples are *The Door in the Wall* by Marguerite de Angeli (1949); *Calico Captive* by Elizabeth George Speare (1957); the Newbery Medal book *The Witch of Blackbird Pond* by Elizabeth George Speare (1958); and *The Cabin Faced West* by Jean Fritz (1958). In 1954, the Laura Ingalls Wilder Award was established to honor an author or illustrator whose books, published in the U.S., have made a substantial and lasting contribution to children's literature. By 1960, the genre of historical fiction was well established.

MILESTONES in the Development of Historical Fiction

Date	Event	Significance
1888	*Otto of the Silver Hand* by Howard Pyle	Early recognized work of historical fiction
1929	*The Trumpeter of Krakow* by Eric Kelly awarded the Newbery Medal	National recognition for an early work of historical fiction
1932–1943	Publication of the first eight books of *Little House* series by Laura Ingalls Wilder	Classic historical fiction
1944	*Johnny Tremain* by Esther Forbes awarded the Newbery Medal	Classic historical adventure set in American Revolution era
1949–1960	Many historical novels published, including *The Witch of Blackbird Pond* by Elizabeth George Speare and *The Lantern Bearers* by Rosemary Sutcliff	Dramatic increase in the quality and quantity of historical novels for children
1954	Establishment of the Laura Ingalls Wilder Award, first awarded to Wilder	Recognition of a historical fiction author for the entire body of her work
1961	Scott O'Dell's *Island of the Blue Dolphins* awarded the Newbery Medal	Landmark book of historical fiction with a strong female protagonist from a minority culture
1971	*Journey to Topaz* by Yoshiko Uchida	Early historical work by a minority (Japanese American)
1975	*The Song of the Trees* by Mildred Taylor	First in a series of books about an African-American family's struggle starting in the Depression era
1982	Establishment of Scott O'Dell Award	Award for outstanding historical novel set in North America
1997	*Out of the Dust* by Karen Hesse awarded the Newbery Medal	Recognition for a novel in verse, new trend in children's fiction

Historical fiction continues to flourish today. Some older historical fiction novels have been criticized for portraying specific cultural groups in a negative light. For example, two Newbery Medal winners, *Caddie Woodlawn* by Carol Ryrie Brink and *The Matchlock Gun* by Walter D. Edmonds, include negative portrayals of Native Americans. Misrepresentations and omissions of Native Americans and other minority groups in history books and historical fiction have been challenged by authors who are insiders to these cultures. These authors have contributed excellent works on the early experiences of their cultural groups in North America, such as *The Birchbark House* and its sequels by Louise Erdrich and *Journey to Topaz* by Yoshiko Uchida.

Definition and Description of Biography

Biography gives factual information about the lives of actual people, including their experiences, influences, accomplishments, and legacies. Biographies are typically more narrative than expository in writing style, adhering to the elements of fiction, and so are included in this chapter rather than as informational books. In addition, biographies are organized by era as is historical fiction and are often related to historical fiction in curricular integration. Biographies differ from historical fiction in that they include books about people who are currently alive so the twenty-year rule for historical fiction does not apply to biography. In the Common Core State Standards, biography are considered informational texts.

An *autobiography* is similar to biography, except that authors tell about their own life. *Memoirs,* although related to autobiographies, focus on the authors' reflections on the meaning of a particular set of past experiences in their lives rather than on the events themselves (Bomer, 2005).

Reading biographies allows children to find inspiration in the lives and accomplishments of people, many of whom overcame hardship in their early years to succeed and make their marks on history. They learn history from the contexts of the lives of historical figures and come to recognize the importance of childhood experiences in shaping who we become as adults.

Biographies can be classified by coverage of the subject's life. In evaluating the following types of biographies, a balance is needed between adequate coverage of the person's life and the tolerance that the children have for detail.

- The *complete biography* covers the entire life of the subject from birth to death. An example is *Napoléon: The Story of the Little Corporal* by Robert Burleigh.

- The *partial biography* covers only part of the life of the subject. Biographies for young children will often be of this type as are biographies of living persons. An example is *The Young Hans Christian Andersen* by Karen Hesse, illustrated by Erik Blegvad.

- The *collected biography* includes the life stories of several people in one book, organized into chapters, such as *Women Daredevils: Thrills, Chills, and Frills* by Julie Cummins, illustrated by Cheryl Harness.

- The *biography series* is a multivolume set of books with each book containing one separate biography, such as the First Biographies series by David A. Adler with books on Thomas Jefferson, Martin Luther King Jr., and Jackie Robinson.

Evaluation and Selection of Biography

In evaluating biography, consider the following criteria:

- **Is the person of interest to children?** Their lives or accomplishments should somehow intersect with young readers' experiences and interests.

- **Is the person presented as a human being with strengths and faults?** The facts should be accurate, with no idealization of the person. Multiple perspectives on their actions and beliefs should be incorporated.

- **Is the depth of coverage at an appropriate level for the intended audience?** Biographers need to select how much to tell of the person's life story and which aspects of their lives will be of interest and meaningful to children.

Excellent Biographies to Read Aloud

Bernier-Grand, Carmen T. *Frida: Viva la Vida! Long Live Life!* Illustrated by David Diaz. Ages 12–18.

Burleigh, Robert. *Napoléon: The Story of the Little Corporal.* Ages 10–14.

Chandra, Deborah, and Madeleine Comora. *George Washington's Teeth.* Illustrated by Brock Cole. Ages 7–11.

Cummins, Julie. *Women Daredevils: Thrills, Chills, and Frills.* Ages 8–12.

Fleischman, Sid. *The Trouble Begins at 8: A Life of Mark Twain in the Wild, Wild West.* Ages 10–15.

Hoose, Phillip. *We Were There, Too! Young People in U.S. History.* Ages 10–13.

Nelson, Vaunda. *Bad News for Outlaws: The Remarkable Life of Bass Reeves, Deputy U.S. Marshall.* Ages 8–12.

Nivola, Claire A. *Planting the Trees of Kenya: The Story of Wangari Maathi.* Ages 6–9.

Hopkinson, Deborah. *Abe Lincoln Crosses a Creek: A Tall Thin Tale.* Illustrated by John Hendrix. Ages 6–9.

Serrano, Francisco. *The Poet King of Tezcoco: A Great Leader of Ancient Mexico.* Illustrated by Pablo Serrano. Ages 10–14.

Stone, Tanya Lee. *Sandy's Circus: A Story about Alexander Calder.* Illustrated by Boris Kulikov. Ages 5–9.

- **Is the documentation of details unobtrusive and integrated into the narrative?** Biographers need to provide documentation supporting their narrative's events and perspectives, but limit the extensive citation within the text, which readers find distracting.

In selecting biographies for a collection, another criterion to consider is whether the collection contains books that reflect people from a range of cultural experiences (e.g., female and male, ethnicities, abilities) as well as backgrounds. Political and entertainment figures along with athletes dominate the field and so teachers need to make careful selections to assure that children have a wide range of biographies available that reflect the many people whose lives are of interest and value to them. Award-winning books are more difficult to locate because there are no awards specific to biography; however, the Orbis Pictus Award for Nonfiction and the Robert F. Sibert Award for Nonfiction have named biographies as award winners.

The evaluation of biographies varies by the type of biography. In biographies for children, more latitude is allowed, and biographers use varying degrees of invention in their narratives. This invention ranges from choosing what aspects of the person's life to emphasize as the theme of the book (e.g., great energy or love of freedom) to actually inventing fictional characters and conversation. Biographies, then, can be classified and evaluated by degree of documentation.

In *authentic biography,* all factual information is documented through eyewitness accounts, written documents, letters, diaries, and audio and video recordings, as found in books such as *Painting the Wild Frontier: The Art and Adventures of George Catlin* by Susanna Reich. Details in the lives of people who lived long ago, such as conversations, are often difficult to document, so biographers use devices to make their writing lively, such as

- interior monologue (telling what someone probably thought or said to himself or herself based on known actions)
- indirect discourse (reporting the gist of what someone said without using quotation marks)
- attribution (interpretation of known actions to determine probable motives)
- inference (reasoning to derive one idea from another)

Fictionalized biography is based on careful research, but the author creates dramatic episodes from known facts using imagined conversation. The conversation is carefully structured around the pertinent facts that are known, but the actual words are invented by the author. An example of this type of biography is *The Dreamer* by Pam Muñoz Ryan.

Much artistic license is allowed in **biographical fiction,** including invented dialogue, fictional secondary characters, and some reconstructed action. The known achievements of the person are reported accurately, but in other respects these works are as much fiction as fact. Due to a trend toward greater authenticity in children's nonfiction, biographical fiction is relatively rare today. An example is *My Uncle Emily* by Jane Yolen in which a young boy spends time with his aunt, the reclusive poet, Emily Dickinson.

The Significance of Point of View in Biography

As with historical fiction, point of view is an important literary element to explore within biography, particularly the point of view of the author toward the person whose life is the focus of that biography. One way to evaluate point of view is to read and compare several biographies on the same person to compare perspectives on that person and to counteract the bias of a particular author. For example, events in the life of Mark Twain can be compared through three perspectives: *The Trouble Begins at 8: A Life of Mark Twain in the Wild, Wild West* is told from a typical narrator voice by author Sid Fleischman; *The Extraordinary Mark Twain (According to Suzy)* by Barbara Kerley is based on a biography written by Twain's thirteen-year-old daughter; and *The Adventures of Mark Twain,* by Robert Burleigh is told from the perspective of Twain's famous character, Huck Finn.

Another excellent set of biographies are four picture books on the life of Wangari Maathai, who started a movement of women to replant trees in Kenya. The books differ in their focus on her life story and in whether her actions are represented as individualistic or as part of a broader social movement. *Mama Miti* (Donna Jo Napoli), *Wangari's Trees of Peace* (Jeanette Winter), *Painting the Trees of Kenya* (Claire Nivola), and *Seeds of Change* (Jen C. Johnson) can be compared to examine what aspects of her life are highlighted and the author's point of view about the her work.

Historical Overview of Biography

Children's biographies reflect the moral, political, and social values of the times in which they are written. Early U.S. biographies were often didactic, providing life lessons for children. In the mid-1800s, Samuel G. Goodrich (Peter Parley) wrote many idealized biographies of famous men and women, treating them as heroic figures rather than as human beings with flaws and imperfections. In 1880, Reverend Mason Weems wrote *The Life and Memorable Acts of George Washington,* a work

MILESTONES in the Development of Biographies

Date	Book	Significance
1939	*Abraham Lincoln* by Ingri and Edgar Parin d'Aulaire	One of the first picture book biographies for younger children; first biography to win the Caldecott Medal
1940	*Daniel Boone* by James H. Daugherty	First biography to win the Newbery Medal
1952	*Diary of a Young Girl* by Anne Frank	Classic autobiography of the Jewish Holocaust
1988	*Lincoln: A Photobiography* by Russell Freedman	First nonfictional photo essay to win a Newbery Medal
1990	First Orbis Pictus Award for Nonfiction (*The Great Little Madison* by Jean Fritz)	Nonfiction as a genre is recognized; first winner is a biography
2001	First Robert F. Sibert Informational Book Medal (*Sir Walter Ralegh and the Quest for El Dorado* by Marc Aronson)	Nonfiction as a genre is recognized; first winner is a biography

that set a long-lasting trend of portraying national leaders as paragons of virtue. It was not until the 1920s that some biographers began to draw on the new fields of psychology and sociology to give more emphasis on understanding people's motivations and examining their early years.

Examples of children's biographies recognized for their merit from 1930 to 1960 are *Abraham Lincoln* by Ingri and Edgar Parin d'Aulaire; *Daniel Boone* by James H. Daugherty; and *Carry On, Mr. Bowditch* by Jean Lee Latham. In the 1960s and 1970s, children's biographies were affected by the more liberal attitudes and relaxed topic restrictions of the new realism that revolutionized children's fiction. Before this time certain subjects (women, ethnic minorities, and infamous people) and topics (personal weaknesses, mistakes, tragedies) were seldom found in children's biographies. By the 1970s, this attitude had changed, as Russell Freedman (1988) pointed out in his Newbery Medal speech: "The hero worship of the past has given way to a more realistic approach, which recognizes the warts and weaknesses that humanize the great" (p. 447).

Topics in Historical Fiction and Biography

Historical fiction and biography can be organized according to universal themes that occur over the course of history or chronologically by historical periods.

Universal Themes in Historical Fiction and Biography

Common themes that extend across time and place in historical stories can be an approach for sharing historical fiction and biography with children. A theme, such as seeking freedom, can be explored through a text set of books set in different times and places. Some possible themes for development are listed here, along with historical fiction and biographies that might be considered for the study of the theme. Other themes may be developed through reading historical fiction and biographies and considering the common themes that go across the books. Once the set is gathered, students read across the books, and then can construct a chart for that theme comparing the books based on time, place, actions, and beliefs.

Searching for Freedom from Persecution

A Boy Named Beckoning: The True Story of Dr. Carlos Montezuma, a Native American Hero by Gina Capaldi. Ages 7–11.
Colonial Voices: Hear Them Speak by Kay Winters. Illustrated by Larry Day. Ages 9–13.
Coolies by Yin. Illustrated by Chris Soentpiet. Ages 7–11.
The Dreamer by Pam Munoz Ryan. Illustrated by Peter Sis. Ages 9–14.
Flight to Freedom by Ana Veciana-Suarez. Ages 11–16. *Henry's Freedom Box* by Ellen Levine. Illustrated by Kadir Nelson. Ages 7–11.
Keeping Corner by Kashmira Sheth. Ages 12–15.
A Long Walk to Water by Linda Sue Park. Ages 12–15.
The Wall: Growing Up behind the Iron Curtain by Peter Sís. Ages 10–15.
Yellow Star by Jennifer Roy. Ages 10–15.

Family Closeness in Times of Adversity

Always Remember Me: How One Family Survived World War II by Marisabina Russo. Ages 8–11.
Between Shades of Gray by Ruta Sepetys. Ages 12–15.
Coming on Home Soon by Jacqueline Woodson. Illustrated by E. B. Lewis. Ages 8–11.
Esperanza Rising by Pam Muñoz Ryan. Ages 9–13.
Going North by Janice N. Harrington. Illustrated by Jerome Lagarrigue. Ages 8–11.
Home to Medicine Mountain by Chiori Santiago. Illustrated by Judith Lowry, Ages 8–11.
House of the Red Fish by Graham Salisbury. Ages 10–14.
Nory Ryan's Song by Patricia Reilly Giff. Ages 9–13.
Show Way by Jacqueline Woodson. Illustrated by Hudson Talbott. Ages 8–11.
Weedflower by Cynthia Kadahota. Ages 10–14.

Presenting Historical Fiction and Biography by Periods of History

The natural relationship of historical fiction and biographies to the study of history and geography suggests building units of study around periods of world and U.S. history. The following descriptions of seven historical periods provide an idea of how these units might be organized. Historical fiction books and biographies for units on other eras and events can be selected from the lists at the end of the chapter, where both historical fiction and biographies are arranged by the seven historical periods beginning in 3000 B.C.

Beginning of Civilization up to 3000 B.C.

This period represents prehistoric cultures and civilizations, including early peoples (Java, Neanderthals, Cro-Magnons) and early civilizations in the Middle East and Asia. Egyptians, Syrians, and Phoenicians developed civilizations; and Hebrews produced a religious faith, Judaism. The subcontinent of India was the site of Aryan civilizations. Chinese dynasties were responsible for excellent works of art and agricultural systems of irrigation. Examples of historical novels set in this time period are Peter Dickinson's *The Kin* and Betty Levin's *Thorn*.

Notable Authors of Historical Fiction and Biographies

Historical Fiction

Avi [Wortis], author noted for historical fiction novels, including the Newbery Award–winning *Crispin: The Cross of Lead* and two Newbery Honor books. www.avi-writer.com

Christopher Paul Curtis, African-American author of historical novels, including the Newbery Medal book *Bud, Not Buddy,* a Depression era novel; Newbery Honor book *The Watsons Go to Birmingham—1963; Elijah of Buxton.* www.christopherpaulcurtis.com

Karen Cushman, author of Newbery acclaimed historical novels set in the Middle Ages. *Catherine, Called Birdy; The Midwife's Apprentice.* www.karencushman.com

Karen Hesse, author of Newbery Medal winner *Out of the Dust,* set in Oklahoma in the 1930s, and the historical fiction picture book *The Cats in Krasinski Square.*

Linda Sue Park, Newbery Award–winning author whose novels focus on historical eras in Korea. *A Single Shard; When My Name Was Keoko; Keeping Score.* www.lindasuepark.com

Richard Peck, Newbery Award–winning author noted for his young adult novels and his historical novels set in rural Illinois. *A Year Down Yonder; The River Between Us.*

Graham Salisbury, author who writes historical and realistic novels set in the Hawaiian Islands where he was raised. *House of the Red Fish; Eyes of the Emperor.* www.grahamsalisbury.com

Gary Schmidt, author of historical fiction novels that focus on difficult social issues and coming-of-age themes. *Lizzie Bright and the Buckminster Boy; Wednesday Wars; Okay for Now.* www .hmhbooks.com/schmidt

Biography

David A. Adler, author of several children's biography series written on different difficulty levels that provide insight to the private and public lives of American leaders and sports figures. *A Picture Book of Dwight David Eisenhower; Frederick Douglas: A Noble Life.* www.davidaadler.com

Carmen Bernier-Grand, author of biographies of Latino artists and activists. *Frida: Viva la vida! Long Live Life; Alicia Alonso: Prima Ballerina; Cesar: Si se puede! Yes, We Can; Diego: Bigger than Life.* www.carmenberniergrand.com

Candace Fleming, author of biographies for middle readers, scrapbook format of photos, maps, and handwritten notes. *The Lincolns: A Scrapbook Look at Abraham and Mary; Our Eleanor: A Scrapbook Look at Eleanor's Roosevelt's Remarkable Life; Amelia Lost: The Life and Disappearance of Amelia Earhart.* www.candacefleming.com

Russell Freedman, author of biographies of famous Americans and of informational books about U.S. history. *Lincoln: A Photobiography; Lafayette and the American Revolution*

Jean Fritz, biographer of political leaders during the U.S. Revolutionary War era. *Can't You Make Them Behave, King George?; And Then What Happened, Paul Revere?*

Jan Greenberg and Sandra Jordan, coauthors of several biographies about renowned artists and their works. *Vincent Van Gogh: Portrait of an Artist; Action Jackson.* www .jangreenbergsandrajordan.com

Civilizations of the Ancient World, 3000 B.C. to A.D. 600

The era of the Greek city-states was followed by Roman rule in Western Europe. Christianity was founded in Jerusalem and spread throughout Europe. Civilizations in ancient Asia produced two remarkable men born about 560 B.C.: the Indian religious leader Buddha and the Chinese philosopher Confucius. Kerrily Sapet's *Cleopatra: Ruler of Egypt* relates the life and times of the legendary Egyptian queen in an illustrated, comprehensive biography. Elizabeth E. Wein's *The Lion Hunter*, a historical novel set in ancient Ethiopia, features King Arthur's half-Ethiopian grandson, who battles political intrigues to survive.

Civilizations of the Medieval World, 600 to 1500

Early African and American civilizations arose independently, while the great civilizations of China and Japan continued to flourish. The eastern part of the Roman Empire maintained its stability and preserved the Byzantine Empire from the capital of Constantinople. The Byzantine Empire created a distinct culture and branch of the Christian Church—the Orthodox Church—which influenced Russia to adopt both the religion and the culture. The rise of the Islamic religion began in the early 600s with Muhammad preaching in Mecca. Following the fall of the Roman Empire, Western Europe dissolved into isolated separate regions without strong governments. Many of the responsibilities of government were carried out by the Christian Church, which dominated the economic, political, cultural, and educational life of the Middle Ages. These feudal societies eventually gave rise to the separate nations of modern Europe. Details about medieval life in France are interwoven in Avi's *Crispin* trilogy with a suspenseful narrative and provocative questions of ethics and morality, while Kathleen Krull's *Kubla Khan: The Emperor of Everything* challenges the stereotype of this Mongol ruler as a barbarian.

The Emergence of Modern Nations, 1500 to 1800

The Renaissance, a literary and artistic movement, swept Western Europe, leading to the invention of the printing press, an emphasis on reason, a reformation of the Christian Church, and advances in science. Central governments throughout Europe increased their power. Spain, and then France, dominated Europe in the 1500s and 1600s. In the 1700s, Russia, Austria, and Prussia rose to power. Europeans explored and settled in Africa, India, and the Americas, with the Portuguese and Spanish taking the lead in exploring and colonizing countries within East Asia, India, Africa, and the Americas along with England, the Netherlands, France, and Russia.

Revolutions created new governments and new nations. The American Revolution (1776–1781) created a new nation; the French Revolution in 1789 affected the direction of governments toward democracy in Europe. Napoleon built an empire across Europe, resulting in the uniting of European nations to defeat Napoleon. Robert Burleigh's richly illustrated biography *Napoléon: The Story of the Little Corporal* describes Napoleon's early childhood in Corsica, his rise to power as a military leader, and his decline. The nations of Latin America also began to gain their independence. China expanded gradually under the Ming and Ch'ing dynasties. Japan prospered under the Tokugawa shogunate. The U.S. and Canada were the sites of rapid population increases due to immigration and settlements along the eastern coast. Some westward expansion was beginning in the U.S. and Canada. Short stories describing the roles of different persons during the Boston Tea Party in 1773 are presented in Kay Winters's *Colonial Voices: Hear Them Speak*.

The Development of Industrial Society, 1800 to 1914

The 1800s were marked by a rapid shift from agricultural societies to industrial societies, with Great Britain as an early site. The factory system developed and prospered, while working and living conditions deteriorated for the worker. Books about life as a millworker are Katherine Paterson's *Bread and Roses, Too;* Katharine Boling's *January 1905;* and Elizabeth Winthrop's *Counting on Grace.* New technology—railroad trains, steamboats, the telegraph, and the telephone—affected transportation and communications. Advances in science and medicine helped to explain the nature of life and improved the quality of life. Education developed into an important institution in Western Europe and North America. Europe underwent revolutions that readjusted boundaries and eventually led to the unification of new nations. The colonization of sub-Saharan Africa by European nations expanded rapidly from 1870 to 1890 so that most of the region was under control of various European nationalism, as depicted in Michaela MacColl's *Promise the Night,* the story of Beryl Markham and British colonists in Kenya.

The westward movement of pioneers was fully realized across the U.S. and Canada, hastened by the building of railroads. Native Americans struggled for survival in the face of these massive population shifts. Slavery had existed in the American colonies from the earliest days, but in the 1800s, slavery became a social and economic issue. Julius Lester's *Day of Tears: A Novel in Dialogue* reconstructs the largest slave auction in American history at Savannah, Georgia, in 1859, through personal accounts of slaves and slave owners. Slavery was abolished as a result of the Civil War (1861–1865) and the Union was preserved at the cost of 600,000 lives and a major rift between the North and the South. Another depiction of the brutality of slavery can be found in Margarita Engle's *The Slave Poet of Cuba.*

The U.S. grew in economic and political strength. An age of imperialism resulted in firm control of large areas of the world by other world powers such as England, France, and Belgium. Great Britain dominated India and parts of Africa and continued its influence over Canada, Australia, and New Zealand, while Japan became a powerful force in East Asia.

World Wars in the Twentieth Century, 1914 to 1945

This era includes World War I (1914–1918) in Europe, in which the U.S. and Canada joined and fought with the Allies (Great Britain, France, Russia, Greece, and Romania) against the Central Powers; the between-wars period that included the Great Depression; Adolph Hitler's rise to power in 1933; and World War II (1939–1945) in Europe and Asia, in which Canada and the U.S. joined forces with England, France, and Russia to battle Germany, Italy, and Japan. In 1917, the Bolshevik Revolution established a Communist government in Russia. *Breaking Stalin's Nose* by Eugene Yelchin conveys the excitement and terror of the Stalinist era of Communism through the eyes of a ten-year-old Russian boy, while *Between Shades of Gray* by Ruta Sepetys portrays the devastating results of Stalin's invasion of Lithuania on a family sent to Siberia.

In 1931, Great Britain recognized Canada, Australia, New Zealand, and South Africa as independent, but each declared its loyalty to the British monarch and continued its cultural ties with Great Britain. The atrocities of the Holocaust during World War II—the persecution and killing of Jewish and other people by the Nazi regime—are portrayed in Jennifer Roy's *Yellow Star,* as a young girl and her family struggle to survive in the Lodz ghetto in Poland during the Nazi occupation. World War II ended shortly after the U.S. dropped nuclear bombs on Hiroshima and Nagasaki, Japan. *Weedflower* by Cynthia Kadahota shows how the fear of Japan created by politicians and the press after the bombing of the U.S. naval station at Pearl Harbor led to the internment of loyal Japanese Americans.

Post–World War II Era, 1945 to 1990

During this era, the U.S. and western European nations were involved in a struggle for world influence with Communist nations, particularly the Soviet Union and China, leading to a massive arms build-up. The Korean War (1950–1953) and the Vietnam War (1965–1973) were major conflicts in which the U.S. fought to contain Communist expansion. The Korean War, combined with the postwar economic recovery of Japan, drew attention to the growing importance of East Asia in world affairs. The Soviet Union launched a series of satellites beginning with Sputnik I in 1957, inaugurating the space age. An explosion of scientific knowledge occurred as a result of increased spending for weapons development and space exploration. The 1950s, 1960s, and 1970s have been described as the Cold War decades because of the increasing hostility between the Soviet Union and the U.S., gradually ending with the break-up of the Soviet republic in the early 1990s. In the 1970s, public pressure mounted in the U.S. to reduce the nation's external military commitments following the Vietnam War. This war also brought major changes in the lives of Vietnamese refugees who fled to the U.S., as depicted in two novels in verse, *All the Broken Pieces* by Ann Burg and *Inside Out and Back Again* by Thanhha Lai.

During the 1960s, a strong Civil Rights Movement, led by Martin Luther King Jr. and other prominent figures, fought for equal treatment of African Americans. The movement led to desegregation of schools, restaurants, transportation, and housing. Another struggle against the policies of racial separation occurred in South Africa in the 1970s and 1980s. The end of apartheid was declared in 1990, followed by free elections in 1994. Equal rights for women were also sought during the feminist movement in the 1970s. Examples of books depicting the civil rights struggle are Robert Sharenow's *My Mother the Cheerleader* and Larry D. Brimner's *Black and White: The Confrontation between Reverend Fred L. Shuttlesworth and Eugene "Bull" Connor*.

Reader Connections:
Understanding Historical Contexts

Children are often limited in their knowledge of history and historical context—the background and environment that surrounded past events, including how people lived and worked. Reading or listening to historical fiction and biography can help students understand the past and appreciate the lives of people who lived in earlier times. Smith, Monson, and Dobson (1992) found that the students in fifth-grade classrooms in which historical novels were used along with the social studies textbooks recalled more historical facts and indicated greater enjoyment in their social studies classes than the students in classrooms that had a similar curriculum without the addition of historical novels.

Past events presented in a purely factual manner can seem irrelevant and sometimes unbelievable to students. By presenting these events as part of a historical story and showing how the events affected the lives of characters much like themselves, students better understand, and are more likely to remember, the events. Historical stories help children connect to the emotions engendered by past events—the fear of combat and the excitement of exploration. In addition, books set in the past allow children to compare their lives with the lives of characters and to better understand and appreciate how context affects people's lives, including their own. Students can also consider how their lives may change in the future.

Teachers can encourage students to read works of historical fiction and biography by displaying these books in the classroom, introducing them in booktalks, selecting them for class read-alouds, and presenting them in text sets for independent reading.

An example of a reader response engagement to build interest, knowledge, and contextual understanding of the time and place is the *jackdaw,* a collection of artifacts or copies of realia from a particular historical period or event. The term *jackdaw* refers to a common European bird that is known to collect colorful objects for its nest. Educators use the term to refer to a collection of concrete artifacts that connect historical books with the real events of the times (Dodd, 1999). For example, as the teacher reads aloud *When My Name was Keoko,* students can research and gather maps of Korea and Asia, time lines of events, old newspaper clippings, examples of the two written languages, images of Korean cultural symbols, newspaper articles on recent negotiations between Korea and Japan related to atrocities toward women during the occupation, and artifacts such as flags and dolls in traditional clothing.

Jackdaws are created by teachers and students working together to collect a wide array of related materials in their original form or in reproductions, including maps, time lines, diary entries, recipes, newspaper clippings, music, clothing, artwork, letters, advertisements, old photographs, and books of the era. These informational materials and objects can be placed in a decorated box or suitcase with labels and explanations or as a museum display. Given the increased emphasis on informational texts in the Common Core State Standards, jackdaws are an excellent means of engaging students in a wide range of types of information focused around a particular historical time period.

Commercial jackdaw kits of reproductions are available, and some museums loan out "heritage trunks" for regional history. The Library of Congress provides access to primary sources at www.loc.gov/teachers as does Primary Source, http://www.primarysource.org/, which has online curriculum units with documents and photographs.

Historical fiction and biography offer children the opportunity to live through the experiences of the past, not just gain knowledge about those events and people. They are able to explore the difficult choices and human contradictions that define our world, while still maintaining hope for making a change in their present and future worlds through imagining the past.

Invitations for Further Investigation

- Read a historical novel and examine the ways in which the setting influences the actions and beliefs of the main character—to clarify conflict, serve as antagonist, illuminate character, establish mood, or to act as symbol (Lukens, 2012).

- Select and read a historical fiction novel, then research the time period and location of its setting. Develop a time line to display and contrast the historical facts and the story events. Create a jackdaw of objects that explore the historical context of this novel.

- Choose one of the seven periods of history listed in this chapter. Select five recommended works of historical fiction and biography set in this era and read them to develop a plan for a unit of study around these books. Analyze the perspectives presented in these books and the authors' backgrounds and methods of research to determine whether they reflect a range of viewpoints on the time period.

- Determine a theme often found in historical fiction novels and biographies. Compare and contrast several books that exemplify the theme and that cut across different time periods. Create a chart to compare the way the theme plays out in the set of books.

References

Bomer, K. (2005). *Writing a life: Teaching memoir.* Portsmouth, NH: Heinemann.

Cohoe, G. (1972). Ancestors. In T. Allen (Ed.), *The whispering wind: Poetry by young American Indians.* New York: Doubleday.

Dodd, E. (1999). Echoes of the past. *Childhood Education, 75*(3), 136–141.

Freedman, R. (1988). Newbery Medal acceptance. *The Horn Book, 64*(4), 444–451.

Lukens, R. (2012). *A critical handbook of children's literature,* 9th ed. New York: Pearson.

Meltzer, M. (1981). Beyond the span of a single life. In B. Hearne (Ed.), *Celebrating children's books.* New York: Lothrop.

Smith, J. A., Monson, J. A., & Dobson, D. (1992). A case study on integrating history and reading instruction through literature. *Social Education, 56,* 370–375.

Recommended Historical Fiction and Biography Books

Ages refer to content appropriateness and conceptual and interest levels. Formats other than novels are coded:

(PI) Picture book
(COL) Short story collection
(GR) Graphic novel
(NV) Novels in verse

Beginning of Civilization up to 3000 B.C.

Historical Fiction

Brennan, J. H. *Shiva.* Lippincott, 1990. Ages 11–15. (Prehistoric Europe, Neanderthal, and Cro-Magnon tribes).

Briggs, Raymond. *Ug: Boy Genius of the Stone Age.* Knopf, 2002. **(PI)**. Ages 9–12. (Stone Age).

Cowley, Marjorie. *Anooka's Answer.* Clarion, 1998. Ages 10–15. (Southern France, Upper Paleolithic era).

Craig, Ruth. *Malu's Wolf.* Orchard, 1995. Ages 9–13. (Stone Age Europe, domestication of wolves).

Dickinson, Peter. *Po's Story.* Putnam, 1998. Ages 8–12. Part of the Kin series. (Prehistoric clans).

Levin, Betty. *Thorn.* Front Street, 2005. Ages 12–16. (Prehistoric times, birth defects).

Civilizations of the Ancient World, 3000 B.C. to A.D. 600

Historical Fiction

Hunter, Mollie. *The Stronghold.* Harper, 1974. Ages 9–14. (British Isles, 100 B.C.).

Lawrence, Caroline. *The Man from Pomegranate Street.* Orion, 2009. Ages 11–14. Roman mystery series. (A.D. 81).

Lawrence, L. S. *Escape by Sea.* Holiday, 2008. Ages 12–18. (Roman Empire, Punic War 218–201 B.C.).

Sutcliff, Rosemary. *The Light beyond the Forest: The Quest for the Holy Grail.* Dutton, 1980. Ages 12–18. (King Arthur and his knights, 520 A.D.).

Wein, Elizabeth E. *The Lion Hunter: The Mark of Solomon.* Viking, 2007. Ages 12–16. (Ethiopia, 6th century).

Williams, Susan. *Wind Rider.* Laura Geringer, 2006. Ages 9–13. (Central Asia, 4000 B.C.).

Winters, Kay. *Voices of Ancient Egypt.* Illus. Barry Moser. National Geographic, 2003. **(PI)**. Ages 8–12. (To 332 B.C.).

Biography

Lasky, Kathryn. *The Librarian Who Measured the Earth.* Illus. Kevin Hawkes. Little, Brown, 1994. **(PI)**. Ages 7–10. (Greece, 200 B.C.).

Sapet, Kerrily. *Cleopatra: Ruler of Egypt.* Morgan Reynolds, 2007. Ages 11–18. (Egypt, 30 B.C.).

Zannos, Susan. *The Life and Times of Socrates.* Lane, 2004. Ages 11–14. Biography series. (Greece to 146 B.C.).

Civilizations of the Medieval World, 600 to 1500

Historical Fiction

Avi. *Crispin: The End of Time.* Balzer & Bray, 2010. Ages 10–15. (France, 14th century). Also *Crispin: At the Edge of the World* (2006) and *Crispin: The Cross of Lead* (2002).

Cushman, Karen. *Catherine, Called Birdy.* Clarion, 1994. Ages 11–15. (England, manor life, 1290s). Also *The Midwife's Apprentice.* (1995). Ages 12–16. (England, Middle Ages). Also *Matilda Bone.* (2000). Ages 11–15. (Medieval England, medical practitioner).

Crossley-Holland, Kevin. *Crossing to Paradise.* Levine, 2006. Ages 12–16. (Great Britain, pilgrimages 1189–1199).

Davis, Tony. *Future Knight.* Illus. Gregory Rogers Delacorte, 2007. Ages 9–12. Series. (England, Middle Ages).

Decker, Timothy. *Run Far, Run Fast.* Front Street, 2007. Ages 9–12. (Black Plague, 1348).

Fern, Tracey E. *Pippo the Fool.* Illus. Paul Estrada. Charlesbridge, 2009. (**PI**). Ages 5–9. (Renaissance, Italy 1400s).

Grant, K. M. *Blue Flame.* Walker, 2008. Ages 11–15. (Languedoc region of France, 1242).

Jinks, Catherine. *Pagan's Crusade.* Candlewick, 2003. Ages 12–15. Sequels. (Templar Knights of Jerusalem, 1187).

Love, D. Anne. *The Puppeteer's Apprentice.* Simon & Schuster, 2003. Ages 9–12. (England, Middle Ages).

McCaughrean, Geraldine. *The Kite Rider: A Novel.* HarperCollins, 2002. Ages 12–16. (China, 13th century).

Millen, C. M. *The Ink Garden of Brother Thophane.* Illus. Andrea Wisnewski. Charlesbridge, 2010. (**PI**). Ages 6–9. (Ireland, 1172).

Napoli, Donna Jo. *Daughter of Venice.* Random, 2002. Ages 11–15. (Venice, Italy, 16th century).

Napoli, Donna Jo. *Breath.* Atheneum, 2003. Ages 14–18. (Germany, late 1200s).

Park, Linda Sue. *A Single Shard.* Clarion, 2001. Ages 9–13. (Korean village, 1100s).

Sedgwick, Marcus. *The Dark Horse.* Random House, 2003. Ages 12–18. (Ancient Britain, Viking tribes).

Yolen, Jane, and Robert Harris. *Girl in a Cage.* Putnam, 2002. Ages 11–16. (England, 1306).

Biography

Demi. *Muhammad.* Simon & Schuster, 2003. (**PI**). Ages 9–13. (Prophet's life and origins of Islam, 570–632).

Demi. *Marco Polo.* Marshall Cavendish, 2008. (**PI**). Ages 9–13. (Trip from Venice to China, 13th century).

Doak, Robin S. *Galileo: Astronomer and Physicist.* Compass Point Books, 2005. Ages 11–15. (Scientist, 1564–1642).

Freedman, Russell. *The Adventures of Marco Polo.* Illus. Bagram Ibatoulline. Scholastic, 2006. Ages 12–15. (Explorer, 1254–1323).

Krull, Kathleen. *Kubla Khan: The Emperor of Everything.* Illus. Robert Byrd. Viking, 2010. (**PI**). Ages 5–10. (China, Mongols 1216–1294).

Krull, Kathleen. *Leonardo da Vinci.* Illus. Boris Kulikov. Viking, 2005. Ages 10–14. Giants of Science series. (Italy, 1452–1519).

Stanley, Diane. *Saladin: Noble Prince of Islam.* HarperCollins, 2002. (**PI**). Ages 9–14. (Egypt and Syria, 1137–1193).

Serrano, Francisco. *The Poet King of Tezcoco: A Great Leader of Ancient Mexico.* Trans. Trudy Balch and Jo Anne Engelbert. Illus. Pablo Serrano. Groundwood, 2007. (**PI**). Ages 10–14. (Mexico, 1400s).

Shulevitz, Uri. *The Travels of Benjamin of Tudela: Through Three Continents in the Twelfth Century.* Farrar, 2005. (**PI**). Ages 10–14. (Jewish world traveller, 1159).

Winter, Jonah. *The Secret World of Hildegard.* Illus. Jeanette Winter. Arthur A. Levine, 2007. (**PI**). Ages 7–12. (Germany, 1100s).

The Emergence of Modern Nations, 1500 to 1800

Historical Fiction

Ahlberg, Allan. *The Baby in the Hat.* Illus. Andre Amstutz. Candlewick, 2008. (**PI**). Ages 4–8. (London, 1688–1697).

Anderson, Laurie Halse. *Chains.* Simon & Schuster, 2008. Ages 11–15. (New York City, enslaved sisters, 1776). Sequel is *Forge,* Atheneum, 2010. (Valley Forge, 1777).

Anderson, M. T. *The Pox Party,* Candlewick, 2006. Ages 12–16. (Slavery, U.S. Revolutionary War, 1775) Also *The Kingdom of Waves* (2008). Astonishing Life of Octavian Nothing series.

Bruchac, Joseph. *The Winter People.* Dial, 2002. Ages 11–16. (French and Indian War, Abenaki village, 1759).

Cushman, Karen. *Alchemy and Meggy Swan.* Clarion, 2010. Ages 11–14. (London, 1558–1603).

Duble, Kathleen Benner. *The Sacrifice.* Simon & Schuster, 2005. Ages 11–15. (U.S., Salem witch hunts, 1692).

Forbes, Esther. *Johnny Tremain.* Houghton, 1943. Ages 10–13. (U.S. Revolutionary War era, 1770s).

Hearn, Julie. *The Minister's Daughter.* Atheneum, 2005. Ages 14–18. (English village, witchcraft, 1645).

Ketchum, Liza. *Where the Great Hawk Flies.* Clarion, 2005. Ages 10–14. (Vermont, Pequot Indians, 1782).

Lawrence, Iain. *The Wreckers.* Delacorte, 1998. Ages 10–14. The trilogy also includes *The Smugglers* (1999) and *The Buccaneers* (2001). (Adventures on the high seas, 1800s; England, Carribean).

McCully, Emily Arnold. *The Escape of Oney Judge: Martha Washington's Slave Finds Freedom.* Farrar, 2007. (**PI**). Ages 9–12. (Washington, DC, late 1800s).

Park, Linda Sue. *The Firekeeper's Son.* Illus. Julie Downing. Clarion, 2003. (**PI**). Ages 8–12. (Korea, 1800s).

Polacco, Patricia. *January's Sparrow.* Philomel, 2009. (**PI**). Ages 8–12. (U.S. Underground Railroad, slavery, 1840's).

Rees, Celia. *Pirates!* Bloomsbury, 2003. Ages 12–16. (Swashbuckling adventure, 1725).

Rockwell, Anne. *They Called Her Molly Pitcher.* Illus. Cynthia Von Buhler. Knopf, 2002. (**PI**). Ages 8–11. (U.S. Revolutionary War, 1778).

Speare, Elizabeth George. *The Witch of Blackbird Pond.* Houghton, 1958. Ages 10–14. (U.S. colonial era, 1680s).

Sturtevant, Katherine. *At the Sign of the Star.* Farrar, 2000. Ages 10–15. (London, 1677).

Winters, Kay. *Colonial Voices: Hear Them Speak.* Illus. Larry Day. Dutton, 2008. (**PI**). Ages 9–13. (Boston Tea Party, 1773).

Biography

Burleigh, Robert. *Napoléon: The Story of the Little Corporal.* Abrams, 2007. (**PI**). Ages 10–14. (France, 1769–1821).

Chandra, Deborah, and Madeleine Comora. *George Washington's Teeth.* Illus. Brock Cole. Farrar, 2003. (**PI**). Ages 7–11. (Humorous story in verse, U.S. president, 1732–1799).

Fleming, Candace. *Ben Franklin's Almanac: Being a True Account of the Good Gentleman's Life.* Atheneum, 2003. Ages 11–14. (U.S. statesman and inventor, 1706–1790).

Fradin, Dennis B. *The Founders: The 39 Stories behind the U.S. Constitution.* Illus Michael McCurdy. Walker, 2005. Ages 10–15. (U.S. politics, 1783–1789) Also *The Signers: The 56 Stories behind the Declaration of Independence* (2002). (U.S. Revolution, 1775–1783).

Freedman, Russell. *Confucius: The Golden Rule.* Illus. Frédéric Clément. Scholastic, 2002. (**PI**). Ages 9–14. (China, philosophers, 5th century B.C.).

Freedman, Russell. *Lafayette and the American Revolution.* Holiday, 2010. Ages 10–18. (U.S. Revolution, 1775–1783). Also *Washington at Valley Forge (*2008). (Winter of 1777–1778).

Fritz, Jean. *And Then What Happened, Paul Revere?* Illus. Tomie dePaola. Coward/McCann, 1973. Ages 8–10. (U.S. Revolution, 1775–1783). Also *Can't You Make Them Behave, King George?* (1976).

Harness, Cheryl. *The Remarkable Benjamin Franklin.* National Geographic, 2005. (**PI**). Ages 7–11. U.S., 1706–1790).

Jurmain, Suzanne Tripp. *George Did It.* Illus. Larry Day. Dutton, 2005. (**PI**). Ages 7–11. (U.S., 1732–1799).

Lasky, Kathryn. *The Man Who Made Time Travel.* Illus. Kevin Hawkes. Farrar, 2003. (**PI**). Ages 8–12. (England, 1693–1776).

Murphy, Jim. *The Real Benedict Arnold.* Clarion, 2007. Ages 11–16. (Revolutionary War era).

Price, Sean. *Ivan the Terrible: Tsar of Death.* Scholastic, 2007. Ages 11–15. (Russia, 1500s).

Reich, Susanna. *Painting the Wild Frontier: The Art and Adventures of George Catlin.* Clarion, 2008. Ages 12–18. (18th Century painter of Native American life).

Schanzer, Rosalyn. *George vs. George: The American Revolution as Seen from Both Sides*. National Geographic, 2004. Ages 9–12. (U.S. Revolution, King George and George Washington, 1775–1783).

Sheinkin, Steve. *The Notorious Benedict Arnold: A True Story of Adventure, Heroism & Treachery*. Roaring Brook, 2010. Ages 10–18. (U.S. Revolution, 1741–1801).

Silvey, Anita. *Henry Knox: Bookseller, Soldier, Patriot*. Illus. Wendell Minor. Clarion, 2010 **(PI)**. Ages 6–9. (U.S., Boston, U.S. Revolution 1775–1783).

Sís, Peter. *Play, Mozart, Play!* Greenwillow, 2006. **(PI)**. Ages 5–8. (Roman Empire, Austria, composer, 1756–1791).

The Development of Industrial Society, 1800 to 1914

Historical Fiction

Avi. *Silent Movie*. Illus. C. B. Mordan. Atheneum, 2003. **(PI)**. Ages 8–12. (New York, Swedish immigrants, 1900s).

Avi. *City of Orphans*, Illus. Greg Ruth. Anthem, 2011. **(PI)**. Ages 10–14. (New York, immigrants, 1865–1898).

Battle-Lavert, Gwendolyn. *Papa's Mark*. Illus. Colin Bootman. Holiday, 2003. **(PI)**. Ages 6–9. (Post–Civil War South).

Boling, Katharine. *January 1905*. Harcourt, 2004. Ages 9–13. (U.S. mill town, child labor, 1905).

Brown, Don. *Kid Blink Beats the World*. Roaring Brook, 2004. **(PI)**. Ages 7–11. (Labor strikes, 1899).

Byars, Betsy. *Keeper of the Doves*. Viking, 2002. Ages 9–13. (Kentucky, 1899).

Carvell, Marlene. *Sweetgrass Basket*. Dutton, 2005. Ages 12–15. (Native American boarding school, early 1900s).

Collins, Pat Lowery. *Daughter of Winter*. Candlewick, 2010. Ages 9–13. (Wampanoag Indians, 1849).

Curtis, Christopher Paul. *Elijah of Buxton*. Scholastic, 2007. Ages 11–14. (Canada, freed slaves, 1849).

Cushman, Karen. *Rodzina*. Clarion, 2003. Ages 9–14. (Orphan train to California, 1881).

DeFelice, Cynthia. *Bringing Ezra Back*. Farrar, 2006. Ages 9–13. (Ohio frontier, 1830s). Sequel to *Weasel* (1990).

Donnelly, Jennifer. *A Northern Light*. Harcourt, 2003. Ages 12–16.(Upstate New York, 1906).

Draper, Sharon M. *Copper Sun*. Atheneum, 2006. Ages 14–18. (Carolinas, slave trade and plantation life, early 1800s).

Engle, Margarita. *The Surrender Tree: Poems from Cuba's Struggle for Freedom*. Henry Holt, 2008. Ages 12–18. (Cuba, 1810–1899).

Erdrich, Louise. *The Porcupine Year*. HarperCollins, 2008. Ages 9–14. (Displaced Ojibwe family, 1852). Sequel to *The Birchbark House* (1999) and *The Game of Silence* (2005).

Frost, Helen. *The Braid*. Farrar, 2006. Ages 12–16. **(NV)**. (Scotland to Canada, 1850s).

Giff, Patricia Reilly. *Nory Ryan's Song*. Delacorte, 2000. Ages 9–13. (Ireland, potato famine, 1845). Sequels are *Maggie's Door* (2003) and *Water Street* (2006).

Holt, Kimberly Willis. *The Water Seeker*. Henry Holt, 2010. Ages 11–14. (U.S. frontier life, 1833–1859).

Holub, Josef. *An Innocent Soldier*. Trans. Michael Hofmann. Scholastic, 2005. Ages 14–18. (Napoleon's Russian campaign, 1812).

Ibbotson, Eva. *Journey to the River Sea*. Dutton, 2002. Ages 11–14. (Brazil, 1910).

Ibbotson, Eva. *The Star of Kazan*. Illus. Kevin Hawkes. Dutton, 2004. Ages 10–14. (Germany and Austria, late 1800s).

Kelly, Jacqueline. *The Evolution of Calpurnia Tate*. Henry Holt, 2009. Ages 10–14. (U.S., Texas, 1899).

LaFaye, A. *Worth*. Simon & Schuster, 2004. Ages 10–14. (Orphan train, Nebraska, late 1800s).

Lee, Milly. *Landed*. Illus. Yangsook Choi. Farrar, 2006. **(PI)**. Ages 7–11. (Southeastern China to Angel Island, San Francisco, early 1900s).

Lester, Julius. *Day of Tears: A Novel in Dialogue*. Hyperion, 2005. Ages 12–18. (Savannah, Georgia, slave auction, 1859).

Levine, Ellen. *Henry's Freedom Box*. Illus. Kadir Nelson. Scholastic, 2007. **(PI)**. Ages 7–12. (Virginia, 1849).

Lewis, J. Patrick. *The Brothers' War: Civil War Voices in Verse*. National Geographic, 2007. Ages 10–14. (Poems about U.S. Civil War).

Lowry, Lois. *The Silent Boy*. Houghton, 2003. Ages 9–15. (New England, autism, 1908–1911).

Lyons, Mary E. *Dear Ellen Bee: A Civil War Scrapbook of Two Union Spies*. Simon & Schuster, 2000. Ages 10–13. (Richmond, Virginia, Civil War era).

McCaughrean, Geraldine. *Stop the Train!* Harper-Collins, 2003. Ages 10–13. (Homesteading, Oklahoma, 1893).

MacColl, Michaela. *Promise the Night.* Chronicle, 2011. Ages 11–15. (British in Kenya, 1912).

McMullan, Margaret. *How I Found the Strong.* Houghton, 2004. Ages 11–15. (Civil War battlefield).

Myers, Anna. *Assassin.* Walker, 2005. Ages 11–15. (Alternating narratives, assassination of Abraham Lincoln, 1865).

Paterson, Katherine. *Bread and Roses, Too.* Clarion, 2006. Ages 10–14. (Massachusetts, mill workers' strike, 1912).

Pearsall, Shelley. *Trouble Don't Last.* Knopf, 2002. Ages 11–15. (Northern Kentucky, slavery, 1859).

Pearsall, Shelley. *Crooked River.* Knopf, 2005. Ages 10–13. (White pioneers and Native Americans, Ohio, 1812).

Peck, Richard. *The River Between Us.* Dial, 2003. Ages 12–18. (Southern Illinois, early Civil War era, 1861).

Peck, Richard. *The Teacher's Funeral: A Comedy in Three Parts.* Dial, 2004. Ages 10–14. (Rural Indiana, 1904).

Philbrick, W. R. *The Mostly True Adventures of Homer P. Figg.* Blue Sky, 2009. Ages 9–14. (U.S. Civil War).

Preus, Margi. *Heart of a Samuai: Based on the True Story of Nakahama Manjiro.* Amulet, 2010. Ages 9–14. (Japan, 1827–1898).

Provensen, Alice. *Klondike Gold.* Simon & Schuster, 2005. (**PI**). Ages 7–10. (Canadian Gold Rush, Yukon, 1890s).

Raven, Margot T. *Night Boat to Freedom.* Illus. E. B. Lewis. Farrar, 2006. (**PI**). Ages 7–10. (Slavery, Kentucky).

Reeder, Carolyn. *Before the Creeks Ran Red.* Harper-Collins, 2003. Ages 11–15. (Beginning of the U.S. Civil War; three linked novellas set in different locations).

Schmidt, Gary. *Lizzie Bright and the Buckminster Boy.* Clarion, 2004. Ages 11–15. (Maine, race relations, 1912).

Siegelson, Kim. *Trembling Earth.* Putnam, 2004. Ages 10–14. (Okefenokee Swamp, Georgia, U.S. Civil War, 1860s).

Stolz, Joelle. *The Shadows of Ghadames.* Tran. Catherine Temerson. Delacorte, 2004. Ages 12–15. (Libya, 1800s).

Tal, Eve. *Double Crossing: A Jewish Immigration Story.* Cinco Puntos, 2005. Ages 11–15. (Ukraine, 1905).

Wells, Rosemary. *Red Moon at Sharpsburg.* Viking, 2007. Ages 12–15. (Virginia, Civil War stories interwoven from North and South, Battle of Antietam, 1862).

Wilson, Diane Lee. *Black Storm Comin'.* Simon & Schuster, 2005. Ages 11–16. (Missouri to California, Civil War era, biracial family, 1860).

Winter, Jonah. *The Fabulous Feud of Gilbert and Sullivan.* Illus. Richard Egielski. Scholastic, 2009. (**PI**). Ages 5–8. (Great Britain, 1842–1901).

Winthrop, Elizabeth. *Counting on Grace.* Random House, 2006. Ages 10–15. (Vermont mill, 1910).

Woodson, Jacqueline. *Show Way.* Illus. Hudson Talbott. Putnam, 2005. (**PI**). Ages 8–11. (African-American women, quilts; slavery to the present).

Yep, Laurence. *Spring Pearl.* Pleasant, 2002. Ages 9–14. (Canton, China, Opium Wars, 1857).

———. *The Traitor.* Farrar, 2003. Ages 10–14. (Chinese and Western coal miners in the Wyoming Territory, 1885).

Yin. *Coolies.* Illus. Chris Soentpiet. Philomel, 2001. (**PI**). Ages 8–12. (Chinese Americans, railroad, 1860s).

Zimmer, Tracie Vaughn. *The Floating Circus.* Bloomsbury, 2008. Ages 11–16. (Circus barge, New Orleans, 1850s).

Biography

Adler, David. *Frederick Douglas: A Noble Life.* Holiday, 2010. Ages 10–16. (U.S., African Americans, 1818–1895).

Armstrong, Jennifer. *Photo by Brady: A Picture of the Civil War.* Atheneum, 2005. Ages 12–14. (Photo essay).

Atkins, Jeannine. *Borrowed Names: Poems About Laura Ingalls Wilder, Madam C. J. Walker, Marie Curie, and their Daughters.* Henry Holt, 2010. (**NV**). Ages 13–18. (U.S. poetry, 1867–1957).

Blumberg, Rhoda. *York's Adventures with Lewis and Clark: An African-American's Part in the Great Expedition.* HarperCollins, 2004. Ages 11–15. (U.S., California, 1804–1806).

Bolden, Tonya. *Maritcha: A Nineteenth-Century American Girl.* Abrams, 2005. Ages 10–14. (1848–1929).

Brown, Don. *A Wizard from the Start.* Houghton Mifflin, 2010. (**PI**). Ages 6–9. (U.S. inventors, 1847–1931).

Brown, Mónica. *My Name Is Gabriela/Me llamo Gabriela: The Life of Gabriela Mistral/La vida de Gabriela Mistral.* Illus. John Parra. Luna Rising, 2005. (**PI**). Ages 5–7. (Bilingual English/Spanish; Chilean author, 1889–1957).

Burleigh, Robert. *Toulouse-Lautrec: The Moulin Rouge and the City of Light.* Abrams, 2005. (**PI**). Ages 8–14. (France, artist, 1864–1901).

Burleigh, Robert. *The Adventures of Mark Twain.* Illus. Barry Blitt. Atheneum, 2011. (**PI**). Ages 7–9. (U.S. author, 1872–1896).

Capaldi, Gina. *A Boy Named Beckoning: The True Story of Dr. Carlos Montezuma, A Native American Hero.* Carolrhoda, 2008. (**PI**). Ages 7–10. (Yavapi Indian, Arizona, late 1800s).

Cohn, Amy L., and Suzy Schmidt. *Abraham Lincoln.* Illus. David A. Johnson. Scholastic, 2002. (**PI**). Ages 7–11. (U.S. president, 1809–1865).

Cummins, Julie. *Women Daredevils: Thrills, Chills, and Frills.* Illus. Cheryl Harness. Dutton, 2007. (**COL**). Ages 8–12. (Stunt performers, 1880–1929).

Debon, Nicolas. *The Strongest Man in the World: Louis Cyr.* Groundwood, 2007. (**GR**). Ages 7–11. (Canada, 1863–1912).

Denenberg, Barry. *Lincoln Shot: A President's Life Remembered.* Illus. Christopher Bing. Feiwel & Friends, 2008. Ages 10–15. (Oversize book with striking newspaper-format pages; U.S. president).

Engle, Margarita. *The Poet Slave of Cuba: A Biography of Juan Francisco Manzano.* Illus. Sean Qualls. Holt, 2006. (**NV**). Ages 12–14. (Cuba, slaves, poetry, 1797–1854).

Fleischman, Sid. *The Trouble Begins at 8: A Life of Mark Twain in the Wild, Wild West.* HarperCollins, 2008. Ages 10–15. (U.S. author, 1835–1910).

Fleming, Candace. *The Lincolns: A Scrapbook Look at Abraham and Mary.* Random House, 2008. Ages 11–15. (Chapters alternate between husband and wife).

Fleming, Candace. *Amelia Lost: The Life and Disappearance of Amelia Earhart.* Schwartz & Wade, 2011. Ages 9–14. (U.S., women, pilot, 1897–1937).

Fradin, Dennis B. *Duel! Burr and Hamilton's Deadly War of Words.* Illus. Larry Day. Walker, 2008. (**PI**). Ages 8–11. (Famous Weehawken, New Jersey, duel, 1804).

Fradin, Judith B., and Dennis B. Fradin. *Jane Addams: Champion of Democracy.* Clarion, 2006. Ages 12–14. (U.S., woman, social reformer, 1860–1935).

Freedman, Russell. *Lincoln: A Photobiography.* Clarion, 1987. Ages 9–12. (U.S. president, 1809–1865).

Giblin, James Cross. *Good Brother, Bad Brother: The Story of Edwin Booth and John Wilkes Booth.* Clarion, 2005. Ages 11–14. (U.S. assassination, 1800s).

Heiligman, Deborah. *Charles and Emma: The Darwins' Leap of Faith.* Holt, 2009. Ages 14–18. (England, 1800s).

Helfer, Ralph. *The World's Greatest Elephant.* Illus. Ted Lewin. Philomel, 2006. (**PI**). Ages 7–12. (Ringling Brothers).

Hesse, Karen. *The Young Hans Christian Andersen.* Illus. Erik Blegvad. Scholastic, 2005. Ages 7–10. (Denmark, 1800s).

Hopkinson, Deborah. *Abe Lincoln Crosses a Creek: A Tall, Thin Tale (Introducing His Forgotten Frontier Friend),* Illus. John Hendrix. Schartz & Wade, 2008. (**PI**). Ages 4–8. (U.S., Kentucky 1809–1865).

Johnson, Dolores. *Onward: A Photobiography of African-American Polar Explorer Matthew Henson.* National Geographic, 2005. Ages 11–14. (U.S. explorer, North Pole, 1866–1955).

Jurmain, Suzanne. *The Forbidden Schoolhouse: The True and Dramatic Story of Prudence Crandall and Her Students.* Houghton, 2005. Ages 12–14. (U.S. educator, 1803–1890).

Keating, Frank. *Theodore.* Illus. Mike Wimmer. Simon & Schuster, 2006. (**PI**). Ages 7–12. (U.S. president, 1858–1919).

Kerley, Barbara. *Walt Whitman: Words for America.* Illus. Brian Selznick. Scholastic, 2006. (**PI**). Ages 9–12. (U.S. poet, Civil War era, 1819–1892).

Kerley, Barbara. *What to Do about Alice? How Alice Roosevelt Broke the Rules, Charmed the World, and Drove Her Father Crazy.* Illus. Edwin Fotheringham. Scholastic, 2008. (**PI**). Ages 5–10. (President Theodore Roosevelt's daughter in the White House, late 1800s).

Kerley, Barbara. *The Extraordinary Mark Twain (according to Susy).* Illus. Edwin Fotheringam. Scholastic, 2010. (**PI**). Ages 7–11. (U.S. author, 1872–1896).

Kraft, Betsy H. *Theodore Roosevelt: Champion of the American Spirit.* Clarion, 2003. Ages 10–14. (1858–1919).

Lutes, Jason, and Nick Bertozzi. *Houdini: The Hand-cuff King.* Hyperion, 2007. (**GR**). Ages 11–15. (Magician, 1908).

McClafferty, Carla Killough. *Something Out of Nothing: Marie Curie and Radium.* Farrar, 2006. Ages 12–16. (U.S. chemist, 1867–1934).

McCully, Emily Arnold. *Marvelous Mattie: How Margaret E. Knight Became an Inventor.* Farrar, 2006. (**PI**). Ages 5–8. (1838–1914).

McGinty, Alice. *Darwin.* Illus. Mary Azarian. Houghton Mifflin, 2009. (**PI**). Ages 5–9. (England, naturalist, 1809–1882).

Nelson, S. D. *Black Elk's Vision: a Lakota Story.* Abrams, 2010. Ages 10–14. (U.S., Black Elk, 1863–1950).

Nelson, Vaunda Micheaux. *Bad News for Outlaws: The Remarkable Life of Bass Reeves, Deputy U.S. Marshal.* Illus. Gregory Christie. Carolrhoda, 2009. (**PI**). Ages 8–12. (U.S., Oklahoma, African American, 1860–1874).

Old, Wendie C. *To Fly: The Story of the Wright Brothers.* Illus. Robert Andrew Parker. Clarion, 2002. (**PI**). Ages 8–11. (Late 1800s, aeronautics).

Place, François. *The Old Man Mad about Drawing: A Tale of Hokusai.* Trans. William Rodarmor. Godine, 2003. Ages 10–14. (Japan, social life and customs, 1760–1849).

Rappaport, Doreen. *Abe's Honest Words: The Life of Abraham Lincoln.* Illus. Gary Kelley. Hyperion, 2008. (**PI**). Ages 6–10. (Lincoln's life with quotations from his speeches and writings).

Ray, Deborah Kogan. *Down the Colorado: John Wesley Powell, the One-Armed Explorer.* Farrar, 2007. (**PI**). Ages 8–11. (Western exploration in U.S., 1869).

Rosen, Michael. *Dickens: His Work and His World.* Illus. Robert Ingpen. Candlewick, 2005. Ages 11–14. (London, 1800s).

Rumford, James. *Sequoyah: The Man Who Gave His People Writing.* Houghton, 2004. (**PI**). Ages 6–10. (Cherokee language, 1770–1843).

Sandler, Martin W. *Lincoln through the Lens: How Photography Revealed and Shaped an Extraordinary Life.* Walker, 2008. Ages 12–15. (Lincoln's life, 1809–1865).

Silverman, Erica. *Sholom's Treasure: How Sholom Alei-chem Became a Writer.* Illus. Mordicai Gerstein. Farrar, 2005. (**PI**). Ages 5–9. (Yiddish author of Jewish life in Russia, 1859–1916).

Sís, Peter. *The Tree of Life.* Farrar, 2003. (**PI**). Ages 12–16. (Charles Darwin, 1809–1888).

Varmer, Hjørdis. *Hans Christian Andersen: His Fairy Tale Life.* Trans. Tiina Nunnally. Illus. Lillian Brøgger. Groundwood, 2005. Ages 10–14. (Danish author, 1805–1875).

Warren, Andrea. *Charles Dickens and the Street Children of London.* Houghton, 2011. Ages 12–15. (1812–1870).

Weatherford, Carole. *Moses: When Harriet Tubman Led Her People to Freedom.* Illus. Kadir Nelson. Jump at the Sun, 2006. (**PI**). Ages 7–11. (Underground Railroad, 1820–1913).

Weatherford, Carole. *I Matthew Henson: A Polar Explorer.* Illus. Eric Velasquez. Walker, 2008. (**PI**). Ages 7–10. (African Americans, exploration, 1901).

White, Linda Arms. *I Could Do That! Esther Morris Gets Women the Vote.* Illus. Nancy Carpenter. Farrar, 2005. (**PI**). Ages 7–10. (U.S. suffragist, 1814–1907).

Wise, Bill. *Louis Sockalexis: Native American Baseball Pioneer.* Illus. Bill Fransworth. Lee & Low, 2007. (**PI**). Ages 9–11. (Penobscot Native American, baseball).

Yolen, Jane. *My Uncle Emily.* Illus. Nancy Carpenter. Philomel, 2009. (**PI**). Ages 5–8. (Amherst, Massachusetts, Emily Dickenson, 1830–1886).

World Wars in the Twentieth Century, 1914 to 1945

Historical Fiction

Bartoletti, Susan Campbell. *The Boy Who Dared.* Scholastic, 2008. Ages 12–18. (Germany, resistance movement, 1933–1945).

Bolden, Tonya. *Finding Family.* Bloomsbury, 2010. Ages 9–12. (West Virginia, African Americans, early 1900s).

Couloumbis, Audrey. *War Games: A Novel Based on a True Story.* Random House, 2009. Ages 9–13. (Greece, Nazi occupation, World War II).

Currier, Katrina Saltonstall. *Kai's Journey to Gold Mountain.* Illus. Gabhor Utomo. Angel Island, 2005. (**PI**). Ages 9–13. (Emigration from China, internment on Angel Island, 1934).

Curtis, Christopher Paul. *Bud, Not Buddy.* Delacorte, 1999. Ages 9–13. (Michigan, Depression era).

Flood, Nancy Bo. *Warriors in Crossfire.* Front Street, 2010. Ages 12–16. (World War II, South Pacific, 1939–1945).

Glatshteyn, Yankev. *Emil and Karl.* Trans. Jeffrey Shandler. Roaring Brook, 2006. Ages 10–15. (Pre–World War II Vienna, Nazi persecution, 1930s).

Hartnett, Sonya. *Thursday's Child.* Candlewick, 2002. Ages 12–16. (Australia, Great Depression).

Havill, Juanita. *Eyes Like Willy's.* HarperCollins, 2004. Ages 12–16. (Austrian and French friends, World War I era).

Hesse, Karen. *Out of the Dust.* Scholastic, 1997. (**NV**). Ages 11–18. (Oklahoma, 1930s).

Hesse, Karen. *Witness.* Scholastic, 2001. (**NV**). Ages 10–18. (Vermont, Ku Klux Klan, 1924). Series of poems in five acts.

Hesse, Karen. *The Cats in Krasinski Square.* Illus. Wendy Watson. Scholastic, 2004. (**PI**). Ages 9–12. (Warsaw, Poland, Jewish ghetto, World War II era).

Holm, Jennifer. *Turtle in Paradise.* Random House, 2010. Ages 9–12. (U.S., Key West, Depression era).

Hull, N. L. *On Rough Seas.* Clarion, 2008. Ages 9–13. (England to Dunkirk, World War II, 1939).

Janeczko, Paul B. *Worlds Afire.* Candlewick, 2004. (**NV**). Ages 12–15. (Hartford, Connecticut, fire, 1944).

Kadohata, Cynthia. *Weedflower.* Simon & Schuster, 2006. Ages 10–14. (Japanese-American internment camp, Arizona, World War II).

Larson, Kirby. *Hattie Big Sky.* Delacorte, 2006. Ages 11–15. (Homesteading in Montana, discrimination toward Germans, World War I, 1918).

Lawrence, Iain. *B for Buster.* Delacorte, 2004. Ages 12–18. (Canadian Air Force, World War II, 1943).

Lisle, Janet Taylor. *The Art of Keeping Cool.* Simon & Schuster, 2000. Ages 10–13. (U.S., Canada, World War II).

Morpurgo, Michael. *Private Peaceful.* Scholastic, 2004. Ages 13–18. (England and France, World War I).

Park, Linda Sue. *When My Name Was Keoko.* Clarion, 2002. Ages 10–14. (Japanese occupation of Korea, 1940s).

Parkinson, Siobhan. *Kathleen: The Celtic Knot.* Pleasant, 2003. Ages 10–14. (Ireland, poverty in Dublin, 1937).

Peck, Richard. *A Year Down Yonder.* Dial, 2000. Ages 10–15. (Southern Illinois, Depression era, 1937). Also *Here Lies the Librarian.* (2006). Ages 11–16. (Rural Indiana, 1914).

Peck, Robert Newton. *Horse Thief.* HarperCollins, 2002. Ages 13–18. (Florida, Depression era, 1930s).

Ray, Delia. *Ghost Girl: A Blue Ridge Mountain Story.* Clarion, 2003. Ages 10–13. (Virginia, 1929–1932).

Roy, Jennifer. *Yellow Star.* Marshall Cavendish, 2006. Ages 10–15. (Poland, Lodz ghetto, 1939–1945).

Ryan, Pam Muñoz. *Esperanza Rising.* Scholastic, 2000. Ages 9–13. (Mexico and U.S., Depression era).

Salisbury, Graham. *Eyes of the Emperor.* Random House, 2005. Ages 12–18. (Japanese Americans in World War II).

Salisbury, Graham. *House of the Red Fish.* Random House, 2006. Ages 10–15. Sequel to *Under the Blood-Red Sun.* (Japanese Americans, Hawai'i, World War II).

Santiago, Chiori. *Home to Medicine Mountain.* Children's Book Press, 1988. (**PI**). Ages 8–11. (Native Americans, boarding schools, 1930s).

Selznick, Brian. *The Invention of Hugo Cabret.* Scholastic, 2007. Ages 9–13. (Paris, 1930s).

Sepetys, Ruta. *Between Shades of Gray,* Philomel, 2011. Ages 13–18. (Lithuania, Siberia, Stalin, 1925–1953).

Sheth, Kashmira. *Keeping Corner.* Hyperion, 2007. Ages 12–18. (India, child widow, 1918).

Shulevitz, Uri. *How I Learned Geography.* Farrar Straus Giroux, 2008 (**PI**). Ages 5–8. (Germany, Warsaw, Poland, World War II).

Spillebeen, Geert. *Kipling's Choice.* Trans. Terese Edelstein. Houghton, 2005. Ages 12–16. (France, World War I).

Spinelli, Jerry. *Milkweed.* Random House, 2003. Ages 11–16. (Warsaw, Poland, persecution of Jews, 1940s).

Uchida, Yoshiko. *Journey to Topaz.* Illus. Donald Carrick. Scribner's, 1971. Ages 10–14. (U.S., internment of Japanese Americans, World War II).

Vanderpool, Clare. *Moon over Manifest.* Delacorte, 2010. Ages 10–14. (U.S., Kansas, Depression era).

Watkins, Yoko Kawashima. *So Far from the Bamboo Grove.* Beech Tree, 1986. Ages 10–15. (Japanese Occupation in Korea, 1939–1945).

Wells, Rosemary. *Wingwalker.* Illus. Brian Selznick. Hyperion, 2002. Ages 8–11. (Oklahoma, Depression era, 1930s).

Wiseman, Eva. *Puppet: A Novel.* Tundra, 2009. Ages 12–18. (Hungary, Hungarian blood libel trial, 1883).

Wolf, Joan M. *Someone Named Eve.* Clarion, 2007. Ages 11–16. (Czechoslovakian survivor, World War II, 1942).

Woodson, Jacqueline. *Coming On Home Soon.* Illus. by E. B. Lewis. Putnam, 2004. (**PI**). Ages 5–9. (African-American family, war effort, World War II).

Zusak, Markus. *The Book Thief.* Knopf, 2006. Ages 13–18. (Munich, Germany, German foster girl, World War II).

Biography

Anderson, M. T. *Strange Mr. Satie.* Illus. Petra Mathers. Viking, 2003. (**PI**). Ages 8–12. (French composer, 1866–1925).

Barbour, Karen. *Mr. Williams.* Holt, 2005. (**PI**). Ages 5–8. (U.S. rural African Americans, oral history, 1930s).

Bartoletti, Susan Campbell. *Hitler Youth: Growing Up in Hitler's Shadow.* Scholastic, 2005. Ages 11–14. (Nazis, Germany, 1939–1945).

Bernier-Grand, Carmen T. *Frida: Viva la Vida! Long Live Life!* Illus. David Diaz. Marshall Cavendish, 2007. (**PI, NV**). Ages 12–18. (Mexican artist, 1907–1954). Also *Diego: Bigger than Life.* Illus. David Diaz. (2009). (**PI, NV**). Ages 13–16. (Mexican painter, 1886–1957).

Bolden, Tonya. *George Washington Carver.* Abrams Books, 2008. (**PI**). Ages 8–12. (African-American scientist and inventor, 1864–1943).

Bryant, Jennifer. *A River of Words: The Story of William Carlos Williams.* Illus. Melissa Sweet. Eerdmans, 2008. (**PI**). Ages 7–10. (U.S. poet and physician, 1883–1963).

Christensen, Bonnie. *Django.* Roaring Brook, 2009. (**PI**). Ages 6–12. (Gypsy jazz musician, disability, 1910–1953).

Denenberg, Barry. *Shadow Life: A Portrait of Anne Frank and Her Family.* Scholastic, 2005. Ages 12–14. (Holocaust, 1939–1945).

de la Peña, Matt. *A Nation's Hope: the True Story of Boxing Legend Joe Louis.* Illus. Kadir Nelson. Dial, 2011. Ages 5–9. (U.S., African-American boxer, World War II).

Fleischman, Sid. *Escape! The Story of the Great Houdini.* Greenwillow, 2006. Ages 10–14. (Magician, 1874–1926).

Fleischman, Sid. *Sir Charlie Chaplin: The Funniest Man in the World.* Greenwillow, 2010. Ages 12–16. (England, comedian 1889–1977).

Fleming, Candace. *Our Eleanor: A Scrapbook Look at Eleanor Roosevelt's Remarkable Life.* Atheneum, 2005. Ages 11–14. (U.S. first lady, 1884–1962).

Grimes, Nikki. *Talkin' about Bessie: The Story of Aviator Elizabeth Coleman.* Illus. E. B. Lewis. Scholastic/Orchard, 2002. (**PI**). Ages 8–13. (African-American female pilot, 1896–1926).

Krinitz, Esther, and Bernice Steinhardt. *Memories of Survival.* Hyperion, 2005. Ages 10–12. (Poland, 1939–1945).

Krull, Kathleen. *Albert Einstein.* Illus. Boris Kulikov. Viking, 2009. Ages 12–15. (German-born physicist, 1879–1955).

Maurer, Richard. *The Wright Sister.* Millbrook, 2003. Ages 12–16. (Katharine Wright Haskell, 1874–1929).

McCarthy, Meghan. *The Story of Charles Atlas, Strong Man.* Knopf, 2007. (**PI**). Ages 6–9. (Bodybuilder, 1893–1972).

Millman, Isaac. *Hidden Child.* Farrar, 2005. (**PI**). Ages 11–14. (Autobiography, Holocaust, France, 1940s).

Nelson, Marilyn. *Carver: A Life in Poems.* Front Street, 2000. Ages 12–16. (**NV**). (African-American scientist, 1900s).

Nobleman, Marc Tyler. *Boys of Steel: The Creators of Superman.* Illus. Ross MacDonald. Knopf, 2008. (**PI**). Ages 6–8. (Inventors of the fictional cartoon character, 1930s).

Parker, Robert Andrew. *Piano Starts Here: The Young Art Tatum.* Schwartz & Wade, 2008. (**PI**). Ages 6–10. (African-American jazz musician, 1910–1956).

Partridge, Elizabeth. *This Land Was Made for You and Me: The Life and Songs of Woody Guthrie.* Viking, 2002. Ages 11–16. (U.S. folk singer and composer, 1912–1967).

Phelan, Matt. *Around the World: Three Remarkable Journeys.* Candlewick, 2011. (**GR**). Ages 10–13. (Thomas Stevens, Nellie Bly, Joshua Slocum, world travel, 1900s).

Poole, Josephine. *Anne Frank.* Illus. Angela Barrett. Knopf, 2005. (**PI**). Ages 11–13. (Netherlands, Holocaust, 1940s).

Rappaport, Doreen. *Eleanor, Quiet No More: The Life of Eleanor Roosevelt.* Illus. Gary Kelley. Disney/Hyperion, 2009. (**PI**). Ages 7–10. (U.S. first lady, 1884–1962).

Rubin, Susan Goldman, with Ela Weissberger. *The Cat with the Yellow Star: Coming of Age in Terezin.* Holiday, 2006. Ages 9–13. (Holocaust, Czech Jews, 1939–1945).

Russo, Marisabina. *Always Remember Me: How One Family Survived World War II.* **(PI)**. Atheneum, 2005. Ages 8–12. (Germany, Holocaust, 1940s).

Stone, Tanya Lee. *Sandy's Circus: A Story about Alexander Calder.* Illus. Boris Kulikov. Viking, 2008. **(PI)**. Ages 5–9. (Calder's wire sculptures, Paris, 1920s).

Sweet, Melissa. *Balloons over Broadway: The True Story of the Puppeteer of Macy's Parade.* Houghton Mifflin, 2012. **(PI)**. Ages 5–9. (Tony Sarg, inventor, helium balloons, 1920s).

Yoo, Paula. *Sixteen Years in Sixteen Seconds: The Sammy Lee Story.* Illus. Dom Lee. Lee & Low, 2005. **(PI)**. Ages 6–10. (Korean immigrant diver, 1932).

Post-World War II Era, 1945 to 1990

Historical Fiction

Addy, Sharon. *Lucky Jake.* Illus. Wade Zahares. Houghton Mifflin, 2007. **(PI)**. Ages 5–8. (U.S. gold rush).

Burg, Ann E. *All the Broken Pieces: A Novel in Verse.* Scholastic, 2009. **(NV)**. Ages 11–15. (Vietnam War era).

Clinton, Catherine. *A Stone in My Hand.* Candlewick, 2002. Ages 11–16. (Palestine, 1980s).

Curtis, Christopher Paul. *The Watsons Go to Birmingham—1963.* Delacorte, 1995. Ages 8–12. (Flint, Michigan, to Birmingham, Alabama, Civil Rights movement).

Cushman, Karen. *The Loud Silence of Francine Green.* Clarion, 2006. Ages 11–15. (McCarthyism, Louisiana, 1950s).

Going, K. L. *The Liberation of Gabriel King.* Putnam, 2005. Ages 9–12. (Georgia, prejudice, 1976).

Edwardson, Debby D. *My Name is Not Easy.* Marshall Cavendish, 2011. Ages 12–15. (Alaska, Inupiaq, Catholic boarding school, five narrators, 1960s).

Gantos, Jack. *Dead End in Norvelt.* Farrar, 2011. Ages 11–14. (Small town, Pennsylvania, 1960s).

Harrington, Janice N. *Going North.* Illus. Jerome Lagarrigue. Farrar, 2004. **(PI)**. Ages 7–11. (African Americans, 1964).

Herrera, Juan Felipe. *Downtown Boy.* Scholastic, 2005. **(NV)**. Ages 10–14. (Migrant workers, California, 1958–1959).

Holt, Kimberly Willis. *When Zachary Beaver Came to Town.* Holt, 1999. Ages 10–14. (Small town, Texas, Vietnam War era, 1971).

Johnston, Tony. *Bone by Bone by Bone.* Roaring Brook, 2007. Ages 11–16. (Race relations in Tennessee, 1950s).

Kadohata, Cynthia. *Kira-Kira.* Simon & Schuster, 2004. Ages 11–18. (Georgia, Japanese Americans, late 1950s).

Lai, Thanhha. *Inside Out & Back Again.* Harper, 2011. Ages 9–14. (Vietnamese immigrants, 1975).

Levine, Ellen. *Catch a Tiger by the Toe.* Viking, 2005. Ages 10–14. (McCarthy congressional hearings, Communism, 1953).

Lorbiecki, Marybeth. *Jackie's Bat.* Illus. Brian Pinkney. Simon & Schuster, 2003. **(PI)**. Ages 6–9. (Jackie Robinson, Brooklyn Dodgers, 1947).

Lyon, George Ella. *Sonny's House of Spies.* Simon & Schuster, 2004. Ages 12–15. (Alabama, 1940–1950).

Mankell, Henning. *Secrets in the Fire.* Trans. Anne Connie Stuksrud. Annick, 2003. Ages 11–14. (Southern Africa, land mines, Mozambique civil war, 1970s and 1980s).

Martin, Ann. *A Corner of the Universe.* Scholastic, 2002. Ages 9–13. (Small town, autism, 1960).

Mason, Margaret H. *These Hands.* Illus Floyd Cooper. Houghton Mifflin, 2010. Ages 5–8. (African Americans, Civil Rights era).

Russell, Ching Yeung. *Tofu Quilt.* Lee & Low, 2009. **(NV)**. Ages 9–12. (Hong Kong, 1960s).

Schmidt, Gary D. *Okay for Now.* Clarion, 2011. Ages 11–14, (U.S., Vietnam War era, 1968).

Selznick, Brian. *Wonderstruck: A Novel in Words and Pictures*. Ages 9–14. **(PI)**. Scholastic, 2011. (New York, 1977).

Sharenow, Robert. *My Mother the Cheerleader.* Harper, 2007. Ages 12–15. (School integration, New Orleans, 1960).

Veciana-Suarez, Ana. *Flight to Freedom.* Orchard, 2002. Ages 11–16. (Cuban immigrant to Miami, 1967).

White, Ruth. *The Search for Belle Prater.* Farrar, 2005. Ages 10–15. Also *Belle Prater's Boy,* 1996. (Kentucky, 1950s).

White, Ruth. *Little Audrey.* Farrar, 2008. Ages 9–13. (Virginia coal mining camp, 1948).

Wiles, Deborah. *Countdown.* Scholastic, 2010. Ages 9–12. (U.S., 1960s).

Williams-Garcia, Rita. *One Crazy Summer.* Amistad, 2010. Ages 8–14. (Oakland, California, Black Panthers, 1968).

Biography

Adler, David A. *A Picture Book of Dwight David Eisenhower.* Holiday, 2002. (**PI**) Ages 7–9. (U.S. president, 1890–1969).

Alcorn, Stephen. *Odetta, The Queen of Folk.* Scholastic, 2010. (**PI**). Ages 5–9. (African Americans, folk singers).

Aldrin, Buzz. *Reaching for the Moon.* Illus. Wendell Minor. HarperCollins, 2005. (**PI**). Ages 7–10. (Autobiography).

Barakat, Ibtisam. *Tasting the Sky: A Palestinian Childhood.* Farrar, 2007. Ages 12–16. (Memoir, military occupation in Palestine, 1961–1987).

Bausum, Ann. *Freedom Riders: John Lewis and Jim Zwerg on the Front Lines of the Civil Rights Movement.* National Geographic, 2005. Ages 12–15. (U.S. South, 1961).

Bernier-Grand, Carmen. *César: ¡Sí, Se Puede!/ Yes, We Can!* Illus. David Diaz.. Cavendish, 2005. (**PI**). Ages 9–12. (Labor rights, migrant farm workers, U.S.).

Bernier-Grand, Carmen. *Alicia Alonso: Prima Ballerina.* Illus. Raul Colon. Cavendish, 2011. (Dance, blindness, Cuba, 1921–2012).

Bridges, Ruby and Margo Lundell. *Through My Eyes.* Scholastic, 1999. Ages 9–16. (Civil rights, school integration, U.S. South, 1960).

Brimner, Larry. *We Are One: The Story of Bayard Rustin.* Boyds Mills, 2007. Ages 11–16. (Civil rights, 1940–1980).

Brimner, Larry. *Black & White: The Confrontation between Reverend Fred L. Shuttlesworth and Eugene "Bull" Connor.* Calkins Creek, 2011. Ages 12–15. (Civil rights, Birmingham, Alabama, 1950s and 1960s).

Chin-Lee, Cynthia. *Amelia to Zora: Twenty-Six Women Who Changed the World.* Charlesbridge, 2005. Ages 9–13. (Women, global cultures).

Cline-Ransome, Lesa. *Young Pelé: Soccer's First Star.* Illus.James E. Ransome. Random House, 2007. (**PI**). Ages 5–9. (Brazilian soccer star, 1950s–1970s).

Delano, Marfé F. *Genius: A Photobiography of Albert Einstein.* National Geographic, 2005. Ages 11–14. (German-born physicist, 1879–1955).

Dendy, Leslie, and Mel Boring. *Guinea Pig Scientists: Bold Self-Experimenters of Science and Medicine.* Holt, 2005. (**COL**). Ages 11–14. (Eighteenth-century Italian scientist Lazzaro Spallanzani).

Ellis, Deborah. *Our Stories, Our Songs: African Children Talk about AIDS.* Fitzhenry & Whiteside (Canada), 2005. Ages 12–15. (Sub-Saharan Africa, orphans).

Fradin, Dennis Brindell. *With a Little Luck: Surprising Stories of Amazing Discovery.* Dutton, 2006. (**COL**). Ages 12–14. (Scientists).

Freedman, Russell. *The Voice That Challenged a Nation: Marian Anderson and the Struggle for Equal Rights.* Clarion, 2004. Ages 11–14. (African-American singer, U.S. Civil Rights era).

Giovanni, Nikki. *Rosa.* Illus. Bryan Collier. Holt, 2005. (**PI**). Ages 8–11. (Civil rights activist).

Golio, Gary. *Jimi: Sounds Like a Rainbow; A Story of the Young Jimi Hendrix.* Illus. Javaka Steptoe. Clarion, 2010. Ages 8–11. (African-American musician, 1960s and 1970s).

Greenberg, Jan, and Sandra Jordan. *Action Jackson.* Illus. Robert Andrew Parker. Millbrook, 2002. (**PI**). Ages 7–10. (U.S. artist, 1912–1956).

Greenberg, Jan, and Sandra Jordan. *Runaway Girl: The Artist Louise Bourgeois.* Abrams, 2003. Ages 12–16. (French modern artist).

Hoose, Phillip. *We Were There, Too! Young People in U.S. History.* Farrar, 2001. Ages 10–13. (A collective biography of sixty young people who influenced their times).

Hoose, Phillip. *Claudette Colvin: Twice Toward Justice.* Melanie Kroupa, 2009. Ages 12–18. (U.S. Civil Rights era).

Johnson, Jen C. *Seeds of Change.* Illus. Sonia Sadler, Lee and Low, 2010. (**PI**). Ages 7–10. (Kenyan conservationist).

Levine, Ellen. *Rachel Carson.* Viking, 2007. Ages 10–16. (Marine biologist, 1962). Up Close biography series.

McDonough, Yona Zeldis. *Hammerin' Hank: The Life of Hank Greenberg.* Illus. Malcah Zeldis. Walker, 2006. (**PI**). Ages 7–12. (Jewish baseball players, 1930s and1940s).

Napoli, Donna Jo. *Mama Miti : Wangari Maathai and the Trees of Kenya.* Illus. Kadir Nelson. Simon & Schuster, 2010. (**PI**). Ages 5–9. (Kenyan environmentalist, 1980s).

Niven, Penelope. *Carl Sandburg: Adventures of a Poet.* Illus. Marc Nadel. Harcourt, 2003. (**PI**), Ages 7–11. (Poet, U.S., 1878-1967).

Nivola, Claire A. *Planting the Trees of Kenya: The Story of Wangari Maathi.* Farrar, 2008. (**PI**). Ages 6–9. (Kenyan environmentalist, 1980s).

Rappaport, Doreen. *Martin's Big Words: The Life of Dr. Martin Luther King, Jr.* Illus. Bryan Collier. Hyperion, 2001. (**PI**). Ages 8–10. (U.S. civil rights activist).

Rembert, Winfred. *Don't Hold Me Back: My Life and Art.* Cricket, 2003. (**PI**). Ages 9–13. (Autobiography, African-American folk artist, Georgia, 1950s).

Ryan, Pam Munoz. *When Marian Sang: The True Recital of Marian Anderson.* Illus. Brian Selznick. Scholastic, 2002. (**PI**). Ages 6–10. (African-American singer, 1897–1993).

Ryan, Pam Munoz. *The Dreamer.* Illus. Peter Sis. Scholastic, 2010. (**PI**). Ages 9–14. (Chile, Pablo Neruda, 1904–1973).

Sís, Peter. *The Wall: Growing Up behind the Iron Curtain.* Farrar, 2007. (**PI/GR**). Ages 10–15. (Autobiography, Czech Republic, Communist era, 1960s).

Tavares, Matt. *Henry Aaron's Dream.* Candlewick, 2010. (**PI**). Ages 5–9. (African American, baseball, 1947).

Wing, Natasha. *An Eye for Color: The Story of Josef Albers.* Illus. Julia Breckenreid. Holt, 2009. (**PI**). Ages 5–9. (German-born American artist, 1975).

Winter, Jeanette. *Wangari's Tree of Peace.* Harcourt, 2008 (**PI**). Ages 5-8. (Kenya, environmentalist, 1980s).

Winter, Jeanette. *The Watcher: Jane Goodall's Life with the Chimps.* Schwartz & Wade, 2011. (**PI**). Ages 7–11. (U.S. primatologists, 1934–present).

Winter, Jonah. *Roberto Clemente: Pride of the Pittsburgh Pirates.* Illus. Raúl Colón. Atheneum, 2005. (**PI**). Ages 7–11. (Puerto Rican baseball player, 1955–1972).

Winter, Jonah. *Dizzy.* Illus. Sean Qualls. Scholastic, 2006. (**PI**). Ages 8–14. (African-American jazz musician, 1917–1993).

Winter, Jonah. *You Never Heard of Sandy Koufax?!* Illus. Andre Carrilho. Schwartz & Wade, 2009. (**PI**). Ages 7–10. (U.S. Jewish baseball players, 1965).

Related Films, Videos, and DVDs

Historical Fiction

The Devil's Arithmetic. (1999). Author: Jane Yolen (1988). 97 minutes.

Grandfather's Journey. (2008). Author: Allen Say (1993). 9 minutes.

Henry's Freedom Box. (2009). Author: Ellen Levin (2007). 12 minutes.

Lyddie. (1995). Author: Katherine Paterson (1991). 90 minutes.

A Midwife's Tale. (1997). Author: Laurel Ulrich (1990). 88 minutes.

My Louisiana Sky. (2001). Author: Kimberly Willis Holt (1998). 98 minutes.

Sarah, Plain and Tall. (1991) and Skylark (1999). Author: Patricia MacLachlan (1985, 1994). 98 minutes.

Seabiscuit. (2003). Author: Laura Hildenbrand (2001). 141 minutes.

So Far from Home. (1999). Author: Barry Denenberg (1997). Dear America Series. 30 minutes.

The Other Side. (2012). Author: Jacqueline Woodson (2001). 8 minutes.

Biography

The Diary of Anne Frank. (1959). Author: Anne Frank (1953). 171 minutes.

John, Paul, George & Ben. (2007). Author: Lane Smith (2006). 12 minutes.

The Man Who Walked between the Towers. (2005). Author/Illustrator: Mordicai Gerstein (2003). 10 minutes.

Snowflake Bentley. (2003). Author: Jacqueline Briggs Martin (1998). Illustrator: Mary Azarian. 16 minutes.

Will You Sign Here, John Hancock? (1997). Author: Jean Fritz (1997). Illustrator: Trina Schart Hyman. 30 minutes.

Chapter Ten

Informational Books

Questions at Night

Why
Is the sky?

What starts the thunder overhead?
Who makes the crashing noise?
Are the angels falling out of bed?
Are they breaking all their toys?

Why does the sun go down so soon?
Why do the night-clouds crawl
Hungrily up to the new-laid moon
And swallow it, shell and all?

If there's a bear among the stars,
As all the people say,
Won't he jump over those pasture-bars
And drink up the Milky Way?

Does every star that happens to fall
Turn into a firefly?
Can't it ever get back to Heaven at all?
And why
Is the sky?

—Louis Untermeyer

Children are naturally curious with an intense interest in the world around them. Informational books nourish this curiosity with interesting facts and explanations along with provocative questions and issues that encourage a thirst for further inquiry. Dry, bland textbooks that fail to engage children as inquirers can be replaced by innovative, colorful, intriguing informational books that are excellent resources for children's interests as well as the school curriculum.

Definition and Description

Informational books give verifiable factual information or explain some aspect of the biological, social, or physical world. These books are literature, not textbooks, and differ in the quality of the writing and illustrations and in their intent. While textbooks are written with the intention of teaching a large body of facts from the view of an expert imparting that knowledge to children, well-written informational literature focuses on a particular topic or issue to engage children's curiosity from the perspective of one enthusiast sharing with another.

Writing in informational books is often referred to as *expository writing,* or writing that explains, whereas fiction writing is called *narrative writing,* or writing that tells a story. This distinction is overly simplistic as fiction and nonfiction both use narrative and expository writing. A science information book such as *The Tarantula Scientist* by Sy Montgomery includes the story of that scientist's life along with information on tarantulas, and Jim Murphy's *An American Plague* tells the stories of people caught up in the panic of the plague as well as historical information. These books introduce readers to the community and practices of science and history; they don't just give facts. The difference is that informational books are about reality and the events, people, places, and ideas are *not* made up, while anything can be made up in fiction writing (Colman, 2007). Another difference is that the main purpose of fiction is to help readers understand what it means to be human, while informational books primarily focus on helping readers discover some aspect of the real world.

Although school and public library records indicate that informational literature makes up 50 to 85 percent of book circulation for children, test scores and research studies indicate that U.S. elementary students score better on literary reading than on informational reading. One reason for this discrepancy is a lack of classroom experience with informational literature in the early grades where fiction is the dominant choice of teachers. This gap is shifting because the Common Core State Standards recommend a 50/50 split between expository and narrative texts, starting in Kindergarten.

Many recent research studies have focused on the reading of informational books in the elementary grades (see Table 10.1). These studies reveal that only through repeated experience with informational books do children learn how to read and write that genre. Children need to learn how to read and enjoy informational books since most day-to-day reading (textbooks, news reports, instructions, recipes, etc.) is expository from middle school through adulthood. A key factor in comprehending expository text is that readers relate new information found in the text to their current understandings and experiences.

Particularly in the early grades, teachers and librarians may have to take the lead in introducing informational literature to students, since parents and caregivers traditionally select fiction for read-alouds. Selecting excellent works of informational literature for reading aloud and suggesting these books to parents for at-home reading is a good way to begin. Calling attention to students' existing

Table 10.1 Important Studies on Reading and Informational Literature		
Researcher(s)	**Subjects**	**Findings**
Jeong, Gaffney, & Choi (2010)	Fifteen grade 2, 3, and 4 classrooms	Examined the availability of informational materials and the time spent with these texts and found only minimal changes at the different grade levels. Teachers did not have a balance of narrative and informational texts at any grade level.
Maloch (2008)	Year-long case study of grade 2 classrooms	Examined the uses of informational text and the support provided by the teacher, and noted the significance of meaningful opportunities to interact with informational texts, mediations of difficulty, vocabulary and discussion, and explicit teaching of text structures.
Mullis, Martin, Kennedy, & Foy (2007)	200,000 fourth-graders from forty countries	U.S. students scored lower in informational reading than in literary reading and ranked fifteenth overall among forty participating countries.
Duke (2000)	Twenty grade 1 classrooms, ten each from very high and very low SES groups	Presence of nonfiction texts and use of nonfiction in class were rare to nonexistent. Consequently, students were unable to read and write informational texts successfully. Findings applied particularly to low-SES students.
Campbell, Kapinus, & Beatty (1995)	National sample of fourth-graders	Students with experience reading magazines and nonfiction had higher average reading proficiencies than those who never read these types of materials.

knowledge on a topic and noting the various text structures while reading will help students learn to read and appreciate this genre. In addition, informational books can be promoted as options in students' self-choice reading, added to classroom library collections, and used across the curriculum.

Types of Informational Books

The types of informational books are based on format and how information is presented on the book page, rather than with the information itself. The most common formats are:

- *Informational chapter book.* This format features a large amount of text that is organized into chapters along with graphics and illustrations, such as *Truce: The Day Soldiers Stopped Fighting* by Jim Murphy and *Life on Earth—and Beyond* by Pamela Turner.

- *Informational picture book.* This format features brief text and large, uncomplicated illustrations that are integral to conveying the information. Examples include *Lady Liberty* by Doreen Rappaport, illustrated by Matt Tavares, and *The Story of Salt* by Mark Kurlansky, illustrated by S. D. Schindler.

- *Concept picture book.* This type of picture book presents only one or two scientific or social concepts through brief, uncomplicated text accompanied by numerous large illustrations. Originally conceived for young children, these books are now also written for older children. *Dogs and Cats* by Steven Jenkins uses a flip-book format to distinguish between cats and dogs, while *Just One Bite* by Lola Schaefer uses life-sized illustrations to show what animals can consume in a single bite.

- *Photo essay.* Presentation of information in the photo essay is equally balanced between text and illustration with excellent information-bearing photographs and a crisp, condensed writing style. Photo essays are generally written for children in the intermediate grades and up, such as *Sneeze!* by Alexandra Siy, with photographs by Dennis Kunkel.

- *Fact books.* Presentation of information in these books is mainly through lists, charts, and tables in almanacs, books of world records, and sports trivia and statistics books, such as *The Guinness Book of World Records.*

- *Informational book series.* Series books consist of multiple books that share a general topic, format, writing style, and reading level. Some series books only convey facts and generalizations about the topic while others, such as HarperCollins' Lets-Read-and-Find-Out Science series, are characterized by careful research and high-quality writing and illustration. A series can have a sole author–illustrator team, as in Scholastic's Magic School Bus series by Joanna Cole and Bruce Degen; or each book can be created by a different author–illustrator team, as in Houghton Mifflin's Scientists in the Field series. Informational series books are published for all age groups and on topics tailored to school curricula. A list of some of the best informational series books is included at the end of the Recommended Books list.

- *Multigenre books.* These books combine elements of both fiction and nonfiction and present accurate factual information alongside an entertaining ribbon of fiction or poetry, such as the well-known Magic School Bus books by Joanna Cole. *Where in the Wild?* by David M. Schwartz and Yael Schy, with fold-out illustrations by Dwight Kuhn, combines poetry with facts about animal camouflage in the wild.

- *Activity books.* This format is organized around directions for activities, such as crafts, recipes, or experiments, as in Vicki Cobb's *See for Yourself: More than 100 Amazing Experiments.*

- *Reference books.* Encyclopedias, dictionaries, and atlases serve as references and provide an overall coverage of a large topic with many facts. An example is Thomas Holtz's *Dinosaurs: The Most Complete, Up-To-Date Encyclopedia for Dinosaur Lovers of All Ages.*

Evaluation and Selection of Informational Books

Children should be offered a variety of books on a particular topic so they can compare across books and consider a range of perspectives. No one book can cover a topic completely, and not every informational book needs to meet every criterion to be worthy. The following selection criteria should be considered:

- **Is the book written in a clear, direct, easily understandable style?** A tight, compressed, but conversational, writing style that is clear, simple, and vivid has become frequent in nonfictional text. We hear the author's enthusiastic voice instead of an impersonal scholarly tone.

- **Is the information accurate, authoritative, and current?** The information can be compared with other recently published sources on the topic. The book should contain information on the sources used by the author, the author's research processes, and acknowledgment of expert consultants. These sources need to be credible and involve multiple perspectives and can be noted in reference lists, further reading suggestions, narratives in the text, author's notes, and end notes.

- **Does the book avoid personification?** Personification involves attributing human qualities to animals, material objects, or natural forces and is considered factually inaccurate.

- **Is the information presented so as to support conceptual understanding and encourage analytical thinking?** The book should not just provide facts but explanations of those facts so that readers can build conceptual understandings. Presentation of information should go from known to unknown, general to specific, or simple to more complex. Reference aids such as tables of contents, indexes, pronunciation guides, glossaries, maps, charts, and tables make information in books easier to find and retrieve, more comprehensible, and more complete. Generalizations must be supported by evidence, such as facts and examples.

- **Does the book introduce readers to strategies for inquiry?** Readers should come to some understandings about the ways in which scientists and historians work together within a community and their inquiry strategies and tools. Books, such as Pamela Turner's *The Frog Scientist* and Scott Nelson's *Ain't Nothing But a Man: My Quest to Find the Real John Henry,* show readers how scientists and historians go about their work and invite students to engage in these processes.

- **Is the book organized around a theme or idea that brings coherence to the information?** Although an informational book may communicate hundreds of facts about a topic, the theme answers the question "What's the point?" The information should lead to ideas that invite readers to invest themselves. Sometimes the theme will be a cognitive concept, such as the way viruses multiply; in other cases it will be an understanding, such as an awareness of the social injustices in the history of the U.S. (e.g., slavery, child labor), as in Larry Dane Brimner's *Birmingham Sunday.*

- **Does the book distinguish between fact, theory, and opinion?** Theories or opinions should be flagged by carefully placed phrases such as "maybe," "is believed to be," or "perhaps." Given the shift to more narrative writing styles and the blending of fact and fiction, a clear distinction in the text between fact and fiction has become increasingly significant.

- **Are the depth and complexity of the topic or concept appropriate for the intended audience?** The author should consider the experiences and understandings that children bring to the topic. Issues include underestimating children's abilities, providing explanations that are beyond children's current understandings or interests, or oversimplifying to the point of inaccuracy. A balance of child-friendly language and scientific rigor is needed.

- **Are the captions and labels clearly written and informative?** The captions should help readers easily access the information included in illustrations, graphs, charts, and maps.

- **Is the book visually attractive to the child?** An intriguing cover, impressive or humorous illustrations, and balance of text and illustrations make books look interesting to a child. Check for the use of interesting visual features and an attractive design format.

- **Are the format and artistic medium appropriate to the content?** The illustrations need to match the intent and level of detail of the text. Child-like illustrations, for example, can fail to provide the detail needed to support the text. Engineered paper or pop-up illustrations are appropriate when three dimensions are required to give an accurate sense of placement of the parts of a whole, as in human anatomy.

Two award programs offer sources of good informational titles. The NCTE's Orbis Pictus Award for Outstanding Nonfiction for Children and the ALA's Robert F. Sibert Informational Book Medal spotlight what are considered to be the best works of nonfiction published in the preceding year (see Appendix A for these lists). Also, the National Science Teacher Association publishes an annual list of Outstanding Science Trade Books for Students K–12 (www.nsta.org /publications/ostb) and the National Council for the Social Studies creates an annual list of Notable Social Studies Trade Books for Young People (www.socialstudies.org/resources/notable).

The Significance of Style in Informational Books

Understanding the parts, or elements, of informational books and how they work together can help you become more analytical in evaluating and selecting informational literature. Style is how authors and illustrators, with their readers in mind, express themselves in their respective media. Sentence length and complexity, word choice, and formal versus conversational tone are part of the expository style, as are use of technical vocabulary, captions, and graphic elements such as tables, charts, illustrations, photographs, diagrams, maps, and indexes. Shelley Tanaka's colorful language and use of large, richly colored photographs, maps, sidebars, and a time line in

---

Excellent Informational Literature to Read Aloud

Bartoletti, Susan Campbell. *Black Potatoes: The Story of the Great Irish Famine, 1845–1850.* Ages 12–16.

Butterworth, Chris. *Sea Horse: The Shyest Horse in the Sea.* Illustrated by John Lawrence. Ages 4–8.

Cowley, Joy. *Chameleon, Chameleon.* Photographs by Nic Bishop. Ages 4–7.

Jenkins, Steve, and Robin Page. *How Many Ways Can You Catch a Fly?* Illustrated by Steve Jenkins. Ages 4–8.

Nelson, Kadir. *We Are the Ship: The Story of Negro League Baseball.* Ages 9–13.

Sayre, April Pulley. *Stars beneath Your Bed: The Surprising Story of Dust.* Ages 5–10.

Schaefer, Lola. *Just One Bite: 11 Animals and Their Bites at Life Size!* Illustrated by Geoff Waring. Ages 5–8.

Schlitz, Laura. *Good Masters! Sweet Ladies! Voices from a Medieval Village.* Illustrated by Robert Byrd. Ages 9–13.

Strauss, Rochelle. *One Well: The Story of Water on Earth.* Illustrated by Rosemary Woods. Ages 9–14.

Mummies: The Newest, Coolest, and Creepiest from Around the World demonstrate how style can make informational literature more interesting.

The *features* used by authors have different purposes that readers need to be able to use as tools in order to understand informational books:

- The *table of contents* overviews the main ideas and organization of the book, while an *index* identifies the specific page where a reader can find a particular topic.
- *Maps*, *diagrams,* and *graphs* provide visual displays of information that show relationships between the parts, while *cut-aways* and *cross-sections* let the reader look inside something.
- *Glossaries* can help readers understand the definitions of important words in comparison to *pronunciation keys* that help readers learn how to say a word.
- Pages often have words in a variety of *fonts* and *type sizes,* with bold and italic words signaling importance.

Each author uses different combinations of these tools, based on their audience and purpose, in ways that affect the accessibility of a book for readers. Readers spend more time studying these features and the illustrations and less time reading text in informational books as compared to fiction.

Another aspect of style is the *structure* of how an author organizes the information to be presented. Many children are familiar and comfortable with the chronological structure of fiction, but not the wide range of structures found in informational texts, which use both narrative and expository styles of writing. Some informational books employ a single text structure; others, particularly longer works, employ several. These structures include:

- *Description.* The author gives the characteristics of the topic, with the main topic organized around related subtopics (e.g., *Spiders* by Nic Bishop).
- *Sequence.* The author lists items in order, usually chronologically or numerically (e.g., *All Stations! Distress! April 15, 1912: The Day the Titanic Sank* by Don Brown).
- *Comparison.* The author juxtaposes two or more components and lists their similarities and differencess (e.g., *Wild Tracks! A Guide to Nature's Footprints* by Jim Arnosky).
- *Cause and effect.* The author states an action and shows the effect, or result, of this action (e.g., *Children of the Great Depression* by Russell Freedman).
- *Problem and solution* or *question and answer*. The author states a problem and its solution or solutions (e.g., *What Do You Do with a Tail Like This*? by Steve Jenkins and Robin Page).

Historical Overview of Informational Literature

The history of children's informational literature is linked to the publication of John Amos Comenius's *Orbis Pictus (The World in Pictures)* in 1657. Not only was this the first children's picture book, but it was also an informational book. This promising beginning was cut short, however, by the Puritan Movement. For nearly 200 years the vast majority of books published for and read by children were intended for moralistic instruction rather than information.

Rapid development of informational literature as a genre began in the 1950s and 1960s in response to the launching of Sputnik, the first artificial space satellite, by the former Soviet Union. Competing in the race for space exploration and new technology, the U.S. Congress funneled money into science education, and publishers responded with new and improved science trade books. Informational picture books for primary grades were introduced, leading to a trend toward more illustrations and less text in informational books for all levels.

As the stature of informational literature rose and more top-flight authors and illustrators were engaged in its production, the quality of research, writing, and art in these books improved. A lighter, yet factual, tone balanced with high-quality, informative illustrations and graphics emerged as the preferred nonfiction style.

In 1990, the National Council of Teachers of English established the Orbis Pictus Award for Outstanding Nonfiction for Children and, in 2001, the American Library Association established the Robert F. Sibert Informational Book Medal, signaling the acceptance of informational literature as an equal player in the field of children's literature. The dull, pedantic fact books that many adults remember from childhood have been replaced with books that have an engaging writing style, an emphasis on visual design, and a focus on accuracy about topics that intrigue children. Another trend is the tremendous growth of informational series books to meet curriculum needs in schools.

Topics of Informational Books

Although informational literature is just one chapter in this book, it is one of the largest single genres in children's literature, in that everything known to humankind is a conceivable topic. Organizing such an enormous variety of topics can be done in a variety of ways, one of which is a scientific approach, dividing the world of information into the biological, the physical, the applied, and the social sciences, along with the humanities.

MILESTONES in the Development of Informational Literature

Date	Book	Significance
1657	*Orbis Pictus* by John Amos Comenius	First known work of nonfiction for children
1683	*New England Primer*	First concept book for American children; reflected didacticism of the Puritan era
1922	*The Story of Mankind* by Hendrik Van Loon	Won the first Newbery Medal; greatly influenced children's books with its lively style and creative approach
1960	Let's-Read-and-Find-Out series by Franklyn Branley and Roma Gans	Introduced the science concept picture book for young children
1990	Orbis Pictus Award for Nonfiction established	Informational literature as a genre is recognized
2001	Robert F. Sibert Informational Book Medal established	Informational literature as a genre is further recognized

Biological Science

Biological science deals with living organisms and the laws and phenomena that relate to any organism or group of organisms. Topics that interest children include dinosaurs, pets, wild animals, ecology, and the environment. An example of such a book is *Extreme Animals: The Toughest Creatures on Earth* by Nicola Davies, illustrated by Neal Layton.

A subtopic of biological science that deserves special attention is human anatomy and sexuality. Young children are naturally interested in their bodies, and as they grow into puberty, they become interested in sex. Experts in the field of sex education suggest honest, straightforward answers to children's questions about their bodies, bodily functions, sex, and sexual orientation. Books on these topics are not necessarily appropriate for use in elementary schools, but are meant for parents who want a resource to share with their children. Teachers and librarians should be able to recommend age-appropriate books, such as Robie Harris's book *It's Not the Stork! A Book about Girls, Boys, Babies, Bodies, Families, and Friends*, illustrated by Michael Emberley.

Physical Science

Physical science, also referred to as ***natural science,*** deals primarily with nonliving materials. Rocks, landforms, oceans, the stars, and the atmosphere and its weather and seasons are topics that children can explore within the fields of geology, geography, oceanography, astronomy, and

Notable Authors and Illustrators of Informational Literature

Susan Campbell Bartoletti, author of informational books about young people during historic periods of oppression. *Hitler Youth: Growing Up in Hitler's Shadow; Black Potatoes: The Story of the Great Irish Famine.* www.scbartoletti.com

Nic Bishop, author/illustrator known for extreme close-up photographs of inhabitants of the natural world. *Spiders; Frogs; Red-Eyed Tree Frog* (with Joy Cowley). www.nicbishop.com

Joanna Cole, author of a variety of informational books for beginning independent readers. Magic School Bus series.

Lynn Curlee, author and illustrator of books about great historical monuments and architectural icons. *Capital; Parthenon; Skyscrapers; Ballparks: The Story of America's Baseball Fields.* http://curleeart.com

Russell Freedman, author of informational books about U.S. history. *Who Was First? Discovering the Americas; Children of the Great Depression; Freedom Walkers; Kids at Work.*

Steve Jenkins, author/illustrator known for colorful, textured cut-paper collage illustrations in informative picture books about living creatures. *Dogs and Cats; Prehistoric: Actual Size; Bones.* www.stevejenkinsbooks.com

David Macaulay, author/illustrator of several books about the construction of monumental buildings and informational picture books for older readers. *Built to Last; The New Way Things Work.* www.davidmacaulay.com

Jim Murphy, author of informational chapter books about events in history, primarily in the U.S. *An American Plague; A Savage Thunder; Truce.* www.jimmurphybooks.com

Pamela Turner, author of photo essays on science and nature and scientists in the field, many in global settings. *The Frog Scientist; Gorilla Doctors; Life on Earth—And Beyond.* www.pamelasturner.com

meteorology. Children can satisfy their curiosity about volcanoes and earthquakes in books such as Catherine Grace's *Forces of Nature,* while teachers can locate books on the solar system , such as Brian Floca's *Moonshot: The Flight of Apollo 11,* for class units.

Applied Science

Applied science deals with the practical applications of pure science devised by people. All machines—from simple levers to supercomputers, from bicycles to space rockets—are part of this field, and many children are interested in finding out how they work. Other aspects of applied science include the use of medicine to cure diseases, the processes by which food is produced, prepared, packaged, and marketed, and the design and manufacture of toys—topics of great interest to children. Children spend hours poring over the details in books, such as David Macaulay's *Built to Last* on architecture and *The New Way Things Work* on machines.

A specific type of book—the **experiment** or **how-to book**—capitalizes on children's desire for hands-on activities, as found in *Chemistry Science Fair Projects Using French Fries, Gumdrops, Soap, and Other Organic Stuff* by Robert Gardner and Barbara G. Conklin. These books range from directions for scientific experiments to cookbooks, guides to hobbies, and directions for small construction projects, like clubhouses.

Social Science

Social science deals with the institutions and functioning of society and the interpersonal relationships of individuals within a society, both in current events and historically. Children can learn about forms of government, religions, countries and cultures, money, and transportation, as well as life-changing historical events. Most children have a natural interest in books about careers, family relationships, and leisure activities. These books range from a focus on young children's interests, in Maya Ajmera's *What We Wear: Dressing Up Around the World,* to those of older readers in *What the World Eats* by Faith D'Aluisio and Peter Menzel, and include depictions of current events, such as Tony O'Brien's *Afghan Dreams: Young Voices of Afghanistan,* as well as historical events, such as Kadir Nelson's *We Are the Ship: The Story of the Negro Baseball League.*

One subtopic is books that name and define problems and problematic behaviors, informing children about actions to take to get help or cope with the problem. The How Can I Deal With . . . series offers case studies and advice on topics such as bullying, new babies, divorce, stepfamilies, death, and racism. Two outstanding series for older students, Issues in Focus Today and Issues That Concern You, discuss the problems associated with abortion, addictions, body image, abuse, bullying, discrimination, gangs, and sexuality.

Humanities

The *humanities* deal with fields that are cultural or artistic. Books of interest include those about the fine arts of drawing, painting, and sculpture; the performing arts of singing, dancing, making instrumental music, and acting; and handicrafts. Since many children are artistically creative and often study dance, music, and drawing, they can be invited to read about the arts and artists to learn new techniques or to draw inspiration from the experiences of others, as in *Ole! Flamenco* by George Ancona. Some might read these books to decide whether they are interested in developing their artistic talents. Books can make the arts more accessible to children by explaining what to look for in an art piece, such as Kimberley Lane's *Come Look with Me: Latin American Art,* or by revealing the hard work required of an artist to achieve a spectacular performance or an intriguing work of art, as in *Chuck Close: Face Book* by Chuck Close.

Reader Connections: Pairing Fact and Fiction

One effective strategy for engaging students with informational books and addressing Common Core State Standards is to pair an informational book with a related fiction book to encourage response and critical thinking. Pairing expository and narrative texts immerses readers into a story world that takes them to another time and place, bringing alive their imaginations, and, at the same time, provides them with information that makes the story "real" and can help them analyze the fiction world.

Examples of possible pairs of novels and informational books include:

- *Nory Ryan's Song* (Patricia Reilly Giff) with *Black Potatoes: The Story of the Great Irish Potato Famine* (Susan Bartoletti)
- *Out of the Dust* (Karen Hesse) with *Children of the Dust Bowl* (Jerry Stanley)
- *Counting on Grace* (Elizabeth Winthrop) with *Kids at Work* (Russell Freedman)
- *Flush* (Carl Hiaasen) with *Tracking Trash* (Loree Griffin Burns)
- *Project Mulberry* (Linda Sue Park) with *The Story of Silk* (Richard Sobol)

For young children, pairing fiction with informational books helps them sort out the characteristics of expository and narrative texts and develop reading strategies for these types of texts. By reading aloud a paired set of books each day, each at a different time of the day, teachers can invite children to discuss and compare the ideas and content as well as note the organizational structures and features that distinguish the two types of texts. Before analyzing the texts, however, children first need time to respond to the books and share their personal connections and what surprised or interested them. In addition, while fiction is meant to be read aloud cover to cover, informational books often do not need to be read aloud in this way. Some shorter books can easily be read in one sitting, but others are designed to read aloud only the relevant portions. Examples of paired picture books and informational books include:

- *Owl Moon* (Jane Yolen) with *All about Owls* (Jim Arnosky)
- *Stellaluna* (Janell Cannon) with *Little Lost Bat* or *Outside and Inside Bats* (Sandra Markle)
- *A Frog in the Bog* (Karma Wilson) with *Frog in a Bog* (John Himmelman)
- *A Color of My Own* (Leo Lionni) with *Chameleon, Chameleon* (Joy Cowley and Nic Bishop)
- *The Doorbell Rang* (Pat Hutchins) with *Fraction Fun* (David Adler)
- *John Henry* (Julius Lester) with *Ain't Nothing but a Man: My Quest to Find the Real John Henry* (Scott Nelson)

Today's nonfiction literature for children meets the needs and interests of young readers in quality, variety, and reader appeal. With these books, children's appetites for learning can be fed, while fueling their curiosity for more information.

Invitations for Further Investigation

- In a small group, select a text set of four to six informational books on a specific social studies or science topic or theme. Read and discuss your responses to the books and web connections and issues. Identify the differences across the books in their approaches and perspectives on the topic.

- Choose an informational book from the text set to analyze. Determine the type, features, and structure and evaluate the book based on the selection criteria. Also list the strategies needed by readers to understand and use the features in the book.

- Investigate the books in one of the informational book series listed in the Recommended Books list. Evaluate these books in terms of their support of the curricular area, their content, quality of writing and illustrations, and likely appeal to children.

- Locate and read several books for young people on a controversial topic such as evolution or sexuality. Examine how these books address the topic and consider in what contexts these books would be appropriate for children.

- Read one of the paired book sets suggested in the chapter with a partner. Develop a comparison chart or Venn diagram to show the similarities and differences in how that topic is explored in the two books. Discuss the ways in which the two books play off of each other for you as readers.

- Investigate pairing informational books with other genres in an inquiry unit. Choose a topic and grade level and generate several paired book sets that could be used to explore information or issues in the unit.

References

Campbell, J. R., Kapinus, B., & Beatty, A. S. (1995). Interviewing children about their literacy experiences. Data from NAEP's integrated reading performance record at grade 4. Washington, DC: U.S. Department of Education.

Colman, P. (2007). A new way to look at literature: A visual model for analyzing fiction and nonfiction texts. *Language Arts, 84*(3), 257–268.

Duke, N. K. (2000). 3.6 minutes a day: The scarcity of informational texts in first grade. *Reading Research Quarterly, 35*(2), 202–225.

Jeong, J., Gaffney, J. & Choi, J. (2010). Availability and use of informational texts in second-, third-, and fourth-grade classrooms. *Research in the Teaching of English, 44*(4), 415–456.

Maloch, B. (2008). Beyond exposure: The uses of informational texts in a second grade classroom. *Research in the Teaching of English, 42*(3), 315–362.

Mullis, I. V. S., Martin, M. O., Kennedy, A. M., & Foy, P. (2007). *IEA's Progress in International Reading Literacy Study in Primary School in 40 Countries: PIRLS 2006 International Report.* Boston, MA: TIMSS & PIRLS International Study Center, Boston College. Retrieved from http://timssandpirls.bc.edu/pirls2006/intl_rpt .html.

Untermeyer, L. (1985). Questions at night. In L. Untermeyer (Selector), *Rainbow in the sky.* San Diego: Harcourt.

Recommended Informational Books

Ages refer to content appropriateness and conceptual and interest levels. Formats other than informational chapter books are coded:

(**PI**) Picture book
(**COL**) Short story collection
(**GR**) Graphic novel

Biological Science

Arnosky, Jim. *Wild Tracks! A Guide to Nature's Footprints.* Sterling, 2008. (**PI**). Ages 7–11.

Aston, Dianna. *An Egg Is Quiet.* Illus. Sylvia Long. Chronicle, 2006. (**PI**). Ages 5–9. Also *A Seed is Sleepy* (2007).

Bishop, Nic. *Frogs.* Scholastic, 2008. (**PI**). Ages 7–10. Also *Spiders* (2007).

Bonner, Hannah. *When Fish Got Feet, Sharks Got Teeth, and Bugs Began to Swarm: A Cartoon Prehistory of Life Long before Dinosaurs.* National Geographic, 2007. (**PI**). Ages 8–11.

Butler, Dori Hillestad. *My Mom's Having a Baby.* Illus. Carol Thompson. Albert Whitman, 2005. (**PI**). Ages 7–9.

Butterworth, Chris. *Sea Horse: The Shyest Horse in the Sea.* Illus. John Lawrence. Candlewick, 2006. (**PI**). Ages 4–8. (England).

Campbell, Sarah. *Growing Patterns: Fibonacci Numbers in Nature.* Photos. Boyds Mills, 2010. (**PI**). Ages 6–9.

Cole, Joanna. *The Magic School Bus and the Climate Change.* Illus. Bruce Degen. Scholastic, 2010. (**PI**). Ages 7–9.

Collard, Sneed. *The Prairie Builders: Reconstructing America's Lost Grasslands.* Houghton, 2005. Ages 10–14.

Collard, Sneed. *Pocket Babies and Other Amazing Marsupials.* Darby Creek, 2007. Ages 8–12.

Cowley, Joy. *Chameleon, Chameleon.* Photos Nic Bishop. Scholastic, 2005. (**PI**). Ages 4–7. Also *Red-Eyed Tree Frog* (1999). (New Zealand).

Davies, Nicola. *Extreme Animals: The Toughest Creatures on Earth.* Illus. Neal Layton. Candlewick, 2006. (**PI**). Ages 8–10.

Doner, Kim. *On a Road in Africa.* Tricylce Press, 2008. (**PI**). Ages 5–8. (Kenya).

Farrell, Jeanette. *Invisible Allies: Microbes That Shape Our Lives.* Farrar, 2005. Ages 12–18.

Fisher, Aileen. *The Story Goes On.* Illus. Mique Moriuchi. Roaring Brook, 2005. (**PI**). Ages 4–7.

Fleischman, John. *Phineas Gage: A Gruesome but True Story about Brain Science.* Houghton, 2002. Ages 12–14.

Frost, Helen. *Monarch and Milkweed.* Illus. Leonid Gore. Atheneum, 2008. (**PI**). Ages 4–7.

Gibbons, Gail. *Ladybugs.* Holiday, 2012. (**PI**). Ages 5–9. Many books on animals for young children.

Harris, Robie H. *It's Not the Stork! A Book about Girls, Boys, Babies, Bodies, Families, and Friends.* Illus. Michael Emberley. Candlewick, 2006. Ages 5–9. For parents to share with children.

Harris, Robie H. *It's Perfectly Normal: A Book about Changing Bodies, Growing Up, Sex, and Sexual Health.* Illus. Michael Emberley. Candlewick, 2009. Ages 11–14.

Harris, Robie H. *Who Has What? All about Girls' Bodies and Boys' Bodies.* Illus. Nadine Bernard Wescott. Candlewick, 2011. (**PI**). Ages 5–9.

Hatkoff, Isabella, Craig Hatkoff, and Paula Kahumbu. *Owen & Mzee: The True Story of a Remarkable Friendship.* Photos Peter Greste. Scholastic, 2006. Ages 5–12. (Photo essay, Kenya).

Holtz, Thomas. *Dinosaurs: The Most Complete, Up-to-Date Encyclopedia for Dinosaur Lovers of All Ages.* Illus. Luis Rey. Random House, 2007. Ages 10–14.

Jenkins, Martin. *Can We Save the Tiger?* Illus. Vicky White. Candlewick, 2011. (**PI**). Ages 5–9.

Jenkins, Steve. *What Do You Do with a Tail Like This?* Houghton, 2003. (**PI**). Ages 4–7.

Jenkins, Steve. *Prehistoric Actual Size.* Houghton, 2005. (**PI**). Ages 5–10.

Jenkins, Steve. *Dogs and Cats.* Houghton, 2007. (**PI**). Ages 5–11.

Jenkins, Steve. *Bones: Skeletons and How They Work.* Scholastic, 2010. (**PI**). Ages 7–11.

Jenkins, Steve, and Robin Page. *How Many Ways Can You Catch a Fly?* Houghton, 2008. (**PI**). Ages 4–8.

Larson, Peter, and Kristin Donnan. *Bones Rock! Everything You Need to Know to Be a Paleontologist.* Invisible Cities, 2004. Ages 11–14.

Markle, Sandra. *Little Lost Bat.* Illus. Alan Marks. Charlesbridge, 2006. (**PI**). Ages 6–10.

Macaulay, David. *The Way We Work: Getting to Know the Amazing Human Body.* Houghton, 2008. Ages 10–15.

Montgomery, Sy. *The Tarantula Scientist.* Photos Nic Bishop. Houghton, 2004. Ages 9–12. (South America).

Montgomery, Sy. *Kakapo Rescue: Saving the World's Strangest Parrot.* Photos Nic Bishop. Houghton, 2010. Ages 9–12. (New Zealand).

O'Connell, Caitlin, and Donna Jackson. *The Elephant Scientist.* Houghton Mifflin, 2011. Ages 11–14. (Namibia).

Page, Robin, and Steve Jenkins. *Sisters and Brothers: Sibling Relationships in the Animal World.* Illus. Steve Jenkins. Houghton, 2008. (**PI**). Ages 7–9.

Pericoli, Matteo. *The True Story of Stellina.* Knopf, 2006. (**PI**). Ages 4–9.

Romanek, Trudee. *Squirt! The Most Interesting Book You'll Ever Read about Blood.* Illus. Rose Cowler. Kids Can, 2006. Ages 9–12.

Sayre, April Pulley. *Stars beneath Your Bed: The Surprising Story of Dust.* Illus. Ann Jonas. Greenwillow, 2005. (**PI**). Ages 5–10.

Schaefer, Lola. *Just One Bite: 11 Animals and Their Bites at Life Size!* Illus. Geoff Waring. Chronicle, 2010. (**PI**). Ages 5–9.

Schlosser, Eric, and Charles Wilson. *Chew on This: Everything You Didn't Want to Know about Fast Food.* Houghton, 2006. Ages 12–14.

Schulman, Janet. *Pale Male: Citizen Hawk of New York City.* Illus. Meilo So. Knopf, 2008. (**PI**). Ages 5–10.

Schwartz, David, and Yael Schy. *Where in the Wild? Camouflaged Creatures Concealed—and Revealed.* Illus. Dwight Kuhn. Tricycle, 2007. (**PI**). Ages 5–9.

Simon, Seymour. *Guts: Our Digestive System.* HarperCollins, 2005. (**PI**). Ages 9–14.

Singer, Marilyn. *What Stinks?* Darby Creek, 2006. (**PI**). Ages 9–12.

Siy, Alexandra. *Sneeze!* Photos Dennis Kunkel. Charlesbridge, 2007. Ages 9–18.

Sloan, Christopher. *The Human Story: Our Evolution from Prehistoric Ancestors to Today.* Photos Kenneth Garrett. Illus. Alfons Kennis and Adrie Kennis. National Geographic, 2004. Ages 11–18.

Turner, Pamela S. *Gorilla Doctors: Saving Endangered Great Apes.* Houghton, 2005. Ages 10–14. (Rwanda).

Turner, Pamela S. *Life on Earth—and Beyond.* Charlesbridge, 2008. Ages 10–13.

Turner, Pamela S. *The Frog Scientist.* Photos Andy Comins. Houghton, 2009. Ages 10–14.

Walker, Sally M. *Fossil Fish Found Alive: Discovering the Coelacanth.* Carolrhoda, 2002. Ages 10–13. (Rwanda).

Physical Science

Arnosky, Jim. *The Brook Book: Exploring the Smallest Streams.* Dutton, 2008. (**PI**). Ages 5–9.

Burns, Loree G. *Tracking Trash: Flotsam, Jetsam, and the Science of Ocean Motion.* Houghton, 2007. Ages 10–13.

Cherry, Lynne. *How We Know What We Know about Our Changing Climate.* Photos Gary Braasch. Dawn, 2008.

Deem, James. *Bodies from the Ice: Melting Glaciers and the Recovery of the Past.* Houghton, 2008. Ages 10–14.

Floca, Brian. *Moonshot: The Flight of Apollo 11.* Atheneum, 2009. (**PI**). Ages 6–9.

Godkin, Celia. *Fire!* Fitzhenry & Whiteside, 2006. (**PI**). Ages 6–9.

Grace, Catherine. *Forces of Nature: The Awesome Power of Volcanoes, Earthquakes, and Tornadoes.* National Geographic, 2004. Ages 11–14.

Harbo, Christopher. *The Explosive World of Volcanoes with Max Axiom, Super Scientist.* Capstone, 2008. (**GR**). Ages 9–12.

Lyon, George Ella. *All the Water in the World.* Illus. Katherine Tillotson. Atheneum, 2011. (**PI**). Ages 5–9.

Sly, Alexandra. *Cars on Mars: Roving the Red Planet.* Charlesbridge, 2009. Ages 9–12.

Strauss, Rochelle. *One Well: The Story of Water on Earth.* Illus. Rosemary Woods. Kids Can, 2007. (**PI**). Ages 9–14.

Treaster, Joseph B. *Hurricane Force: In the Path of America's Killer Storms.* Kingfisher, 2007. Ages 9–13.

Wick, Walter. *A Drop of Water: A Book of Science and Wonder.* Scholastic, 1997. Ages 8–11.

Applied Science

Abramson, Andra S. *Heavy Equipment Up Close.* Sterling, 2008. (**PI**). Ages 7–9.

Ball, Johnny. *Go Figure! A Totally Cool Book about Numbers.* DK Publishing, 2005. Ages 10–14.

Carlson, Laurie. *Thomas Edison for Kids: His Life and Ideas; 21 Activities.* Chicago Review, 2006. Ages 10–14.

Carson, Mary Kay. *Exploring the Solar System: A History with 22 Activities.* Chicago Review, 2006. Ages 10–14.

Cobb, Vicki. *See for Yourself: More than 100 Amazing Experiments.* Illus. Dave Klug. Skyhorse, 2010. Ages 9–12.

Curlee, Lynn. *Capital.* Atheneum, 2003. (**PI**). Ages 7–11. Also *Parthenon* (2004) and *Skyscrapers* (2007).

Fisher, Valorie. *How High Can a Dinosaur Count? And Other Math Mysteries.* Random House, 2006. (**PI**). Ages 6–10.

Gardner, Robert, and Barbara G. Conklin, *Chemistry Science Fair Projects Using French Fries, Gumdrops, Soap, and Other Organic Stuff.* Enslow, 2004. Ages 11–14.

Hakim, Joy. *The Story of Science: Aristotle Leads the Way.* Smithsonian, 2004. Ages 11–14. Story of Science series.

Jackson, Donna M. *ER Vets: Life in an Animal Emergency Room.* Houghton, 2005. Ages 12–14.

Katzen, Mollie. *Salad People and More Real Recipes.* Tricycle Press, 2005. Ages 5–8.

Leedy, Loreen. *The Great Graph Contest.* Holiday, 2005. (**PI**). Ages 6–8.

Levine, Shar. *The Ultimate Guide to Your Microscope.* Sterling, 2008. Ages 9–12.

Macaulay, David. *The New Way Things Work.* Houghton, 1998. Ages 10–15.

Macaulay, David. *Built to Last.* Houghton, 2010. Ages 10–15.

Mills, Andrea, and Phil Hunt. *Go! The Whole World of Transportation.* Dorling Kindersley, 2006. Ages 8–12.

Ridley, Sarah. *A Metal Can.* Gareth Stevens, 2006. Ages 7–9.

Ross, Val. *The Road to There: Mapmakers and Their Stories.* Tundra, 2003. Ages 12–16.

Skurzynski, Gloria. *Are We Alone? Scientists Search for Life in Space.* National Geographic, 2004. Ages 10–14.

Sullivan, George. *Built to Last: Building America's Amazing Bridges, Dams, Tunnels, and Skyscrapers.* Scholastic, 2005. Ages 12–16.

Walsh, Melanie. *10 Things I Can Do To Help My World.* Candlewick, 2008. (**PI**). Ages 5–8.

Social Science

Ajmera, Maya, Elise H. Derstine, and Cynthia Pon. *What We Wear: Dressing Up Around the World.* Photos. Charlesbridge, 2012. (**PI**). Ages 5–8. Also *Our Grandparents: A Global Album* (2010).

Allen, Thomas B. *George Washington, Spymaster: How the Americans Outspied the British and Won the Revolutionary War.* National Geographic, 2004. Ages 11–14.

Armstrong, Jennifer. *The American Story: 100 True Tales from American History.* Illus. Roger Roth. Knopf, 2006. Ages 9–13.

Aronson, Marc, and Marina Budhos. *Sugar Changed the World: A Story of Magic, Spice, Slavery, Freedom, and Science.* Clarion, 2010. Ages 12–15.

Barnard, Bryn. *The Genius of Islam: How Muslims Made the Modern World.* Knopf, 2011. (**PI**). Ages 10–14.

Bartoletti, Susan Campbell. *Black Potatoes: The Story of the Great Irish Famine, 1845–1850.* Houghton, 2001. Ages 12–16.

Bausum, Ann. *Denied, Detained, Deported: Stories from the Dark Side of American Immigration.* National Geographic, 2009. Ages 10–14.

Bial, Raymond. *Tenement: Immigrant Life on the Lower East Side.* Houghton, 2002. Ages 9–14.

Blacklock, Dyan. *The Roman Army: The Legendary Soldiers Who Created an Empire.* Illus. David Kannett. Walker, 2004. (**PI**). Ages 11–14.

Blumenthal, Karen. *Let Me Play: The Story of Title IX, The Law That Changed the Future of Girls in America.* Atheneum, 2005. Ages 12–14.

Brimner, Larry Dane. *Birmingham Sunday*. Calkins Creek, 2010. Ages 10–14. (Photo essay).

Brown, Don. *All Stations! Distress! April 15, 1912: The Day the Titanic Sank*. Roaring Brook, 2008 (**PI**). Ages 6–12.

D'Aluisio, Faith, and Peter Menzel. *What the World Eats*. Tricycle, 2008. Ages 9–13.

Deem, James M. *Bodies from the Ash: Life and Death in Ancient Pompeii*. Houghton, 2005. Ages 10–14.

Ellis, Deborah. *Our Stories, Our Songs: African Children Talk about AIDS*. Fitzhenry, 2005. Ages 12–14.

Floca, Brian. *Lightship*. Atheneum, 2007. (**PI**). Ages 5–7.

Fradin, Dennis Brindell. *Let It Begin Here! Lexington and Concord: First Battles of the American Revolution*. Illus. Larry Day. Walker, 2005. (**PI**). Ages 6–10.

Frank, Mitch. *Understanding the Holy Land: Answering Questions about the Israeli-Palestinian Conflict*. Viking, 2005. Ages 12–14.

Freedman, Russell. *Kids at Work: Lewis Hine and the Crusade against Child Labor*. Clarion, 1994. Ages 9–12.

Freedman, Russell. *Children of the Great Depression*. Clarion, 2005. Ages 11–14.

Freedman, Russell. *Freedom Walkers: The Story of the Montgomery Bus Boycott*. Holiday, 2006. Ages 9–13.

Freedman, Russell. *Who Was First? Discovering the Americas*. Clarion, 2007. Ages 10–14.

Giblin, James Cross. *Secrets of the Sphinx*. Illus. Bagram Ibatoulline. Scholastic, 2004. Ages 9–12.

Hill, Laban C. *Harlem Stomp! A Cultural History of the Harlem Renaissance*. Little, Brown, 2004. Ages 11–14.

Hoose, Phillip. *We Were There, Too! Young People in U.S. History*. Farrar, 2001. Ages 10–13.

Hoose, Phillip. *The Race to Save the Lord God Bird*. Farrar, 2004. Ages 11–14.

Hopkinson, Deborah. *Shutting Out the Sky: Life in the Tenements of New York*. Scholastic, 2003. Ages 11–14.

Hopkinson, Deborah. *Up Before Daybreak: Cotton and People in America*. Scholastic, 2006. Ages 9–14.

Janeczko, Paul B. *Top Secret: A Handbook of Codes, Ciphers, and Secret Writing*. Illus. Jenna LaReau. Candlewick, 2004. Ages 9–14.

Kennett, David. *Pharaoh: Life and Afterlife of a God*. Holtzbrinch, 2008. Ages 10–14. (Egypt).

Kerley, Barbara. *One World, One Day*. Photos. National Geographic, 2009. (**PI**). Ages 5–9.

Konrad, Marla S. *I Like to Play*. Photos. Tundra, 2010. (**PI**). Ages 5–8. (Global). World Visions series.

Kuklin, Susan. *Families*. Hyperion, 2006. (**PI**). Ages 5–10.

Kurlansky, Mark. *The Story of Salt*. Illus. S. D. Schindler. Putnam, 2006. (**PI**). Ages 8–11. (Also physical science).

Lauber, Patricia. *Who Came First? New Clues to Prehistoric Americans*. National Geographic, 2003. Ages 10–14.

Levinson, Cynthia. *We've Got a Job: The 1963 Birmingham Children's March*. Peachtree, 2012. Ages 10–14.

Macy, Sue. *Swifter, Higher, Stronger: A Photographic History of the Summer Olympics*. National Geographic, 2004. Ages 11–14.

Macy, Sue. *Wheels of Change: How Women Rode the Bicycle to Freedom*. National Geographic, 2011. Ages 10–14.

Markle, Sandra. *Rescues!* Lerner, 2006. Ages 9–13.

Marrin, Albert. *Oh, Rats! The Story of Rats and People*. Illus. C. B. Mordan. Dutton, 2006. Ages 8–12.

McWhorter, Diane. *A Dream of Freedom: The Civil Rights Movement*. Scholastic, 2004. Ages 10–14.

Meyer, Don, editor. *The Sibling Slam Book: What It's Really Like to Have a Brother or Sister with Special Needs*. Woodbine, 2005. Ages 12–14.

Morris, Ann. *Families*. HarperCollins, 2000. Ages 4–7. (Photo essay). Series of photo essays for young children.

Murphy, Jim. *An American Plague: The True and Terrifying Story of the Yellow Fever Epidemic of 1793*. Clarion, 2003. Ages 9–14.

Murphy, Jim. *A Savage Thunder: Antietam and the Bloody Road to Freedom*. M. K. McElderry, 2009. Ages 10–14.

Murphy, Jim. *Truce: The Day the Soldiers Stopped Fighting*. Scholastic, 2009. Ages 10–14. (World War I, Europe).

National Children's Book and Literary Alliance. *Our White House: Looking In and Looking Out.* Candlewick, 2008. (**PI**). Ages 9–13.

Nelson, Kadir. *We Are the Ship: The Story of the Negro League Baseball.* Hyperion, 2008. (**PI**). Ages 9–13.

Nelson, Scott. *Ain't Nothing but a Man: My Quest to Find the Real John Henry.* National Geographic, 2008. Ages 11–14.

Nevius, Carol. *Karate Hour.* Illus. Bill Thomson. Marshall Cavendish, 2004. (**PI**). Ages 5–10.

O'Brien, Anne S. *After Gandhi: One Hundred Years of Nonviolent Resistance.* Charlesbridge, 2009. Ages 10–14.

O'Brien, Tony, and Mike Sullivan. *Afghan Dreams: Young Voices of Afghanistan.* Bloomsbury, 2010. Ages 9–12.

Olson, Tod. *How to Get Rich in the California Gold Rush: An Adventurer's Guide to the Fabulous Riches Discovered in 1848.* Illus. Scott Allred. National Geographic, 2008. Ages 9–13.

Osborne, Mary Pope. *Pompeii: Lost and Found.* Illus. Bonnie Christensen. Knopf, 2006. (**PI**). Ages 7–12.

Patent, Dorothy Henshaw. *The Buffalo and the Indians: A Shared Destiny.* Illus. William Muños. Clarion, 2006. Ages 9–14. (Photo essay).

Philip, Neil. *The Great Circle: A History of the First Nations.* Clarion, 2006. Ages 11–15.

Rappaport, Doreen. *Lady Liberty: A Biography.* Illus. Matt Tavares. Candlewick, 2008. (**PI**). Ages 7–10.

Robb, Don. *Ox, House, Stick: The History of Our Alphabet.* Illus. Anne Smith. Charlesbridge, 2007. (**PI**). Ages 9–12.

Sandler, Martin. *The Dust Bowl through the Lens: How Photography Revealed and Helped Remedy a National Disaster.* Walker, 2009. Ages 10–14. (Photo essay).

Schanzer, Rosalyn. *Witches! The Absolutely True Tale of Disaster in Salem.* National Geographic, 2011. Ages 9–14.

Schlitz, Laura A. *Good Masters! Sweet Ladies! Voices from a Medieval Village.* Illus. Robert Byrd. Candlewick, 2007. Ages 9–13.

Shoveller, Herb. *Ryan and Jimmy: And the Well in Africa that Brought Them Together.* Kids Can, 2006. Ages 9–12. (Uganda).

Sloan, Christopher. *Bury the Dead: Tombs, Corpses, Mummies, Skeletons and Rituals.* National Geographic, 2002. Ages 10–14.

St. George, Judith. *So You Want to Be President?* Illus. David Small. Philomel, 2012, updated. (**PI**). Ages 7–10.

Tanaka, Shelley. *Mummies: The Newest, Coolest, and Creepiest from Around the World.* Abrams, 2005. Ages 9–13.

Walker, Sally M. *Secrets of a Civil War Submarine: Solving the Mysteries of the H. L. Hunley.* Carolrhoda, 2005. Ages 12–14.

Winters, Kay. *Colonial Voices: Hear Them Speak.* Illus. Larry Day. Dutton, 2008. Ages 9–12.

Humanities

Aliki. *Ah, Music!* HarperCollins, 2003. (**PI**). Ages 6–9.

Ancona, George. *Capoeira: Game! Dance! Martial Art!* Lee & Low, 2007. Photos. Ages 10–14. (Brazil).

Ancona, George. *Ole! Flamenco.* Lee & Low, 2010. Ages 9–12. (Photo essay).

Close, Chuck. *Chuck Close: Face Book.* Abrams, 2012. Ages 9–12.

Cummings, Pat, compiler–editor. *Talking with Artists,* Vols. 1, 2, 3. Bradbury, 1992, 1995, 1999. Ages 8–12.

Eric Carle Museum of Picture Book Art. *Artist to Artist: 23 Major Illustrators Talk to Children about Their Art.* Philomel, 2007. Ages 9–18.

Govenar, Alan. *Extraordinary Ordinary People: Five American Masters of Traditional Arts.* Candlewick, 2006. Ages 12–15.

Greenberg, Jan, and Sandra Jordan. *Ballet for Martha: Making Appalachian Spring.* Illus. Brian Flores. Flash Point, 2010. (**PI**). Ages 9–12.

Helsby, Genevieve. *Those Amazing Musical Instruments!* Sourcebooks, 2007. Ages 9–14. (Includes CD).

Lane, Kimberley. *Come Look with Me: Latin American Art.* Charlesbridge, 2007. Ages 10–14. Come Look with Me series books include African-American, Asian, and American Indian art as well as women artists.

Levine, Gail Carson. *Writing Magic: Creating Stories That Fly.* HarperCollins, 2006. Ages 9–12.

Marcus, Leonard S. *The Wand in the Word: Conversations with Writers of Fantasy.* Candlewick, 2006. Ages 11–14.

Raczka, Bob. *Here's Looking at Me: How Artists See Themselves.* Lerner, 2006. Ages 8–11.

Ruggi, Gilda W. *The Art Book for Children.* Phaidon, 2005. Ages 7–9.

Sayre, Henry. *Cave Paintings to Picasso: The Inside Scoop on 50 Art Masterpieces.* Chronicle, 2004. Ages 11–14.

Strum, James, Andrew Arnold, and Alexis Frederick-Frost. *Adventures in Cartooning.* First Second, 2009. Ages 9–12.

Swett, Sarah. *Kids Weaving: Projects for Kids of All Ages.* Photos Chris Hartlove. Illus. Lena Corwin. Stewart, Tabori & Chang, 2005. Ages 7–13.

Thompson, Lauren. *Ballerina Dreams.* Photos James Estrin. Feiwel & Friends, 2007. Ages 5–8. (Cerebral palsy, dance).

Warhola, James. *Uncle Andy's: A Faabbbulous Visit with Andy Warhol.* Putnam, 2003. (**PI**). Ages 5–8.

Wolf, Allan. *Immersed in Verse: An Informative, Slightly Irreverent & Totally Tremendous Guide to Living the Poet's Life.* Illus. Tuesday Mourning. Lark Books, 2006. Ages 12–14.

Informational Book Series

Art

Learn to Draw. Walter Foster. Ages 6–10.

Start-Up Art and Design. Cherrytree. Ages 7–10.

Bilingual

Animal Clues/¿Adivina de quién es? Rosen. Ages 4–7.

Animal Opposites/Animales opuestos. Capstone. Ages 4–7.

Everyday Wonders/Maravillas de todos los días. Rosen. Ages 4–7.

Environment

One Small Step. Smart Apple Media. Ages 7–10.

Saving Earth's Animals. Rosen. Ages 9–12.

Saving Our Living Earth. Lerner. Ages 10–14.

Geography

Meet Our New Student. Mitchell Lane. Ages 7–9.

World of Colors. Capstone. Ages 5–7.

Global Issues

Changing World. Arcturus. Ages 10–13.

Troubled Treasures: World Heritage Sites. ABDO. Ages 9–12.

Health and Personal Problems

Head-to-Toe Health. Cavendish. Ages 7–9.

How Can I Deal With? Smart Apple. Ages 7–10.

Issues in Focus Today. Enslow. Ages 12–18.

Issues That Concern You. Greenhaven. Ages 12–16.

History

America's Living History. Enslow. Ages 9–14.

Captured History. Compass Point. Ages 12–16.

Children in History. Sea-to-Sea. Ages 9–12.

Mathematics

Count the Critters. ABDO. Ages 5–7.

Real World Math. Cherry Lake. Ages 9–11.

Sir Cumference Math Adventures. Charlesbridge. Ages 9–11.

Science

Animals Working Together. Capstone. Ages 5–8.

Face to Face with Animals. National Geographic. Ages 7–10.

How It's Made. Gareth Stevens. Ages 7–9.

Let's Read and Find Out Science, HarperCollins, Ages 5–9.

Nic Bishop Science. Scholastic. Ages 5–7.

Scientists in the Field. Houghton. Ages 8–12.

The Real Scientist Investigates. Sea-to-Sea. Ages 9–12.

Social Studies

Cultures of the World. Cavendish. Ages 10–13.

People in the Community. Heinemann. Ages 4–6.

Wide Range of Topics

Eyewitness Books. Dorling Kindersley. Ages 11–15.

Related Films, Videos, and DVDs

Building Big. (2000, miniseries). Author: David Macaulay. 327 minutes.

Dinosaur Bones. (2006). Author: Bob Barner (2001). 12 minutes.

The Emperor's Egg. (2005). Author: Martin Jenkins (1999). 10 minutes.

Magic School Bus. Author: Joanna Cole. 52 videos based on the book series, Scholastic videos online.

Open Wide: Tooth School Inside . . . and Other Stories. (2007). Author: Laurie Keller (2000). 54 minutes.

What Do You Do with a Tail Like This? (2008). Authors: Robin Page and Steve Jenkins (2005). 8 minutes.

Chapter Eleven

iterature for
a Diverse
Society

Oh, the Places You'll Go

Uh-huh, I've travelled
By car, train, boat, plane
To Kenya, Uganda
France, Italy, Spain.

Still many a country
I plan to explore
Here's how you do it
I've done it before.

Weather won't stop you
Nor cost of the flight
You'll fly the world over
By day and by night.

The means are at hand
You've not far to look
Oh, the places you'll go
When you travel by book.

—*Ashley Bryan*

We live in a global society, filled with the richness of cultural diversity as well as the devastation of violence and racism. Literature can provide a pathway to understanding diverse ways of living, valuing our connections as human beings, and challenging inequities. The first part of this chapter, An Education That Is Multicultural and Intercultural, focuses on ways teachers can make their teaching relevant to students and to the interconnected world in which they live. The second part, Multicultural and International Literature, identifies literature that supports a culturally based curriculum.

Section One: An Education That Is Multicultural and Intercultural

A serious mismatch exists in U.S. schools today. School curricula and textbooks present predominantly mainstream, European-American perspectives. Moreover, the cadre of U.S. teachers is predominantly (83%) from European-American, suburban backgrounds (U.S. Department of Education, 2012). They have been taught to teach in ways that work best with people with similar backgrounds and often have not had close, sustained relationships with individuals from ethnic, cultural, and socioeconomic backgrounds that differ from their own. On the other hand, school populations in the U.S. are becoming increasingly diverse; 46 percent of the students in public schools during 2010 were from minority populations, indicating that the minority will soon become the majority (U.S. Department of Education, 2012).

The resulting mismatch has contributed to an education system that is not working for many students. The Office of National Assessment for Educational Progress reports a continuing reading achievement gap between whites and Native Americans, Latinos, and African Americans. In 2009, 22 percent of white fourth-graders and 20 percent of Asian-American fourth-graders scored below the basic level in reading, which stands in sharp contrast to the percentages for other ethnic groups—52 percent of African Americans, 51 percent of Latinos, and 50 percent of American Indians were below the basic level as fourth-graders and the numbers are much higher for those below proficiency (80–85%). Clearly, teachers need to become more familiar with the influence of culture on teaching and learning.

At the same time, U.S. classrooms are experiencing the largest influx of immigrants since the early 1900s, further increasing the diversity of students. More than 14 million immigrants (legal and illegal) settled in the U.S. between 2000 and 2010, coming from all parts of the world, with the majority from Mexico, China and Taiwan, India, Philippines, Vietnam, El Salvador, Cuba, and Korea (U.S. Census Bureau, 2010).

Teachers in all parts of the country are increasingly likely to have students from diverse ethnic, racial, national, and language groups in their classrooms, whether in urban, suburban, or rural areas. This diversity is reflected in the global nature of our lives. Children will live and work in a world that is vastly different from the one in which we grew up. Rapid economic, technological, and social changes are connecting us across the globe. Knowledge of the world and of diverse cultures is no longer a luxury, but a necessity. Children need understandings of both the diverse cultural groups within their own country and of global cultures that cross outside of their borders.

An education that is multicultural and intercultural is one in which diverse cultural perspectives are woven throughout the curriculum and school life instead of being the focus of a special book or unit (Sleeter & Grant, 1987). This orientation includes the following:

- Understanding one's own personal cultural identity
- Valuing the unique perspectives of diverse cultural groups
- Connecting to the universal experiences that are shared across cultures
- Critiquing the inequities and injustices experienced by specific cultural groups
- Developing a commitment to taking action for a more just and equitable world

An education that is multicultural and intercultural is culturally responsive, culturally expansive, and culturally critical. Children's literature plays a crucial role by providing students with the opportunity to immerse themselves into story worlds and gain insights into how people feel, live, and think. They go beyond a tourist's perspective of simply gaining information about particular cultures to living *within* these cultures through their experiences with literature.

Culturally Responsive Curriculum

All students need to find their lives and cultural experiences reflected within classrooms and the books they read, but this is much more likely to occur for students from mainstream, European-American families. Culturally responsive curriculum focuses on the need to develop teaching strategies and materials that are more consistent with the cultural orientations of ethnically and globally diverse students. Geneva Gay (2010) points out that using the cultural knowledge, experiences, frames of reference, and performance styles of ethnically diverse students makes learning more relevant and effective.

Teachers are culturally responsive in their use of literature when they:

- **Find reading materials that are relevant to students' lives.** Supporting all students as learners means becoming personally acquainted with students and knowledgeable about books that are culturally relevant to their lives. For ethnically and globally diverse students this may be literature about young people whose lives and cultures are similar to their own. For second-language learners this may be bilingual literature in the student's native tongue, so as to make learning English easier and to signal the value of the student's first language. Students who rarely find their lives reflected in a book may dismiss literacy as irrelevant or even a threat to their cultural identities.

- **Ensure that school and classroom literature collections reflect the cultural diversity of the classroom, school, community, and world.** Even when schools and communities are culturally homogeneous, librarians and teachers should select books that reflect the diversity of the greater world. To do so, they may need to search for books from small presses that focus on particular ethnic groups and for translated books originating from other countries.

- **Give students a choice in their reading material.** Giving students a choice in what they read acknowledges their lives and interests as significant and relevant within the classroom. Include less conventional formats in selecting reading materials, such as picture books for older readers, audiobooks, and graphic novels, as well as nonfiction materials such as manuals and magazines.

- **Conference with students about their reading as often as possible.** One-on-one discussions give teachers an opportunity to learn about students' reading interests and needs, express their curiosity about what students are currently reading, and suggest other books.

The search for culturally relevant literature recognizes that all children have multiple cultural identities, including gender, social class, family structure, age, religion, and language, as well as ethnicity and nationality. This broad understanding of culture as ways of living and being in the world that influence our actions, beliefs, and values is essential to understanding why culture matters in our lives. Culture influences how each of us thinks about ourselves and the world around us. Students from all cultures, including the mainstream, must recognize that they have a particular perspective on the world in order to value as well as critically examine that perspective. This understanding, in turn, supports them in exploring other cultural perspectives.

Culturally Expansive Curriculum

A culturally expansive curriculum builds from awareness of students' own cultural identities to considering points of view that go beyond their own. Literature provides a window to ethnic and global cultures through in-depth inquiries into a particular culture and the integration of multiple cultural perspectives into every classroom study.

An inquiry into a particular culture should include a range of books that reflects the diversity and complexity of that culture. In exploring Diné (Navajo) culture, for example, students can read historical fiction, such as *Little Woman Warrior Who Came Home* by Evangeline Parsons-Yazzie, along with traditional literature, such as *Ma'ii and Cousin Horned Toad* by Shonto Begay. They can also examine images of contemporary Diné life both off and on the reservation in *Alice Yazzie's Year* by Ramona Maher and *Racing to the Sun* by Paul Pitts. This range of literature challenges students to go beyond stereotypes to examine the shared values and beliefs within a culture as well as the diversity of views and lives that are integral to every cultural group.

A culturally expansive curriculum becomes inclusive of multiple cultural perspectives across all content areas through the integration of literature. The perspectives of those long neglected—Native Americans, African Americans, Latinos, and Asian Americans, to name a few—can be included in the social studies and history curriculum. Important contributions by scientists, such as Elijah McCoy, whose inventions revolutionized steam engines, can be included in the science curriculum. Works by authors who reflect a range of ethnic and global backgrounds can be included in the reading and literature curriculum. For example, a literature unit could focus on Francisco Jiménez, a Mexican American whose books describe the struggles of immigrants and their families who work in the California fields. One strategy is to read aloud one of the featured author's works while students discuss others by that author in literature circles.

The goal of those who write, publish, and promote multicultural and international children's literature is to help young people learn about, understand, and ultimately accept those different from themselves, thus breaking the cycles of prejudice and oppression among peoples of different cultures. Progress toward this goal may well begin when young people read multicultural or international literature and realize how similar they are to children of different cultures and how interesting their differences are. They are also challenged not to consider their own culture as the "norm" against which others are judged as strange or exotic. These books help build bridges and cross borders between people of different nationalities and cultures (Lehamn, Freeman, & Scharer, 2011).

The books that are selected for read-alouds, booktalks, book displays, and text sets for classroom studies or independent reading should reflect the diversity of cultural experiences in the classroom as well as invite exploration of broader ethnic and global cultures.

Booktalks, for example, might be used to connect students who read mainstream books with literature from a wider range of cultures that have a similar theme or genre. A collection of picture books on families, a common topic investigated in the primary grades, might include the following.

Families by Ann Morris and *Families* by Susan Kuklin (Cross-cultural)
I Love Saturdays y Domingos by Alma Flor Ada, illustrated by Elivia Savadier
    (Mexican-American, biracial)
Hot, Hot Roti for Dada-ji, F. Zia, illustrated by Ken Min (Indian-American)
Molly's Family by Nancy Garden, illustrated by Sharon Wooding (two mothers)
My Mei Mei by Ed Young (Chinese-American, adoption)
Where's Jamela? by Niki Daly (South African)
A New Year's Reunion by Yu Li-Qiong, illustrated byZhu Cheng-Liang (Chinese)
My Two Grannies by Floella Benjamin, illustrated by Margaret Chamberlain (British, biracial)

Culturally Critical Curriculum

Although multicultural education celebrates diversity and cross-cultural harmony, its more important goal has always been to transform society and ensure greater voice, equity, and social justice for marginalized groups (Gay, 2010). Raising issues of inequality, power, and discrimination is central to an education that is multicultural and intercultural. Paulo Freire (1970) believes that students need to critically read the world by questioning "what is" and "who benefits," instead of accepting inequity as just the way things work. Students need to examine why these social problems exist and who benefits from keeping inequities in place. They also need to consider new possibilities by asking "what if" and taking action for social change. Through these questions, students develop a critical consciousness about their everyday world and the ways in which power plays out in their relationships and society.

Literature plays a significant role in social justice education by documenting the history and contemporary stories of marginalized peoples, presenting their perspectives, and providing a way for their voices to be heard. These perspectives are rarely included within textbooks and the standard curriculum. Literature can support students in considering multiple perspectives on complex social issues such as undocumented immigrants, as in *Friends from the Other Side* by Gloria Anzaldúa, *The Circuit* by Francisco Jiménez, *La línea* by Ann Jaramillo, *Ask Me No Questions* by Maria Budhos, *A Time of Miracles* by Anne-Laure Bondoux, and *The Arrival* by Shaun Tan.

A critical literacy or social justice curriculum has four dimensions (Lewison, Leland, & Harste, 2008), all of which can be supported by literature:

- Disrupting the commonplace by looking at the everyday through new lenses that challenge assumptions (e.g., *The Other Side* by Jacqueline Woodson or *Wringer* by Jerry Spinelli)

- Considering multiple perspectives that may be contradictory or offer alternative interpretations of history or current issues (e.g., *Voices in the Park* by Anthony Browne or *Seedfolks* by Paul Fleischman)

- Focusing on sociopolitical issues to examine societal systems and unequal power relationships and to get at the root causes of social problems (e.g., *The Good Garden* by Katie Smith Milway or *The Absolutely True Diary of a Part-Time Indian* by Sherman Alexie)

- Taking action and promoting social justice by taking a stand against oppression and acting to create change (e.g., *The Lady in the Box* by Ann McGovern or *Iqbal* by Francesco D'Adamo)

Section Two:
Multicultural and International Literature

Multicultural literature and international literature are not separate genres; rather, they occur in all genres. You will have noted many references to these books and authors throughout the previous chapters in discussions of trends and issues, notable author and illustrator lists, and recommended booklists. In an ideal, culturally integrated world, this integration of multicultural and international literature would be sufficient. But the groups and perspectives represented in multicultural literature have, until recently, been absent or misrepresented in books for children and remain underrepresented today. Furthermore, neither multicultural nor international literature is well known or fully recognized by the educational mainstream. We highlight these books in this chapter so that they are not underrepresented in your classroom collections and engagements. Changing demographics in the U.S. and globalization of society require school curricula and materials that will prepare young people to live in a changing and ever more diverse world.

Definitions and Descriptions

Multicultural literature is defined in various ways by educators and scholars. Some define it broadly as all books about people and their individual or group experiences within a particular culture, including mainstream cultures. Most define it more specifically as literature by and about groups that have been marginalized and disregarded by the dominant European-American culture in the U.S. This definition includes racial, ethnic, religious, and language minorities, those living with physical or mental disabilities, gays and lesbians, and people living in poverty. In this chapter, we highlight literature by and about the racial, religious, and language groups in the U.S. that have created a substantial body of children's literature. This includes literature by and about African Americans, Asian/Pacific Americans (including people of Chinese, Hmong, Japanese, Korean, and Vietnamese descent), Latinos (including Cuban Americans, Mexican Americans, Puerto Ricans, and others of Spanish descent), religious cultures (including Buddhist, Hindu, Jewish, and Muslim), and Native Americans (a general term referring to the many tribes of American Indians). Examples of books about other marginalized groups are found throughout the genre chapters, especially in the lists of recommended books.

International literature in the U.S. refers to books that are set in countries outside of the U.S. The focus of this chapter is on books originally written and published in countries other than the U.S. for children of those other countries and then published in this country. These books can be subdivided into three categories:

- *English language books.* Books originally written in English in another country and then published or distributed in the U.S.. Examples include *How to Heal a Broken Wing* by Bob Graham (Australia) and the Harry Potter series (United Kingdom).

- *Translated books.* Books written in a language other than English in another country, then translated into English and published in the U.S. Examples include *While We Were Out* by Ho Baek Lee (South Korea) and *Inkheart* by Cornelia Funke (Germany).

- *Foreign language books.* Books written and published in a language other than English in another country, then published or distributed in the U.S. in that language. One example is *Le Petit Prince* by Antoine de Saint-Exupéry (France).

Many authors and illustrators of books set in international contexts are from the U.S. These books are written and published in the U.S. primarily for an audience of U.S. children rather than written for children of that specific culture. These books, often referred to as *global literature,* have been integrated into other chapters and so are not highlighted in this chapter. Categories of global literature include:

- Books written by immigrants from another country who now reside in the U.S. and write about their country of origin; for example, *The Red Scarf Girl* by Ji-Li Jiang (China).

- Books written by authors who move between global cultures on a regular basis, such as Baba Wagué Diakité who lives in the U.S. and regularly spends time in Mali, his culture of origin.

- Books written by American authors who draw from their family's heritage in their country of origin, but whose own experiences have been in the U.S.; for example, *When My Name Was Keoko* by Linda Sue Park (Korea).

- Books written by an author who lived in another country for a significant period of time; for example, *Colibrí* by Ann Cameron (Guatemala).

- Books written by authors who research a particular country and who may or may not have visited that country as part of their research; for example, *The Breadwinner* by Deborah Ellis (Afghanistan).

- Books written by an author in collaboration with someone from that country; for example, *A Little Piece of Ground* by Elizabeth Laird with Sonia Nimr (Palestine).

The Value of Multicultural and International Literature for Children

Multicultural and international literature builds bridges of understanding across countries and cultures, connecting children to their home cultures and to the world beyond their homes. This literature benefits children in the following ways:

- Gives young people who are members of marginalized groups or recent immigrants the opportunity to develop a better sense of who they are and of their agency.

- Develops an understanding of and appreciation for diverse cultures, bringing alive those histories, traditions, and people.

- Addresses contemporary issues of race, religion, poverty, exceptionalities, and sexual orientation from the perspectives of members of those groups to provide a more complete understanding of current issues and of the people who belong to these groups, thus challenging prejudice and discrimination.

- Adds the perspective of marginalized groups and global cultures to the study of history, thereby giving students a more complete understanding of past events.

- Helps young people realize the social injustices endured by particular peoples in the U.S. and around the world, both now and in the past, to build a determination to work for a more equitable future.

- Builds students' interest in the people and places they are reading about and paves the way to a deeper understanding and appreciation of the geographical and historical content encountered in textbooks and later content-area studies.

- Provides authenticity through literature written by insiders to a country, region, or ethnic group and allows members of that group to define themselves. These portrayals challenge the typical media coverage of violence and crises.

- Develops a bond of shared experience with children of other ethnicities and nations and enables students to acquire cultural literacy with a global perspective.

While both textbooks and books can provide students with information about a country, literature invites them into the world of children from that culture and provides rich details about daily life, human emotions, and relationships, answering the questions that are significant to children. The textbook may provide facts about the country, but novels about the country show the implications of the facts for children's lives and help readers "live in" the country for a time (Lehman, Freeman, & Scharer, 2011).

Evaluation and Selection of Multicultural and International Literature

In addition to the requirement that literature have high literary merit, multicultural and international books need to be examined for *cultural authenticity:* the extent to which a book reflects the core beliefs and values and depicts the details of everyday life and language for a specific cultural group. Given the diversity within all cultural groups, there is never one image of life within any culture and so underlying world views are often more important to consider. Readers from the culture depicted in a book need to be able to identify and feel affirmed that what they are reading rings true in their lives; readers from another culture need to be able to identify and learn something of value about cultural similarities and differences (Fox & Short, 2003). The following criteria should be considered when evaluating and selecting multicultural and international books for school and classroom libraries:

- **Authenticity of cultural beliefs and values from the perspective of that group.** Research the background of the author and illustrator to determine their experiences or research related to this story (check their websites). Examine the values and beliefs of characters and whether they connect to the actual lives of people from within that culture.

- **Accuracy of cultural details in text and illustrations.** Examine the details of everyday life, such as food, clothing, homes, and speech patterns, represented in the book and whether they fit within the range of experiences of that culture.

- **Integration of culturally authentic language.** Look for the natural integration of the language or dialect of a specific cultural group, especially within dialogue. Some terms or names in the original language of translated books, for example, should be retained. Check whether a glossary is included if needed.

- **Power relationships between characters.** Examine which characters are in roles of power or significance in a book, with a particular focus on how the story is resolved and who is in leadership and action roles.

- **Perspectives and audience.** Look at whose perspectives and experiences are portrayed and who tells the story. In particular, consider whether the story is told from a mainstream or European-American perspective about ethnically or globally diverse characters. Also consider whether the intended audience is children from within that culture or if the book was written to inform a mainstream audience about a particular culture.

- **Balance between historic and contemporary views of groups.** The majority of literature about global and ethnic cultures is found in the genres of traditional literature and historical fiction, creating stereotypes of these cultures as dated and set in the past. Search for books that reflect contemporary images.

- **Adequate representation of any group within a collection.** No one book can definitively describe a culture or cultural experience. Look for a range of books that provide multiple representations of a culture and be aware of particular images that are overrepresented—for example, almost all of the picture books on Korean Americans depict them as newly arrived immigrants to the U.S. and most books depict the Middle East as a rural landscape of sand and camels. These overrepresentations reflect and create stereotypes of a particular group.

Book awards can guide teachers and librarians toward high-quality multicultural and international books. The best known of these is the Coretta Scott King Award, given annually to an African-American author and illustrator whose books are judged to be the most outstanding inspirational and educational literature for children. The Américas Award and the Pura Belpré Award, which honor outstanding Latino authors and illustrators of children's books, are good resources for locating authentic literature for this rapidly growing population. Other awards include the Asian/ Pacific American Award for Literature, honoring outstanding work of Asian-American authors and illustrators, and the American Indian Youth Literature Award, honoring the best writing and illustrations by and about American Indians. Awards such as these encourage the publication of more and better quality literature highlighting the experiences of diverse cultures.

Awards for international literature are plentiful but often more difficult to locate. The Mildred L. Batchelder Award is given to a U.S. publisher of the most distinguished translated children's book, thus, encouraging the translation and publication of international books in the U.S. (see Appendix A). The Outstanding International Books List (www.usbby.org) and Notable Books for a Global Society (www.tcnj.edu/~childlit) are annual award lists. Also, many countries have their own national awards, similar to the Newbery and Caldecott awards in the U.S. The Hans Christian Andersen award winners and nominees are a good source of the most outstanding authors and illustrators from around the world (www.ibby.org). Worlds of Words (www.wowlit .org) has a searchable database of international literature available in the U.S. and several online journals with book reviews of cultural authenticity and the use of this literature in classrooms.

In addition, small presses have become a source of multicultural and international books that are particularly valuable for their cultural points of view.

Asian American Curriculum Project. Publishes and distributes Asian-American books from small presses. www.asianamericanbooks.com. (Also see Asia for Kids at www.afk.com).

Children's Book Press. Publishes folktales and contemporary picture books, often bilingual, for Latino, Native American, and Asian-American children. www.childrensbookpress.org.

Cinco Puntos. Focuses on stories of the U.S.–Mexico border region, the Southwest, and Mexico. www.cincopuntos.com.

Piñata Books/Arte Público. Publishes children's books with a Latino perspective, including many bilingual books. www.latinoteca.com/arte-publico-press/pinata-books.

Just Us Books. Produces Afrocentric books that enhance the self-esteem of African-American children. www.justusbooks.com.

Lee & Low Books. Stresses authenticity in stories for Asian-American, Latino, and African-American children. Asian-American-owned small press. www.leeandlow.com.

Oyate. Evaluates books with Native themes and distributes books, particularly those written and illustrated by Native people. Native American evaluators and organization. www.oyate.org.

Salina Bookshelf. Focuses on the Diné tribe. http://www.salinabookshelf.com.

Evaluating and selecting multicultural and international literature for your classroom, although essential, is not enough to ensure that students will actually read the books. Without adult guidance, children tend to choose books about children like themselves, so invite students to explore these books through reading them aloud, giving booktalks, and encouraging discussion in literature circles.

Multicultural Literature

Historical Overview of Multicultural Literature

Many cultures living in the U.S. were ignored within children's books or portrayed as crudely stereotyped characters, objects of ridicule, or shadowy secondary characters. Books with blatant racism, such as Helen Bannerman's *The Story of Little Black Sambo* (1900) and Hugh Lofting's *The Voyages of Dr. Dolittle* (1922), have today either been rewritten to eliminate the racism or have disappeared from libraries.

The first indication of change came in 1949 when an African-American author, Arna Bontemps, became the first member of a minority group to win a Newbery Honor Award, for *Story of the Negro*. A more sympathetic attitude toward diverse ethnic cultures emerged in the 1950s through the positive, yet still patronizing, treatment of multicultural characters in Newbery Medal books such as *Amos Fortune, Free Man* by Elizabeth Yates (1950) and *. . . And Now Miguel* by Joseph Krumgold (1953).

The Civil Rights Movement of the 1960s focused attention on the social inequities and racial injustices that prevailed in the U.S. and resulted in two landmark publications. The first of these was *The Snowy Day* by Ezra Jack Keats (1962), the first Caldecott Medal book with an African-American protagonist. The second publication was a powerful article in 1965 by Nancy Larrick, "The All-White World of Children's Books," which reported that African Americans were omitted entirely or scarcely mentioned in nearly all U.S. children's books. American trade book publishers, the education system, and the public library system were called on to fill this void.

MILESTONES in the Development of Multicultural Literature

Date	Event	Significance
1932	*Waterless Mountain* by Laura Armer wins Newbery Medal	One of the few children's books about minorities in the first half of the twentieth century
1946	*The Moved-Outers* by Florence C. Means wins Newbery Honor	A departure from stereotyped depiction of minorities begins
1949	*Story of the Negro* by Arna Bontemps wins Newbery Honor	First minority author to win a Newbery Honor
1950	*Song of the Swallows* by Leo Politi wins Caldecott Medal	First picture book with a Latino protagonist to win the Caldecott Medal
1963	*The Snowy Day* by Ezra Jack Keats wins Caldecott Medal	First picture book with an African-American protagonist to win the Caldecott Medal
1965	"The All-White World of Children's Books" by Nancy Larrick	Called the nation's attention to the lack of multicultural literature
1969	Coretta Scott King Award founded	African-American literature and authors begin to be promoted
1975	*M. C. Higgins, the Great* by Virginia Hamilton wins Newbery Medal	First book by a minority author to win the Newbery Medal
1976	*Why Mosquitoes Buzz in People's Ears* illustrated by Leo and Diane Dillon wins Caldecott	First picture book by an African-American illustrator to win the Caldecott Medal
1990	*Lon Po Po: A Red-Riding Hood Story from China* translated and illustrated by Ed Young wins Caldecott Medal	First picture book by a Chinese-American illustrator to win the Caldecott Medal
1993	Américas Award founded	Encouraged authors and illustrators to publish books portraying Latin America, the Caribbean, and Latinos in the U.S.
1994	*Grandfather's Journey* written and illustrated by Allen Say wins Caldecott Medal	First picture book by a Japanese-American illustrator to win the Caldecott Medal
1996	Pura Belpré Award founded	Promotes Latino literature, authors, and illustrators

The Coretta Scott King Award was established in 1969 to recognize African-American authors, but it was not until 1975 that an author of color, Virginia Hamilton, won a Newbery Medal. The prevailing opinion among U.S. children's book publishers and professional reviewers shifted to focus on members of a group as the ones most able to write authentically about their own cultures and experiences. European-American authors were no longer as likely to win major awards for writing about minorities as they were in the early 1970s.

The late 1990s saw the long overdue development of Latino literature. Bilingual books published in response to the demands of ESOL/ELL (English for speakers of other languages/English language learners) programs and the founding of the Américas Award and the Pura Belpré Awards contributed to this growth.

Although the last several decades have seen positive changes in the status of multicultural literature in the U.S., there is still a marked shortage of books and of authors and illustrators from within those cultures. The Cooperative Children's Book Center (Horning, Lindgren, & Schliesman, 2012) reported the following statistics based on their review of approximately 3,400 new children's and young adult books in 2011:

- 3.6 percent (123 books) had significant African or African-American content (64% created by black authors/illustrators)

- 2.6 percent (91 books) had significant Asian/Pacific or Asian-/Pacific-American content (84% created by authors/illustrators of Asian/Pacific heritage)

- 1.7 percent (58 books) had significant Latino content (90% created by Latino authors/illustrators)

- 8 percent (28 books) featured American Indian themes, topics, or characters (43% created by American Indian authors/illustrators)

A broader indication of the shortage is that approximately 9 percent of the new books published for children in 2011 were by or about people of color, even though these groups represent more than 38 percent of the population (U.S. Census Bureau, 2010). Another problematic indicator is the recent decrease in books depicting people of color, from 13 percent of the new books in 2008 to 9 percent in 2011. In addition to not enough books, subtle issues of racism and stereotypes continue to be problematic. All children have the right to see themselves within a book: to find the truth of their experiences, rather than misrepresentations. Many challenges remain in the writing and publication of multicultural literature.

Types of Multicultural Literature

Each ethnic group contains subgroups that differ from one another in country of origin, language, race, traditions, and present location. Teachers must be especially conscious of and sensitive to these differences and guard against presenting these groups as uniform or selecting literature that does so. Gross overgeneralization is not only inaccurate but also a form of stereotyping.

African-American Literature Of all multicultural groups living in the U.S., African Americans have produced the largest and most rapidly growing body of children's literature (Bishop, 2007). Every genre is well represented in African-American literature, but none better than poetry, such as *The Blacker the Berry* by Joyce Carol Thomas and *Sweethearts of Rhythm* by Marilyn Nelson. Because it is so personal, poetry digs deep within a culture, as is evident in

Excellent Multicultural Literature to Read Aloud

Brown, Monica. *Marisol McDonald Doesn't Match.* Illustrated by Sara Palacios. Ages 5–8. (Biracial)

Curtis, Christopher Paul. *Elijah of Buxton.* Ages 9–12. (African-American)

Jaramillo, Ann. *La línea.* Ages 11–15. (Mexican-American)

Levine, Ellen. *Henry's Freedom Box.* Illustrated by Kadir Nelson. Ages 5–8. (African-American)

Look, Lenore. *Alvin Ho: Allergic to Girls, School, and Other Scary Things.* Ages 9–12. (Chinese-American)

Morales, Yuyi. *Just a Minute.* Ages 5–8. (Mexican-American)

Nelson, Kadir. *Heart and Soul: The Story of America and African Americans.* Ages 9–12. (African-American)

Nislick, June Levitt. *Zayda Was a Cowboy.* Ages 9–13. (Jewish)

Park, Linda Sue. *Mulberry Project.* Ages 10–14. (Korean-American)

Tingle, Tim. *Crossing Bok Chitto.* Illustrated by Jeanne Rorex Bridges. Ages 8–11. (Choctaw/Native American)

the sensitive yet powerful work of Nikki Giovanni, Nikki Grimes, Eloise Greenfield, Langston Hughes, Marilyn Nelson, and Joyce Carol Thomas.

Tapping into their rich oral tradition, African Americans have contributed Anansi the Spider, Brer Rabbit, and John Henry to the list of favorite U.S. folklore characters. Authors, such as Ashley Bryan in *Beautiful Blackbird,* continue to bring folktales from Africa. African Americans have also reclaimed their tales by retelling (without racist elements) stories that were first written by European-American authors, as Julius Lester has done in his retelling of Joel Chandler Harris's *The Tales of Uncle Remus: The Adventures of Brer Rabbit.* In addition, authors are creating modern folktales and tall tales, such as *Thunder Rose* by Jerdine Nolen and *Porch Lies* by Patricia McKissack.

African Americans have told the stories of their lives in the U.S. through both historical and realistic fiction. The stories for older readers often include painfully harsh but accurate accounts of racial oppression, as in *Elijah of Buxton* by Christopher Paul Curtis or Mildred Taylor's historical fiction saga of the close-knit Logan family, including *Roll of Thunder, Hear My Cry.* Teachers can balance these stories with contemporary novels of African American lives, such as Jacqueline Woodson's *Locomotion,* Angela Johnson's *Bird,* and Walter Dean Myers's *The Cruisers.*

Many picture books focus on stories based on historical events, particularly slavery or civil rights, but the range of themes and topics in historical and contemporary picture books is expanding, as evidenced in books such as *Wind Flyers,* by Angela Johnson, illustrated by Loren Long, and *The Moon over Star* by Dianna H. Aston, illustrated by Jerry Pinkney. Outstanding illustrators include Leo and Diane Dillon, Jerry Pinkney, Brian Pinkney, E. B. Lewis, Bryan Collier, and Kadir Nelson.

African-American nonfiction is mainly informational books focused on the Civil Rights era, such as Elizabeth Partridge's *Marching for Freedom,* and biographies featuring sports heroes as well as those from a broader spectrum of achievement; for example, see *Becoming Billie Holiday* by

Carole Boston Weatherford, illustrated by Floyd Cooper, and *Best Shot in the West: The Adventures of Nat Love* by Pat McKissack. Kadir Nelson's *Heart and Soul* combines historical information and biography to create powerful narratives and dramatic images that depict the complex ways in which African Americans contributed to and shaped the history of America.

Asian-/Pacific-American Literature Asian-American and Pacific-American children's literature consists primarily of stories about Chinese Americans, Japanese Americans, and Korean Americans, possibly because these groups have lived in this country longer than others. A major theme in much of the fiction and nonfiction for older readers is the oppression that drove the people out of their homelands or the prejudice and adjustments that they faced as newcomers in this country. More recently, books have focused on bicultural identify, learning to appreciate one's cultural heritage as well as developing a strong identity as an American, such as Thanhha Lai's *Inside Out and Back Again* and Wendy Wan Long Shang's *The Great Wall of Lucy Wu*.

Notable Authors and Illustrators of Multicultural Literature

African-American

Leo and Diane Dillon, illustrators of two Caldecott Medal books. Leo was the first African American to win a Caldecott Medal. *Why Mosquitoes Buzz in People's Ears; Ashanti to Zulu; Never Forgotten.*

Angela Johnson, author of books on family relationships, longing, and loss. *Heaven; Bird; Wind Flyers.*

Patricia McKissack, author of modern African-American folktales and historical books. *Goin' Someplace Special; Best Shot in the West: The Adventures of Nat Love; Porch Lies.*

Walter Dean Myers, author of contemporary realistic fiction about African Americans growing up. Many of his picture books are illustrated by his son, Christopher Myers. *Scorpions; The Cruisers; Looking Like Me.* www.walterdeanmyers.net

Kadir Nelson, illustrator and author of historical picture books with dramatic expressive paintings. *We Are the Ship; Henry's Freedom Box; Heart and Soul.* www.kadirnelson.com

Brian Pinkney, illustrator who uses swirling lines and intricate scratchboard renderings. *Cendrillon: A Caribbean Cinderella; Boycott Blues; Sit-In: How Four Friends Stood Up by Sitting Down.* www.brianpinkney.net

Mildred Taylor, award-winning author of historical fiction about growing up black in the southern U.S. in the 1940s and 1950s. *Roll of Thunder, Hear My Cry; Song of the Trees; The Land; The Gold Cadillac.*

Jacqueline Woodson, author of introspective novels dealing with adversity and loss. *Miracle's Boys; Locomotion; The Other Side; Show Way, After Tupac and D. Foster.* www.jacqueline woodson.com

Asian-/Pacific-American

Cynthia Kadohata, author of historical fiction about Japanese-American experiences as well as Vietnam. *Kira-Kira* (Newbery Medal); *Weedflower; Outside Beauty; Cracker; A Million Shades of Gray.* www.kira-kira.us/index.html

Grace Lin, author/illustrator of picture books and novels on Taiwanese-American experiences and Chinese traditional literature. *Where the Mountain Meets the Moon; The Year of the Dog; Ling & Ting.* http://www.gracelin.com

Linda Sue Park, author of historical and contemporary fiction about Korean and Korean-American experiences. *Keeping Score; Project*

Mulberry; When My Name Was Keoko; The Single Shard. www.lindasuepark.com

Allen Say, illustrator and author of picture books who uses soft, evocative watercolors to focus on the cultural struggles of Japanese-American and Japanese characters. *Grandfather's Journey; Drawing from Memory* (memoir).

Kashmira Sheth, author of historical and contemporary fiction about India and the experiences of Indian Americans. *Keeping Corner; Blue Jasmine; My Dadima Wears a Sari.* www.kashmirasheth.typepad.com

Latino

Francisco Jiménez, author of autobiographical stories as an undocumented Mexican immigrant farm worker. *The Circuit; Breaking Through; Reaching Out.* www.scu.edu/cas /modernlanguages/facultystaff/jimenezhomepage

Rafael Lopez, illustrator who uses a strong graphic style and visual symbols based in Mexican traditions. *The Cazuela That the Farm Maiden Stirred; My Name is Celia; Book Fiesta.* www.rafaellopez.com

Yuyi Morales, illustrator and author of picture books combining storytelling and glowing images from Mexican traditions. *Just a Minute; Just in Case.* www.yuyimorales.com

Pam Muñoz Ryan, author of novels drawn from her Mexican-American heritage and her background in bilingual education. *Becoming Naomi Leon; Esperanza Rising.* www.pammunozryan.com

Gary Soto, author of contemporary stories about the Mexican-American experience. *Chato and the Party Animals; Baseball in April; Worlds Apart: Traveling with Fernie and Me.* www.garysoto.com

Native American

Joseph Bruchac, Abenaki author of Native American historical and contemporary novels as well as traditional literature. *Buffalo Song; Hidden Roots; Code Talker.* www.josephbruchac.com

Louise Erdrich, author of historical fiction about an Ojibwa tribe on Lake Superior. *The Birchbark House; The Game of Silence; The Porcupine Year.*

S. D. Nelson, illustrator and author of traditional and historical picture books using Lakota images and stories. *Black Elk's Vision; Quiet Hero: The Ira Hayes Story; Walking on Earth and Touching the Sky.* www.sdnelson.net

Virginia Driving Hawk Sneve, author of picture books, both informational books and traditional literature, with a focus on Sioux and Lakota peoples. *The Christmas Coat: Memories of My Sioux Childhood.*

Religious Cultures

Eric Kimmel, author of traditional literature based in Jewish traditions as well as from around the world. *Wonders and Miracles: The Passover Companion; The Golem's Latkes.* www.erickimmel.com

Asma Mobin-Uddin, Pakistani-American author of picture books about Muslim-American experiences and Islamic religious traditions. *My Name Is Bilal; A Party in Ramadan.* www.asmamobinuddin.com

Traditional stories from Asia retold in English have contributed many interesting folktales and folktale variants. Characters who are generally thought of as European, such as Little Red Riding Hood and Cinderella, have their Asian counterparts, as exemplified in *Lon Po Po: A Red-Riding Hood Story from China,* translated and illustrated by Ed Young, and *Yeh-Shen: A Cinderella Story from China* by Ai-Ling Louie, illustrated by Ed Young.

Asian-American artists have brought the sophisticated style and technical artistry of Asia to their illustrations. Ed Young's use of screenlike panels and exotic, textured paper and Allen Say's precision in his oil paintings are noteworthy in *My Mei Mei by Ed Young and Grandfather's Journey* by Allen Say. Both have also written picture book autobiographies of their childhoods.

The body of Asian-/Pacific-American children's literature is rapidly expanding, particularly in realistic and historical fiction, through authors such as Linda Sue Park, Cynthia Kadohata, Lenore Look, Grace Lin, and Kashmira Sheth. The Asian/Pacific American Award for Literature, along with small presses and distributors, has also expanded this body of literature. The Pacific is still not represented well, although Hawai'i has a history of small presses and traditional literature. A notable recent Hawaiian title is *Surfer of the Century* by Ellie Crowe, illustrated by Richard Waldrep.

Latino Literature   Few Latino children's books are published in the U.S. despite the fact that Latinos represent an estimated 13 percent of the population and are considered the fastest-growing segment of the population (U.S. Census Bureau, 2010). The books that are available mainly focus on the experiences of Mexican Americans and Puerto Ricans, with a few books based on Cuban-American experiences. This body of literature continues to be filled with stereotyped portrayals of Latinos living in poverty and struggling to learn English, with their problems typically solved by European Americans. Many of the books focus on superficial aspects of culture, such as festivals and food, rather than the everyday lives and struggles of Latino children. A recent development has been the natural integration of Spanish phrases and words into books written in English to reflect the cognitively complex codeswitching of bilingual speakers.

One exciting development is the number of outstanding Latino authors and illustrators who are creating books for children, including Alma Flor Ada, George Ancona, Lulu Delacre, Gary Soto, Yuyi Morales, Francisco Jiménez, Juan Felipe Herrera, Maya Christina González, Monica Brown, Pam Muñoz Ryan, and Margarita Engle. Their books include *Just in Case* by Yuyi Morales, *Becoming Naomi Leon* by Pam Muñoz Ryan, and *Marisol McDonald Doesn't Match* by Monica Brown.

The Américas Award (honoring a U.S. work that authentically presents Latino experiences in Latin America, the Caribbean, or the U.S.) and the Pura Belpré Award (honoring outstanding Latino authors and illustrators) promote high-quality Latino literature for children.

Native American Literature   Almost from the moment that European explorers landed on this continent some 500 years ago, Native Americans have suffered at the hands of European Americans. Consequently, books written from a Native American perspective often focus on oppression and racism, ranging from historical novels, such as *Sweetgrass Basket* by Marlene Carvell, to contemporary novels, such as *The Absolutely True Diary of a Part-Time Indian* by Sherman Alexie. *Shin-Chi's Canoe* by Nicola I. Campbell, illustrated by Kim LaFave, from Canada, is an example of these themes in picture books. Appreciation, celebration, and protection of nature—central tenets of Native American cultures—are other recurrent themes in books such as *Buffalo Song* by Joseph Bruchac, illustrated by Bill Farnsworth, and *The Birchbark House* by Louise Erdrich.

Although much has been written about Native Americans, relatively little has been written by members of these cultures, and so this body of literature is dominated by outsider perspectives and issues of authenticity. Another imbalance is that the majority of books continue to be traditional literature and historical fiction, with few contemporary books to challenge stereotypes that Native Americans lived "long ago." A further issue is that many tribal nations have few or no children's books available about their specific nation, while others, such as the Diné (Navajos), have a larger body of work. Small tribal presses are producing books for their own children but many of these are difficult to access. Oyate (www.oyate.org) provides an online catalog of books from small tribal presses.

Native Americans who are known for their children's books include Joseph Bruchac for his historical and realistic novels and retold stories, Tim Tingle for his retold stories, and S. D. Nelson and Shonto Begay for their illustrations. Examples are *Hidden Roots* by Joseph Bruchac, *Black Elk's Vision* by S. D. Nelson, and *Crossing Bok Chitto* by Tim Tingle, illustrated by Jeanne R. Bridges.

Religious Cultures Literature   As the mainstream religious culture in the U.S., Christianity dominates children's books. Books that portray other religious cultures, including Buddhist, Hindu, Jewish, and Muslim cultures, are difficult to find. Contemporary children's fiction set within the context of a religious culture and written from the perspective of a member of that religion is especially scarce. Asma Mobin-Uddin's *My Name Is Bilal* is a picture book for older readers, illustrated by Barbara Kiwak, which explores fitting into the mainstream while remaining true to one's Islamic culture. Maha Addasi's *Time to Pray,* a picture book for younger readers, focuses on a young Muslim girl who visits her grandmother and learns the rituals for prayer. Nonfiction and folklore on religion are somewhat more plentiful. Author–illustrator Demi, for example, is known for her picture book biographies and story collections about Buddha and Muhammed.

The body of Jewish children's literature is by far the largest produced by any nonmainstream religious culture in this country and mainly focuses on the Jewish Holocaust in Europe during the 1930s and 1940s. The prejudice and cruelty that led to the Holocaust and the death camps are recurring themes in fiction and nonfiction for older readers. Since many Jewish people immigrated to the U.S. as the Nazi threat grew in Europe, much Holocaust literature has been written by eyewitnesses or by authors who base their stories on real people and events, such as *Black Radishes* by Susan Meyer and *Always Remember Me* by Marisabina Russo. Another recent trend is Holocaust novels set in other parts of the world, such as *Tropical Secrets: Holocaust Refugees in Cuba* by Margarita Engle and *A Faraway Island* by Annika Thor about Holocaust refugees in Sweden.

Illustrated Jewish folktales offer excellent, witty stories of high literary quality to complement the strong informational books about Jewish holidays and traditions. One major concern is the lack of picture books and novels reflecting contemporary Jewish-American experiences, although a few are emerging, such as *Gathering Sparks* by Howard Schwartz and *I Wanna Be Your Shoebox* by Cristina García. Barry Deutsch's *Hereville: How Mirka Got Her Sword* is particularly interesting as a graphic novel which is a fantasy about a modern Orthodox Jewish girl who wants to fight dragons.

The Jewish community has promoted literary excellence through the National Jewish Book Awards and the Association of Jewish Libraries' Sydney Taylor Awards.

Bilingual Literature   *Bilingual books* provide the text in two languages, frequently English/Spanish to reflect the rapid growth of the Latino population in the U.S. Picture books and shorter chapter books predominate, since longer books in two languages would be bulky and costly and are not generally useful for advanced readers. These books, if well done, are helpful to children in ESOL/ELL and world language programs. They also provide a way to value and maintain literacy in a child's first language. However, not all bilingual books have artful or even accurate translations, so careful selection is advisable. The concept book *My Colors, My World/Mis colores, mi mundo* by Maya Christina González involves a child's search for the colors hidden in her desert environment through poetic text in English and Spanish. Bilingual books reflecting Asian languages, such as *Cooper's Lesson* by Sun Yung Song, in Korean/English, are also being published.

International Literature

Historical Overview of International Literature

Much of the children's literature that was available in the U.S. during the seventeenth, eighteenth, nineteenth, and early twentieth centuries came from Europe. These early children's books are an important part of our cultural heritage, but we seldom think of the fact that they were originally published in other countries and languages. They are so familiar that we consider them our children's classics, and indeed they have become so.

With the rapid growth in the U.S. children's book field in the twentieth century, the flow of books from other countries became overshadowed by large numbers of U.S. publications. In addition, during World War II, little cultural exchange occurred across international borders. The end of World War II saw a change in the international mood, leading to the establishment of the field of international children's literature and a global increase in children's books in translation. This movement was supported by the establishment of the International Board on Books for Young People (www.ibby.org), an organization involving people from many nations who are involved in all aspects of the children's book field. IBBY publishes *Bookbird: Journal of International Children's Literature*. The U.S. affiliate is the USBBY (www.usbby.org).

We are all citizens of an ever-changing world. Our lives are going global, connected by the stories we share across cultures. International literature immerses children in stories to gain insights into how people live, think, and feel in other times and places. We need to promote more literary exchanges with countries whose bodies of literature are growing rapidly to bring more of the world's best literature to our children's attention. We also must encourage the development of stronger literature from countries that have not had the resources to support the writing and publication of their own national literature.

Excellent International Literature to Read Aloud

Boyce, Frank Cottrell. *Millions.* Ages 11–14. (England)

Brun-Cosme, Nadine. *Big Wolf and Little Wolf.* Ages 6–9. (France)

Chen, Zhiyuan. *Guji, Guji.* Ages 5–8. (Taiwan)

de Mari, Silvana. *The Last Dragon.* Ages 10–14. (Italy)

Dowd, Siobhan. *The London Eye Mystery.* Ages 8–11. (United Kingdom)

Graham, Bob. *April and Esme: Tooth Fairies.* Ages 4–8. (Australia)

Skármeta, Antonio. *The Composition.* Illustrated by Alfonso Ruano. Ages 8–12. (Chile)

Valckx, Catharina. *Lizette's Green Sock.* Ages 3–6. (France)

Wild, Margaret. *Fox.* Illustrated by Ron Brooks. Ages 6–8. (Australia)

Yumoto, Kazumi. *The Friends.* Ages 10–14. (Japan)

International Literature by World Regions

The international books that are most often available in the U.S. have been and continue to be books from English-speaking countries, with the largest numbers from Great Britain, Australia, and Canada. Although the books do not require translation, they are often published in the U.S. with changes in spelling, character and place names, and sometimes titles and cover

MILESTONES in the Development of International Children's Literature

Date	Event	Signficance
1657	*Orbis Pictus* by John Amos Comenius	Earliest nonfiction picture book
1697	*Tales of Mother Goose* by Charles Perrault	Earliest folktales from France
1719/ 1726	*Robinson Crusoe* by Daniel Defoe/ *Gulliver's Travels* by Jonathan Swift	Two early adult adventure books from England adopted by children
1812	*Nursery and Household Tales* by Jakob and Wilhelm Grimm	Traditional folktales from Germany
1836	*Fairy Tales* by Hans Christian Andersen	Early modern folktales from Denmark
1846	*Book of Nonsense* by Edward Lear	Early humorous poetry from England
1865	*Alice's Adventures in Wonderland* by Lewis Carroll	Classic English modern fantasy
1880	*Heidi* by Johanna Spyri	Early realistic story from Switzerland
1881	*The Adventures of Pinocchio* by Carlo Collodi	Modern fantasy from Italy
1883	*Treasure Island* by Robert Louis Stevenson	Adventure tale by a Scottish author
1885	*A Child's Garden of Verses* by Robert Louis Stevenson	Classic collection of Golden Age poems from England
1894	*The Jungle Book* by Rudyard Kipling	Animal stories set in India by an English author
1901	*The Tale of Peter Rabbit* by Beatrix Potter	Classic English picture book
1908	*The Wind in the Willows* by Kenneth Grahame	Animal fantasy from England
1908	*Anne of Green Gables* by Lucy Maud Montgomery	Realistic family story from Canada
1926	*Winnie-the-Pooh* by A. A. Milne	Personified toy story from England
1928	*Bambi* by Felix Salten	Personified deer story from Germany
1931	*The Story of Babar* by Jean de Brunhoff	Personified elephant story from France
1945	*Pippi Longstocking* by Astrid Lindgren	Classic fantasy from Sweden

illustrations. The major awards and award winners from English-speaking countries are in Appendix A.

Translated books come to the U.S. from around the world, but the largest numbers are from Western Europe. Today, many books come from Sweden, Norway, Denmark, Switzerland, the Netherlands, Germany, France, and Belgium. A few books come from Italy and Spain, such as the Italian fantasy *The Last Dragon* by Silvana de Mari.

Most translated children's books from the Middle East are novels for middle-graders or young adults and come to the U.S. from Israel. Books from or set in other countries in this region—such as *Tasting the Sky* by Ibtisam Barakat, set in Palestine, and *Persepolis* by Marjane Satrapi, set in Iran—are all the more welcome for their rarity.

Translated children's books from Asia were mostly from Japan, but books from Korea, China, and Taiwan are increasingly available. Japan and Korea have a sophisticated field of book illustrating, and many beautifully illustrated picture books are making their way to the U.S., such as *While We Were Out* by Ho Baek Lee and *New Clothes for New Year's Day* by Hyun-Joo Bae.

Notable Authors and Illustrators of International Literature

Bodil Bredsdorff, Danish author of the Children of the Crowe Cove series, translated into English. *The Crow-Girl; Eidi; Tink; Alek.*

Anthony Browne, British author and illustrator whose stark surrealism reveals modern social ills. Children's Laureate. *Voices in the Park; Little Beauty; Me and You; The Tunnel; Willy the Wimp; The Shape Game.*

Mem Fox, Australian author of picture storybooks for beginning readers. *Wilfrid Gordon McDonald Partridge; Ten Little Fingers and Ten Little Toes; Koala Lou; Possum Magic.* www.memfox.com

Cornelia Funke, German author of award-winning fantasy novels, including the Inkheart trilogy. *The Dragon Rider; The Thief Lord; Inkheart; Ghost Knight; Reckless.* www.corneliafunke.de

Bob Graham, Australian author and illustrator of whimsical picture books. *How to Heal a Broken Wing; April and Esme: Tooth Fairies; "Let's Get a Pup," Said Kate; A Bus Called Heaven; Oscar's Half Birthday.*

Emily Gravett, British author and illustrator of picture books full of intricate details and dry humor. *Little Mouse's Big Book of Fears; Wolves; Orange Pear Apple Bear; The Rabbit Problem.* www.emilygravett.com

Suzy Lee, Korean illustrator of wordless books that celebrate imagination and play. *Mirror; Shadow; Wave; The Zoo.* www.suzyleebooks.com

Beverley Naidoo, South African author and Carnegie Medalist whose novels deal with the effects of political injustice on children. *The Other Side of Truth; Burn My Heart; Journey to Jo'burg.* www.beverleynaidoo.com

Phillip Reeve, British author of fantasy, including the Larklight, Hungry City Chronicles, and Fever Crumbs series, known as steampunk. *Here Lies Arthur; Fever Crumb; A Web of Air; Mortal Engines.* www.philip-reeve.com

Shaun Tan, Malaysian-Australian author and illustrator who explores social and political issues through surreal, dreamlike imagery. *The Arrival; Tales from Outer Suburbia; Lost and Found.* www.shauntan.net

Margaret Wild, Australian author of picture books about friendship and its power to heal. *Fox; The Very Best of Friends; Woolvs in the City; Harry and Hopper; Our Granny; Old Pig; Lucy Goosey.*

Tim Wynne-Jones, Canadian author of humorous and suspenseful novels for middle-graders and young adults. *The Maestro; Rex Zero, King of Nothing; Rex Zero and the End of the World.* www.timwynne-jones.com

African nations, with the exception of the Republic of South Africa, have produced little children's literature that has been exported to the U.S., primarily due to economics. Publishing books is expensive, especially in full color; therefore, the publishing industry is not firmly established in these countries. Books of realistic fiction in which contemporary life in an African country is portrayed are rare and those that are available are typically written by British authors, such as *City Boy* by Jan Michael. British authors are also writing historical fiction about English children growing up in African countries, such as Trilby Kent's *Stones for My Father,* set in South Africa.

One of the challenges for those who work with children is combating the ignorance that is at the root of racial, cultural, and religious prejudice and intolerance. Children's literature, particularly the rich multicultural and international selections that are currently available, is a powerful tool in this effort for it shows that the similarities between all people bring us together as human beings. We are connected by a shared humanity and by the uniqueness that each culture contributes to a richly diverse world, providing unity within difference. Children need to find their own lives reflected within a book as well as imagine cultural ways of living and thinking beyond their own. Integrating a literature that is multicultural and intercultural into classrooms builds bridges of understanding across cultures.

Invitations for Further Investigation

- Select a minority group whose perspectives have been omitted or inadequately covered in the study of U.S. history. Examples include Native Americans and their forced removal to reservations in the 1800s, Japanese Americans and their internment in prison camps during World War II, and Chinese Americans and their role in the construction of the transcontinental railroad in the 1860s. Read several works of age-appropriate historical fiction or nonfiction about that era written from the perspective of that group. Discuss the perspectives offered by these books as compared to a U.S. history textbook.

- Choose a global issue, such as violence, conservation, child labor, or hunger, and pull together a text set of ten to twelve books that explore this issue across multiple cultures. Compare the various perspectives on this issue from these different cultures.

- Select a country or region outside the U.S. that you would like to explore with children. Compile an annotated bibliography of ten to fifteen children's books, both fiction and nonfiction, that could promote interest in and help young people learn more about the country or region.

References

Bishop, R. S. (2007). *Free within ourselves: The development of African American children's literature.* Portsmouth, NH: Heinemann.

Bryan, A. (1998). Oh, the places you'll go. In *Book poems.* New York: Children's Book Council.

Fox, D., & Short, K. (2003). *Stories matter: The complexity of cultural authenticity in children's literature.* Urbana, IL: National Council of Teachers of English.

Freire, P. (1970). *Pedagogy of the oppressed.* New York: Continuum.

Gay, G. (2010). *Culturally responsive teaching* (2nd ed.). New York: Teachers College Press.

Horning, K. T., Lindgren, M. V., & Schliesman, M. (2012). *CCBC Choices, 2011.* Madison, WI: University Publications.

Larrick, N. (1965, September 11). The all-white world of children's books. *Saturday Review,* 63–65, 84–85.

Lehman, B., Freeman, E., & Scharer, P. (2010). *Reading globally, K–8*. Thousand Oaks, CA: Corwin.

Lewison, M., Leland, C., & Harste, J. (2008). *Creating critical classrooms*. New York: Erlbaum.

Sleeter, C., & Grant, C. (1987). An analysis of multicultural education in the U.S. *Harvard Education Review, 57*, 421–444.

U.S. Census Bureau. (2010). www.census.gov.

U.S. Department of Education. (2012). The Condition of Education 2012. Washington, DC: NCES.

Recommended Multicultural Books

Ages refer to content appropriateness and conceptual and interest levels. Formats other than chapter books are coded:

(PI) Picture book
(COL) Short story collection
(GR) Graphic novel
(NV) Novel in verse

African-American Literature

Aston, Dianna H. *The Moon over Star*. Illus. Jerry Pinkney. Dial, 2008. (**PI**). Ages 5–8.

Bolden, Tonya. *Wake Up Our Souls*. Abrams, 2004. Smithsonian Art Museum. Ages 10–14. (African-American artists).

Bryan, Ashley. *Ashley Bryan: Words to My Life's Song*. Photos Bill Meguinness. Atheneum, 2009. (**PI**). Ages 8–12.

Cline-Ransome, Lesa. *Words Set Me Free: The Story of Young Frederick Douglass*. Illus. James Ransome. Simon & Schuster, 2012. (**PI**). Ages 6–9. Also *Young Pele: Soccer's First Star* (2007).

Curtis, Christopher Paul. *Elijah of Buxton*. Scholastic, 2007. Ages 9–12.

English, Karen. *Hot Day on Abbott Avenue*. Illus. Javaka Steptoe. Clarion, 2004. (**PI**). Ages 5–8.

Evans, Shane. *Underground*. Roaring Brook, 2011. (**PI**). Ages 6–9.

Grimes, Nikki. *Bronx Masquerade*. Dial, 2002. Ages 12–18.

Hamilton, Virginia. *The People Could Fly: The Picture Book*. Illus. Leo and Diane Dillon. Knopf, 2004. Ages 10–14. Also *Many Thousand Gone: African Americans from Slavery to Freedom* (Random, 1992).

Johnson, Angela. *Bird*. Puffin, 2006. Ages 11–14. Also *Heaven* (1998).

Johnson, Angela. *Wind Flyers*. Illus. Loren Long. Simon & Schuster, 2007. (**PI**). Ages 6–9. (Tuskegee Airmen of World War II).

Levine, Ellen. *Henry's Freedom Box*. Illus. Kadir Nelson. Scholastic, 2007. (**PI**). Ages 5–8.

McKissack, Patricia, and Fred McKissack. *Porch Lies: Tales of Slicksters, Tricksters, and Other Wily Characters*. Illus. André Carrilho. Schwartz & Wade, 2006. (**PI**). Ages 7–10.

McKissack, Patricia, and Fred McKissack. *Never Forgotten*. Illus. Leo and Diane Dillon. Schwartz & Wade, 2011. (**PI**).. Ages 9–12.

McKissack, Patricia, and Fred McKissack. *Best Shot in the West: The Adventures of Nat Love*. Illus. Randy DuBurke. Chronicle, 2012. (**GR**). Ages 12–15.

Myers, Walter Dean. *Looking Like Me*. Illus. Christopher Myers. Egmont, 2009. (**PI**). Ages 6–9. Also *Jazz* (2006).

Myers, Walter Dean. *The Cruisers*. Scholastic, 2010. Ages 10–14. Series.

Nelson, Kadir. *We Are the Ship: The Story of Negro League Baseball*. Jump at the Sun/Hyperion, 2008. (**PI**). Ages 7–10.

Nelson, Kadir. *Heart and Soul: The Story of America and African Americans*. Balzer & Bray, 2011. Ages 9–12.

Nelson, Marilyn. *Sweethearts of Rhythm: The Story of the Greatest All-Girl Swing Band in the World*. Illus. Jerry Pinkney. Dial, 2009. (**PI**). Ages 10–14. (Poetry and biography).

Partridge, Elizabeth. *Marching for Freedom: Walk Together, Children, and Don't You Grow Weary*. Viking, 2009. Ages 10–14.

Pinkney, Andrea D. *Boycott Blues: How Rosa Parks Inspired a Nation*. Illus. Brian Pinkney. Greenwillow,

2008. (**PI**). Ages 5–8. Also *Sit-In: How Four Friends Stood Up by Sitting Down* (Little Brown, 2010).

Shange, Ntozake. *Coretta Scott.* Illus. Kadir Nelson. Amistad, 2009. (**PI**). Ages 5–8.

Taylor, Mildred. *Roll of Thunder, Hear My Cry.* Dial, 1976. Ages 9–12.

Thomas, Joyce Carol. *The Blacker the Berry.* Illus. Floyd Cooper. Joanna Cotler, 2008. (**COL**). Ages 5–8.

Weatherford, Carole Boston. *Becoming Billie Holiday.* Illus. Floyd Cooper. Wordsong, 2008. Ages 12–15.

Wiles, Deborah. *Freedom Summer*. Illus. Jerome Lagarrigue. Atheneum, 2001. (**PI**). Ages 7–10.

Williams-Garcia, Rita. *One Crazy Summer*. Amistad, 2010. Ages 11–14.

Woodson, Jacqueline. *Locomotion.* Putnam, 2003. (**NV**). Ages 9–12. Also *Peace, Locomotion* (2009).

Woodson, Jacqueline. *The Other Side.* Illus. E. B. Lewis. Putnam, 2001. (**PI**). Ages 5–8.

Woodson, Jacqueline. *Show Way.* Illus. Hudson Talbott. Putnam, 2005. (**PI**). Ages 7–12.

Woodson, Jacqueline. *After Tupac and D. Foster*. Putnam, 2008. Ages 10–14.

Asian-/Pacific-American Literature

Barasch, Lynne. *Hiromi's Hands.* Lee & Low, 2007. (**PI**). Ages 5–8. (Japanese-American).

Budhos, Marina. *Ask Me No Questions.* Atheneum, 2006. Ages 10–14. (Bangladeshi-American).

Crowe, Ellie. *Surfer of the Century: The Life of Duke Kahanamoku.* Illus. Richard Waldrep. Lee & Low, 2007. (**PI**). Ages 8–11. (Hawaiian).

Heo, Yumi. *Ten Days and Nine Nights: An Adoption Story.* Schwartz & Wade, 2009. (**PI**). Ages 5–8. (Korean-American).

Hirahara, Naomi. *1001 Cranes*. Delacorte, 2008. Ages 10–14. (Japanese-American).

Kadohata, Cynthia. *Kira-Kira.* Atheneum, 2004. Ages 11–14. (Japanese-American).

Kadohata, Cynthia. *Weedflower.* Atheneum, 2006. Ages 11–14. (Japanese-American).

Krishnaswami, Uma. *Chachaji's Cup.* Illus. Sumeya Sitaraman. Children's Book Press, 2003. (**PI**). Ages 5–9. (Indian-American).

Lazo Gilmore, Dorina. *Cora Cooks Pancit.* Illus. Kristi Valiant. Shen's, 2009. (**PI**). Ages 5–9. (Filipino-American).

Lin, Grace. *The Year of the Dog.* Little Brown, 2006. Ages 8–11. (Taiwanese-American).

Look, Lenore. *Ruby Lu: Empress of Everything.* Atheneum, 2006. Illus. Anne Wildsorf. Ages 6–9. (Chinese-American).

Look, Lenore. *Alvin Ho: Allergic to Girls, School, and Other Scary Things*. Illus. LeUyen Pham. Schwartz & Wade, 2008. Ages 9–12. (Chinese-American).

Ly, Many. *Roots and Wings.* Delacorte, 2008. Ages 12–16. (Cambodian-American).

Mochizuki, Ken. *Baseball Saved Us.* Illus. Dom Lee. Lee & Low, 1993. (**PI**). Ages 7–10. (Japanese-American).

Park, Linda Sue. *Project Mulberry.* Clarion, 2005. Ages 10–14. (Korean-American).

Park, Linda Sue. *Keeping Score.* Clarion, 2008. Ages 9–12. (Korean-American).

Salisbury, Graham. *Night of the Howling Dogs.* Wendy Lamb Books, 2007. Ages 8–11. (Hawaiian).

Say, Allen. *Grandfather's Journey.* Houghton, 1993. (**PI**). Ages 7–9. (Japanese-American).

Shang, Wendy Wan-Long. *The Great Wall of Lucy Wu.* Scholastic, 2011. Ages 9–12. (Chinese-American).

Shea, Pegi Deitz. *Tangled Threads: A Hmong Girl's Story*. Clarion, 2003. Ages 10–14. (Hmong).

Senzai, N. H. *Shooting Kabul.* Simon & Schuster, 2010. Ages 9–12. (Afghan-American).

Sheth, Kashmira. *Blue Jasmine.* Hyperion, 2004. Ages 11–14. (Indian-American).

Uchida, Yoshiko. *Journey to Topaz.* Scribner's, 1971. Ages 9–12. (Japanese-American).

Wong, Janet S. *Alex and the Wednesday Chess Club.* Illus. Stacey Schuett. M. K. McElderry, 2004. (**PI**). Ages 5–8.

Yep, Laurence. *Dragon's Gate.* HarperCollins, 1993. Ages 12–14. Also *Dragonwings* (1975).

Yep, Laurence. *The Dragon's Child: A Story of Angel Island*. HarperCollins, 2008. Ages 9–12. (Chinese-American).

Young, Ed. *My Mei Mei.* Philomel, 2006. (**PI**). Ages 4–7. (Chinese-American).

Zia, F. *Hot, Hot, Roti for Dada-ji.* Illus. Ken Min. (**PI**). Ages 5–8. (Indian-American).

Latino Literature

Ada, Alma Flor. *I Love Saturdays y domingos.* Illus. Elivia Savadier. Atheneum, 2002. (**PI**). Ages 4–8. (Mexican-American).

Ancona, George. *Capoeira: Game! Dance! Martial Art!* Lee & Low, 2007. Ages 10–14. (Brazilian-American).

Alvarez, Julia. *How Tia Lola Learned to Teach.* Knopf, 2010. Ages 9-12. (Dominican-American). Series.

Brown, Monica. *Marisol McDonald Doesn't Match.* Illus. Sara Palacios. (**PI**). Ages 5–8. (Peruvian/Scottish/American).

Canales, Viola. *The Tequila Worm.* Random, 2005. Ages 12–15. (Mexican-American).

González, Lucia M. *The Storyteller's Candle.* Illus. Lulu Delacre. Children's Books Press, 2008. (**PI**). Ages 5–8. (Puerto Rican–American).

Hayes, Joe. *Dance, Nana, Dance/Baila, Nana, baila: Cuban Folktales in English and Spanish.* Illus. Mauricio Trenard Sayago. (**COL**). Ages 8–11. (Cuban-American).

Jaramillo, Ann. *La línea.* Roaring Brook, 2006. Ages 11–15. (Mexican-American).

Jiménez, Francisco. *The Circuit: Stories from the Life of a Migrant Child.* Houghton, 1999. (**COL**). Ages 10–14. Also *Breaking Through* (2001) and *Reaching Out* (2008). (Mexican-American).

Mora, Pat. *Book Fiesta! Celebrate Children's Day, Book Day/Celebremos el día de los niños, el día d los libros.* Illus. Rafael Lopez. Rayo, 2009. (**PI**). Ages 5–8. (Mexican-American).

Morales, Yuyi. *Just a Minute.* Chronicle, 2003. (**PI**). Ages 5–8. Also *Just in Case.* (2008). (Mexican-American).

Riech, Susanna. *Jose! Born to Dance.* Illus. Raul Colon. Simon & Schuster, 2005. (**PI**). Ages 6–9. (Mexican-American).

Ryan, Pam Muñoz. *Becoming Naomi León.* Scholastic, 2004. Ages 11–15. (Mexican-American).

Soto, Gary. *Chato and the Party Animals.* Illus. Susan Guevara. Putnam, 2000. (**PI**). Ages 5–8. (Mexican-American).

Soto, Gary. *Worlds Apart: Traveling with Fernie and Me.* Illus. Greg Clarke. Putnam, 2005. Ages 10–14. (Mexican-American).

Tafolla, Carmen. *What Can You Do with a Rebozo?* Illus. Amy Cordova. Tricycle, 2008. (**PI**). Ages 5–8. (Mexican-American).

Vamos, Samantha. *The Cazuela That the Farm Maiden Stirred.* Illus. Rafael Lopez. Charlesbridge, 2011. (**PI**). Ages 5-8. (Mexican-American).

Veciana-Suarez, Ana. *Flight to Freedom.* Orchard, 2002. Ages 12–14. (Cuban-American).

Velasquez, Eric. *Grandma's Records.* Walker, 2004. (**PI**). Ages 6–9. (Puerto Rican-American).

Native American Literature

Alexie, Sherman. *The Absolutely True Diary of a Part-Time Indian.* Little, Brown, 2007. Ages 14–16. (Spokane/Coeur d'Alene).

Begay, Shonto. *Ma'ii and Cousin Horned Toad.* Scholastic, 1992. (**PI**). Ages 6–9. (Diné/Navajo).

Bruchac, Joseph. *Code Talker.* Dial, 2005. Ages 12–15. (Diné/Navajo).

Bruchac, Joseph. *Hidden Roots.* Scholastic, 2006. Ages 8–11. (Abenaki).

Bruchac, Joseph. *Buffalo Song.* Illus. Bill Farnsworth. Lee & Low, 2008. (**PI**). Ages 8–11. (Nez Percé).

Campbell, Nicola I. *Shin-Chi's Canoe.* Illus. Kim LaFave. Groundwood, 2008. (**PI**). Ages 5–8. (Interior Salish/Métis/Canada).

Carvell, Marlene. *Sweetgrass Basket.* Dutton, 2005. Ages 10–14. (Mohawk).

Erdrich, Louise. *The Birchbark House.* Hyperion, 1999. Ages 8–12. Also *The Game of Silence* (2005), *The Porcupine Year* (2008), *Chickadee* (2012). (Ojibwe).

Maher, Ramona. *Alice Yazzie's Year.* Illus. Shonto Begay. Tricycle, 2003. (**PI**). (Diné/Navajo).

McLaughlin, Timothy. *Walking on Earth and Touching the Sky: Poetry and Prose by Lakota Youth at Red Cloud Indian School.* Illus. S.D. Nelson. Abrams, 2012. Ages 9–12. (Lakota).

Medicine Crow, Joseph. *Counting Coup: Becoming a Crow Chief on the Reservation and Beyond.* National Geographic, 2006. Ages 10–14. (Absarokee).

Messinger, Carla, and Susan Katz. *When the Shadbush Blooms.* Illus. David K. Fadden. Tricycle, 2007. (**PI**). Ages 5–8. (Lenape).

Nelson, S. D. *Quiet Hero: The Ira Hayes Story.* Lee & Low, 2006. (**PI**). Ages 8–11. (Pima).

Nelson, S. D. *Black Elk's Vision: A Lakota Story*. Abrams, 2010. (**PI**). Ages 9–12. (Lakota).

Nicholson, Caitlin Dale, and Leona Morin-Neilson. *Niwechihaw = I Help*. Illus. Caitlin Dale Nicholson. Groundwood, 2008. (**PI**). Ages 5–8. (Cree).

Parsons-Yazzie, Evangeline. *Dzani Yazhi Naazbaa': Little Woman Warrior Who Came Home; A Story of the Navajo Long Walk*. Illus. Irving Toddy. Salina Bookshelf, 2005. (**PI**). Ages 8–11. (Diné/Navajo).

Pitts, Paul. *Racing to the Sun*. HarperCollins, 1988. Ages 9–12. (Diné/Navajo).

Simermeyer, Genevieve. *Meet Christopher: An Osage Indian Boy from Oklahoma*. Photos Katherine Fogden. Council Oaks Books, 2008. (**PI**). Ages 9–12. (Osage).

Sneve, Virginia Driving Hawk. *The Christmas Coat: Memories of My Sioux Childhood*. Illus. Ellen Beier. Holiday House, 2011. (**PI**). Ages 6–9. (Sioux).

Tingle, Tim. *Crossing Bok Chitto: A Choctaw Tale of Friendship and Freedom*. Illus. Jeanne Rorex Bridges. Cinco Puntos, 2006. (**PI**). Ages 8–11. (Choctaw). Also *Saltpie: A Choctaw Journey from Darkness into Light* (2010).

Religious Cultures Literature

Addasi, Maha. *Time to Pray*. (Bilingual). Illus. Ned Gannon. Boyds Mills, 2010. (**PI**). Ages 6–9. (Muslim).

Buller, Laura. *A Faith Like Mine: A Celebration of the World's Religions through the Eyes of Children*. DK, 2005. (**PI**). Ages 9–12. (World religions).

Cooper, Helen. *The Golden Rule*. Illus. Gabi Swiatkowska. Abrams, 2007. (**PI**). Ages 5–8. (Multiple religions).

Demi. *Buddha*. Holt, 1996. (**PI**). Ages 5–8. (Buddhist). Also *Muhammad* (2003). (Muslim).

Deutsch, Barry. *Hereville: How Mirka Got Her Sword*. Illus. J. Richmond. Amulet, 2010. (**GR**). Ages 9–12 (Jewish).

Engle, Margarita. *Tropical Secrets: Holocaust Refugees in Cuba*. Holt, 2009. (**NV**). Ages 12–15. (Jewish).

Ferber, Brenda. *Julia's Kitchen*. Farrar, 2006. Ages 10–14. (Jewish).

García, Cristina. *I Wanna Be Your Shoebox*. Simon & Schuster, 2008. Ages 8–11. (Jewish).

Gershator, Phillip. *Sky Sweeper*. Illus. Holly Meade (**PI**). Farrar, 2007. (Buddhist).

Haynes, Emily. *Ganesha's Sweet Tooth*. Chronicle, 2012. (**PI**). Ages 5–8. (Hindu).

Hesse, Karen. *The Stone Lamp: Eight Stories of Hanukkah through History*. Illus. Brian Pinkney. Hyperion, 2003. (**COL**). Ages 9–13. (Jewish).

Khan, Hena. *Night of the Moon*. Illus. Julie Paschkis. Chronicle, 2008. (**PI**). Ages 4–8. (Muslim).

Kimmel, Eric. *Wonders and Miracles: A Passover Companion*. Scholastic, 2004. (**COL**). Ages 11–14. (Jewish).

Kimmel, Eric. *The Golem's Latkes*. Illus. Aaron Jasinski. Cavendish, 2011. (**PI**). Ages 6–9. (Jewish).

Krishnaswami, Uma. *The Closet Ghosts*. Illus. Shiraaz Bhabha. Children's Book Press, 2005. (**PI**). Ages 6–8. (Hindu).

Littman, Sarah. *Confessions of a Closet Catholic*. Dutton, 2005. Ages 10–14. (Jewish).

Meyer, Susan. *Black Radishes*. Delacorte, 2010. Ages 9–12. (Jewish).

Millman, Isaac. *Hidden Child*. Farrar, 2005. Ages 9–14. (Jewish).

Mobin-Uddin, Asma. *My Name Is Bilal*. Illus. Barbara Kiwak. Boyds Mills, 2005. (**PI**). Ages 9–12. (Muslim).

Mobin-Uddin, Asma. *The Best Eid Ever*. Illus. Laura Jacobsen. Boyds Mills, 2007. (**PI**). Ages 5–8. (Muslim).

Mobin-Uddin, Asma. *A Party in Ramadan*. Illus. Laura -Jacobsen. Boyds Mills, 2009. (**PI**). Ages 5–8. (Muslim).

Nislick, June Levitt. *Zayda Was a Cowboy*. Jewish Publication Society, 2005. Ages 9–13. (Jewish).

Russo, Marisabina. *Always Remember Me: How One Family Survived World War II*. Atheneum, 2005. (**PI**). Ages 8–11. (Jewish).

Schwartz, Howard. *Gathering Sparks*. Ill. Kristina Swarner. Roaring Brook, 2010. (**PI**). Ages 5–9. (Jewish).

Vernick, Shirley. *The Blood Lie*. Cinco Puntos, 2011. Ages 11–14. (Jewish).

Wayland, April Halprin. *New Year at the Pier: A Rosh Hashanah Story*. Illus. Stephane Jorisch. Dial, 2010. (**PI**). Ages 5–9. (Jewish).

Bilingual Literature

Alarcón, Francisco X. *Poems to Dream Together/ Poemas para soñar juntos*. Illus. Paula Barragán.

Lee & Low, 2005. (**COL**). Ages 8–12. (English/Spanish).

Alarcón, Francisco X. *Animal Poems of the Iguazú/Animalario del Iguazú: Poemas*. Illus. Maya Christina González. Children's Book Press, 2008. (**COL**). Ages 9–12. (English/Spanish).

Ancona, George. *Mi barrio/My Neighborhood*. Children's Press, 2004. (**PI**). Ages 5–8. We Are Latinos series.

Argueta, Jorge. *Arro con leche: Un poema para cocinar*. Illus. Fernando Vilela. Goundwood, 2010. (**PI**). Ages 6–9. Also *Sopa de frijoles: Un poema para cocinar* (2009). (English/Spanish).

Brown, Mónica. *My Name Is Celia: The Life of Celia Cruz/Me llamo Celia: La vida de Celia Cruz*. Illus. Rafael López. Rising Moon, 2004. (**PI**). Ages 8–11. (English/Spanish).

Brown, Mónica. *Pelé, King of Soccer/Pelé, el rey del fútbol*. Trans. Fernando Gayesky. Illus. Rudy Gutierrez. Rayo, 2009. (**PI**). Ages 5–8. (English/Spanish).

Brown, Mónica. *Clara and the Curandera*. Trans. Gabriela Baeza Ventura. Illus. Thelma Muraida. Piñata, 2011. (**PI**). Ages 5–9. (English/Spanish).

Colato Laínez, René. *Playing Lotería/El juego de la lotería*. Illus. Hill Arena. Luna Rising, 2005. (**PI**). Ages 5–8. (English/Spanish).

Colato Laínez, René. *René Has Two Last Names: René tiene dos apellidos*. Trans. Gabriela Baeza Ventura. Illus. Fabiola Grauller. Piñata, 2009. (**PI**). Ages 5–8.

Carlson, Lori, editor. *Red Hot Salsa: Bilingual Poems on Being Young and Latino in the U.S.* Holt, 2005. (**COL**). Ages 10–14. (English/Spanish).

Cumpiano, Ina. *Quinito, Day and Night/Quinito, día y noche*. Illus. José Ramírez. Children's Book Press, 2008. (**PI**). Ages 5–8. Also *Quinito's Neighborhood/El vecindario de Quinito*. (2005). (English/Spanish).

Dumas Lachtman, Ofelia. *Pepita and the Bully/Pepita y la peleonera*. Trans. Gabriela Baeza Ventura. Illus. Alex Pardo DeLange. Piñata, 2011. (**PI**). Ages 5–8. (English/Spanish).

Garza, Carmen Lomas, with Harriet Rohmer. *In My Family/En mi familia*. Trans. Francisco X. Alarcón. Children's Book Press, 1996. (**PI**). Ages 5–12. (English/Spanish).

Garza, Xavier. *Lucha Libre: The Man in the Silver Mask*. Trans. Luis Humberto Cristhwaite. Cinco

Puntos, 2005. (**PI**). Ages 8–11. Also *Maximillian and the Mystery of the Guardian Angel* (2011). (English/Spanish).

Gonzales Bertrand, Diane. *The Party for Papa Luis/La fiesta para Papa Luis*. Trans. Gabriela Baeza Ventura. Illus. Alejandro Galindo. Piñata, 2010. (**PI**). Ages 5–8. (English/Spanish).

González, Maya Christina. *My Colors, My World/Mis colores, mi mundo*. Children's Book Press, 2007. (**PI**). Ages 5–8. (English/Spanish).

Guy, Ginger Foglesong. *Siesta*. Illus. René King Moreno. Greenwillow, 2005. (**PI**). Ages 3–6. (English/Spanish).

Hayes, Joe. *Don't Say a Word, Mama/No digas nada, mama*. Illus. Esau Andrade Valencia. Cinco Puntos, 2012. (**PI**). Ages 6–9. (English/Spanish).

Herrera, Juan Felipe. *Grandma and Me at the Flea/Los meros meros remateros*. Illus. Anita DeLucio-Brock. Children's Book Press, 2002. (**PI**). Ages 4–8. (English/Spanish).

Lee-Tai, Amy. *A Place Where Sunflowers Grow*. Trans. Marc Akio Lee. Illus. Felicia Hoshino. Children's Book Press, 2006. (**PI**). Ages 5–8. (English/Japanese).

Medina, Jane. *The Dream on Blanca's Wall/El sueño pegado en la pared de Blanca*. Illus. Robert Casilla. Boyds Mills/Wordsong, 2004. Ages 8–11. (English/Spanish).

Robles, Anthony. *Lakas and the Makibaka Hotel/Si Lakas at ang Makibaka Hotel*. Trans. Eloisa D. de Jesús. Illus. Carl Angel. Children's Book Press, 2006. Ages 7–9. (English/Tagalog).

Shin, Sun Yung. *Cooper's Lesson*. Trans. Min Paek. Illus. Kim Cogan. Children's Book Press, 2004. (**PI**). Ages 5–8. (English/Korean).

Song, Ha. *Indebted as Lord Chom: The Legend of the Forbidden Street/No nhu Chua Chom*. Illus. Ly Thu Ha. East West Discovery Press, 2006. (**PI**). Ages 5–8. (English/Vietnamese).

Stewart, Mark, and Mike Kennedy. *Latino Baseball's Finest Fielders/Los más destacados guantes del béisbol latino*. Trans. Manuel Kalmanovitz. Millbrook, 2002. (**COL**). Ages 9–13. (English/Spanish).

Tran, Truong. *Going Home, Coming Home/Ve Nha, Tham Que Huong*. Illus. Ann Phong. Children's Book Press, 2003. (**PI**). Ages 5–8. (English/Vietnamese).

Zepeda, Gwendolyn. *Growing Up with Tamales/Los tamales de Ana*. Trans. Gabriela Baeza Ventura. Illus. April Ward. Piñata, 2008. (**PI**). Ages 5–8. (English/Spanish).

Recommended International Books

Ages refer to content appropriateness and conceptual and interest levels. Country of original publication is noted. Formats other than chapter books are coded:

(**PI**) Picture books
(**COL**) Short story collection

English-Language Books

Ahlberg, Janet, and Allan Ahlberg. *The Jolly Postman.* Little, Brown, 1986. Ages 5–8. (England).

Almond, David. *My Name is Mina.* Delacorte, 2010. Ages 10–14. Prequel to *Skellig* (1998). (England).

Asare, Meshack. *Sosu's Call.* Kane/Miller, 2002. (**PI**). Ages 6–9. (Ghana).

Baker, Jeannie. *Home.* Greenwillow, 2004. (**PI**). Ages 5–8. (Australia).

Base, Graeme. *The Legend of the Golden Snail.* Abrams, 2010. (**PI**). Ages 5–8. (Australia).

Bateson, Catherine. *Stranded in Boringsville.* Holiday House, 2005. Ages 10–14. (Australia).

Benjamin, Floella. *My Two Grannies.* Illus. Margaret Chamberlain. Francis Lincoln, 2008. (**PI**). Ages 6–9. (England).

Boyce, Frank Cottrell. *Framed.* HarperCollins, 2006. Ages 11–14. Also *Millions* (2004). (England).

Briggs, Raymond. *The Snowman.* Random House, 1978. (**PI**). Ages 5–8. (England).

Browne, Anthony. *Voices in the Park.* DK, 2001. (**PI**). Ages 8–11. Also *Me and You* (Farrar, 2009). (England).

Browne, Anthony. *Little Beauty.* Candlewick, 2008. (**PI**). Ages 5–8. (England).

Brugman, Alyssa. *Being Bindy.* Delacorte, 2006. Ages 12–15. (Australia).

Child, Lauren. *Clarice Bean Spells Trouble.* Candlewick, 2006. Ages 8–12. (England).

Clarke, Judith. *Kalpana's Dream.* Front Street, 2005. Ages 12–15. (Australia).

Colfer, Eoin. *Artemis Fowl.* Hyperion, 2001. Ages 10–12. (Ireland). Series.

Crossley-Holland, Kevin. *Crossing to Paradise.* Scholastic, 2008. Ages 10–15. (England). Series.

Croza, Laurel. *I Know Here.* Illus. Matt James. Groundwood, 2010. (**PI**). Ages 5–8. (Canada).

Daly, Niki. *Once Upon a Time.* Farrar, 2003. (**PI**). Ages 4–8. (South Africa).

Daly, Niki. *Where's Jamela?* Farrar, 2004. (**PI**). Ages 5–8. (South Africa).

Diakité, Baba Wagué. *A Gift from Childhood: Memories of an African Boyhood.* Groundwood, 2010. Ages 9–12. (Mali).

Dhami, Narinder. *Bindi Babes.* Delacorte, 2004. Ages 11–14. (England).

Dowd, Siobhan. *The London Eye Mystery.* David Fickling, 2008. Ages 8–11. (England).

Fensham, Elizabeth. *Helicopter Man.* Bloomsbury, 2005. Ages 12–14. (Australia).

Fine, Anne. *The Jamie and Angus Stories.* Illus. Penny Dale. Candlewick, 2002. Ages 7–9. (England).

Foreman, Michael. *Saving Sinbad.* Kane/Miller, 2002. (**PI**). Ages 4–8. (England).

Fox, Mem. *Wilfrid Gordon McDonald Partridge.* Illus. Julie Vivas. Kane/Miller, 1985. (**PI**). Ages 5–8. (Australia).

Fox, Mem. *Ten Little Fingers and Ten Little Toes.* Illus. Helen Oxenbury. Harcourt, 2008. (**PI**). Ages 5–8. (Australia).

French, Jackie. *Hitler's Daughter.* HarperCollins, 2003. Ages 9–12. (Australia).

Gardner, Lyn. *Into the Woods.* Illus. Mini Grey. Random House, 2007. Ages 8–11. Also *Out of the Woods* (2010). (England).

Gay, Marie-Louise. *Caramba.* Anansi, 2005. (**PI**). Ages 5–8. (Canada).

Gleeson, Libby. *Half a World Away.* Illus. Freya Blackwood. Scholastic, 2007. (**PI**). Ages 5–8. (Australia).

Graham, Bob. *How to Heal a Broken Wing.* Candlewick, 2008. (**PI**). Ages 5–8. Also *April and Esme, Tooth Fairies.* (2010). (Australia).

Gravett, Emily. *Wolves.* Simon & Schuster, 2006. (**PI**). Ages 5–8. Also *Little Mouse's Big Book of Fears.* (2008). (England).

Grey, Mini. *Traction Man Meets Turbodog.* Knopf, 2008. (**PI**). Ages 5–8. (England).

Hartnett, Sonya. *The Midnight Zoo.* Candlewick, 2010. Ages 10–14. (Australia).

Horacek, Petr. *Silly Suzy Goose.* Candlewick, 2006. (**PI**). Ages 4–6. (England).

Ibbotson, Eva. *The Star of Kazan.* Dutton, 2004. Ages 11–13. Also *The Dragonfly Pool* (2008). (England).

Ihimaera, Witi. *Whale Rider.* Harcourt, 2003. Ages 12–15. (New Zealand).

Jeffers, Oliver. *Stuck.* Philomel, 2011. (**PI**). Ages 5–8. (Ireland).

Jordan-Fenton, Christy, and Margaret Pokiak-Fenton. *Fatty Legs.* Annick, 2011. Ages 9–12. (Canada, Inuit).

Kent, Trilby. *Stones for My Father.* Tudra, 2011. Ages 10–14. (South Africa).

Laird, Elizabeth, with Sonia Nimr. *A Little Piece of Ground.* Haymarket, 2006. Ages 10–14. (Palestine).

Lightfoot, Gordon. *Canadian Railroad Trilogy.* Illus. Ian Wallace. Groundwood, 2010. (**PI**). Ages 9–12. (Canada).

Little, Jean. *Willow and Twig.* Viking, 2003. Ages 11–14. (Canada).

Lester, Alison. *Are We There Yet? A Journey around Australia.* Kane/Miller, 2005. (**PI**). Ages 5–8. (Australia).

Lofthouse, Liz. *Ziba Came on a Boat.* Illus. Robert Ingpen. Kane/Miller, 2007. Ages 8–12. (**PI**). (Australia).

Loyie, Larry, with Constance Brissenden. *As Long as the Rivers Flow.* Illus. Heather D. Holmlund. Douglas & McIntyre, 2002. (**PI**). Ages 8–12. (Canada, Cree).

Lunn, Janet. *Laura Secord: A Story of Courage.* Illus. Maxwell Newhouse. Tundra, 2001. Ages 9–12. (Canada).

Matas, Carol. *Sparks Fly Upward.* Clarion, 2002. Ages 9–13. (Canada).

McCaughrean, Geraldine. *The Death-Defying Pepper Roux.* Harper, 2009. Ages 10–14. (England).

McKay, Hilary. *Saffy's Angel.* M. K. McElderry, 2002. Ages 9–12. (England).

Michael, Jan. *City Boy.* Clarion, 2009. Ages 10–14. (United Kingdom, set in Malawi).

Milway, Katie Smith. *The Good Garden: How One Family Went from Hunger to Having Enough.* Illus. Sylvie Daigneault. Kids Can Press, 2010. (**PI**). Ages 9–12. (Honduras). Also *One Hen* (2008). (Ghana).

Morpurgo, Michael. *Kensike's Kingdom.* Scholastic, 2003. Ages 8–11. (England).

Murray, Martine. *The Slightly True Story of Cedar B. Hartley (Who Planned to Live an Unusual Life).* Scholastic, 2003. Ages 9–13. (Australia).

Naidoo, Beverley. *Out of Bounds: Seven Stories of Conflict and Hope.* HarperCollins, 2003. Ages 10–14. (South Africa).

Naidoo, Beverley. *Burn My Heart.* Amistad, 2009. Ages 10–14. (Kenya).

Ness, Patrick. *A Monster Calls.* Illus. Jim Kay. Candlewick, 2011. Ages 12–15. Inspired by Siobhan Dowd. (England).

Newman, John. *Mimi.* Candlewick, 2010. Ages 9–12. (Ireland).

Nicholls, Sally. *Ways to Live Forever.* Scholastic, 2008. Ages 8–11. (England).

Parkinson, Siobhan. *Something Invisible.* Roaring Brook Press, 2006. Ages 10–13. (Ireland).

Pendziwol, Jean. *Marja's Skis.* Illus. Jirina Marton. Groundwood, 2007. (**PI**). Ages 5–8. (Canada).

Pratchett, Terry. *Nation.* HarperCollins, 2008. Ages 12–15. (England).

Pullman, Philip. *The Golden Compass.* Knopf, 1996. Ages 12–15. His Dark Materials trilogy. (England).

Ravishankar, Anushka. *Elephants Never Forget.* Illus. Christiane Pleper. Houghton, 2010. (**PI**). Ages 5–8. (India).

Reeve, Philip. *Fever Crumb.* Scholastic, 2009. Ages 12–15. Series. Also *A Web of Air* (2010). (England).

Rodda, Emily. *The Key to Rondo.* Scholastic, 2008. Ages 8–11. (Australia).

Rosen, Michael. *Michael Rosen's Sad Book.* Illus. Quentin Blake. Candlewick, 2005. (**PI**). Ages 8–11. (England).

Rosoff, Meg. *Meet Wild Boars.* Illus. Sophie Blackall. Holt, 2005. (**PI**). Ages 4–8. (England).

Rowling, J. K. *Harry Potter and the Sorcerer's Stone.* Scholastic, 1998. Ages 9–13. (England). Harry Potter series.

Stanley, Elizabeth. *The Deliverance of Dancing Bears.* Kane/Miller, 2002. (**PI**). Ages 5–9. (Australia).

Tan, Shaun. *The Arrival.* Scholastic, 2007. (**PI**). Ages 10–14. (Australia).

Tan, Shaun. *Tales from Outer Suburbia.* Scholastic, 2009. (**PI**). Ages 13–16. (Australia).

Trottier, Maxine. *Migrant.* Illus. Isabelle Arsenault. Groundwood, 2011. (**PI**). Ages 5–9 (Canada).

Waddell, Martin. *Captain Small Pig.* Illus. Susan Varley. Peachtree, 2009. (**PI**). Ages 5–8. (England).

Wallace, Ian. *The Naked Lady.* Roaring Brook, 2002. (**PI**). Ages 6–12. (Canada).

Wild, Margaret. *Fox.* Illus. Ron Brooks. Kane/Miller, 2001. (**PI**). Ages 6–8. (Australia).

Wild, Margaret. *Woolvs in the Sitee.* Illus. Anne Spudvilas. Front Street, 2007. (**PI**). Ages 10–14. (Australia).

Williams, Michael. *Now Is the Time for Running.* Little, Brown, 2011. Ages 12–15. (South Africa).

Wilson, Jacqueline. *Candyfloss.* Illus. Nick Sharratt. Roaring Book Press, 2007. Ages 10–14. (England).

Wynne-Jones, Tim. *Rex Zero and the End of the World.* Farrar, 2007. Ages 8–11. (Canada).

Translated Books

Akbarpur, Ahmad. *Good Night, Commander.* Trans. from Farsi by Shadi Eskandani. Illus. Morteza Zahedi. Groundwood, 2010. (**PI**). Ages 6–9. (Iran).

Baasansuren, Bolormaa. *My Little Round House.* Trans. from Japanese by Helen Mixter. Groundwood, 2010. (**PI**). Ages 5–8. (Mongolia).

Bae, Hyun-Joo. *New Clothes for New Year's Day.* Trans. from Korean. Kane/Miller, 2007. (**PI**). Ages 5–8. (South Korea).

Bluitgen, Kåre. *A Boot Fell from Heaven.* Illus. Chiara Carrer. Kane/Miller, 2003. (**PI**). Ages 5–9. (Denmark).

Bondoux, Anne-Laure. *A Time of Miracles.* Trans. from French by Y. Maudet. Delacorte, 2011. Ages 10–14. (France). Also *The Killer's Tears* (2006). (Chile).

Bredsdorff, Bodil. *The Crow-Girl: The Children of Crow Cove.* Trans. from Danish by Faith Ingwersen. Farrar, 2004. Ages 11–12. (Denmark). Also *Eidi* (2010).

Brun-Cosme, Nadine. *Big Wolf & Little Wolf.* Trans. from French by Claudia Bedrick. Illus. Olivier Tallee. Enchanted Lion, 2009. (**PI**). Ages 6–9. (France).

Combres, Elizabeth. *Broken Memory: A Novel of Rwanda.* Trans. from French by Shelley Tanaka. Groundwood, 2009. Ages 12–15. (Rwanda).

Chen, Jiang Hong. *Mao and Me: The Little Red Guard.* Trans. from French by Claudia Zoe Bedrick. Enchanted Lion, 2008. (**PI**). Ages 9–12. (Memoir, China).

Chen, Zhiyuan. *Guji, Guji.* Trans. from Chinese. Kane/Miller, 2004. (**PI**). Ages 5–8. (Taiwan).

Choung, Eun-Hee. *Minji's Salon.* Trans. from Korean. Kane/Miller, 2007. (**PI**). Ages 5–8. (South Korea).

D'Adamo, Francesco. *Iqbal: A Novel.* Trans. from French by Ann Leonori. Atheneum, 2003. Ages 9–12. (Pakistan).

de Mari, Silvana. *The Last Dragon.* Trans. from Italian by Shaun Whiteside. Hyperion, 2006. Ages 10–14. (Italy).

Duman Tak, Bibi. *Soldier Bear.* Illus. Philip Hopman. Trans. from Dutch by Laura Watkinson. Eerdmans, 2011. Ages 9–12. (Poland/Europe).

Eriksson, Eva. *A Crash Course for Molly.* Trans. from Swedish by Elisabeth Dyssegaard. Farrar, 2005. (**PI**). Ages 5–7. (Sweden).

Filipovic, Zlata. *Zlata's Diary: A Child's Life in Wartime Sarajevo.* Trans. From French by Christina Pribichevich-Zoric. Penguin, 1994/2006 (revised edition). Ages 12–18. (Bosnia).

Funke, Cornelia. *The Thief Lord.* Trans. from German by Oliver Latsch. Scholastic, 2002. Ages 10–14. (Germany).

Funke, Cornelia. *Inkheart.* Trans. from German by Anthea Bell. Scholastic, 2003. Ages 10–14. (Germany).

Funke, Cornelia. *Dragon Rider.* Trans. from German by Anthea Bell. Scholastic, 2004. Ages 10–14. (Germany).

Goscinny, René. *Nicholas.* Trans. from French by Anthea Bell. Illus. Jean Jacques Sempé. Phaidon, 2005. (**COL**). Ages 9–12. (France).

Harel, Nira. *The Key to My Heart.* Illus. Yossi Abulafia. Kane/Miller, 2002. (**PI**). Ages 4–7. (Israel).

Hole, Stian. *Garmann's Summer.* Trans. from Norwegian by Don Bartlett. Eerdmans, 2008. (**PI**). Ages 5–8. (Norway).

Jung, Reinhard. *Dreaming in Black and White.* Trans. from German by Anthea Bell. Phyllis Fogelman Books, 2003. Ages 10–14. (Germany).

Konnecke, Ole. *Anton Can Do Magic.* Trans. from German by Catherine Chidgey. Lerner, 2011. (**PI**). Ages 5–8. (Germany).

Kruusval, Catarina. *Ellen's Apple Tree.* Trans. from Swedish by Joan Sandin. R & S Books, 2008. (**PI**). Ages 5–8. (Sweden).

Landström, Lena. *Boo and Baa Have Company.* Illus. Olof Landström. Trans. from Swedish by Joan Sandin. Farrar, 2006. (**PI**). Ages 4–7. (Sweden). Boo and Baa series.

Lat. *Kampung Boy.* First Seconds, 2006. Ages 10–12. Also *Town Boy* (2007). (Malaysia).

Lee, Ho Baek. *While We Were Out.* Kane/Miller, 2003. (**PI**). Ages 3–6. (South Korea).

Lee, Suzy. *The Zoo.* Kane/Miller, 2007. (**PI**). Ages 5–8. Also *Mirror* (2003), *Wave* (2008), *Shadow* (2010). (Korea).

Liu, Jae Soo. *Yellow Umbrella.* Kane/Miller, 2002. (**PI**). Ages 2–6. (Companion CD with music composed by Sheen Dong Il). (South Korea).

Matti, Truus. *Departure Time.* Trans. from Dutch by Nancy Florest-Flier. Namelos, 2011. Ages 10–14. (Netherlands).

Metselaar, Menno, and Ruud van der Rol. *Anne Frank: Her Life in Words and Pictures*. Trans. from Dutch by Arnold Pomerans. Roaring Brook, 2009. Ages 10–14. (Netherlands).

Muggenthaler, Eva. *Fish on a Walk*. Trans. from German. Enchanted Lion, 2011. (**PI**). Ages 5–9. (Germany).

Nakagawa, Chihiro. *Who Made This Cake?* Illus. Junji Koyose. Trans. from Japanese. Front Street, 2008. (**PI**). Ages 5–8. (Japan).

Nayar, Nandini. *What Should I Make?* Illus. Proiti Roy. Trans. from Hindi. Tricycle, 2009. (**PI**). Ages 5–8. (India).

Orlev, Uri. *Run, Boy, Run.* Trans. from Hebrew by Hillel Halkin. Houghton, 2003. Ages 10–13. (Israel).

Rasmussen, Halfdan. *A Little Bitty Man and Other Poems for the Very Young.* Trans. from Danish by Marilyn Nelson and Pamela Espeland. Illus. Kevin Hawkes. Candlewick, 2011. (**PI**). Ages 5–8. (Denmark).

Sakai, Komako. *Emily's Balloon.* Trans. from Japanese. Chronicle, 2006. (**PI**). Ages 3–5. (Japan).

Satrapi, Marjane. *Persepolis.* Pantheon, 2003. (**GR**). Ages 10–14. (Iran).

Sellier, Marie. *Legend of the Chinese Dragon.* Trans. from French by Sibylle Kazeroid. Illus. Catherine Louis. NorthSouth, 2007. (**PI**). Ages 5–8. (Set in China).

Singh, Vandana. *Younguncle Comes to Town.* Illus. B. M. Kamath. Viking, 2006. Ages 8–11. (India).

Skármeta, Antonio. *The Composition.* Trans. from Spanish by Elisa Amado. Illus. Alfonso Ruano. Groundwood, 2000. (**PI**). Ages 8–12.

Stolz, Joelle. *The Shadows of Ghadames.* Trans. from French by Catherine Temerson. Delacorte, 2004. Ages 11–14. (Set in Libya).

Thor, Annika. *A Faraway Island*. Trans. from Swedish by Linda Schenck. Delcorte, 2009. Ages 9–12. Also *The Lily Pond* (2011). (Sweden).

Uehashi, Nahoko. *Morbito: Guardian of the Spirit.* Trans. from Japanese by Cathy Hirano. Illus. Yuko Shimizu. Scholastic, 2008. Ages 10–14. Also *Morbito II: Guardian of the Darkness* (2010). (Japan).

Valckx, Catharina. *Lizette's Green Sock.* Trans. from French. Clarion, 2005. (**PI**). Ages 3–6. (France).

Van Mol, Sine. *Meena*. Trans. from Dutch. Illus. Carianne Wijffels. Eerdmans, 2011. Ages 5–8. (Belgium).

Vejjajiva, Jane. *The Happiness of Kati.* Trans. from Thai by Prudence Borthwick. Atheneum, 2006. Ages 10–12. (Thailand).

Xiong, Kim. *The Little Stone Lion.* Trans. from Chinese. Heryin, 2006. (**PI**). Ages 4–7. (China).

Yan, Ma. *The Diary of Ma Yan: The Struggles and Hopes of a Chinese Schoolgirl.* Trans. from Mandarin by He Yanping. HarperCollins, 2005. Ages 10–14. (China).

Yu, Li-Qiong. *A New Year's Reunion*. Trans. from Chinese. Illus. Zhu Cheng-Liang. Candlewick, 2011. (**PI**). Ages 6–9. (China).

Yumoto, Kazumi. *The Friends.* Trans. from Japanese by Cathy Hirano. Farrar, 1996. Ages 10–14. (Japan).

Related Films, Videos, and DVDs

I Hate English! (2006). Author: Ellen Levine (1989). 14 minutes. (Asian-American).

I Love Saturdays y Domingos. (2002). Author: Alma Flor Ada. Illustrated by Elvivia Savadier (2002). 18 minutes. (Bilingual).

Inkheart. (2009). Author: Cornelia Funke (2003). 106 minutes. (Germany).

Millions. (2005). Author: Frank Cottrell Boyce (2004). 98 minutes. (England).

The Thief Lord. (2006). Author: Cornelia Funke (2002). 99 minutes. (Germany/Australia).

War Horse (2011). Author: Michael Morpugo (2007/ 1982). 146 minutes.

Part Three

Literature
in the
School

Finding a range of compelling books for children is only a first step. The ways in which we use those books can either invite children to enthusiastically immerse themselves as readers or lead them to dread the questions and worksheets they will have to complete once they finish reading the book.

Chapters 12 and 13 focus on curriculum and teaching strategies. Chapter 12 begins with a discussion of the political context that influences the use of literature in schools, particularly highlighting the Common Core State Standards. The two main approaches to teaching reading—basal reading programs and literature-based reading—are discussed in terms of strategies for incorporating literature into the teaching of reading. Features such as sample planning webs, evaluation checklists, and literature-related activities to help preservice

teachers in school practicums gain experience with literature provide practical procedural suggestions and advice.

Chapter 13 presents strategies for engaging children with literature and eliciting their responses. The chapter and strategies are organized around three types of experiences with literature that have different purposes for readers. Reading Widely for Personal Purposes includes strategies for teacher read-alouds, student independent reading, booktalks, readers' theatre, and experiencing literature as multimodal texts. Reading Critically to Inquire about the World includes literature discussions, a variety of literature response engagements, using drama as response, and literature across the curriculum. Reading Strategically to Learn about Literacy focuses on using literature to learn about writing.

Chapter Twelve

Literature in the Curriculum

In Sight

Close your eyes and look inside.
A mirror shines within;
To find where you are going,
First see where you have been.

—*Charles Ghigna*

This chapter highlights the political context that surrounds the use of literature in classrooms as well as broader issues of planning for literature instruction. More specific instructional strategies related to the integration of literature into literacy are shared in Chapter 13. This chapter begins with a discussion of the Common Core State Standards and their impact on the ways in which schools are planning for literature and literacy. Different organizational structures for organizing a literature curriculum with students, such as genres, themes or topics, authors or illustrators, literary and visual elements, and notable books are overviewed along with strategies for planning literature units. Literature plays an important role in the teaching of reading and writing, either as a supplement to a basal reader program or through a literature-based approach. The latter part of the chapter includes sections on evaluating a literature program and gaining experience with observing the use of literature in classrooms as a preservice teacher.

The Politics of Literacy and Literature

The teaching of reading has been a controversial and contested area of debate among both educators and politicians. Calls for higher literacy standards are the focus of intense national and international interest and have led to the imposition of "one size fits all" models of national literacy standards and high stakes testing through legislation and policy initiatives. Although initiatives on the teaching of reading have long evolved from public pressure, the increasing involvement of federal and state governments in specific decisions about literacy instruction in order to raise standards is a more recent development. These public debates and government initiatives have often resulted in punitive legislation aimed at controlling teachers.

Congress created the ***National Reading Panel*** (NRP) in 1997 to assess the status of research-based knowledge about reading. The *Report of the National Reading Panel* (2000) was met with great controversy and skepticism because of the panel's narrow definition of scientific research that excluded the majority of research studies conducted over a thirty-year period and resulted in a highly skewed set of recommendations. This report narrowed the teaching of reading to instruction in phonemic awareness, phonics, reading comprehension, fluency, and vocabulary. A large body of research studies on reading aloud and independent silent reading were not included because they did not meet the NRP's narrow definition of scientific research.

The ***No Child Left Behind Act*** (NCLB) was passed in 2001 and ***Reading First*** programs were established to implement the NRP components of reading instruction. By 2008, reading comprehension tests indicated that Reading First did *not* have statistically significant impacts on reading comprehension test scores in grades 1–3, and other national testing indicated that reading achievement scores for intermediate students either had not increased or were decreasing. These findings called into question the assumption that a phonics-based approach to reading instruction would produce better readers than other approaches.

Many schools adopted basal reader programs with highly controlled and stilted stories for young children, not recognizing that carefully selected literature can support students in developing the reading skills identified in NCLB and Reading First. Nursery rhymes, predictable books, and poems can help children develop phonemic awareness. Teacher read-alouds, paired reading, readers' theatre, and choral reading can increase children's reading fluency. Shared reading and repeated oral reading can teach children sound–symbol relationships and increase their reading fluency. Independent silent reading of good literature, especially if followed by reflection, can increase children's vocabulary and conceptual knowledge, as well as develop their reading comprehension.

Overemphasis of any one component of reading instruction, such as phonics, to the exclusion of the others in beginning reading instruction as mandated by NCLB is detrimental to students. Programs advocating heavy emphasis on phonics but no daily teacher read-aloud or daily independent silent reading of excellent books of the students' own choosing often produce resistant readers. Daily read-alouds and independent silent reading demonstrate fluency, build meaningful vocabulary and conceptual knowledge, offer reading practice, and improve attitudes toward reading.

Accountability is a demand by government agencies and the public for school systems and teachers to improve students' school achievement as demonstrated by test scores. The NCLB Act expanded accountability by requiring annual testing of reading and mathematics achievement for all students in grades 3 to 8. NCLB also required that performance data be disaggregated according to race, gender, income, and other criteria to demonstrate progress in closing the achievement gap between students viewed as "disadvantaged" and other groups of students. This data was used to grade schools as Pass or Fail, depending on student achievement by averages for the grade and by subgroups. Schools that receive failing grades are given a period of time to improve student achievement. Failure of a school to do so results in reduced federal and state funding for the school, vouchers for students to attend another public school or charter school in the case of repeated failures by the school, or replacement of administrators and teachers, depending on state and local policies. States developed the actual tests used, the procedures for implementation of the policy, and timetables for implementation according to federal requirements.

Critics point out that the focus on multiple choice tests has dumbed down the curriculum and led to "drill and kill" approaches to teaching isolated skills as well as to pushing low-scoring students out of public schools to boost scores. The National Association of Educational Progress tracks trends in reading achievement and issues a report called the "Nation's Report Card." Data shows that reading comprehension scores for 2011 remained unchanged at grade 4, with a slight improvement at grade 8, after several years of decline that seem to be associated with NCLB. Many educators believe that the major reason for this decline was a decrease in voluntary reading among students. As a result of NCLB, a large amount of class time was spent on basic beginning reading skills, diminishing curricular efforts in other subjects, including the enjoyment and appreciation of literature. As is often the case with policy initiatives, the failure and shortcomings of NCLB and Reading First has led to a new initiative based on a new set of standards and assessments.

Common Core State Standards

The current focus of national and state efforts is the *Common Core State Standards*, which have been adopted by almost all of the states. These K–12 standards were developed by a group appointed by the National Governor's Association and the Council of Chief State School Officers. They examined research on the levels of literacy needed for success in college and careers and worked backward to determine the literacy knowledge they believed students needed to have at each grade level to be college and career ready by the end of high school. These grade-specific standards in reading, writing, speaking, listening, and language also set requirements for literacy in history/social studies, science, and technical content areas. These standards are having a significant impact on instruction due to state mandates, and schools are under tremendous pressure to make changes in their instruction. National performance-based assessments are being developed to measure student achievement and to evaluate teachers and schools on the standards.

Aspects of the Common Core State Standards that impact the use of literature and the myths associated with each aspect include:

- An increase in the use of informational texts in classroom instruction, beginning in kindergarten with a 50/50 split between literary and informational texts. Since informational text is only 10 to 15 percent of the texts in most primary classrooms, schools need to greatly increase the availability and use of informational texts.

  - Myth—narrative and literary fiction are not valued in the standards. The standards have a strong focus on literary texts and argue for a better balance of the types of texts used in classrooms, not an overbalance in the other direction.

- An emphasis on continual increases across grade levels in the complexity of texts that students are reading. CCSS provides a list of text exemplars for each grade level along with excerpts from these texts to demonstrate this increase in text complexity.

  - Myth—these lists are of core books to be read by all students instead of being exemplars to help teachers consider the complexity of texts in their school.

  - Myth—text complexity is determined by quantitative measures, specifically by lexile levels. Text complexity in CCSS is determined by lexile levels along with teacher judgment about the difficulty of a text related to the readers in that classroom and the task in which they are engaged.

- A focus on the close reading of texts and text analysis where students are required to find and cite evidence in the text as they discuss key ideas and details, craft and structure, and knowledge and ideas from these texts. Text analysis is viewed as bringing rigor to reading with an emphasis on higher level critical reading skills.

  - Myth—reader response does not include text analysis and stays at a simple level of personal connections that do not lead to critical thinking. This myth reflects a misunderstanding of reader response that has been incorporated into CCSS. Reader response begins with personal connections and interpretations, and then moves readers into analyzing their response through dialogue based on evidence from their lives and the text to develop their interpretations.

  - Myth—the focus on close text-based reading in CCSS mandates a return to narrow definitions of what and how students read. Many policy makers are interpreting close reading as in-depth, step-by-step analysis of each part of the text to examine literal and inferential meanings. History indicates that this type of textual criticism turned off several generations of students as readers because it lacked purpose, meaning, and connections to ideas and issues that students cared about (Langer, 2010).

Resources to support you in meeting the Common Core State Standards are integrated throughout this text—titles of books across a range of categories, discussions of the structures and types of informational texts, information about literary elements and text structures, methods for measuring text complexity, and ways to integrate text analysis with reader response.

CCSS emphasize reading across multiple texts to compare ideas and information. Examples of reader connections to facilitate this reading across texts and perspectives are included in the genre chapters.

You should also be aware of research findings about the value of literature for children in relation to literacy to counter misunderstandings. Research studies summarized in Table 12.1 indicate that two engagements are especially important in teaching children to read: regularly reading aloud excellent literature, and time for silent independent reading of free-choice material. Research studies in Table 12.2 show that reading and writing strategies and skills go hand in hand—a strong focus with CCSS as well.

Table 12.1 Important Studies on Literature and Reading

Researchers(s)	Participants	Findings
Fullerton & Colwell (2010)	Content analysis of multiple studies	Ethnographic content analysis of research on literature discussion 1989–2009. The analysis identifies the benefits of small group discussions, the role of the teacher, and the influence of gender and student power and status on discussion.
Maloch (2008)	Second grade classroom	Documented teacher support to build student knowledge about informational texts through multiple opportunities with the texts, supportive encounters, and learning text features.
Santoro, Chard, Howard, & Baker (2008)	First-grade students across multiple classrooms	Read-alouds when combined with comprehension instruction and student discussions promoted growth in comprehension and vocabulary.
Arya, Martens, Wilson, Altwerger, Jin, Laster, & Lang (2005)	One hundred urban, low SES second-graders in four schools; two classes used commercial phonics-based reading programs; two classes used literature-based instruction	No significant difference was found in measures of students' phonics use, reading accuracy, or comprehension, contradicting the National Reading Panel's predictions that phonics-based reading programs produce better readers.
Wilson, Martens, Arya, & Altwerger (2004)	Eighty-four urban, low SES second-graders taught reading with three different reading programs: Direct Instruction and Open Court, scripted phonics-based reading programs; and Guided Reading, a literature-based reading program	No significant difference was found in measures of students' phonics use; Guided Reading students could describe settings and characters, retell stories cohesively, form inferences, and make connections. These findings contradict the National Reading Panel recommendations on phonics.

(Continued)

Table 12.1 Continued

Researchers(s)	Participants	Findings
Worthy, Patterson, Salas, Prater, & Turner (2002)	Twenty-four struggling, resistant readers in grades 3 through 5	The most effective factor in increasing these students' motivation to read was a reading instructor who tailored instruction to each student's unique needs, found materials that fit each student's interests, and took time to inspire students to read.
Ivey & Broaddus (2001)	1,765 sixth-graders in twenty-three diverse schools in mid-Atlantic and northeastern U.S.	When asked what made them want to read in the classroom, students ranked as most important: • Free reading time and teacher read-alouds of literature • Quality and diversity of reading materials and a choice in selecting these materials
Anderson (1996)	Elementary-grade students	Even slight increases (10 minutes a day) in time spent reading independently lead to gains in reading achievement. Amount of free reading in early grades helps determine reading ability in grades 5 and 6.

Given the political context surrounding literacy and literature and the research on literature, literature can become a planned component of classroom life through two types of curricular frameworks. The first framework is a literature curriculum where instruction is planned around literature as a discipline with a particular content of literary knowledge. The second framework involves the integration of literature into the literacy curriculum as reading materials to support the teaching of reading and writing in a basal reader program.

Table 12.2 Important Studies on Literature and Writing

Researcher(s)	Participants	Findings
Journal of Children's Literature, Fall 2008	Series of case studies by different researchers on the use of literature mentor texts to support writing	Each group of researchers presents a case study of the kinds of text structures found in literature and strategies for learning from these mentor texts to support comprehension and writing.
Jarvey, McKeough, & Pyryt (2008)	Two classes of fourth-grade students	Comparison of two approaches to teaching students to write trickster tales. Documents the strategies within a genre approach of reading and analyzing literature that supported students in their writing of that genre.
Barrs (2000)	Eighteen fourth-graders in five elementary schools in London whose reading and writing were analyzed over one school year	Children use the language and writing styles of books they read in their writing. Writing development was closely linked to reading development and vice versa.

Researcher(s)	Participants	Findings
Cantrell (1999)	Twenty-one children in four third-grade classrooms where teachers used recommended literacy practices (explicit skill instruction and meaning-centered activities) to a high degree and nineteen children in four classrooms where teachers used these practices to a low degree	In classrooms where teachers frequently used children's literature, integrated reading and writing, and taught reading and writing skills in context, students developed reading and writing skills at higher levels than students in classrooms where teachers provided more isolated skill instruction.
Lancia (1997)	Second-graders	Students "borrowed" plots, plot elements, characters, stylistic devices, and information from books to use in their own writing. Good books were good models for writing.
Dressel (1990)	Fifth-graders	Student writing was directly affected by the characteristics of the stories they heard and discussed, regardless of the students' reading abilities. The better the quality of the read-aloud, the better the quality of the student writing.

Planning a Literature Curriculum

Literature is more than a collection of well-written stories and poems and has its own body of knowledge. A term that is sometimes used to label this treatment of literature is *discipline-based literature instruction.* The object of such a course of study is to teach children *about* literature—the terms used to define it, its components or elements and genres, and the craft of creating literature. The terms and elements of fiction are presented in Chapter 3; the terms and elements of illustrations are presented in Chapter 4; the terms and elements of nonfiction are presented in Chapter 10; and the genres and their characteristics are presented in Chapters 5 through 11.

Some schools use a *traditional approach* to literature that focuses on mastery of content. This approach places the teacher at the center, in that the teacher decides the agenda, dispenses the information, asks the questions, and often supplies the answers. The goal of this approach is for students to learn what the teacher tells them about the literature under study.

Our focus is on an *inquiry approach,* which is grounded in problem-based learning and constructivist learning and focuses on how one learns. Teachers who choose this approach want their students to be actively engaged in posing questions that are significant to them as they explore the power of literature to examine the human condition. In an inquiry approach:

- Students' inquiry is guided by their *own* questions related to a piece of literature—questions they find compelling and honestly care about. During the inquiry process, students revise their questions as they learn and discuss, debate, and share information with other students. Collaborative learning, team projects, and small group discussions are emphasized.

- Emphasis is placed on the process of how to search for and make sense of information about literature so that the knowledge gained is conceptual and has wide application.

- Teachers are facilitators rather than dispensers of knowledge who think collaboratively with students instead of providing answers.

Elementary and middle-school teachers can organize a literature curriculum by genre, theme or topic, author or illustrator, literary element or device, or notable books. An alternative is to create a hybrid literature curriculum by including aspects of several of these approaches.

Genres

By organizing a literature curriculum around literary genres, teachers provide a context for students to learn about the various types of literature and the characteristics of each. An inquiry approach to genre typically begins by immersing students in exploring a wide range of books from that genre to develop a list of characteristics for that genre; for example, that works of historical fiction are always set in the past or that characters in folktales are two-dimensional. Students then move to in-depth explorations of specific books within the genre and of the ways these characteristics play out differently across the genre.

Cruz and Pollock (2004) share their experiences of immersing students in an inquiry around the genre of fantasy. Their approach reflects an excellent structure for engaging students in exploring literary elements and genre within a meaningful context through:

- Gathering and sorting a range of texts to determine which belong to the genre
- Reading aloud picture books and novels to discuss excellent examples of the genre
- Independently reading many books in the genre
- Charting student observations about the genre in various ways
- Discussing selected books from the genre in small group literature circles
- Writing their own stories based on their knowledge of the genre

One advantage of this plan is that students are exposed to a wide variety of literature across the school year. Knowledge of different genres gives students useful frameworks for understanding story types that support their comprehension as readers and their use of genre structures as writers. Planning involves choosing a genre, gathering a wide range of books, and selecting several representative books. Most teachers choose to do one or two genre studies a year, selecting genres that will expand children's reading or that relate to state standards for a particular grade level.

Themes or Topics

Organizing a study of literature by theme or topic is the most frequent and effective way to engage students with literature. Focusing on the multiple connections and interpretations of issues and themes in a book gives students an opportunity to relate what they learn to their own lives. Themes and topics will vary according to ages and experiences of students. Often, primary children are most interested in themes and topics having to do with school and family life, while middle-grade students are often intrigued by themes and topics related to difficult social and global issues and to their own need for inner resources as they transition into adulthood.

Examples of themes include:

- Taking action can make a difference
- Force creates movement

- Systems organize our lives and world
- Decisions have consequences
- Belonging creates relationships and conformity
- Difference is a resource, not a problem
- Life is a journey across many kinds of pathways

Children often read or listen to a particular book or set of books related to the theme and explore the theme through questioning, journaling, reflecting, discussing, writing, responding through drama and art, and further reading. Strategies to support discussion and response are in Chapter 13.

Books can also be organized around topics like animals, friendship, family, transportation, and careers as a way to support students in locating books for independent reading. Organizing by topic, however, does not facilitate discussion and thoughtful connections across books because topics stay on the surface of the book and do not engage students with issues around which they can engage in dialogue with each other.

Authors or Illustrators

The goal of a curriculum in literature organized by author or illustrator is to acquaint students with the books and styles of children's authors and illustrators. Students also gain knowledge of authors' or illustrators' lives and how these life experiences influenced their books as well as how they use particular literary or visual elements to tell their stories. This type of inquiry influences students' choices as readers, their comprehension and reading strategies, and their writing processes and strategies. Many times, these authors and their books become mentors for students as writers, an important focus of the anchor standards for writing in the Common Core State Standards.

The choice of authors and illustrators will naturally be guided both by students' reading interests and the teacher's desire to introduce students to notable authors and illustrators and their books. As children experience a sampling of the chosen author's or illustrator's work, attention will be focused on trademark stylistic elements such as unusual use of words, color, or media, as well as themes, characters, character types, or settings common to these works. Later, information about the person's life can be introduced through published or online interviews and even guest appearances by the author or illustrator. Websites, biographies, and biographical reference sources, such as *Something about the Author* (Gale, 2012) and *Children's Literature Review* (Gale, 2011), provide information about children's book authors and illustrators. Many biographies and autobiographies of children's book authors and illustrators are available, both as individual books, such as *The House That Baba Built: An Author's Childhood in China* by Ed Young and *Drawing from Memory* by Allan Say, as well as books that are part of a series, such as Richard C. Owen's Meet the Author series.

Literary and Visual Elements and Devices

Organizing around literary elements usually refers to the elements of fiction and nonfiction as presented in Chapters 3 and 10, such as character, plot, theme, and setting. Visual elements, such as artistic styles, media, and book format, can be addressed as well. A *literary device* is a technique used to achieve a specific effect, such as using irony, symbolism, parody, and foreshadowing to add richness to stories. For example, several authors have published parodies of the classic *Goodnight Moon* by Margaret Wise Brown, a long-time favorite of young children who demand that it be read over and over. *Goodnight Goon* by Michael Rex and *Goodnight iPad* by Anne Droyd are parodies for older readers who recognize the way the author has played on a classic text from their childhoods.

The goal of a literature curriculum organized by literary elements and devices is to give students a better understanding of the craft of writing so that they can read more perceptively and appreciatively and apply this knowledge to their own writing. Since this approach is analytical and somewhat abstract, it is more appropriate for older students and is often integrated into minilessons as part of a writing workshop rather than as a separate unit of study.

Careful selection of children's books to facilitate the investigation of each literary element or device is crucial. The featured element must be prominent and be used by the author with extraordinary skill to captivate readers. Books of various genres can be grouped to demonstrate the same literary element. Picture books are particularly good at presenting literary elements and devices clearly and in relatively simple contexts so that they can be understood more easily. One resource for selecting picture books for this use is Susan Hall's *Using Picture Storybooks to Teach Literary Devices*, Vols. 1–4 (1990, 1994, 2001, 2007).

Students' acquaintance with the literary elements and devices should go far beyond mere definition and include close reading of key passages. These passages can be used to examine the author's craft at developing character, establishing mood, authenticating setting, or using such devices as inference, symbolism, or foreshadowing. Students can then explore these elements and devices in their own art, drama, and writing to give a personal and more complete understanding of these concepts, providing an evaluation of students' grasp of these concepts.

Notable Books

Notable books are exemplary books for children that can be classic or contemporary and can include books from different genres and award-winning lists. The books are read and analyzed for the features that contribute to their excellence, such as their relevance to readers, unique perspectives or insights, treatment of topics, memorable characters, or illustrations.

In the primary grades, teachers will most likely read notable books aloud to students, since most will be too difficult for independent reading. Reading aloud by teachers is important in the intermediate and middle grades as well, but the books can also be read independently by students. Analysis of notable books can occur through discussion (whole class or small group), dialogue journal writing (with the teacher or a friend who is reading the same book), or reading logs. Regardless of the method students use to respond to these books, they should be encouraged to relate the books to their own lives and to compare them to other books. Even if students are responding in more independent ways, such as journal writing, it is a good idea to invite them to share their thoughts with one another.

Teachers who organize their literature curriculum by notable books must be careful to remain flexible in book selections from year to year so that the list of notable books reflects students' current interests and reading preferences. A list of notable books that never varies can result in student disinterest and stale teaching.

Developing Literature Units

Initial planning for literature units includes establishing your goals for what students will explore or learn through the unit, selecting several books that will receive in-depth focus (often called touchstone books), and gathering a collection of many books related to the unit focus. For example, initial planning for a science fiction unit on future worlds could involve identifying these core books:

- Independent reading—*The City of Ember* by Jeanne DuPrau (2003), *Turnabout* by Margaret Peterson Haddix (2000), *The House of the Scorpion* by Nancy Farmer (2002), *The Hunger Games* by Suzanne Collins (2008), *Mortal Engines* by Phillip Reeve (2003), *The Green Book* by Jill Paton Walsh (1986)
- Read-aloud touchstone text—*The Giver* by Lois Lowry (1993)
- Small group literature circle books—*Gathering Blue* (2000), *Messenger* (2004), *Son* (2012) by Lois Lowry
- Featured author—*Looking Back: A Book of Memories* by Lois Lowry (2000)

Collecting, brainstorming, and organizing the activities are the final steps in planning for a literature curriculum. Two helpful tools in organizing the details of literature units are webs and lesson plans.

Webs   A *web* is a graphic planning tool that reveals relationships between ideas and so creates a visual overview of a literature unit, including its focus, concepts, related book titles, and activities. A web is a map that helps teachers and students find their way to their goals and can be changed easily to encompass new ideas and adapted for different uses or to meet special needs and circumstances. Teachers can use the web as a source for daily or weekly lesson plans as the unit unfolds.

Ideas for a web are generated through brainstorming. The main advantage of webbing is that the process clarifies and creates ideas for connections between concepts, books, and activities. Activities can be drawn across content areas and skill areas—writing, reading, listening, thinking, speaking, art, crafts, drama, and music. Involving students in creating webs gives them a voice in planning and can provide original ideas and relationships that the teacher had not considered. The web in Figure 12.1 shows ideas for a unit of study on the literary element of character. The web in Figure 12.2 is built around concepts relating to forced journeys and refugees. This web begins with literature to develop a conceptual understanding of journeys as movement along a pathway (physical, emotional, cultural, psychological, etc.) as a frame for an exploration of the topic of refugees.

Lesson Plans   Lesson plans vary according to the needs and experience of the teacher, but lessons plans for each day or week usually include the following components:

- *Goals or objectives* are the conceptual ideas or issues for a particular set of activities, essentially the "why" behind those activities. These goals give a focus for the activities but also leave space for students to pursue their inquiries. A teacher planning a literature unit on refugees might have the goal that students understand the complex issues of documentation and of legal and illegal entry into a country by refugees.

- *Activities and materials* indicate the preparation that the teacher needs to do for the experience, the materials needed, and the tasks or engagements for students. Teachers wanting students to understand the complex issues of documentation could read aloud the informational book *Denied, Detained, Deported* by Ann Bausum while students select from novels to read in small groups, such as *La Linea* by Ann Jamarillo, *Ask Me No Questions* by Marina Budhos, and *A Time of Miracles* by Anne-Aaure Bondoux.

Figure 12.1 Web Demonstrating Investigation of a Literary Element, Grades 2–4

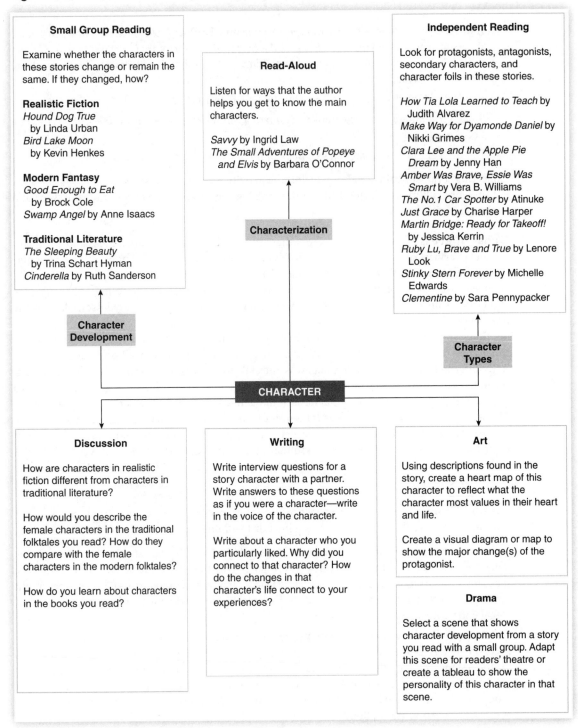

Figure 12.2 Conceptual Web on Forced Journeys, Grades 4–8

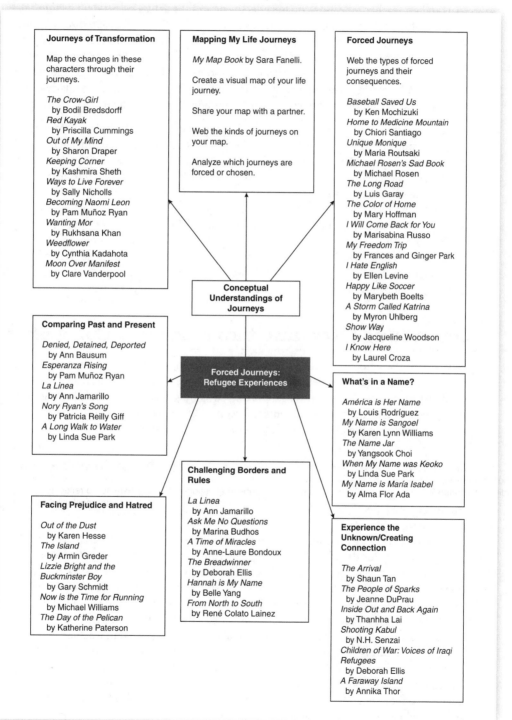

Journeys of Transformation

Map the changes in these characters through their journeys.

The Crow-Girl
  by Bodil Bredsdorff
Red Kayak
  by Priscilla Cummings
Out of My Mind
  by Sharon Draper
Keeping Corner
  by Kashmira Sheth
Ways to Live Forever
  by Sally Nicholls
Becoming Naomi Leon
  by Pam Muñoz Ryan
Wanting Mor
  by Rukhsana Khan
Weedflower
  by Cynthia Kadahota
Moon Over Manifest
  by Clare Vanderpool

Mapping My Life Journeys

My Map Book by Sara Fanelli.

Create a visual map of your life journey.

Share your map with a partner.

Web the kinds of journeys on your map.

Analyze which journeys are forced or chosen.

Forced Journeys

Web the types of forced journeys and their consequences.

Baseball Saved Us
  by Ken Mochizuki
Home to Medicine Mountain
  by Chiori Santiago
Unique Monique
  by Maria Routsaki
Michael Rosen's Sad Book
  by Michael Rosen
The Long Road
  by Luis Garay
The Color of Home
  by Mary Hoffman
I Will Come Back for You
  by Marisabina Russo
My Freedom Trip
  by Frances and Ginger Park
I Hate English
  by Ellen Levine
Happy Like Soccer
  by Marybeth Boelts
A Storm Called Katrina
  by Myron Uhlberg
Show Way
  by Jacqueline Woodson
I Know Here
  by Laurel Croza

Conceptual Understandings of Journeys

Comparing Past and Present

Denied, Detained, Deported
  by Ann Bausum
Esperanza Rising
  by Pam Muñoz Ryan
La Linea
  by Ann Jamarillo
Nory Ryan's Song
  by Patricia Reilly Giff
A Long Walk to Water
  by Linda Sue Park

Forced Journeys: Refugee Experiences

What's in a Name?

América is Her Name
  by Louis Rodríguez
My Name is Sangoel
  by Karen Lynn Williams
The Name Jar
  by Yangsook Choi
When My Name was Keoko
  by Linda Sue Park
My Name is María Isabel
  by Alma Flor Ada

Challenging Borders and Rules

La Linea
  by Ann Jamarillo
Ask Me No Questions
  by Marina Budhos
A Time of Miracles
  by Anne-Laure Bondoux
The Breadwinner
  by Deborah Ellis
Hannah is My Name
  by Belle Yang
From North to South
  by René Colato Lainez

Facing Prejudice and Hatred

Out of the Dust
  by Karen Hesse
The Island
  by Armin Greder
Lizzie Bright and the Buckminster Boy
  by Gary Schmidt
Now is the Time for Running
  by Michael Williams
The Day of the Pelican
  by Katherine Paterson

Experience the Unknown/Creating Connection

The Arrival
  by Shaun Tan
The People of Sparks
  by Jeanne DuPrau
Inside Out and Back Again
  by Thanhha Lai
Shooting Kabul
  by N.H. Senzai
Children of War: Voices of Iraqi Refugees
  by Deborah Ellis
A Faraway Island
  by Annika Thor

- *Evaluation and reflection* involve plans for evaluating students' understandings around the goals and for teacher reflections on the effectiveness of the activities. *Student evaluation* can take the form of written reflections, oral questions, whole class or small group discussions, entries in student journals, and written, oral, artistic, and dramatic responses to literature. *Self-evaluation by the teacher* can focus on student interest in the activities, student understandings related to the goals, and the plan's success in predicting time and materials needed and the effectiveness of the activities and materials. During the literature unit, teachers will want to regularly evaluate their students' understandings and questions and make adjustments in the plans.

Because literature units are several weeks long, they usually include a culminating activity that gives students an opportunity to reflect on what they have learned, review major ideas, and celebrate the focus of the unit or share their own inquiries. An overall unit evaluation is valuable to teachers, particularly if they intend to use the unit with another group of students.

Online sources of lesson plans created by teachers include ReadWriteThink (www.readwrite think.org) and Web English Teacher (www.webenglishteacher.com). Students can use the Internet to research topics for literature units of study, locate websites for author studies, or identify sources for further research on a theme. Students often enjoy finding books on topics of interest and read-ing others' comments on these books. Links to several of these sites can be found on the American Library Association's Great Sites for Kids (www.ala.org/gwstemplate.cfm?section=greatwebsites& template=/cfapps/gws/default.cfm) in the Literature and Languages category.

Integrating Literature into a Literacy Curriculum

Nowhere in the school curriculum is literature more important than in the teaching of reading and writing. Literature can be instrumental in helping children learn to read as well as keeping children's interest in reading alive, supporting struggling readers in strengthening their reading strategies, and encouraging all students to become lifelong readers. Two common approaches to teaching reading in the U.S. involve different roles for literature.

Basal Reading Program Supplemented by Children's Literature

Teachers bring a variety of teaching styles and needs to teaching: no single approach fits all teachers or students. The most common approach to the teaching of reading is the basal reading approach supplemented by children's literature.

The basal reading program has been the traditional approach to teaching reading in U.S. ele-mentary schools for decades. These programs consist of a series of readers that are supposedly written at successively more difficult levels. The core materials include a student reader, a teach-er's manual, student workbooks, and tests. The strength of the basal program is that it provides teachers with an organized instructional framework on which to build and for which the reading selections and related activities are already provided. Basal reading programs offer teachers consid-erable guidance and help with the decisions and challenges involved in teaching children to read.

Guided reading consists of small group instruction, close attention to assessment of stu-dents' reading levels, matching students with books that are incrementally "leveled" by reading difficulty, explicit instruction on reading strategies to improve comprehension, and short-term intervention for students who struggle. One widely used guided reading program is the Fountas and Pinnell Leveled Books Program, K–8, published by Heinemann.

The learning theory on which basal reading materials are based holds that learning complex skills begins with mastering the simplest components of that skill before attempting the next larger components, and so on until the whole skill is learned. In terms of learning to read, this means that the letters of the alphabet are learned first, followed by letter-sound patterns, words, and then sentences. Finally, when the components of reading are learned, whole works of literature, such as stories, plays, and poems, are read. This theory is challenged by those who believe that reading is a meaning-based process rather than a skill that is mechanical and additive.

In the 1980s, U.S. publishers of basal readers made an effort to improve the quality of stories in basal readers and integrated more multicultural stories and excerpts from high-quality trade books, such as a chapter or episodes from a longer children's book. These changes were incorporated while retaining the skill-based instruction and the belief that reading is learned from part to whole.

Basal readers, however, are not a substitute for real books. Even though some basal stories are good literature, not excerpted or adapted, the brevity of these selections is a problem for intermediate grades. Most students in these grades are capable of reading novel-length chapter books and should be doing so regularly in their school reading program. Students in classes where anthologies and basal readers are used exclusively are denied the all-important self-selection of reading material from a wide variety of books.

Another issue is that the focus on in-depth text analysis, which is at the heart of the Common Core State Standards, requires complex texts and novels in order for characters and issues to develop and change over time. Students need whole texts with multiple layers of meaning, not simplified stories and excerpts, if they are to engage in critical reading and search for intertextual connections across and within texts.

Ideally, each teacher should be allowed to choose the approach to teaching reading that best suits his or her philosophy of learning and teaching style. In many school districts across the U.S., however, the use of a basal approach to teach reading is mandated. Even more restrictive is the use of lockstep methods of teaching reading that rely on highly scripted, prescribed teacher plans that must be followed with no accommodation. In a three-year study on methods of teaching reading, Ryder, Sekulski, and Silberg (2003) found that this type of direct instruction has limited applicability, should not be used as the main method of reading instruction, and is not as effective as methods that allow teachers to engage in a more flexible approach.

Many teachers, despite mandates, have moved away from a slavish "read-every-page-or-bust" attitude toward these programs. They have found ways to improve their teaching of reading by using their basal programs in innovative ways that eliminate some of the skills exercises and allow time for literature. Some guidelines drawn from the example of these teachers are:

- Use only the best literary selections in the basal and substitute good literature for the rest.

- Let students read the better-written basal selections for enjoyment or discussion, and eliminate some of the skill, drill, and comprehension lessons that take the focus away from meaning.

- Eliminate the workbooks and worksheets that are used to keep children busy while the teacher meets with small groups. Students can read self-choice books until their group meets.

- Eliminate the stigma of ability grouping through whole-class studies of a particular story or by forming heterogeneous small groups to read and discuss a story. Use the time saved for individual student conferences.

- Use phonics and skills lessons from the basal reader only when you have identified a particular student or group of students who need those skills. Children do not learn according to an imposed schedule, but when they need that skill and so are ready to learn. Use the time saved from ineffective exercises to read aloud or for students to read self-choice books.

- Avoid comprehension questions at the end of basal reading lessons that trivialize the stories or demean the students. Use the time saved to invite children to share their personal responses or to respond to the story in writing, drama, or art.

- Make phonics instruction or word study a regular but brief (10–15 minutes) part of primary-grade reading instruction instead of taking the majority of time. Use that time to read and talk about good stories.

- The basal readers for older students contain individual chapters excerpted from different novels. Have the students read these chapters as a preview to decide which novel to read.

- Create a text set of literature that builds from the themes, topics, and authors in the basal and that extends the basal units into real books.

Basal readers are most effective when used in concert with a wide variety of trade books that reflect students' interests and reading abilities. The basal reader can provide guidance and structure for teachers, while trade books provide the variety, self-selection, and interest that motivate children to want to read. The role of literature as supplemental materials will be increasingly important for classrooms using these programs in order to encourage the level of thinking and text complexity required by the Common Core State Standards.

Reading Incentive Programs   Some schools have purchased commercially produced ***reading incentive programs*** to motivate students to read more widely as a supplement to a basal reader program. These programs have computerized management components to track students' progress. These programs, such as *Accelerated Reader,* include a pretest for assigning a reading level to each student for a certain level of books that have a predetermined number of points according to their difficulty as determined by the program developers. After students finish reading a book silently, they complete a multiple-choice test to assess literal comprehension and earn points and prizes based on their score.

Reports on the success of such programs are mixed. Many teachers and schools report disappointment in the programs and concerns about whether such programs are having a positive impact on their students' interest in reading due to the following:

- Students' free choices for reading are limited.
- Students only value books in the program's database due to the reward system.
- Extrinsic rewards can diminish the desire of students to read for pleasure.
- Personal enjoyment of literature and reading is often deemphasized.
- Testing students' literal comprehension can interfere with reading books to experience the world of that story.
- Tests of literal comprehension often emphasize inconsequential material to the detriment of the development of critical thinking in students.
- Many students find ways to gain the rewards without reading the books by asking other students for the answers, skimming the books for frequently tested details, or seeing the movie.

- These programs are very costly and could be replaced by purchasing trade books for class-rooms and school libraries. The program selections can soon become dated, necessitating additional expenditures.

Teachers can design their own reading incentive programs where students keep a record of their own free-choice silent reading, have opportunities to respond to books in a variety of ways, and work toward individual silent reading goals set by the student and the teacher together. Rewards, such as a special celebration party, are provided for the class for reaching goals.

Literature-Based Reading

Literature-based reading is an approach to teaching reading through the use of trade books. The learning theory in which literature-based reading is grounded holds that children learn by searching for meaning in the world around them and engaging in inquiry into ideas and issues from their reading as well as examining their strategies as readers.

Teachers using a literature-based approach to reading structure a classroom environment to immerse children in good literature. In these classrooms, children hear literature read aloud several times a day, see good readers reading voluntarily, discover that good books can entertain them and tell them things they want to know, and constantly engage in reading books that they themselves have chosen because they are interested in the topics. Frequent student–teacher conferences allow teachers to check comprehension, assess reading strategies, and form small groups or create class lessons around strategies that need explicit attention and teaching to support reading development.

As in basal reading programs, explicit reading instruction is an important feature of literature-based reading, particularly in the primary grades. Phonics, concepts of print, vocabulary, and comprehension strategies are taught in literature-based reading, but within the context of interesting literature. Unlike basal reading programs, these skills are never taught in isolation, where they have no real meaning, are never the focus of the entire reading period, and are taught only when needed.

Literature-based reading instruction addresses the components of instruction considered essential to the teaching of reading by the Common Core State Standards: engaging with text to analyze key ideas and details, craft and structure, and the integration of knowledge and ideas. By including daily teacher read-alouds and self-choice independent reading, students are more likely to also develop positive attitudes toward reading, self-motivation to read, and a lifelong reading habit.

Key elements of the literature-based reading classroom include the following:

- Daily reading aloud of good literature by the teacher
- Reading skills taught when needed and within meaningful contexts, never in isolation
- Quantities of good trade books in the classroom (five or more books per child), selected to match specific interests and approximate reading abilities of the students in the class
- Daily silent reading by students of self-selected books
- Daily opportunities for students to share their responses to books orally
- Daily opportunities for students to respond to literature in a variety of ways, including writing, drama, and art
- Frequent individual student–teacher reading conferences

Decisions about what to teach, when to teach it, and what materials to use are made by the teacher in the literature-based reading classroom based on the specific students in that classroom. These decisions and the responsibility for materials selection and acquisition may make literature-based reading more demanding of teachers' professional judgment than other reading methods; however, this approach has proven to be effective not only in teaching students to read but also in creating a positive attitude toward reading and lifelong reading habits. Moreover, the focus on provocative materials and students' personal responses makes teaching more exciting and enjoyable.

The absence of a prescribed, lockstep program is one of the greatest strengths of literature-based reading, but it also makes this approach vulnerable to many abuses. The following practices have no place in literature-based reading approaches:

- Using mediocre literature in the reading program solely on the basis of what is on hand with no regard to its appeal to students or its suitability to curricular goals
- Regularly using class sets of single trade books with a predetermined reading schedule and fill-in-the-blank worksheets (a practice referred to as the "basalization of literature")
- Round-robin reading where each child takes a turn reading a section aloud to the group (and everyone else pays no attention).
- Selecting and assigning every book read by students
- Assigning book reports under the guise of a book response to check comprehension

There is no one right way to teach literature-based reading. The method cannot be packaged, and so teachers need to understand the theory behind the practices as well as create an effective set of engagements and structures. Several practical resources include *Igniting a Passion for Reading* by Steven L. Layne (2009), *Reading for Real* by Kathy Collins (2008), *The Wonder of It All* by Nancy Johnson and Cyndi Giorgis, and *The Daily Five* by Gail Boushey and Joan Moser.

Resources for a Literature-Based Curriculum

An effective literature-based curriculum is based on resources that include the school library media center, bookfairs, parents, guest authors and illustrators, and local public libraries as well as a strong classroom library collection.

- *School library media center.* The well-stocked, efficiently run library media center is the heart of a school. Ideally, library media specialists and teachers work collaboratively, with teachers informing librarians of their resource needs and librarians identifying and locating appropriate resources, keeping teachers updated with the newest literature, and suggesting ways to present books to students.

- *Bookfairs.* A bookfair is a book sale organized by a book vendor and held in the school building for several days. Bookfairs call attention to reading and send strong messages to children and parents about a school's stance on the importance of quality literature.

- *Parent partnerships.* Partnerships honor the resources and expertise of the home and the school. Instead of sending home worksheets and homework that interferes with family life, parents can read to their children, listen to their children read aloud, and take their children to the library to select books. Some parents may be able to come to the classroom to listen to or read with children, read aloud to small groups or individuals, and record stories and poems. Teachers can honor home cultures by inviting children and families to share oral stories, such as the origin of a child's name, birthday traditions, bedtime rituals, and favorite family activities and games.

- *Guest authors and illustrators.* Professional children's authors and illustrators often visit schools to share about their creative processes and books. Such visits are powerful experiences that influence children as readers. Publisher websites and marketing departments have information on arranging author visits in person or through electronic media.

- *Local public library.* Public libraries provide many services in addition to loaning books, including interlibrary loan, summertime reading programs, and story hours for young children that can be useful information for parents.

Most of the responsibility for acquiring a large and varied collection of books in your classroom will be yours. Classroom libraries usually have a permanent collection as well as a collection that is checked out from the school or public library and changes regularly to provide depth and breadth to units of study and appeal to students' interests.

Your classroom library collection can be built inexpensively by:

- Requesting an allocation from your principal or PTO for the purchase of books.
- Submitting a small grant proposal to your school district, professional organization, or local foundations (banks, local businesses, etc).
- Involving students in paperback book clubs and taking advantage of bonus books.
- Asking parents for donations of children's books that they plan to discard.
- Establishing a "give a book to the classroom" policy for parents who want to celebrate their child's birthday or a holiday at school in some way.
- Frequenting garage sales and library book sales, where good books are often quite cheap.
- Taking advantage of discounts offered by some bookstores to teachers. You might also check with your librarian to see if there is a book jobber, or wholesale dealer for a publisher, in your area.

You will need to devise a coding system for your permanent collection to streamline shelving and record keeping, such as color coding books by genre with colored tape on the spines. If possible, students should have the responsibility for color coding, checking in/out, repairing, and reshelving books. Some teachers have students create book bins or baskets in the classroom library where students sort books by topics that fit their interests and ways of thinking about books. A collection that provides easy access to great books is essential to creating a culture of reading in your classroom.

Evaluating the Literature Program

Ongoing evaluation is part of responsible teaching because it reveals the strengths and needs of students and teachers and indicates where to focus instruction. In today's schools, reading and mathematics dominate standardized tests, and so little or no attention is paid to children's growth in literary understanding. Portfolio assessment, conferencing, and observation can be used to evaluate how well a literature program is meeting children's needs. Observation, when carefully directed, can provide a full description of student progress, teacher strengths and needs, and the literature program. It is also the most efficient method of assessment, since it can be done while one is engaged in other tasks.

Observation and Assessment of Student Learning

Evaluation of students in a literature curriculum will focus mainly on the curriculum's effect on student actions as readers. Experienced teachers often develop checklists to use in observation and assessment of various aspects of their literature programs.

Checklists need to reflect differences in student interactions with literature by grade level and experiences. For example, preschool or first-grade teachers are likely to look for evidence that their students use the terms *author* and *illustrator* in their discussions of books and recognize the work of specific authors and illustrators. Middle-grade teachers would be more likely to look for evidence that students have developed an understanding of why specific authors and illustrators appeal to them and are using their literary structures as mentors for their writing. Teachers at all grade levels will look for evidence that students are enjoying reading and voluntarily choosing to read. Figure 12.3 gives an example of a possible evaluation instrument.

Figure 12.3 Checklist for Student Involvement with Literature

Evaluator: _____   Date: _____

Actions	Yes	No	Comment
Reading and Listening			
Student reads voluntarily and willingly	——	——	_____
Student enjoys reading and listening to literature	——	——	_____
Student reads during silent reading time	——	——	_____
Student reads and listens to literature for entertainment	——	——	_____
Student reads for information	——	——	_____
Student reads and listens to a variety of fiction, nonfiction, and poems	——	——	_____
Response to Literature			
Student talks thoughtfully about books read or heard	——	——	_____
Student shares responses to books with peers	——	——	_____
Student is attentive during read-aloud sessions	——	——	_____
Student can discuss a fiction book in terms of			
character	——	——	_____
plot	——	——	_____
setting	——	——	_____
theme	——	——	_____
style	——	——	_____

Actions	Yes	No	Comment
Student can discuss an informational book in terms of			
structure	____	____	_____
theme	____	____	_____
style	____	____	_____
Student accepts that different people have different responses to the same story	____	____	_____
Student relates stories to personal experiences	____	____	_____
Student compares and contrasts stories, authors' writing styles, and illustrators' artistic styles	____	____	_____
Selection of Literature			
Student knows how to select appropriate books for independent reading	____	____	_____
Student knows how to use a computer to find, read about, and select books from the school library	____	____	_____
Student keeps a log of books read independently	____	____	_____
Student is developing personal preferences in literature	____	____	_____
Student tries new book genres	____	____	_____

Observation and Assessment of Teacher Effectiveness

Regular self-assessment is an important part of a teacher's professional development. The following checklists were conceived with preservice teachers in mind, mainly for the purposes of self-evaluation and guiding their observation of the classrooms they visit as part of their coursework.

Checklist for Classroom Environment The environment of a classroom is determined mainly by what the classroom teacher values in learning and teaching. These values determine how the classroom is arranged, which materials are available, and what sorts of events and activities are regularly scheduled as noted in Figure 12.4.

Checklist for Teaching Activities Success in engaging children as lifelong readers does not depend on generous supplies of equipment or a certain physical layout, although these can be useful. It is what the teacher does with literature that makes the biggest impression on children. Activities that create a positive and nonthreatening learning environment are the most successful with children as evaluated in Figure 12.5.

Figure 12.4 Checklist for Promoting Literature through Classroom Environment

Evaluator: _____ Date: _____

Observations	Yes	No	Comment
Physical Layout			
Desks are arranged to promote student discussion	___	___	_____
Classroom has a computer center	___	___	_____
Room has quiet areas for reading and thinking	___	___	_____
Reading area is well lit with comfortable seating and shelves	___	___	_____
Displays of student response projects	___	___	_____
Classroom library materials are			
easy for students to reach and reshelve	___	___	_____
coded and organized logically	___	___	_____
Materials			
Classroom has a trade book and audiobook library	___	___	_____
Classroom library is adequate in			
scope (variety of genres, both fiction and nonfiction)	___	___	_____
depth (variety of books within a genre)	___	___	_____
quality (light reading for entertainment to excellent quality for study)	___	___	_____
varying difficulty and reading abilities	___	___	_____
recent books along with old favorites	___	___	_____
multicultural and international books	___	___	_____
poetry collections	___	___	_____
Classroom has a temporary collection from the library to			
provide for varying student interests	___	___	_____
support classroom units of study	___	___	_____
Scheduling			
Time is provided for self-choice reading every day	___	___	_____
Time is provided for browsing and selecting books regularly	___	___	_____
Time is provided for response to literature	___	___	_____

Figure 12.5   Checklist for Promoting Literature through Teaching Activities

Evaluator: _____   Date: _____

Actions/Activities	Yes	No	Comment
Making Literature Enjoyable			
Daily read-aloud of high-quality literature	___	___	_____
Select books for read-aloud that			
reflect students' interests	___	___	_____
represent a wide variety of genres	___	___	_____
represent outstanding examples of each genre	___	___	_____
Share poetry orally on a regular basis	___	___	_____
Range of poets from popular, notable, and Golden Age	___	___	_____
Share stories through storytelling	___	___	_____
Motivating Students to Read			
Introduce books regularly through booktalks	___	___	_____
Introduce interactive digital books and audiobooks	___	___	_____
Encourage listening to audiobooks and reading along in print versions	___	___	_____
Encourage student response to literature			
by asking open-ended or divergent questions	___	___	_____
by encouraging varied responses	___	___	_____
through oral response	___	___	_____
through written response	___	___	_____
through graphic response	___	___	_____
Invite students to choose books for independent reading	___	___	_____
Offer fiction and nonfiction options for independent reading	___	___	
Take class to school library weekly for book browsing	___	___	_____
Take class to public library for a field trip	___	___	_____
Invite a librarian to booktalk and tell stories in classroom	___	___	_____

(Continued)

Figure 12.5 Continued

Actions/Activities	Yes	No	Comment
Demonstrating Reading Behaviors			
Read during silent reading time	——	——	————————
Talk enthusiastically about books read	——	——	————————
Show students how to select books	——	——	————————
Showing the Relevance of Literature			
Include literature that is culturally relevant to students			
in read-aloud selections	——	——	————————
in booktalks	——	——	————————
in text sets for group reading	——	——	————————
Integrate literature across the curriculum			
in health/science	——	——	————————
in social studies/history	——	——	————————
in language arts/reading	——	——	————————
in mathematics	——	——	————————
Encouraging Literature Appreciation			
Create literature units	——	——	————————
Reaching beyond the Classroom			
Send read-aloud suggestions to parents	——	——	————————
Encourage parents to visit library with their children	——	——	————————
Invite parents and community leaders to read-aloud	——	——	————————
Evaluation			
Record student growth			
in understanding literary concepts	——	——	————————
in choices of books to read	——	——	————————
in attitude toward reading	——	——	————————
in quality of responses (verbal, written, artistic)	——	——	————————

 ## Invitations for Further Investigation

Many elementary and early childhood education programs include school-based practicum experiences. These school experiences give preservice teachers opportunities to observe teaching and classroom management styles, acquire firsthand experience working with children, and explore theories and ideas from their methods courses, such as the use of good literature. The following invitations are possible literature activities that we have found to work in school-based practicums, particularly when shared with other preservice teachers to discuss similarities and differences.

Learning about Children as Readers

1. Interview three children in the classroom, preferably at different levels of reading ability, to find their exposure to literature, attitudes toward reading, purposes for reading, and sources of reading material.

2. Interview several students about their reading interests. Based on your findings, suggest appropriate titles to the students for independent reading from books available in the school.

3. Conduct a class survey of reading interests, using the ideas described in Chapter 2. Compile and analyze findings to suggest titles for independent reading.

Learning to Engage Children with Literature

1. Booktalk a set of four or five books appropriate for students in the class. Be sure to include informational, global, and multicultural literature. After the booktalk, display the books in the classroom and observe students' interest in reading them.

2. Read aloud one or two picture books and a chapter book. After each read-aloud session, invite students to respond with their connections and thoughts. Compare your experiences of reading aloud from the two types of books and students' responses to the two types of books.

3. Select a poem, work with students in arranging it for choral reading, rehearse, and present the choral reading to any available audience. Note students' response to the activity and poem.

4. Introduce students to a specific author or illustrator by demonstrating how to give an author or illustrator profile. *Author and illustrator profiles* usually include interesting facts about the author, a recent picture, one or two distinguishing characteristics of the author's work (such as favorite topics, themes, style of illustration or writing), the presenter's interests in the author's work, and other books written by the author. A one-page handout summarizing this information and listing major books is useful to other preservice teachers and the classroom teacher. Children presenting author or illustrator profiles can post their summary sheets on the class bulletin board or website. Variations to presenting author and illustrator reports orally to the class include:

   - Presenting the profile in first-person as the author or illustrator (costumes or props)
   - Presenting the profile as a biographical skit about the author (pairs or small group)
   - Creating a poster or bulletin board display about the author or illustrator
   - Presenting the profile as an interview, with one student as the interviewer and the other taking the role of the author

Learning about Student Response to Literature

1. Select a picture book or a chapter from a novel that involves four to six characters. Read it aloud to a group of students and then engage them in a creative drama, readers' theatre, or

graphic arts response to the book (see Chapter 13 for ideas). Note students' insights into the book through their responses.

2. Help students design and construct a literature-related bulletin board, such as a mural based on a whole-class read-aloud selection or a response to books read independently by students in the class. This display can be mounted in the school hallway for observation by students in other classrooms.

References

Ada, A. F. (1995). *My name is María Isabel.* New York: Aladdin.

Alvarez, J. (2010). *How Tía Lola learned to teach.* New York: Knopf.

Anderson, R. C. (1996). Research foundations to support wide reading. In V. Greaney (Ed.), *Promoting reading: Views on making reading materials accessible to increase literacy levels* (pp. 55–77). Newark, DE: International Reading Association.

Anderson, R. C., Hiebert, E. H., Scott, J. A., & Wilkinson, I. A. (1985). *Becoming a nation of readers: The report of the commission on reading.* Champaign, IL: Center for the Study of Reading.

Atinuke. (2011). *The No. 1 car spotter.* LaJolla, CA: Kane/Miller.

Arya, P., Martens, P., Wilson, G. P., Altwerger, B., Jin, L., Laster, B., & Lang, D. (2005). Reclaiming literacy instruction: Evidence in support of literature-based programs. *Language Arts, 83*(1), 63–72.

Barrs, M. (2000). The reader in the writer. *Reading, 34*(2), 54–60.

Bausum, A. (2009). *Denied, detained, deported.* New York: National Geographic.

Boelts, M. (2012). *Happy like soccer.* Castillo, L. (Illus.). Somerville, MA: Candlewick.

Bondoux, A. (2009). *A time of miracles.* New York: Delacorte.

Boushey, G., & Moser, J. (2006). *The daily five.* Portland, ME: Stenhouse.

Bredsdorff, B. (2004). *The Crow-Girl.* New York: Farrar.

Budhos, M. (2006). *Ask me no questions.* New York: Atheneum.

Cantrell, S. C. (1999). The effects of literacy instruction on primary students' reading and writing achievement. *Reading Research and Instruction, 39*(1), 3–26.

Children's literature review: Excerpts from reviews, criticism, and commentary on books for children and young people, Vols. 1–158. (1976–2011). Farmington Hills, MI: Thomson Gale.

Choi, Y. (2001). *The name jar.* New York: Dell.

Cole, B. (2007). *Good enough to eat.* New York: Farrar.

Collins, K. (2008). *Reading for real.* Portland, ME: Stenhouse.

Collins, S. (2008). *The hunger games.* New York: Scholastic.

Croza, L. (2010). *I know here.* James, M. (Illus.). Toronto, ON: Groundwood.

Cummings, P. (2004). *Red kayak.* New York: Dutton.

Cruz, M., & Pollock, K. (2004). Stepping into the wardrobe: A fantasy genre study. *Language Arts, 81*(3), 184–195.

Draper, S. (2010). *Out of my mind.* New York: Atheneum.

Dressel, J. H. (1990). The effects of listening to and discussing different qualities of children's literature on the narrative writing of fifth graders. *Research in the Teaching of English, 24*(4), 397–414.

Droyd, A. (2011). *Goodnight iPad: A parody for the next generation.* New York: Blue Rider.

Duprau, J. (2003). *The city of Ember.* New York: Random House.

Duprau, J. (2004). *The people of Sparks.* New York: Random House.

Edwards, M. (2005). *Stinky Stern forever.* New York: Harcourt.

Ellis, D. (2009). *Children of war: Voices of Iraqi refugees.* Toronto, ON: Groundwood.

Fanelli, S. (1995). *My map book.* New York: HarperCollins.

Farmer, N. (2002). *The house of the scorpion.* New York: Simon & Schuster.

Fullteron, S. K., & Colwell, J. (2010). Research on small-group discussions of literature: An analysis of three decades. In Jimenez, R., Risko, V., Hundley, M., & Rowe, D., 59th Yearbook of the National Reading Conference (pp. 57–74). Oak Creek, WI: NRC.

Garay, L. (1997). *The long road.* Toronto, ON: Tundra.

Ghigna, C. (2003). In sight. In *A fury of motion: Poems for boys.* Honesdale, PA: Boyds Mills.

Giff, P. R. (2000). *Nory Ryan's song.* New York: Delacorte.

Greder, A. (2008). *The island.* Chicago, IL: Allen & Unwin.

Grimes, N. (2009). *Make way for Dyamonde Daniel.* Christie, R. G. (Illus.). New York: Putnam.

Haddix, M. P. (2000). *Turnabout.* New York: Simon & Schuster.

Hall, S. (1990). *Using picture storybooks to teach literary devices: Recommended books for children and young adults* (Vol. 1). Phoenix, AZ: Oryx. (Vol. 2, 1994; Vol. 3, 2001; Vol. 4, 2007; Santa Barbara, CA: Libraries Unlimited.)

Han, J. (2011). *Clara Lee and the apple pie dream.* Kao, J. (Illus.). New York: Little, Brown.

Hancock, J., & Hill, S. (1987). *Literature-based reading programs at work.* Portsmouth, NH: Heinemann.

Harper, C. M. (2007). *Just Grace.* Boston, MA: Houghton.

Hesse, K. (1997). *Out of the dust.* New York: Scholastic.

Hoffman, M. (2002). *The color of home.* Littlewood, K. (Illus.). New York: Dial.

Hyman, T. S. (1977/2001). *Sleeping beauty.* New York: Little, Brown.

Isaacs, A. (1994). *Swamp Angel.* Zelinsky. P. (Illus.). New York: Schwartz & Wade.

Ivey, G., & Broaddus, K. (2001). "Just plain reading": A survey of what makes students want to read in middle school classrooms. *Reading Research Quarterly, 36*(4), 350–377.

Jaramillo, A. (2006). *La línea.* New York: Roaring Brook.

Jarvey, M., McKeough, M., & Pyryt, M. (2008). Teaching trickster tales: A comparison of instructional approaches. *Research in the Teaching of English, 43*(1), 42–73.

Johnson, N., & Giorgis, C. (2007). *The wonder of it all.* Portsmouth, NH: Heinemann.

Journal of Children's Literature (2008). Special Issue: Children's books as mentor texts. *34*(2), 31–67.

Kadohata, C. (2006). *Weedflower.* New York: Atheneum.

Kerrin, J. S. (2005). *Martin Bridge: Ready for takeoff!* Kelly, J. (Illus.). Toronto, ON: Kids Can.

Khan, R. (2009). *Wanting Mor.* Toronto, ON: Ground-wood.

Lai, T. (2011). *Inside out and back again.* New York: Harper.

Lainez, R. C. (2010). *From north to south/Del norte al sur.* San Francisco, CA: Children's Book Press.

Lancia, P. J. (1997). Literary borrowing: The effects of literature on children's writing. *The Reading Teacher, 50*(6), 470–475.

Langer, J. (2010). *Envisioning literature: Literary understanding and literature instruction.* New York: Teachers College.

Law, I. (2008). *Savvy.* New York: Dial.

Layne, S. (2009). *Igniting a passion for reading.* Portland, ME: Stenhouse.

Levine, E. (1995). *I hate English.* Bjorkman, S. (Illus.). New York: Scholastic.

Look, L. (2004). *Ruby Lu, brave and true.* Wilsdorf, A. (Illus.). New York: Simon & Schuster.

Lowry, L. (1994). *The giver.* Boston, MA: Houghton. Also *Gathering blue* (2000), *Messenger* (2004), and *Son* (2012).

Lowry, L. (2000). *Looking back: A book of memories.* Boston, MA: Houghton.

Maloch, B. (2008). Beyond exposure: The uses of informational texts in a second grade classroom. *Research in the Teaching of English, 42*(3), 315–362.

McEwan, J. (2007). *Rufus the scrub does not wear a tutu.* Margeson, J. (Illus.). Plain City, OH: Darby Creek.

Mochizuki, K. (2004). *Baseball saved us.* New York: Lee & Low.

National Association of Educational Progress (2011). *The Nation's Report Card: Reading 2011.* Washington, DC: National Center for Education Statistics, Institute of Education Sciences, U.S. Department of Education.

Nicholls, S. (2008). *Ways to live forever.* New York: Scholastic.

O'Connor, B. (2009). *The small adventures of Popeye and Elvis.* New York: Farrar.

Park, F., & Park, G. (19998). *My freedom trip.* Jenkins, D. (Illus.). Honesdale, PA: Boyds Mills.

Park. L. S. (2010). *A long walk to water.* New York: Clarion.

Paterson, K. (2009). *The day of the pelican.* New York: Clarion.

Pennypacker, S. (2006). *Clementine.* Frazee, M. (Illus.). New York: Hyperion.

Reeve, P. (2003). *Mortal engines.* New York: HarperCollins.

Rex, M. (2008). *Goodnight goon: A parody.* New York: Putnam.

Rodriquez, L. (1997). *América is her name.* Willimantic, CT: Curbstone.

Rosen, M. (2008). *Michael Rosen's sad book.* Blake, Q. (Illus.). Somerville, MA: Candlewick.

Routsaki, M. (2008). *Unique Monique.* Papaniklaou, P. (Illus.). LaJolla, CA: Kane/Miller.

Ryan, P. M. (2000). *Esperanza rising.* New York: Scholastic.

Ryan, P.M. (2004). *Becoming Naomi Leon.* New York: Scholastic.

Russo, M. (2011). *I will come back for you: A family in hiding during World War II.* New York: Schwartz & Wade.

Ryder, R. J., Sekulski, J. L., & Silberg, A. (2003). Results of direct instruction reading program evaluation longitudinal results: First through third grade, 2000–2003. Madison, WI: Wisconsin Department of Public Instruction.

Sanderson, R. (2002). *Cinderella.* New York: Little, Brown.

Santiago, C. (2002). *Home to Medicine Mountain.* Lowery, J. (Illus.). San Francisco, CA: Children's Book Press.

Say, Allen. (2011). *Drawing from memory.* New York: Scholastic.

Schmidt, G. (2004). *Lizzie Bright and the Buckminster boy.* New York: Clarion.

Senzai, N. H. (2010). *Shooting Kabul.* New York: Simon & Schuster.

Sheth, K. (2007). *Keeping corner.* New York: Hyperion.

Something about the author: Facts and pictures about authors and illustrators of books for young people, Vols. 1–239 (1971–2012). Detroit: Gale.

Santoro, L., Chard, D., Howard, L., & Baker, S. (2008). Making the very most of classroom read-alouds to promote comprehension and vocabulary. *The Reading Teacher, 61*(5), 396–408.

Tan, S. (2006). *The arrival.* New York: Scholastic.

Thor, A. (2009). *A faraway island.* New York: Delacorte.

Uhlberg, M. (2011). *A storm called Katrina.* Bootman, C. (Illus.). Atlanta, GA: Peachtree.

Urban, L. (2011). *Hound dog true.* New York: Harcourt.

Vanderpool, C. (2010). *Moon over Manifest.* New York: Delacorte.

Walsh, J. P. (1986). *The green book.* New York: Farrar.

Williams, K. L. (2009). *My name is Sangoel.* Stock, C. (Illus.). New York: Erdmans.

Williams, M. (2011). *Now is the time for running.* New York: Little, Brown.

Williams, V. B. (2001). *Amber was brave, Essie was smart: The story of Amber and Essie told here in poems and pictures.* New York: Greenwillow.

Wilson, G. P., Martens, P., Arya, P., & Altwerger, B. (2004). Readers, instruction, and the NRP. *Phi Delta Kappan, 86*(3), 242–246.

Woodson, J. (2005). *Show way.* New York: Putnam.

Worthy, J., Patterson, E., Salas, R., Prater, S., & Turner, M. (2002). "More than just reading": The human factor in reaching resistant readers. *Reading Research and Instruction, 41*(2), 177–202.

Yang, B. (2004). *Hannah is my name.* Somerville, MA: Candlewick.

Young, E. (2011). *The house that Baba built: An artist's childhood in China.* New York: Little Brown.

Chapter Thirteen

 ngaging Children with Literature

I Meant to Do My Work Today

I meant to do my work today—
But a brown bird sang in the apple tree,
And a butterfly flitted across the field,
And all the leaves were calling me.

And the wind went sighing over the land
Tossing the grasses to and fro,
And a rainbow held out its shining hand—
So what could I do but laugh and go?

—*Richard LeGallienne*

Engagement with literature highlights the potential of a book to capture children's attention and invite their participation in a story world. Authentic, well-written books are the first step, but they must be supported by significant experiences that bring children and books together for a variety of purposes. These experiences include reading widely for personal purposes, reading critically to inquire about the world, and reading strategically to learn about literacy.

Teachers are the key to effectively engaging children in these three types of experiences with literature throughout the school day. Gabriela, a 9-year-old, begins her day by pulling *To Dance: A Ballerina's Graphic Novel* (Siegel, 2006) out of her desk to pursue her personal inquiry on becoming a ballerina. After independent reading, the class moves into reading instruction and guided reading. The teacher works with Gabriela's group in a guided inquiry to analyze how authors use dialogue for character development in *Bink and Gollie* (DiCamillo, 2010). After lunch, the teacher reads aloud *Iqbal* (D'Adamo, 2001), the fictionalized story of a boy who led an influential movement against child labor in Pakistani carpet factories, as part of a collaborative inquiry on human rights. Students discuss the protagonist's anger and fear and his willingness to take action for freedom, despite the risks. They explore his strategies for taking action and their concerns about whether kids can really make a difference in a world controlled by adults.

Balancing these experiences supports children's development as readers and as human beings. The emphasis across these three dimensions may shift as children become proficient readers and gain life experiences. Older readers may primarily focus on using reading to inquire, whereas young children focus more on reading for personal purposes and to learn about literacy. This shift in emphasis does not exclude the other types; all three should be integrated into the experiences offered to children, no matter what their age. Each serves a different purpose and highlights different books and roles for adults and children.

Reading Widely for Personal Purposes

Reading literature widely for personal purposes highlights choice and extensive reading for purposes that are significant to children's own lives, ranging from enjoyment to personal inquiries on topics of interest. Reading widely involves engagement and demonstration; students are not focused on writing or talking about the book or using it for an activity. They just immerse themselves in reading alongside other readers. The goal is to create a lifelong habit of reading for purposes that matter to the reader—not because the teacher said so.

Students should have the opportunity to choose from a wide range of reading materials. Wide reading provides children with a broad background from which to develop comprehension and interpretation strategies, promotes positive attitudes about reading, and encourages the development of lifelong reading habits. Many adults stop engaging with books once they leave school and view reading as boring because of the lack of choice in schools. In addition, reading many materials with ease increases children's fluency and the integration of reading strategies.

The experiences that encourage reading widely for personal purposes include reading aloud, independent reading, shared reading, and experiencing literature through multimodal texts. The role of the teacher is to provide a regularly scheduled time for reading and a variety of materials for students to read.

Reading Aloud by Teachers

Reading aloud to children by family members and teachers is essential for children's acquisition of reading strategies and positive attitudes toward reading. Read-alouds are the centerpiece of a literature curriculum. Beginning in their infancy and throughout the elementary and middle-school years, children should hear books and poems read aloud on a daily basis. This teaching strategy is just as important in the intermediate grades as it is in primary grades.

Some important reasons that teachers read aloud are:

- To increase students' abilities to think critically and comprehend connected discourse
- To help students understand literary devices and the conventions of story, such as genres, characters, settings, themes, and plot
- To expand and enrich vocabulary
- To provide a model of expressive, fluent reading
- To build knowledge and interest in topics and issues related to classroom inquiries and units
- To share exciting and stimulating literature that is beyond students' reading ability, but well within their listening ability
- To encourage students to love reading and literature

Three distinct aspects of the read-aloud experience are essential to make it effective as a teaching strategy. Those aspects are (1) selecting the literature to read, (2) preparing the students for read-aloud time, and (3) reading the book aloud. Each aspect needs to be taken into consideration for a successful read-aloud experience.

Book Selection   No matter which book you choose to read aloud, it is essential that you first read the book to determine whether the story is enjoyable and worthy of children's time and whether it is appropriate for your students. You also can note ways in which the story lends itself to student response.

Over the course of a school year you will want to read aloud a variety of poems, short stories, picture books, and chapter books of different genres and moods. You will also want to ensure that there is a balance of males and females as main characters in the books and that the main characters come from different backgrounds and cultural settings.

Lists of Excellent Books to Read Aloud are provided in Chapters 4 through 11. You may also want to look at references that suggest books for reading aloud: Judy Freeman's *Books Kids Will Sit Still For, 3: A Read-Aloud Guide* (2006), Jim Trelease's *The Read-Aloud Handbook* (2006), and Lester Laminack and Reba Wadsworth's *Learning Under the Influence of Language and Literature: Making the Most of Read-Alouds across the Day* (2006).

The most recognized books for children, though sometimes complex, deserve to be shared with students over the course of their elementary school years. When a book or poem is challenging for students, you need to be prepared to support their understanding. Without this help, many children would never experience and enjoy some of the more difficult but worthwhile pieces of literature. Conversely, you will want to avoid choosing books for reading aloud that students can and will consume eagerly on their own, reserving those books for students' independent reading.

When first reading aloud to a new class, however, you may need to start with shorter and easier books that are popular with students and gradually build to longer and more challenging books as you become better acquainted with your students, their interests, and their abilities.

Preparation   You can prepare students for reading aloud by having them remove distractions, such as pencils and other objects, from their immediate vicinity; by having them sit quietly in the designated place for read-aloud time; and by asking them to be ready to listen. If the book has concepts that you believe will baffle your students, you may want to quickly establish a context for the book before beginning to read.

Introduce the book by stating the title, author, and illustrator of the book, even with the smallest children. This will teach children that books are written and illustrated by real people called authors and illustrators. For international and multicultural literature use the book jacket to briefly tell students how the author's and illustrator's backgrounds relate to the book's focus— for example, "This author lives in the U.S., but her parents are from Korea, so she talked with them about their experiences and did research in libraries." You may need to look at the author's website to get this information, but first check the book jacket and look for an author's note or acknowledgment.

Sometimes you may want to ask the students to predict what they believe the story will be about from looking at the cover and the title; other times you may want to explain briefly why you chose this book to read. For example, you may say that you are going to read this book because "it's another story by one of our favorite authors, Anthony Browne" or that "the book will tell us more about what it was like to live in Korea right after World War II." Some teachers read aloud several picture books by the same author over the course of a week to make students aware of a notable author. Book introductions should be short. They serve the purpose of inviting students to enter into the world of the story with you.

Reading Picture Books Aloud Effectively   Consider the following steps:

- Position yourself close to the class so that all students can see the pictures.

- Show the pictures as you read the book. Remember that the text and pictures are carefully integrated in a picture book to convey the story as a whole. Hearing and seeing picture books should be simultaneous.

- After the introduction, read the book aloud, placing emphasis on the meaning of the story. Think of reading aloud as a type of dramatic performance.

- Your body movements and facial expressions can enhance the drama of the read-aloud experience. Leaning forward during a scary, suspenseful part of a story and smiling or chuckling during a funny part can convey your involvement in the story.

- Maintain eye contact with your students. Be sure you are aware of their nonverbal responses to this reading experience to determine if a word of explanation is needed.

- Read fiction from beginning to end without interruptions except on an as-needed basis. Some books, such as concept books, informational books, and interactive books, do call for interruptions in the read-aloud process.

Reading Chapter Books Aloud Effectively   Many of the same considerations hold true with chapter book read-alouds. Of course, chapter books have few, if any, illustrations, so holding the book for students to see the pictures is not necessary. Some students may therefore enjoy sketching the images in their heads as they listen. In addition, chapter books are usually read aloud over a relatively long period of time, from a few days to many weeks.

Practices that teachers have used successfully during chapter book read-alouds to hook the students on the book and to keep them tuned in and involved include:

- Keeping a chart of the characters—their names, relationships, and roles in the story—as the characters appear. This strategy is especially helpful if the story has a large number of characters.

For example, in *The Westing Game* (1978) by Ellen Raskin, the many characters must be remembered for the mystery plot to make sense.

- Designing and displaying a map of the story setting to track the events of the story in sequence. In most quest fantasies this visual aid can assist students in following the characters' journey.

- Developing a time line on which the dates are set at intervals above the line and the story events placed below the line at the appropriate date. For historical fiction and biographies, a time line can also include a third tier of historic events.

Sharing Literature from Oral Traditions through Storytelling

Telling stories to students is particularly important for sharing literature from oral traditions. Many Native American tribal nations, for example, have long traditions of oral literature. Some traditional stories are meant to be told only at certain times of the year or to particular audiences, and so it is not appropriate for these stories to be published as a book that could be read at the wrong time or place. These stories should be shared in their oral form.

Teachers bring oral stories to life through personal expression and interpretation and can use them to establish a close connection with students. Oral storytelling should be a regular part of classroom read-aloud experiences. Suggestions and resources for storytelling are in the chapter on traditional literature.

Independent Reading by Students

Another way for students to experience good literature is to read it themselves. Indeed, the ultimate goal of a literature program is to turn students into readers who, of their own free will, read self-selected literature with enjoyment, understanding, and appreciation. To assist students in becoming independent, lifelong readers, teachers in grades K–8 need to set aside time each day for students to read independently. Kindergarten and first-grade students may spend only five to ten minutes reading independently, and often a quiet hum occurs as beginning readers say the words aloud as they read or tell their own stories based on the illustrations. Older students will often read silently for up to an hour.

Some schools have instituted *sustained silent reading (SSR)* programs on a schoolwide basis to promote the reading habit in students. A certain time each day is set aside for all students, teachers, librarians, coaches, principals, custodians, and office and kitchen staff to take a "reading break." The philosophy behind SSR programs is that students need to see adults who read and who place a high priority on reading. Students read materials of their own choosing and are not usually required to write book reports or give oral reports on these materials.

If your school utilizes a commercial reading incentive program, you may take advantage of the availability of the literature that is provided as part of the program. Use the program flexibly in ways that develop intrinsic motivation for reading, avoid the negative competitive aspects of the program, and help students achieve individual goals set for their independent reading.

Whether or not your school has an SSR program, you will want to provide your students with an independent reading time each day. Remember that the goal is to have the students read as many different books and materials as possible, so they should not be required to write long responses. At most, they might be asked to keep a simple record sheet of what they have read. Tips for establishing a successful independent reading time include:

- Have a well-stocked classroom collection of books—poetry, plays, picture books, novels, and information books, along with graphic novels and magazines.
- Conduct booktalks regularly so that students become aware of books they may wish to read.
- Display new books attractively in the classroom and show videos of notable authors talking about their books and craft. These techniques are effective in "selling" books to children.
- Schedule the same time each day for independent reading. Allow enough time for students to get well into their books and to achieve some level of satisfaction from the reading.
- Insist on attentiveness to books during this time. With primary-grade students, quiet talking in pairs about books or individual lipreading aloud may be on-task behavior. Children in intermediate grades can read silently and usually prefer to do so, although recent research indicates some boys prefer social interaction while reading.
- Spend the independent reading period engrossed in books, setting yourself as an example of a reader. Be knowledgeable of and interested in the books that students are reading.

Retellings and dramatic play are another way that students engage in independent exploration of literature to make stories their own. As young children tell and retell stories, they develop their concept of story and expand their oral language. Teachers can encourage retellings by creating a conducive environment in one area of the classroom with props, such as story puppets, feltboards with cut-out story figures, toys that can be used as characters (stuffed animals, dolls, plastic figures), wordless books, and favorite picture books. Some children take a book shared by the teacher during a class read-aloud and page through it, retelling the story from the pictures; others take puppets and recreate the story or make up an entirely new adventure with the same characters.

Audio or video recorders can inspire younger students to record and listen to their favorite stories, and older students can develop radio or television shows based on favorite books or record their readers' theatre performances.

Booktalks

A *booktalk* is an oral presentation by a teacher, a librarian, or a student who tells about a book to interest other students in reading it. Booktalks are not book reports, analyses of the author's style, or old-fashioned discussions of characters, setting, theme, and plot. Booktalks have been used effectively for years by librarians who developed this strategy into an art for the purpose of encouraging students to check out books from the library. Each week teachers can give booktalks on five to ten books from their classroom and school library collections; in this way, they can entice students to read and experience good literature.

Some teachers who give frequent booktalks also encourage students to give booktalks to induce other students to read the suggested books. A regular feature of *Reading Rainbow,* the public television program about children's books, is children giving booktalks. You can tape two or three of these *Reading Rainbow* booktalks and show them in class to help students learn how to give good booktalks. For more tips on booktalks, see www.thebooktalker1.com and www.nancykeane.com/booktalks.

The following are our recommendations for conducting booktalks:

- Choose books that you like or that you think your students will enjoy. Sincere enthusiasm for a book is stimulating and infectious.

• Have the book available to show to the students as you give the booktalk. Format aspects—such as cover illustrations, length, size, and shape of the books—which also influence book choices, can be weighed by students only if they can see the book.

• Keep the booktalk brief, no more than two or three minutes. Do not tell too much about the book or the students will see no reason to read it. For most books, four to six sentences will suffice.

• Tell the topic and something about the action in the story, but *do not tell the plot*. Feature a scene or character that the story revolves around, but do not discuss a scene that gives away the ending.

• Booktalk a group of books that share the same theme; in this case you will want to talk briefly about each book and how it fits with the others.

The following is an example of a booktalk on *The House of the Scorpion* (2002) by Nancy Farmer:

If you ever think about what life will be like in the future, 100 years from now, you will enjoy reading *The House of the Scorpion,* a novel about young Matt, who has spent his life locked away in a hut because he is a clone and clones are outcasts hated by human society. As Matt comes of age he discovers that he is the clone of El Patrón, the cruel ruler of Opium, a drug kingdom farmed by "eejits," brain-dead clones. Opium is located between the U.S. and Aztlán, once called Mexico. In El Patrón's household, Matt finds support from a cook and a bodyguard, and eventually Maria, who begins to care about Matt. When Matt realizes that his life is at risk, he makes a break for freedom and escapes to Aztlán, only to face more hardships and adventures. Matt wonders who he is, why he exists, and whether, as a clone, he has free will. *The House of the Scorpion* by Nancy Farmer has received many honors, including winning the National Book Award for young people's literature.

After you have given the booktalk, place the book on the reading table for students to peruse and to consider. Over time, give booktalks on a variety of books at different levels of reading difficulty, on different topics, and with male and female protagonists from many cultures. In this way, you will appeal to the wide range of interests and abilities that exist among students in a classroom.

Shared Reading

Shared reading is a term used to describe teaching strategies that draw on the natural processes of literacy learning that have long occurred in book-loving homes. These various strategies—*shared-book experience, choral reading,* and *paired reading*—provide children with opportunities to experience good literature as they are learning to read. The strategies have in common a modification of the parent–child interaction with repeated readings of favorite books as the child gradually acquires an understanding of print and its relationship to our sound system or to the words we speak. A list of pattern books suitable for use in shared reading activities can be found in the picture book chapter.

The *shared-book experience* is an adaptation of a natural home-learning strategy used with groups of beginning readers in school settings. Enlarged-text books of 24" × 30" or larger, called *Big Books,* usually well-loved and predictable books like Eric Carle's *The Very Hungry Caterpillar* (1968), are presented to groups of beginning readers in a sequence proposed by Holdaway (1982).

First, favorite, well-known poems and songs are repeated in unison by the students and the teacher while the teacher points to the text of the Big Book. A review of the story is then used to teach skills in context. Following this activity, the teacher involves the students in language play, such as alphabet games, rhymes, and songs that use letter names. Then a new story in Big Book format is presented by the teacher. Students participate by repeating the story, line by line, after the teacher. Later, students read independently from a wide selection of favorite books and compose original stories, often modeled after the new story.

Choral reading is reading aloud in unison or parts with a whole class, small group, or individual students so that students hear the text at the same time they read it. Choral reading can involve arranging a poem into speaking parts as a way to enjoy and interpret the poem (see Chapter 4). Choral reading a range of texts can provide support for students who are struggling as readers, typically by having less proficient students read in unison with more fluent readers or having a struggling student read chorally with a recorded version of the text. Teachers can also read one-on-one with a child, so that the teacher initially takes the lead in the choral reading and then gradually quiets her/his voice as the child gains confidence and takes over the lead.

Paired reading, also known as partner reading or buddy reading, involves two people sharing the reading of a text in some way. Two children can share a text by reading back and forth to each other, changing off every other page or section of the book or taking different voices or parts of the text. Another variation, often used with struggling readers, involves the teacher and child reading side by side. The child reads aloud until she or he has difficulty, at which point the adult supplies the word so that the reading can continue fluently.

In all of these strategies, well-chosen literature is important; the nature of the experience is companionable, not authoritative; and the child reader must see the text and hear the words simultaneously. Sometimes, the adult places a finger under each word as it is being read to draw the child's attention to the print. Selecting favorite, loved stories as well as meaningful, predictable stories is essential because the success of these strategies is contingent on frequent rereadings of the same book.

These variations of shared reading focus on the role of fluent reading experiences and multiple rereadings in learning to read. As students read stories over and over, they are able to attend to different aspects of the print and the story, learning something different about the text each time. They also develop a feeling of competence in themselves as readers, which is especially important for struggling readers who may not have experienced fluent reading.

Readers' Theatre

Readers' theatre is the oral presentation of literature by two or more actors, and usually a narrator, reading from a script. Unlike plays, there is little or no costuming or movement, no stage sets, and no memorized lines. Literature becomes a living experience for readers through the use of facial expressions, voice, and a few gestures. Students engage in multiple rereadings of the script to develop a fluent, expressive interpretation of the story to share with an audience. Features typically associated with readers' theatre include:

- The readers and narrator typically remain on the "stage" throughout the production.
- Readers use little movement; instead, they suggest action with gestures and facial expressions.
- Readers and narrator sit on chairs or stools, and performers usually remain seated throughout the performance. Sometimes, readers sit with their backs to the audience to suggest that they are not in a particular scene.

- No costumes or stage settings are necessary and, at most, should be suggestive, rather than complete or literal, to encourage the imaginations of the audience. The use of sound effects may enhance the performance and give the impression of a radio play.

Scripts can be developed for readers' theatre by the teacher or by older students adapting a work of literature enjoyed by the class. Picture books readily lend themselves to adaptation, as do short stories. Some teachers have successfully adapted well-selected scenes from a favorite chapter book for readers' theatre (see Figure 13.1). Alan Armstrong's novel *Whittington* (2005), a Newbery Honor Book, is an animal fantasy that intertwines three plots: the contemporary barn-yard, the medieval folktale, and Ben's reading problems. The qualities to seek in a promising story

Figure 13.1   Sample Page of a Script Developed for Readers' Theatre

---

Whittington
(adapted from Chapter 1, pp. 2–5)
by Alan Armstrong
Random House, 2005

CHARACTERS:

Narrator

Whittington (cat)

The Lady (duck)

Other characters appear later in the story

Narrator:	This scene takes place in the barnyard.
Whittington:	Hello.
The Lady:	Who are you?
Whittington:	Whittington.
The Lady:	Whittington? That's a funny name for a cat. It's more like the name of a town.
Whittington:	Doesn't it mean anything to you?
The Lady:	No.
Whittington:	Then you don't know history. Whittington is a person in history. He's in books. Anyway, what's your name?
The Lady:	They call me Lady because I'm in charge.
Narrator:	Whittington, the cat, explains that he needs a place to live.
The Lady:	You don't have a home?
Whittington:	I did. A boy took me in when I was a kitten. Then they sent him away because he read things backwards. They were ashamed. They sent him to a special school out west. He was going to take me along but they said no.
The Lady:	So what do you want from me?
Whittington:	A place in the barn.

Etc. . . .

---

are natural-sounding dialogue, strong characterization, drama or humor, and a satisfactory ending. If the original work has extensive dialogue, the script writing is an easy activity. The script begins with the title of the book, the name of the author, a list of characters, and usually an opening statement by the narrator. Following the introduction, the dialogue is written into script form, with the narrator scripted for the remaining nondialogue, narrative parts.

Scripts can also be purchased, but finding scripts that are both well written and adapted from the literature you are using in your classroom may prove difficult. If you decide to develop readers' theatre scripts from the literature you are using, remember that developing the first script is the most difficult. Once you have created the first one, you will find out how easy the process is. Intermediate-grade students take readily to script development once they have a model to imitate. Aaron Shepard's RT Page (www.aaronshep.com/rt) is a website guide to readers' theatre with tips on scripting, staging, and performing.

Choice of literature can include virtually any literary genre—picture storybooks, novels, biographies, long poems, letters, diaries, and journals. See Figures 13.2 and Figures 13.3 for books suitable for script development. Another example, Paul Fleischman's *Bull Run* (1993), a historical novel set during the Civil War, is written as a series of episodes told by different characters at different stages of the war. At the end of the book, the author provides a list of each character's entries that can be used to produce readers' theatre performances. Variations on readers' theatre can be accomplished through the addition of background music, choral poems, and brief scenes from different stories tied together by a common theme.

Figure 13.2 Picture Books Adaptable for Readers' Theatre Scripts

Bink and Gollie by Kate DiCamillo
Buttons by Brock Cole
Chrysanthemum by Kevin Henkes
Dog and Bear: Two Friends, Three Stories by Laura Vaccaro Seeger
Duck on a Bike by David Shannon
Frog and Toad Are Friends by Arnold Lobel
The Great Kapok Tree: A Tale of the Amazon Rainforest by Lynne Cherry
I Am the Dog, I Am the Cat by Donald Hall
The Three Little Wolves and the Big Bad Pig by Eugene Trivizas

Figure 13.3 Novels Adaptable for Readers' Theatre Scripts

Bud, Not Buddy by Christopher Paul Curtis
Ella Enchanted by Gail Carson Levine
The Giver by Lois Lowry
One Day and One Amazing Morning on Orange Street by Joanne Rocklin
Seedfolks by Paul Fleischman
The Small Adventure of Popeye and Elvis by Barbara O'Connor
Whittington by Alan Armstrong
Witness by Karen Hesse

Preparation for a readers' theatre presentation gives students an opportunity to strengthen their oral reading abilities and to try out their expressive skills. The group typically reads through the script once or twice and then works on refining the interpretive aspects of each performer. Decisions need to be made on the arrangement of chairs and speakers for greatest visual effect. Following each presentation, an evaluation is made by the group with the goal of improving future performances.

Readers' theatre is well suited to classroom reenactments of literary experiences. Students have the opportunity to construct meaning for a literary work in a new medium—the medium of drama—with considerable ease and pleasure.

Experiencing Literature as Multimodal Texts

Children in today's world are immersed in mass media, including video games, iPods, and the Internet, that provide them with interactive digital, visual, auditory, and dramatic texts. Children's literature is increasingly available in a range of media, providing important points of access for many children. These multimodal texts include audiobooks, films, and digital books.

Audiobooks of children's literature, available on CDs or as downloadable formats, provide readings by well-known actors and professional readers. Reviews of excellent-quality audiobooks can be found in the major review journals (listed in Chapter 3). The following are websites of publishers of substantial numbers of audiobooks:

www.randomhouse.com

www.recordedbooks.com

www.scholastic.com

Audiobooks are an excellent teaching tool. Consider some of the following uses:

• Listen to an audiobook as a class instead of using a teacher read-aloud. The novelty of the performance—something different from the teacher's reading—may add interest.

• Use audiobooks at a center where a group of children can work independently. Provide each child with a copy of the book to follow the narration.

• When assigning homework reading to students, offer students who have difficulties in reading the option of listening to the audiobook while following the narration in a copy of the book. Students who otherwise would be unable to participate in class discussions of the book with their peers will be able to contribute.

• Students can access free audiobooks through public libraries or websites such as www.librivox .org and www.gutenberg.org.

• Auditory learners especially appreciate audiobooks.

Films based on children's books provide students with a multimedia experience of a story. Teachers can engage students in comparing how film is similar to and different from text. Both have plots, characters, settings, themes, styles, and points of view. Both are edited and both can have dialogue and narration. However, film differs from text in that it has sound (spoken words, music, and sound effects) and photography (color or black and white, angles, close-ups, and panoramas). Additionally, films have actual people or animated characters inhabiting the character roles and actual settings, whereas books ask readers to form their own images of characters and settings.

With this quick background in the elements of cinema, students can become better "readers" of film, equipped to discuss or write their personal responses to films based on literature. Films that support or contradict the content of the book may be suitable for classroom use depending on the teacher's intent. Usually teachers show a film based on a book after the book has been read and discussed. The film then provides an opportunity to compare and contrast the book and the film while considering the advantages and limitations of the two media. For some students the movie experience may be motivation to read the book or others in the same series or by the same author.

At the end of Chapters 5 through 11, lists of films related to book categories are provided. The American Library Association has an annual award, the Andrew Carnegie Medal for Excellence in Children's Video, given to the producer of the video. Teachers will want to select films based on children's books that are appropriate to the age level and are connected to classroom inquiries.

Some sources for films, videos, and DVDs are as follows:

- *The Video Source Book* (Edited by James Craddock), published by Cengage Gale, Detroit, MI. This annual reference lists media and provides sources for purchase and rental.
- Two websites of video distributors are www.libraryvideo.com and www.knowledgeunlimited .com.
- The Internet Movie Database (www.imdb.com) is a large film database with production, ratings, and other movie details with links to external reviews.

Digital books are an increasingly popular format for accessing literature. Digital books are available on websites such as the International Children's Digital Library (www.en.childrenslibrary. org), which makes books available in different languages, as well as from a range of children's publishers and software suppliers (see www.childrenssoftwareonline.com). Many of these books provide interactive components, allowing children to click on a particular character or part of the setting to get additional information, dialogue, or sound effects, as well as narration that students can read along with. Scholastic has developed Storia, interactive applications for e-books, a trend by other publishers as well.

Electronic book (e-book) readers are not yet widely used in schools, but are growing in popularity and will be integrated into classrooms as the technology develops and becomes more affordable. E-books are generally cheaper than paper books, take up less space, are environmentally less wasteful to produce, and are more easily distributed. They have the potential to make the concept of an out-of-print book obsolete and to make virtually any book available to readers who have access to the Internet. Access to full-text books is also possible on smartphones.

E-book readers provide access not only to books but also to newspapers, magazines, and blogs and so can be an important source of informational materials as required by the Common Core State Standards. As a result, teachers have greatly expanded choices of reading materials for students and literature for text sets and in-class reading. A disadvantage of some e-book readers is the lack of color graphic capability, making picture books, illustrated informational books, and graphic novels using color ineffective as e-books.

Capabilities of e-book readers that may facilitate reading include:

- A built-in dictionary so that readers can get a definition of a word simply by clicking on it
- Automatic searching and cross-referencing of text for finding earlier references to characters or events

- Nonpermanent highlighting
- Text-to-speech software that can automatically convert e-books to audiobooks

The benefits of e-books appear to be stronger with older children. A recent study by the Cooney Center (2012) found that parents and their 3- to 6-year-old children engaged *less* with the content of the story when reading an e-book and the children recalled fewer narrative details than when reading the print book.

Plays, as a literary genre, are written, dramatic compositions or scripts intended to be acted. A play may be divided into parts called *acts;* in turn, each act may be divided into *scenes.* The script usually has set design, costumes, and stage directions, as well as dialogue provided for each actor. Plays are usually published in *playbooks* that can be purchased as a set for use in group reading situations.

A good play has a subject that appeals to children, an interesting character or two, and a problem that worsens before being resolved satisfactorily. Humor always appeals to children, and conflict between characters is needed for interest and drama. Some children's plays are adaptations of children's books, while others are *original plays*—stories originating in play form. The following resources can be used to locate plays:

- *Children's Book and Play Review,* an online journal of play reviews (http://cbpr.lib.byu.edu)
- International Association of Theatre for Children and Young People (U.S. national section is Theatre for Young Audiences, www.assitej-usa.org)
- American Alliance for Theatre and Education (www.aate.com)
- Smith and Kraus, publisher of plays and play anthologies (www.smithandkraus.com)
- Eldridge Publishing, one of the oldest children's play publishers (www.histage.com)

Several children's authors have written play scripts. Examples include *Skellig: The Play* by David Almond (2005), *Zap* by Paul Fleischman (2005), *Monster* by Walter Dean Myers (1999), *Novio Boy: A Play* by Gary Soto (2006), and *Pushing Up the Sky* by Joseph Bruchac (2000). Sharon Creech's *Replay* (2005) has a play included at the end of the novel.

Children create a unique literary experience by performing a drama, one that immerses them in creating a story while building on their natural enjoyment of play. Plays can be read independently or in small groups, performed as readers' theatre, or performed as a drama for an audience.

Reading Critically to Inquire about the World

Reading literature critically to inquire about the world involves reading to consider issues and ideas in children's lives, the broader society, and the content areas. These experiences support children in becoming critical and knowledgeable readers and thinkers. Readers are encouraged to engage deeply with the text and then to step back to share their connections and reflect critically with others about the text and their responses.

This intensive reading of a few books to think deeply and critically balances the extensive reading of many books. The books chosen for intensive reading have multiple layers of meaning and invite readers to linger longer. These books invite social interaction and discussion, as students need others to help them think about what they have read as they struggle with interpretation and understanding. Because the focus is on dialogue and thinking, the literature may be beyond their reading ability, so the text should be read aloud to them, particularly in the case of young children and struggling readers.

When students experience a story, they often want to respond or express their reactions to the experience in some way. Sharing their responses can involve thinking about the experience through a new form or medium; they develop a better understanding of what they experienced by organizing and deepening their feelings and thoughts, and they discover that other readers' experiences with the same book may have been different. Although it is important to give students opportunities to respond to books, not every book needs or merits a lengthy response. Rosenblatt (1978) reminds us that no two people have the same life experiences and that it is the transaction that occurs between the text, the reader, and the present context that provokes a particular response. Teachers can offer opportunities for students to respond to their literary experiences in many different ways.

In addition, children can engage with literature as part of thematic studies or inquiries within content areas, such as math, science, and social studies. They read critically to compare information and issues across these books, learn facts about the topic, and consider conceptual issues. Literature becomes a tool for understanding the world and considering broader social and scientific issues, as well as a means of facilitating children's interest in a topic.

Literature Discussion

Whole-class discussion usually accompanies a read-aloud. In these discussions, comprehension is assumed and the discussion centers on the different ways students feel and think about the book, characters, events, themes, and outcome. Teachers invite students to share their connections by asking "What are you thinking?" instead of asking questions to check comprehension. In a class discussion, the teacher often has the pivotal role as discussion leader. However, only some of the students will have an opportunity to express their viewpoints because of the group size.

Another format for students to discuss their responses to literature is a *literature circle,* where students meet in small groups to share their responses about a book they have read as a group or a book read aloud by the teacher to the whole class. One of the goals of literature circles is for children to learn to work and think with one another and to value the opinions and views of others. The small group format is student led and provides more opportunities for dialogue. Teachers do not need to be members of the groups, but if they do join a group, they participate as a reader and share their responses and thoughts. The following features are typically found in literature circles:

- The books are organized around a particular theme as either *shared book sets* (multiple copies of the same text) or *text sets* (ten to fifteen conceptually related picture books). Each small group reads a different shared book or text set related to the same broad theme (see Figures 13.4 and Figures 13.5).

- Students are introduced to the selections through short booktalks and given time to browse the books. They list their first and second choices on ballots that are used to organize students into heterogeneous groups of four to six.

- Students read the books and prepare for literature discussion.

  - Students reading chapter books determine how many pages to read a day in order to finish the book in one or two weeks. Reading goals that are not completed at school are considered homework. Students meet in a mini-circle for ten to fifteen minutes daily to check in with each other on their reading goals and share connections and confusions.

Figure 13.4 Shared Book Sets on Journeys for Literature Circles

Picture Books

Each literature circle has multiple copies of one of these titles.

Amelia's Road by Linda Altman
Fox by Margaret Wild
Goin' Someplace Special by Patricia McKissack
Going Home by Eve Bunting
John Patrick Norman McHennessy: The Boy Who Was Always Late by John Burningham
The Pink Refrigerator by Tim Egan
Sebastian's Roller Skates by Jeanne de Déu Prats
Something Beautiful by Sharon Wyeth

Chapter Books

Each literature circle has multiple copies of one of these titles.

Becoming Naomi León by Pam Muñoz Ryan
Elijah of Buxton by Christopher Paul Curtis
The Golden Compass by Philip Pullman
Journey by Patricia MacLachlan
The Last Dragon by Silvana de Mari
Lizzie Bright and the Buckminster Boy by Gary Schmidt
When My Name Was Keoko by Linda Sue Park
Wringer by Jerry Spinelli

Figure 13.5 Text Sets on War and Conflict for Literature Circles

Conditions That Lead to War

Baseball Saved Us by Ken Mochizuki
The Butter Battle Book by Dr. Seuss
First Come the Zebras by Lynne Barasch
In the Rainfield by Isaac Olaleye
The Island of the Skog by Steven Kellogg
The Mightiest by Keiko Kasza
Terrible Things by Eve Bunting
Tusk Tusk by David McKee
When I Grow Up, I Will Win the Nobel Peace Prize by Isabel Pin
The Wild Wombat by Udo Weigelt

War as an Institution

The Araboolies of Liberty Street by Sam Swope
The Conquerors by David McKee
The Day Gogo Went to Vote by Eleanor Sisulu
The End of War by Irmela Wendt
The Monkey Bridge by Rafe Martin
The Roses in My Carpets by Rukhsana Khan
Sami and the Time of the Troubles by Florence P. Heide and Judith Heide Gilliland
The War by Anais Vaugelade
War and Peas by Michael Foreman
When the Horses Ride By: Children in the Times of War by Eloise Greenfield

Consequences of War

The Bracelet by Yoshiko Uchida
Faithful Elephants by Yukio Tsuchiya
Gleam and Glow by Eve Bunting
My Secret Camera by Mendel Grossman
The Orphans of Normandy by Nancy Amis
Rose Blanche by Roberto Innocenti
Sadako by Eleanor Coerr
Shin's Tricycle by Tatsuharu Kodama
So Far from the Sea by Eve Bunting
Star of Fear, Star of Hope by Jo Hoestlandt

Overcoming War

Alia's Mission: Saving the Books of Iraq by Mark Stamaty
The Brave Little Parrot by Rafe Martin
The Cello of Mr. O by Jane Cutler
Gandhi by Demi
Hiroshima No Pika by Toshi Maruki
Let the Celebrations Begin! by Margaret Wild
Oasis of Peace by Laurie Dolphin
A Place Where Sunflowers Grow by Amy Lee-Tai
Rebel by Allan Baillie
Good Night, Commander by Ahmad Akbarpour

Students who are struggling with the book can partner with another student from the group or listen to an audiorecording of the book.

- Young children may not be able to independently read the more complex picture books that support literature discussion. The books can be read aloud to them by a teacher, an older buddy reader, or a family member, or they can listen to an audiorecording. Young children benefit from hearing the book read aloud several times. One option is to have the books read aloud at home for several days before the school discussion.

- As students read, they respond by writing or sketching their connections, questions, and concerns. The responses may be in a literature log, on sticky notes placed in the book, on a graffiti board, or on a closed Internet network.

- Encourage students who finish reading ahead of the rest of the group to read an independent reading book thematically related to their literature circle books.

- Students complete the book and meet in literature circles for extended discussions, typically after students have read the entire book. Students may need to meet in literature circles along the way if a chapter book is particularly difficult or if students are struggling readers or English language learners. Literature circles can last anywhere from two days to two weeks, depending on the length of the book and the depth of the discussion. The discussions are open-ended and provide time for readers to share their initial responses and then dialogue about several issues in more depth.

  - Students create a web or consensus board to brainstorm the issues that they could explore further, based on their initial sharing.

  - Students identify a focused anomaly or concern that they want to inquire about together as a group.

  - Students prepare for the discussion of the identified issue by rereading sections of the book, writing or sketching in their logs, marking relevant quotations with sticky notes, engaging in further research, or using a particular response engagement.

  - Students share their ideas and connections related to the identified issue and engage in dialogue around differing interpretations and perspectives.

  - Students can continue their literature circles by returning to their web multiple times to identify another issue for discussion.

- Text set discussions begin with each student reading one or two books from the set and meeting to share their books. Students often move between reading and sharing for a week or two and then web the connections and differences across the books in their set. They choose one of these issues to discuss in greater depth through inquiry and critique.

- When students complete their literature circles, they can present the key ideas from their discussions to pull together their thinking about the book or text set. They can informally talk about their books and share their webs with classmates. Another option is to create a formal presentation by first listing the most important ideas they want to share about their book. They then brainstorm different ways to present these ideas (murals, skits, posters, dioramas, etc.) and choose the one that best fits the ideas they want to share.

A third option is to create a classroom newsletter/newspaper in which each literature group writes about the books they are reading and includes visual sketches, webs, or charts.

The discussions in literature circles are more complex and generative if teachers embed these circles within a broad class theme, such as identity or journeys, around which they have planned a range of engagements, including class read-alouds and browsing of other books on that theme. This theme may be connected to a unit of inquiry within the curriculum or to issues students are exploring in their lives.

When students have the opportunity to converse and dialogue about what they are reading, they explore their "in-process" understandings, consider alternative interpretations, and become critical inquirers. Literature circles support reading as a transactional process in which readers actively construct understandings of a text by bringing meaning to, as well as from, that text. They come to understand that there is no one meaning to be determined, but many possible interpretations to explore and critique. The primary intent of these discussions is to provide a space for readers to think about life from multiple perspectives, not to learn about literary elements or comprehension strategies.

Literature Response Engagements

Requiring students to list the author, title, date, genre, setting, main characters, and summary of the plot seldom causes students to delve more deeply into literature. Students usually view traditional book reports as tedious busywork and as a punishment for reading a book. Although teachers assign book reports to get students to read, students often report that they never read the book, but instead read the bookflap and a page or two at the beginning and end.

Recently, some so-called literature response forms or worksheets have been published for use by teachers who adopt literature-based reading approaches. These worksheets are often little more than disguised book report forms. Such comprehension assessment may be occasionally useful for reading instruction, but is of no use if your interest is students' responses to literature.

Readers deepen and extend their interpretations of literature when they respond in a variety of ways. When readers move from reading to writing, art, or drama, they take a new perspective on the piece of literature. In the process of exploring their thinking about a book through various sign systems, they discover new meanings and expand their understandings of that book.

The following response engagements provide structures to encourage students to push their thinking about a book. These engagements stand in contrast to activities where students write a summary, retell a book, answer comprehension questions, or make a "cute" art project. Response engagements challenge students to find and explore the issues that they find significant within a book, rather than answer the teacher's questions about the book. (See *Creating Classrooms for Authors and Inquirers* by Kathy G. Short and Jerome Harste, 1996, for more information and examples of these engagements.)

- *Freewrites*. At the beginning of a group meeting, set a timer for five minutes and write continuously about your thoughts on the book, then turn and talk in the group. If the group is still not sure how to begin, one person can read aloud all or part of their freewrite. The group discusses the ideas in that freewrite and then moves on to the next person.

- *Post-ful thinking*. Put sticky notes on pages where you have a significant connection as you read and jot a quick comment. Share these when your group meets to find issues to discuss together. You can also use sticky notes to revisit the book when the group decides to examine a particular issue. Mark pages relevant to the issue as a way to prepare for the discussion.

• *Literature logs.* Stop periodically as you read and respond to what you are thinking about, including questions and connections. These entries can take the form of a written response, a sketch, a web, a chart, quotes you want to remember, and so on. Reread your literature log right before beginning a group discussion so the issues are fresh in your mind.

• *Collage reading/text rendering.* Mark quotes that are significant to you as you read. In collage reading, group members read aloud quotes to each other. One person reads a quote, then someone else reads another quote, and the reading continues in no particular order. Readers choose when to read a quote in order to build off of what someone else has read, but no comments are made about the quotes. Text rendering is similar, except the reader states why they chose the quote. There is no discussion until after the text rendering is finished.

• *Graffiti boards.* Put a large sheet of paper on the table. Each group member takes a corner of the paper to write, web, and sketch their thoughts about the book or text set. The comments, sketches, quotes, and connections are not organized; the major focus is on recording initial responses during or immediately after reading a book. Group members share from their graffiti to start the discussion. Webbing or charting can then be used to organize the connections.

• *Save the last word for me.* As you read, note passages or quotes that catch your attention because they are interesting, powerful, confusing, or contradictory and put the quote on a 3" × 5" card. On the back of the card, write why you found that particular passage noteworthy. In the group, one person shares a quote and the group briefly discusses their thinking while the initial person remains silent. When the discussion dies down, the person who chose the quote tells why he/she chose it. That person has the last word, then the group moves on to the next person. Young children can show a page from a picture book instead of reading a quote.

• *Sketch to stretch.* After reading a book, make a sketch (a quick graphic/symbolic drawing) of what the story meant to you or your connections to the book (not an illustration of the story). In the group, show your sketch and discuss its symbols and ideas. After sharing the sketches, choose issues to explore in more depth as a group.

• *Webbing what's on my mind.* After sharing initial responses to a book, your group brainstorms a web of issues, themes, and questions that could be discussed from the book or text set. Using the web, your group decides on the one issue that is most interesting or causes the most tension to begin discussion. You can continue your discussion by choosing from other ideas on the web. New ideas are added as they develop from the discussion.

• *Consensus board.* Divide a large board into four sections with a circle in the middle. The circle contains the book's title or key theme. In the individual sections, each of you writes or sketches personal connections to the book or theme. The group discusses these individual connections and comes to consensus on the issues or big ideas to explore further. These are written in the middle of the board for further discussion.

• *Comparison charts/Venn diagrams.* Read a text set and discuss similarities and differences across the books. From these discussions, develop broad categories that you want to compare more closely. Make a chart with the books listed on the side and the categories across the top. Both pictures and words are used to make the comparisons in the boxes. A Venn diagram (two circles that overlap in the center) focuses the comparison on one major issue at a time.

- *Story ray.* You each receive a three-foot strip of paper (a ray) on which to create a visual essence of a selected chapter using colors, images, and a few words, with various art media and little or no white space. Share your rays in the groups and explain their symbolism. The rays are then assembled on a large mural or wall in the shape of sun rays to reflect the unfolding of the novel.

- *Mapping.* Maps provide a way to organize your thinking and explore relationships among ideas, people, and events. They can take a range of forms to show visual relationships, explore processes and change, and record movement of people or ideas. Consider using maps to show the following:

  - The journey of change for a character within a book or of an idea/issue over the course of the book
  - Symbols that show the heart (the values and beliefs) or the mind (the thoughts and ideas) of a particular character
  - A cultural "X-ray" in the shape of a person that shows a character's inner values and beliefs and outer actions and qualities
  - A flowchart that explores how certain decisions made by a character create particular consequences

- *Time lines and diagrams.* Time lines can help you think about how particular historical events influenced the characters in the story. Draw a line on a long strip of paper, placing the dates below the line on scaled intervals. Note the story events above the line and the events from history below the line. Time lines are also useful with text sets of historical sources.

Students who are new to working in groups often find that working in pairs is an easier way to become comfortable with discussion. Any of these response engagements may be used with partners rather than in a small group. There are also several response engagements that are particularly designed for partners. Here are two possibilities:

- *Say something.* Two people share the reading of a short story. The first person reads aloud a chunk of text (several paragraphs or a page) to the other person. When the reader stops, both of them "say something" by making a prediction, sharing personal connections, asking questions, or commenting on the story. The second person then reads aloud a chunk of text and again both "say something." The two readers continue alternating the reading of the story, commenting after each reading, until the story is completed.

- *Written conversation.* Have a silent conversation by talking on paper. Two people share a piece of paper and a pencil, talking about a book by writing back and forth to each other. No talking is allowed, except with young children, who often need to write and then read what they have written aloud in order for the other child to write back.

Drama as Response

Creative drama is informal drama that involves the reenactment of story experiences (McCaslin, 1990). It is improvisational and involves the actors creating dialogue and movement as they engage in the drama. Props may be used, but not scenery or costumes. Because of its improvisational nature and simplicity, creative drama places importance on the experience of the participants, not on performance for an audience.

A picture book, short story, or single scene from a chapter book may be dramatized. The most suitable stories to start with are relatively simple, involving two to six characters and high action. Many folktales fit this description. The steps in guiding creative drama in the classroom are:

- Students select a story they want to act out and listen to or read it independently several times, paying attention to the characters and story scenes.

- Students list the characters and the scenes on the board or on chart paper.

- Students assign parts to actors. If enough students are interested in dramatizing the same story, two or more casts of actors can be assigned. Each cast of characters can observe the performances of the others and learn from them.

- Each cast uses the list of scenes to review the plot, ensuring that all actors recall the events. Discuss the characters, having students describe the actions, dialogue, and appearance for each.

- Give the cast of characters a few minutes to decide how to handle the performance. Then run through it several times to work out the bumpy parts. Lines are improvised, not memorized.

The Fantastic Plays for Kids website (www.childdrama.com) has useful ideas and lesson plans for creative drama.

Dramatic inquiry, also known as ***Drama in Education,*** involves the use of drama to create an imaginative space or drama world around critical moments in a story, rather than acting out a story (Heathcote, 1984). Students develop characters and situations and take on diverse perspectives that go beyond the book. Discussion supports readers in standing back and talking about events that happened to other people in a different world. Dramatic inquiry puts students in the middle of events and within the world of the story as they explore their tensions and issues. Students explore multiple perspectives within and beyond the story boundaries through strategies such as the following:

- *Tableaus.* Each small group of students creates a frozen image without talk or movement to represent an idea or moment related to the story.

- *Writing-in-role.* Students assume the identity of a character and write a text from that perspective, such as a reflection on events or a journal entry.

- *Hot seat.* Students take on the roles of different characters and sit on the hot seat to respond to questions about their perspective on an issue from the story.

- *News program.* Students take on the role of television or newspaper reporters and interview characters from the book to retell an event from a range of perspectives.

- *Perspective switch.* Each student shifts perspectives, trying out the perspectives of characters who are opposed, supportive, or ambivalent to an issue.

These drama strategies take readers beyond reenactments of a story to their own drama worlds, giving them a lens for critically examining the events and margins of a story. *Action Strategies for Deepening Comprehension* (Wilhelm, 2002) offers examples of these drama strategies in responding to literature.

Literature across the Curriculum

Literature across the curriculum refers to the use of literature to replace or supplement textbooks in social studies, science, health, and mathematics. Literature provides more interesting and well-written accounts and perspectives on historical events and scientific information. In addition, textbooks often superficially cover large amounts of information, whereas nonfiction literature focuses on a particular topic in more depth, providing a context for inquiry into broader social and scientific issues. Students who struggle as readers can benefit from attractively illustrated and more accessible nonfiction literature. A collection of nonfiction literature of varying lengths and difficulties can meet the needs of students at different reading levels, unlike textbooks written on a single readability level.

Literature makes social studies content more memorable because the stories are presented from a child's point of view, allowing children to see the world through a narrative framework. Children are more likely to understand and remember history when it is presented as a story with characters, settings, and events. They can then move from an interest in the narrative to an interest in the historical information.

Literature also permits students to examine multiple perspectives on a topic, which helps develop critical thinking. By comparing historical information from various sources, students encounter differing perspectives on a particular era of history. In addition, literature often relates political and social events to relevant moral issues. Children can see how these events affected the lives of real people and understand the morality underlying their choices. Unlike textbook authors, who must write to satisfy all viewpoints, authors of children's literature are more likely to face controversial issues head-on. For ideas on planning a unit around the forced journeys of refugees see the web in Figure 12.2. Examples of literature offering a range of perspectives for a social studies inquiry on Japanese-American internment camps and for a science unit about the moon can be found in Figure 13.6.

Figure 13.6 Text Sets for Multiple Perspectives in Science and Social Studies Units

The Moon

And if the Moon Could Talk by Kate Banks, illustrated by Georg Hallensleben (Realistic fiction)

Comets, Stars, the Moon, and Mars: Space Poems and Paintings by Douglas Florian (Poetry)

The Dog Who Loved the Moon by Cristina Gárcia, illustrated by Sebastia Serra (Fantasy, Cuba)

A Full Moon Is Rising: Poems by Marilyn Singer, illustrated by Julia Cairns (Poetry, global)

If You Decide to Go to the Moon by Faith McNulty, illustrated by Steven Kellogg (Fantasy/science)

The Moon by Seymour Simon (Science)

Moon Man by Tomi Ungerer (Fantasy, France)

The Moon over Star by Dianna H. Aston, illustrated by Jerry Pinkney (Historical fiction)

Moon Plane by Peter McCarty (Fantasy)

Moonshot: The Flight of Apollo 11 by Brian Floca (History)

Moontellers: Myths of the Moon from Around the World by Lynn Moroney, illustrated by Greg Shed (Myths, world)

One Giant Leap by Robert Burleigh, illustrated by Mike Wimmer (History)

Thanking the Moon: Celebrating the Mid-Autumn Moon Festival by Grace Lin (Festival, Chinese American)

Japanese-American Internment Camps/ World War II

Baseball Saved Us by Ken Mochizuki, illustrated by Dom Lee (Historical fiction picture book)

Bat 6: A Novel by Virginia Euwer Wolff (Historical fiction novel)

The Children of Topaz: The Story of a Japanese American Internment Camp by Michael Tunnell and George Chilcoat (History)

(Continued)

Figure 13.6 Continued

Dear Miss Breed: True Stories of the Japanese American Incarceration during World War II and a Librarian Who Made a Difference by Joanne Oppenheim (History)

A Diamond in the Desert by Kathryn Fitzmaurice (Historical fiction novel)

Fighting for Honor: Japanese Americans and World War II by Michael Cooper (History)

Flowers from Mariko by Rick Noguchi, illustrated by Michelle R. Kumata (Historical fiction picture book)

Home of the Brave by Allen Say (Modern fable, picture book)

Journey to Topaz and *Journey Home* by Yoshiko Uchida (Historical fiction novels, memoir)

A Place Where Sunflowers Grow by Amy Lee-Tai, illustrated by Felicia Hoshino (Historical fiction picture book)

Under the Blood-Red Sun by Graham Salisbury (Historical fiction novel, Hawai'i)

Weedflower by Cynthia Kadohata (Historical fiction novel)

Trade books in science and health present different sources of information as a means to verify facts. Students can compare the facts presented in the textbook with those found in various books on the same topic. Global warming, a topic frequently in the news, is addressed in a number of books. For example, David Laurie and Cambria Gordon's *The Down-to-Earth Guide to Global Warming* (2007) and *How We Know What We Know about Our Changing Climate* by Lynne Cherry and Gary Braasch (2008) are two short, well-written informational books, while Marcus Sedgwick's science fiction novel *Floodland* (2001) features a girl who searches for her parents after the sea has risen as a result of global warming, causing cities to become islands. Another work of science fiction, *The House of the Scorpion* (2002) by Nancy Farmer, can become the basis for investigations into cloning and its ramifications.

Many nonfiction books on health and science present information in interesting ways through graphs, tables, figures, photographs, and other visual presentations, coupled with a lively writing style. Comparison of information from different sources can be readily provided when students are not limited to a single source for their information. Teachers who draw on various types of texts for their instruction have discovered that literature has the power to educate the mind while enlightening the spirit.

Content-area reading is the ability to read to acquire, understand, and connect to new content in a particular discipline. In content-area classes students are often assigned textbooks, a type of expository text, which they frequently have more difficulty reading and understanding than narrative texts. Teachers can make reading textbooks easier if they teach students how such texts are structured and explain their specialized features. In Chapter 10, the elements and structures of informational texts are explained with examples. Heard and McDonough (2009), Stead (2005), and Hoyt, Mooney, and Parkes (2003) provide many practical ideas on teaching reading strategies for informational texts.

Reading Strategically to Learn about Literacy

Reading literature to learn about literacy creates strategic readers who reflect on their reading processes and text knowledge. Adults should encourage these engagements by helping children develop a repertoire of strategies to use when they encounter difficulty, either in figuring out words or in comprehending, and to gain knowledge of text structures and literary elements.

Adults guide children's reflections on their reading processes by teaching lessons on strategies, literary elements, and text structures and by having students read literature that highlights particular reading strategies based on teacher knowledge of children's needs. Students who have a range of effective reading strategies and text knowledge can problem solve when encountering difficulty so as to develop reading proficiency.

Many schools use commercial materials for reading instruction rather than literature. Although children are taught how to read through these materials, they do not necessarily develop the desire or habit of reading. They are capable of reading but are not engaged readers who are motivated, knowledgeable, and strategic.

Engagements with literature that focus on learning about literacy include guided reading, guided comprehension, conferencing, and mini-lessons in which students read books in order to examine their current reading strategies and develop new strategies. Teachers carefully assess which readers are on the "edge of knowing" a particular strategy and form small groups of students who share similar needs for guided reading. Reading strategies are taught within the context of reading a book for meaning and then pulling back to talk about the strategies students used to make sense of that book or to figure out unfamiliar words.

Often literary instruction takes the form of worksheets where students list story elements, such as character, plot, and conflict, rather than thoughtfully considering how these elements influence meaning. Recently there has been a strong emphasis on genre studies. Some of these genre studies are formulaic, whereas others involve students in an inquiry approach to construct their understandings of the genre. These genre studies provide a way for students to explore literary elements and genres within a meaningful context. Author studies, in which students immerse themselves in reading and examining an author's whole body of work, are another meaningful context in which students can examine particular literary elements and genres to learn about literature.

Writing often provides an effective way for students to explore language and text structure, particularly if they use literary works as writing models. When children read and listen to stories, they accumulate vocabulary, sentence structures, stylistic devices, and story ideas and structures. Well-written stories and poems, such as those in Tables 13.1 and Tables 13.2, serve as models for

Table 13.1   Using Literary Works as Writing Models in Grades 1–3

Literary Device or Element	Suggested Books
Characterization	***Marisol McDonald Doesn't Match*** by Monica Brown ***Sheila Rae, the Brave*** by Kevin Henkes ***Farmer Duck*** by Martin Waddell ***Duck on a Bike*** by David Shannon
Dialogue	***I Want My Hat Back*** by Jon Klassen ***John Patrick Norman McHennessy*** by John Burningham ***The Wild Wombat*** by Udo Weigelt
Episodic Plot	***Bink and Gollie*** by Kate DiCamillo ***Dog and Bear: Two Friends, Three Stories*** by Laura V. Seeger ***Tales for Very Picky Eaters*** by Josh Schneider

(Continued)

Table 13.1 Continued	
Literary Device or Element	**Suggested Books**
Journal Writing	*Pictures from Our Vacation* by Lynne Rae Perkins *Diary of a Fly* by Doreen Cronin
Setting	*Art & Max* by David Wiesner *A New Year's Reunion* by Yu Li-Qiong *Goin' Someplace Special* by Patricia McKissack

Table 13.2 Using Literary Works as Writing Models in Grades 4–7	
Literary Device or Element	**Suggested Books**
Characterization	*The Watsons Go to Birmingham* by Christopher Paul Curtis *Lizzie Bright and the Buckminster Boy* by Gary Schmidt *Alvin Ho: Allergic to Dead Bodies, Funerals and Other Fatal Circumstances* by Lenore Look
Dialogue	*Ruby Holler* by Sharon Creech *My Name Is Not Easy* by Debby Dahl Edwardson *Better than Weird* by Anna Kertz
Mood	*The Dreamer* by Pam Muñoz Ryan *A Monster Calls* by Patrick Ness *Fox* by Margaret Wild
Journal Writing	*Diary of a Wimpy Kid* by Jeff Kinney *Ways to Live Forever* by Sally Nicholls *Hound Dog True* by Linda Urban
Point of View	*Faith and the Electric Dogs* by Patrick Jennings *When My Name Was Keoko* by Linda Sue Park *Mockingbird* by Kathryn Erskine
Flashbacks	*So Far from the Sea* by Eve Bunting *Hush* by Jacqueline Woodson *Pictures of Hollis Woods* by Patricia Reilly Giff

children in their own writing. When an 8-year-old boy who wrote extremely well-developed, interesting stories was asked how he learned to make up such good stories, he replied, "It's really a secret, but I'll tell you if you won't tell my teacher. I don't really make up the stories. When I was little, my mother read lots of books to me; then in school my teachers read a lot more. So what I do is take a beginning from one of the stories, a middle from another, and the end from another.

And then I make up a title." Children who have a rich literary background have a well-stocked storehouse of ideas and structures to put to use in their storytelling and writing.

Writing a story modeled after another story can be an enjoyable way to explore constructing meaning through particular text structures. The student adapts a story form or idea into a new creation. Examples include the following:

- Students create another episode using the same characters.
- Students write a different ending to the story.
- Students recast the story from the perspective of another character. Examples of a change in point of view can be found in Jon Scieszka's *The True Story of the 3 Little Pigs by A. Wolf* (1989), which gives the Big Bad Wolf's version, and Scieszka's *The Frog Prince Continued* (1991), which tells the shocking truth about "happily ever after."
- Students write a prequel to a story.
- Students take a story set in the past and rewrite it with a modern-day setting. Alternatively, a character from the historical narrative can become a visitor to modern times.

Many cultures view reading as necessary to a well-ordered society and to the moral well-being of the individual. Engagement with literature invites children to make meaning of texts in personally significant ways in order to facilitate learning of content and to develop positive lifelong reading attitudes and habits. In addition, children gain a sense of possibility for their lives and for society, along with the ability to consider others' perspectives and needs. Engagement with literature thus allows them to develop their own voices and, at the same time, go beyond self-interest to an awareness of broader human consequences.

Invitations for Further Investigation

- Select a picture book or scene from a novel to rewrite into a script for readers' theatre. If possible, try the piece with a group of children and reflect on their engagement.
- Read aloud a picture book to a group of students and engage them in a discussion using one of the literature response engagements. Reflect on this experience and what you learned from the students' responses. Read teacher vignettes from *WOW Stories* (www.wowlit.org /on-line-publications/stories), in which teachers reflect on their use of these engagements with students.
- Put together a group of text sets around a theme, such as power, conflict, change, journeys, identity, or relationships. Include a range of perspectives, genres, and cultures within your set of books. You might also include multimodal texts and oral literature as well as written literature.

References

Akbarpour, A. (2010*). Good night, Commander.* Illus. M. Zahedi. Toronto, ON: Groundwood.

Almond, D. (2005). *Skellig: The play.* New York: Delacorte.

Altman, L. J. (1995). *Amelia's road.* Sanchez, E. (Illus.). New York: Lee & Low.

Amis, N. (2003). *The orphans of Normandy.* New York: Atheneum.

Armstrong, A. (2005). *Whittington*. New York: Random House.

Aston, D. (2008). *The moon over star*. Pinkney, J. (Illus.). New York: Dial.

Baillie, A. (1994). *Rebel*. Wu, D. (Illus.). Boston, MA: Houghton Mifflin.

Banks, K. (1998). *And if the moon could talk*. Hallensleben, G. (Illus.). New York: Frances Foster.

Barasch, L. (2009). *First come the zebras*. New York: Lee & Low.

Brown, M. (2012). *Marisol McDonald doesn't match*. Palacios, S. (Illus.). San Francisco, CA: Children's Book Press.

Bruchac, J. (2000). *Pushing up the sky: Seven Native American plays for children*. New York: Dial.

Bunting, E. (1989). *Terrible things*. Gammell, S. (Illus.). Philadelphia, PA: Jewish Publication Society.

Bunting, E. (1998). *Going home*. Diaz, D. (Illus.). New York: HarperCollins.

Bunting, E. (1998). *So far from the sea*. Soentpiet, C. (Illus.). New York: Clarion.

Bunting, E. (2001). *Gleam and glow*. Sylvada, P. (Illus.). San Diego, CA: Harcourt.

Burleigh, R. (2009). *One giant leap*. Wimmer, M. (Illus.). New York: Philomel.

Burningham, J. (1987). *John Patrick Norman McHennessy: The boy who was always late*. New York: Knopf.

Carle, E. (1968). *The very hungry caterpillar*. New York: Philomel.

Cherry, L. (1990). *The great kapok tree: A tale of the Amazon rainforest*. San Diego, CA: Harcourt.

Cherry, L. (2008). *How we know what we know about our changing climate*. Barusch, G. (Photos). New York: Dawn.

Coerr, E. (1993). *Sadako*. Young, E. (Illus.). New York: Putnam.

Cole, B. (2000). *Buttons*. New York: Farrar.

Cooper, M. (2000). *Fighting for honor: Japanese Americans and World War II*. New York: Clarion.

Cooney Center. (2012). *Print books vs. E-books*. Joanganzcooneycenter.org/Reports-35.htmloutlines

Creech, S. (2002). *Ruby Holler*. New York: HarperCollins.

Creech, S. (2005). *Replay: A new book*. New York: Joanna Cotler Books.

Cronin, D. (2007). *The diary of a fly*. Bliss, H. (Illus.). New York: Joanna Cotler Books.

Curtis, C. P. (1995) *The Watsons go to Birmingham—1963*. New York: Delacorte

Curtis, C. P. (1999). *Bud, not Buddy*. New York: Delacorte.

Curtis, C. P. (2007). *Elijah of Buxton*. New York: Scholastic.

Cutler, J. (1999). *The cello of Mr. O*. Couch, G. (Illus.). New York: Puffin.

D'Adamo, F. (2001). *Iqbal*. New York: Aladdin.

David, L., & Gordon, C. (2007). *The down-to-earth guide to global warming*. New York: Orchard.

De Deu Prats, J. (2005). *Sebastian's roller skates*. Rovira, F. (Illus.). LaJolla, CA: Kane/Miller.

de Mari, S. (2006). *The last dragon*. New York: Hyperion.

Demi. (2001). *Gandhi*. New York: M. K. McElderry.

DiCamillo, K. (2010). *Bink and Gollie*. Fucile, T. (Illus.). New York: Candlewick.

Dolphin, L. (1993). *Oasis of peace*. Dolphin, B. (Illus.). New York: Scholastic.

Dr. Seuss. (1984). *The butter battle book*. New York: Random House.

Edwardson, D. (2011). *My name is not easy*. Tarrytown, NY: Cavendish.

Erskine, K. (2010). *Mockingbird*. New York: Philomel.

Farmer, N. (2002). *The house of the scorpion*. New York: Atheneum.

Fleischman, P. (1993). *Bull Run*. New York: HarperCollins.

Fleischman, P. (1997). *Seedfolks*. New York: HarperCollins.

Fleischman, P. (2005). *Zap*. New York: Candlewick.

Floca, B. (2009). *Moonshot: The flight of Apollo 11*. New York: Atheneum.

Florian, D. (2007). *Comets, stars, the moon, and Mars: Space poems and paintings*. New York: Harcourt.

Foreman, M. (2002). *War and peas*. Atlanta, GA: Andersen Press.

Freeman, J. (2006). *Books kids will sit still for, 3: A read-aloud guide*. Portsmouth, NH: Libraries Unlimited.

Gaiman, N. (2003). *The wolves in the walls.* New York: HarperCollins.

Garcia, C. (2008). *The dog who loved the moon.* Serra, S. (Illus.). New York: Atheneum.

Giff, P. R. (2002). *Pictures of Hollis Woods.* New York: Wendy Lamb.

Greenfield, E. (2006). *When the horses ride by: Children in the times of war.* Gilchrist, J. S. (Illus.). New York: Lee & Low.

Grossman, B. (1989). *Tommy at the grocery store.* Chess, V. (Illus.). New York: Harper.

Grossman, M. (2000). *My secret camera.* San Diego, CA: Gulliver.

Hall, D. (1994). *I am the dog, I am the cat.* Moser, B. (Illus.). New York: Dial.

Heard, G., & McDonough, J. (2009). A *place for wonder: Reading and writing nonfiction in primary grades.* Portland, ME: Stenhouse.

Heathcote, D. (1984). *Dorothy Heathcote: Collected writings on education and drama.* London, England: Hutchinson.

Heide, F. P., & Gilliland, J. H. (1992). *Sami and the time of the troubles.* Lewin, T. (Illus.). New York: Clarion.

Henkes, K. (1987). *Sheila Rae, the brave.* New York: Greenwillow.

Henkes, K. (1991). *Chrysanthemum.* New York: Greenwillow.

Hesse, K. (2001). *Witness.* New York: Scholastic.

Holdaway, D. (1982). Shared book experience: Teaching reading using favorite books. *Theory into Practice, 21,* 293–300.

Hoyt, L., Mooney, M., & Parkes, B. (2003). *Exploring informational texts.* Portsmouth, NH: Heinemann.

Innocenti, R. (1985). *Rose Blanche.* Minneapolis, MN: Creative Education.

Jennings, P. (1996). *Faith and the electric dogs.* New York: Scholastic.

Kadohata, C. (2006). *Weedflower.* New York: Atheneum.

Kasza, K. (2001). *The mightiest.* New York: Putnam.

Kellogg, S. (1973). *The island of the Skog.* New York: Dial.

Kertz, A. (2011). *Better than weird.* Toronto, ON: Orca.

Khan, R. (1998). *The roses in my carpets.* Himler, R. (Illus.). New York: Holiday.

Kinney, J. (2007). *Diary of a wimpy kid.* New York: Amulet.

Klassen, J. (2011). *I want my hat back.* Somerville, MA: Candlewick.

Kodama, T. (1992). *Shin's tricycle.* Ando, N. (Illus.). New York: Walker.

Laminack, L., & Wadsworth, R. (2006). *Learning under the influence of language and literature: Making the most of read-alouds across the day.* Portsmouth, NH: Heinemann.

Laurie, D., & Gordon, C. (2007). *The down-to-earth guide to global warming.* New York: Orchard.

Lee-Tai, A. (2006). *A place where sunflowers grow.* Hoshino, F. (Illus.). San Francisco, CA: Children's Book Press.

LeGallienne, R. (1969). I meant to do my work today. In L. Untermeyer (Ed.), *The Golden treasury of poetry.* Anglund, J.W. (Illus.). New York: Golden Press.

Levine, G. C. *Ella enchanted.* New York: HarperCollins.

Li-Quiong, Yu. *A New Year's reunion.* Cheng-Liang, Z. (Illus.). Somerville, MA: Candlewick.

Lin, G. (2010). *Thanking the moon: Celebrating the Mid-Autumn Moon Festival.* New York: Knopf.

Lobel, A. (1970). *Frog and Toad are friends.* New York: Harper.

Look, L. (2011). *Alvin Ho: Allergic to dead bodies, funerals, and other fatal circumstances.* New York: Schwartz & Wade.

Lowry, L. (1993). *The giver.* New York: Houghton.

MacLachlan, P. (1993). *Journey.* New York: Yearling.

Martin, R. (1997). *The monkey bridge.* Amiri, F. (Illus.). New York: Knopf.

Martin, R. (1998). *The brave little parrot.* Gaber, S. (Illus.). New York: Putnam.

Maruki, T. (1980). *Hiroshima no pika.* New York: Lothrop, Lee & Shepard.

McCarty, P. (2006). *Moon plane.* New York: Holt.

McCaslin, N. (1990). *Creative drama in the classroom* (5th ed.). New York: Longman.

McKee, D. (1990). *Tusk tusk.* LaJolla, CA: Kane/Miller.

McKee, D. (2004). *The conquerors.* New York: Handprint.

McKissack, P. (2001). *Goin' someplace special*. Pinkney, J. (Illus.). New York: Atheneum.

Mochizuki, K. (1993). *Baseball saved us*. Lee, D. (Illus.). New York: Lee & Low.

Moroney, L. (1995). *Moontellers: Myths of the moon from around the world*. Shed, G. (Illus.). Flagstaff, AZ: Northland.

Myers, W. D. (1999). *Monster*. New York: Harper Collins.

Ness, P. (2011). *A monster calls*. Kay, K. (Illus.). Somerville, MA: Candlewick.

Nicholls, S. (2008). *Ways to live forever*. New York: Scholastic.

Noguchi, R. (2001). *Flowers from Mariko*. Kumata, K. R. (Illus.). New York: Lee & Low.

O'Connor, B. (2009). *The small adventure of Popeye and Elvis*. New York: Farrar.

Olaleye, I. O. (2000). *In the rainfield*. Grifalconi, A. (Illus.). New York: Blue Sky.

Oppenheim, J. (2006). *Dear Miss Breed: True stories of the Japanese American incarceration during World War II and the librarian who made a difference*. New York: Scholastic.

Park, L. S. (2002). *When my name was Keoko*. New York: Clarion.

Perkins, L. R. (2007). *Pictures from our vacation*. New York: Greenwillow.

Pin, I. (2005). *When I grow up, I will win the Nobel Peace Prize*. New York: Farrar.

Pullman, P. (1996). *The golden compass*. New York: Knopf.

Raskin, E. (1978). *The westing game*. New York: Dutton.

Rocklin, J. *One day and one amazing morning on Orange Street*. New York: Amulet.

Rosenblatt, L. M. (1978). *The reader, the text, the poem: The transactional theory of the literary work*. Carbondale, IL: Southern Illinois University Press.

Ryan, P. M. (2010). *The dreamer*. Sis, P. (Illus.). New York: Scholastic.

Salisbury, G. (1994). *Under the blood-red sun*. New York: Delacorte.

Say, A. (2002). *Home of the brave*. New York: Houghton Mifflin.

Schmidt, G. (2004). *Lizzie Bright and the Buckminster boy*. New York: Clarion.

Schneider, J. (2011). *Tales for very picky eaters*. New York: Clarion.

Scieszka, J. (1989). *The true story of the 3 little pigs by A. Wolf*. Smith, L. (Illus.). New York: Viking.

Scieszka, J. (1991). *The frog prince continued*. Johnson, S. (Illus.). New York: Viking.

Sedgwick, M. (2001). *Floodland*. New York: Delacorte.

Seeger, L. V. (2007). *Dog and bear: Two friends, three stories*. New York: Roaring Brook.

Shannon, D. (2002). *Duck on a bike*. New York: Blue Sky.

Short, K., & Harste, J. (1996). *Creating classrooms for authors and inquirers*. Portsmouth, NH: Heinemann.

Siegel, S. (2006). *To dance: A ballerina's graphic novel*. Siegel, M. (Illus.). New York: Simon & Schuster.

Simon, S. (2003). *The moon*. New York: Simon & Schuster.

Singer, M. (2011). *A full moon is rising: Poems*. Cairns, J. (Illus.). New York: Lee & Low.

Sisulu, E. B. (1996). *The day Gogo went to vote*. Wilson, S. (Illus.). Boston, MA: Little, Brown.

Soto, G. (1997). *Novio boy: A play*. New York: Harcourt.

Spinelli, J. (2004). *Wringer*. New York: Harper.

Stamaty, M. A. (2004). *Alia's mission: Saving the books of Iraq*. New York: Knopf.

Stead, T. (2005). *Reality checks: Teaching reading comprehension with nonfiction K–5*. Portland, ME: Stenhouse.

Swope, S. (1989). *The Araboolies of Liberty Street*. Root, B. (Illus.). New York: Sunburst.

Trelease, J. (2006). *The read-aloud handbook* (6th ed.). New York: Penguin.

Trivizas, E. (1993). *The three little wolves and the big bad pig*. Oxenbury, H. (Illus.). New York: Macmillan.

Tsuchiya, Y. (1988). *Faithful elephants*. Lewin, T. (Illus.). Boston, MA: Houghton Mifflin.

Tunnell, M., & Chilcoat, G. (1996). *The children of Topez: The story of a Japanese American internment camp*. New York: Holiday.

Uchida, Y. (1971). *Journey to Topaz*. New York: Aladdin.

Uchida, Y. (1978). *Journey home*. New York: Aladdin.

Uchida, Y. (1993). *The bracelet.* Yardley, J. (Illus.). New York: Philomel.

Ungerer, T. (2009). *Moon man.* London: Phaidon.

Urban, L. (2011). *Hound dog true.* New York: Harcourt.

Vaugelade, A. (2001). *The war.* Minneapolis, MN: Carolrhoda.

Waddell, M. (1992). *Farmer Duck.* Oxenbury, H. (Illus.). Cambridge, MA: Candlewick.

Weigelt, U. (2001). *The wild wombat.* Piepenbrink, A. K. (Illus.). New York: North-South.

Wendt, I. (1991). *The end of war.* Boratynski, A. (Illus.). New York: Pitspopany.

Wiesner, D. (2010*). Art & Max.* New York: Clarion.

Wild, M. (1991). *Let the celebrations begin!* Vivas, J. (Illus.). New York: Orchard.

Wild, M. (2006). *Fox.* Brooks, R. (Illus.). LaJolla, CA: Kane/Miller.

Wilhelm, J. (2002). *Action strategies for deepening comprehension.* New York: Scholastic.

Wolff, V. (1998). *Bat 6: A novel.* New York: Scholastic.

Woodson, J. (2002). *Hush.* New York: Putnam.

Yan, M. (2005). *The diary of Ma Yan.* New York: HarperCollins.

Appendix A

Children's Book Awards

Some of the following awards were established prior to 1988. For access to the complete lists of winners and honor books for these awards, go to the websites as indicated.

National, General Awards

The United States

Caldecott Medal

This award, established in 1938 by the Association for Library Service to Children division of the American Library Association, is given to the illustrator of the most distinguished picture book for children published in the U.S. during the preceding year. Only U.S. residents or citizens are eligible. Award winners and honor books since 1991 are listed here. For the complete list of winners and honor books, go to http://www.ala.org/alsc/awardsgrants/bookmedia/caldecottmedal/caldecotthonors/caldecottmedal.

2012 *A Ball for Daisy* by Chris Raschka. Schwartz & Wade. Ages 3–7. (Realism/wordless).

HONOR BOOKS

Blackout by John Rocco. Disney-Hyperion. Ages 4–8. (Realism).

Grandpa Green by Lane Smith. Roaring Brook. Ages 5–11. (Realism).

Me . . . Jane by Patrick McDonnell. Little, Brown. Ages 5–8. (Biography).

2011 *A Sick Day for Amos McGee* by Philip C. Stead. Illustrated by Erin E. Stead. Roaring Brook. Ages 3–8. (Animal fantasy).

HONOR BOOKS

Dave the Potter: Artist, Poet, Slave by Laban Carrick Hill. Illustrated by Bryan Collier. Little, Brown. Ages 6–10. (Biography).

Interrupting Chicken by David Ezra Stein. Candlewick Press. Ages 4–6. (Animal fantasy).

2010 *The Lion & the Mouse* by Jerry Pinkney. Little, Brown. Ages 3–8. (Folklore).

HONOR BOOKS

All the World, by Liz Garton Scanlon. Illustrated by Marla Frazee. Beach Lane Books. Ages 3–7. (Poetry).

Red Sings from Treetops: A Year in Colors, by Joyce Sidman. Illustrated by Pamela Zagarenski. Houghton Mifflin Books for Children. Ages 4–8. (Poetry).

2009 *The House in the Night* by Susan Marie Swanson. Illustrated by Beth Krommes. Houghton Mifflin. Ages 3–5. (Fantasy).

HONOR BOOKS

A Couple of Boys Have the Best Week Ever by Marla Frazee. Harcourt. Ages 5–8. (Realism).

How I Learned Geography by Uri Shulevitz. Farrar. Ages 5–8. (Mixed genre).

A River of Words: The Story of William Carlos Williams by Jen Bryant. Illustrated by Melissa Sweet. Eerdmans. Ages 3-5. (Biography).

2008   *The Invention of Hugo Cabret* by Brian Selznick. Scholastic. Ages 8–12. (Fantasy, novel-length).

HONOR BOOKS

Henry's Freedom Box: A True Story from the Underground Railroad by Ellen Levine. Illustrated by Kadir Nelson. Scholastic. Ages 7–10. (Biography [1849], multicultural [African-American]).

First the Egg by Laura Vaccaro Seeger. Roaring Brook. Ages 3–5. (Pattern, concept, easy-to-read, toy book).

The Wall: Growing Up Behind the Iron Curtain by Peter Sís. Farrar. Ages 8–14. (Autobiography, partial graphic novel).

Knuffle Bunny Too: A Case of Mistaken Identity by Mo Willems. Hyperion. Ages 3–6. (Realism).

2007   *Flotsam* by David Wiesner. Clarion. Ages 5–9. (Fantasy, wordless).

HONOR BOOKS

Gone Wild: An Endangered Animal Alphabet by David McLimans. Walker. Ages 8–14. (ABC, nonfiction).

Moses: When Harriet Tubman Led Her People to Freedom by Carole Boston Weatherford. Illustrated by Kadir Nelson. Hyperion/Jump at the Sun. Ages 7–11. (Biography).

2006   *The Hello, Goodbye Window* by Norton Juster. Illustrated by Chris Raschka. Hyperion. Ages 4–7. (Realism).

HONOR BOOKS

Rosa by Nikki Giovanni. Illustrated by Bryan Collier. Holt. Ages 8–11. (Biography).

Zen Shorts by Jon J. Muth. Scholastic. Ages 5–9. (Traditional, religious).

Hot Air: The (Mostly) True Story of the First Hot-Air Balloon Ride by Marjorie Priceman. Atheneum. Ages 4–8. (Historical fiction [1783]).

Song of the Water Boatman and Other Pond Poems by Joyce Sidman. Illustrated by Beckie Prange. Houghton. Ages 7–12. (Poetry).

2005   *Kitten's First Full Moon* by Kevin Henkes. Greenwillow. Ages 3–5. (Animal fantasy).

HONOR BOOKS

The Red Book by Barbara Lehman. Houghton. Ages 4–9. (Fantasy, wordless).

Coming on Home Soon by Jacqueline Woodson. Illustrated by E. B. Lewis. Putnam. Ages 5–8. (Historical fiction [rural United States, World War II]).

Knuffle Bunny: A Cautionary Tale by Mo Willems. Hyperion. Ages 3–6. (Realism).

2004   *The Man Who Walked between the Towers* by Mordecai Gerstein. Roaring Brook/Millbrook. Ages 5–9. (Realism).

HONOR BOOKS

Ella Sarah Gets Dressed by Margaret Chodos-Irvine. Harcourt. Ages 3–5. (Realism).

What Do You Do with a Tail Like This? by Steve Jenkins and Robin Page. Houghton Mifflin. Ages 4–7. (Informational).

Don't Let the Pigeon Drive the Bus! by Mo Willems. Hyperion. Ages 4–7. (Fantasy).

2003   *My Friend Rabbit* by Eric Rohmann. Roaring Brook/Millbrook. Ages 4–8. (Animal fantasy).

HONOR BOOKS

The Spider and the Fly by Mary Howitt. Illustrated by Tony DiTerlizzi. Simon & Schuster. Ages 6–12. (Poetry).

Hondo and Fabian by Peter McCarty. Holt. Ages 3–6. (Realism).

Noah's Ark by Jerry Pinkney. SeaStar/North-South. Ages 6–10. (Traditional).

2002   *The Three Pigs* by David Wiesner. Clarion/Houghton Mifflin. Ages 5–7. (Traditional).

HONOR BOOKS

The Dinosaurs of Waterhouse Hawkins by Barbara Kerley. Illustrated by Brian Selznick. Scholastic. Ages 7–10. (Informational).

Martin's Big Words: The Life of Dr. Martin Luther King, Jr. by Doreen Rappaport. Illustrated by Bryan Collier. Hyperion. Ages 5–9. (Biography).

The Stray Dog by Marc Simont. HarperCollins. Ages 4–7. (Realism).

2001 *So You Want to Be President?* by Judith St. George. Illustrated by David Small. Philomel. Ages 7–10. (Informational, biography).

HONOR BOOKS

Casey at the Bat: A Ballad of the Republic Sung in the Year 1888 by Ernest L. Thayer. Illustrated by Christopher Bing. Handprint. Ages 7–12. (Poetry).

Click, Clack, Moo: Cows That Type by Doreen Cronin. Illustrated by Betsy Lewin. Simon & Schuster. Ages 6–9. (Animal fantasy).

Olivia by Ian Falconer. Atheneum. Ages 4–8. (Animal fantasy).

2000 *Joseph Had a Little Overcoat* by Simms Taback. Viking. Ages 4–7. (Traditional, pattern).

HONOR BOOKS

When Sophie Gets Angry—Really, Really Angry . . . by Molly Bang. Scholastic. Ages 4–6. (Realism).

A Child's Calendar by John Updike. Illustrated by Trina Schart Hyman. Holiday. Ages 5–9. (Poetry).

The Ugly Duckling adapted and illustrated by Jerry Pinkney. Morrow. Ages 4–7. (Modern folktale).

Sector 7 by David Wiesner. Clarion. Ages 5–9. (Modern fantasy, wordless).

1999 *Snowflake Bentley* by Jacqueline Briggs Martin. Illustrated by Mary Azarian. Houghton. Ages 8–12. (Biography).

HONOR BOOKS

Duke Ellington: The Piano Prince and His Orchestra by Andrea Davis Pinkney. Illustrated by Brian Pinkney. Hyperion. Ages 8–10. (Biography).

No, David! by David Shannon. Scholastic. Ages 3–5. (Realism, pattern).

Snow by Uri Shulevitz. Farrar. Ages 4–6. (Realism).

Tibet through the Red Box by Peter Sís. Farrar. Ages 7 and up. (Biography, magic realism).

1998 *Rapunzel* by Paul O. Zelinsky. Dutton. Ages 7–10. (Traditional).

HONOR BOOKS

The Gardener by Sarah Stewart. Illustrated by David Small. Farrar. Ages 7–10. (Realism).

Harlem by Walter Dean Myers. Illustrated by Christopher Myers. Scholastic. Ages 10–14. (Poetry).

There Was an Old Lady Who Swallowed a Fly by Simms Taback. Viking. Ages 5–7. (Folk poem, engineered).

1997 *Golem* by David Wisniewski. Clarion. Ages 6–12. (Traditional).

HONOR BOOKS

Hush! A Thai Lullaby by Minfong Ho. Illustrated by Holly Meade. Orchard. Ages 2–6. (Poetry).

The Graphic Alphabet by David Pelletier. Orchard. Ages 7–10. (ABC, art).

The Paperboy by Dav Pilkey. Orchard. Ages 8–10. (Realism).

Starry Messenger by Peter Sís. Farrar. Ages 9–14. (Biography).

1996 *Officer Buckle and Gloria* by Peggy Rathmann. Putnam. Ages 5–7. (Animal fantasy).

HONOR BOOKS

Alphabet City by Stephen T. Johnson. Viking. Ages 7–9. (Concept).

The Faithful Friend by Robert D. San Souci. Illustrated by Brian Pinkney. Simon & Schuster. Ages 10–14. (Traditional).

Tops & Bottoms by Janet Stevens. Harcourt. Ages 6–8. (Traditional).

Zin! Zin! Zin! A Violin by Lloyd Moss. Illustrated by Marjorie Priceman. Simon & Schuster. Ages 5–7. (Concept).

1995 *Smoky Night* by Eve Bunting. Illustrated by David Diaz. Harcourt. Ages 6–8. (Realism, multicultural).

HONOR BOOKS

Swamp Angel by Anne Isaacs. Illustrated by Paul O. Zelinsky. Dutton. Ages 6–9. (Modern folktale).

John Henry by Julius Lester. Illustrated by Jerry Pinkney. Dial. Ages 6–9. (Traditional).

Time Flies by Eric Rohmann. Crown. Ages 6–9. (Wordless).

1994 *Grandfather's Journey* by Allen Say. Houghton. Ages 7–9. (Biography).

HONOR BOOKS

Peppe the Lamplighter by Elisa Bartone. Illustrated by Ted Lewin. Lothrop. Ages 7–9. (Realism).

In the Small, Small Pond by Denise Fleming. Holt. Ages 5–7. (Pattern).

Owen by Kevin Henkes. Greenwillow. Ages 5–7. (Animal fantasy).

Raven: A Trickster Tale from the Pacific Northwest by Gerald McDermott. Harcourt. Ages 7–9. (Traditional, Native American).

Yo! Yes? by Chris Raschka. Orchard. Ages 5–7. (Realism, multicultural).

1993 *Mirette on the High Wire* by Emily Arnold McCully. Putnam. Ages 7–9. (Realism).

HONOR BOOKS

Seven Blind Mice by Ed Young. Philomel. Ages 6–10. (Modern folktale).

The Stinky Cheese Man and Other Fairly Stupid Tales by Jon Scieszka and Lane Smith. Illustrated by Lane Smith. Viking. Ages 7–11. (Modern folktales).

Working Cotton by Sherley Anne Williams. Illustrated by Carole Byard. Harcourt. Ages 7–9. (Realism, African-American).

1992 *Tuesday* by David Wiesner. Clarion. Ages 7–10. (Fantasy, wordless).

HONOR BOOKS

Tar Beach by Faith Ringgold. Crown. Ages 6–9. (Multicultural, African-American).

1991 *Black and White* by David Macaulay. Houghton. Ages 8–12. (Mystery).

HONOR BOOKS

Puss in Boots by Charles Perrault. Illustrated by Fred Marcellino. Farrar. Ages 5–7. (Traditional).

"More, More, More," Said the Baby: 3 Love Stories by Vera Williams. Greenwillow. Ages 3–5. (Realism).

Newbery Medal

This award, established in 1922 and sponsored by the Association for Library Service to Children division of the American Library Association, is given to the author of the most distinguished contribution to children's literature published during the preceding year. Only U.S. citizens or residents are eligible for this award. Award winners and honor books since 1991 are listed here. For the complete list of winners and honor books, go to www.ala.org/ala/mgrps /divs/alsc/awardsgrants/bookmedia/newberyhonors /newberymedal.cfm.

2012 *Dead End in Norvelt* by Jack Gantos. Farrar Straus Giroux. Ages 8–14. (Historical fiction).

HONOR BOOKS

Inside Out & Back Again by Thanhha Lai. HarperCollins Children's Books. Ages 8–12. (Historical fiction).

Breaking Stalin's Nose by Eugene Yelchin. Henry Holt. Ages 9–12. (Historical fiction).

2011 *Moon over Manifest* by Clare Vanderpool. Delacorte. Ages 11–16. (Historical fiction).

HONOR BOOKS

Turtle in Paradise by Jennifer L. Holm. Random House Children's Books. Ages 11–14. (Historical fiction).

Heart of a Samurai by Margi Preus. Amulet Books. Ages 10–14. (Historical fiction).

Dark Emperor and Other Poems of the Night by Joyce Sidman. Illustrated by Rick Allen. Houghton Mifflin Books for Children. Ages 6–10. (Poetry).

One Crazy Summer by Rita Williams-Garcia. Amistad. Ages 9–12. (Historical fiction).

2010 *When You Reach Me* by Rebecca Stead. Wendy Lamb Books. Ages 9–14. (Fantasy).

HONOR BOOKS

Claudette Colvin: Twice Toward Justice by Phillip Hoose. Melanie Kroupa Books. Ages 11–15. (Biography).

The Evolution of Calpurnia Tate by Jacqueline Kelly. Henry Holt. Ages 9–12. (Historical fiction).

Where the Mountain Meets the Moon by Grace Lin. Little, Brown and Company Books for Young Readers. Ages 8–11. (Fantasy).

The Mostly True Adventures of Homer P. Figg by Rodman Philbrick. Blue Sky Press. Ages 9–12. (Historical fiction).

2009 *The Graveyard Book* by Neil Gaiman. Illustrated by Dave McKean. HarperCollins. Ages 10–14. (Fantasy).

HONOR BOOKS

The Underneath by Kathi Appelt. Illustrated by David Small. Atheneum. Ages 9–13. (Animal fantasy).

The Surrender Tree: Poems of Cuba's Struggle for Freedom by Margarita Engle. Holt. Ages 11–18. (Poetry).

Savvy by Ingrid Law. Dial. Ages 10–12. (Fantasy).

After Tupac & D Foster by Jacqueline Woodson. Putnam. Ages 11–14. (Realism, multicultural [African-American]).

2008 *Good Masters! Sweet Ladies! Voices from a Medieval Village* by Laura Amy Schlitz. Candlewick. Ages 9–13. (Informational).

HONOR BOOKS

Elijah of Buxton by Christopher Paul Curtis. Scholastic. Ages 9–13. (Historical fiction [mid-eighteenth-century Ontario], multicultural [African-American]).

The Wednesday Wars by Gary D. Schmidt. Clarion. Ages 10–13. (Realism).

Feathers by Jacqueline Woodson. Putnam. Ages 9–12. (Historical fiction [1971]).

2007 *The Higher Power of Lucky* by Susan Patron. Illustrated by Matt Phelan. Simon & Schuster. Ages 9–12. (Realism).

HONOR BOOKS

Penny from Heaven by Jennifer L. Holm. Random House. Ages 11–14. (Mixed genre: realism/autobiography/historical fiction [Brooklyn, 1953]).

Hattie Big Sky by Kirby Larson. Delacorte. Ages 12–16. (Historical fiction [Montana, 1918]).

Rules by Cynthia Lord. Scholastic. Ages 9–13. (Realism, special challenges [autism]).

2006 *Criss Cross* by Lynne Rae Perkins. Greenwillow. Ages 12–15. (Realism).

HONOR BOOKS

Whittington by Alan Armstrong. Illustrated by S. D. Schindler. Random House. Ages 9–14. (Traditional, animal fantasy, special challenges [dyslexia]).

Hitler Youth: Growing Up in Hitler's Shadow by Susan Campbell Bartoletti. Scholastic. Ages 11–15. (Collected biography).

Princess Academy by Shannon Hale. Bloomsbury. Ages 12–14. (Modern fantasy).

Show Way by Jacqueline Woodson. Illustrated by Hudson Talbott. Putnam. Ages 7–12. (Multicultural [African-American]).

2005 *Kira-Kira* by Cynthia Kadohata. Atheneum. Ages 11–14. (Historical fiction [Georgia, 1950s], multicultural [Japanese-American]).

HONOR BOOKS

Al Capone Does My Shirts by Gennifer Choldenko. Putnam. Ages 11–14. (Realism, special challenges [autism]).

The Voice That Challenged a Nation: Marian Anderson and the Struggle for Equal Rights by Russell Freedman. Clarion. Ages 11–14. (Photobiography).

Lizzie Bright and the Buckminster Boy by Gary D. Schmidt. Clarion. Ages 13–16. (Historical fiction [Maine, 1912]).

2004 *The Tale of Despereaux: Being the Story of a Mouse, a Princess, Some Soup, and a Spool of Thread* by Kate DiCamillo. Illustrated by Timothy Basil Ering. Candlewick. Ages 5–8. (Modern fantasy).

HONOR BOOKS

Olive's Ocean by Kevin Henkes. Greenwillow. Ages 9–12. (Realism).

An American Plague: The True and Terrifying Story of the Yellow Fever Epidemic of 1793 by Jim Murphy. Clarion. Ages 9–14. (Informational).

2003 *Crispin: The Cross of Lead* by Avi. Hyperion. Ages 8–12. (Modern fantasy).

HONOR BOOKS

The House of the Scorpion by Nancy Farmer. Atheneum. Ages 11–14. (Modern fantasy).

Pictures of Hollis Woods by Patricia Reilly Giff. Random House. Ages 10–13. (Realism).

Hoot by Carl Hiaasen. Knopf. Ages 9–12. (Realism).

A Corner of the Universe by Ann M. Martin. Scholastic. Ages 11–14. (Realism).

Surviving the Applewhites by Stephanie S. Tolan. HarperCollins. Ages 12–16. (Realism).

2002 *A Single Shard* by Linda Sue Park. Clarion/Houghton. Ages 10–14. (Realism).

HONOR BOOKS

Everything on a Waffle by Polly Horvath. Farrar. Ages 12–14. (Realism).

Carver: A Life in Poems by Marilyn Nelson. Front Street. Ages 12–14. (Poetry, biography).

2001 *A Year Down Yonder* by Richard Peck. Dial. Ages 10–14. (Historical fiction [United States, 1930s]).

HONOR BOOKS

Because of Winn-Dixie by Kate DiCamillo. Candlewick. Ages 8–12. (Animal realism).

Hope Was Here by Joan Bauer. Putnam. Ages 12–14. (Realism).

Joey Pigza Loses Control by Jack Gantos. Farrar. Ages 9–12. (Realism).

The Wanderer by Sharon Creech. HarperCollins. Ages 12–14. (Realism).

2000 *Bud, Not Buddy* by Christopher Paul Curtis. Delacorte. Ages 9–12. (Multicultural [African-American]).

HONOR BOOKS

Getting Near to Baby by Audrey Couloumbis. Putnam. Ages 10–12. (Realism).

26 Fairmount Avenue by Tomie dePaola. Putnam. Ages 7–9. (Biography).

Our Only May Amelia by Jennifer L. Holm. HarperCollins. Ages 10–14. (Historical fiction [United States, 1899]).

1999 *Holes* by Louis Sachar. Farrar. Ages 10–13. (Realism).

HONOR BOOKS

A Long Way from Chicago by Richard Peck. Dial. Ages 9–12. (Historical fiction [United States, 1930s]).

1998 *Out of the Dust* by Karen Hesse. Scholastic. Ages 13–16. (Historical fiction [United States, 1920–1934]).

HONOR BOOKS

Lily's Crossing by Patricia Reilly Giff. Delacorte. Ages 9–11. (Historical fiction [United States, 1944]).

Ella Enchanted by Gail Carson Levine. HarperCollins. Ages 9–12. (Modern fantasy).

Wringer by Jerry Spinelli. HarperCollins. Ages 9–12. (Realism).

1997 *The View from Saturday* by E. L. Konigsburg. Atheneum. Ages 9–12. (Realism).

HONOR BOOKS

A Girl Named Disaster by Nancy Farmer. Orchard. Ages 12–14. (Realism, multicultural [Mozambique/Zimbabwe]).

The Moorchild by Eloise McGraw. McElderry/Simon & Schuster. Ages 9–12. (Modern fantasy).

The Thief by Megan Whalen Turner. Greenwillow. Ages 12–16. (Modern fantasy).

Belle Prater's Boy by Ruth White. Farrar. Ages 10–12. (Realism).

1996 *The Midwife's Apprentice* by Karen Cushman. Clarion. Ages 10–14. (Historical fiction [England, 1200s]).

HONOR BOOKS

The Great Fire by Jim Murphy. Scholastic. Ages 9–13. (Informational).

The Watsons Go to Birmingham—1963 by Christopher Paul Curtis. Delacorte. Ages 10–14. (Historical fiction [Southern United States, 1960s; African-American]).

What Jamie Saw by Carolyn Coman. Front Street. Ages 10–14. (Realism).

Yolanda's Genius by Carol Fenner. McElderry. Ages 10–14. (Realism, multicultural [African-American]).

1995 *Walk Two Moons* by Sharon Creech. HarperCollins. Ages 11–14. (Realism, Native American).

HONOR BOOKS

Catherine, Called Birdy by Karen Cushman. Clarion. Ages 10–14. (Historical fiction [England, 1200s]).

The Ear, the Eye, and the Arm by Nancy Farmer. Orchard. Ages 10–13. (Modern fantasy).

1994 *The Giver* by Lois Lowry. Houghton. Ages 10–12. (Modern fantasy).

HONOR BOOKS

Crazy Lady by Jane Leslie Conly. HarperCollins. Ages 10–12. (Realism).

Dragon's Gate by Laurence Yep. HarperCollins. Ages 12–14. (Historical fiction [China, western United States, 1860s]).

Eleanor Roosevelt: A Life of Discovery by Russell Freedman. Clarion. Ages 10–14. (Biography).

1993 *Missing May* by Cynthia Rylant. Orchard. Ages 10–13. (Realism).

HONOR BOOKS

The Dark-Thirty: Southern Tales of the Supernatural by Patricia McKissack. Knopf. Ages 8–12. (Modern fantasy, ghost stories, multicultural [African-American]).

Somewhere in the Darkness by Walter Dean Myers. Scholastic. Ages 11–14. (Realism, multicultural [African-American]).

What Hearts by Bruce Brooks. HarperCollins. Ages 11–14. (Realism).

1992 *Shiloh* by Phyllis Reynolds Naylor. Atheneum. Ages 8–10. (Animal realism).

HONOR BOOKS

Nothing but the Truth by Avi. Orchard. Ages 10–14. (Realism).

The Wright Brothers: How They Invented the Airplane by Russell Freedman. Holiday. Ages 9–12. (Informational, biography).

1991 *Maniac Magee* by Jerry Spinelli. Little, Brown. Ages 9–13. (Realism).

HONOR BOOK

The True Confessions of Charlotte Doyle by Avi. Orchard. Ages 10–13. (Historical fiction [England, United States, 1830]).

Boston Globe–Horn Book Awards

These awards, established in 1967 and sponsored by *the Boston Globe* and *Horn Book Magazine,* are given to an author for outstanding fiction or poetry for children, to an illustrator for outstanding illustration in a children's book, and, since 1976, to an author for outstanding nonfiction for children. Award winners and honor books since 1991 are listed here. For the

complete list of award winners, go to http://archive
.hbook.com/bghb/past/past.asp.

2012 FICTION: *No Crystal Stair: A Documentary
Novel of the Life and Work of Lewis
Michaux, Harlem Bookseller* by Vaunda
Micheaux Nelson. Illustrated by R. Gregory
Christie. Carolrhoda Lab.

NONFICTION: *Chuck Close: Face Book,* by
Chuck Close. Abrams Books for Young Readers.

ILLUSTRATION: *Extra Yarn* by Mac Barnett.
Illustrated by Jon Klassen. Balzer + Bray.

2011 FICTION: *Blink & Caution* by Tim Wynne-
Jones. Candlewick.

NONFICTION: *The Notorious Benedict
Arnold: A True Story of Adventure, Heroism,
& Treachery* by Steve Sheinkin. Flash Point/
Roaring Brook.

ILLUSTRATION: *Pocketful of Posies: A
Treasury of Nursery Rhymes* by Salley Mavor.
Houghton.

NONFICTION: *Talking with Artists* by Pat
Cummings. Bradbury.

ILLUSTRATION: *Seven Blind Mice* by Ed
Young. Philomel.

2010 FICTION: *When You Reach Me* by Rebecca
Stead. Random House.

NONFICTION: *Marching for Freedom* by
Elizabeth Partridge. Vikinge.

ILLUSTRATION: *I Know Here* by
Laurel Croza. Illustrated by Matt James.
Groundwood.

2009 FICTION: *Nation* by Terry Pratchett.
HarperCollins.

NONFICTION: *The Lincolns: A Scrapbook
Look at Abraham and Mary* by Candace
Fleming. Random House.

ILLUSTRATION: *Bubble Trouble* by Margaret
Mahy. Illustrated by Polly Dunbar. Clarion.

2008 FICTION AND POETRY: *The Absolutely
True Diary of a Part-Time Indian* by
Sherman Alexie. Little, Brown.

NONFICTION: *The Wall: Growing Up
Behind the Iron Curtain* by Peter Sís. Farrar.

ILLUSTRATION: *At Night* by Jonathan Bean.
Farrar.

2007 FICTION AND POETRY: *The Astonishing
Life of Octavian Nothing, Traitor to the
Nation, Volume I: The Pox Party* by M. T.
Anderson. Candlewick.

NONFICTION: *The Strongest Man in
the World: Louis Cyr* by Nicolas Debon.
Groundwood.

ILLUSTRATION: *Dog and Bear: Two
Friends, Three Stories* by Laura Vaccaro
Seeger. Roaring Brook.

2006 FICTION AND POETRY: *The Miraculous
Journey of Edward Tulane* by Kate DiCamillo.
Illustrated by Bagram Ibatoulline. Candlewick.

NONFICTION: *If You Decide to Go to the
Moon* by Faith McNulty. Illustrated by Steven
Kellogg. Scholastic.

ILLUSTRATION: *Leaf Man* by Lois Ehlert.
Harcourt.

2005 FICTION AND POETRY: *The Schwa Was
Here* by Neal Schusterman. Dutton.

NONFICTION: *The Race to Save the Lord
God Bird* by Phillip Hoose. Farrar.

ILLUSTRATION: *Traction Man Is Here!* by
Mini Grey. Knopf.

2004 FICTION AND POETRY: *The Fire-Eaters* by
David Almond. Delacorte.

NONFICTION: *An American Plague: The
True and Terrifying Story of the Yellow Fever
Epidemic of 1793* by Jim Murphy. Clarion.

ILLUSTRATION: *The Man Who Walked
between the Towers* by Mordicai Gerstein.
Roaring Brook.

2003 FICTION AND POETRY: *The Jamie and
Angus Stories* by Anne Fine. Illustrated by
Penny Dale. Candlewick.

NONFICTION: *Fireboat: The Heroic
Adventures of the John J. Harvey* by Maira
Kalman. Putnam.

ILLUSTRATION: *Big Momma Makes the World* by Phyllis Root. Illustrated by Helen Oxenbury. Candlewick.

2002 FICTION AND POETRY: *Lord of the Deep* by Graham Salisbury. Delacorte.

NONFICTION: *This Land Was Made for You and Me: The Life and Songs of Woody Guthrie* by Elizabeth Partridge. Viking.

ILLUSTRATION: *"Let's Get a Pup!" Said Kate* by Bob Graham. Candlewick.

2001 FICTION AND POETRY: *Carver: A Life in Poems* by Marilyn Nelson. Front Street.

NONFICTION: *The Longitude Prize* by Joan Dash. Illustrated by Dušan Petricic. Farrar.

ILLUSTRATION: *Cold Feet* by Cynthia DeFelice. Illustrated by Robert Andrew Parker. DK Ink.

2000 FICTION: *The Folk Keeper* by Franny Billingsley. Atheneum.

NONFICTION: *Sir Walter Ralegh and the Quest for El Dorado* by Marc Aronson. Clarion.

ILLUSTRATION: *Henry Hikes to Fitchburg* by D. B. Johnson. Houghton.

1999 FICTION: *Holes* by Louis Sachar. Farrar.

NONFICTION: *The Top of the World: Climbing Mount Everest* by Steve Jenkins. Houghton.

ILLUSTRATION: *Red-Eyed Tree Frog* by Joy Cowley. Illustrated with photographs by Nic Bishop. Scholastic.

1998 FICTION: *The Circuit: Stories from the Life of a Migrant Child* by Francisco Jiménez. University of New Mexico Press.

NONFICTION: *Leon's Story* by Leon Walter Tillage. Illustrated by Susan L. Roth. Farrar.

ILLUSTRATION: *And If the Moon Could Talk* by Kate Banks. Illustrated by Georg Hallensleben. Farrar.

1997 FICTION: *The Friends* by Kazumi Yumoto. Farrar.

NONFICTION: *A Drop of Water: A Book of Science and Wonder* by Walter Wick. Scholastic.

ILLUSTRATION: *The Adventures of Sparrow Boy* by Brian Pinkney. Simon & Schuster.

1996 FICTION: *Poppy* by Avi. Illustrated by Brian Floca. Orchard.

NONFICTION: *Orphan Train Rider: One Boy's True Story* by Andrea Warren. Houghton.

ILLUSTRATION: *In the Rain with Baby Duck* by Amy Hest. Illustrated by Jill Barton. Candlewick.

1995 FICTION: *Some of the Kinder Planets* by Tim Wynne-Jones. Orchard.

NONFICTION: *Abigail Adams: Witness to a Revolution* by Natalie S. Bober. Atheneum.

ILLUSTRATION: *John Henry* retold by Julius Lester. Illustrated by Jerry Pinkney. Dial.

1994 FICTION: *Scooter* by Vera B. Williams. Greenwillow.

NONFICTION: *Eleanor Roosevelt: A Life of Discovery* by Russell Freedman. Clarion.

ILLUSTRATION: *Grandfather's Journey* by Allen Say. Houghton.

1993 FICTION: *Ajeemah and His Son* by James Berry. Harper.

NONFICTION: *Sojourner Truth: Ain't I a Woman?* by Patricia and Fredrick McKissack. Scholastic.

ILLUSTRATION: *The Fortune-Tellers* by Lloyd Alexander. Illustrated by Trina Schart Hyman. Dutton.

1992 FICTION: *Missing May* by Cynthia Rylant. Orchard.

NONFICTION: *Talking with Artists* by Pat Cummings. Bradbury.

ILLUSTRATION: *Seven Blind Mice* by Ed Young. Philomel.

1991 FICTION: *The True Confessions of Charlotte Doyle* by Avi. Orchard.

NONFICTION: *Appalachia: The Voices of Sleeping Birds* by Cynthia Rylant. Illustrated by Barry Moser. Harcourt.

ILLUSTRATION: *The Tale of the Mandarin Ducks* retold by Katherine Paterson. Illustrated by Leo and Diane Dillon. Lodestar.

National Book Award for Young People's Literature

This award, sponsored by the National Book Foundation, is presented annually to recognize the outstanding contribution to children's literature, in terms of literary merit, published during the previous year. The award committee considers books of all genres written for children and young adults by U.S. writers. The award carries a $10,000 cash prize.

2011 *Inside Out & Back Again* by Thanhha Lai. Harper.

2010 *Mockingbird* by Kathryn Erskine. Philomel Books.

2009 *Claudette Colvin: Twice Toward Justice* by Phillip Hoose. Farrar, Straus and Giroux.

2008 *What I Saw and How I Lied* by Judy Blundell. Scholastic.

2007 *The Absolutely True Diary of a Part-Time Indian* by Sherman Alexie. Little, Brown.

2006 *The Astonishing Life of Octavian Nothing, Traitor to the Nation, Vol. 1: The Pox Party* by M. T. Anderson. Candlewick.

2005 *The Penderwicks* by Jeanne Birdsall. Knopf.

2004 *Godless* by Pete Hautman. Simon & Schuster.

2003 *The Canning Season* by Polly Horvath. Farrar.

2002 *The House of the Scorpion* by Nancy Farmer. Atheneum.

2001 *True Believer* by Virginia Euwer Wolff. Atheneum.

2000 *Homeless Bird* by Gloria Whelan. HarperCollins.

1999 *When Zachary Beaver Came to Town* by Kimberley Willis Holt. Holt.

Great Britain

Kate Greenaway Medal

This award, established in 1955 by the Chartered Institute of Library and Information Professionals, is given to the illustrator of the most distinguished work in illustration in a children's book first published in the United Kingdom during the preceding year. Award winners since 1992 are listed here. The complete list is at www.carnegiegreenaway.org.uk/greenaway/full_list_of_winners.php.

2012 *A Monster Calls* by Jim Kay. Walker Books.

2011 *FArTHER* by Grahame Baker-Smith. Templar.

2010 *Harry & Hopper* by Freya Blackwood. Scholastic.

2009 *Harris Finds His Feet* by Catherine Rayner. Little Tiger Press.

2008 *Little Mouse's Big Book of Fears* by Emily Gravett. Macmillan.

2007 *The Adventures of the Dish and the Spoon* by Mini Grey. Jonathan Cape.

2006 *Wolves* by Emily Gravett. Macmillan.

2005 *Jonathan Swift's "Gulliver"* by Martin Jenkins. Illustrated by Chris Riddell. Walker.

2004 *Ella's Big Chance* by Shirley Hughes. Bodley Head.

2003 *Jethro Byrd—Fairy Child* by Bob Graham. Walker.

2002 *Pirate Diary* by Chris Riddell. Walker.

2001 *I Will Never Not Ever Eat a Tomato* by Lauren Child. Orchard.

2000 *Alice's Adventures in Wonderland* by Lewis Carroll. Illustrated by Helen Oxenbury. Walker.

1999 *Pumpkin Soup* by Helen Cooper. Farrar.

1998 *When Jessie Came Across the Sea* by Amy Hest. Illustrated by P. J. Lynch. Candlewick.

1997 *The Baby Who Wouldn't Go to Bed* by Helen Cooper. Doubleday.

1996 *The Christmas Miracle of Jonathon Toomey* by Susan Wojciechowski. Illustrated by P. J. Lynch. Walker.

1995 *Way Home* by Libby Hathorn. Illustrated by Gregory Rogers. Random House.

1994 *Black Ships before Troy* retold by Rosemary Sutcliff. Illustrated by Alan Lee. Frances Lincoln.

1993 *Zoo* by Anthony Browne. Julia MacRae.

1992 *The Jolly Christmas Postman* by Janet and Allan Ahlberg. Heinemann.

Carnegie Medal

This award, established in 1936 by the Chartered Institute of Library and Information Professionals, is given to the author of the most outstanding children's book first published in English in the United Kingdom during the preceding year. Award winners since 1992 are listed here. The complete list of winners is at www.carnegiegreenaway.org.uk/carnegie/full_list_of_winners.php.

2012 *A Monster Calls* by Patrick Ness. Walker Books.

2011 *Monsters of Men* by Patrick Ness. Walker Books.

2010 *The Graveyard Book* by Neil Gaiman. Bloomsbury.

2009 *Bog Child* by Siobhan Dowd. David Fickling.

2008 *Here Lies Arthur* by Philip Reeve. Scholastic.

2007 *Just in Case* by Meg Rosoff. Penguin.

2006 *Tamar* by Mal Peet. Walker.

2005 *Millions* by Frank Cottrell Boyce. Macmillan.

2004 *A Gathering Light* by Jennifer Donnelly. Bloomsbury.

2003 *Ruby Holler* by Sharon Creech. Bloomsbury/HarperCollins.

2002 *The Amazing Maurice and His Educated Rodents* by Terry Pratchett. Doubleday/HarperCollins.

2001 *The Other Side of Truth* by Beverly Naidoo. Puffin/HarperCollins.

2000 *Postcards from No Man's Land* by Aidan Chambers. Bodley Head.

1999 *Skellig* by David Almond. Delacorte.

1998 *River Boy* by Tim Bowler. Oxford.

1997 *Junk* by Melvin Burgess. Andersen.

1996 *His Dark Materials: Book 1, Northern Lights* by Philip Pullman. Scholastic.

1995 *Whispers in the Graveyard* by Theresa Bresling. Methuen.

1994 *Stone Cold* by Robert Swindells. Hamish Hamilton.

1993 *Flour Babies* by Anne Fine. Hamish Hamilton.

1992 *Dear Nobody* by Berlie Doherty. Hamish Hamilton.

Canada

The Governor General's Literary Awards

The Governor General's Literary Awards were inaugurated in 1937, with prizes for children's literature (text and illustration) added in 1987. The Canada Council for the Arts administers the awards and added prizes for books written in French. The current prize to winners in each category—$15,000—dates from 2000. In addition, publishers of the winning books receive $3,000 to assist with promotion.

2011 ILLUSTRATION: *Ten Birds* by Cybèle Young. Kids Can.

TEXT: *From Then to Now: A Short History of the World* by Christopher Moore. Illustrated by Andrej Krystoforski. Tundra Books.

2010 ILLUSTRATION: *Cats' Night Out* by Caroline Stutson. Illustrated by Jon Klassen. Simon & Schuster Books for Young Readers.

TEXT: *Fishtailing* by Wendy Phillips. Coteau Books.

2009 ILLUSTRATION: *Bella's Tree* by Janet Russell. Illustrated by Jirina Marton. Groundwood Books.

TEXT: *Greener Grass: The Famine Years* by Caroline Pignat. Red Deer Press.

2008 ILLUSTRATION: *The Owl and the Pussycat* by Edward Lear. Illustrated by Stéphane Jorisch. Kids Can.

TEXT: *The Landing* by John Ibbitson. Kids Can.

2007 ILLUSTRATION: *The Painted Circus* by Wallace Edwards. Kids Can.

TEXT: *Carnation, Lily, Lily, Rose: The Story of a Painting* by Hugh Brewster. Kids Can.

2006 ILLUSTRATION: *Ancient Thunder* by Leo Yerxa. Groundwood.

TEXT: *Pirate's Passage* by William Gilkerson. Trumpeter.

2005 ILLUSTRATION: *Imagine a Day* by Sarah L. Thomson. Illustrated by Rob Gonsalves. Atheneum.

TEXT: *The Crazy Man* by Pamela Porter. Groundwood.

2004 ILLUSTRATION: *Jabberwocky* by Lewis Carroll. Illustrated by Stéphane Jorisch. Kids Can.

TEXT: *Airborn* by Kenneth Oppel. HarperCollins.

2003 ILLUSTRATION: *The Song within My Heart* by Dave Bouchard. Illustrated by Allen Sapp. Raincoast.

TEXT: *Stitches* by Glen Huser. Groundwood.

2002 ILLUSTRATION: *Alphabeasts* by Wallace Edwards. Kids Can.

TEXT: *True Confessions of a Heartless Girl* by Martha Brooks. Groundwood.

2001 ILLUSTRATION: *An Island in the Soup* by Mireille Levert. Groundwood.

TEXT: *Dust* by Arthur Slade. HarperCollins Canada.

2000 ILLUSTRATION: *Yuck, a Love Story* by Don Gillmore. Illustrated by Marie-Louise Gay. Stoddart Kids.

TEXT: *Looking for X* by Deborah Ellis. Groundwood.

1999 ILLUSTRATION: *The Great Poochini* by Gary Clement. Groundwood.

TEXT: *A Screaming Kind of Day* by Rachna Gilmore. Fitzhenry & Whiteside.

1998 ILLUSTRATION: *A Child's Treasury of Nursery Rhymes* by Kady MacDonald Denton. Kids Can.

TEXT: *The Hollow Tree* by Janet Lunn. Knopf Canada.

1997 ILLUSTRATION: *The Party* by Barbara Reid. Scholastic Canada.

TEXT: *Awake and Dreaming* by Kit Pearson. Viking.

1996 ILLUSTRATION: *The Rooster's Gift* by Pam Conrad. Illustrated by Eric Beddows. Groundwood.

TEXT: *Ghost Train* by Paul Yee. Groundwood.

1995 ILLUSTRATION: *The Last Quest of Gilgamesh* by Ludmila Zeman, reteller. Tundra.

TEXT: *The Maestro* by Tim Wynne-Jones. Groundwood.

1994 ILLUSTRATION: *Josepha: A Prairie Boy's Story* by Jim McGugen. Illustrated by Murray Kimber. Red Deer College Press.

TEXT: *Adam and Eve and Pinch-Me* by Julie Johnston. Lester.

1993 ILLUSTRATION: *Sleep Tight, Mrs. Ming* by Sharon Jennings. Illustrated by Mireille Levert. Annick.

TEXT: *Some of the Kinder Planets* by Tim Wynne-Jones. Groundwood.

1992 ILLUSTRATION: *Waiting for the Whales* by Sheryl McFarlane. Illustrated by Ron Lightburn. Orca.

TEXT: *Hero of Lesser Causes* by Julie Johnston. Lester.

1991 ILLUSTRATION: *Doctor Kiss Says Yes* by Teddy Jam. Illustrated by Joanne Fitzgerald. Groundwood.

TEXT: *Pick-Up Sticks* by Sarah Ellis. Groundwood.

1990 ILLUSTRATION: *The Orphan Boy* by Tololwa Mollel. Illustrated by Paul Morin. Oxford.

TEXT: *Redwork* by Michael Bedard. Lester & Orpen Dennys.

Australia

Australian Children's Books of the Year Awards

The Children's Book Council of Australia sponsors five awards for excellence in children's books: the Picture

Book of the Year Award (established in 1956); the Book of the Year for Early Childhood Award (established in 2001); the Book of the Year for Younger Readers Award (established in 1982); the Book of the Year for Older Readers Award (established in 1946); and the Eve Pownall Award for Information Books. Award winners since 1991 are listed here. For the complete list of winners, go to www.cbca.org.au/awardshistory.

Australian Picture Book of the Year Award
(May be for mature readers.)

2011 *Mirror* by Jeannie Baker. Walker Books.
      Hamlet by Nicki Greenberg. Allen & Unwin.

2010 *The Hero of Little Street* by Gregory Rogers. Allen & Unwin.

2009 *Collecting Colour* by Kylie Dunstan. Lothian.

2008 *Requiem for a Beast* by Matt Ottley. Lothian.

2007 *The Arrival* by Shaun Tan. Lothian.

2006 *The Short and Incredibly Happy Life of Riley* by Colin Thompson. Illustrated by Amy Lissiat [AKA Colin Thompson]. Lothian.

2005 *Are We There Yet? A Journey Around Australia* by Alison Lester. Viking.

2004 *Cat and Fish* by Joan Grant. Illustrated by Neal Curtis. Lothian.

2003 *In Flanders Fields* by Norman Jorgensen. Illustrated by Brian Harrison-Lever. Sandcastle.

2002 *An Ordinary Day* by Libby Gleeson. Illustrated by Armin Greder. Scholastic.

2001 *Fox* by Margaret Wild. Illustrated by Ron Brooks. Allen & Unwin.

2000 *Jenny Angel* by Margaret Wild. Illustrated by Anne Spudvilas. Penguin.

1999 *The Rabbits* by John Marsden. Illustrated by Shaun Tan. Lothian.

1998 *The Two Bullies* by Junko Morimoto. Translated by Isao Morimoto. Crown.

1997 *Not a Nibble* by Elizabeth Honey. Allen & Unwin.

1996 *The Hunt* by Narelle Oliver. Lothian.

1995 *The Watertower* by Gary Crew. Illustrated by Steven Woolman. Era.

1994 *First Light* by Gary Crew. Illustrated by Peter Gouldthorpe. Lothian.

1993 *Rose Meets Mr. Wintergarden* by Bob Graham. Viking/Penguin.

1992 *Window* by Jeannie Baker. Julia MacRae.

1991 *Greetings from Sandy Beach* by Bob Graham. Lothian.

Australian Book of the Year
for Early Childhood Award

2011 *Maudie and Bear* by Jan Ormerod. Illustrated by Blackwood, Freya. Little Hare Books.

2010 *Bear & Chook by the Sea* by Lisa Shanahan. Illustrated by Emma Quay. Lothian.

2009 *How to Heal a Broken Wing* by Bob Graham. Walker Books.

2008 *Pearl Barley and Charlie Parsley* by Aaron Blabey. Viking.

2007 *Amy & Louis* by Libby Gleeson. Illustrated by Freya Blackwood. Scholastic.

2006 *Annie's Chair* by Deborah Niland. Viking.

2005 *Where Is the Green Sheep?* by Mem Fox. Illustrated by Judy Horacek. Viking.

2004 *Grandpa and Thomas* by Pamela Allen. Viking.

2003 *A Year on Our Farm* by Penny Matthews. Omnibus/Scholastic Australia.

2002 *"Let's Get a Pup!" Said Kate* by Bob Graham. Walker/Candlewick.

Australian Children's Book of the Year
for Younger Readers Award

2011 *The Red Wind* by Isobelle Carmody. Viking.

2010 *Darius Bell and the Glitter Pool* by Odo Hirsch. Allen & Unwin.

2009 *Perry Angel's Suitcase* by Glenda Millard. Illustrated by Stephen Michael King. ABC Books.

2008 *Dragon Moon* by Carole Wilkinson. Black Dog.

2007 *Being Bee* by Catherine Bateson. University of Queensland Press.

2006 *Helicopter Man* by Elizabeth Fensham. Bloomsbury.

2005 *The Silver Donkey* by Sonya Hartnett. Viking.

2004 *Dragonkeeper* by Carole Wilkinson. Black Dog.

2003 *Rain May and Captain Daniel* by Catherine Bateson. University of Queensland Press.

2002 *My Dog* by John Heffernan. Illustrated by Andrew McLean. Scholastic Australia.

2001 *Two Hands Together* by Diana Kidd. Penguin.

2000 *Hitler's Daughter* by Jackie French. HarperCollins.

1999 *My Girragundji* by Meme McDonald and Boori Pryor. Illustrated by Meme McDonald. Allen & Unwin.

1998 *Someone Like Me* by Elaine Forrestal. Penguin.

1997 *Hannah Plus One* by Libby Gleeson. Illustrated by Ann James. Penguin.

1996 *Swashbuckler* by James Moloney. University of Queensland Press.

1995 *Ark in the Park* by Wendy Orr. HarperCollins.

1994 *Rowan of Rin* by Emily Rodda. Omnibus.

1993 *The Bamboo Flute* by Garry Disher. Collins/ Angus & Robertson.

1992 *The Magnificent Nose and Other Marvels* by Anna Fienberg. Illustrated by Kim Gamble. Allen & Unwin.

1991 *Finders Keepers* by Emily Rodda. Omnibus.

Australian Children's Book of the Year for Older Readers Award (For mature readers.)

2011 *The Midnight Zoo* by Sonya Hartnett. Viking.

2010 *Jarvis 24* by David Metzenthen. Penguin Group Australia.

2009 *Tales from Outer Suburbia* by Shaun Tan. Allen & Unwin.

2008 *The Ghost's Child* by Sonya Hartnett. Viking.

2007 *Red Spikes* by Margo Lanagan. Allen & Unwin.

2006 *The Story of Tom Brennan* by J. C. Burke. Random House.

2005 *The Running Man* by Michael Gerard Bauer. Omnibus.

2004 *Saving Francesca* by Melina Marchetta. Viking.

2003 *The Messenger* by Markus Zusak. Pan Macmillan Australia.

2002 *Forest* by Sonya Hartnett. Viking.

2001 *Wolf on the Fold* by Judith Clarke. Allen & Unwin.

2000 *48 Shades of Brown* by Nick Earls. Penguin.

1999 *Deadly, Unna?* by Phillip Gwynne. Penguin.

1998 *Eye to Eye* by Catherine Jinks. Penguin.

1997 *A Bridge to Wiseman's Cove* by James Moloney. University of Queensland Press.

1996 *Pagan's Vows* by Catherine Jinks. Omnibus.

1995 *Foxspell* by Gillian Rubinstein. Hyland House.

1994 *The Gathering* by Isobelle Carmody. Penguin.

Angel's Gate by Gary Crew. Heinemann.

1993 *Looking for Alibrandi* by Melina Marchetta. Penguin.

1992 *The House Guest* by Eleanor Nilsson. Viking.

1991 *Strange Objects* by Gary Crew. Heinemann Australia.

Awards for a Body of Work

Hans Christian Andersen Award

This international award, sponsored by the International Board on Books for Young People, is given every two years to a living author and to a living illustrator whose complete works have made important international contributions to children's literature. Awards prior to 1980 can be found at www.ibby.org.

2012 AUTHOR: Maria Teresa Andruetto (Argentina)
ILLUSTRATOR: Peter Sís (Czech Republic)

2010 AUTHOR: David Almond (United Kingdom)
ILLUSTRATOR: Jutta Bauer (Germany)

2008 AUTHOR: Jürg Schubiger (Switzerland)
ILLUSTRATOR: Roberto Innocenti (Italy)

2006 AUTHOR: Margaret Mahy (New Zealand)
ILLUSTRATOR: Wolf Erlbruch (Germany)

2004 AUTHOR: Martin Waddell (Ireland)
ILLUSTRATOR: Max Velthuijs (Netherlands)

2002 AUTHOR: Aidan Chambers (United Kingdom)
ILLUSTRATOR: Quentin Blake (United Kingdom)

2000 AUTHOR: Ana Maria Machado (Brazil)
ILLUSTRATOR: Anthony Browne (United Kingdom)

1998 AUTHOR: Katherine Paterson (United States)
ILLUSTRATOR: Tomi Ungerer (France)

1996 AUTHOR: Uri Orlev (Israel)
ILLUSTRATOR: Klaus Ensikat (Germany)

1994 AUTHOR: Michio Mado (Japan)
ILLUSTRATOR: Jörg Müller (Switzerland)

1992 AUTHOR: Virginia Hamilton (United States)
ILLUSTRATOR: Kveta Pacovská (Czechoslovakia)

1990 AUTHOR: Tormod Haugen (Norway)
ILLUSTRATOR: Lisbeth Zwerger (Austria)

1988 AUTHOR: Annie M. G. Schmidt (Netherlands)
ILLUSTRATOR: Dušan Kállay (Czechoslovakia)

1986 AUTHOR: Patricia Wrightson (Australia)
ILLUSTRATOR: Robert Ingpen (Australia)

1984 AUTHOR: Christine Nöstlinger (Austria)
ILLUSTRATOR: Mitsumasa Anno (Japan)

1982 AUTHOR: Lygia Bojunga Nunes (Brazil)
ILLUSTRATOR: Zbigniew Rychlicki (Poland)

1980 AUTHOR: Bohumil Riha (Czechoslovakia)
ILLUSTRATOR: Suekichi Akaba (Japan)

Laura Ingalls Wilder Award

This award, sponsored by the Association for Library Service to Children of the American Library Association, is given to a U.S. author or illustrator whose body of work has made a lasting contribution to children's literature. Between 1960 and 1980, the Wilder Award was given every five years. From 1980 to 2001, it was given every three years. Beginning in 2001, it has been given every two years.

2011 Tomie dePaola
2009 Ashley Bryan
2007 James Marshall
2005 Laurence Yep
2003 Eric Carle
2001 Milton Meltzer
1998 Russell Freedman
1995 Virginia Hamilton
1992 Marcia Brown
1989 Elizabeth George Speare
1986 Jean Fritz
1983 Maurice Sendak
1980 Theodor S. Geisel (Dr. Seuss)
1975 Beverly Cleary
1970 E. B. White
1965 Ruth Sawyer
1960 Clara Ingram Judson

NCTE Excellence in Poetry for Children Award

For the list of award winners, see Chapter 5.

Awards for Specific Genres or Groups

Mildred L. Batchelder Award

This award, established in 1968 by the Association for Library Service to Children of the American Library Association, is given to the American publisher of a children's book considered to be the most outstanding of those books originally published in a country other than the U.S. in a language other than English and subsequently translated and published in the U.S. during the previous year. Award winners since 1991 are listed here. The complete list of winners is at www.ala.org/alsc/awardsgrants /bookmedia/batchelderaward/batchelderpast.

2012 *Soldier Bear* by Bibi Dumon Tak. Translated from Dutch by Laura Watkinson. Illustrated by Philip Hopman. Eerdmans.

2011 *A Time of Miracles* by Anne-Laure Bondoux. Translated from French by Y. Maudet. Delacorte.

2010 *A Faraway Island* by Annika Thor. Translated from Swedish by Linda Schenck. Delacorte.

2009 *Moribito: Guardian of the Spirit* by Nahoko Uehashi. Translated from Japanese by Cathy Hirano. Scholastic.

2008 *Brave Story* by Miyuki Miyabe. Translated from Japanese by Alexander O. Smith. VIZ Media.

2007 *The Pull of the Ocean* by Jean-Claude Mourlevat. Translated from French by Y. Maudet. Delacorte.

2006 *An Innocent Soldier* by Josef Holub. Translated from German by Michael Hofmann. Arthur A. Levine.

2005 *The Shadows of Ghadames* by Joëlle Stolz. Translated from French by Catherine Temerson. Delacorte.

2004 *Run, Boy, Run* by Uri Orlev. Translated from Hebrew by Hillel Halkin. Houghton Mifflin.

2003 *The Thief Lord* by Cornelia Funke. Translated from German by Oliver Latsch. Scholastic.

2002 *How I Became an American* by Karin Gündisch. Translated from German by James Skofield. Cricket.

2001 *Samir and Yonatan* by Daniella Carmi. Translated from Hebrew by Yael Lotan. Levine/Scholastic.

2000 *The Baboon King* by Anton Quintana. Translated from Dutch by John Nieuwenhuizen. Walker.

1999 *Thanks to My Mother* by Schoschana Rabinovici. Translated from German by James Skofield. Dial.

1998 *The Robber and Me* by Josef Holub. Translated from German by Elizabeth D. Crawford. Holt.

1997 *The Friends* by Kazumi Yumoto. Translated from Japanese by Cathy Hirano. Farrar.

1996 *The Lady with the Hat* by Uri Orlev. Translated from Hebrew by Hillel Halkin. Houghton.

1995 *The Boys from St. Petri* by Bjarne Reuter. Translated from Danish by Anthea Bell. Dutton.

1994 *The Apprentice* by Pilar Molina Llorente. Translated from Spanish by Robin Longshaw. Illustrated by Juan Ramón Alonso. Farrar.

1993 No award.

1992 *The Man from the Other Side* by Uri Orlev. Translated from Hebrew by Hillel Halkin. Houghton.

1991 *A Hand Full of Stars* by Rafik Schami. Translated from German by Rika Lesser. Dutton.

Coretta Scott King Awards

These awards, founded in 1970, are given to an African-American author and an African-American illustrator whose children's books, published during the preceding year, made outstanding inspirational and educational contributions to literature for children and young people. The awards are sponsored by the Social Responsibilities Round Table of the American Library Association. Award winners since 1991 are listed here. For the complete list of winners, go to www.ala.org/emiert/cskbookawards/recipients.

2012 AUTHOR: *Heart and Soul: The Story of America and African Americans* by Kadir Nelson. Balzer + Bray.

ILLUSTRATOR: *Underground: Finding the Light to Freedom* by Shane W. Evans. Roaring Brook Press.

2011 AUTHOR: *One Crazy Summer* by Rita Williams-Garcia. Amistad.

ILLUSTRATOR: *Dave the Potter: Artist, Poet, Slave* by Laban Carrick Hill. Illustrated by Bryan Collier. Little, Brown.

2010 AUTHOR: *Bad News for Outlaws: The Remarkable Life of Bass Reeves, Deputy U.S. Marshal* by Vaunda Micheaux Nelson. Illustrated by R. Gregory Christie. Carolrhoda Books.

ILLUSTRATOR: *My People* by Langston Hughes. Illustrated by Charles R. Smith, Jr. Atheneum.

2009 AUTHOR: *We Are the Ship: The Story of Negro League Baseball* by Kadir Nelson. Jump at the Sun.

ILLUSTRATOR: *The Blacker the Berry* by Joyce Carol Thomas. Illustrated by Floyd Cooper. HarperCollins.

2008 AUTHOR: *Elijah of Buxton* by Christopher Paul Curtis. Scholastic.

ILLUSTRATOR: *Let It Shine* by Ashley Bryan. Atheneum.

2007 AUTHOR: *Copper Sun* by Sharon Draper. Simon & Schuster/Atheneum.

ILLUSTRATOR: *Moses: When Harriet Tubman Led Her People to Freedom* by Carole Boston Weatherford. Illustrated by Kadir A. Nelson. Jump at the Sun/Hyperion.

2006 AUTHOR: *Day of Tears: A Novel in Dialogue* by Julius Lester. Jump at the Sun/Hyperion.

ILLUSTRATOR: *Rosa* by Nikki Giovanni. Illustrated by Bryan Collier. Holt.

2005 AUTHOR: *Remember: The Journey to School Integration* by Toni Morrison. Houghton.

ILLUSTRATOR: *Ellington Was Not a Street* by Ntozake Shange. Illustrated by Kadir A. Nelson. Simon & Schuster.

2004 AUTHOR: *The First Part Last* by Angela Johnson. Simon & Schuster.

ILLUSTRATOR: *Beautiful Blackbird* by Ashley Bryan. Atheneum.

2003 AUTHOR: *Bronx Masquerade* by Nikki Grimes. Dial.

ILLUSTRATOR: *Talkin' about Bessie: The Story of Aviator Elizabeth Coleman* by Nikki Grimes. Illustrated by E. B. Lewis. Orchard/Scholastic.

2002 AUTHOR: *The Land* by Mildred D. Taylor. Fogelman/Penguin Putnam.

ILLUSTRATOR: *Goin' Someplace Special* by Patricia McKissack. Illustrated by Jerry Pinkney. Atheneum.

2001 AUTHOR: *Miracle's Boys* by Jacqueline Woodson. Putnam.

ILLUSTRATOR: *Uptown* by Bryan Collier. Holt.

2000 AUTHOR: *Bud, Not Buddy* by Christopher Paul Curtis. Delacorte.

ILLUSTRATOR: *In the Time of the Drums* retold by Kim L. Siegelson. Illustrated by Brian Pinkney. Hyperion.

1999 AUTHOR: *Heaven* by Angela Johnson. Simon & Schuster.

ILLUSTRATOR: *I See the Rhythm* by Toyomi Igus. Illustrated by Michele Wood. Children's Book Press.

1998 AUTHOR: *Forged by Fire* by Sharon M. Draper. Atheneum.

ILLUSTRATOR: *In Daddy's Arms I Am Tall: African Americans Celebrating Fathers* by Javaka Steptoe. Lee & Low.

1997 AUTHOR: *Slam!* by Walter Dean Myers. Scholastic.

ILLUSTRATOR: *Minty: A Story of Young Harriet Tubman* by Alan Schroeder. Illustrated by Jerry Pinkney. Dial.

1996 AUTHOR: *Her Stories: African American Folktales, Fairy Tales, and True Tales* by Virginia Hamilton. Illustrated by Leo and Diane Dillon. Blue Sky.

ILLUSTRATOR: *The Middle Passage: White Ships/Black Cargo* by Tom Feelings. Dial.

1995 AUTHOR: *Christmas in the Big House, Christmas in the Quarters* by Patricia C. McKissack and Fredrick L. McKissack. Illustrated by John Thompson. Scholastic.

ILLUSTRATOR: *The Creation* by James Weldon Johnson. Illustrated by James E. Ransome. Holiday.

1994 AUTHOR: *Toning the Sweep* by Angela Johnson. Orchard.

ILLUSTRATOR: *Soul Looks Back in Wonder* compiled and illustrated by Tom Feelings. Dial.

1993 AUTHOR: *The Dark-Thirty: Southern Tales of the Supernatural* by Patricia McKissack. Knopf.

ILLUSTRATOR: *Origins of Life on Earth: An African Creation Myth* by David A. Anderson. Illustrated by Kathleen Atkins Smith. Sight Productions.

1992 AUTHOR: *Now Is Your Time! The African-American Struggle for Freedom* by Walter Dean Myers. HarperCollins.

ILLUSTRATOR: *Tar Beach* by Faith Ringgold. Crown.

1991 AUTHOR: *The Road to Memphis* by Mildred D. Taylor. Dial.

ILLUSTRATOR: *Aïda* retold by Leontyne Price. Illustrated by Leo and Diane Dillon. Harcourt.

Gryphon Award for Transitional Books

The Gryphon Award is given annually to a book published in the preceding year in recognition of an English-language work of fiction or nonfiction for which the primary audience is children in kindergarten through grade 4. The title exemplifies those qualities that successfully bridge the gap in difficulty between books for reading aloud to children and books for practiced readers. The award, established in 2004, is sponsored by the Center for Children's Books at the Graduate School of Library and Information Science at the University of Illinois in Urbana–Champaign.

2012 *Like Pickle Juice on a Cookie* by Julie Sternberg. Illustrated by Matthew Cordell. Amulet/Adams.

2011 *We Are in a Book!* by Mo Willems. Hyperion.

2010 *Adventures in Cartooning* by James Sturm, Andrew Arnold, and Alexis Frederick-Frost. First Second.

2009 *Frogs* by Nic Bishop. Scholastic.

2008 *Billy Tartle in Say Cheese!* by Michael Townsend. Knopf.

2007 *The True Story of Stellina* by Matteo Pericoli. Knopf.

2006 *Stinky Stern Forever* by Michelle Edwards. Harcourt.

2005 *Little Rat Rides* by Monika Bang-Campbell. Harcourt.

2004 *Bow Wow Meow Meow: It's Rhyming Cats and Dogs* by Douglas Florian. Harcourt.

Pura Belpré Award

The Pura Belpré Award honors Latino writers and illustrators whose work best portrays, affirms, and celebrates the Latino cultural experience in a work of literature for youth. This award is sponsored by the Association for Library Service to Children and the National Association to Promote Library Service to the Spanish Speaking.

2012 AUTHOR: *Under the Mesquite* by Guadalupe Garcia McCall. Lee and Low.

ILLUSTRATION: *Diego Rivera: His World and Ours* by Duncan Tonatiuh. Abrams Books for Young Readers.

2011 AUTHOR: *The Dreamer* by Pam Muñoz Ryan. Illustrated by Peter Sís. Scholastic.

ILLUSTRATION: *Grandma's Gift* by Eric Velasquez. Walker.

2010 AUTHOR: *Return to Sender* by Julia Alvarez. Alfred A. Knopf.

ILLUSTRATION: *Book Fiesta! Celebrate Children's Day/Book Day; Celebremos El día de los niños/El día de los libros.* by Pat Mora. Illustrated by Rafael López. Rayo.

2009 AUTHOR: *The Surrender Tree: Poems of Cuba's Struggle for Freedom* by Margarita Engle. Henry Holt.

ILLUSTRATION: *Just In Case* by Yuyi Morales. Roaring Brook Press.

2008 AUTHOR: *The Poet Slave of Cuba: A Biography of Juan Francisco Manzano* by Margarita Engle. Illustrated by Sean Qualls. Holt.

ILLUSTRATOR: *Los Gatos Black on Halloween* by Marisa Montes. Illustrated by Yuyi Morales. Holt.

2006 AUTHOR: *The Tequila Worm* by Viola Canales. Random House.

ILLUSTRATOR: *Doña Flor: A Tall Tale about a Giant Woman with a Great Big Heart* by Pat Mora. Knopf.

2004 AUTHOR: *Before We Were Free* by Julia Alvarez. Knopf.

ILLUSTRATOR: *Just a Minute: A Trickster Tale and Counting Book* by Yuyi Morales. Chronicle.

2002 AUTHOR: *Esperanza Rising* by Pam Muñoz Ryan. Scholastic.

ILLUSTRATOR: *Chato and the Party Animals* by Gary Soto. Illustrated by Susan Guevara. Putnam.

Distinguished Play Award

This award, sponsored by the American Alliance for Theatre and Education, honors the playwright(s) and the publisher of the work voted as the best play for young people published during the past calendar year (January to December) in three categories: Category A (plays primarily for upper and secondary school–age audiences), Category B (plays primarily for elementary and middle school–age audiences), and Category C for adaptations. Award winners since 2000 are listed here. The complete list is at www.aate.com/?page=awardwinners#Dist_Play.

2011 Category A: *The K of D* by Laura Schellhardt. Dramatic Publishing.

Category B: *A Best Friends Story* by Sandra Fenichel Asher. Dramatic Publishing.

Category C: *The Giver* adapted by Eric Coble from the novel by Lois Lowry. Dramatic Publishing.

2010 Category A: *Somebody's Children* by Jose Casas. Dramatic Publishing.

Category B: *Three* by Colleen Neuman. Baker's Plays.

Category C: *Bud, Not Buddy* adapted by Reginald Andre Jackson from the novel by Christopher Paul Curtis. Dramatic Publishing.

Iqbal adapted for the stage by Jerome Hairston, story by Francesco D' Adamo, with translation by Ann Leonori. Plays for Young Audiences, a partnership of Seattle Children's Theatre and Children's Theatre Company–Minneapolis.

2009 Category A: No award.

Category B: *Kindness* by Dennis Foon. Dramatic Publishing.

Category C: *Treasure Island* adapted by Ken Ludwig from the novel by Robert Louis Stevenson. Samuel French.

2008　Category A: *Brave No World: Community, Identity, Stand-Up Comedy* by Laurie Brooks. Dramatic Publishing.

Category B: No award.

Category C: *The Bluest Eye* adapted by Lydia R. Diamond from the novel by Toni Morrison. Dramatic Publishing.

2007　Category A: *Kara in Black* by Max Bush. Dramatic Publishing.

Category B: *La ofrenda* by Jose Casas. Dramatic Publishing.

Category C: *Roald Dahl's Danny the Champion of the World* adapted by David Wood. Samuel French.

2006　Category A: No award.

Category B: *The Forgiving Harvest* by Y York. Dramatic Publishing.

Category C: No award.

2005　Category A: *Eric and Elliot* by Dwayne Hartford. Dramatic Publishing.

Category B: *In the Garden of the Selfish Giant* by Sandra Fenichel Asher. Dramatic Publishing.

Category C: *The Rememberer* by Steven Dietz, based on *As My Sun Now Sets* by Joyce Simmons Cheeka as told to Werdna Phillips Finley. Dramatic Publishing.

2004　Category A: *The Music Lesson* by Tammy Ryan. Dramatic Publishing.

Category B: No award.

Category C: *Sarah, Plain and Tall* adapted by Joseph Robinette from the book by Patricia MacLachlan. Dramatic Publishing.

2003　Category A: *Paper Lanterns, Paper Cranes* by Brian Kral. Anchorage Press Plays.

Category B: *Salt and Pepper* by Jose Cruz Gonzalez. Dramatic Publishing.

Category C: *Spot's Birthday Party* adapted for the stage by David Wood, based on the book by Eric Hill. Samuel French.

2002　Category A: *Belongings* by Daniel Fenton. Dramatic Publishing.

Category B: No award.

Category C: *Ezigbo, the Spirit Child* dramatized by Max Bush. Anchorage Press Plays.

Category C: *A Village Fable* by James Still, music by Michael Keck. Dramatic Publishing.

2001　Category A: *The Wrestling Season,* by Laurie Brooks. Dramatic Publishing.

Category B: No award.

Category C: *Afternoon of the Elves* by Y York. Dramatic Publishing.

2000　Category A: *And Then They Came for Me: Remembering the World of Anne Frank* by James Still. Dramatic Publishing.

Category A: *The Taste of Sunrise* by Suzan Zeder. Anchorage Press.

Category B: *The Wolf Child* by Edward Mast. Anchorage Press.

Category C: No award.

Edgar Allan Poe Award (Mystery)—
Best Juvenile Novel Category

This award, established in 1961 and sponsored by the Mystery Writers of America, is given to the author of the best mystery of the year written for young readers. Award winners since 1991 are listed here. For the complete list of winners, go to www.theedgars.com /edgarsDB/index.php and select "Best Juvenile" from the award category.

2012　*Icefall* by Matthew J. Kirby. Scholastic.

2011　*The Buddy Files: The Case of the Lost Boy* by Dori Hillestad Butler. Albert Whitman.

2010　*Closed for the Season* by Mary Downing Hahn. Houghton Mifflin.

2009　*The Postcard* by Tony Abbott. Little, Brown.

2008　*The Night Tourist* by Katherine Marsh. Hyperion.

2007　*Room One: A Mystery or Two* by Andrew Clements. Simon & Schuster.

2006　*The Boys of San Joaquin* by D. James Smith. Simon & Schuster.

2005　*Chasing Vermeer* by Blue Balliett. Scholastic.

2004 *Bernie Magruder & the Bats in the Belfry* by Phyllis Reynolds Naylor. Atheneum.

2003 *Harriet Spies Again* by Helen Ericson. Random House/Delacorte.

2002 *Dangling* by Lillian Eige. Atheneum.

2001 *Dovey Coe* by Frances O'Roark Dowell. Simon & Schuster.

2000 *The Night Flyers* by Elizabeth McDavid Jones. Pleasant Company.

1999 *Sammy Keyes and the Hotel Thief* by Wendelin Van Draanen. Knopf.

1998 *Sparrows in the Scullery* by Barbara Brooks Wallace. Atheneum.

1997 *The Clearing* by Dorothy R. Miller. Atheneum.

1996 *Looking for Jamie Bridger* by Nancy Springer. Dial.

1995 *The Absolutely True Story . . . How I Visited Yellowstone Park with the Terrible Rupes* by Willo Davis Roberts. Atheneum.

1994 *The Twin in the Tavern* by Barbara Brooks Wallace. Atheneum.

1993 *Coffin on a Case* by Eve Bunting. HarperCollins.

1992 *Wanted . . . Mud Blossom* by Betsy Byars. Delacorte.

1991 *Stonewords* by Pam Conrad. Harper.

Scott O'Dell Award for Historical Fiction

This award, donated by the author Scott O'Dell and established in 1984, is given to the author of a distinguished work of historical fiction for children or young adults set in the New World and published in English by a U.S. publisher. The author must be a citizen of the U.S. Award winners since 1991 are listed here. For the complete list of winners, go to www.scottodell.com/odellaward.html.

2012 *Dead End in Norvelt* by Jack Gantos. Farrar, Straus & Giroux.

2011 *One Crazy Summer* by Rita Williams Garcia. Amistad.

2010 *The Storm in the Barn* by Matt Phelan. Candlewick.

2009 *Chains* by Laurie Halse Anderson. Simon & Schuster.

2008 *Elijah of Buxton* by Christopher Paul Curtis. Scholastic.

2007 *The Green Glass Sea* by Ellen Klages. Viking.

2006 *The Game of Silence* by Louise Erdrich. HarperCollins.

2005 *Worth* by A. LaFaye. Simon & Schuster.

2004 *The River between Us* by Richard Peck. Dial.

2003 *Trouble Don't Last* by Shelley Pearsall. Knopf.

2002 *The Land* by Mildred D. Taylor. Fogelman/Penguin Putnam.

2001 *The Art of Keeping Cool* by Janet Taylor Lisle. Atheneum.

2000 *Two Suns in the Sky* by Miriam Bat-Ami. Front Street/Cricket.

1999 *Forty Acres and Maybe a Mule* by Harriette Gillem Robinet. Atheneum.

1998 *Out of the Dust* by Karen Hesse. Scholastic.

1997 *Jip: His Story* by Katherine Paterson. Dutton.

1996 *The Bomb* by Theodore Taylor. Harcourt Brace.

1995 *Under the Blood-Red Sun* by Graham Salisbury. Delacorte.

1994 *Bull Run* by Paul Fleischman. HarperCollins.

1993 *Morning Girl* by Michael Dorris. Hyperion.

1992 *Stepping on the Cracks* by Mary Downing Hahn. Clarion.

1991 *A Time of Troubles* by Pieter van Raven. Scribner's.

Orbis Pictus Award

This award, established in 1990 and sponsored by NCTE's Committee on Using Nonfiction in the Elementary Language Arts Classroom, is given to an author in recognition of excellence in writing of nonfiction for children published in the U.S. in the preceding year.

2012 *Balloons over Broadway: The True Story of the Puppeteer of Macy's Parade* by Melissa Sweet. Houghton Mifflin.

2011 *Ballet for Martha: Making Appalachian Spring* by Jan Greenberg and Sandra Jordan. Illustrated by Brian Floca. Roaring Brook.

2010 *The Secret World of Walter Anderson* by Hester Bass. Illustrated by E. B. Lewis. Candlewick.

2009 *Amelia Earhart: The Legend of the Lost Aviator* by Shelley Tanaka. Illustrated by David Craig. Abrams.

2008 *M.L.K.: Journey of a King* by Tonya Bolden. Abrams.

2007 *Quest for the Tree Kangaroo: An Expedition to the Cloud Forest of New Guinea* by Sy Montgomery. Photos by Nic Bishop. Houghton.

2006 *Children of the Great Depression* by Russell Freedman. Clarion.

2005 *York's Adventures with Lewis and Clark: An African-American's Part in the Great Expedition* by Rhoda Blumberg. HarperCollins.

2004 *An American Plague: The True and Terrifying Story of the Yellow Fever Epidemic of 1793* by Jim Murphy. Clarion.

2003 *When Marian Sang* by Pam Muñoz Ryan. Illustrated by Brian Selznick. Scholastic.

2002 *Black Potatoes: The Story of the Great Irish Famine, 1845–1850* by Susan Campbell Bartoletti. Houghton.

2001 *Hurry Freedom: African Americans in Gold Rush California* by Jerry Stanley. Crown.

2000 *Through My Eyes* by Ruby Bridges and Margo Lundell. Scholastic.

1999 *Shipwreck at the Bottom of the World: The Extraordinary True Story of Schackleton and the Endurance* by Jennifer Armstrong. Crown.

1998 *An Extraordinary Life: The Story of a Monarch Butterfly* by Laurence Pringle. Illustrated by Bob Marstall. Orchard.

1997 *Leonardo da Vinci* by Diane Stanley. Morrow.

1996 *The Great Fire* by Jim Murphy. Scholastic.

1995 *Safari beneath the Sea* by Diane Swanson. Photographs by the Royal British Columbia Museum. Sierra Club.

1994 *Across America on an Emigrant Train* by Jim Murphy. Clarion.

1993 *Children of the Dustbowl: The True Story of the School at Weedpatch Camp* by Jerry Stanley. Random House.

Robert F. Sibert Informational Book Medal

This award, established by the Association for Library Service to Children of the American Library Association, is awarded annually to the author of the most distinguished informational book published during the preceding year.

2012 *Balloons over Broadway: The True Story of the Puppeteer of Macy's Parade* by Melissa Sweet. Houghton Mifflin Books for Children.

2011 *Kakapo Rescue: Saving the World's Strangest Parrot* by Sy Montgomery. Photographs by Nic Bishop. Houghton Mifflin.

2010 *Almost Astronauts: 13 Women Who Dared to Dream* by Tanya Lee Stone. Candlewick.

2009 *We Are the Ship: The Story of Negro League Baseball* by Kadir Nelson. Jump at the Sun.

2008 *The Wall: Growing Up behind the Iron Curtain* by Peter Sís. Farrar.

2007 *Team Moon: How 400,000 People Landed Apollo 11 on the Moon* by Catherine Thimmesh. Houghton.

2006 *Secrets of a Civil War Submarine: Solving the Mysteries of the H. L. Hunley* by Sally M. Walker. Carolrhoda.

2005 *The Voice That Challenged a Nation: Marian Anderson and the Struggle for Equal Rights* by Russell Freedman. Clarion.

2004 *An American Plague: The True and Terrifying Story of the Yellow Fever Epidemic of 1793* by Jim Murphy. Clarion.

2003 *The Life and Death of Adolf Hitler* by James Cross Giblin. Clarion.

2002 *Black Potatoes: The Story of the Great Irish Famine, 1845–1850* by Susan Campbell Bartoletti. Houghton.

Other Notable Book Awards

New York Times Best Illustrated Children's Books of the Year

Sponsored by the *New York Times,* this list of ten books appears annually in the *Times.* A three-member panel of experts chooses the books.

International Reading Association Children's Book Award

Sponsored by the Institute for Reading Research and administered by the International Reading Association, this international award is given annually to an author for a first or second book that shows unusual promise in the children's book field.

International Board on Books for Young People Honour List

Sponsored by the International Board on Books for Young People (IBBY), this biennial list is composed of three books (one for text, one for illustration, and one for translation) from each IBBY National Section to represent the best in children's literature published in that country in the past two years. The books selected are recommended as suitable for publication worldwide.

State Children's Choice Award Programs

Nearly all states have a children's choice book award program. Usually, a ballot of about twenty-five titles is generated from children's or teachers' nominations. Children from all over the state then vote for their favorite title. For information about your state children's choice award program, contact your state library association.

Appendix B

Professional Resources

Books

Barr, C., & Thomas, R. L. (2008). *Popular series fiction for K–6 readers* (2nd ed.). Santa Barbara, CA: Libraries Unlimited.

——. *Popular series fiction for middle school and teen readers* (2nd ed.). Santa Barbara, CA: Libraries Unlimited.

Guides to the best and most popular series, including series titles, all books in a given series, and suggestions for similar series.

Barstow, B., Riggle, J., & Molnar, L. (2007). *Beyond picture books: Subject access to best books for beginning readers* (3rd ed.). Santa Barbara, CA: Libraries Unlimited.

Subject guide to 3,600 titles for beginning readers ages 4 to 7. Includes a list of 200 outstanding first readers.

Bedford, A., & Albright, L. (Eds.) (2011). *A master class in children's literature: Trends and issues*. Urbana, IL: NCTE.

Each chapter focuses on a contemporary issue in children's literature and provides suggestions, strategies, and resources.

Bishop, R. S. (2007). *Free within ourselves: The development of African-American children's literature.* Westport, CT: Greenwood.

The evolution of fiction written for black children and by black authors and illustrators within the context of African-American social and literary history. Profiles of contemporary African-American authors and illustrators conclude the book.

The children's catalog (2009). New York, NY: H. W. Wilson.

Part 1 lists books and magazines recommended for preschool children through sixth-graders, as well as useful professional resources. Part 2 helps the user locate entries through one alphabetical, comprehensive key that includes author, title, subject, and analytical listings.

De Las Casas, D. (2006). *Kamishibai story theater: The art of picture telling.* Santa Barbara, CA: Libraries Unlimited.

Practical information on developing a kamishibai program using large illustrated cards based on the street art form seen from the 1920s to 1950s in Japan. See Allen Say's *Kamishibai Man* (Houghton, 2005) for a story about an itinerant storyteller.

Duke, N., Caughlan, S., & Juzwik, M. (2011). *Reading and writing genre with purpose in K–8 classrooms*. Portsmouth, NH: Heinemann.

Identifies the problems in commonly used approaches to teaching genre and provides examples of alternative practices along with five guiding principles for instruction. Provides a range of tools for managing a genre approach in the classroom.

Evans, D. (2008). *Show & Tell: Exploring the fine art of children's book illustration*. San Francisco, CA: Chronicle.

Examines the work of twelve illustrators to teach the elements of art and composition as they relate to picture book illustration.

Fox, D. L., & Short, K. G. (Eds.). (2003). *Stories matter: The complexity of cultural authenticity in children's literature.* Urbana, IL: NCTE.

Social responsibility of authors, cultural sensitivity and values, authenticity of content and images, and authorial freedom addressed by many contributors, including authors, illustrators, editors, publishers, educators, librarians, and scholars.

Freeman, J. (2007). *Once upon a time: Using storytelling, creative drama, and reader's theater with children in grades pre-K–6.* Santa Barbara, CA: Libraries Unlimited.

Tried-and-true stories, ideas, and activities for storytelling with children, including a bibliography of over 400 children's books to adapt for creative drama and/or readers' theatre.

Garcha, R., & Russell, P. Y. (2006). *The world of Islam in literature for youth: A selective bibliography for K–12.* Lanham, MD: Scarecrow.

Sixteen chapters present various aspects of Islam and the Muslim culture with annotated books; video and audio resources and teaching suggestions are included in separate chapters.

Gebel, D. J. (2006). *Crossing boundaries with children's books.* Lanham, MD: Scarecrow.

Includes annotations of nearly 700 international children's books published between 2000 and 2004, as well as selected American books set in countries other than the United States.

Hall, S. (1990, 1994, 2001, 2007). *Using picture storybooks to teach literary devices: Recommended books for children and young adults* (Vols. 1, 2, 3 & 4). Phoenix, AZ: Oryx Press.

Offers strategies for using picture books to teach complex literary devices.

Jobe, R., & Dayton-Sakari, M. (1999). *Reluctant readers: Connecting students and books for successful reading experiences.* Markham, ON: Pembroke.

Activities and books for teachers and librarians to engage reluctant readers.

Layne, S. (2009). *Igniting a passion for reading.* Portland, ME: Stenhouse.

Ways of engaging students to become readers who love a good book and to create a reading culture in a classroom.

Leeper, A. (2006). *Poetry in literature for youth.* Lanham, MD: Scarecrow.

Innovative ways to integrate poetry into the K–12 curriculum and annotations of over 900 poetry books are included in this guide.

Lehman, B. (2007). *Children's literature and learning: Literary study across the curriculum.* New York, NY: Teachers College Press.

Theories and methods for teaching literature across the curriculum.

Lehman, B., Freeman, E., & Scharer, P. 2010. *Reading globally, K–8.* Thousand Oaks, CA: Corwin.

The use of global literature across subject areas with numerous examples of outstanding books and teaching strategies.

Lehr, S. S. (Ed.). (2008). *Shattering the looking glass: Challenge, risk and controversy in children's literature.* Norwood, MA: Christopher-Gordon.

Politics, controversial issues, and recent change in the world of children's literature.

Leland, C. (2012). *Teaching children's literature: It's critical.* New York, NY: Routledge.

Practical strategies for a critical approach to engaging children with literature in ways that build from children's lives and cultural knowledge to question the world, explore power relationships, and consider actions to promote social justice.

Lima, C. W., & Lima, J. A. (2010). *A to zoo: Subject access to children's picture books* (8th ed.). Westport, CT: Libraries Unlimited.

This index indicates the subject matter of 14,000 picture books for children with access through author, illustrator, and title, as well as 800 subjects.

Lukenbill, W. B. (2006). *Biography in the lives of youth: culture, society and information.* Englewood, NJ: Libraries Unlimited.

Varied uses of biography, types of biographies, their changes over time, and an extensive bibliography are presented, with age appropriateness indicated.

Lukens, R., Smith, J., & Coffel, C. (2013). *A critical handbook of children's literature* (9th ed.). New York, NY: Pearson.

Contains separate chapters on each literary element along with examples from children's books; also focuses on other aspects of literary concepts, such as genres and formats.

Marcus, L. (2012). *Show me a story! Why picture books matter*. Somerville, MA: Candlewick.

Interviews with twenty-one illustrators of children's picture books.

Naidoo, J. C. (Ed.) (2010). *Celebrating cuentos: Promoting Latino children's literature and literacy in classrooms and libraries*. Wesport, CT: Libraries Unlimited.

Strategies and research on integrating Latino children's literature into classrooms and libraries, interviews with Latino authors and illustrators, and information on evaluating and selecting quality Latino literature.

Nichols, M. (2006). *Comprehension through conversation*. Portsmouth, NH: Heinemann.

Issues and strategies to consider in engaging students in purposeful booktalks to lead them to deeper understandings of fiction and nonfiction. Talk as a way to encourage students to think about text through comprehension, conversation, and collaboration.

Pavonetti, L. (Ed.) (2011). *Bridges to understanding: Envisioning the world through children's books*. Lanham, MD: Scarecrow.

A guide to international children's books published in the United States from 2005 to 2010, with descriptions of 700 books from more than 70 countries in an annotated bibliography.

Stan, S. (Ed.). (2002). *The world through children's books.* Lanham, MD: Scarecrow.

A guide to international children's books published in the United States from 1996 to 2000, including a selection of children's books written by U.S. authors but set in other countries. An annotated bibliography is included.

Sullivan, M. (2003). *Connecting boys with books: What libraries can do.* Chicago, IL: American Library Association.

Suggestions for program changes to address the problem of low reading skills among preadolescent boys.

Sullivan, M. (2009). *Connecting boys with books 2: Closing the reading gap.* Chicago, IL: American Library Association.

A strategic plan for boys and reading through stimulating a sense of excitement in reading.

Tatum, A. W. (2005). *Teaching reading to black adolescent males: Closing the achievement gap.* Portland, ME: Stenhouse.

Practical suggestions for providing meaningful and culturally responsive reading strategies and assessment for black males and guidelines for selecting and discussing nonfiction and fiction texts with them.

Van Orden, P. (2000). *Selecting books for the elementary school library media center: A complete guide.* New York, NY: Neal-Schuman.

An essential tool for new school libraries and useful for most libraries in balancing collections.

Vardell, S. M. (2008). *Children's literature in action: A librarian's guide.* Santa Barbara, CA: Libraries Unlimited.

Practical information for the preservice school or public librarian.

Books about the History of Children's Literature

Bingham, J., & Scholt, G. (1980). *Fifteen centuries of children's literature: An annotated chronology of British and American works in historical context.* Westport, CT: Greenwood.

Gillespie, M. C. (1970). *History and trends: Literature for children.* Dubuque, IA: Brown.

Hunt, P. (1995). *Children's literature: An illustrated history.* Oxford, England: Oxford University Press.

Hunt, P., & Ray, S. G. (1996). *International companion encyclopedia of children's literature.* London: Routledge.

Marcus, L. (2008). *Minders of make-believe: Idealists, entrepreneurs, and the shaping of American children's literature.* Boston. MA: Houghton.

A 300-year history of children's book publishing, showing the evolution from a local endeavor to an international business.

Marshall, M. R. (1988). *An introduction to the world of children's books: Books about the history of children's literature* (2nd ed.). Aldershot, England: Gower.

Bibliographies: Annual Lists

"CCBC Choices"

An annual spring annotated booklist published by and for the members of the Friends of the CCBC, Inc. (Cooperative Children's Book Center). For information about CCBC publications and/or membership in the Friends, send a self-addressed stamped envelope to CCBC Choices, Friends of the CCBC, Inc., P.O. Box 5189 Madison, WI 53705.

"Children's Choices"

This yearly list of newly published books, chosen by young readers themselves, appears in the October issue of *The Reading Teacher* as a project of the International Reading Association/Children's Book Council Joint Committee.

"Notable Children's Books"

This annual American Library Association list appears in the March issue of *School Library Journal* and also in the March 15 issue of *Booklist.*

"Notable Children's Books in the Language Arts (K–8)"

This annual list of outstanding trade books for enhancing language awareness among students in grades K–8 appears in each March issue of *Language Arts.*

"Notable Social Studies Trade Books for Young People"

This list appears in the May/June issue of *Social Education* and at www.socialstudies.org/notable.

"Outstanding International Book List"

This annual list of outstanding books for K-12 is sponsored by USBBY and highlights books that were first published in another country. The list appears in the February issue of *School Library Journal.*

"Outstanding Science Trade Books for Students K–12"

This list appears in the March issue of *Science and Children* and at www.nsta.org/publications/ostb/.

"Teachers' Choices"

This yearly list includes books recommended by teachers. It appears each November in *The Reading Teacher* and at www.reading.org.

"Young Adults' Choices"

The books on this annual list are selected by readers in middle, junior high, and senior high schools. It appears in the November issue of *Journal of Adolescent and Adult Literacy* and at www.reading.org.

Appendix C

Children's Magazines

The following list includes some of the most popular children's magazines available to young people, organized by primary emphasis.

Drama

Plays, the Drama Magazine for Young People. Scripts for plays, skits, puppet shows, and round-the-table readings (a type of readers' theatre). 8–10 scripts per issue. Ages 6–17. 7 issues/year. Order at www.playsmagazine.com

Health

Turtle. Articles, fiction, and activities with an emphasis on health, nutrition, and fitness. Ages 3–5. 6 issues/year. Similar magazines for different age groups include *Humpty Dumpty Magazine* (ages 5–7) and *Jack and Jill* (ages 8–12). Order at www.cbhi.org

History

Calliope. Articles, stories, time lines, maps, and authentic photos to generate an interest in world history. Themed issues. Ages 9–14. 9 issues/year. Order at www.cobblestonepub.com

Cobblestone. Articles about U.S. history. Themed issues. Ages 9–14. 9 issues/year. Order at www.cobblestonepub.com

Language

Allons-Y. Topics of interest to 12- to 18-year-olds in French. Information and cultural details of French-speaking countries. Read-aloud plays and language CDs. 6 issues/year. Order at http://classroommagazines.scholastic.com

Das Rad. Topics of interest to 12- to 18-year-olds in German. Information and cultural details of German-speaking countries. Read-aloud plays and language CDs. 6 issues/year. Order at http://classroommagazines.scholastic.com

¿Qué Tal? Topics of interest to 12- to 18-year-olds in Spanish. Information and cultural details of Spanish-speaking countries. Read-aloud plays and language CDs. 6 issues/year. Order at http://classroommagazines.scholastic.com

Language Arts

Read. Classic and contemporary fiction and nonfiction, plays, personal narratives, poetry; readers' theatre plays; articles on developing writing skills. Ages 11–16. 16 issues/year. Order at www.weeklyreader.com

Scholastic Scope. Plays, short stories, nonfiction, writing exercises, and skill builders. Ages 11–15. 17 issues/year. Order at http://classroommagazines.scholastic.com

Stone Soup: The Magazine by Young Writers and Artists. Stories, poems, book reviews, and art by children. Ages 8–13. 6 issues/year. Order at www.stonesoup.com

Storyworks. Focuses on development of grammar, writing, vocabulary, test-taking. Includes read-aloud plays. Ages 8–11. 6 issues/year. Order at http://classroommagazines.scholastic.com

Literature

Cricket. Fiction, nonfiction, book reviews, activities. Features international literature. Ages 9–14. 9 issues/year. Order at www.cricketmag.com

Lady Bug. Fiction, poems, songs, and games. Ages 3–6. 9 issues/year. Order at www.cricketmag.com

Spider. Fiction, poems, songs, and games for the beginning reader. Ages 6–9. 9 issues/year. Order at www.cricketmag.com

Mathematics

DynaMath. Humorously formatted word problems, computation, and test preparation; careers in mathematics feature. Ages 8–11. 8 issues/year. Order at http://classroommagazines.scholastic.com

Scholastic Math. Math problems, computation, statistics, consumer math, real-life applications, career math, critical reasoning. Ages 11–15. 12 issues/year. Order at http://classroommagazines.scholastic.com

Nature

National Geographic Explorer. Classroom magazines featuring nonfiction and nature photography aligned with science and social studies curriculum. Four levels (grades K–1, 2–3, 4–6, 6–12). 7 issues/year. Order at www.magma.nationalgeographic.com/ngexplorer

National Geographic Kids. Nonfiction articles and nature photography. Promotes geographic awareness. Ages 6–14. 10 issues/year. Order at www.kids.nationalgeographic.com/kids

Ranger Rick. Fiction and nonfiction, photo essays, jokes, riddles, crafts, plays, and poetry promoting the appreciation of nature. Superlative nature photography. Ages 7–12. 12 issues/year. Order at www.nwf.org/kids

Big Backyard. Animal and nature stories and photography for the preschooler. Ages 3–7. 12 issues/year. Order at www.nwf.org/News-and-Magazines.aspx

Recreation

Boys' Life. News, nature, sports, history, fiction, science, comics, Scouting, colorful graphics, and photos. Published by the Boy Scouts of America. Ages 7–18. 12 issues/year. Order at www.boyslife.org

Electronic Gaming Monthly. Gaming software and hardware previews and reviews. Ages 12 and up. 12 issues/year. Order at www.egmmag.com/subscribe

Highlights. General-interest magazine offering fiction and nonfiction, crafts, poetry, and thinking features. Ages 6–12. 12 issues/year. Order at www.highlights.com

Junior Baseball Magazine. Articles on baseball skills, sportsmanship, safety, and physical fitness. Ages 10–14. 6 issues/year. Order at www.juniorbaseball.com

New Moon: The Magazine for Girls and Their Dreams. An international magazine by and about girls. Builds healthy resistance to gender inequities. Ages 8–12. 6 issues/year. Order at www.newmoon.com/magazine

Nick Magazine. Nickelodeon television channel entertainment and humor magazine with television-related celebrity interviews, comics, puzzles, and activities. Ages 6–14. 10 issues/year. Order at www.nick.com/shows/nick_mag

Sports Illustrated for Kids. Stories about sports and sports celebrities, amateur sports, trivia. Poster included with each issue. Ages 6–10. 12 issues/year. Order at www.sikids.com

Science

Current Science. News in science, health, and technology; science activities; U.S. national science projects; science mystery photos; and kids in the news. Ages 11–16. 16 issues/year. Order at www.weeklyreader.com/current-science-magazine

Odyssey. Theme-based issues explore the latest science news. Ages 9–14. 9 issues/year. Order at www.odysseymagazine.com

Science World. Articles, experiments, and news to supplement the science curriculum. Ages 11–16. 14 issues/year. Order at http://classroommagazines .scholastic.com

SuperScience. Science concepts, critical thinking, and reasoning through hands-on activities and experiments; science news stories; interviews with scientists. Themed issues. Ages 8–11. 8 issues/year. Order at http://classroommagazines.scholastic.com

Social Studies

Faces. Articles and activities exploring world cultures. Ages 9–14. 9 issues/year. Order at www .cobblestonepub.com

Junior Scholastic. Features U.S. and world history, current events, world cultures, map skills, and geography. Ages 11–14. 18 issues/year. Order at http://classroommagazines.scholastic.com

Muse. Wide-ranging articles exploring ideas in science, history, and the arts. Ages 10–15. 9 issues/ year. Order at www.cricketmag.com

Skipping Stones: An International Multicultural Magazine. Articles by, about, and for children about world cultures and cooperation. Multilingual. Ages 7–17. 5 issues/year. Order at www.skipping stones.org

Index to Children's Books and Authors

Subject Index

Credits and Acknowledgments

Text Credits

Page ii: Peck, Richard, "A Story is a Doorway." Reprinted by permission of the author.

Page 3: "Reading," by Elizabeth Barrett Browning. From *Aurora Leigh*, London: J. Miller, 1864.

Page 15: "My Book," from *Somebody Catch My Homework*, by David L. Harrison. Illustrated by Betsy Lewin. Copyright © 1993 by David L. Harrison and Betsy Lewin. Published by Boyds Mills Press. Reprinted by permission.

Page 31: "A Reading," by Hannah More, from *The Works of Hannah More*, Vol. II, London, T. Cadell, Strand.

Page 49: "Picture This," from *BOOKSPEAK!: Poems About Books*, by Laura Purdie Sales. Text copyright © 2011 by Laura Purdie Sales. Reprinted by permission of Clarion Books, an imprint of Houghton Mifflin Harcourt Publishing Company. All rights reserved.

Page 62: Shannon, David (1998). *No, David!* New York, New York. Scholastic Books, Age 2–5.

Page 83: "What's a Poem?," from *A Fury of Motion*, by Charles Ghigna. Copyright © 2003, by Charles Ghigna. Published by Wordsong, an imprint of Boyds Mills Press. Reprinted by permission.

Page 88: "The Pickety Fence," from *One at a Time* by David McCord. Copyright renewed © 1980 by David McCord. By Permission of Little, Brown and Company. All rights reserved.

Page 88: "Slowly," © James Reeves from *Complete Poems for Children* (Heinemann). Reprinted by permission of the James Reeves Estate.

Page 89: Taylor, Jane, "The Star," Philadelphia: G. S. Appleton; New York: D. Appleton & Co. 1851.

Page 89: G. Orr Clark.

Page 90: "The Sun Has a Tail," by Emanuel di Pasquale. Copyright by author, Emanuel di Pasquale. Permission granted by author.

Page 90: "Speed Adjustments," from *The Monster Den*, by John Ciardi. Copyright © 1963 by John Ciardi. Published by Wordsong, an imprint of Boyds Mills Press. Reprinted by permission.

Page 93: "Giraffes," a poem, by Sy Kahn in *TRIPTYCH: A Collection of Poems*, 1966. Reprinted by permission of the author.

Pages 93–94: Lindsay, Vachel, "The Little Turtle," from *The Golden Whales of California and Other Rhymes in the American Language*. New York. The Macmillan Company, 1920.

Page 94: Goodrich, Samuel G. "Higglety, Pigglety, Pop," 1846.

Page 94: "There Was an Old Man with a Beard," Edward Lear, *A Book of Nonsense*, London: Frederick Warne and Co; New York: Scribner, Welford, and Co., 1870.

Page 94: "The Wind and I Play," from *GUYKU: A Year of Haiku for Boys* by Bob Rackzka. Text copyright © 2010 by Bob Rackza. Reprinted by permission of Harcourt Children's Books, an imprint of Houghton Mifflin Harcourt Publishing Company. All rights reserved.

Page 95: "Pockets," from *Tap Dancing on the Roof: Sijo (Poems)* by Linda Sue Park. Text copyright © 2007 by Linda Sue Park. Reprinted by permission of Clarion Books, an imprint of Houghton Mifflin Harcourt Publishing Company. All rights reserved.

Page 95: "Autumn Leaves," from *In the Spin of Things: Poems of Motion*, by Rebecca Kai Dotlitch. Copyright © 2003 by Rebecca Kai Dotlitch. Published by Wordsong, an imprint of Boyds Mills Press. Republished by permission.

Page 95: "Concrete Cat," by Dorthi Charles, from *Knock at a Star: A Child's Introduction to Poetry*, revised edition (Little, Brown and Co.) © 1999, by X. J. Kennedy and Dorothy M. Kennedy. Used with permission.

Page 107: "There Is a Land," Copyright © 1985 by Highlights for Children, Inc., Colombus, Ohio. Reprinted by permission.

Page 123: "Magic Words," Anonymous Inuit Poet, as translated by Edward Field. Reprinted by permission of Edward Field.

Page 145: "Listening to Grownups Quarreling," from *The Marriage Wig and Other Poems,* by Ruth Whittman. Copyright © 1968 and renewed 1996 by Ruth Whittman. Reprinted by permission of Houghton Mifflin Harcourt Publishing Company. All rights reserved.

Page 165: "Ancestors" by Grey Cohoe, from *Whispering Wind* by Terry Allen, copyright © 1972 by the Institute of American Indian Arts. Used by permission of Doubleday, a division of Random House, Inc. Any third party use of this material, outside of this publication, is prohibited. Interested parties must apply directly to Random House, Inc. for permission.

Page 193: "Questions at Night," from *Rainbow in the Sky,* by Louis Untermeyer. Copyright © 1935 by Houghton Mifflin Harcourt Publishing Company. Copyright renewed 1963 by Louis Untermeyer. Reprinted by permission of Houghton Mifflin Harcourt Publishing Company. All rights reserved.

Page 213: Bryan, Ashley (1998). "Oh the Places You'll Go." New York. Children's Book Council. Reused by permission.

Page 247: "In Sight," from *A Fury of Motion,* by Charles Ghigna. Copyright © 2003 by Charles Ghigna. Published by Wordsong, an imprint of Boyds Mills Press. Reprinted by permission.

Page 275: Richard Le Gallienne, "I Meant to Do My Work Today," *The Lonely Dancer, and Other Poems,* London: John Lane; New York: John Lane Company, 1914.

Illustration Credits

Illustration 1: From *No, David!* by David Shannon. Scholastic Inc./The Blue Sky Press. Copyright © 1998 by David Shannon. Reprinted by permission.

Illustration 2: Image used by permission of Barefoot Books, 2013.

Illustration 3: From *Chester* by Ayano Imai, copyright © 2007 by Ayano Imai. Used by permission of minedition rights & licensing AG/Switzerland. All rights reserved.

Illustration 4: Illustration by Bill Thomson, used with permission of Amazon Publishing, all rights reserved.

Illustration 5: From *Knuffle Bunny* by Mo Willems. Illustrations copyright © 2004 by Mo Willems. Reprinted by permission of Disney • Hyperion, an imprint of Disney Children's Book Group, LLC. All rights reserved.

Illustration 6: From *Rapunzel's Revenge*. Illustration copyright © 2008 by Nathan Hale. Reprinted with permission of Bloomsbury USA. All rights reserved.

Illustration 7: Illustration copyright © 2004 by Stephen Savage from *Polar Bear Night* by Lauren Thompson.

Scholastic Inc./Scholastic Press. Reprinted by permission.

Illustration 8: From *The Hello, Goodbye Window* by Norton Juster. Pictures copyright © 2005 by Chris Raschka. Reprinted by permission of Disney • Hyperion, an imprint of Disney Children's Book Group, LLC. All rights reserved.

Illustration 9: Illustration from *Song of the Water Boatman and Other Pond Poems* by Joyce Sidman, illustrated by Beckie Prange. Illustrations copyright © 2005 by Beckie Prange. Reprinted by permission of Houghton Mifflin Harcourt Publishing Company. All rights reserved.

Illustration 10: From *Officer Buckle and Gloria* by Peggy Rathmann, copyright © 1995 by Peggy Rathmann. Used by permission of G. P. Putnam's Sons, a division of Penguin Group (USA) Inc.

Illustration 11: Illustration from *The Subway Mouse*. Copyright © 2003 by Barbara Reid. Reproduced by permission of Scholastic Canada.

Illustration 12: From *A Drop of Water* by Walter Wick. Scholastic Inc./Scholastic Press. Copyright © 1997 by Walter Wick. Reprinted by permission.

Design Image Credits

Chapter opener background, lower right corner and A-head flag icons: David Wiesner.

Section opener banner: Pixel Bunneh/Fotolia.

Part and chapter opener drop caps: Drizzd/Fotolia.

Further Investigations icon: Andrew Buckin/Fotolia.

References icon: Pixel Embargo/Fotolia.

Read Aloud icon: Verte/Fotolia.

Notable Authors icon: Oleksandr Moroz/Fotolia.

Recommended Books icon: Anterovium/Fotolia.

Related Films icon: Hana76/Fotolia.